PSYCHOLOGY

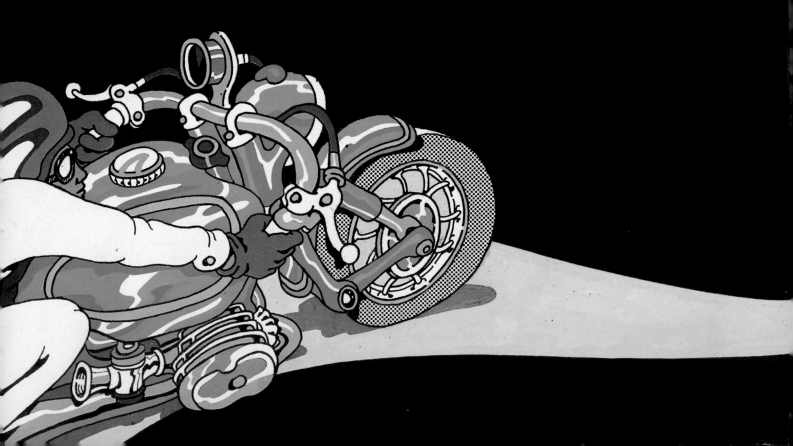

ILLUSTRATION BY
EDWARD BADAJOS

PSYCHOLOGY

RICHARD W. MALOTT
Western Michigan University

DONALD L. WHALEY
North Texas State University

BEHAVIORDELIA
Kalamazoo, Michigan

HARPER'S COLLEGE PRESS
A department of Harper & Row, Publishers
New York / Hagerstown / San Francisco / London

Psychology. Copyright © 1976 by Harper & Row, Publishers, Incorporated.

Printed in the United States of America. All rights reserved. No part of this book may be used or reproduced in any manner whatsoever without written permission except in the case of brief quotations embodied in critical articles and reviews. For information address Harper & Row, Publishers, Inc., 10 East 53rd Street, New York, N.Y. 10022.

International Standard Book Number: 0-06-168401-5
Library of Congress Catalog Card Number: 75-25946

Edited by Elizabeth L. C. Wolf, Caroline Eastman, Raleigh Wilson, Barbara E. Swart
Designed by Ben Kann
Composition by Susan Wiltse
Color work by Kevan Miller
Mechanically prepared by Sharon Sattler
Produced by Behaviordelia and Ben Kann
Printed by Kingsport Press

PREFACE

We've had a great deal of fun in writing and producing this book, as you can tell by just glancing at it. But we've also put our most serious intellectual efforts into it, though you may need to go beneath its surface before that becomes apparent. It's our heaviest work, in spite of our attempt at a light style. And in trying to deal with much of the field of current psychology, we've regressed to nineteeth century functionalism. That is, we look at what others may treat as mental phenomena, instead treating them as processes or actions. We ask what functions these processes serve in helping the species survive and in rewarding the actions of the individual.

We start with a biological and evolutionary view of psychology which plays a role throughout the book. Then we look at the learning, sensory, and perceptual processes. We've also found a functional framework useful in looking at much of the cognitive work in developmental psychology by Jean Piaget, as well as much of the cognitive work in social psychology. That same functionalist view allows us to look at a good deal of the work of Sigmund Freud as processes resulting from the inherited structure of the individual, and as rewards and punishers from the individual's past and present environment.

So we've covered much of the standard field of psychology, though not from an eclectic point of view — one that often results in a set of unrelated topics. Rather, we've taken a unified approach showing how many of the topics of psychology relate to each other; and, at the same time, showing how this unified view, the functionalist view, can unite some of these approaches — evolutionary, biological, behavioral, cognitive, social, and dynamic.

ABOUT THE CONTENT OF PSYCHOLOGY

We stress the knowledge the science of psychology has given us, trying to show how this knowledge allows us to understand our own everyday world, and trying to show how we can use it to help ourselves and others lead better lives. You may also wish to use the book, *Introduction to the Science of Psychology*, to study the methods used to find that knowledge. That book was written to go along with this one, and presents the science of psychology in a useful, clear, and pleasant manner.

WRITTEN WITH STUDENTS IN MIND

In many ways, we've tried to create a text designed for you students. First we present psychology so you can relate to it. We present most of the topics in terms of events selected to be of interest to you. Throughout, the book weaves a story about the lives of six students at Big State University, involved in the intro psych course, who portray concepts covered in this book through events in their lives. They reflect features of people we all know, including ourselves. In some cases, they seem a little extreme — much better, or much worse, than real life — in fact, we often picked extremes to make our points; but those extremes do exist. Look around you.

Besides showing some basic concepts, and some of our human features, we hope the story also makes the book more rewarding to read. We've written in an informal and personal style, hoping to make your studying easy and pleasant. We've made an effort not to fill the book with unused technical terms, while at the same time we've brought in key concepts, dealing with them as needed. We've wanted to avoid making the concepts of psychology appear simpler than they really are, as many of the concepts are indeed quite complex; instead, we've attempted to present these complex concepts in an informal and personal manner. In the same manner, Ed Badajos created the art to achieve these three goals, and to illustrate the basic concepts in a helpful way.

You can read more of what we have to say about writing style in the first part of the Notes section at the back of the book, where you'll also find the bibliography and occasional comments we've made about each chapter.

Though written and designed for students, we hope teachers, our colleagues, will also find this book of value, since we thought the things we put in the book are of value to us as professional psychologists as well as to you students.

SEXISM AND RACISM

We've hoped to give you some tools that may be of use to you in your efforts to help yourself and our society move toward a more just position. We've tried to do this by looking at some of the reasons for why things are as they are, rather than merely presenting things as we feel they should be. For instance, we mention the problem that not all women, or men, or Blacks, or Whites are indeed free from harmful cultural constraints in how they treat themselves and others. And those people who seem to be, may have mixed motives, coming as we all do from our traditional culture. The people in our story are often involved in these problems, sometimes as the present source of the problem, sometimes as the victim, sometimes as both the source and the victim, and sometimes as the solver.

We've also made an effort to write in a non-sexist, non-rascist style, by avoiding male words as generic pronouns (e.g., the reader..., he...), while showing people in roles other than the standard way they're stereotyped for their sex or race.

BASED ON INSTRUCTIONAL TECHNOLOGY

Instructional technology is the art and science of using what we know from psychology and other areas to develop improved ways of helping people learn. This book is a product of such instructional technology.

We've already mentioned some of the features of this technology. For instance, we've made the book as rewarding as we were able so you'll more likely read it, since you need to read it before you can learn from it.

We've tried to be fairly practical as we planned this book, putting aside many of our prejudices about what a book should be like, how much knowledge and how many facts it should contain, and how much you should learn from it. Instead we've gotten a rough idea of how much students really can learn from a single course, and used that as a guide to determine how much material we presented.

It seems best to present many of the key concepts of psychology, spending a good deal of time trying to get a feel for those concepts. We've avoided making a superficial sweep at all of the hundreds of concepts of psychology, knowing full well you'd only be able to master a small portion of those; and besides people forget most of those superficially presented concepts shortly after the final exam anyway. So rather than leave that whole process to chance, we selected some of the most crucial concepts, presenting them in a way we hope will help you make use of many of them long after this course is over. We hope this book and this course will have a great effect on your life and the way you look at your life.

We've also profited by the large amount of useful feedback from many students as well as teachers who were good enough to read parts of our work. The student feedback was of great value in helping us decide how to present psychology so you'll understand, value, and enjoy it.

We've also seen that you can learn best, if you don't have to play the guessing game: What am I supposed to learn? Learning works much better when everyone's up front about the course or text goals — what they expect you to learn. So we've given you a road map of sorts: all of the major concepts in each chapter are set off in bold face followed by a definition of that concept — a fact you'll find of immense value as you review for quizzes and exams. The concepts are also defined in the Glossary at the end of this book.

And we've placed study objectives at the end of each section, pointing to the crucial concepts. They're of great value in helping you find out whether you've gotten the key points from each chapter. These study objectives are the numbered questions at the end of each of the sections. You should answer them as you read the text, rereading any sections where you're not sure you've made the correct answer. You may also wish to use the workbook, *Introduction to the Concepts of Psychology,* to be even more certain of mastering the material or concepts of the present text. That book goes along with this one, as it's designed to help you master the study objectives for this text.

We hope that you'll enjoy this text, that you'll learn from it, and that you'll find something of use in it.

ACKNOWLEDGMENTS

We would like to thank the following academic reviewers for their very generous and helpful comments, though, of course, the point of view and any shortcomings the book may contain are our responsibility:

Galen Alessi, Western Michigan University; Gordon Anderson, Jamestown Community College; Peter J. Behrens, Pennsylvania State University (Allentown); Joseph A. Besso, Jr., North Texas State University; Kathy Buckheit, Southeast Community College; Roy E. Cain, Pan American University; Thomas D'Andrea, Haverford College; Erhard Eimer, Wittenberg University; Howard Farris, Western Michigan University; Nancy Faulk, Western Michigan University; Barb Fulton, Western Michigan University; William H. Glaze, North Texas State University; Ralph W. Hansen, Augustana College; Curt Hulteen, Blackhawk Community College; Marilyn Gilbert Komechak, North Texas State University; James Kopp, University of Texas (Arlington); Thomas Lawson, Western Michigan University; John Lelak, Sinclair Community College; Kass Lockhart, Western Michigan University; James R. Lott, North Texas State University; Kay Malott, Western Michigan University; Richard P. McGlynn, Texas Technological University; Jack Michael, Western Michigan University; George R. Mount, Mountainview College; Steve Mozara, Galveston Junior College; James A. Newell, Galveston Junior College; Ron Olson, Western Michigan University; Dan G. Perkins, Richland Community College; LeRoy P. Richardson, Montgomery County Community College; Arthur Snapper, Western Michigan University; Travis Thompson, University of Minnesota; Richard V. Wagner, Bates College; Robert J. Weber, Oklahoma State University; Mary Peterson Sojourner Weiss, University of Rochester; Scott Wood, Drake University.

To make this a student-oriented text, we've also found it very helpful to get feedback from students and others. In addition to the students involved in classroom validation, we would like to thank the following people for their knowledgeable suggestions:

Sharian Deering, Janet Ellis, Roy Elrod, Franklin Fordham, J. Michael Gautney, Dale General, Sigrid Glenn, Lyle Grant, Donna Hicks, Harvey Jacobs, Beverly Louisell, Susan Rucker, Walter Scott, Vivian Snapper, Greg Stikeleather, Tim Trainor, Suanne Williams.

The following clerical and research staff gave us truly excellent help beyond the reasonable call of duty:

June Asselin, Sharian Deering, Jan Delger, Sue O'Connor, Susan Rucker, Mary Anne Slomski, Marilyn Walker, Elizabeth Whaley.

We'd also like to thank our proofreaders, Frank Galloway and Mary Ann Bowman.

17 SOCIAL VALUES

Social factors cause us to have certain learned rewards and punishers. In turn, those learned values affect much of what we do and who we like.

18 ATTITUDE CHANGE

Women's liberation provides many good examples of the factors affecting our attitudes about crucial issues.

19 MORALITY

Unlike lower animals, we civilized creatures **need** moral control to survive. But moral control is a fragile process, sometimes causing problems. Various levels of moral control affect how we respond to the chance to cheat in college.

20 SOCIAL ROLES

We tend to play the same social roles in the same setting, though we may switch roles when the setting changes. This depends on what roles are rewarded — whether we're rewarded for being the scientist or the theologian, the model child or the college radical.

21 SIGMUND FREUD AND PERSONALITY

We can still learn much from Freud's classic theory with its stress on sexual and aggressive rewards, social-moral control, and rational control.

22 CONSCIOUSNESS: MEANINGS AND DEFINITIONS

We learn self-awareness from the people who affect how we use our language.

23 CONSCIOUSNESS AS PRIVATE ACTIVITY

We learn from and are rewarded by our fantasies, by what we say to ourselves in private. Those fantasies can control what we do later in reality.

24 CONSCIOUSNESS AND ITS LIMITS

Pain, hypnosis, and meditation are all related to self-awareness, and much confusion is eliminated in the process.

25 EMOTIONS

Emotions are our physiological reactions to crucial events in our world. Often emotions prepare us to deal with those events though sometimes they may harm us. Such reactions may also function as unlearned and learned rewards and punishers.

PSYCHOLOGICAL PROBLEMS

26 HANS SELYE AND STRESS

In coping with stress, we may find ways that give us longer, more healthy, less stressful, lives, but it's always risky business.

27 NEUROSES

Inept patterns of handling stress take many forms called neuroses. These neuroses often fail to fade away, persisting throughout a person's life, sometimes leading to psychoses and confinement.

28 BEHAVIOR PROBLEMS

Problem behaviors occur because of the strong control of immediate rewards. Better actions may not occur, though they pay off more in the long run, because, at best, distant rewards exert weak control.

29 PSYCHOSES

Often an environment may do much to produce and maintain psychotic actions, though it seems warm and loving. It's always worthwhile to insure that normal actions are the ones that get the rewards, even with psychoses that may have organic roots.

30 RETARDATION

New and powerful training techniques provide the greatest help for the retarded as they help overcome some of the problems caused by brain damage and genetic and congenital factors.

THERAPIES

31 B. F. SKINNER AND BEHAVIOR MODIFICATION

Behavior mod, a useful new approach, deals with human problems, ranging from the training of the retarded, to the bizarre actions of the psychotic, to the little, everyday trials we all confront.

32 JOSEPH WOLPE AND BEHAVIOR THERAPY

This new therapy helps get rid of many problems, such as those involving sex, test anxiety, and lack of assertiveness.

CONTENTS

BIOSOCIAL BASES

PSYCHOLOGICAL PROBLEMS

THERAPIES

PSYCHOLOGY

CHAPTER 1 INTRODUCTION

OF MICE AND SYSTEMS

"Present your yellow top card . . .
Present your yellow top card . . .
Present your yellow top card . . .
Present your yellow top card . . ."
A yellow sign flashed the message
as the transcribed voice droned
on. "Present your yellow top
card."

Sid looked at the yellow
top card he had clutched for the
fifty or so minutes he had been
waiting in line: FIELDS SIDNEY
W. 2 201 NR DUM *The letters
and numbers meant something,
of course, but what? The "2" he
guessed meant that he was a
sophomore. The NR? Hmmm —
could mean non-resident. Too
bad, if he was a resident, he
wouldn't have to pay such high
fees. The "201"? He had heard
that it stood for your major. In
Sid's case, "201" would have to
mean Psychology.*

Sid closed his eyes. Sounds
were all around; voices — faceless
like himself, caught in the
torment of registration.

PSYCHOLOGY

Definition

Yes, Sid Fields, one of the characters that we'll stay with through the pages of this book, is a psychology major. He plans to earn a degree in that subject — as perhaps many who are reading this book intend to do. Less than a century ago neither Sid, nor you for that matter, could have majored in psychology. At that time psychology was not a separate field of study. It was part of philosophy. People who studied psychology were still called philosophers.

But what is psychology in our day and age? What do psychologists do? Like most people, Sid isn't quite sure. Sure, he's heard that psychology is "the study of the mind" — whatever that means. The truth is that it doesn't mean much at all. Today, most psychologists wouldn't go along with such a dated description of what they're supposed to be doing. Their big complaint would likely involve the term, "mind". As it turns out, it's a vague term that so many people take to mean such different things that in net result, it means little or nothing.

What do psychologists study then if they don't study the mind? As you will see, they study behavior, and a wide range of events dealing with behavior in both humans, and other creatures. We'll talk about most of these events. Some in more detail than others.

Psychology: the study of behavior.

- 1 Within what discipline did psychology first begin?
- 2 Why do most modern psychologists object to defining psychology as "the study of the mind"?
- 3 What is psychology?

Order

"Hey, move up!" Sid's eyes snapped open. There was a gap in the line in front of him.

"Sorry." There were only two in front of him now. Sid could see the girl who was taking the ID pictures. *Why was she taking so long?* Sid thought to himself. *Why did it all have to be such a pain? If enough planning and time went into it, it could be worked out — no standing in line, no hassles — smooth as silk. But then, didn't he expect too much?* Sid thought of Uncle Jason, his father's oldest brother. Uncle Jason had studied to be a rabbi; then stricken by polio when he was eighteen, he gave up his studies — but not his wisdom. Sid smiled. He could almost see Uncle Jason now; his head twisted to the side, chin cocked outward like a bulldog — scars of the illness.

"Order — psht! What do we know about order? A fable, a story we tell ourselves. If things run well, if they go smooth, it is a mistake, a freak. Mark my words, there's too much to the cosmos, too much to run, too much to ever know. What farce to presume to run the world!"

At last it was Sid's turn — he was next. *But what was wrong?* The girl was fooling around with the machine, a grim and harried look on her face. It seemed to Sid that her tinkering was endless. *Would he spend the rest of his life here in the men's gym — grow old and die, here at registration?*

The girl walked over to Sid. She looked very upset. "Look," she said, "something's wrong with the machine. It happens — it just gets messed up." Sid gulped in spite of himself.

"What do I do now?" he asked.

"I'll just mark your card, so you can go on," the girl said. "Keep looking for a notice in the *Daily.* It should let you know about getting an ID picture made later — okay?"

"Okay," Sid said. He tried to look friendly and unbothered.

"I'm sorry," she said. "God, what a hassle!"

"Yeah," Sid said. She left him to go break the bad news to the long line of students.

Sid had seen enough carnage for one day — he moved quickly away, following the arrows to station seven. Maybe Uncle Jason was right — maybe the idea that there was order was a lie — a lie we tell each other that lets us go on putting up with this topsy-turvy, rag-tag mess, without rhyme or reason, that doesn't give a good diddle about any of us! Sidney laughed and looked around him at the chaos. *Better not ask us poor schnooks about it just now.*

The nature of it all

Is it as Sid's Uncle suggests — are all outcomes merely by chance? Perhaps. But for now it appears otherwise — some events lead in a quite regular fashion to others. Dark clouds precede rain; a seed planted in the soil brings forth a plant. The study of how some events seem to produce others is called "science".

Science: the systematic study of how events or occurrences are related to the production of other events or occurrences.

When one group of events always yields the same outcome, we say they cause it to happen. "Cause" is the key word here. Once all the conditions are there, the outcome is bound to occur. This used to be called 'cause and effect', but nowadays we speak of it as "determinism". When the correct conditions are there, the outcome is determined.

Determinism: the notion that an event is produced or results from the active presence of a precise set of conditions.

The science of psychology is like other sciences in terms of the logic it's based on. What people do is just as much "caused" as any other event in nature. Thus, like other sciences, psychology has two main parts: analysis, where the tie-ins among events — causes and effects — are found; and application, where these facts are used to control outcomes, making desired results occur.

Analysis: the task of finding out and describing the precise set of conditions that give rise to specific events.

Application: the bringing together of the needed conditions in order to produce certain desired events or outcomes.

- ■ 4 What is meant by the notion that what happens to us is merely by chance?
- ■ 5 How did science originate?
- ■ 6 Define science.
- ■ 7 Briefly outline what is meant by "cause and effect".
- ■ 8 What is the modern term that has replaced cause and effect?
- ■ 9 How is the science of psychology like all other sciences?
- ■10 What are the two main parts or efforts in the science of psychology?
- ■11 Describe the first branch or part of the science of psychology.
- ■12 Describe the second branch of the science of psychology.
- ■13 Can you think of an example of how analysis and applied psychology interact?

The haves and have nots

As Sid moved toward his destiny at station seven, he passed by a group of five husky students in the midst of a heavy rap.

"You're fulla it, Red!" Liggit said. All the men wore T-shirts marked "Property of BSU", and the emblem of Big State University. Coach Purvis' plan was to have the football squad sign up for classes at the same time. "Group reliance", he called it. The team would eat, sleep, study as a unit — take the same courses when they could.

"I ain't gonna take no chemistry course, not this nigger!"

"Come on man," Red coaxed. "It'll be a blast. We get ta mix up them chemicals and stuff like that. We can make us a bomb!"

"Yeah," Ragsdale said, "you do that Red. You do that and blow your honky head off."

"You know, I sure would like ta make one a them potents," Curly said. "You drink a glass a that an' it turns you inta one a them mean muthas."

"Whada' you mean, Curly; you already Dr. Goof-off!"

Someone came from the crowd to join the group. He was dressed like the others. Standing at the edge of the huddle of burly athletes, he was among them, but apart. His name was Juke.

"John Henry Jackson!" Liggit said, as he caught a glimpse of Juke. All heads snapped toward him. "Welcome to the goin's on, my man!"

"Hey," Red said after things had died down. "Let's ask Juke."

"Yeah, Juke," Liggit said. "This guy here wants us to sign up for chem."

"What about it, Juke?" Okie asked.

"Chemistry — no man." Juke shook his head. "No way!"

"Why'n the hell not!" Red said.

"Cause they'll flunk you out sure as my butt's black — that's why!"

"Come on, Juke. Hell, so maybe we'll have to study a little."

"Study? What's wrong with this cat? Hey, man, what you been putting in your Gatoraide?" Ragsdale said.

"Study won't get it, Red. You gotta be a brain to pass that course. You can work your tail off, get a tutor, start going ta Sunday School, and that still won't cut it. I'm talkin' about knowin' what's goin' on — dig? Smart is something you gotta have in front — gotta be born that way. There's things some people never can learn!"

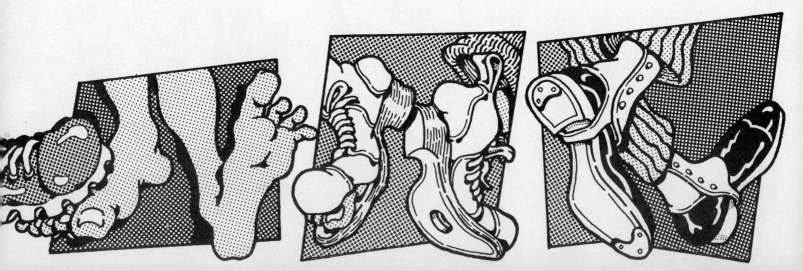

Individual differences

Juke's turned on to a fact about people that has kept psychology busy right from the start: We're all different from each other. Our looks or features, what we like and dislike, the size and shape of our bodies — simply aren't the same.

Another basic difference involves skills. In our culture the worth of people is measured in terms of what they can do — skills they can perform, problems they can solve. Skill in jumping, running, and making your body work, make a good athlete. Other skills — and the degree to which they can be performed — are basic to making a passing mark in chemistry or other college courses — even psych.

Juke's telling his friends and brothers to stay out of courses that call for skills they're not likely to have. He's telling them that there are individual differences between them and others who will pass the course with little trouble. These individual differences Juke suggests are crucial.

Individual differences: the idea that people differ in very basic ways along various characteristics.

***

After awhile, Juke left the team, working his way alone through the morass of warm bodies to the class card tables. He took a trial class slip from his pocket and checked the list of courses. There it was; big as life: Chem 100. The same course he'd hassled about a few minutes ago. Seeing it on his list gave Juke a twinge of guilt. He'd been rough on old Red, but he was tryin' to tell it straight. Red, Rags, Okie,

Liggit, they'd all flunk. So why was he different? Well, he just was. His dad never got out of high school — his mother only went to the fifth grade. It didn't matter.

Juke looked again at the list of courses. Some pretty heavy stuff there — could he make it? No, it wouldn't be like high school. *Hell. Man, I just gotta find out what this here nigger can do!*

Just then he became aware that he was staring at a girl who walked toward him from the other end of the aisle. She was tall and slight. She stopped for an instant before going into the women's room and glanced up — just long enough to see Juke staring at her. Turning without a flicker, she went through the door.

- ■14 The fact that people are not alike in many respects has provided the basis for a topic of study in psychology. What is it?
- ■15 What is probably more important in terms of how people are different than physical characteristics — at least as far as the study of psychology is concerned?

INHERITANCE, LEARNING, AND EVOLUTION

Another topic closely tied to skills, and their lack or ample supply, has to do with how the person got them. Some things — color of eyes, body features, etc. — we acquire when we're born. They are inherited — passed on at conception. But what about memory? Recalling phone numbers, words, ways to do things? Some believe these skills are likewise passed on from parents. Juke's idea is "you either got it or you don't". In this sense Juke is a "nativist", meaning he also seems to believe that if "you don't have it, you can't get it." What's the answer? Is Juke right — or wrong? In later pages, we will try to find out what skills can be acquired and separate them from those

that only the "right" parents can give us.

Nativist: a person who tends to believe that people are born with basic skills that cannot be acquired through learning or experience.

But sometimes there's a basic change from parent to offspring. A child may be able to do things his parents never could. When life forms change in a gradual way across time and generations in their skill to get along or survive, it is called evolution. The term is most often applied to biology, where it refers to changes in a species structure that occur from parent to offspring. But

this is far too narrow a way to look at it. We will also discuss other kinds of evolution in this book.

Evolution: a change, that occurs across generations, in the ability of a type of creature to deal with its environment.

- ■16 What is another area in psychology that's closely tied to skills and how they differ from person to person?
- ■17 What are the two ways mentioned in this chapter that a person acquires skills?
- ■18 What is a nativist?
- ■19 Define evolution.

The real things in life

Mae Robinson was at last safe behind the door of the women's room. "Damn him! He had no right to look at me that way. If he thinks I'm just another black woman waiting like a melon to be plucked from the vine, well . . ." Mae stopped short. "But that's what I am — another black woman. Wasn't that the point? Wasn't that why I came to BSU in the first place?"

Last year, Mae had gone to Christian College, a small private liberal arts college, across town. They treated her well there — a full ride, tuition, room — they paid it all. Pretty and bright, Mae was catered to, wined and dined. She could see what they thought. It was in their faces. "See — see how liberal we are! We love black people, too!"

It was fine for a time. At mid-term she'd had second and third thoughts. She loved English — her major — but wanted an active hand in shaping the future, in helping to solve the problems that black people — her people — had to face. By the end of the spring term she had decided to leave Christian, to go to BSU in the fall. There were many blacks there — she could learn their problems and try to help. She would change her major to psych.

Mae looked at herself in the mirror. "Well, Miss Hotshot Do-Good. Now what?" Mae said aloud to herself. She looked around to see if she had been overheard. Voices came from the lounge area.

"So I said to her, 'Well, Mom, what do you think the "real" thing is in college?' and she said, real huffy and bent outa shape, 'Obviously, Catherine, it's to get something in your head besides pot and sex; like for instance, we'd like you to learn enough to get a job someday! At least, Catherine, that's what your father and I think we're sacrificing for!'"

"Hell," another voice said.

"It really burned me. I got ticked at her. 'Look', I said, 'no matter what you think about it, mother, there's more to life than just saying back a bunch of dumb facts so you can get some dippy job! Like — I'd like to find myself; you know — wisdom, knowledge, learn something about people and relationships — because frankly, Mother, I don't want to grow up to be the same uptight bitch you are!'"

Mae winced. Had she really said that to her mother? But there was more to it than coarse talk. It was the way the girl felt about school. It was a new idea for Mae, and there was a lot of it here. This morning in line she had heard two students talking.

"But what's so great about Lit 200? You just said you don't learn anything," one of them said.

"A 'C' man! No study, no tests, and it's in the bag to begin with."

Mae couldn't help it. She got mad at these people. "School" — she even liked the way the word sounded. Books, teachers — these were sacred to her; they always had been. It wasn't true for others — that much was clear. Yes, there was a lot to learn about here at BSU. Not all about blacks, and not all would be pleasant.

She left the women's room. There was only one more course she needed. Classes started Monday. The transfer had been hectic. Oh, to have the weekend off! She would go to a movie or two, read some good fiction, maybe sew on the dress she was making. That was out. Reading lists were handed out with class cards in four of her classes. There was work due Monday. Some of the profs here sure didn't waste time. Her weekend would be spent in the library. Mae felt a little sad. *A new campus, new places to see and explore, and I'm going to be stuck in the library. Do I always have to do what I'm supposed to?*

Function and feeling

Most of us break the world down into what goes on in it — what happens around us and to us — and how we feel about it. Some ask: Which is more crucial — what we do or how we feel? Mae is surprised at some of her fellow students because they seem to think that feeling good, being happy, finding themselves, is the only goal. Things they are told to do — study, plan, work, tote that briefcase, lift that book — are seen as a drag and a bore. Mae could be right in putting them down at that. But on the other hand, even Mae, tough as she is, still feels the strain of her chores. She often longs to be free of the yoke. Well, what should she, they, we, do? We've got to do what it takes to make things go — but can we risk shutting out feelings?

■20　Briefly summarize the conflict many people have in terms of functioning and feelings.

Human vs. the system

If Mae had seen the clenched fists and red face of the man she passed at the English table, she would know that not all BSU students take school lightly.

"But I don't think you understand . . ."

"On the contrary, Mr. uh, Mr. . . ."

"LaPorte."

"Yes, Mr. LaPorte, it's not I who fails to understand, I dare say, but you. One cannot take 102 unless one has first gained an acceptable mark in 101. It is what is known as a 'prerequisite'. You do know what the word means, I trust, Mr. uh . . ."

Chet felt his ears burn, students were looking at him. He took a deep breath, and set his feet.

"Look, it's this way. I got a wife and family and a job at the Central Street Standard Station. I'd like to keep my wife and family, so I gotta keep my job. The only course I can take is 102."

"This may come as a surprise to you, but I, too, have a wife and I sympathize to the utmost with your struggle for an education, God knows. But none of these data alter the fact that 101 must be completed before one can be enrolled in 102."

"But I just . . ."

"I don't want to think you're a dullard, but you must grasp the simple truth that if one were allowed to take 102 before having 101, he or she would undoubtedly flunk it with all possible alacrity!"

Chet turned his face downward and glared at his shoetops. He fought back the choking sounds that wanted to eek from his throat. He couldn't think of anything else to say. *Picky little gnats, little people pulling him down. Was everyone out to get him? Would Mickey Mouse never die?*

"Would you please tell me where I can find the Department Chairman?" Chet asked solemnly.

"Surely you're not going to bother him with this?"

"I want to see the Chairman."

The man behind the desk looked at Chet for perhaps the first time. The tenseness, the grim set of his jaw — an older student — these were things he hadn't noticed. He became afraid of Chet. It showed in the way his eyes began to dart around as though looking for help. "If you must absolutely have it your way, I'll oblige you." He reached for the proper card. "However, I think it only fair to say that I'm not doing you a favor, as you'll all too soon discover."

Chet grabbed the card and turned to walk to a nearby standing table where he would fill it out.

"I'm not doing any favors for the instructor, either," the professor yelled, his courage bolstered as Chet walked away.

SYSTEM INSENSITIVITY AND INDIVIDUAL NEEDS

Is nature on our side? Does it care about us humans? Sorry, but "no" to both questions. We've come to accept the fact that nature is not on ours — or anyone's — side. Nature is. That's all. We're on our own. If we were foolish enough to leave it up to nature we could end up in a bad way. Clearly, our job is to improve on the odds that nature gives. This often involves getting around our own (human) natures. When people try to build a way of doing something better than it would be done by nature or chance, it's called a system.

System: the placing of tasks, personnel, and machines into a unit to achieve a somewhat complex end result or function.

As you might suspect, a university is a system for educating and training people. It does much more than that, and is thus really many systems within a system.

Both Chet and Sid have figured out that there's a lot of slop in the BSU system. This is true to some extent of all systems. How people relate to the system is a topic we will court throughout this book.

- ▪21   Whose side is nature on?
- ▪22   What have humans built to improve on nature?
- ▪23   Define system.
- ▪24   There were two aspects of the relationship between the individual and the system that we will discuss in this book. What were they?

THE SEXES

Chet looked at his watch, almost three. Carol said she would meet him at the snack bar. She was on her afternoon break from the Mental Health Clinic where she worked as a receptionist.

When inside the snack bar, Chet spotted Carol at once. She was smiling; her hand in the air waving to him. "Hi babe," Chet said. He kissed Carol quickly on the cheek.

"How'd it go?" Carol asked. "Did you get all the courses you wanted?"

"Yeah," Chet said. "But it took some doin'. This jerk from English wasn't going to let me into 102. I talked him into it, though."

"But aren't you supposed to take 101 first?"

"That's what that little twerp gave me such a hard time about."

"But 102's hard, Chet! You'll never pass; you know how bad you were at comp in high school!"

"I'm not goin' to flunk! What the hell do you know about it?"

"Chet, I've had the course.

I wasn't always a typist. I was almost a senior when I quit to get married, remember?"

"Here we go again. You were on your way to being a big hot-shot scholar but I spoiled all of that, right? So maybe I'll take your job and you go to school!"

Here comes Dawn!

Dawn Baker started to feel better. The whole thing had been a shock — not the lines and the mass of people. She liked crowds — she liked watching them, wondering about them. Where were they coming from? Where were they going? Would they be fun to know? Would she impress them? Could she get them to like her? No, it wasn't the crowds that bothered her. It wasn't the system either. That was simple. All you had to do was read and do what it said; easy as pie. It was her hurt feelings. So many people didn't even seem to know she was there; didn't treat her special. It made her feel strange; empty inside — like she was lost. Maybe that's the way it was when you're dead. Dawn shuddered.

She looked around her at the crowd in the student union. They were relaxed, not running scared, hassled, harried. There was time, now.

At Central High she'd been head cheerleader, a big cheese in the student council, prom queen, homecoming queen — a hotshot. But what now? Little fish in a big pond? A lot of pretty faces and nice bods in the big U? Sure, she'd heard that. So what? It was time to make her play. The group around the soda fountain had thinned out. There was room for them to see her. Now. The camera in her head started to roll. She could see herself get up slowly; not too fast, easy, relaxed, poised — that's it. Now, smooth the skirt — good! Perfect! Shoulders back, not too far. Careful; walk loose like she was strolling down by a country stream. That's it. It was working. Little fish in a big pond, huh? Maybe not. The boy at the fountain came to take her order. She wetted her lips and opened her eyes wider.

"A small coke please — very little ice — if you can manage it." She smiled — a slight trick with her lips. She could see her words lilting from her lovely mouth, hanging like silver puffs in the air.

Female-male, male-female roles

There are many things to look into when the roles of the sexes in the culture are the topic — history, for instance. How did the roles get to be the way they have been up to now? What part does and did biology play? To what extent are roles merely learned or products of culture? And lastly, what about the future?

How will being equal work? What about the struggle itself — will it cost more than it gains?

■25 What are some important issues regarding female-male, male-female roles that will be discussed in this book? (Name three.)

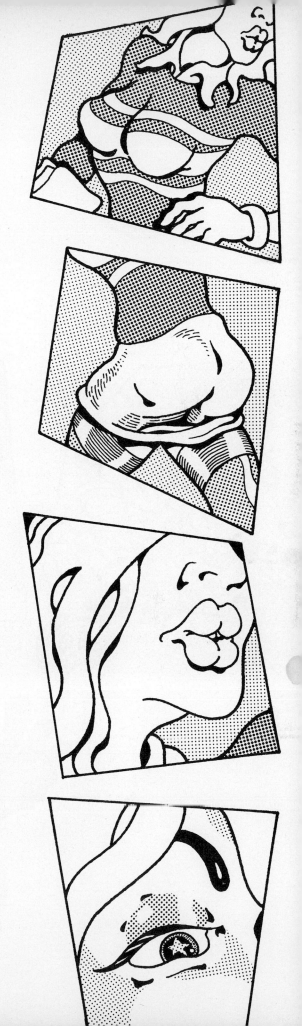

It's a new year

The football hung in the air for a month. *Come on, Christmas!* Juke said to himself. *Ain't you never gonna' get here?*

When it came, it fell lightly, like an angel cake in his arms. Juke hugged the ball. His cleats caught tight in the turf, the muscles of his legs strained, plunging him forward, shooting him past the red jerseys, grasping hands betrayed by the motion of their bodies. Seconds later, Juke was in the end zone.

"Ohwee!" Juke said. "This is goin' ta be some kind of a year!"

***

Mae came back to the dorm at 8:30. She pushed the elevator button and waited. A few yards from her three fellows, two of them in tweedy coats, a third wearing a BSU letter sweater, talked to a girl. Mae looked away at first, but her eyes returned to gather in more detail on the girl. She was striking. In fact, she was gorgeous. She could have been the co-ed in a TV ad — she was perfect — if you liked that kind of thing. Mae didn't.

"If you really mean that, you could go have a few beers and a pizza with us," one of the men said.

"Beer! I couldn't do that. After all those cokes I'd wet my pants for sure." They all laughed.

Just then the elevator came. Mae got on fast. The scene with the girl turned her off. *High school stuff,* she thought.

***

Mae took a shower and changed into jeans. She was making a list of what she had to do in the library when she heard a key turn in the door.

"Hi there," a tousled head of blond hair poked through the doorway. "I'm Dawn — Dawn Baker. I guess I'm your roommate." It was the girl Mae'd just seen in the lobby. She was struggling with a key that was caught in the lock, trying to balance an armload of new books, a frown on her face. She turned and beamed at Mae, the frown gone in a split second. "Could you give me a hand here?"

Mae took the books without reply, and put them on the table.

Dawn looked at Mae, puzzled by her silence. "I am in the right room — 526?"

"Yes — I guess so. I'm Mae Robinson."

"Good to meet you, Mae. Are you a freshman, too?"

"Soph — transfer student."

"Oh," Dawn said. "And you're black. I mean — of course you're black; anyone can . . . I mean, I always wanted a black roommate." Dawn was happy with what she'd said. She waited like a puppy that thought it was about to get petted.

"Yes," Mae said. There was an awkward pause as Dawn waited for her to say more.

"Well — I guess I better go; these dudes're waiting downstairs. It's gonna be a great year, Mae." Dawn took Mae's hand and shook it. "I know we're going to be the best of friends."

***

For some unknown reason Sid had been given a room in the wing of the dorm that housed the BSU athletes. All those jocks and Sid. Well, maybe it'd be okay. His roommate seemed like a good man — a footballer they called "Juke". Seemed kinda quiet, really. Sid liked him. Oh well, time to take a look at the new books he'd just paid a fortune for.

The pages crackled as Sid opened one of them. Holding the book at arm's length, he read the title softly aloud: "*Psychology.* Well, *Psych,* we'll just see what I know after I've read you that I don't know now!"

BIOPHYSICAL BASES

We set our stage in the first chapter. And, no doubt, you set yours too: you survived your registration hassels; maybe you're through drops-and-adds; and your psych class has met once or twice. You've just met our six main characters: Mae, Dawn, Sid, Juke, Chet, and Carol; and you've also met some of the main characters in the new drama of your own life.

So now we'll work through the rest of the term together. We'll look at psychology — which concerns what we do and why we do it — we'll do this so you can see what's going on in your own life. This way you'll understand both psych and yourself better.

In the chapters of this first section we'll look at some of the basic facts of psychology — facts that apply to simpler creatures as well as to all of us. We'll look at the way our biology and physical structure affect what we do and why we do it. In other words, we'll look at the biophysical bases of behavior — we'll look at psychology as a branch of biology.

Much of biology is based on the notion of evolution, often with complex forms of life evolving from simpler forms. So we'll look at how evolution applies to psych, seeing that the creature's biology causes it to act in certain ways. But we'll also see that the ways the creature's actions affect its world, in turn cause that creature's structure to evolve in certain ways. Structure affects action, action affects structure, structure affects action, etc. We'll ask: how did our actions evolve, how did we get to be the way we are today? And we'll discover there are always reasons for the way we've come to act as we do, though those reasons may be a challenge to find.

In this biophysical section we'll look at the evolution of behavior from basic to complex forms. We'll also cite many facts about behavior; and they're just that — facts — statements so well-proven that most experts agree about them. But we'll also tie them together with a theory of the evolution of behavior; and the theory is also just that — a theory — a guess good enough to help you make sense out of this host of facts, and to help you look at your world. So in this section, we'll bounce back and forth between the actions of simple creatures and the actions of us complex humans; we hope you enjoy the ride.

CHAPTER 2
BIOPHYSICAL
STRUCTURE

COMPLEXITY AND INSTABILITY OF STRUCTURE

When atoms collide

". . . on and on it goes — the same process; atoms collide, neutrons fuse, and there emerges from this strife, a grander, more eloquent structure. A more complex atom, a new wealth of electrons whirling about its center. Atomic evolution? Biology? Life? Call it that or call it falling in love — for in some way it all seems the same." Dr. Burt paused, the bell sounded, the period was over.

Sid Fields burst loose from the spell that had held him fast for the past fifty minutes. Possessed with courage foreign to him, he leaped to his feet and started to applaud. Others joined in at once. Soon the lecture hall was filled with the sound of two hundred intro physics students paying tribute. Professor Burt smiled, bowed slightly, and left the podium. Sid started up the ramp toward the exit, still looking back at Dr. Burt who'd not left the stage. Then something stopped his progress — something soft and yielding.

"'Scuse me," Sid said. He jumped back, like he'd done something dreadful. The woman he'd just knocked into was turned toward him but her eyes went past him, down front toward Professor Burt. Sid saw a cardboard badge pinned on her sweater. It said: "Back the Bulldogs! BSU BOOSTERS. My name is Dawn Baker." She didn't seem to notice that Sid had slammed into her; made no sign to show that she'd heard his apology.

"Isn't Dr. Burt just marvelous!" she said, looking at Sid for the first time.

"She's a brilliant woman," Sid mumbled.

"That was a fine thing you did," she said. "You were the first, you know. They all followed you."

"The first?" Sid asked.

"Yes — I was sitting behind you. You were the first to stand and applaud."

"Oh — yeah . . . uh . . . thanks." *Was it true? Maybe it was. Good thing he hadn't known it at the time.*

"It was a great lecture. She had a way of making it all fit — you know what I mean?"

"Uh . . . yeah, I think so. Relevant."

"Yes! Relevant, that's it."

"Well . . . look," Dawn said. "I've got to get back to the dorm — I live at Co-ed. You aren't going that way are you?"

"I live there too," Sid said. "Come to think of it there is a book I forgot to get," he lied. "Might as well go get it now."

"Perfect!" Dawn said. "Now what was it you were saying?"

When people first started to observe the heavens, the world, life and matter all around, they wanted to know what was going on. What was nature up to? What was it trying to do? Not that it was a person or anything like that — but where was it going? Some looked and saw only motion. Matter was restless, ever changing. Order — or what appeared to be order — was only a phase in this eternal flux. Others also saw change, but believed it went in a certain direction. All things moved toward peace, stability, a state of rest.

If you choose to support either of the notions above, you'll have no trouble finding facts, and others who see things that way, to support you. But in this chapter, we're going to try to get you to consider still another aspect of nature — that all around us, even at this instant, some parts of nature are moving toward ever greater complexity.

Even now our sun, a "young" star, is in the first simple stage of what may be called "atomic evolution".

Atomic evolution: a process occurring in nature where, through fusion of nuclei, simple atoms evolve into more complex ones.

The sun is called a young star because it's almost pure hydrogen. Hydrogen is the simplest element, having only one electron whirling around its nucleus. When nuclei of two hydrogen atoms collide, their neutrons fuse under intense heat, releasing energy that comes to us as sunshine. What remains is a more complex atom — no longer hydrogen, but helium. There are now two electrons that surround a slightly altered nucleus. As the process goes on, nuclei of these helium atoms will collide, creating more complex atoms still — beryllium, carbon, oxygen. So it goes, right on down the line, each new atom more complex than the atoms from which it fused. Is there no limit — can we expect the sun will one day become a ball of pure uranium, the most complex atoms found in nature — uranium with ninety-two busy electrons whirling about a heavy complex nucleus?

- 1 What do we imply about the composition of our sun by calling it a "young" star?
- 2 What atomic process is going on with our sun?
- 3 Define atomic evolution.

Atomic complexity and instability

But what's so great about uranium? Why does it end there? Is there something magic about the atomic number ninety-two? In order to answer these questions, a new concept — instability — is needed. As atoms become complex they reach a point where they become unstable. The nuclei of these atoms become so loaded with protons and other sub-atomic parts that they can't remain intact — they start to break apart. Too much complexity. When atoms split or break apart, it's called "atomic fission".

Physicists have shown how greater complexity leads to splitting by producing elements in the atomic lab that are more complex than uranium. These atoms are so unstable that they last for only a fraction of a second — then break apart.

These two concepts, complexity and instability, may help us make more sense out of nature. We've seen how they apply at the atomic level. Since they also apply elsewhere, they can be thought of as two basic principles of structure.

Principle of Complexity: as matter exists and survives at any level (atoms, molecules, cells, creatures, cultures, etc.) changes occur that tend to make some units at that level more complex.

Principle of Instability: as a system reaches a certain point in complexity, it becomes unstable which tends to limit further complexity — at least at the level of that system.

- 4 If scientists have created more complex elements than uranium where are they now?
- 5 What are the two concepts that have been called basic principles of structure?
- 6 State the Principle of Complexity.
- 7 State the Principle of Instability.

The soup of creation

"Cummere, Jackson, I got somethin' to show you!"

Juke saw that it was that LaPorte guy — Chet LaPorte. *Musta found something new to gripe about.* Though he'd only been at it a short while, Juke liked the job with the P.E. department. He was assigned to help Coach Krub conduct the freshman Physical Conditioning classes. As it turned out, Coach Krub left it all up to Juke. Juke found it wasn't a bad deal. For the most part, the guys were okay, but a few of them — like this LaPorte . . .

"Dammit, snap it up!" Chet said. "This's somethin' you and the rest of this screwed up P.E. bunch should see." Juke felt a rush of anger.

When they reached the showers, Chet stopped and pointed inside. "Look at that!" he ordered. Juke peered inside. Two huge centipedes wriggled on the dimly lighted floor. There were three or four small slugs, a half dozen other long-legged spider-looking things. "All the money I gotta pay to take this jerk course I didn't want to take in the first place — and then I gotta take a shower in the middle of some damn chamber a' creepy horrors!"

Juke scowled, rubbed his nose. "You're right, man," he said.

"What?" Chet said — it was like he hadn't heard.

"I don't blame you — I wouldn't go in there either. Look, go down the hall and shower up in the staff room. It's okay. I'll see the man 'bout this. Somethin' gotta be done."

"Well, I just thought I'd let you . . . Down the hall?"

"Yeah, to the right."

"Jackson, you're okay."

Juke stood for some time looking at the creatures in the damp, warm, concrete shower. *Don't want 'em to tear this place down,* Juke thought. *Save it for tourists. This shower's so old — I wouldn't be surprised to find this's where it all started — where life began!*

Chemical evolution

Matter becomes more complex when elements come together to form compounds. Atoms of one element unite with atoms of other elements to form a new unit of matter — the molecule. The study of how elements combine to form compounds is called "chemistry". Compounds, too, vary in how simple or complex they are. Numbers of single elements join, but the limit of instability crops up again. Compounds of simple elements can only go so far before they become unstable. At this point instability is surmounted as single elements start to combine with existing compounds — and compounds combine with other compounds.

Molecules that contain carbon often bind together in large groups or chains to which molecules of simple compounds attach themselves. Vast chains and networks of molecules are formed in this manner. These carbon compounds are called "organic compounds". Their study is, of course, the subject of organic chemistry.

Compounds that contain hydrogen and oxygen can become monster size, highly complex organic groups. There's no theoretical limit to how complex they could get — yet there seems to be a practical one. When they grow too large they tend to break apart — instability.

■ 8 Atoms of different elements come together to form a new unit called _____.
■ 9 The most complex chemical compounds are called _____ compounds. They always contain _____. When they also contain _____ and _____, they have no theoretical limit to size or complexity.

Molecular evolution

Organic compounds are of great concern to us all because food we eat is made of organic compounds; also, fuels — coal, oil, wood — are organic. But others study complex organic molecules for the sake of basic science. They presume that the simple protein substance emerged from amino acids and that throughout this time these molecules evolved, assuming many new forms and becoming more complex. This process, called "molecular evolution", generated the first primitive cells that led to the contemporary cell's basic unit of life.

Molecular evolution: evolution of the molecular structure.

■10 Why are organic compounds of interest to all people?
■11 Why are organic compounds of interest to scientists who are trying to pinpoint the origin of life?
■12 Thought question: What are living things made of?
■13 From what organic compounds are protein substances made?
■14 Define molecular evolution.

Life created in the lab

There was a time when everyone's idea of a mad scientist was a person trying to create life in a test tube. But for decades many tough-minded scholars and technicians have been working hard to do just that — generate life — trying to chart the likely course or courses of molecular evolution. These scientists must keep their methods simple — processes that involve heat, elements, and water and other compounds that were around when the earth first formed. It has to be an open system, too — no pressure cooker or other fancy gear. Nature didn't have it, so neither can they.

From what they've learned, it looks like the stages of this

evolution must have gone something like this: first, simple non-organic compounds formed into organic compounds — organic mass. As the organic matter became more complex, it yielded the first amino acids — at first only a few, but then as many as twenty or so types or kinds. The amino acids combined to form the protein-like substance, or proteinoid — the forebear of all protein. All of these steps have been done in the lab under the same conditions as must have obtained on the new planet Earth.

The newest finding coming from the molecular evolution lab is the formation of cell-like structures from proteinoid. One type of these cell things (there are several types of protocells, as they're called) is a microsphere. Microspheres appear to do most of the same things cells do, although not always in the same way. They look like cells; little spheres with an outside membrane that encloses them. They grow until they reach a mature form. But do they reproduce — and do they move?

There's no doubt that microspheres help make more of their kind. They need more assistance — more ready made substances and intact energy from the environment — than cells we're used to dealing with. Yet the microspheres are and must be constant midwives in the process. Without their effort there'd be no crop of little microspores, who do, by the way, grow up to look like their parents. Movement has been noted in microspheres, and there's some reason to believe this movement is directed, not random — as though they're moving toward or away from something.

- 15 Briefly sketch the various likely stages of molecular evolution.
- 16 What is the forebear of modern protein called?
- 17 Name one type of model cell (protocell) produced in the lab. What function does it perform?

Nature never sleeps

Still the microsphere just isn't a true cell. No one's satisfied so far. So it's back to the lab for the molecular evolution bunch, to try again. Meanwhile, in a damp clump of black rock near a volcano in Hawaii, and in perhaps thousands of other places, the raw stuff that life's made of is forming.

This should remind us that there's one great difference between the lab and nature. Only a few labs are working on the problem of molecular evolution — a few dozen quite human people. They have to stop work to care for their families, to eat, to sleep. Nature has thousands of labs, ten million hands, and all the time there is — and nature never, never sleeps.

- 18 How do nature's experiments differ from ours?

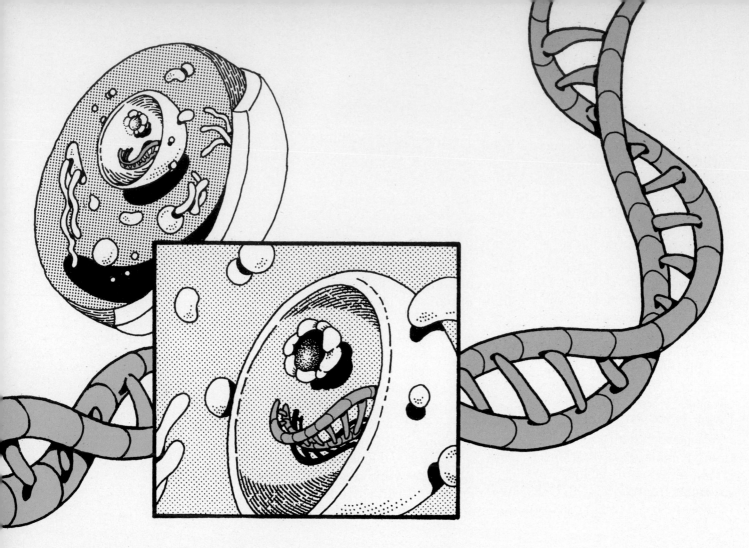

SINGLE CELL REPRODUCTION

The cell

Nature just keeps it up. It will sooner or later produce the most complex microsphere, or other protocells, it can — then instability. Microspheres as such can only go so far, get so complex.

But a lot could happen along the way. For instance, every once in a while a special microsphere is going to pop up — one with a slightly different structure, a structure that allows it to reproduce in a more efficient way and not depend so much on the outside for help — one whose reproduction process could be more self-contained. But why should this matter?

When we're talking about the most simple cells it probably doesn't. When a cell reproduces, it produces a new unit of life that is basically identical to its parent self. No new cell is ever the precise copy of its parent. But then — when such a simple form of life is concerned — when it is made of such a small number of simple parts — there are only a fixed few ways an offspring could differ from its parent.

This isn't true when more complex cells are concerned. The offspring of a complex cell could differ a great deal, for there's more room for all kinds of things to happen. All the fine complex structure of the parent could be lost. Fickle fortune would thus limit the chance for complexity to maintain — and build across generations. There it is again — up pops the devil — instability, the arch-enemy of complexity.

■19 We don't have to worry about simple cells being too different from their parents. Why? This doesn't hold true when cells become more complex. Why not?

The gene

But if chance keeps doing complex cells in, maybe this same chance will create a cell that has a new structure: some gimmick that acts like an insurance policy — limits chance, protects the complexity that one cell has and makes sure its heirs get it. This is exactly what did happen. At some point in evolving, a cell hit upon a structure that acts to keep the form more or less constant from parent to offspring. This structure is called a "gene". A gene is a substructure of the cell. It was talked about for a long time before it was found and analyzed.

Gene: substructure of a cell that functions to maintain more or less constant form or structure between parent and offspring.

It's the DNA you've heard so much about — deoxyribonucleic acid — simple molecules that hook one to the next in a chain or thread. Two such threads form side by side in a helix or spiral shape — the "double helix". It's this double helix structure that's the gene. In transferring structure, order of the molecules of the parent cell is kept intact in the offspring. Of course, it's transferred from parent to offspring during reproduction.

The gene governs things like size, shape, and other features of the offspring — tending to keep the offspring like the parent.

- ■20 There's a feature that saves the cell from instability; how does it work? What is it called?
- ■21 Define gene.
- ■22 What is a gene constructed of? Give initials. Give full name.
- ■23 Draw a double helix.

The gene and mutation: nature's one-two punch

Sometimes there's a change in the structure of the gene — the way the simple building blocks are arranged on the two threads. It can happen to a parent when things like severe temperatures, contact with harsh chemicals, or stray rays make contact with a cell. This change in the structure of the gene may change future growth of the parent cell but most important is the fact that it's passed on to the offspring. Since the gene governs what kind of structure the cell will have, the new cell will turn out somewhat unlike other cells of its species. A change that results when the structure of the gene is altered is called a "mutation".

Mutation: change in the composition of the gene that results in altered structure in offspring as compared to the parent.

The one-two punch of the gene and the change allowed by mutation are a tough pair to beat. Both work to create cells that are ever different, unique, complex. Genes keep complexity (once it arises and proves to help the cell survive) constant. Meanwhile, mutation keeps on making subtle changes in the offspring that'll be passed on if the offspring survives long enough to reproduce. In this way mutation keeps polishing, making the species better able to survive.

It was without doubt the hand-in-hand work of the gene and mutation that beat the instability trap. It cleared the way and caused life to explode on the small planet Earth. It was this move that prepared the way for great creatures — the human among them — to evolve.

- ■24 How do genes and mutation work to provide great complexity?
- ■25 Define mutation.

THE LIFE EXPLOSION

The Glop That Kidnapped Kalamazoo

The guard sat at the metal desk eating a sandwich and reading a newspaper; beyond him, the thick lead-lined door that led to the plutonium vault. More than a ton of the awesome stuff was kept there. The guard was not destined to dine alone that night. For at that very instant, the "Glop" — slimy freak from the swamp — oozed forward. Bigger at this moment than a small truck, it would grow to the size of a football field once it devoured the plutonium feast inside. Meanwhile, the guard, unknowing, with no hint of the gooey death that stalked him, started to nod. A ray of gray, viscous matter flowed under the door, a pseudopod that belonged to the Glop.

"Look out!" Red bellowed. "The Glop's put out a testicle!" Down the row Liggit, Ragsdale, Curly, all guffawed.

"No man — the word's 'tentacle'," Curly rumbled in a low-pitched voice.

Friday night at the campus flick. Twenty-five cents and a student I.D. got you in. Half the football squad was there, Juke Jackson among them.

"Hey, Red. That the woman you been messin' round with down there?" Juke asked.

Red strained to see who it was Juke was talking about. "Oh — yeah, that one. We went to the same high school. Crystal Burke. In the green — that who you mean?"

"That's her. What about the one sittin' by her? You know her?"

"Met her once when she's with Crystal. Name's Mae. Mae Robinson. She's cool okay, but she acts a little uppity."

"Yeah?" Juke said.

Just then the final reel began, the suspense-filled climax of "The Glop That Kidnapped Kalamazoo".

Limit of the single cell

Thus, single-celled creatures found a new function made possible by the structure of the gene. They could pass on new structure to offspring. At the same time cells retained the tendency to mutate. This meant that some offspring would have structure that differed slightly from the parent. In many cases this made their chances to survive far better. With these two great skills there would be no stopping this single-celled life from taking new shapes, forms, and acquiring new functions. They would venture as far and as wide as limits would allow, moving ever more toward complexity. But above all, these single-celled creatures would endure. They seemed to have a means to second guess nature — a ready counter for its cruel whims. It didn't seem to matter what new challenge the environment mustered — changes in heat, cold, shortage of food, an influx of caustic substance into the life space. Somehow the creature or its cousins — some number of its kind — survived. These mutants were for the most part just like their fallen kin. They differed only slightly, but differed enough in ways that mattered in survival.

The proof that these creatures were hardy and robust is seen in the fact that they are with us today in great scope and number. They are called "microorganisms".

Microorganism: simple life forms; often single-celled creatures.

Some microorganisms are helpful to humans. They degrade wastes, turning them into rich soil, help convert milk into cheese, fruit juice into wine. But some are a curse. We call these germs. They invade our bodies and cause disease and death.

But what about the "Glop" — the single-celled creature that "kidnapped" Kalamazoo — worked complex vault locks, outwitted an entire army, humbled a thousand computers with its lightning fast logic? Need we fear such a mutant? No. Not at all. Such a single-celled marvel just couldn't be. For one thing, a single cell that large would have a tough time moving fuel in, and just as tough a time getting wastes out. The point is that there's a limit to the number and kind of functions that can be performed by a single cell. The complex functions the Glop performed simply couldn't be done without more moving parts, sensors and other structural features that couldn't be packed into a single cell — instability again, the end of the line for the single cell.

■26 In what sense do single cells second-guess nature?
■27 What is a microorganism?
■28 Why is it impossible for single cells to develop the highly complex functions often credited them in science fiction movies?

ORIGIN OF MULTI-CELLED CREATURES

Cells — the building blocks of life

There's a limit to what a single cell can do — a limit to complexity — a point of instability. But what about many such cells taken as a whole? Think of a cell as a brick. A group of bricks apart from each other are still just bricks. But when they are fastened to each other — fitted — they become something else — assume new function. They become a wall, a house, a walkway. Cells are much the same. When they're put together, a new structure can occur — the old limit to complexity is gone.

It often works out that cells that live together have a better chance to survive than those who go it alone. Cells at the center of a cluster may grow larger and stronger than those on the outside. Outside cells get the full brunt of harmful stimuli — friction, cold and heat, and stray rays that damage structure. It's only at the expense of their cousins, pushed outside, that the inside cells, shielded and safe, reproduce to keep the species alive. Does nature in its "wisdom" provide that some should die so that a greater purpose will be served? No such thing. It just happens that greater complexity pays off sometimes and up to a point.

- ■29 Why would cells ever begin to exist in clusters or groups?
- ■30 What factor tended to give a cluster of cells an advantage over single cells in some situations?

Cell differentiation

Cells that congregate, even join, are still just cells — they function the same, have the same needs as when they were loners. And, of course, one feature that all cells in the cluster retain is the ability to mutate. As at other levels, this provides the way for greater complexity.

Suppose two cells exist side by side. They both need oxygen to burn fuel and to stay alive. They expel carbon dioxide as a waste product. But oxygen is in short supply — hard times are upon them. They both scrape through — live just long enough to reproduce. One produces offspring just like itself — oxygen eaters, givers of carbon dioxide. The other cell gives rise to mutant offspring, with a new structure. These mutants take in carbon dioxide as waste. Just the reverse of their parent and of offspring of the other cell.

There should be no problem in seeing that if the two parent cells were good neighbors, their offspring are going to be even better ones. Each type of cell now has a better chance of surviving because of the mutation. As long as they stay close, they'll have an edge on cells that don't have such helpful neighbors. When two organisms survive through such joint advantage it is called "symbiosis".

Symbiosis: situation where two or more organisms have a greater mutual chance to survive as a result of the function they provide for each other.

Groups of cells thus have an even greater edge when some of them mutate and as a result of their new structure, provide a function that helps all members of the group. Don't be fooled into thinking that a cell mutates in a certain way because the group needs help and nature steps in to help.

There's no way to tell if a mutant cell's going to help or not. Sometimes mutants arise that hinder the group. They feed off the group, weaken it, make it work harder to survive — and they give nothing in return. Cells who exist at the expense of others and don't help out are called "parasites".

Parasite: an organism that exists because of functions provided by others, but does not contribute to their survival.

Once cells join, and some mutate in ways that help the group survive, the way is once again paved for great leaps in complexity. As time and mutation go on there's a trend for multi-celled organisms to grow cells that add to the whole. This process is called "cell differentiation". But the key thing here is not that cells are different — not that they have a new structure. It's the fact that their new structure allows them to provide a function that helps the whole survive. Thus, it's "differentiation of function" that we're really talking about.

Differentiation of function: as single-celled organisms develop into multiple-celled ones, some cells develop specialized structure which allows them to provide a function that helps the total organism survive.

■31 When a cell or other creature mutates in such a manner that it and another creature have a greater chance to survive, this is called _____.

■32 When a cell or other creature mutates in such a way that it makes use of function provided by others but does not contribute to their survival, it is called a _____.

■33 Define symbiosis. Define parasite.

■34 Define differentiation of function.

Centralization of function

Before they joined the club — became a multi-celled organism — single cells used to absorb fuel, gasses, and other things they needed directly from the life space that engulfed them. Wastes were dumped into the same medium. In complex organisms, single cells no longer do this for themselves. Fuel and oxygen are delivered by organs and physiological systems — clusters of like cells that have differentiated and are now equipped to serve that function. For instance, when it was a loner a cell had to detect, and then move away from, harmful stimuli. Now when contact is made a special system of differentiated cells (nerves) carries the stimulus to a central area (the spinal cord or brain) where it's transferred to muscles (cells differentiated to produce movement) that transport the entire complex of cells out of danger.

   Thus, as multi-celled creatures become more complex, we find differentiated cells form substructures called "organs". Organs in turn connect to form "physiological systems". Special functions that cells provide are thus centralized. They've evolved at new locations within the creature that seem to serve all cells best — "centralization of function".

Organ: substructure of a complex creature where cells form together to provide a function or functions that help the entire organism survive.

Physiological system: group of organs and supporting structures, that provide a special function for a creature.

Centralization of function: as multi-celled organisms become more complex, cells specialize in a new function, and give up old functions. Functions given up are taken on by other cells specialized in those functions. Cells that provide like function tend to be located at places in the organism best suited to serve the whole.

■35 What is an organ? Define.
■36 What is a physiological system? Define.
■37 Define centralization of function.

COMPLEXITY AND MUTATION IN MULTI-CELLED CREATURES

The end of mutation

In the first part of this chapter we said that the gene acted to maintain a level of complexity across the generation gap. If a cell got to the point that it was making out pretty well, it'd be too bad if chance would wipe it all out. The gene kept this from taking place. It kept the structure of the offspring very much like the parent's. But there was still room for change — through mutation. The problem is that there's no way to tell if the new structure will help or hinder survival. If it hinders, the cell could die or just produce fewer offspring, and lose out in that manner.

But if we're talking about one cell, what's the worry? What's one cell more or less? Those that didn't mutate, or those that changed in ways that helped or at least didn't hurt chances — will survive. There'll be enough of them so that the species goes on. But as single cells combine to form more complex forms — as cells are differentiated and functions centralized — mutation gets a little risky. Just think of a creature lucky enough to have cells differentiated to form a liver. A liver's a fine piece of machinery — it sifts out poisons, and provides other functions that help all the cells survive. Then one fine day a "rebel" liver cell isn't content just to stay a liver cell — it wants to be something else. It mutates to become a skin cell. Skin cells reproduce fast, and pretty soon things get out of hand. The next thing you know, the creature's liver turns into a fingernail — or a big toe. You can see that wouldn't make the creature — or the rest of the cells — very happy. As a result, when creatures become complex, cells don't mutate so easily. And as you might suspect, more complex cells tend to mutate less often than simple ones. How? Because complex cells don't reproduce as often. Less chance for mutation.

Law of Complexity and Mutation: as multiple-celled creatures tend to develop complex differentiated cells and systems of centralized function, mutations become less likely.

Thus, when complexity reaches a certain point, the same mechanism that created that complexity in the first place — mutation — threatens the creature. Instability again! When this level of complexity is reached change must occur more slowly — not be so drastic as mutation might allow.

Mutation had to go — and so it did. The human as perhaps the most complex model nature's made to date, is a case in point. Humans have specialized cells, organs, systems and central functions. Yet, for all the trillions of complex human cells, mutation is a rare event.

But without mutation, how can the move toward complexity go on in humans and other multi-celled creatures? Or does it go nowhere, is this the end? Have we reached the final limit — the final limit this side of instability?

- ■38 Mutation is always good for the creature. Discuss.
- ■39 Why is mutation a problem with complex organisms?
- ■40 What would happen to a complex organism if mutation weren't held in check?
- ■41 What is the law that states the relationship between complexity and mutation in complex organisms?
- ■42 Define the Law of Complexity and Mutation.
- ■43 How common is mutation in human cells?

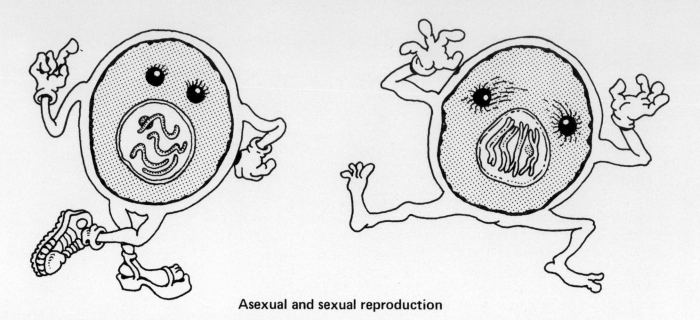

Asexual and sexual reproduction

The storyline was plodding, the dialogue stilted, the acting bad beyond belief — and as Mae knew from the biology course she'd had at Christian College, there were downright errors in the biological facts portrayed. The movie was so bad, it might well become a classic. Students roared loudest at the clumsy attempts to lace a scene here and there with sex. At one point the hero was forced to tear away the heroine's lab smock, saving her from a Glop spore that had taken root on her bosom. This contrived bit of near-porn brought the house down, with hoots, yells, and whistles.

Sex, Mae thought. *Why are people so intrigued by it? For other creatures it's only a very minor part of life; something they do to reproduce. Some don't need sex at all; they reproduce without it — do it all themselves; asexual reproduction it's called. Suppose humans were that way — asexual reproducers. Now that would be something! What would the filmmakers do then? For that matter, what about commerce? Ad agents would have to find something besides sex to sell their wares — it could wreck the economy!*

* * *

Indeed, reproduction need not involve sex. All the reproduction we've talked about thus far has occurred without it — "asexual reproduction", as it's called.

Asexual reproduction: reproduction process that produces an offspring with one parent.

In asexual reproduction, the creature produces offspring without joining with another creature. The most common form of asexual reproduction is called "mitosis".

Mitosis: asexual reproduction where the creature divides to form two identical organisms.

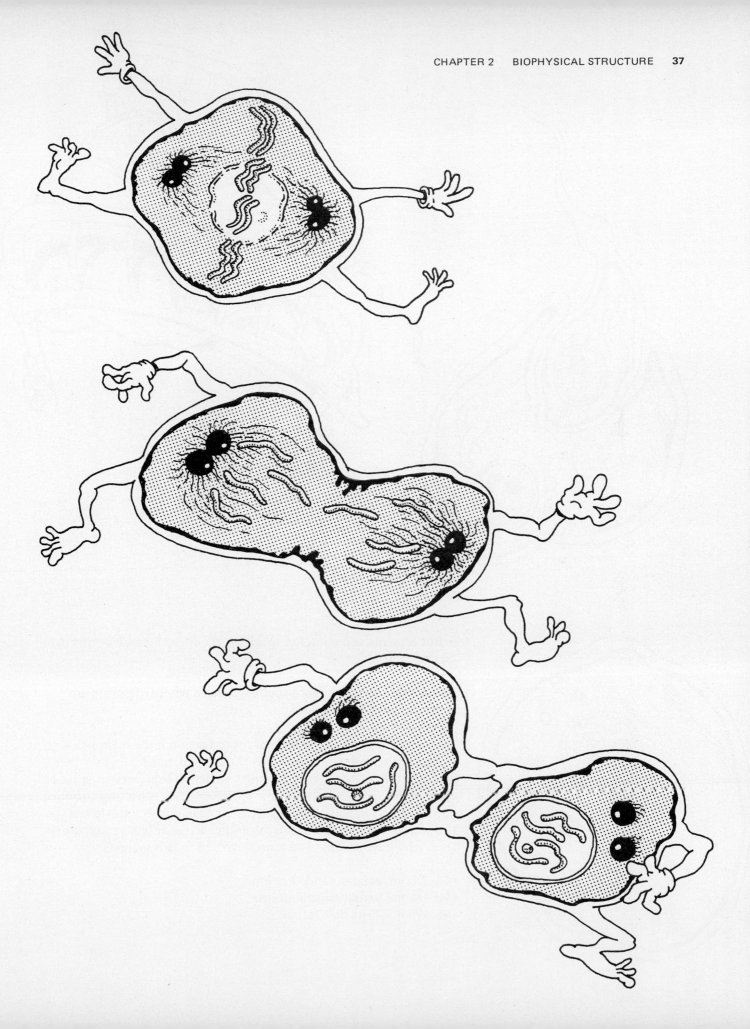

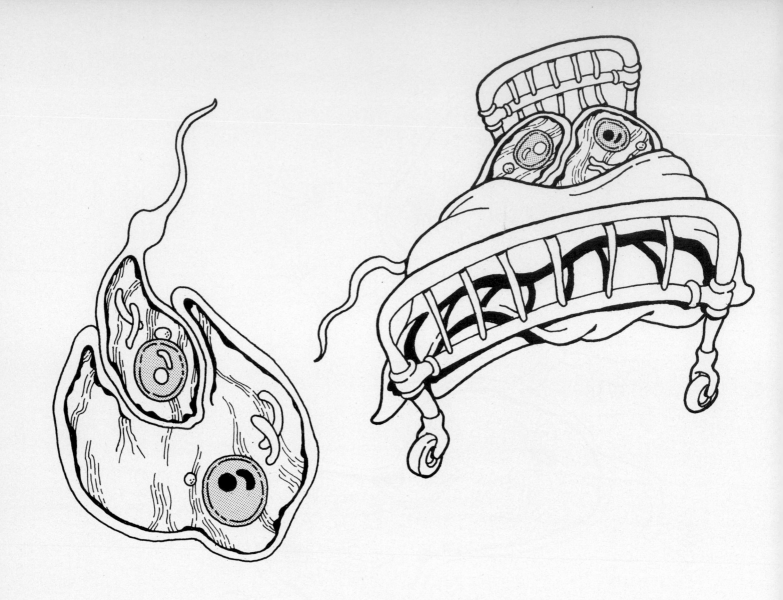

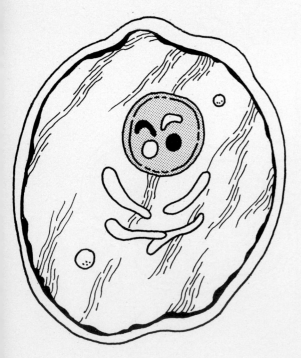

But humans and complex species reproduce themselves through "sexual reproduction".

Sexual reproduction: reproduction process where offspring are produced with two parents.

To a non-partial viewer, sexual reproduction must seem like a great deal of bother when compared to the asexual act. It requires that two creatures of life spaces that may differ to some extent great or small, must meet and spend time together. They must also produce germ cells and in some way insure their fusion into a single cell. The whole thing would be much simpler to do at leisure and alone. Then why have complex creatures evolved in this manner?

- ▪44 Define asexual reproduction.
- ▪45 Define sexual reproduction.
- ▪46 What is mitosis? Define.

Sexual reproduction and complexity

We've pointed out in a past section that mutation isn't likely to yield
a good outcome when the creature is a complex one; one with organs
and physiological systems that must all work in concert. A mutant
cell could reproduce to form a mutant organ, giving up old function
in the process, and leaving the rest of the creature in the lurch. The
entire mass of cells — the creature itself — would perish. Again, as
we've pointed out, when creatures therefore reach a certain stage of
complexity, mutation becomes a rare event.

But this poses a problem. If the environment were to change in a
manner that was hostile to the species, there would be no mutants —
no creatures who could survive. The trend toward new structure,
toward new complexity, would have ended as the power to mutate
ceased. All creatures would have long since developed identical
structure — identical strengths and faults.

It's just this problem that sexual reproduction gets around. With
this type of reproduction, a new level is reached; the way is cleared
for further complexity. Human sexual reproduction shows this quite
well. Sperm are released in the medium of fluid that is the major
part of male reproductive matter, semen. A sperm is not an adequate
cell, as it will disintegrate unless it finds a partner cell. When the
sperm makes contact with the female reproductive matter, the egg, it
penetrates, the egg and sperm are joined. The two cells combine to
form a stable cell. The entire structure of the offspring will grow
from this single cell. But what will the structure be like?

Egg: female reproductive cell that will unite with male sperm to form
a new creature.

Sperm: male reproductive cell that will unite with female egg to form
a new creature.

▪47 Define egg.
▪48 Define sperm.

The gene lottery

We learned when dealing with simple creatures that structure is controlled by the gene. In humans the gene likewise controls structure. A single gene gives rise to a discrete feature of structure such as eye color, hair texture, size and shape of limb, etc. Dozens of genes are contained in a kind of gene package called a "chromosome".

Chromosome: package that contains genes; each human cell has 46 chromosomes, half of which are represented in reproductive cells (sperm or egg).

A sperm or egg is supplied with half (23) of each of the donor's 46 chromosomes. The exact 23 chromosomes the sperm or egg will have of the possible 46 is governed by chance — there's no way to know in front. Eggs and sperm are formed when the complete reproductive cell splits. Each sperm and egg is given half of the complement of chromosomes. This splitting of the reproductive cell is called "meiosis".

Meiosis: the splitting of the human reproductive cell to form sperm and eggs with half (23) of the full complement of chromosomes of the parent.

In this sense sexual reproduction is a sort of biological lottery. The mother and father each select half of their genes in random fashion and toss them together. The offspring receive their genetic complement from these two random selections.

It's clear that sexual reproduction is a good system. It gives plenty of room for further complexity. By sampling only half the genes from each parent, creatures with features and structures never seen before can well occur. Sisters and brothers may share certain features, but differ greatly in others. Only in the rare case where a fertilized egg breaks into two or more separate cells (forming identical twins, triplets, etc.) do creatures have the same genes, and therefore the same structure. Aside from this no two are alike. A new threat from the environment is now more likely to find some who survive it.

Mae failed to see the survival features of sexual reproduction. It isn't just a new way to reproduce that humans just happen to have acquired. It's a giant leap ahead, one that beats the instability trap of mutation, and provides for complex structure. Without it the human could never have evolved.

- ■49 Define chromosome. How many does the human have? How many of each partner's are present at conception?
- ■50 Define meiosis.
- ■51 How do meiosis and mitosis differ?
- ■52 In what sense can conception be thought of as a biological lottery?
- ■53 Sexual reproduction has no great advantages over asexual reproduction. Attack or defend.

CONCLUSIONS — THE GREAT MUTATION

Sid looked over at Juke who was now heavy into the books, studying. Sid envied Juke at this moment. He wished he could get into his studies, but somehow it just wouldn't work. He kept thinking about the girl he'd met in physics class. *Dawn — Dawn Baker. Sure would like to get a date with her — but how? Can't just walk right up and ask her. Maybe Juke could give me some hints.*

"Hey Juke."

"Yeah, man."

"How do you go about asking a girl out on this campus?"

"Out?" Juke said.

"On a date."

"Oh. Ask her, man. Jus' walk right up and ask her."

"I don't know. I don't know if I'm her type. I think she goes for big guys with muscles, good looks, flashy — you know."

"Oh," Juke said. "Only one thing to do then."

"Yeah! What is it?"

"Mutate, man."

"Mutate?"

"Sure, mutate." There was a long pause.

"Thanks a lot, Jackson."

Muffled laughter came from behind Juke's book.

***

We've come far in this chapter. We started with the most simple of atoms, hydrogen, showing how it gained step by step in complexity — but that complexity at that level ended when structure reached the breaking-up point — so complex that it became unstable. This same theme was played upon at chemical, molecular, cellular, multi-cellular, and complex-creature levels.

But our account wouldn't be complete if we didn't mention a quite special mutation that occurred somewhere along the way. The structure that resulted is of utmost concern for the survival of all higher creatures, and of the very greatest concern for humans. It deserves to be called the "Great Mutation". The change in structure that it produced allows creatures to adapt to changes in their surroundings, even those that are extreme and happen all at once. Creatures with this structure can adapt without mutation or breeding — each creature doing so within its own lifetime. The Great Mutation occurred, and at once all creatures with the new structure gained a vast edge on those without it. The function this structure allowed is called **learning.** In the next chapter we will take an in-depth look at the anatomy and physiology that allow us and similar creatures to engage in this fantastic process.

CHAPTER 3
PHYSIOLOGICAL PROCESSES

INTRODUCTION

There are one hundred trillion cells that make up the human body. All of these came from the single cell formed by the union of a sperm and an egg. But there's more to the feat than just the simple splitting and resplitting of cells. As the embryo grows, cells emerge that are quite unlike that first cell. Some form nerve and brain tissue, others hair and skin, still others organs, glands, and blood vessels — billions of years of evolution crammed into one small cell. In this chapter we'll attempt to cover the highlights of those aspects of human structure and function that relate most to behavior.

STRUCTURE AND FUNCTION

There are, of course, many things we could observe when we study life forms. Just dissecting them to learn their parts and how they're put together is both an important and respectable pursuit. But this alone doesn't seem to make most people happy for long. Sooner or later they get around to asking: "But what does it do?" They want to know about function. The study of the gross structure of the human body is called "anatomy"; the study of its function is "physiology".

Anatomy: study of the structure of plants and animals.

Physiology: study of the function of living things and their organs.

Many structures or substructures may take part in providing a function. For this reason physiologists speak of physiological systems. A physiological system consists of a group of structures that are related in that they work together to provide a function or functions.

- 1 Define anatomy.
- 2 Define physiology.
- 3 Review: Define physiological system.

SIMPLE STIMULUS TRANSFER, ABSORPTION, AND TRANSFORMATION

Simple stimulus transfer

As we pointed out in the last chapter, the first multi-celled creatures were scarcely more than globs of single-celled organisms. Are we wrong to call such a loose conglomerate of cells a creature? Perhaps. Still, they lived and thrived because they were a unit, having advantage in some environments over single-celled structures. But if cells live as a unit, it follows that at some point they started to respond as a unit. How did this come about?

Think of such a clump of cells adrift in liquid space — all around it stimuli — energy of many forms and in many strengths. At this instant let's say a sharp piece of rock or harmful chemical makes contact somewhere on the outside surface of the group. How can the presence of this stimulus affect other cells, cells not making contact, cells far removed from the scene?

If contact is with a rock or other solid object, then the mechanical force of the contact — kinetic energy — would be transferred from cells at the impact point to the cells touching them, and so on down the line. As you can see, this doesn't require that cells react or even be alive. It would work just as well with balls on a billiard table, or a row of dominoes.

There exist today groups of single cells living together and responding as a unit to events in their life space in just such a way. But problems arise when we rely on such a simple system. Energy is lost as it passes through and between cells — it decays quickly and dies. If the cluster of cells is too large, those furthest from the point of contact may never get the message. The result — a creature that doesn't have itself together. Time of transfer is also a factor. Survival could well depend on a quick response to harmful stimuli or the presence of fuel. Too slow could be too late — the food gone, the cluster destroyed or engulfed by a predator. A better means of stimulus transfer would have to evolve if multi-celled creatures were to grow larger, use their many cells to advantage, and develop more complex functions.

Stimulus transfer: conduction of a stimulus energy from one part or structure of a creature to other parts or structures.

- ■ 4 Define stimulus transfer.
- ■ 5 How might the effects of contact with an object on the part of some cells be transferred to the rest of the cells in the group?
- ■ 6 What two problems might the transfer method described above present?

Absorption

We and all other creatures are immersed in a constant bath of energy — energy of many kinds, forms, and strengths. We call these various energy forms "stimuli" when we talk about types of energy and the effect they have on living matter.

Stimulus: any event in our physical world.

A stimulus must first be absorbed before it can affect any other substance — living or not. When a stimulus is absorbed it changes the structure of the matter it impinges on, altering its physical or chemical make-up — although the matter may quickly change back once the stimulus has gone. Yet the change does occur — this is what is meant by "absorption".

Absorption: change in physical or chemical structure when a stimulus makes contact.

Whether or not energy is absorbed depends on its form and strength, and on the chemical and physical make-up of the creature it strikes. Once absorbed, a stimulus may fail to cause a creature to act. Whether or not responses are produced by a stimulus once it's absorbed depends on a number of factors. The amount of energy absorbed is one. Others relate to the setting — where the creature is and the task at hand. In a broader sense, both absorption and action relate to the role that a given type of energy played in the survival of the species as it evolved.

- ▪ 7 Define absorption.
- ▪ 8 What is a stimulus?
- ▪ 9 What current factors and what species factors govern whether or not a stimulus is absorbed by a particular creature?

Receptors

Many kinds of stimuli — chemical, mechanical, sound and light waves — may relate to survival. No stimulus stands a chance of being effective — causing a creature to respond — unless it is first absorbed. Whether a creature responds to minute traces of fuel or escapes from harmful stimuli (that could prove lethal in large doses), depends very much on how readily some of its cells absorb small amounts of these forms of energy. As a result, complex creatures have evolved cells with structures well-suited to absorb certain forms of stimulus energy. Such specialized cells are called "receptors".

Creatures seem to develop receptor cells that are as good at absorbing that energy as they can be whenever being sensitive to a form of energy is crucial to survival. For instance, receptor cells in the human eye will absorb the very smallest package or unit that light can be broken down to — a single photon.

Receptors: specialized cells well-suited to absorb certain forms of energy.

Some animals have receptor cells that are sensitive to stimuli or features of stimuli for which others have no receptor cells at all. Color is an instance of such a stimulus feature. Humans, apes, and most birds have receptor cells that specialize to absorb different wave lengths of light. Creatures that don't depend on fruits and vegetables for food, or creatures that come out only at night, don't seem to have evolved such receptor cells — they don't respond to color stimuli.

- 10 Define receptors.
- 11 Review: When cells mutate to take on a new function, it is called d_____ of f_____. How does this relate to receptors?
- 12 How sensitive are human light-receptor cells?
- 13 Cite an instance of receptor cells found in some species but not in others.

Stimulus transformation

When stimuli are absorbed they're changed into a new form of energy; but not just any new form. All stimuli must sooner or later be changed or "transformed" into forms that fit in with those special structures that have evolved to perform stimulus transfer.

Stimulus transform: a change of stimulus from one form of energy to another.

In the human, stimuli must first be transformed into chemical or electrochemical energy before they can be transferred. Transformation between the two modes also occurs. A stimulus makes contact with the surface, is transformed into electro-chemical energy by a receptor cell lying nearby. This resulting energy makes contact with a gland that reacts by secreting chemicals — transforming the electrochemical energy to chemical energy. Packages of chemical energy secreted by the gland circulate through the bloodstream until they reach tissue or an organ that's sensitive to them.

Some structures making the initial transform of stimuli coming from the outside are quite simple. Contact stimuli give rise to pain, touch, cold, heat, and vision; and chemical stimuli are involved in taste and smell. They are all transformed at once into electrochemical energy by receptor cells. Hearing requires a complex transformation involving many steps before stimuli are changed to electrochemical energy and transferred throughout the body.

- 14 Define stimulus transform.
- 15 Into what two forms of energy must stimuli be transformed before they can be transferred throughout the human system?
- 16 Give four examples of the simplest form of stimulus transfer.

MAJOR STIMULUS TRANSFER SYSTEMS

There are two major human stimulus transfer systems. One, the "endocrine system", allows for more or less global contact with body tissue by circulating packages of chemical energy in the bloodstream. Though contact with these stimuli is global, their effects can be selective. Organs and structures are sensitive to some of these chemical substances and not to others.

Endocrine system: stimulus transfer system that involves chemicals dispersed by glands into the bloodstream, where contact is made with other tissues through blood circulation.

The second important human stimulus transfer system is the "nervous system". It's made up of specialized cells that connect to form pathways that are enclosed or self-contained to a greater or lesser extent. This system is suited for rapid and selective stimulus transfer. One specialized part of this general nervous system — the somatic nervous system — connects the outside world to the brain and spinal cord — the central nervous system. The somatic nervous system then transfers stimuli back from the central nervous system to muscles that cause adaptive responses to occur. A special part of the nervous system — the autonomic nervous system — performs the task of working with the endocrine system, allowing these two systems to function as a unit.

Nervous system: stimulus transfer system made of specialized cells that form pathways through which electrochemical energy is conducted.

- ▪17 Define endocrine system.
- ▪18 How do chemicals make contact with the body structures — how are they distributed?
- ▪19 Define nervous system.
- ▪20 What transfer system allows for rapid and selective action?
- ▪21 What special part of the nervous system connects with the endocrine system?

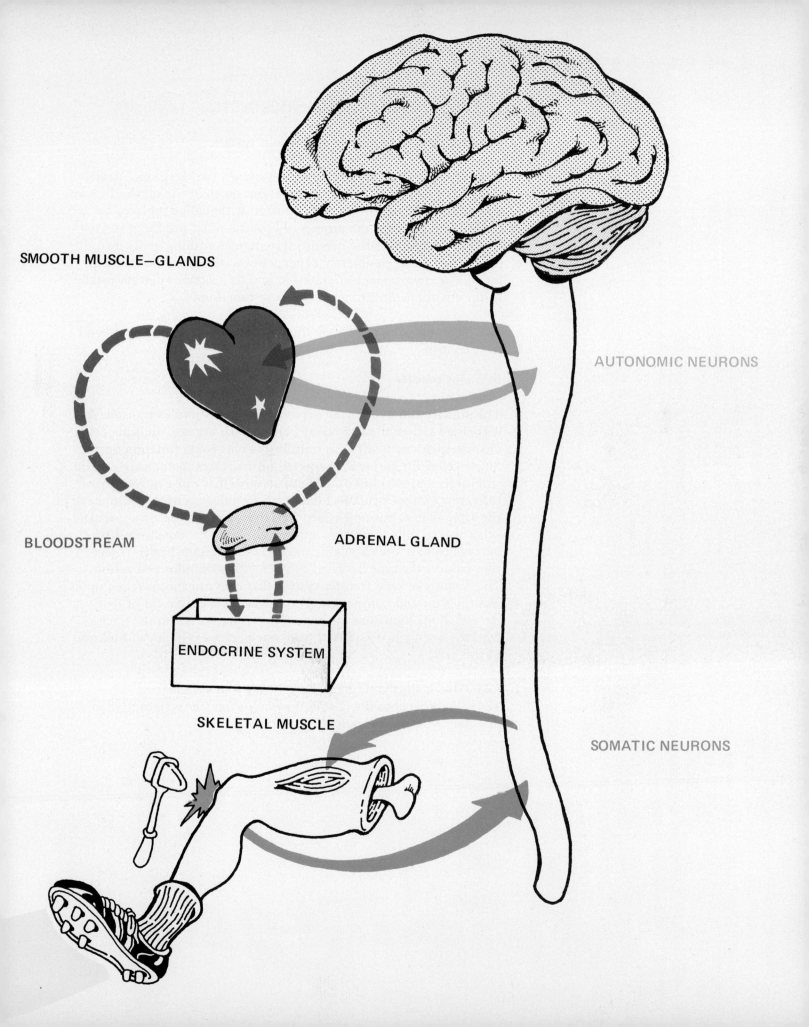

SMOOTH MUSCLE–GLANDS

AUTONOMIC NEURONS

BLOODSTREAM

ADRENAL GLAND

ENDOCRINE SYSTEM

SKELETAL MUSCLE

SOMATIC NEURONS

THE FUNCTION OF THE NERVOUS SYSTEM

Evolution and functions of the nervous system

If we are to understand the nervous system — the receptors, nerves, spinal cord, and brain — we must toss out much of the myth, the awe and presumed magic often ascribed to it. It should be replaced by respect — respect for the process of evolution that produced it. We shouldn't forget that the nervous system does nothing on its own. It is a passive guest, completely dependent on its host — the environment. The environment produced it, and its functions pertain totally to the environment. But what are these functions?

■22 What does it mean to say the nervous system does nothing on its own?

Stimulus transfer

The primary function of the nervous system is stimulus transfer. As we've said earlier, the nervous system evolved because multiple-celled creatures with such stimulus transfer systems could function better. Single-celled life forms have special substructures that absorb certain stimuli (receptors), and other substructures that cause movement (effectors). Other structures suited for stimulus transfer developed at the same time as multiple-celled organisms evolved receptor cells and other special cells to provide movement. As a rule, creatures survive best which have the most efficient receptor-effector bridge — one that reduces the time between contact with a stimulus and action. The simple chemical transfer system that early organisms relied upon was too slow and nonspecific. Yet, it was never gotten rid of — it persists in the human as the endocrine system. It is also the means whereby energy is transferred from one nervous system cell (neuron) to the next.

■23 What is the main function of the nervous system?
■24 What role does the chemical stimulus transfer system have in human stimulus transfer?

Relay function

Stimulus transfer became a greater problem as species grew larger, evolving more complex organs and systems. Interplay among these units was crucial — but there was a limit to how much of a creature's tissue could be specialized for stimulus transfer. As a result, nervous systems became better arranged. Cells came together to form relay centers where stimulus transfer proceeded with greater speed and economy. In the human, the spinal cord and the greater portion of the brain itself are devoted to the simple routing of impulses.

Stimulus selection function

Once contact is made with a stimulus, a receptor has no choice but to absorb this energy. But responding to a stimulus isn't always best — not at all times and in all settings. It would be well if there were some way a stimulus could be selected from among the many absorbed at a given instant. A creature that is starving would fare best if it responded to the smell of nearby food, not reacting to other stimuli that suggest the presence of harmful but far from lethal conditions.

The nervous system helps provide this stimulus selection function — making it likely that stimuli most relevant to survival are responded to. It acts in both direct and indirect ways to achieve this result. Some reflex movements reduce the strength of stimuli by blocking them from reaching the receptor. When sound is too loud, small muscles that connect to the series of bones conducting eardrum movement relax. The same strength of sound stimuli produces less movement in the middle ear, causing us to experience less sound. Blinking or squinting our eyes in intense light also reduces stimuli reaching receptors.

The nervous system acts on its own to select stimuli that are responded to through a process called inhibition. Inhibition accounts for the fact that we see objects with a very dark border which makes them stand out against their background. Cells adjacent to the border inhibit the production of electrochemical energy at the border — as though no light at all was present in that region. Impulses going to the brain are reduced to near zero. The result — a crisp and clear object, distinct from the background.

Inhibition also occurs at relay areas and other large structures of the spinal cord and brain. For some parts of the system to function at peak, others must remain idle. Centers in the brain not only help distribute inputs — they do so selectively, acting as gatekeepers. This is made possible through the complex interconnections among all parts of the nervous system.

Stimulus selection by the nervous system changes as a result of past rewards and punishers. Stimuli having little effect under one condition gain great control as new experience dictates. Sights, sounds, tastes, and smells leap out at us after they've been linked to outcomes that relate to our well-being, though in the past we may never have noticed them.

■25 Why is stimulus selection a crucial function?
■26 Give one direct and one indirect way the nervous system helps provide stimulus selection function.

Arousal function

Sometimes it's best that even a weak stimulus input has the effect of calling many parts of the body into quick and intense action. The nervous system provides for this arousal in two ways. The first involves its action on the endocrine system. One segment of the nervous system — the autonomic nervous system (ANS) — connects to the glands and major structures of the endocrine system. Impulses coming from the ANS cause glands to secrete chemicals into the bloodstream. All tissues and structures are reached as blood circulates and relevant organs can respond to the crisis.

A faster method of massive arousal of a short term nature is achieved by the structures of the nervous system itself. Alone and within an intact bundle of axons, one nerve cell supplies only a small contained current. But large structures of the brain have hundreds of thousands of neurons whose single currents may sum together — the result, a huge rush of electrical action that can flood into all structures — gross arousal in an instant. One part of the nervous system that provides the power for this massive call to arms is the reticular formation. It comprises what may be thought of as the inner core of the brain — a structure about the size of your little finger. It extends up from the spinal cord into the deep center of the brain — a good location to receive sensory input and to mobilize the entire brain.

■27 Briefly describe what's meant by the term "arousal function".
■28 The nervous system creates arousal in two main ways. Describe them.

Feedback

An event taking place on your scalp causes disturbance to nearby receptor cells. They respond, producing current that makes adjacent neurons fire, their impulses leading down the axon bundle to the spinal cord. Once there, impulses are relayed to a motor nerve that services arm muscles. You respond — you scratch your head. If you hit the right spot and the scratching works, the receptors that signaled the disturbance will stop action. If not, they'll keep it up. The muscles that controlled the response may or may not be called on again. This is a type of feedback, because in a sense, the muscle is informed of its success or failure.

But there's one thing it wasn't informed of — what it did to produce the outcome. If they're to work, muscles must not only respond to inputs from other structures — they must also respond to themselves. Evolution took care of this nicely by providing muscles with small structures that generate current when they act. When a muscle moves, it acts not only in response to impulses coming from other sources — it also responds to impulses produced by its own movement. This is another type of feedback.

Feedback from muscles is also crucial for other reasons. Movement from one muscle sends impulses that inhibit action of an opposing muscle or other part of the body that would interfere with its action and successful result. Much of the nervous system is devoted to feedback function. Organs, muscles, glands, the many parts of the brain itself, must come under the control of their own action as well as the outcomes they produce — two types of feedback.

▪29 Describe at least two instances where feedback function is important for muscle function.

STRUCTURE OF THE NERVOUS SYSTEM

The neuron

The "neuron" is a cell. It evolved to assume the special function of stimulus transfer. It is the building block of the nervous system. Neurons form nerves, and the intricate structures of the spinal cord and brain. But, first of all, neurons are cells. They have cell membranes enclosing a nucleus. The nucleus and other structures burn fuel, keep the cell alive, and produce other substances it needs to function.

Neurons come in many shapes and sizes. Some, for instance, are drawn out in long thin strands many feet in length. A sensory neuron — a single cell — goes from your big toe all the way up to the middle of your back. The long drawn-out part of the cell is called the "axon". It's the part of the neuron that provides a path for stimuli to travel long distances. The other end of the neuron has many tree-like branches called "dendrites". Impulses flow into dendrites, then travel down the axon. Nerves are axons that run alongside each other in bundles.

Nerves that transfer sensory stimuli to the central nervous system are called "afferent", or sensory nerves. They deal with the senses: hearing, sight, touch, temperature, taste, and smell. "Efferent", or motor neurons, provide transfer in the other direction. Impulses from inner structures are transferred to muscles, causing them to contract, moving some of the creature's body parts. Other neurons are relays shunting impulses caused by outside stimuli to other parts, often to motor neuron pathways that lead back out to muscles. These relay neurons are sometimes called "interneurons". They connect to other neurons, making chains or networks that are quite complex and whose function is only partly understood. The point where neurons connect with each other is called a "synapse".

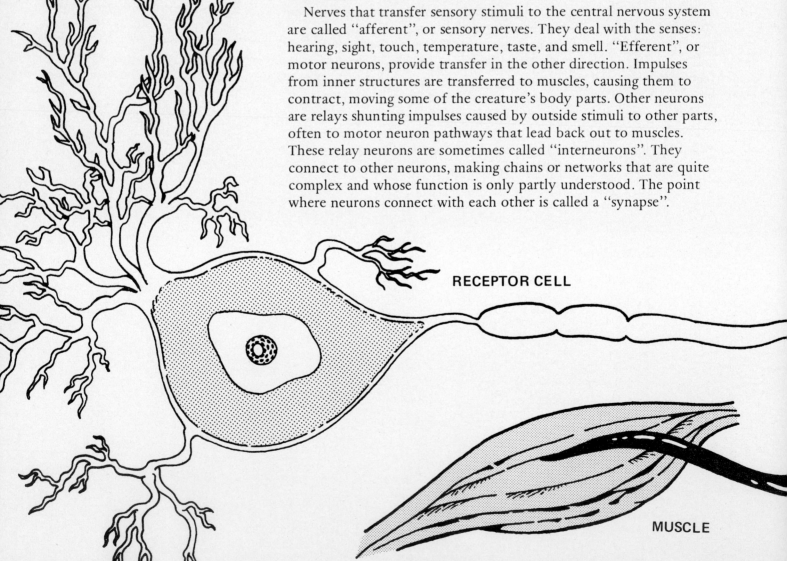

RECEPTOR CELL

MUSCLE

Neuron: cell specialized for rapid and far reaching stimulus transfer.

Axon: part of the neuron cell body that transfers stimuli across the greatest distances.

Dendrite: that part of the neuron that receives a stimulus input.

Nerves: axons that run in bundles alongside each other.

Afferent nerves: nerves that transfer sensory stimuli coming from the outside, to inside structures.

Efferent nerves: nerves that transfer stimuli to muscles or glands, causing them to respond.

Interneurons: neural cells that form pathways to serve a relay function in stimulus transfer.

Synapse: connection between two neurons.

- ■30 Define neuron.
- ■31 What is an afferent neuron? An efferent neuron?
- ■32 What does an interneuron do?
- ■33 Define synapse.

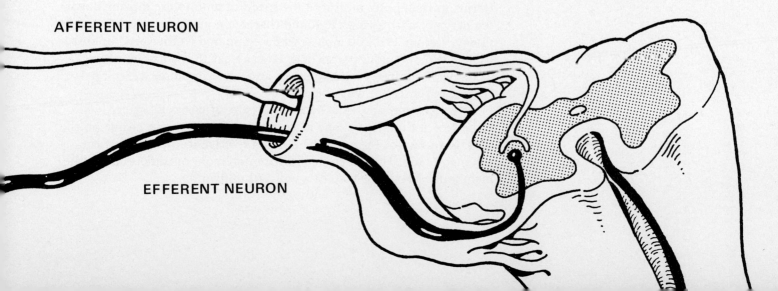

SPINAL COLUMN

AFFERENT NEURON

EFFERENT NEURON

How neurons conduct

Receptor cells absorb stimuli, converting the stimulus energy into a new form — electrochemical energy. This energy contacts the dendrites of an adjacent neuron, causing this cell to send energy down its axon. This is nerve conduction. But what is the nature of this flowing energy and how is it produced?

Quite early in the game, workers found that an electric current was always present when nerves were active. At that moment in history electricity was a newly discovered miracle — something so amazing it just had to play a great role in the scheme of things. Why not in the human nervous system? Nerves were merely wires carrying electric current — the nerve impulse. This answer made most people feel content about nerve conduction until a famous scientist named Hermann Helmholtz measured the speed of an impulse moving down the nerve of a frog's leg. He found that nerve impulses traveled quite slowly — from 2 to 200 mph — when compared to the speed of electricity, 186,300 miles per second. It was clear that whatever they were, nerves didn't work like wires, and nerve impulses weren't just electric current. But why the current at all?

As we know today, each neuron is a sort of wet cell battery — in principle, not unlike the one in your car, with a positive charge on the outside surface of the axon membrane, relative to the inside of the cell membrane. The difference in potential from outside to inside the membrane is roughly 1/10 of a volt (70 millivolts).

This is how it is when a neuron is at rest. It will stay that way until something happens to the cell membrane — something such as contact with chemicals or electric current — to change its permeability ever so slightly. When this happens, the nerve fires. To "fire" means that positive ions come rushing through the weakened membrane and reverse the charge on both sides — making the inside positive and the outside negative. This action affects the next part of the nerve, causing the same change in polarity to occur — then on it goes down the length of the axon, a moving negative wave. Once the wave has passed a point in the axon, the state of the axon behind it starts to return to normal. Positive ions from inside pass outward to restore the outside positive charge. Within a thousandth of a second it's loaded (back to normal), and ready to fire again.

■34 Why was it first thought that neural axons were like wires and impulses electricity?

■35 Who first measured the speed of nerve conduction?

■36 Describe the resting state, firing, and return to resting state of a neuron.

The All or None Law

Stimuli differ in strength as well as in form. Further, strength or intensity is far from being a neutral or inert feature of stimuli, as the effects a stimulus has on living tissue depend in large part upon how strong it is. For this reason, a creature has an edge in survival if its actions are controlled by stimulus strength as well as form. But if this is to occur, stimulus strength must somehow be coded in neural action. How is this achieved? This may appear a simple problem for someone who's not aware of how neurons conduct. "Nothing to it! A small amount of a stimulus causes a small wave of negative current down the neural axon — a larger stimulus, a larger current, and so on." Quite simple. But there's one problem: neurons don't work that way. A neuron either fires — sending the largest current it can muster down the axon — or it doesn't fire at all; and there's nothing in between. This is called the "All or None Law" of nerve conduction.

All or None Law: neurons either fire as totally as they are capable or they don't fire at all. There is no graded response.

Yes, the All or None Law holds for all neurons. But the receptor saves the day — allowing the strength of a stimulus to be retained in the nature of the nerve impulse. As we already know, receptors transform raw stimulus energy into electrochemical energy. Unlike the action of a nerve with its all-or-none wave of current, receptor energy is a graded electrochemical output that grows larger as the amount or strength of stimulus contact increases.

Receptor endings connect to the dendrites of nearby neurons. If the current reaching its dendrites is strong enough, a neuron will fire, and then restore itself — ready to fire again. All of this takes only a thousandth of a second. After firing, the neuron remains at rest until the current coming from the receptor is again large enough to make it fire. More intense and lasting stimuli make the rate of neuron firing increase, until, at last, it's firing as often as it can. No sooner does it restore itself than it's called on to expend its charge. In theory this would result in the neuron firing as often as a thousand times per second — if enough current reached its dendrites. Less intense stimuli and/or shorter lasting stimuli would produce less receptor current and cause the neuron to fire less often. So, the more intense the stimulus that reaches the receptor, the more current it sends to the dendrites and the more often the neuron puts out impulses.

But we often respond to more intense stimuli than a single neuron can code, or respond differently to. What happens then? Well, then the neurons work together as a team. When stimuli become intense, groups or nets of receptors converge on clusters of dendrites belonging to many neurons. As stimulus strength at a point of contact increases or as the area of contact grows, currents from increased numbers of receptors come into play. These currents become stronger as they reach the dendrites of the neuron bundle. This causes the neurons to fire. As receptor currents mount, more neurons in a bundle join in until scores are involved. This is called "recruitment". As more neurons fire, the result is a nerve discharge that's the summated total of the current from all the single neurons recruited.

Recruitment: as summated action of receptors grows, more neurons in a bundle begin to fire.

Receptor currents also increase and affect greater numbers of neurons in a bundle as energy coming from the outside increases. The final upshot is that a greater amount of energy reaching receptors results in a greater number of neurons being involved — all firing in terms of the All or None Law — but making a total nerve discharge that keeps up with the strength of the input.

- ■37 State the All or None Law.
- ■38 What apparent problem does the All or None Law suggest?
- ■39 How can intensity of a stimulus be coded by a single neuron?
- ■40 How is intensity and/or area of stimulus contact reflected where groups of receptors and neurons are involved?

Synaptic transfer

As mentioned before, neurons connect to other neurons at special junctions called synapses. Transfer taking place at the synapse involves a unique chemical exchange between the axon of one neuron and the dendrite of another. Axons end in an enlarged structure called the end bouton. The impulses are received by a special nodule on the adjacent dendrite called the dendritic spine. End boutons contain many small island-like structures called "synaptic vesicles". They release chemicals when an impulse reaches the end of the axon. These chemicals or chemical transfer agents, as they are called, play a prime role in synaptic transfer. Some chemicals released by the synaptic vesicles promote transfer across the synapse while others retard it, or stop it altogether.

Synaptic vesicles: clumps of matter occurring in the end bouton that release chemicals when an impulse comes down the axon.

Transmitter agents: chemicals released at the synapse that govern the nature of synaptic transfer.

- ■41 What are the synaptic vesicles? Define.
- ■42 Define transmitter agents.

CONCLUSIONS

In this chapter we've remained true to the theme of evolution in dealing with human anatomy and physiology. Although we've paid due respects to the human nervous system, we've not treated it like some deity deserving of worship. Instead we've taken a simpler view — that it represents a highly complex and efficient solution to the problem of putting a creature in contact with its environment. As such, it's a fine piece of work, one slowly and subtly crafted through eons by the demands of survival. Now we're better prepared to view the human in action, having at least a passing knowledge of inner structure and function. It's time to look at behavior, and how it came about.

CHAPTER 4
EVOLUTION
AND BEHAVIOR

INTRODUCTION

Since psychology is the science of behavior, we ask why do we behave or act as we do? And we find one reason we act as we do is because of the way we're built, because of our structure. So then we ask, why are we built that way? And we find one reason we're built as we are is that we inherit much of our structure from our ancestors, and that this is a structure that evolved over many generations due to natural selection — the selection of those mutations that helped creatures survive long enough to produce more of their own kind. As we'll see, this notion of natural selection applies to the evolution of learned response patterns — as well as to the evolution of structure — to patterns handed down through our culture as well as to structures handed down through our genes. And we'll find features such as active life helping us survive whether we are the simpler or the more complex creatures.

So we'll assume most of our current actions are caused by the structures we inherit; and we'll assume that those structure-caused actions helped our ancestors survive — they fit the circumstance. Therefore, we'll try to figure out how such patterns of action helped them survive and see if they're still useful to us.

PASSIVE LIFE

Evolution and animals

Dodo is a tiny creature — so tiny you need a microscope to see it. But if you did see Dodo, you'd think it has it made — the good life, lying there in that nice, warm fluid, not working, just absorbing the food it's lying on. Pretty good — but what happens when it has absorbed all the food around; does it then go to work for more food? No. It just lies there absorbing food as the food happens to drift by, the fluid carrying its meals to the creature.

But of course there's a problem with this drifting food since it might bump into Dodo and then drift on before Dodo has time to absorb it. And things can get even worse if the fluid stops carrying the small bits of food to Dodo. Does the little creature go to work to get more food then? No, it just starves to death, because Dodo can't move on its own since it never acquired the function of motion. It will die if food isn't near at hand. Dodo does pretty well when there's food aplenty, but it will starve during the famine. So it goes. And passive creatures do exist more or less like Dodo, with some bacteria, virus, and algae being passive forms of life — passive at least as far as motion from place to place is concerned.

- 1 What is the danger of the passive life?
- 2 What are examples of passive life?

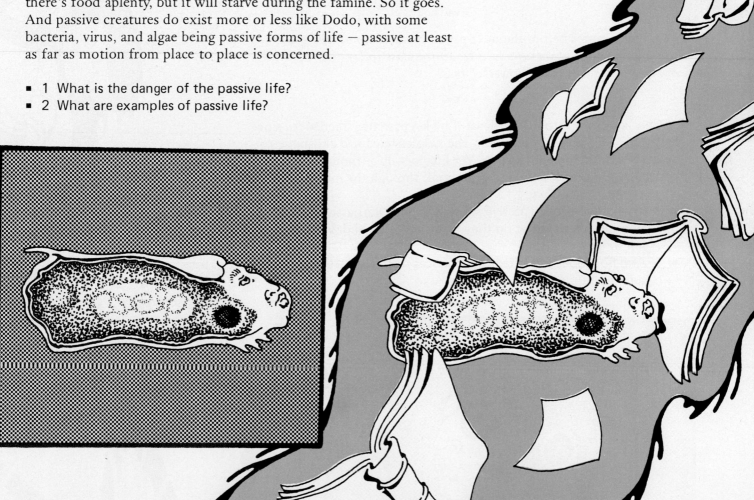

Humans

Simple life forms like Dodo can be passive, but so can complex life forms, passive at least with regard to some crucial acts, causing much the same problems for the human as for the bacterium.

***

Chet sat in the back row having some trouble staying awake during the first meeting of the psych class. *Just sit here behind that girl's afro so prof can't see me catching a few z's. Damn, he moved. Why can't he stay in one place?*

What's he doin' now? Tellin' us what he's assigned for the next class. Puttin' it on the blackboard. His writing's worse than mine. Can't read it too well. Now I can't even see what he's writing either. Wish that girl'd wear her hair like normal people do; then I could see the blackboard. What the hell. Bag it.

***

A few minutes before the next psych class: *Damn it, there was some homework I was supposed to do for class today. Can't remember what it was. Oh well, bag it.*

***

Chet may be in trouble, at least if he keeps acting like Dodo, since hard times did come Dodo's way, the helpless creature did starve to death when the food got scarce. Yet life goes on — though mainly active life. So now it's time to again look through the microscope.

- 3 In what way does a passive student act like the passive bacterium? In other words, what do they both fail to do and what do they fail to get?
- 4 And how does this affect the chances of the passive student to succeed in college?

ACTIVE LIFE

Evolution and animals

As the dead carcass of Dodo drifts off, another little creature swims by. And this new creature, Gore, has a crucial feature helping it survive as its world changes — it can move on its own, not having to wait for food to come its way. So Gore's more likely to bump into food since it's on the move. If there's not enough food in one place, Gore keeps on the move until it runs into more food someplace else. When the going gets tough, the tough get going. Now, this doesn't mean that Gore is looking for food. No, it's just that it does move around a lot and so is more likely to happen to bump into food.

While Gore is active in moving from place to place, it's also active in another way: it surrounds its food — just like a pillow struck by a baseball. And since it gets ahold of its food, the food can't drift away before Gore absorbs it. Thus Gore loses much less food than Dodo. And those two types of action helped Gore survive the big famine.

We saw that some bacteria are passive life forms, like our Dodo; they don't locomote. And do fairly simple yet active creatures like Gore also really exist? As you've no doubt guessed, the answer is yes. Amoebas have active motion; they move from place to place and they "hold onto" the food they contact.

- 5 What are two types of action that help creatures get food?
- 6 What's a real example of fairly simple, active life?

Humans

Not all simple creatures are like the passive Dodo as Gore shows us. And not all complex creatures are like the passive Chet as Sid will show us, since some active response patterns work — for humans as well as amoebas.

***

Damn! Another PhD who writes like a gradeschool kid, Sid thought. After class he went to the front of the room, where he could make out most of the words on the blackboard, except for . . . "Sir, Dr. . . . ah . . ." Sid glanced at the top of the blackboard finding the psych teacher's name, "Ah . . . Harper, what's that say there?" he asked pointing to the blackboard.

"Page 1."

"Of course, thank you, Sir." Sid wrote the assignment in his notebook and headed back to the dorm.

- 7 In what two ways might an active student behave like the active amoeba?
- 8 How does this action affect the student's chances to survive?

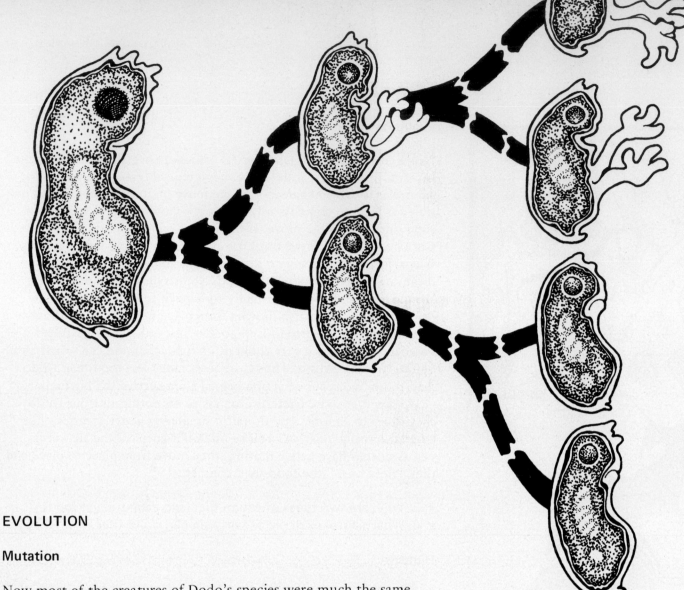

EVOLUTION

Mutation

Now most of the creatures of Dodo's species were much the same, but once in a while one was born that differed from the rest. That happens in two ways for simpler creatures: The area around the parent might change and in turn cause a chemical change in the parent, with its offspring inheriting that new chemical structure. And this chemical change might affect the outside structure of the offspring though it only affected the inner chemical make-up of the parent. Or, the area around the parent might change during birth causing a chemical change in the offspring only, so that it differed from the parent, causing a mutation.

Some mutations give the offspring a better chance to survive, while some make it harder for them to survive since in the delicate balance of life even slight changes can be fatal — whether these are changes in the environment or in the structure of the creature. However, for the most part, mutations have no great effect at all on the creature.

- ▪ 9 Review: What is a mutation?
- ▪10 What are two ways a mutation occurs?
- ▪11 Does a mutation most often help the offspring survive?

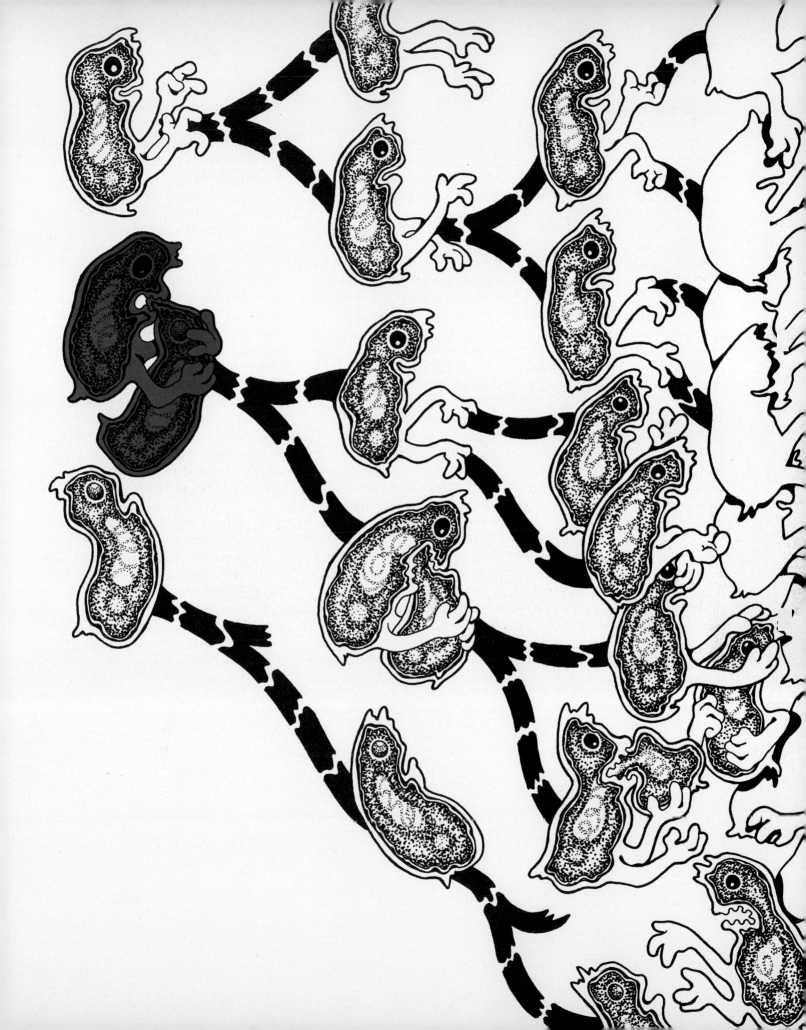

Natural selection

As we've just seen, creatures that mutate differ from others. And once in a while one of these changes helps the new creature survive, with the world of nature letting it live longer than the others that are almost, but not quite, the same. We call this "natural selection".

Natural selection: features of a creature help it survive in the world of nature, allowing the creature to pass that feature on to its offspring.

And how does natural selection affect the way a species evolves? When a famine comes along those mutants with useful features will have a better chance since creatures will get more of the food if they move about or latch onto that food when they bump into it. But also there will be even less food left for the passive ones that didn't adapt so well, since the movers and grabbers will have more than their share, so the passive may starve to death, instead of inheriting the earth. And the creatures left will have at least one new feature helping them survive — allowing them to produce more offspring that keep the species alive.

And what about the offspring of these new creatures? A few of them will also mutate, with some mutating in ways that make it harder to survive. For instance, a creature might mutate back to an early form that has less motion. But sometimes a creature will mutate a new feature — one improving even further its chances of getting food or getting away from harm; for instance, a feature like greater speed. And this latest model will be more likely to survive than its parent. This swifter creature will win the race when things get rough again. When food gets scarce it may stand in the field alone amidst the dead hulks of friends and family. So it goes.

So the years pass, with one helpful mutation piling on top of the next until a very hardy creature comes forth — at least hardy in the world where this species evolved. Thus, natural selection plays a crucial role in the way species do evolve. Creatures mutate and nature selects — the two processes working together, hand in hand, combining to produce a strong species.

Theory of evolution by natural selection: the process of mutation causes a variety of life forms, with some forms surviving, while others die as the state of nature selects among them. And the offspring of those that survive may inherit some of these helpful structural changes. Thus a species acquires more and more helpful new features over time, with creatures evolving that are well suited for their world.

- ■12 Define natural selection.
- ■13 Cite a case where the forces of nature select out creatures that mutated a good feature — and reject another that mutated a poor feature.
- ■14 Does evolution by natural selection tend to produce creatures well designed for their world?

Sickle cell anemia

Juke put his book down to comment to Sid. "You know this evolution by natural selection is right on. It explains what's goin' down with sickle cell anemia."

"How do you figure that?" Sid asked.

"Well, I always wondered why us Blacks got to hassel with it when whitey don't. But I can get next to it when I look at it in terms of natural selection. Here's why we evolved that way in Africa; it's because that trait helped us survive in that environment, since it makes us immune to the sleeping sickness that some of the local flies carry. And that sleeping sickness really wasted the white colonials.

Now here's something else bothered me: forty percent of the Blacks in West Africa inherit the sickle cell anemia trait, but only ten percent of us Blacks in the States inherit it. But Blacks can survive just as well over here without that trait so the amount of Blacks without the trait rose from sixty percent to ninety percent. And that's how a group can evolve in a way that helps them survive one place but they may lose that trait if it don't help them some when their environment changes."

■15 Why did Blacks evolve sickle cell anemia in West Africa, and why are they losing it in America?

Natural selection in human social systems

We've seen how natural selection works to produce new forms of biological structure in the animal world; what about your world? Can natural selection also produce new forms of learned acts in complex social systems? Let's look at a case affecting you to get an answer.

What causes you to survive in college? How smart you are? We doubt it. Most likely you're smart enough to get through college, if you're smart enough to get here in the first place.

What about how hard you work? We think that's one of the major factors, since students often do poorly if they don't study. There's a close relation between the amount of time you put into something and how well you do at it, even though once in a while you may work hard and goof up, or take it easy and do well. So by and large, college wipes out people who haven't learned to work.

Now you'll probably work hard and graduate from college; so any offspring you produce will be more likely to go to college, more likely than will the offspring of parents who did not graduate from college, since college grads are more likely to have children who also go to college. (Note: This social selection differs from biological selection, as we're not saying college grads are more likely to produce offspring — in fact, they're less likely to; we're just saying they're more likely to encourage their offspring to go to college.)

So what'll happen when your offspring get into college? They will probably work hard and survive, since they're likely to learn your style of hard work. Therefore, all things equal (which they never are), more and more students should work hard and survive in college.

To sum up: college students differ in how hard they work. Natural social selection causes hard workers to survive college. The offspring may learn this style of hard work from their parents. And these offspring are more likely to go to college (for other causes). So there we have it; a new breed of hard working college student may be evolving, if no other factors come into play. A case of natural selection of learned acts in complex social systems.

■16 Cite a case where natural selection can affect the way people perform in college.
■17 Show how that case might result in the evolution of more students who perform well.

PURPOSIVISM

Thus far we've gotten a good feel for the following notions: The world of nature dictates which acts help a creature survive. We call this "natural selection". The creature's structure affects how it will act. How it acts affects whether there will be offspring to inherit that structure. And the whole process combines with mutation to affect the structure and actions of the creatures that evolve.

That's a useful way of looking at evolution and behavior. Now let's check out a less useful way.

***

Juke and Sid sat in their room reading this chapter. As Juke put his book down he said, "This evolution stuff's heavy business. But seems almost like they're sayin' nature's tryin' to build better and better creatures; an' I think nature don't give a damn. I hope they aren't sayin' nature has a purpose. Can you dig that?"

"Right. The problem comes when people talk about 'natural selection'. You almost get the picture that Mother Nature's out there picking out this little creature and casting that one aside. But there's no Mother Nature, and there's no purpose."

"Nature may be a motha, but they ain't no Motha Nature. An' nature don't have a purpose. Nature ain't a person or a thing; it's just what's out there in the world: the wind, air, water, weather, plants, animals, and you and me. And when it all comes together, some creatures survive and some don't. And it stands to reason: the ones best suited to their world survive. And if their kids inherit their strengths, then their kids'll survive. And some will even mutate more strengths. And it's got to be — the species just keeps gettin' better and better. But they ain't no Mama plannin' the whole thing out. And they ain't no goal out there that the forces of nature tryin' to get to."

***

The notion Juke and Sid object to is called "purposivism". (The first part is pronounced like "purpose" and you can take it from there.)

Purposivism: the notion that events have purposes causing them to occur.

People often fall into the purposivism trap, when thinking about why things occur as they do. This is even more true when there seems to be a logical progression of events leading from some lesser state of affairs to some greater state. But Juke is correct: evolution often does result in an improved state of affairs simply due to the structure of nature and not because of some plan or purpose.

But we err just as much when we suggest creatures have a purpose just because they act in a way that produces good results. A creature does not move so that it can get food, because it does not have a purpose — not even the purpose of surviving; instead the species has evolved that move at certain times, because those creatures that did move that way happened to get food and thus survived to produce offspring.

We often quit before we really find the causes of things, when we rely on purpose to explain nature, an easy cop-out, leaving us with the notion that the cause of an event can occur after that event has taken place. But most scientists agree that the causes of an event must be present at the time of the event. For instance, the causes of evolution are there while the creatures evolve — the future can't cause things to happen now. In the same way, the cause of a behavioral act can not be its future results; but it might be the effect of its past results on the current condition of the creatures.

It is tempting to think in terms of purpose when dealing with simpler creatures; but it is even more tempting to resort to "purpose" when we look at complex creatures — a temptation we do well to resist.

- ■18 Define purposivism and cite an instance of it in statements about evolution and about behavior.
- ■19 State a better way of talking about causes than an appeal to purpose, and give an instance.

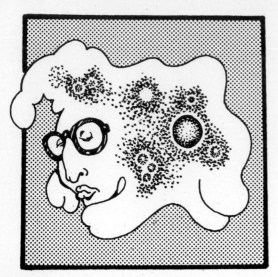

BASIC CAUSES OF ACTION

Our biophysical structure provides all of us creatures with the capacity for our actions whether we are passive or active, whether we fail or survive. But those creatures that did survive passed on their biophysical capacity for action as the inheritance they left their offspring. Thus we act because action helped our ancestors survive — because we inherited their structure for action.

Evolution with animals

We'll sometimes pause to look back at the simpler creatures while looking at our own complex lives. This may help us deal with our complex world. Thus, we hope to see what gets us moving by looking at the causes of action of the simple planarian.

We discussed Gore's moving about, latching onto food, bumping into things. But Gore's not always in motion, since motion is not the "natural" state of most creatures — something must prod them into action. And two things cause Gore to move: lack of fuels such as food, and threat of harm. Gore will start to move about if it's been some time since the creature has eaten. That way it'll be more likely to run into food. But Gore slows way down again after eating its fill. And this slowing down also helps it survive since motion uses up that food; so Gore gets by with less food when it slows down. Thus creatures may survive even when fuel is scarce, if they don't waste their fuel with excess motion.

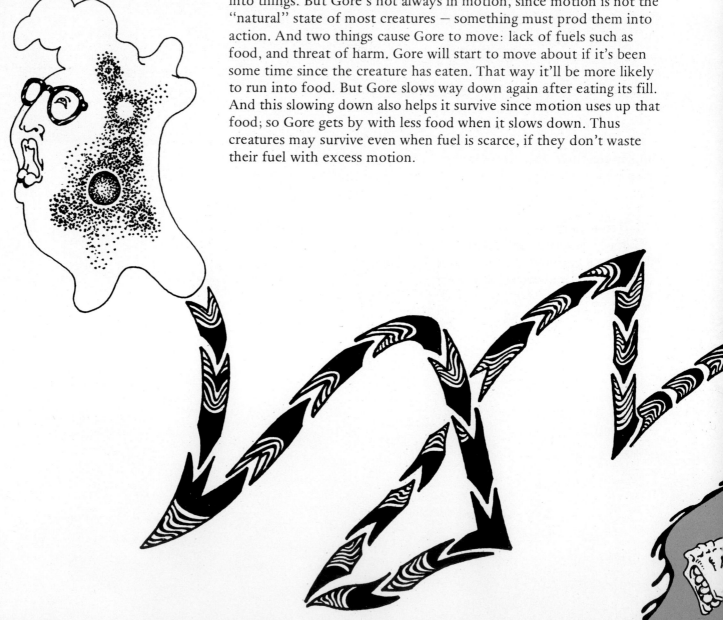

Gore will also start moving if there is threat of harm. Too much light, too much acid in its fluid medium, or too much heat. Such harmful conditions (states) cause the creature to move. And a Gore on the move is more likely to escape this harm.

Another instance of harm-induced motion is shown by the wood louse, often found sheltered in the dampness beneath fallen logs. Research workers have shown this creature will die after only a few hours exposure to dry air — clearly a harmful state of affairs. And they also showed the wood louse will greatly increase its rate of moving about when exposed to that harmful dry air. Thus it will be more likely to happen into damp safety beneath a log if it keeps moving about instead of just lying there drying up.

Perhaps some creatures evolved that didn't get more active when they ran low on fuel or were in a harmful state. But they'd have been more likely to die off. So it goes. But other creatures — those responding like Gore — were more likely to survive, since they began moving around when they ran low on fuel or made contact with a harmful state.

■20 What two classes of events cause creatures to move?
■21 How does motion help the creature survive when it's running low on fuel and also when it's in a harmful state?
■22 Why would a creature that was always in motion be less likely to survive?

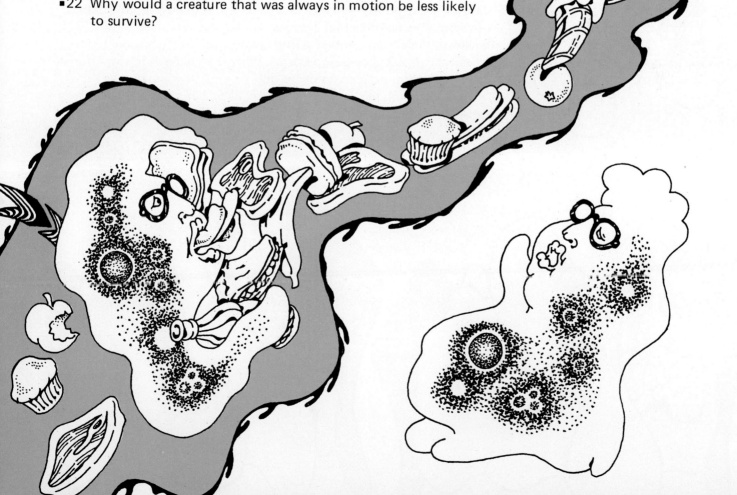

How it is now with humans

Getting up from the lunch table, Chet stretched with the air of a satisfied man. He thought to himself, *What a meal. I ate so much I could bust. Good thing Carol agreed to come home from work to fix me a decent lunch. Bad for a man not to get a good, hot lunch.* Stretching one more time, he belched and laid down on the couch.

As Carol rushed out the door for work, she asked, "Don't you need to study your psych?"

"No sweat; plenty a' time; so get off my back an' let me rest." Though Chet soon fell asleep he was tossing and turning in a short time, at last waking up. *Damn it's hot in here. Why can't that woman keep it a little cooler? She knows I'm trying to sleep . . .* "Carol, where the hell are you?" *. . . Oh, yeah, she went back to work.* Chet lay there a couple more minutes before getting up to open the window. Soon he was back asleep.

But he woke up with a start at 1:45. *Damn it; why the hell didn't she set that damned alarm clock. She knows I got a two o'clock class. Damn, I only got 15 minutes to study and get over to class.*

***

Now this scene with Chet shows three things. First, well-fed Chet slowed way down, just like other creatures. Second, too-hot Chet stirred into action, just like other creatures. And third, potential danger (doing poorly in psych) failed to get him moving, just like other simple creatures that get into trouble because there's no backward link from a future harmful event to Chet's current action (recall the problem of purposivism). What may happen in the future can't affect him now; so he sleeps on.

Lack of action in the face of danger (like Chet's failing psych) causes severe problems for many of us. But sometimes our culture

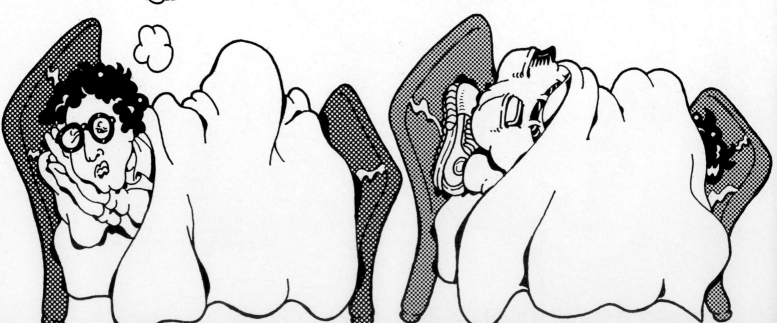

instills in us a way of dealing with such problems. Let's see how this affects Sid, waiting until a later chapter to go into the details.

***

Leaving the dining hall, Sid went up to his room for a brief nap. *Food's sure not like Mom's, but it still makes me feel like grabbing a quick snooze. I'll just stretch out for a few z's before I re-read the psych chapter.*

Laying down, Sid started to doze off, only to have a fitful sleep. He pulled the covers over his head to no avail. *Hell with it. I can't ever sleep when I've got something I need to do. I'll worry about this quiz 'til I know I've got it down cold. So I might as well start studying now. Maybe I can sleep for a few minutes when I'm done studying.*

***

This sort of worrying is not likely to be found in creatures as simple as Gore. But it serves much the same function as events that cause direct harm; it gets people moving; it makes them more likely to take action — action that will get them out of harm's way — that will help them survive — help them stay in college and avoid failing their courses. We'll read more about such complex causes in future chapters.

- ■23 Cite a case where the two basic causes of motion affect human action.
- ■24 Cite a case where a person doesn't take action even though a harmful event may be on its way.
- ■25 Cite a case where a person does take action.

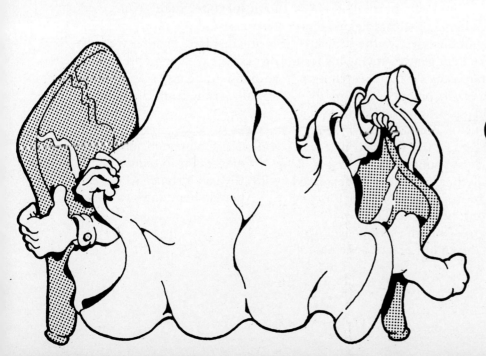

HABITUATION

Evolution with animals

Sometimes a creature finds itself in a bind. Its rate of motion rises since it's exposed to a harmful state. Yet it doesn't escape the harm no matter where it moves. If that happens, it may slow down or stop moving altogether. Fatal? Not always. Maybe the harm will go away. Maybe a cloud will come over the sun, so it won't be too bright. Then the creature that stopped moving may still have enough fuel left to go on living after the harmful state has passed. A tricky balance. Keep moving — will the creature escape before the fuel runs out? Stop moving — will the harmful state go away before it kills the creature? This is habituation. And those creatures whose response to harmful states habituates are sometimes a little more likely to survive since they don't use up all of their fuel. And that's why such creatures have evolved.

Habituation: decreased motion or response to a state of affairs (often a harmful state) due to prolonged exposure to that state.

Note that the harmful state may keep causing tissue damage, even though responses to it habituate; it's just that the harmful state stops causing the creature to move around once it habituates.

- ■26 Define habituation and cite an instance.
- ■27 How can habituation help a creature survive?

Humans and pain

Juke felt good catching that football, running down the field; twisting, turning, leaving those guys behind; it felt good to . . . Wham! *Where in the hell did Big Red come from? It don't matter, I can't lay here all day. Damn that shoulder hurts . . . guess if I just hold my shoulder back a bit . . . like this . . . yeah, that's it . . . now it don't . . . oops, yes it does . . . just a little forward . . . that's it . . . still hurts, but not so much.* Juke had kept moving his shoulder until he found a position that reduced the pain.

The next play: Juke was off; there's the ball; he caught it. *Got to look out for Red. Where is that big son-of-a . . . Damn, there he is. He move too fast for such a big dude. I'll just do my famous jukestep and . . .* "Ohh . . ."

Down again. But it wasn't Big Red's tackle that hurt so much this time. As Juke tried to sidestep Big Red, he also favored his shoulder; that threw him off balance. So he twisted his ankle as his cleats dug into the turf. Now he was on the ground again and really hurting. Red gave him a hand and helped him hop-hobble over to the bench. Juke kept gently moving his foot about as he sat there watching the others practice — trying to find a position that didn't hurt so much; but nothing worked. He'd twist this way and that way — always futile. And at first it really hurt. As the pain decreased Juke stopped moving his foot about; he just sat there — engrossed in the scrimmage. And by the end of practice the pain had all but gone away, though his ankle had swollen. Juke was puzzled by this until he recalled a section he had just read in his psych text — a section about habituation.

Note that in this case at least two responses habituated to the harmful state: Juke's pain response and the motion of his foot. (In a later chapter we will discuss the pain response — the response of being aware of the stimuli arising from the tissue damage.)

- ■28 Cite a human instance of movement to reduce pain.
- ■29 Give an instance where a human habituates to pain.

Humans and distraction

Mae found the chapter on evolution and behavior hard reading. She could read it all right as long as she had a little peace and quiet. But that was just when Dawn turned on her radio — and loud too. Didn't seem to bother Dawn, but Mae kept reading the same sentence over and over. She'd hate to hurt her new roommate — Dawn was trying so hard; she'd turned on WSOL, the only all soul station within range.

Dawn even leaned back and clapped her hands in time to the music — not too loud — just loud enough to let Mae know she had a real feeling for that kind of music. Dawn expressed this feeling by moving her hands way back right after each clap, where she held them waiting for the next beat — "Hee-Haw" style. At first she tried clapping with the off-beat, but that didn't work too well; so she shifted over to the beat itself — a little easier to handle.

"I just love soul music, don't you!" Dawn said. Mae nodded and kept on trying to read.

Dawn got back on the beat and clapped for twelve more bars — too bad Mae failed to notice her feeling for the music. In fact, worse than that, Mae cleared her throat, and asked, "Would you mind turning it down a little; I can't keep my mind on this book."

Without looking up, Dawn reached for the volume knob and turned it down — but not enough to suit Mae. Mae tried but still kept reading "active life" over and over.

And it says, "When the going gets tough, the tough get going." So she picked up her book and headed for the lounge. The dorm staff told them the lounge was kept as a quiet area so they could study there. But when she got to the lounge she saw why some of the sophomore skeptics had snickered. A madhouse. People coming and going, talking and laughing, but not studying. Mae didn't even go in. It was back to her room, hoping Dawn had noticed her plight and would "turn it down just a bit more"; but no such luck.

Mae tried to read, resting her head on one hand, covering one ear with her hand in a vain effort to cut the noise in half. But there she was; still reading the same thing over and over. Yet little by little she did stop noticing the music as she began getting into her psych — she could hear the sounds, but they didn't distract her so much. She had habituated to the music; no longer trying to escape it, and no longer being distracted by it. Ten minutes later the news came on; so Dawn turned the radio off, causing Mae's reading rate to double.

■30 Cite an instance where a human habituates to distraction.

BASIC STIMULUS CONTROL

Thus far we've looked at two causes of Gore's motion — lack of fuel, and harm. Both control the amount of Gore's motion, and both directly affect whether Gore will survive. But a third class of events also affects Gore's motion. These new events don't cause Gore to increase or decrease its motion; they affect the course of motion. And, they have only an indirect effect on whether Gore survives.

But let's look at a new Gore — a new model, a new species, a zoo-plankton swimming along the top of the water. And let's see how this new type of control affects our new Gore.

Sometimes food is more likely to be found in one spot than another; for instance, zoo-plankton eat algae. And the algae plant needs light. So where does Gore find its meal? Where there's light. And sure enough, that creature evolved so that it moves toward the light if it hasn't eaten for a while. Does the light cause Gore to move? Not really. No, the light doesn't cause it to move; but the absence of food does. Gore will start moving even in the dark if it's low on food. What does the light do? The light directs the course of the motion. It guides Gore.

Of course, there've been creatures that didn't mutate that way, creatures like the amoeba with its random motion, not under the stimulus control of the light, bumping into food only by chance, and less likely to survive when food gets scarce. So it goes. But other creatures did mutate so that the light stimulus controls the path of their motion, and such creatures, like the zoo-plankton, are more likely to survive.

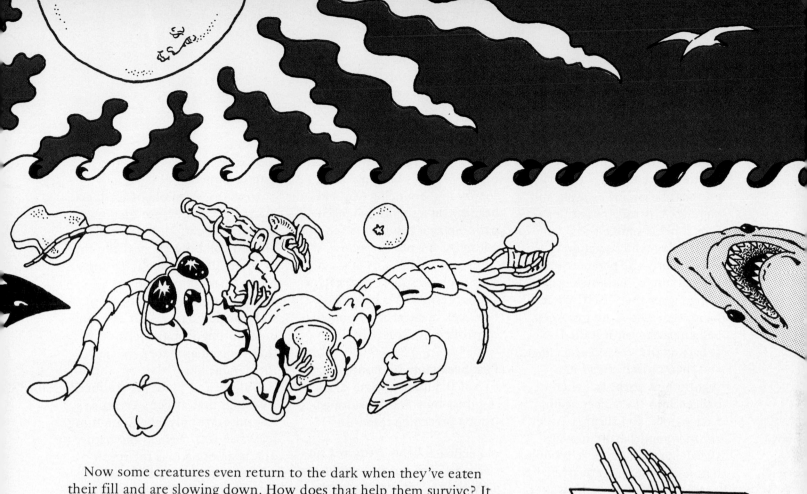

Now some creatures even return to the dark when they've eaten their fill and are slowing down. How does that help them survive? It gets them away from bigger creatures that might eat them in turn. Thus, light can direct the course of motion of well-fed animals as well, sending them back to the safety of the dark. In both cases, we call this control "basic stimulus control". And, of course, creatures under proper stimulus control are more likely to survive.

Basic stimulus control: control exerted by a stimulus over the form or path of a response.

Let's look at another instance of basic stimulus control — this time control with a much more complex creature — the female tick. After mating she climbs to the tip of a bush, clinging there, perhaps for months, until some creature chances to wander beneath her. Then she lets go of the branch, falling on the creature's back to feast on its blood. And what unique stimulus controlled her release, guiding her to her meal? The odor of butric acid from the glands in the skin of the mammal strolling beneath the bush. So odor as well as light can exert basic stimulus control over a creature's responses.

- ■31 State the two ways basic stimulus control differs from the basic causes of motion.
- ■32 How does stimulus control help creatures survive? Give one instance based on fuel and one based on harm.
- ■33 Define basic stimulus control.

FEEDBACK STIMULUS CONTROL

Evolution with animals

Now let's look at one more form of stimulus control — feedback — one that helps both simple and complex creatures. First, let's see how it helps simple ones.

One day while swimming along, Gore, the paramecium, banged into something — something bigger than itself. What happened? Did Gore just keep banging away until it died? No. It backed off, turned at an angle, and then moved ahead in a slightly new path. But then it banged into the object again, backing off, and turning at yet another angle before moving ahead one more time. After doing that a few times, Gore arrived at a free course and swam away.

***

Let's look more closely at this. Gore made a response — a forward motion. The response produced a result — Gore's banging into something, bouncing off, and heading on a slightly changed path. So that result changed the nature of the next response, with Gore moving along its new path. This cycle (response-results-altered response) is called a feedback cycle. The response is controlled by its feedback.

Feedback stimulus control: control of the form or path of a response by stimuli resulting from a preceding response.

Feedback helps creatures survive since without it they'd keep making the same error time and time again until it killed them. So we're not surprised that all moving creatures that have survived seem to be under feedback control — even the simple amoeba.

Now this example of feedback control involves more than mere mechanical action. It's not like a billiard ball bouncing off the side of the table it strikes at an angle. Even if Gore hits the thing straight on, it still moves off at some angle, that way of responding resulting from the structure that evolved as Gore's species, the paramecia.

But we don't label as feedback all things that affect a creature's response. We only label something feedback if it changes the nature of a response and is the result of an earlier response. For instance, Gore swam along a clear path after getting free of the object standing in its way. But then a current came along pushing Gore onto a new course, changing its

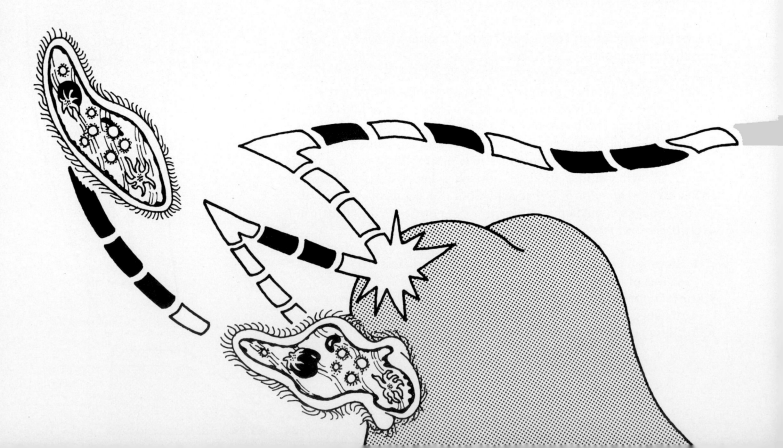

response. Does that mean the current was feedback? No. Merely changing the response is not enough. This change must result from another response. And being hit by the current was not a result of Gore's response. That current would have affected Gore no matter what it was doing — and no matter where it was doing it, since it swept into the whole area. The current would have been feedback only if Gore had run into it as a result of its swimming. But this didn't happen — therefore it isn't feedback.

Not all feedback is the result of external stimuli; response-produced stimuli from within the body (proprioceptive stimuli) can also act as feedback to control the form of the next response. To see this let's look at

another swimming creature, but one much more complex than the zoo-plankton and the planaria. Let's look at the dogfish, a fish that swims by wiggling its body much like a snake crawling through the grass.

The dogfish starts to undulate at the head, with the posture of undulation passing down the body. The front muscles cause the front of the body to undulate, producing proprioceptive feedback stimuli. These stimuli control the muscles of the mid-section, causing that part of the body to undulate. This in turn controls the next set of muscles, causing the next part of the body to undulate, and so on. Research workers studied the role of feedback by cutting all the afferent nerves from the

proprioceptors. Without those pathways of feedback, the dogfish could not perform its rhythmic swimming movements, proving that response-produced stimuli from within the body can also act as feedback.

Proprioceptive stimuli: inner stimuli produced by the tension (or position) of the muscles.

- ∎34 Be able to cite cases of feedback and non-feedback stimulus control.
- ∎35 Define feedback stimulus control.
- ∎36 What creatures have feedback stimulus control?
- ∎37 What would happen to a moving creature not controlled by feedback stimulus control?

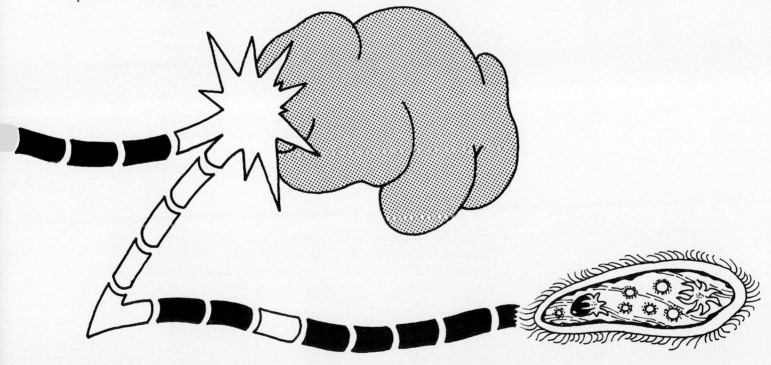

Human uses of feedback

But what about human beings? Feedback stimulus control plays an even larger role in complex creatures such as us, where it seems nearly all of our actions are under feedback control, with the stimuli from one response controlling the form of the next.

Scientists show this in the lab in several ways. For instance, the sound of your own voice provides crucial feedback in the control of the way you talk, with the nature of each sound controlled by the ones that came just before it. You can see this through the use of delayed feedback where the sound of your voice gets back to you a fraction of a second after you've spoken. This delayed feedback shows how crucial normal feedback is since you can hardly talk under these conditions.

You can do this yourself with a three-headed tape recorder, by talking into the mike which is picked up on the first head (the record head) and getting your feedback from the third head (playback head) through earphones. This causes delayed feedback since it takes a fraction of a second for the tape to get from the record head to the playback head. The effect can be enhanced by playing the tape deck at its slowest speed.

We also control how loudly we speak with feedback from the sound of our own voice. This is often shown when someone tries to talk while listening to a stereo through a pair of earphones. The sound of the music masks the sound of people's voices causing them to speak much more loudly than normal and causing a mild amount of condescending mirth among those being spoken to.

***

Chet hurried to class. *Ten minutes early. Good, somebody already here.* "Hi. We supposed to hand something in today?"

Dawn smiled. "Yeah, a paper about how this chapter applies to humans."

"Gosh, I don't know what I'm gonna do." Chet paused, hoping the young woman would let him glance at her work — just to get a few ideas. But when she kept smiling and that was all, Chet rushed to the back row and started writing. *I suppose this'd be easier if I'd read the chapter, but maybe the prof won't ask for 'em 'til the end of the hour.*

***

Dr. Harper paused, the class period over, with him only halfway through his lecture. "That does it for today. See you Friday." Notebooks slammed shut. Students rose from their seats causing much noise and commotion. Chet was relieved until Juke shouted out, "Hey, Harper, you forgot to get our homework," causing Chet to sink back down in his seat.

"Oh yeah. Everybody, hold it a minute. Put your homework here on my desk as you leave the room."

"One more thing," Dr. Harper shouted, stopping the noise and commotion once more. The students were eager to get going — to get to the next class. "Do the same kind of homework for the next chapter and turn it in at the next class."

Sid raised his hand.

"Yeah?" the harried teacher nodded toward Sid.

"How can we do the next chapter, 'til we see the way you marked this one? We'll just keep making the same mistakes."

Damn that kid. I don't want to postpone the homework; we'll have enough trouble getting it all done this term anyway. To the class: "I'll have them graded by tomorrow, and I'll put comments on them. Pick 'em up at my office." Class ended amidst mild groans.

The next day: Sid walked over to Dr. Harper's office. *It's a drag to make a special trip to get that paper. But I'd better follow up on it since I caused such a fuss.*

When Sid got back his paper: *Wow, he doesn't just want examples, he wants us to show how they relate to the concepts. Well at least I should do better than a "C" on this next one.*

***

Without giving it much thought, Chet knew he didn't need to go all the way over to the office. He'd do okay without seeing Harper's comments.

***

And that's the real world you, dear reader, must deal with — in and out of college. Often it's not clear what you're supposed to do — what's needed to survive. Your teacher assigns something, but things are vague. The teacher implies college students should know what to do — just use their own good judgement. So you do, but your own good judgement isn't good enough. At least it wasn't like your teacher's judgement. Perhaps you couldn't read your teacher's mind. And who suffers when the teacher isn't clear? Not the teacher.

Now how is this an instance of feedback type stimulus control? Well first, your teacher's remarked about what you did right and wrong and what you should do in the future; that can exert stimulus control over your efforts the next time — it can guide or direct your future actions. And second, the remarks are feedback since they resulted from what you did earlier.

***

But others fail to be clear too. So when you get a new job, the odds are your boss won't give you clear enough guidance. You'll have a better chance to survive in your job if you go after feedback — feedback about how well you're doing your job. Go after that feedback even though it may be even harder to get the feedback from your boss than from your teachers.

But suppose you are the boss; does that mean you don't need feedback anymore? No, you really need it now. Companies and other groups often fail because of lack of feedback. Suppose things aren't going well with a business you're running. Don't just keep plodding down the same old path to failure. Get feedback by asking your customers how you should change your product, your services, and your marketing, by asking your employees how you should change your operations. Then you'll much more likely survive.

Or maybe you'll become a teacher yourself. You will also need feedback to do a good teaching job. And things are changing in the teaching field since doing a good job teaching may play a bigger role in helping the teacher survive nowadays. So as a teacher you'll need to get feedback from your students: How much are they learning? Can you change the way you teach so they'll learn more? Do they like your course? What can you do to improve it?

So both company managers and college teachers supervise others, with the manager overseeing employees and the teacher helping students. And both should look to the results of their efforts for cues to help them improve. These results should exert stimulus control over their future efforts. And since this control is a product of their earlier actions it is feedback from those actions — feedback needed for success.

If you get and use feedback, you too will be more likely to succeed — more likely whether you're an amoeba, student, worker, business manager, or teacher.

- ■38 What is an example of feedback stimulus control in college?
- ■39 Cite a case of a person using feedback stimulus control and a person failing to use it.
- ■40 Which person will be more likely to survive? Why?
- ■41 Cite three areas where feedback will help you survive.
- ■42 Recognize sources and types of feedback useful for a business manager.
- ■43 Do the same for a college teacher.

CONCLUSIONS

Biological structures evolve through natural selection, with structures that function better surviving while others die out. Now there is chemical function, biological function, and behavioral function all affecting the creature's chances to survive. We looked at the behavioral function — how a creature acts and how its actions might affect its chances to survive. So the forces of nature select biological structures that cause creatures to act in useful ways allowing those to evolve whose actions are well suited to their world.

But this notion of natural selection applies to the evolution of learned response patterns — as well as to the evolution of structure — to patterns handed down through our culture as well as to structures handed down through our genes. And we find features such as active life helping us survive whether we are the simpler or the more complex creatures.

But we must always be wary of purposive answers to our questions since we don't act as we do so we can survive in the future; instead we act as we do because we and our ancestors survived by acting that way in the past. We must be on our guard against making false purposive statements since we'll have many chances to make such errors as we look at the rest of psychology.

We've also looked at some basic facts about the ways creatures act, seeing that those ways of acting may have widespread survival value since they're needed by lower creatures like the amoeba and zoo-plankton as well as higher creatures like you and me. They help us all survive. And here are some of those very basic facts:

We're most active when we need to be.
Our actions may decrease when they're fruitless — behavior habituates.
Our actions come under stimulus control.
And some of these stimuli feed back from our own actions.

Those are some of the basic facts of psychology — the science of behavior; some of the facts that help us see why we do what we do. In the next chapters, we'll look deeper into the causes of our actions; and we'll also keep asking how those actions help us survive in a biological world and in a social world.

CHAPTER 5
MOTIVATION OF LEARNED ACTS

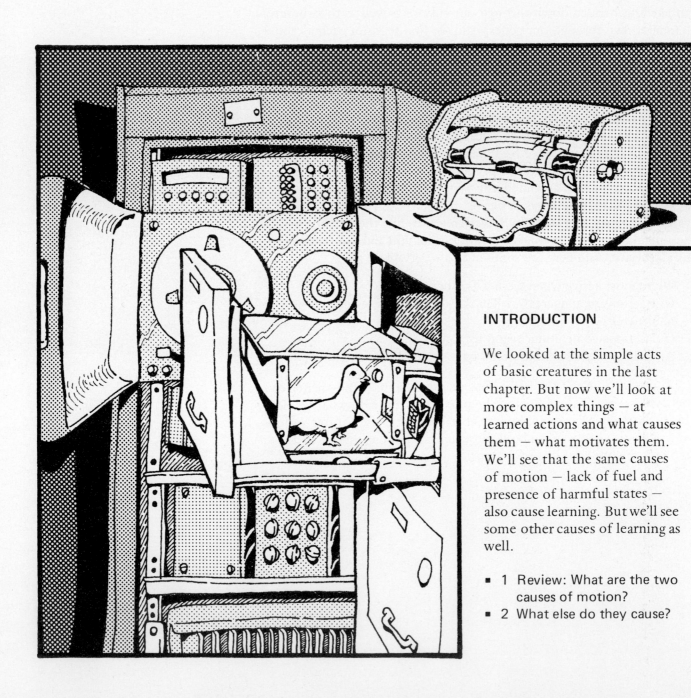

INTRODUCTION

We looked at the simple acts of basic creatures in the last chapter. But now we'll look at more complex things — at learned actions and what causes them — what motivates them. We'll see that the same causes of motion — lack of fuel and presence of harmful states — also cause learning. But we'll see some other causes of learning as well.

- 1 Review: What are the two causes of motion?
- 2 What else do they cause?

OPERANT CONDITIONING

A visit to the research laboratory

Mae had stopped by Dr. Harper's office to discuss some questions she had about the chapter, but found the office closed and a note taped to the door: "I'm in my lab — room 272." *I guess this means it's okay for me to go to his lab. Now where's room 272?*

She finally found it, this time a room with the door wide open, looking more like an electronics lab than a psych lab. *Where were all the people, or at least the animals?* She saw Dr. Harper bending over a maze of wires; and at the same time smelled the telltale odor pervading the area letting her know the animals were not too far away!

"Hi, Dr. Harper."

The teacher-scientist jumped, startled from his work. "Ah . . . oh . . . hi. Come on in."

"Hi, I'm Mae Robinson. I'm in your intro psych class."

"Of course, you're in the two o'clock section. What can I do for you, Mae?"

"I had a couple questions about this Motivation chapter, but what're you doing with all that stuff?"

"Oh, I use it to program my research."

"What do you mean?"

"Well, I've got some animals in these two chambers here, a rat in one and a pigeon in the other, and . . ." At that point a little buzzing noise occurred, causing Harper to spring into action. "My session timer. Got to take the subjects out of the chamber."

He opened the doors to the two chambers, deftly picking up the pigeon with one hand while grasping the rat with the other. Then he pushed open the door to the animal colony room giving Mae a chance to see the source of the animal smells. Harper placed each animal in its home cage after weighing it on a small pair of scales. Then he returned to the control room where Mae waited.

"Here, let me show you what I'm doing, since it might make this chapter a little clearer. See, I put the subjects of my experiments, the rat and the pigeon, in these two Skinner boxes. Now sometimes my rat can get a drop of water from this water dipper when it presses this little response lever here. So the rat learns to press the lever, since the drops of water act as a reward for that response when the animal is deprived of water. And the same thing works with my pigeon. It can get birdseed from this food-hopper when it pecks this response key, here. So the pigeon learns to peck the key since the food acts as a reward when the animal runs low on food."

"That's far out. But does it work that way, every time with every rat or pigeon you put in there?"

"Yeah, I've never found a rat or pigeon that couldn't learn to press the lever or peck the key when that response produced a needed food. There don't seem to be too many individual differences, when you deal with basic learning and motivation processes under fairly constant conditions. And these creatures seem to learn almost any response you'd care to use, whether it's bar pressing, key pecking, chain pulling, panel pushing, or turning in circles — it doesn't matter. And it also seems to work with any species too, whether they're our standard albino lab rats, pigeons, monkeys, fish; turtles, or even planaria."

"What about people?"

"Sure it works with people — people learn don't they? At first we did research with people in settings almost like our Skinner box for animals, where we saw that their learning process didn't differ much from the learning process for lower animals. We found that retarded as well as normal children could learn to push levers for food reward, such as M & M's. Adults would also learn such acts working with more complex rewards involving visual stimuli. Then we moved on to more complex conditions with humans learning more complex responses such as smiling, talking, reading, writing and cooperation, in more complex settings such as the home, classroom, hospital, and even college."

- 3 What is a Skinner box?
- 4 What's it used for?
- 5 When is food a reward?
- 6 What animal species learn because of rewards?
- 7 What does research say about the role of individual differences within the same species?
- 8 How does the learning process for humans compare to that process for animals?
- 9 What sort of responses and settings have been used to study human learning?

Science and its applications

"But why are you still messin' around with your rats and pigeons if you can do all that heavyweight stuff with people? I don't understand that 'cause I care a lot more about them than I do about animals."

"Sure, so do I. But we can study the basic processes of learning and motivation much better in the lab, where we have control of all those outside factors, factors that might confuse the results of our research. We can raise our experimental subjects under constant conditions so we can know where they're coming from, so to speak."

"But it seems like there's only so much you can learn from a rat in your Skinner box. Seems like you'd want to stop messing around with animals and just get on with it."

"I know what you mean," Harper nodded, "but it often doesn't work that way. We never stop learning from the basic research lab even after we've begun to have a great deal of success in applying our knowledge to helping people. Though I'll have to admit we often succeed in applications to humans with methods we still haven't really studied that much in the lab. But we keep thinking we'll make the most progress in applying our knowledge to humans, if we stay in close touch with the science of psychology as we get it from the lab."

"So you're spending all this time in the lab so you can learn things to help people."

"Well, that's one of the reasons, but there's another one too. Just learning how nature works is a big reward in itself. And that keeps me hanging in with my lab research too. It's sort of science for the sake of science. Knowledge for the sake of knowledge."

"Well, I'm mainly into people, but I can get next to that too."

■10 Why is it sometimes easier to do research in the lab rather than in applied settings?

■11 What reason (other than to help people) do scientists give for doing basic research in the lab?

Why learning?

Now in the last chapter we looked at some basic factors in the psychology of all creatures from the amoeba to human beings; we've looked at active responses, causes of motion, habituation, basic or unlearned stimulus control, and feedback stimulus control.

These factors all help creatures survive. They work well in a constant world — a world that doesn't change. But much of the world does change. Perhaps there's no longer any food in the lighted area. The creature that keeps moving toward the light will starve. And maybe there's a new source of food in a shaded area. The creature that starts heading toward the shade every time it's without food will be more likely to survive. The old stimulus control must break down and a new stimulus control must be set up.

Motion toward the light no longer results in food. Thus movement in the presence of the light drops out. But motion toward the shaded area does result in food. Therefore that new response is picked up. The creature "learns" to go toward the shaded area because that act is rewarded with food. The light no longer exerts stimulus control over the response of movement, but the shaded area does. This is a major type of learning — "operant conditioning".

Operant conditioning: a change in the likelihood of a response due to the results of that response.

Generally whenever you use the word "learning" you're talking about something that can be understood as an example of operant conditioning. And the concept of operant conditioning is an attempt to give a more precise definition of one form of learning where we specify, with a little more detail, the type of experience that produces the learning — mainly a type of experience where the response produces some specific results (usually a result that helps the creature).

Learning: a change in behavior that occurs as a result of experience.

We've studied another concept that's fairly close to the notion of operant conditioning — a concept that may cause some confusion — the concept of "feedback stimulus control". Recall how we defined it: "a stimulus resulting from a response that changes the form or path of the next response". So how does feedback stimulus control differ from operant conditioning? It differs in the effects of the result of the response. For feedback control, the results of the response provide a stimulus that acts as a cue guiding the response along one path or another. While for operant conditioning the results of the response act as a reward or punisher for that response, making it more or less likely to occur again the next time the creature's in that same situation. Another way to put it is that feedback stimulus control changes the situation and controls the next response; whereas, operant conditioning somehow changes the creature itself a little bit, and controls how the creature will respond again in the same situation.

It's clear that creatures that can learn will adapt better to a changing world, surviving where others die. And, in fact, all moving creatures, even the simplest show at least some signs of operant conditioning or learning. Perhaps, there once were complex moving creatures that couldn't learn. But if there were, that handicap, no doubt, caused them to die off.

So the results of our actions can serve two functions. They can exert stimulus control — provide cues that guide our actions. And they can also cause us to learn. As we'll see, these latter results work as rewards and punishers.

- ■12 Define operant conditioning and compare and contrast it with learning and feedback stimulus control.
- ■13 State the conditions where learning helps creatures survive, and cite an instance.

Animals that learn

Gore, the infant mountain lion, awoke. It was running low on fuel as a few hours had passed since the last time it ate. So it became more active, crawling nearer Mother, as it wandered aimlessly about. Gore lowered its head to the ground and moved along Mother's belly. Nothing happened. Then Gore raised its head but kept moving along the belly. After awhile Gore's mouth made contact with a nipple. It went back to sleep only when it had nursed itself full.

***

What were the results of Gore's raising its head and moving along Mother's belly? It made contact with a fuel supply — Mother's milk-filled breast. Gore soon learned to raise its head and move along Mother's belly, since such acts obtained the needed milk. Learned acts are controlled by their results. Deprive a creature of fuel, and it will learn actions that get that fuel. In other words the creature will be more likely to make a response in the future if that response has been rewarded in the past.

***

Something else can also come into play here. One other time Gore awoke though it had plenty of food. What was the matter? A cold night wind blew over it causing Gore to shiver and raise itself slightly. It started crawling around and after a few minutes, it ended up on the other side of Mother. Then Gore settled back down to sleep since the wind couldn't reach it there. And so Gore also soon learned that response, because it had escaped harm. Whenever Gore got cold, it rushed to the other side of Mother to snuggle up in comfort. Expose the creature to harm and it will learn acts removing it from that harm.

- ■14 Cite an instance of operant conditioning with a creature motivated by lack of fuel.
- ■15 Cite an instance of operant conditioning with a creature motivated by a harmful state.

Animals that do not learn

Dodo, the infant mountain lion, awoke, starting to move around since it was running out of fuel, finally by chance bumping into one of Mother's nipples where it drank its fill. But later whenever it ran low on fuel, it spent the same long time crawling around before bumping into a nipple; getting fuel didn't change what it did; it didn't learn.

Each time Dodo awoke cold it crawled around for awhile before reaching the warm side of Mother. Getting away from harm didn't cause Dodo to learn either, as it took Dodo the same amount of time to reach its mother even after several chances to learn, while Gore soon learned to get to its mother's side with no wasted time. Dodo died of lack of fuel and exposure. So it goes.

***

Thus, there are two basic motives for action: lack of a needed fuel, and presence of harm.

Now, here was Dodo's problem: it did not inherit a biophysical structure that would allow getting fuel and escaping harm to cause learning. So Dodo couldn't learn since creatures only learn when they are affected by the results that follow right after their actions. And it didn't get enough fuel and was exposed to too much harm (since it couldn't learn the acts that got fuel and escaped harm). As you can see, it would be hard for any complex species to evolve if it couldn't learn — it wouldn't survive long enough to evolve.

■16 Cite an instance where a creature didn't learn when motivated by lack of fuel.

■17 Cite an instance where a creature didn't learn when motivated by a harmful state.

■18 What would be the likely result for creatures that often do not learn?

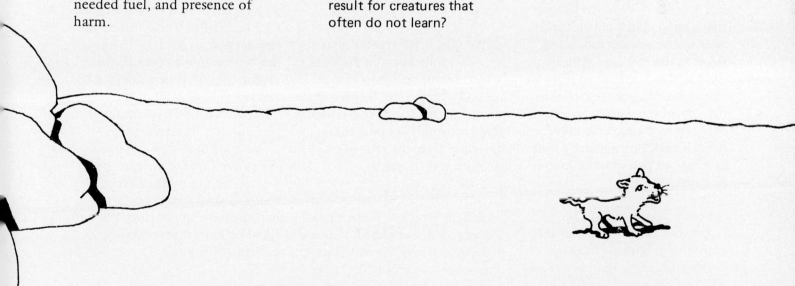

REINFORCERS

Reinforcers vs. rewards

Reinforcer: a change in conditions, stimuli, or events occurring right after a response and causing that response to be learned.

Reward: an everyday term meaning roughly the same thing as reinforcer.

We'll often use the simple word "reward" rather than the term "reinforcer" just for the sake of smooth reading; but keep in mind: by "reward" we mean the precise technical term "reinforcer". And something is only a reinforcer if it causes the creature to learn the act that came right before that thing.

So it might not really be a reinforcer, even though we think it may be desirable enough to be one. There's only one way we can find out if it is — we must see if the creature or person learns the act that precedes that thing. And these same constraints also apply to our use of "reward". But the everyday use of the term "reward" differs somewhat from our use. The everyday use means simply a thing given as a payment or prize for something done. For that use, it doesn't matter whether or not that thing is valued by the person getting the reward, or whether or not it can cause the person to learn the act being rewarded. But for our use, it's crucial that the reward cause the person to learn the act being rewarded.

- ■19 Define reinforcer and reward.
- ■20 How can we find out if something is in fact a reinforcer?

Human learning

Humans also learn in much the same way as lower creatures like Gore. We humans will tend to learn an act if a reward follows that action, and we won't learn an act if no reward follows it. Also, much the same type of reward also causes us to learn as causes lower creatures to learn — for instance, we learn actions that reduce harm or produce needed fuel. But now let's look at a case or two of basic human learning.

* * *

Dawn awoke because of the cool breeze blowing through her window. *Is it time to get up? No, still dark out. Sure cold. No wonder, I must've kicked the sheets down to the foot of the bed.* But she fell fast asleep soon after she had pulled the sheet up around her.

* * *

We take it for granted that you cover up when you're cold. Why? Because it seems like second nature — we learned that complex act so long ago; and we had no trouble learning that response since the reward of warmth was so quick.

* * *

A little later the alarm caused Dawn to bolt out of bed. *Where'd I put that thing?* She still didn't know her way around her new room, but at last finding the noisy alarm clock she shut it off. Dawn went to breakfast alone since Mae could sleep in that day. But she hadn't yet learned her way around the dining room too well either. *Now let's see, I think I walked right by the butter tray, yes, there it is.* And, "Oh, excuse me, where do you get the milk?"

The student gave a sleepy nod toward the east wall of the room. "Thanks a lot," Dawn strained to give an early morning smile.

Now the last time I tried to get coffee I ended up with a cup full of hot water. But I think that's it. And sure enough, she had the right spigot since her cup filled up with that rewarding caffeine this time.

* * *

Dawn was learning. And she'd keep learning until her actions seemed perfect — second nature again. After all, look at the strong rewards that quickly followed her correct actions: by pushing the correct button in the correct place, she shut off an aversive noise. By keeping her eyes open, she'd get food she needed — butter and milk. By pressing the right handle, she got one of her favorite drugs — caffeine. She won't have much trouble learning how to survive the dining room jungle.

■21 Cite cases of humans learning due to rewards based on harmful states.
■22 Also cite cases based on fuel.

Needed fuels that do not act as reinforcers

We've seen a close relation between biological needs and the rewards that control learning. But is there always that close relation? Are there things we need that don't function as rewards? Yes. Some vitamins, for instance, may not work as rewards for some species. Basic research has been done with monkeys showing that they can not learn acts if the only reward for those acts is vitamin A, even though that vitamin is needed for them to stay healthy and survive.

But how can it be that some needed fuels do act as rewards while others fail to? As with all basic biological processes, we should look to the evolution of the species, to find our answer. We should look at the environment in which the species evolved. In that environment vitamin A was plentiful, always present in the foods the monkeys found rewarding in their own right, so they got all the vitamin A they needed when they consumed those foods. Therefore; they were able to keep healthy and survive, even though that needed vitamin didn't function as a reward. And they never evolved a biophysical structure that caused vitamin A to function as a reward. In fact, many, if not most creatures evolved like that with some of their vitamins not acting as rewards even though they might now run low on that vitamin due to the fact that the substance is no longer common in their normal diet.

How can it be that a needed fuel that is now scarce does not act as a reward causing the creature to learn responses that produce that needed fuel? This occurs because a biological structure can't adapt to a rapidly changing world, in a single generation, since evolution requires many generations for major structure changes to occur.

But evolution could take place if the changed conditions were to persist. For instance, a whole strain or species of monkeys might evolve for whom vitamin A would be a strong reward. This could happen if an occasional monkey mutated so that vitamin A was a reward for it, and if those monkeys were much more likely to survive, and if those conditions persisted for many generations so that the early strain of monkeys would have time to die off leaving the vitamin-A-rewarded monkeys as the sole survivors.

■23 Under what conditions could a species evolve without a needed fuel acting as a reward?

Evolution of non-biological reinforcers

In the last chapter, we looked at the notion of basic stimulus control where a creature's actions are guided by some non-biological stimulus such as light. Because of the low intensity of the light it was itself neither a fuel nor harmful — it didn't affect any biological need. Yet it did control actions. And this basic stimulus control evolved because it directed the creature's actions toward fuel and away from harm, thus having only an indirect effect on the creature's biological needs. That's stimulus control — cues that guide actions. But there are also non-biological events that act as reinforcers — that don't act as fuels or reduce harmful conditions — reinforcers that cause actions to be learned without serving any direct biological needs.

* * *

Gore, the mountain lion, stopped nursing and started eating as it grew older; it ate small, living creatures. One day it went walking through the woods behind Mother. A slight motion occurred on the ground just to the right causing Gore to stop and stare. Nothing. Wait. There it was again. Now nothing. Now motion. There. Gore pounced on the small creature — a tasty lunch. Then Gore ran, catching up with Mother.

Gore soon learned the response of looking at moving things since the sight of such motion was a reward. And that learned response helped it locate food.

Gore walked behind its mother, still looking at the bright shiny grass along the path — rarely looking into the dark forest, since bright things were a big reward for Gore — like motion, rewarding the looking response. And looking at bright things helped Gore see food, since Gore could see better in bright light, and since the creatures it ate moved about more in bright light. So Gore also learned to look at bright things.

* * *

But other stimuli may also function as non-biological rewards or punishers. For instance, harm is often found in the presence of other stimuli. There may be harmful food, where there's a putrid odor. So complex creatures learn acts that help them escape or avoid the odor (perhaps by getting themselves away from the odor). Let's look at this in terms of natural selection.

First note that seeing motion and light and getting away from putrid odors are non-biological rewards. They have their value for creatures because they direct the creature's learned actions toward fuel and away from harm. Such non-biological rewards function in much the same way as basic stimulus control — basic stimulus control directs the unlearned actions of simpler creatures toward the fuel and away from harm. In both cases, creatures will more likely survive if they are under the control of these non-biological conditions. And their offspring will also more likely survive, if such control is passed on to them. So natural selection can account for such control by stimuli that in themselves are neither needed nor harmful.

That accounts for the unlearned acts of simple creatures but what about the learned actions of complex creatures? Such creatures learn acts that move them toward or produce stimuli paired with fuel. And they learn acts that direct them away from or get rid of stimuli paired with harm. So they, too, will more often get to the needed fuel and avoid the harm. And if their offspring inherit this tendency to learn acts that produce stimuli, then those offspring will more likely survive. Otherwise, they'll have a harder time surviving. So we're saying that many species are born with the tendency to be rewarded by bright moving stimuli and perhaps punished by certain odors. And they're born that way because these rewards and punishers helped their ancestors survive.

***

Another day, another Dodo: this Dodo was never distracted by the bright lights or bustle of life, always staying right behind Mother, failing to go after the bright lights and motion, failing to get the food it might find there, getting only the food that was unlucky enough to cross its path. And since not much food did cross Dodo's path, the poor creature starved to death. So it goes. Natural selection works again. For most complex creatures light and motion reward the act of looking.

***

Gore inherited a biophysical structure that caused bright, moving things to act as rewards; Dodo had not inherited this structure. And since those rewards help creatures survive, Gore will live though Dodo might die. This doesn't mean Dodo is dumb and Gore smart; it just means one creature inherited a structure that helps it survive. Creatures without those structures are much less likely to survive. So it goes.

To sum up, natural selection may have caused events like light and motion to affect learning. So we learn acts that result in events which, in themselves, are neither fuel nor harmful. Thus, rewards need not always be fuel or the removal of harm.

■24 How can non-biological reinforcers help a creature survive? Cite an instance.

Non-biological reinforcers and human actions

And, like most other creatures, we also inherit the biophysical structures that cause bright, loud, moving, changing things to act as rewards. However, we've greatly changed our world causing much of it to differ from the world in which these structures evolved. So what helped us survive then may sometimes help and sometimes hurt our chances to survive now.

Freshmen get the eight o'clock classes since they register last. So Dawn returned to the dorm, after her eight o'clock class. She'd stop by the lounge since no one would be there now; then she could study without waking Mae. But she heard voices as she approached the lounge. *What is it? Oh, just the TV. And no one there watching it.* She was relieved. Unfortunately, she, herself sat down to watch the tube — instead of turning it off. *Just for a minute though.*

What is that show? Ah, The Electric Company. *It's so cute. I just love it, even if it is for kids.* And Dawn didn't turn off those audio-visual stimuli until the show's credits started rolling by.

***

Children's TV Workshop, the show's producer, put much effort into it, trying hard to make it rewarding for kids — bright lights, bright colors, motion, changing sounds, changing everything, always changing, constant action, always moving. A big reward for Gore, for kids, and for college students. What does it reward? The act of looking at the tube. And that's TV — a machine for giving out audio-visual rewards — rewards for staring at the tube. Often looking at moving, changing events, may help us survive — just like it did Gore. It helps us, even though not directly. But we get into trouble when someone puts those rewards in the wrong place — like a TV show that may hinder our chances to survive — *The Electric Company* won't help Dawn though it does help children. Not that TV will be a life or death matter but it may be just one more factor holding us back from doing something worthwhile — one more hurdle in the road of our accomplishments — our objectives in life.

■25 Cite a case where human acts are controlled by non-biological rewards — acts that might help one person and yet hurt another.

RESPONDENT CONDITIONING

We've looked at one kind of learning called operant conditioning — a change in response due to the reward that follows that response. Creatures will move toward light if that response is rewarded with fuel. An infant will move toward a mother's breast if that response is rewarded by milk and comfort. A human will cover up if that response is rewarded by warmth. College students will learn their way around the dining hall with amazing speed if those responses are rewarded by the delicious dorm food. We even learn to do such things as watch TV shows if those responses are rewarded by the right sort of audio-visual events. But there also seems to be another kind of learning — respondent conditioning.

***

Mae was quite pleased that Professor Harper took the time to show her around his lab since he was so busy. She was pleased since he had talked to her about his research as well as about her specific class problems, though she was also feeling somewhat guilty at taking so much of his time. On the other hand, Harper was also pleased that an intro psych student took an interest in his research, as he found that most (even many of his colleagues) had some trouble seeing the value of basic scientific research.

The role of the experimental psychologist — the intellectual — is sometimes a lonely one. Mae's interest in his research reinforced Harper's telling her about it, yet he didn't want to bore her if she was just being polite; so, "You said you had some questions about this chapter?"

"Yeah, well you've pretty well cleared it up about operant conditioning; I didn't know you were doing research in that field. But I guess that's not what I thought it was all about. I thought you guys always rang a bell and got dogs to drool because they thought food was coming."

"Well we do do some work like that. It's called 'respondent conditioning', but I think the Russian scientists may be doing a little more of that work than we are; I suppose it's because Ivan Pavlov, the Russian physiologist, was the first to do a thorough study of it, toward the end of the last century."

"I guess I don't really see what it's all about," Mae probed.

"Okay, here's the way respondent conditioning works: Creatures salivate whenever food touches their tongue. Now Pavlov observed that the dogs he was working with also produced saliva whenever their feeder walked into their room. So he did some research on the subject. He rang a bell just before putting a small amount of food in a dog's mouth. He did this for several trials, until the dog salivated to the sound of the bell, without the food being present. The dog had learned to salivate to the sound of the bell, because of its pairing with the food."

"Yeah, that's the study I was thinking about. So you're saying respondent conditioning is a form of learning also?"

"Yes, respondent conditioning

and operant conditioning are the two major types of learning, if not the only types, though most often we mean 'operant conditioning' when we use the term 'learning' outside the lab. Most of the time you're thinking of operant conditioning when you say you learned something."

"Got it. But here's another thing's been bugging me: I don't see how you guys are using the word 'stimulus'. Like, to me 'stimulus' means some kind of force or prod that pushes things along. You know, like when you push a kid in a swing, like you're pushing is the stimulus. So I don't get it when you say a reward is a stimulus that comes after the response it rewards. Like that doesn't fit in with my

notion that a stimulus is a sort of prod or a pusher."

"Well, that way of using the word is fairly common," Harper agreed. "But we use it to mean something a little more general — mainly to mean any thing or event in the physical world. Any change in our world is a stimulus whether it comes before or after a response. It doesn't have to be a stimulus for something; it's just any event in our environment."

"Okay, that makes a little more sense now."

- ▪26 Who was the first to do a thorough study of respondent conditioning?
- ▪27 Describe Pavlov's experiment.
- ▪28 Review: Define stimulus.

Respondent conditioning compared with evolution

Mae thought for a moment, "Well, I think I see how operant and respondent conditioning relate. But it looks like respondent conditioning and evolution are pretty much the same thing, since something like a sight or a sound can get control over a creature's actions through pairing with something like food."

"You've got a good point there," Harper replied, "but they're not quite the same process though they may serve much the same function. In respondent conditioning a neutral stimulus acquires the power of another stimulus, through the pairing of those two stimuli. This happens in the presence of a single creature. And . . ."

"What about that creature's offspring? Will the stimulus with its new power affect the off-spring? Will the pups of Pavlov's dogs salivate when they hear the bell too?"

"No, that's just the point. We can't inherit what our parents learned. But in evolution, a non-biologically important stimulus may become important in helping the species survive because it is often paired with some stimulus that's more biologically important. Yet, in the case of evolution, the pairing of the two events — the biologi-cally important and unimportant stimuli — in no way changes any individual creature. It's just that some creatures happen to be reinforced by these biologically unimportant stimuli due to the peculiar nature of the creature's biological structure. And those creatures are then more likely to survive since being controlled by this new reward puts them into better contact with the biologi-cally significant rewards or events.

■29 In what way do respondent conditioning and evolution serve the same function?
■30 How do they differ?

Evolution of respondent conditioning

Gore bit down on the dried carcass twisting and pulling until it had ripped off a chunk of flesh. And the young creature started salivating the instant the flesh touched its tongue. Now the saliva in Gore's mouth served two functions: it helped Gore chew the dried meat and it also helped the creature swallow the food.

For several days after that, Gore kept going back to the remains of the carcass and eating its daily fill. Now after a few days of this, Gore's saliva ducts started flowing at the mere sight of its next meal. Having the fluid in its mouth in advance also helped, allowing Gore to more quickly chew and swallow the small bits of meat, since it no longer had to wait for the saliva to start flowing.

Gore and Dodo got to the scant remains of the carcass at about the same time, but Gore managed to eat most of the remaining food before Dodo had barely gotten started, since that poor creature had not learned to salivate at the sight of food and was therefore not able to consume dry meat with Gore's speed. Learning to salivate will help Gore survive in the competition over scarce food. Poor Dodo. And we're not surprised that creatures have evolved that can learn to salivate at the sight of food.

■31 How might early salivation help a creature survive?

Definition

Now three events were involved in that instance in Gore's life: the food in Gore's mouth, the salivation, and the sight of the stimulus for salivation — no past learning was required for the food in the mouth to cause Gore to salivate as he was most likely born with that response to food in the mouth. But the sight of food had no effect at first. The sight itself caused Gore to salivate only after the food in the mouth had followed that sight several times. The sight got its effect only as a result of Gore's experience — namely, a few pairings of the sight with the food in the mouth. So the sight of the food became a learned stimulus or "conditioned stimulus", whereas the food was the unlearned stimulus or "unconditioned stimulus".

Unconditioned stimulus: something that evokes a response without prior experience.

Conditioned stimulus: something that evokes a response after a few pairings with another stimulus that already causes that response.

The notion of control by an unconditioned stimulus is about the same as the notion of basic stimulus control. Consider the light causing the food deprived creature to approach it. That's an instance of basic or unlearned stimulus control and the light is working as an unconditioned stimulus causing the approach response.

But what about the response itself? We call the response an "unconditioned response" when Gore salivates to the taste of food in the mouth (unconditioned stimulus). And we call the response a "conditioned response" when it responds to the sight of the food (conditioned stimulus). So the following definitions will come as no surprise to you.

Unconditioned response: response evoked by a stimulus even without prior experience.

Conditioned response: response evoked by a stimulus only after pairing that stimulus with one that already causes the response.

And finally, we have respondent conditioning — the technical name for the pairing of those two stimuli.

Respondent conditioning: the procedure of pairing two stimuli with the result that one stimulus (conditioned stimulus) acquires the power to cause the response already caused by the other stimulus (unconditioned stimulus).

■32 Define and cite instances of the following concepts: unconditioned stimulus, conditioned stimulus, unconditioned response, conditioned response, and respondent conditioning.

OPERANT VS. RESPONDENT CONDITIONING

Dawn put down her book. "Well, it looks like there are supposed to be two kinds of learning — operant conditioning and respondent conditioning, but they look the same to me. They both involve stimuli like rewards or like conditioned and unconditioned stimuli; but they call food a reward one time and an unconditioned stimulus another time. And both procedures involve actions too."

"Harper got me straight on it," Mae said. "First look at operant conditioning: There food follows the response. Then look at respondent conditioning: There the response follows the food. So with operant conditioning the response goes before the reward (e.g., food), and with respondent conditioning, the response goes after the unconditioned stimulus (e.g., food), or the conditioned stimulus."

"And in the case of operant conditioning, the pairing of the reward with the response is the main thing; but for respondent conditioning, the pairing of the unconditioned and conditioned stimuli is the main thing."

"Okay, let me try to put it another way to see if I've got it. With operant conditioning, we learn to make the response that gets the reward that follows it. And with respondent conditioning we learn to make the same response to a new stimulus that we already make to an old stimulus. Is that it?"

"I think you got it," Mae answered, both women happy to have mastered a set of fairly complex concepts.

■33 Which comes first, stimulus or response, in operant and in respondent conditioning?

■34 What pairings are most important in operant and in respondent conditioning?

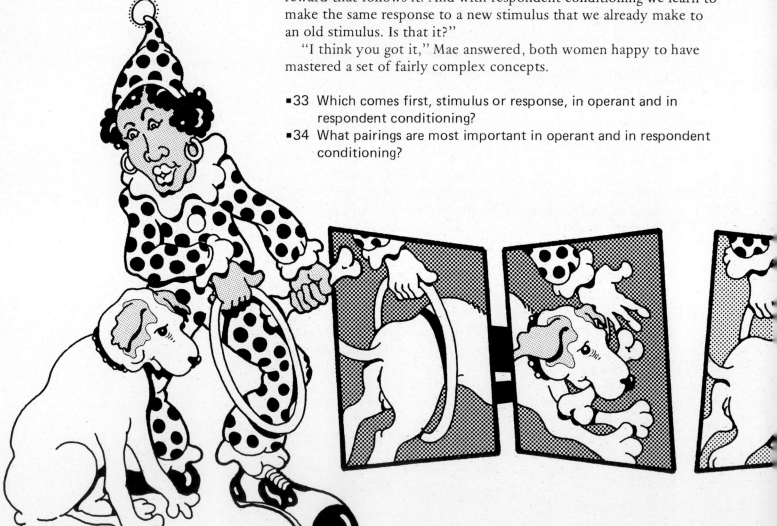

CONCLUSIONS

In this chapter we've dealt with the causes of learning, seeing that all
learning seems to be based on events that have helped the creature's
ancestors survive — getting fuel and escaping harm. Even non-
biological reinforcers are at least tied to such helpful conditions
though in an indirect manner. In the next chapter, we'll see instances
of other sorts of reinforcers, reinforcers that also help the species
survive. And these events cause both types of learning — respondent
as well as operant conditioning. We suggest that non-biological events
— bright, loud, moving things — became reinforcers, as the species
evolved, because they were paired with food or harm; but take care
— don't confuse this sort of evolution with respondent conditioning.
Respondent conditioning occurs during the life of a single creature
while evolution occurs throughout the generations of a species.

Now, in this chapter we've looked at the motivation for learning;
in the next chapter we'll look at how learning itself can account
for the motives of some very complex actions — actions that puzzled
humankind for hundreds of years.

CHAPTER 6
MOTIVATION INDIRECTLY RELATED TO BIOLOGICAL NEED

INTRODUCTION

In this chapter, our treatment of motivation will be somewhat unique — differing from the standard heredity approach and from the standard learning approach as well. The heredity approach says creatures inherit complex response patterns — patterns they perform when such responses are needed; while the learning approach says creatures inherit nothing that prepares them for any specific responses they may need to make, instead they learn those responses after conception. We agree with the learning view: all complex acts are learned; while we also agree with the heredity view: creatures inherit structures that help them learn those specific acts. What the creature inherits is the capacity to be reinforced by certain events that result if it responds in the right ways when need be.

- 1 What are the heredity and learning approaches to motivation? And how does the approach to this book relate to them?

IMPRINTING

We saw that light by itself can be a reward even though it isn't a fuel. Note that simple stimuli such as light are the same for offspring as for parents. But now we will see other non-biological stimuli that function as rewards though they are more complex and vary from one creature to the next.

***

Peck . . . peck . . . peck, peck — crack. Gore's beak broke through the egg, as little by little it chipped away its shell. And then, at last, it was hatched — a new duckling in a new world. It stood up, stumbled, stood up again, stumbled, took a step, stumbled, took another step and didn't stumble any more. Eyes wide open, the first thing Gore saw was MOTHER, standing near by. Mother all brown and black with little white speckles, a white ring around her eye, and a little green in her tail feathers — Mother with the yellow webbed feet — Mother with the flat yellow bill. The very sight of her was a big reward for Gore. And the sight of her was an even stronger reward when Gore was closer to her. So Gore soon learned to follow when Mother started to wander away from the nest. Good for Gore; because Mother went straight to the riverside — the riverside with all that food. And then Gore followed her back to the safety of their nest after they had eaten their fill.

Gore's mother had learned the acts that find fuel and avoid harm. But it might take Gore a while to learn all that; and it might also just walk into trouble since Gore could walk soon after birth. So Gore would be more likely to survive if it stayed near good old, safe old Mom. That should happen if the sight of Mom was a reward. Then Gore would just need to learn a few actions that produced this lovely reward. Not too difficult. A turn of the head gets a prompt reward — the sight of Mom. Or suppose Mom goes behind a bush while Gore's looking? Good-looking Gore will soon see Mom, if it just starts walking her way. Gore had no trouble learning to stay very close to her; that always got its reward — a big beautiful view of Mom.

But what do we mean "view of Mom"? The side view? Profile? Rear end? Front end? Running? Walking? Swimming? Stretching? Preening? No two sights the same.

Suppose you saw only a profile view of a stranger, then later you met the stranger face-to-face — a front view. It might not look like the same person to you. That's why police mug shots contain both views. Yet what about poor Gore? It has the same problem. Many views of Mom must act as a reward if Gore is to approach her under all conditions. And it doesn't seem likely that all those many complex views could be inherited as rewards; our genetic mechanisms

don't seem up to that task. Besides, some mothers don't look like other mothers; so Gore's acts should be reinforced by the unique views of its unique mother and not some other duckling's mother as well. But there seems to be no way for Gore to inherit that. We need something else to turn the unique sights of Mom into a reward.

Well, most often, the first moving thing ducklings see is their mothers. Now suppose ducklings were born with the tendency to be reinforced by their first moving view. This would solve the problem since the duckling would be reinforced by its mother no matter how odd she looked. And indeed this does happen; we call it "imprinting".

Imprinting: changing a neutral stimulus into a reinforcer by exposing the newborn to that stimulus.

But this imprinting process kept going for the first several hours of Gore's young life, not stopping with the first thing Gore saw. And Gore saw many views of Mom, during those hours, causing all those views to become imprinted rewards.

* * *

But our fictional Dodo remained behind when its mother left the nest, as it had not inherited the ability to acquire imprinted reinforcers. But later it did wander off by itself. And it began to starve to death, barely able to move, giving a young fox no trouble catching it.

* * *

Thus many species that might wander into trouble are born so they acquire rewards through imprinting. No doubt early species didn't survive over the ages if they failed to develop this tendency to imprint. Of course you should realize that the evolution of one characteristic, even a simple one, requires thousands of years — no quick process.

- 2 Define imprinting.
- 3 For most creatures, what is the first thing seen and therefore the most common imprinted stimulus?
- 4 What type of response is most often rewarded by the imprinted stimulus, in the creature's normal world?
- 5 What types of species show imprinting?
- 6 How does imprinting help the infant survive?

LABORATORY RESEARCH

A good deal of research has been done showing that the imprinted stimulus need not be the bird's mother. Some of the first work was done outside the lab by Konrad Lorenz, the European ethologist. He showed imprinting in geese, with a very strange stimulus, at least strange for geese. They imprinted on him, as he was the first thing the newly hatched geese saw. So Lorenz could often be found walking down a dirt path toward the pond with a gaggle of geese close behind. He clearly showed the stimulus didn't have to look like the bird's normal mother for it to be imprinted.

Since then, many workers have brought the study of imprinting from the natural settings of Lorenz into the research laboratory, where they can study the factors that affect imprinting in a more precise manner. They have found the birds can imprint only during a critical period of time, a period shortly after the birds have hatched. This most likely helps the creatures survive, since it insures that they can't imprint on the wrong thing after mother has become an imprinted stimulus.

Other work has shown that there are some limits — limits in the nature of the stimuli to which a bird can imprint. For instance, ducklings are less likely to imprint to a yellow stimulus object. This constraint may help them survive since it would limit imprinting to other ducklings as they are often yellow. If they imprinted on each other, rather than wise old Mother, they might wander off to their death. So they may have evolved structures preventing them from imprinting on the stimuli likely to cause problems — mainly other yellow ducklings — with no need to evolve structures to prevent them from imprinting on Lorenz or any other passing Pied Piper.

Some laboratory scientists have clearly shown that the imprinted stimulus does indeed act as a reward, controlling almost any response that will produce it. For instance, birds will learn the operant response of pecking a response key if that response causes the imprinted stimulus to appear. This is why it is so important to do lab research in addition to field research in the creature's normal environment. Such lab studies allow the scientist to get at the crucial features of a process by getting rid of those features that are not crucial; by getting rid of features that may have played a role as the species evolved — features determined only by the structure of the creature's normal world, not by the biological structure the creature inherits.

For instance, scientists seemed to feel that the response of following the imprinted stimulus was part of the inherited biological structure of the creature. In other words, they thought the "following" response was biologically locked into the imprinted stimulus. This could be shown to be wrong only in the research laboratory. And the results from such research form the basis of our analysis throughout this chapter — the notion that rewards are determined by the biological structures creatures inherit, but the sequence of responses is not inherited.

- 7 Who did some of the first work on imprinting? And what did he find?
- 8 What features of imprinting were demonstrated in the lab?
- 9 When do birds imprint? How would that help them survive?
- 10 How can limits on the nature of the imprinted stimulus help a species survive?
- 11 Why didn't those limits prevent the birds from imprinting on Lorenz?
- 12 What reason for doing lab research was discussed?

INSTINCT — INSTINCTIVE REINFORCERS

We've looked at biological rewards, non-biological rewards, and imprinted rewards, all having one thing in common — they all help each individual, itself, to survive. But for the species to survive more is needed — the parent must often respond in ways that help not itself but its offspring. These responses are often called instinctive responses with the notion that the specific response patterns are inherited. However, we would like to present a different view: the creature does not inherit specific response patterns, instead it inherits the tendency for certain events to act as rewards at just the right times, rewarding actions that help the species survive.

Sex

It starts with the sex act which, for most creatures, is a reward only at certain times, since the proper season, producing its chemical changes in the creature, is needed to cause this contact to act as a reward.

* * *

One of the males had tried to mount Gore, the mammal, that winter — very painful; the sexual contact was not a reward, hurting so much it made Gore fight back, fending off her suitor.

But that was winter, and now spring had come, bringing biochemical changes in Gore. Another male mounted her — he more assertive when he mounted her, she much less so. The sexual contact was now a reward, where it had once been a punisher. Gore mated, getting pregnant, and giving birth to her first litter that spring.

* * *

Creatures learn to engage in acts that get rewards. The female gets pregnant only as a side effect of the sex act — a side effect that just happens to result in offspring. Creatures don't engage in the sex act if their nature is such that sexual contact is never a reward; if such creatures exist, the side effect would be that they wouldn't procreate, leaving that species to die off without much ado.

For many creatures, sex is a reward only during one season (like spring), causing the offspring to be born at a time (like summer) when they're most likely to survive. A weak species or strain may die off if they do otherwise, due to the harsh conditions of other seasons.

Infant care

Yet the offspring need more than mild conditions to survive. For instance, the parents may have to build a nest. However, they don't build the nest because they want to house their offspring. Instead, they build the nest because those actions get reinforced at that moment. A case in point is the female rat whose feet become more sensitive when it's time to build a nest. Perhaps touching the nesting material is more rewarding than touching other things at that time. But a creature doesn't spend all its life building complex nests as that would waste fuel. The stimuli from the responses of nest building become rewards only at certain times — times just prior to the birth of the offspring. This is due to biochemical changes in the animal — changes that result from being pregnant.

Again lab research pinpointed some of the crucial factors. For instance, scientists showed that the hormone, progesterone, is a biochemical that can cause nest building. They showed this by injecting it in canaries who in turn built nests at times when such actions were otherwise not called for.

Note that nest-building is a fragile process, though a crucial one. It depends on the animal being in a world like the one in which its species evolved — a world that contains things to build nests with, things like the material present when the species evolved. Otherwise, the creature doesn't build the nest.

And even more may be required for the offspring to survive, since some creatures need a long time for their complex sensory and response systems to develop. Such creatures must be kept from harm and must be fed by the parent. The female mammal nurses its offspring — not because she wants to get food to her young but because nursing can produce rewards for the mother.

***

Gore's breasts were swollen and sore. The very first time one of the infants began to nurse, the pain decreased. Gore escaped this pain by letting the infant keep on nursing. Other stimuli also reinforced Gore's nursing. Gore's biochemistry (hormones) produced changes in Gore that made nursing (suckling) very rewarding causing her to learn to be a good breast feeder, learning to lie in positions that gave the infants easy access to her nipples.

***

The infant managed to get a hold of one of Dodo's nipples and start nursing; but then it lost its grip and fell off. Dodo never learned to breast feed as nursing produced no rewards for her. And her babies, since they nursed catch as catch can, all died of starvation sooner or later.

***

And again, this analysis is supported by lab research. In one experiment milk cows learned to make an operant response reinforced by the nursing action of a milking machine. The research also showed that the reward involved more than escaping from the pressure of an engorged udder since the cows would make the response rewarded by the nursing action of the milking machine, even within a few hours after they had been milked and even though their udders had not yet refilled.

This whole nursing process works on a tight natural cycle with the infant's suckling response rewarded by the milk, with that response acting as a stimulus that activates the milk-producing glands, with those glands causing the breasts to fill, with the full breasts causing nursing to become a reward for the mother, with the rewards causing her to make learned responses that result in the infant suckling. And so life's support system goes on and on, based not on an instinct for raising children but on the learning of acts that produce rewards for the actor at the moment of action.

The problem

Here's the general problem we've looked at. The species will survive, only if its members perform some special acts that may not help the specific individual survive at that moment — but acts that do help the individual or the species as a whole survive in the long run. These are acts such as mating and nest building. What motivates such acts? What causes each creature to engage in such acts? The answer for many species is: change in the creature's world produces chemical changes within the creature — changes that convert neutral stimuli into rewards. Then the creature learns the acts that produce those rewards at that time; and it keeps doing that as long as the stimuli are rewarding. Those acts also help that creature, itself, to survive in the future, or its offspring to survive now or in the future. This is what we mean by "instinct".

Instinctive reinforcer: a reinforcer for a response that either helps a creature survive in the future or helps its offspring survive. Most often the reinforcer acts only during certain crucial times — times when some events in the creature's world trigger biochemical changes within the creature, and those biochemical changes in turn alter the effect some neutral event has on the creature, causing the neutral event to stop being neutral and start acting as a reinforcer.

- ■13 Define instinctive reinforcer.
- ■14 What events cause neutral stimuli to become reinforcers?
- ■15 How does this help the species survive?
- ■16 How do instinctive reinforcers for sex acts help the species survive?
- ■17 How do instinctive reinforcers for infant care help the species survive?

Instinct vs. instinctive

Psychologists explained many things with their concept, "instinct", during the first part of this century: Why do birds build nests? Because of their nest-building instinct. Why do mothers suckle their young? Because of their mothering instinct. Why do squirrels store nuts? Their survival instinct. Why did the famous Hollywood movie actress take an overdose of sleeping pills? "Because of her death wish" (read instinct), her lover was reported to have said in quoting her psychiatrist. And here's the problem: we may feel no need to look further for other causes, once we say an instinct causes an act, since we've answered the "why" question.

And of course, we can explain anything in terms of instincts. We invent the "life" instinct if they live and the "death" instinct if they die; the "fighting" instinct if they fight and the "peace" instinct if they don't. The "do" instinct and the "don't" instinct. Therefore most psychologists came to reject the term "instinct" when they saw it being used as the easy way out in our pursuit of knowledge — knowledge about why creatures act as they do.

But many psychologists still held on to the essence of instinct, though throwing away the term itself: Why do birds build nests? Because they inherit the complex response pattern of nest building. Why do mothers suckle their young? Because they inherit the complex response pattern of nursing. Yet the two views don't differ that much. It doesn't greatly matter whether they say we inherit a complex response pattern (like a very complex unconditioned response), or whether they say we inherit a response-causing instinct. And besides, we haven't been able to find direct evidence that we can inherit any response patterns that complex.

Think about that complex response sequence needed to build a nest — a sequence that must vary a great deal as the layout of the world around that creature varies — with trees and hills and streams and bushes and grass being one place for one creature and other places for other creatures. It's hard to imagine that the creature could inherit the large number of response patterns needed to mesh with any of the large number of arrangements it ran into. It would be better if it inherited the capacity to be reinforced by certain events — events the creature would make contact with — simply as a result of its normal actions.

Yet creatures clearly do inherit biochemical structures causing them to be rewarded by certain stimuli like food, water, and warmth. So we've stressed the following notions: Creatures do inherit the tendency to be reinforced by certain events. They inherit the ability to learn. And they do not inherit the complex response patterns themselves (not even complex unconditioned responses). So: Why do birds build nests? Because they inherit the tendency to be rewarded by stimuli that result from acts involved in nest building. Why do mothers suckle? Because they inherit the tendency to be rewarded by stimuli that result from acts involved in nursing.

So the nest builder could then learn those acts that result in the rewarding events, with the crucial side effect that the acts would also result in its building the nest. But of course we need much more research — psychological research to find the rewards controlling the complex response patterns — those involved in actions such as nest building and nursing; and biochemical research to trace the chain of events causing certain stimuli to become instinctive rewards at certain times. We hope this new way of looking at instinctive rewards may set the stage for such research.

And note that non psychologists may use the term "instinct" in a way that differs slightly from the ways we discussed. In fact, the same people may not always mean the same thing when they use the term "instinct". Sometimes they mean a complex response pattern the creature inherits, while at other times they mean something much simpler — only that the creature inherits a factor that affects its actions. For instance, they might say, "It's instinctive that creatures like food." But we won't deal with that use of the word, since we already get at that notion of inherited factors affecting rewards with the concept of unlearned rewards. But you should keep in mind that "instinct" means different things to different people, as you read the rest of this book and in talking with others.

- 18 What's wrong with the original use of the term "instinct"?
- 19 How did psychologists deal with the issue while holding on to the essence of instinct? What's wrong with that approach?
- 20 What approach do the authors take?

PURPOSIVISM REVISITED

Once again Juke and Sid sat in their room studying psych. Sid laid his book aside, hoping Juke would notice his signal for starting a chat; but Juke kept on reading; so Sid was forced to clear his throat: "Here's another place where people could get into that purposivism thing."

"Yeah, I was thinkin' the same thing. All you got to do is say, 'Gore mates so she can have kids'; or 'she nurses her kids so they'll stay alive'; or 'she builds a nest to protect her kids'. That's sayin' she has a purpose. And it's sayin' something in the future can affect something now. But something that don't exist yet can't cause anything to happen."

"Yeah," Sid added, "the cause of what a creature does now contacts the creature now — not in the future; those rewards are at work right now — future benefits to the creature or its offspring don't affect anything happening now."

"But seem like there is a problem with what you just said."

Sid frowned, not liking to be wrong.

But Juke went on, "You said the reward cause the response; but the reward don't exist 'til Gore respond. The reward don't come before the response; it come after. So it look to me like that's another case of purposivism — saying the cause come after the effect."

Sid thought a minute. "Okay, but the reward comes right after the response — not way off in the future."

Juke made a valid point — the reward following a response can't control that instance of the response, since events in the future can't affect events in the present. So future rewards don't affect current actions. In fact, you can't even be sure your current actions will get their future reward. But Gore responded because that response did get a reward sometime in the past. The past rewards for Gore's actions cause its currect acts. In the past it just happened to make some response, and bingo, a reward came along; so the next chance it got, Gore might repeat that response. So the cause for Gore's actions — or our actions — lies in the past and the present, not in the future.

■21 Cite three cases where you could make a purposive statement about instinct control. Describe the same thing in a correct way.

■22 Give a purposive and a correct way of talking about the effects of rewards on learning.

AGGRESSION

In this section, we'll study acts that are called aggressive, acts that harm others. We'll look at the way aggression helps creatures survive, the forms aggression may take, and the causes of aggression. We will look at aggression as a learned operant response controlled by inherited reinforcers.

Evolution and harm

As we've seen, harmful states increase the rate of motion. But sometimes a creature can't just run, it must struggle and fight to get out of harm's way. And what if nothing more prompt than escape from harm rewarded this struggle? Then the creature might not learn good defense skills in time, since it would often die first. But suppose some built-in events reinforced each correct struggle or fighting response as soon as it occurred — even before that response got the creature free. Such prompt rewards would really help the creature learn better ways of fighting for its life.

***

Out of the nest and on its own for the first time. Watch out! That often spells danger. But Gore scampered off. And didn't have to scamper far before WHAM! Gore was on its back. Never before? What was this? Blood running down its side. Gore gnashed its teeth and flailed its claws. Though it twisted and squirmed it couldn't get off its back. At last the huge thing lifted its paw off Gore's chest; Gore needed no more; it righted itself, reared up on its hind legs, and stood there shaking and trembling. But it kept on gnashing its teeth.

The creature moved closer, a killer who would eat Gore. And Gore flailed wildly in the air until its claws chanced to scratch Killer's own flesh; then it kept scratching. Gore gnashed its teeth until it also happened to bite Killer. Then it bit and bit and clawed and clawed, hurting more and biting harder. And after one such hard bite Killer backed off slightly. But Gore stayed on its hind legs gnashing its teeth and clawing the air. Then it dropped back to the ground with its forepaws — never taking its eyes off Killer. Killer tensed and sprang at its victim. But, too late — Gore took off as fast as it could go. Through the grass and into a hollow log. The creature stalked around the log for some time before wandering off to lick its small, Gore-caused wounds. Gore's heart kept beating hard for a long time. But after awhile the creature ventured out again.

***

Let's do an instant replay on the Killer-Gore fight: Gore's rate of motion increased (it flailed and gnashed), due to a harmful event (Killer's biting). Yet increased activity by itself wouldn't help Gore escape. But what happened when Gore's actions made contact with Killer, when it started biting and clawing Killer instead of thin air? Those actions allowed Gore to escape the harmful state of being bitten by Killer.

One creature bites another. The harmful event will raise the rate of motion of the bitten creature; yet more motion by itself may not suffice to allow the victim to escape. But suppose the victim turns and bites its attacker instead of running? That response might cause the attacker to loosen its grip — loosen its grip just enough to allow the victim to escape. So creatures that bite, strike out, or hit, when in pain, may be more likely to survive. This response to pain is called "aggression".

Now, here's a tricky point: We don't say animals are born prone to aggress when in pain. Rather, they're born with a tendency for certain events to act as rewards when they are in pain. For instance, when in pain, we're told to bite the bullet, grit our teeth, or clench our fists and bear it. We believe these acts are learned, since they produce some internal events which function as unlearned rewards. For instance, it might be that internal events coming from the pressure of gritting our teeth produce just such rewards.

Now understand that the victim isn't trying to hurt its attacker. It may not even be trying to escape. It just acts in ways that produce those internal rewards since the creature is rewarded by such events due to its biochemical structure — a structure inherited because ancestors with the same structure survived long enough to reproduce. And, in fact, most surviving creatures do inherit that tendency to be rewarded by internal stimuli resulting from counter-attack during times of pain.

Some actions happen to have results that help creatures survive. Some of those actions also produce events that are unlearned rewards. Suppose the capacity to be rewarded by those events is inherited. Then the offspring will also more likely survive. And those actions are likely to become part of the normal survival kit of that species.

Now let's look a little closer at how aggressive acts can come to be learned, under the control of built-in aggressive results. We're saying certain events act as rewards whenever harmful events affect the creature, even though those events may be only slightly harmful. So what? Think about the very first time Gore made contact with a harmful event. At that point it had no well-developed pattern of aggressive actions — those acts had to be shaped up through their results — the rewards of the moment.

For instance, suppose Gore was bumped, or bruised, or snapped at, as an infant. Gore might have kept moving, more or less as it was before, at least for an instant; but perhaps one movement was made with slightly more vigor than the others. Perhaps a movement of its paw in the air or a slight closing of its mouth. Then all of a sudden that response produced stimuli that were just a little more rewarding, and so Gore kept making that response, closing its mouth even further, as its mouth was already partly closed; causing even more rewarding results through the proprioceptive stimuli arising from its muscles; causing the response to keep being made, with its mouth closing even further until its teeth chanced to touch; causing tactual (touch) stimuli to come into play as rewards, and on and on — in a spiral until Gore's actions were shaped into a well-developed set of gnashing and chewing acts triggered by the slightest contact with a harmful state of affairs. Gore might learn such acts, to some extent, during the first few seconds of the first contact with a harmful event, as we've tried to show; but it may take a few contacts before Gore acquires the standard, viscious, attack responses it will later show.

Each creature learns aggressive acts. And at first glance, it might seem like those acts they learn would differ from creature to creature, because the precise nature of the response would depend on what just happened to produce the rewards, while the creature was learning that response. But this may not be so, as the physical structure of the creature may limit the ways its movements can produce those rewards. For instance, the rat may have only one way to get the most of such rewards, by standing on its hind legs with its front paws in the air — the classic aggression response seen in all rats. But it may take a few times for each rat to acquire that standard response pattern.

Let's see how this ties in with the research on imprinting. Recall that we saw the inherited biological structure determined the process of imprinting with only slight limits as to what sorts of stimuli would be most easy to imprint. In turn, the imprinting process determined the events that would act as rewards but not the acts that would produce those rewards. The nature of the acts was determined by physical structure of the creature's world and its own mechanical structure. We're saying the same thing might be true with aggression, where the inherited biological structure determined the process of harmful events causing certain response-produced stimuli to be rewards. But that inherited structure doesn't determine the form of those acts that will produce those rewards. The nature of those acts is determined by the physical structure of the creature's world and its own mechanical structure.

* * *

Keep this in mind: the results of aggression produce prompt rewards — rewards that don't themselves help the creature survive, in any direct manner. Gore does not aggress in order to survive; it aggresses because of the prompt rewards (perhaps stimuli like pressure on its teeth and claws). Repeat: It doesn't aggress to survive. Yet it does survive because it aggressed. But we'll also see how being rewarded by stimuli that result from aggression may sometimes hurt our chances to survive; yet because of those prompt aggression rewards we may aggress just the same.

***

Later that day Killer saw the little creature again. It crouched, ready to pounce, but hesitated a moment; the last time it got hurt when it attacked. But then — WHAM! Again the little creature was on its back, but this time not acting the same way, squealing a lot, but no gnashing or clawing. It righted itself when Killer took its paw off, but then just started running around; it didn't get in a defense posture. The creature stumbled when Killer gave it another side swipe with its paw. On its side after one more blow. Then Killer pounced on it with its front paws, quickly biting the back of its neck, leaving Dodo to dangle, dead, from Killer's mouth.

***

Such creatures will be less likely to survive if stimuli resulting from counter attack do not become rewards, when the creatures are under attack. But they would also be less likely to survive, if they were always reinforced by the stimuli resulting from fighting, since they might then spend all their time fighting. They are better off if fighting produces such rewards when and only when fighting helps them survive, for instance, when they are being attacked. And of course that is the way creatures have evolved, so that the results of fighting are more rewarding when the conditions warrant fighting.

- ▪23 Cite an instance of harm-produced attack.
- ▪24 How does this help the counter-attacker survive?
- ▪25 What is the alternative to the notion that creatures inherit the response of attacking or aggressing when in pain?
- ▪26 Is the victim who counter-attacks trying to hurt the attacker? Please explain.
- ▪27 Do creatures aggress so they can survive? Please explain.

Humans and harm

Because we evolved in much the same world as Gore did, we tend to respond like Gore — with pain making certain acts rewarding.

* * *

Chet couldn't see the chair in his way since daylight had not yet come when he got out of bed. But he felt it with his shin. "Damn that thing; that hurts!" And he kicked it with his bare foot (second mistake). "Ouch!"

Carol woke up. "What's the matter, Chet?"

"Can't you keep anything in the right place? I almost killed myself because of your damn chair," he complained.

* * *

Notice that Chet is one up on Gore, since he can do more with his mouth than bite, he can also say things that hurt. We'll talk more about the rewards for that sort of action in a later chapter.

* * *

Carol lay there more hurt than Chet. It wouldn't help to tell Chet that he left the chair in the middle of the room.

Her marriage wasn't working out like she had hoped. She wondered if every marriage went like this or was it just Chet? When things weren't going his way, he became awfully hard to get along with; and this caused real problems as things often weren't going his way.

* * *

Though our species evolved under much the same conditions as Gore's, we no longer live under those conditions. So our biophysical structure often causes us trouble in our new human world. Pain-produced rewards for attack helped us survive during the times when we evolved; but now it often makes it harder for us to survive, since we rarely need to deal with direct physical attack; yet the least little pain causes us to find aggression rewarding — often causing us to hurt people we love — making it hard for them to get along with us. Our biophysical structure evolves more slowly than our culture; so we may need to develop ways of working around the limits of our inherited structure if we are to prevent harmful aggression. But it often takes special efforts to oppose the biophysical rewards for aggression. And our culture may need our help with those efforts.

■28 Cite a case where pain caused a human to aggress. What caused the pain? What actions resulted? Did the actions do any good? What harm did they do?

■29 Why do humans aggress if it no longer helps them survive?

■30 Under what conditions did the human biophysical basis for aggression evolve?

Evolution and frustration

There's yet another time when stimuli from aggression become rewards: when normal rewards are withheld. You've heard the old saying: "Don't take food away from an eating dog."

* * *

Gore just brought down its first rabbit — Gore's big score. And a tasty one indeed. Gore's brother came up alongside and started gnawing on the other end. As it chewed, it yanked the rabbit out of Gore's mouth. Gore growled, snapping at its brother. The brother yelped, letting the rabbit fall from his own mouth. Gore grabbed the meat with a vicious bite and held tight. All further efforts of the brother were in vain. It took a much bigger creature than that to make Gore share its meal.

* * *

Gore's food (reward) was removed. This affected Gore, making the results of aggression act as a reward, with the stimuli from growling, biting, etc. becoming a reward. This aggression helped Gore retrieve its food; the food helped Gore survive.

* * *

When Dodo's brother jerked the rabbit from its mouth, Dodo whimpered a bit. Then waited around but couldn't get back at its meal — not until there was nothing left but the bones. Dodo lost a lot of weight that way; so much that it died a few months later. Natural selection.

* * *

So we've seen two events that produce aggressive rewards, presenting a harmful state or taking away a fuel source, and both events may be bad for the creature. We have a name for the act of causing stimuli to become rewards by stopping other rewards — we call it "frustration".

Frustration: withholding reinforcers where they have been obtained before.

As we will see, frustration causes aggression in humans as well as lower creatures.

■31 Define frustration.
■32 How would frustration-caused aggression help a creature survive?

Humans and frustration

Often we're not too far removed from Gore and its fighting brother, since we humans aggress just like they do when something frustrates our getting our rewards.

* * *

Chet hurried home from his last class — hot, tired, and hungry — he was no one to mess around with. He could hardly wait for dinner as he had skipped lunch. Now, sharp reader that you are, you see it coming don't you? That's right: dinner wasn't ready.

"Wha' da ya mean it's not ready?" he protested.

"I'm sorry, Chet. Since there was such a mob at the store, it just took a long time that's all; it's always that way after work on Friday."

"Damn it, Carol, when I pay for the food around here, I expect you to serve it on time and without a lot of crap about crowded stores." He shouted, stamped, and pounded his fist.

* * *

Why did Chet pound his fist? To show how much his wife abused him; or, because the action was rewarding in his current frustrated state?

Carol didn't bother to point out the cold truth — that she paid for more of the food than he did. He'd just shout back at her if she answered him.

■33 Cite a case of human aggression caused by frustration. What reward was interfered with? And how did the person aggress?

Non-biological causes of aggression and non-harmful forms of aggression

Non-biological events, events other than harm and frustration, also set up aggressive reinforcers for some species. And these rewards are sometimes produced by acts other than direct attack, unlike the rewards of pressure on the teeth and claws. For instance, the sight of a member of the same species can set up such aggressive rewards, with the result that the creatures do the harmless acts that produce them. For instance, the male Siamese fighting fish will aggress with the harmless act of extending its gill membranes to the non-biological event of the sight of other males of the same species. And they are even more likely to aggress that way when those other males also aggress in that manner. Fighting cocks do much the same thing, ruffling neck feathers, raising hackles, and bobbing their heads up and down in an aggressive display, while monkeys may open their mouths, bare their fangs and snarl. In all cases this is the first stage in a stimulus-response chain leading to direct fighting contact with the other creature if the chain isn't broken by the flight of one of the two fighters. And, in fact, it often happens that one of the two will turn tail and run, thus preventing the harm that would result to one or both of the fighters if the stimulus-response chain reached the fighting stage.

But how would creatures evolve to respond to such non-biological events and with acts that don't even harm the other creature? Well, we've seen other non-biological events exert control over a creature's actions. For instance, light exerts unlearned stimulus control by guiding the unlearned acts of simple creatures. And light, motion, and smell are non-biological rewards controlling the learned acts of more complex creatures. So non-biological control is common, but why would non-biological events cause creatures to aggress? Why did these creatures evolve so that those events controlled their actions?

By now, our first guess should always be that such control may have helped their species survive. And the next question, "How?", should evoke the standard answer. The non-biological event must be tied to some biological event, though perhaps not in a direct manner, tied to some biological event such as fuel, harm, producing and caring for offspring, etc.

And so we ask, what biological events of that sort might follow the sight of a member of their species? And the answer is clear: that other creature might take their food or attack them. This is even more likely if that other creature is showing the first stages of the stimulus-response chain leading to direct attack. Then we ask how does such control help them deal with the related biological event? And we answer loud and clear: going through the first stages of the attack chain may cause the other creature to flee, thus avoiding harm from the fight and any loss of fuel that might be involved. So both non-biological causes of aggression and harmful forms of aggression would seem to have clear value in helping the species survive.

Aggressive reinforcer: an event that becomes a reinforcer when the creature is exposed to conditions that may be bad for it — either (1) the removal of a fuel source, (2) a harmful state, or (3) events that have been paired with such conditions in the history of the species.

■34 Describe non-biological events that set up aggressive reinforcers and harmless acts that may result.
■35 How might they have evolved?
■36 Define aggressive reinforcer.

DEFINING MOTIVATION

What do most people mean when they say "someone is motivated to do something"? They mean the person has a reason for doing that thing. "What is their motive", means what is their reason. How will it help them? What's the cause? We will try to define the term so it's in keeping with this common sense approach, as well as the precise notions arising from the science of psychology. So we need to define motivation in a way that deals with three types of acts — learned operant acts, learned and unlearned respondent acts, and the unlearned motion of simple creatures.

In the case of operant acts, motivation raises the value of rewards. This can be done in several ways: The reward value of fuel rises, if the creature is deprived of that fuel. The reward value of escape from harm rises, if the creature is exposed to that harmful state. The value of aggressive rewards rises, if the creature is exposed to frustration or harm. And the value of instinctive rewards rises according to the season and the creature's biochemistry.

In the case of respondent acts, motivation raises the strength of the stimulus to evoke the response. The strength of a conditioned or unconditioned, fuel-based stimulus rises, if the creature is deprived of that fuel. While the strength of a harmful stimulus is effective as soon as it is presented.

And in the case of unlearned motion, motivation increases motion. This occurs if the creature is deprived of fuel or exposed to a harmful state.

So we must define motivation in a way that gets at the essence of the factors that motivate these response systems.

Motivation: factors that: 1) increase the effect stimuli have as reinforcing stimuli; 2) increase the effect they have as unconditioned or conditioned stimuli; and 3) simply raise the overall rate of motion.

However, we should look at some other issues in the motivation of operant acts. For instance, it is less clear what factors affect the value of imprinted rewards and non-biological rewards such as light and sound. But you might be able to affect their reward values, if you deprived the creatures of either those rewards themselves or of the biological conditions on which they're based, the needed fuels. And deprivation also affects sexual rewards.

But you can affect the value of a reward in another way — by short-circuiting the normal methods. You can go directly inside the creature through the use of chemicals, electrical stimulation, or surgery. For instance, some drugs can raise the value of many instinctive rewards, electrical brain stimulation can raise the value of aggressive rewards, and destroying certain areas of the brain can increase the reward value of food to the point where a lab rat will eat so much it grows to many times its normal weight.

■37 What three types of acts must be taken into account when we define motivation?

■38 In general what does motivation do in the case of operant acts?

■39 In the case of respondent acts?

■40 And in the case of the simple response of motion?

■41 List at least three ways to motivate operant acts.

■42 Define motivation.

EMOTIONS

Example

Let's replay Gore vs. Killer one more time: Watch out, Gore, here it comes — WHAM! On its back with Killer hulking above. The blow, the fall, the pain, the blood, the sight of that huge thing getting larger as it moved closer, the growl, the sudden shock of it all — this had quite an effect on Gore — an effect like nothing before — causing Gore's small brain to fire tiny electric pulses at a high rate; causing Gore's blood pressure to rise, as new chemicals began flowing through its blood stream; causing the blood to rush to Gore's skin as its surface blood vessels expanded and others contracted; causing Gore to breathe faster and faster; causing its muscles to tense; in short, causing Gore to be ready for action. And none too soon.

Killer pulled back and then sprang at the young rat. But Gore was on its feet, ready to fight. The rat struck out with one vicious blow after another — with one tearing bite after another. Gore fought with more vigor than ever before — not like he and the rat pups playing in their nest — striking and nibbling; now he was moving fast and biting hard. Again Killer backed off for an instant, the instant Gore needed to escape, running faster than it ever had in its young life.

Analysis

These body changes, or emotions, helped Gore respond with greater vigor and greater speed at times when vigor and speed were useful. And when were they useful? When Gore was in a harmful state or when it was in danger of losing a meal. Then Gore must act with utmost vigor and speed to survive, whether it's to fight or to flee. Emotional reactions function to help creatures respond better under times of stress — times when action is really useful. So harmful events and frustration cause emotional physiological reactions to occur, at the same time they're causing aggressive reinforcers to come into effect.

And what triggers these emotional reactions? Stimuli can cause emotional reactions if they're either tied in a direct or in an indirect manner to biological needs. Harmful states as well as frustration produce emotional reactions. But so do things like sudden noises and moving objects, events not tied in a direct manner to biological need. Gore's likely to find either a prey or a predator where there's a sudden noise or motion — eat or be eaten. In either case Gore will more likely survive if it's ready for action. So creatures that have an emotional reaction to such things, either biological or non-biological, will more likely survive.

Emotions: temporary physiological changes due to stimulus changes in the creature's world — both the internal and external world.

- ▪43 Define emotion.
- ▪44 What are two physical reactions that might be called emotional?
- ▪45 What are four types of events that cause emotional reactions?
- ▪46 What function do emotional reactions serve?
- ▪47 How do emotional reactions to non-biological events help creatures survive?

CONCLUSIONS

We've looked at more and more complex acts throughout this section of our book. In the last chapter, we studied the process that allows us to build these complex acts — we studied the process of learning. There we saw the motivation for learning — its causes.

And in this chapter, we saw how the concepts of reinforcer and learning help us understand some puzzling acts — acts based on imprinted, aggressive, and instinctive reinforcers. Perhaps these acts puzzle us because of the unique ways their reinforcers come into play. And, of course, purposivism doesn't help clear things up either. But in any case, we solve the puzzle when we see the following: those puzzling acts are learned acts whose rewards function only under certain conditions — proper exposure for imprinting, pain or frustration for aggression, and seasonal or other chemical changes for instinctive actions.

We also looked at how motivation and emotion relate. There we saw that emotional reactions are not themselves motives or causes but rather they help the actions that will achieve rewards — the rewards.

Now in the next three chapters we'll look at even more complex learning — learning that allows for advanced human actions — actions that make up much of our everyday lives — actions that get us humans into trouble and, perhaps more often, get us out of trouble.

CHAPTER 7
LEARNING: BASIC ELEMENTS

WHEN CREATURES FIRST LEARNED

Pig Out

Anchovies. Sid loved the salty little fish — at least he thought he did. He ordered a large pizza from Tony's — students do not live by books alone. You've got to eat if you're gunning for a chem mid-term the next morning. Sid figured Juke would come in at the same time he always did, and they'd split the giant cartwheel of pizza. But by the time Juke arrived there wasn't so much as a soggy crust left. Sid ate it all — a pig out!

It was past one before Sid turned in. He'd studied all that week, but it seemed there was just too much to nail down — too many terms, formulas, concepts. Sid covered what he felt was crucial — the rest got a kiss and a promise. It was risky. If Sid'd picked the wrong things to study, he could bomb the exam. Sid felt panic for the first time since he'd entered college.

***

When Sid woke up there was a horrid taste in his mouth; his bloated stomach churned with torment. The anchovies had struck back. It was 6:30 — only an hour of sack time before his eight o'clock class and the chem exam. Had he learned the right things?

Learning

At one time in the course of evolution, none of the earth's tenants
could learn. None yet possessed the structure that allowed response
patterns to alter as a result of contact with new forces. The sole
method that living forms had to adapt to the environment was
mutation.

So it went on and on for eons. Species lived and thrived only to be
expunged by still a new threat from the environment — save a few
mutants who survived.

Then one day a special mutant appeared. Its structure allowed it
to learn. Learning proved a vast boon — rather than relying solely on
mutation, these creatures could come up with new ways of coping —
new responses. As things around them changed, their actions changed
in turn. As a group, the learners lived longer and produced more offspring, winning by default over species that didn't have this structure
— natural selection. Thus began the reign of creatures that learn.

The apex of this great thrust of nature is seen in human beings.
They can learn to change their actions to suit the world. And, unlike
all other creatures, they can learn to mold the world to adhere to
their unique form. How do they do it? What controls what they
learn? Of all responses they could make, why are some learned and
others not?

- 1 Review: What is a mutation?
- 2 Review: What is natural selection?

THE LAW OF IMMEDIATE RESULTS

Learning what's best to learn

Young Gore roams the woods. Going somewhere, after something? No. At this point in its new life, Gore's acting from a script chosen by evolution — doing things newborn Gores have done for thousands of years; gross actions that will be replaced with precise ones as soon as Gore learns them.

Gore pokes a bush, sniffs a rock, takes time to groom, smoothing down shiny fur with paws and tongue. Next, Gore turns over a dead branch. A juicy grub! Gore gobbles it down.

***

On this day, Gore found food under a dead limb. We, with our knowledge of nature, are aware that grubs frequent the damp regions beneath dead tree limbs. Gore doesn't share our knowledge of the ways of grubs — has no such awareness. It would help if finding the grub made poking under dead limbs one of Gore's more frequent actions. If so, Gore would be more likely to look under dead branches in the future, thus finding needed fuel. And this is, in fact, what happens. The presence of food rewards Gore's actions of looking under dead limbs. Henceforth, Gore's actions will be a bit less aimless, and Gore will be more likely to survive in the hostile forest.

But suppose this happened instead? Suppose the food rewarded one of the other responses? This could spell trouble for Gore. Poking a bush or sniffing a rock is far less likely to yield a grub. Grooming and primping have their place, but they're useless in the quest for food. If one of these actions had somehow been rewarded, Gore would have learned to do something that wouldn't help it find food. Starving could be the outcome. What's best for Gore seems clear enough: a reward should strengthen the response that comes immediately before it — the response that most likely has something solid to do with producing it.

So you can see what's important about the response that directly precedes the reward: that response is a good bet to be the one that did the trick — produced the reward. Earlier actions may have had little or nothing to do with it.

Gore's the kind of creature that's going to survive. Gore's actions are described by the "Law of Immediate Results".

The Law of Immediate Results: a result has the most effect on the response that came just before it (a response is most controlled by the results that occurred just after it).

- 3 Review: If they aren't learned, how are these first behaviors of the organism acquired?
- 4 If a creature makes six different responses, and the last is followed by reward, which one is likely to be strengthened?
- 5 Why would it matter if some other response was rewarded by the food instead?
- 6 What is the law called which governs the response that will be rewarded in this instance?
- 7 State the Law of Immediate Results.

Punishment

Dodo had been long without fuel. Rib bones showed clearly beneath thin skin — bare patches where feathers had lost their sheen, turned dull, and fallen out. Dodo was dying. In the past, Dodo had found a feast of ripe larvae under these rocks. Dodo moved one of the larger ones — it was covered with moss. There was a hissing sound as a snake coiled and flattened its head. A stream of white fluid sprayed from the snake's gaping mouth, spewing into Dodo's eyes. Blinded, Dodo whirled, stumbled, and careened in circles. After a time the effects of the venom wore off. Dodo could see again. The rocks were still there. Dodo tried the large mossy one. There was a hissing noise . .

* * *

Survival depends on learning what to do to gain fuel. Creatures must look in the right places and make the correct follow-through responses once a fuel source is found. But survival also depends in equal measure on learning what **not** to do. Natural selection has provided most complex animals with a structure which makes it likely that responses that lead to harmful outcomes will occur less often. This result is called "punishment".

Punishment: a reduction in actions that takes place when these actions lead to outcomes that harm tissue or remove reinforcers.

The event, whether it be a form of energy or other outcome in the environment, that causes the punishment effect to occur, is called a "punisher".

Punisher: an outcome (often a harmful one) that reduces the occurrence of actions it closely follows.

Two basic kinds of stimuli have the native or unlearned power to act as punishers for most creatures: events that cause tissue damage (those that produce cuts, bruises, burns, etc.,) and the loss of rewards.

Loss of reward as a punisher

Gore, now a soaring eagle, swooped down on the small rodent. The force of the strike pushed Gore's prey into the dust, half covering it. It lay quiet and still within the strong cage of Gore's talons. Gore relaxed the vice-like grip. Feathers had been ruffled in the swift descent. Gore started to preen, turning from the catch. The rodent lifted its small head. It moved in silence, soon lost in the tall grass nearby. When Gore returned to the task at hand, the meal had vanished. There was nothing. Gore would be less likely to stop to groom next time. That response had been well punished.

■ 8 What happens to make it less likely that organisms will continue actions that lead to harmful outcomes?

■ 9 How did creatures acquire this feature of their behavior?

■10 Define punishment.

■11 Define punisher.

■12 What are two kinds of events mentioned that act as punishers?

■13 Cite an instance of how stimuli that damage tissue serve as punishers.

■14 Cite an instance of how loss of reward serves as a punisher.

Punishment and the Law of Immediate Results

In a previous section we pointed out that rewards strengthen those actions they·are closest to in time — those they follow right behind. Other responses that are more removed from the reward are affected less or not at all.

The Law of Immediate Results also applies to punishment. Actions that most closely precede a punisher are those most affected by it. These responses will be the ones knocked out or suppressed. Others that happened farthest before the punisher suffer little if any from the power of the punisher. Again, it's easy to see why things evolved this way. The response that comes just before the reward or punisher is the one that likely played a major role in causing it to occur. The creature will be helped most if this response is the one most strengthened (in the case of a reward), or the one most suppressed (in the case of a punisher).

■15 How does the Law of Immediate Results apply to punishment?

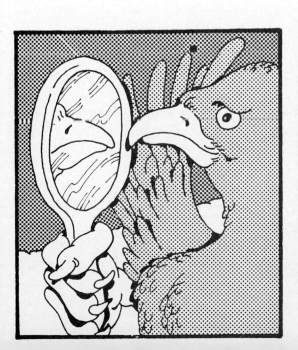

AWARENESS AND LEARNING

Good time Sidney's got the blahs

Sid was hustling to the chem exam. He was going to be late by five or ten minutes — putting him even more under the gun. As ill-prepared as he felt, he figured he'd need each precious second he could eke out to spend on the questions. When he'd first gotten up his head was a dull ache. Now it was alive — a three-alarm throbbing torture. Crashing waves of nausea pounded the tender shores of his stomach. *Was he ill or was it the panic?*

Sid had to slow down when he reached the entrance to the building. Student traffic was still filing out. Someone touched him on the shoulder.

"Hi, Sid." It was Dawn and Mae. Dawn had got a walk, her eight o'clock had been called off. Mae was always up and out by that time — class or no.

"Oh, hello," Sid said. He wanted to smile. Instead he just stood there, looking first at them and then to the door.

"Is something wrong, Sid? You look so pale," Dawn said. Both Dawn and Mae began to look him over, frowning slightly with concern.

"Everything! Everything's wrong!" Sid blurted out. "Got this chem exam I'm gonna get creamed on. It's a bi . . . I mean, it's tough." Sid was appalled by his voice. It was pitched higher than he liked — had a nasal whine to it, like a whipped pup. "Look, I gotta go. Okay? See you later." Sid rushed through the door and into the building. Dawn and Mae looked at each other.

"That dude's in bad shape. Never saw him like that before," Mae said.

"Something's wrong for sure. He's so uptight," Dawn said. "Poor baby — I guess he's got problems just like the rest of us, but this's the first time I ever heard him complain. It must be bad. We're all so busy talking about our bad breaks — I guess we think he's okay since he doesn't gripe all the time."

"You're dead right," Mae agreed. "We take him for granted. I got a flash. Let's do something nice for Sid — show him we think he's special!"

"Fantastic idea! Let's do something really fine." Dawn paused. "But what?"

"We'll think of something. Two of the greatest brains around are bound to come up with a stellar deed or two that'll turn old Sid's head clean around!"

Super Sid

When Sid left the Science Building forty minutes later, he was slightly
over ten feet tall. The exam had been a wipe-out all right. But it was
Sid who'd done all the wiping. He'd aced it. There was a good chance
he'd missed only one or two questions, maybe none at all. A perfect job!

Thinking back on the questions, Sid was amazed at how well he'd
recalled answers from the readings and class notes. Formulas and
other precise facts that he'd not even tried to memorize jumped out
at him, sharp and crystal clear. Somehow he'd learned the right
things; and he'd done it without being aware he was doing it. Must be
a word for people like him. *"Genius" — nice word, had a good ring to it.*

Self-awareness: knowing and knowing that you know

Sid points out a fact that new students of behavior often fail to
grasp: you don't need to be aware that you're learning — and
therefore of what you're learning — to learn. Being able to make the
right responses (the ones that will yield reward) when the time comes,
and self-awareness (knowing that you know what to do), can be two
distinct things. Further, this learning without self-awareness isn't
strange, odd or unique — in fact it's the rule.

All learning done by non-humans, that done by children before
they master language, and the greater part of learning done by us all,
proceeds without self-awareness. All that's needed for learning to
occur is for a response to be followed by a strong result — a reward
or punisher. Being aware that you've made the response; being aware
that you were rewarded or punished; and having the self-awareness
that there was some cause and effect tie between response and result
— these may or may not occur. They will, of course, under the right
conditions, as we shall see in a later chapter.

- ■16   Contrast "knowing what to do" with "knowing that you know".
- ■17   Which of the two options above would be called self-awareness?
- ■18   What is needed for learning to occur?
- ■19   Who can learn without self-awareness?

THE LAW OF REPEATED DELAYED RESULTS

The dust rose in clouds, reaching into Gore's humanoid nostrils, causing sneezing, and blinking of small, but human-like eyes. Each gust brought more dust, tinted red from the glare of the sun. The dry season was upon them. Gore cracked open the large nuts and chewed the pulp inside. There was some moisture there, but precious little, scarcely worth the effort. Thwarted, Gore threw the halves of the opened nuts into the dirt. Some of the shells landed open side down, making small domes. Others landed open side up — bowls facing up to the cloudless sky.

That night it rained. A shower, brief but intense. By the time Gore made it from its lair, the rain was over. It had gone, swallowed by the greedy dust. When Gore awoke the next morning, the smell of water was still strangely fresh. A glimmer coming from one of the shells caught Gore's eye. It and others had captured some of the rain! But those with the round part pointing up had not. Gore licked the bowls until all traces of moisture were gone. He survived that day and the next. A shower came again, and again after that. And so it went for weeks. Gore rushed to the upturned shells each morning. During the day, more nuts were cracked open, the pulp removed and sucked dry. And at some point Gore's actions changed. Now Gore always placed them in the dirt open side up — facing the sky.

***

From what we know of the Law of Immediate Results, we know that learning depends on rewards or punishers that must follow right after the actions that produce them. But in preparing for a test, the reward or punishment for study actions doesn't come right away. Hours, days, weeks may go by before scores are posted or the test is returned. How then can learning occur? The answer is a somewhat

complex one. It is given in part by reference to a new law — the Law of Repeated Delayed Results.

The Law of Immediate Results provides that the response that occurs just before the reward or punisher will be the one that receives the greatest effect. For the most part, a good thing. Acts that come an instant before the result are likely the ones that caused it.

But other cases arise where the act that produces the result occurs some time before the result appears. Much time and many acts may take place between the response that did the trick and the result it produced. Lucky for us and other creatures, our structure has evolved in a way that takes care of this. The way it works is described by the Law of Repeated Delayed Results.

The Law of Repeated Delayed Results: a result occurring some time after the response that produces it, may gain control over that response if the delayed pairing of response with result occurs often enough.

Because of this law at work, Gore survived. Gore learned to place the shells in a manner that would retain the most water from the showers. The time between placing the shells and drinking their contents was a matter of many hours and sometimes days. Although delayed, reward was time and again paired with the same actions of placement.

- ■20 What is the law that allows for repeated delayed results to affect the response that produces them?
- ■21 State the law alluded to above.
- ■22 Cite an instance of the Law of Repeated Delayed Results at work.

DELAYED RESULTS AND MEDIATION

All actions produce some type of outcome — some reward or punisher. But a reward occurring long after a response, leaves a space in time for many other actions and their outcomes to take place — all this happening after a response is made and before the delayed result appears. In light of this, let's take a new look at the actions of the humanoid Gore in dealing with the coconut shells.

At first Gore tossed the empty shells aside, letting them land on the ground as they might. Later — after the rain — Gore found water in the shells that had chanced to fall open-side up. Gore must have seen the position of the shells as he picked them up to drink their contents. It is likely, therefore, that seeing shells in this position in the future would be more rewarding than seeing them placed in other positions. Why? Because shells placed in the sand that way were the ones that contained precious water.

Perhaps this sight was enough of a reward to control Gore's actions. It caused the creature to place them open-side up — just seeing them was a mild reward. Placing shells in this manner also insured more water; making the sight of shells facing upward an even greater reward. Now, can we say that the delayed result — water — controlled placement actions? Only indirectly. It was really the mildly rewarding outcome of seeing the shells placed a certain way that controlled Gore, and not, strictly speaking, the delayed result of water.

This way of looking at Gore's actions involves far more than a simple response controlled by a delayed result. In this instance we can't say whether simple delayed results could account for Gore's learning or if events occurring between must also be taken into account — the incident with Gore is fiction, but one that could have happened.

It's still true, though, that many of the acts humans must learn would never be learned if other actions and outcomes didn't bridge the gap between act and delayed reward. We call it "mediation" when sequences of actions and mildly rewarding outcomes provide this function.

Mediation: sequences of more or less standard responses and events that fill the time between a response that produces a reinforcer and the occurrence of that reinforcer.

Often the actions that provide mediation are verbal — simple chains of words we say to ourselves. This form of mediation occurs when we look in the phone book for a number, and then say that sequence of digits over and over until we get across the room to the telephone. Being able to say the number correctly after you've put the book down is a mild reward, and also serves as a cue to repeat the number again. So it goes until you've reached the phone. The big reward comes when the number is dialed. It's this reward that maintains looking in the phone book in the first place and also keeps the outcomes of other actions mildly rewarding. Without the big reward all these responses would no longer be maintained by their outcomes. With this in mind, let's speculate about the role mediation plays in bringing study behavior under the control of the delayed result of test scores.

Before the first test, Sid didn't know what to study for that course and that professor. Of course he'd taken tests in other courses, so he studied pretty much the same way he had for them. He took the test, and some days later got back the results. He'd done well. When it came time to study for the second exam, Sid went over the chapters and pages of notes the test would cover. This situation gave cues for Sid to make certain responses — to recall how he'd studied on the test, and to recall the result he'd received for his effort.

To "recall" means to "call" or "say" again — to talk to yourself about what happened in the past. Like the rest of us, Sid had to learn the skills of recall; he wasn't born with them. When we're youngsters, grown-ups insist that we give an account of what we've done and what has happened. They bombard each of us with never-ending questions like: What are you doing now? What did you do yesterday? What happened at the zoo? Who did you see at the store? . . . In the process they teach us how to recall. They reward us when we answer their questions the way they want us to; but they aren't so cordial if we don't come up with the right answers. So, over the years we develop the skills of recall.

Today, when we try to solve a problem, we ask ourselves what we did when we faced a problem like it before and what happened as a result. Our answers — the recall — allow us to alter new actions so that results will be even better in the future. Of course, recall is a form of mediation — verbal mediation — chains of single responses, each one maintained by the mildly rewarding outcome it produces. Verbal mediation helps glue current responses to delayed rewards so that in the end, success controls our behavior, even if success is a long time coming.

Mediation responses don't have to be verbal. Any sequence of actions and their outcomes can help delayed reward to gain control over a response — just as long as mediation actions occur in regular ways, a standard bridge between response and delayed reward. Creatures other than humans may come under the control of delayed reward when they make sequences of movements that serve the mediation function. Of course, mediation of this type is not nearly as effective as human recall. But it does lead to mildly rewarding outcomes, which in turn lead to other mediated actions until the reward is reached. We'll learn more about how neutral outcomes become rewards in a later chapter.

- ■23 Define mediation.
- ■24 Cite an instance of mediation.
- ■25 Explain how mediation might work to make test study behavior more effective.

THE BAIT-SHY EFFECT

Bait-shy Sid

It was nine o'clock. "Just get over one test and I gotta start toolin' up for a new one," Sid grumbled to himself as he turned the pages in the poly sci text. There was a knock on the door. "It's open!" Sid yelled gruffly.

"Hello, Sidney," Dawn poked her blond head through the doorway.

"Dawn?" Sid said. "That you — uh, gosh, come on in." Sid's tone changed.

"Yeah — sure, Sid. Will in a minute." Dawn turned to whisper something to someone in the hall. Sid heard snickers and hoarse whispers — a man's voice. Sounded like Juke.

"What's going on out there?"

"Nothing, Sid." Dawn turned back to Sid. "Sid — will you do me a big favor? Will you close your eyes?"

"Do what? Why?"

"Close your eyes — puleese."

"Why should . . ."

"Pretty puleese." Sid closed his eyes.

"We know it's not your birthday, Sid, but . . ."

"Happy birthday to yew, happy birthday to yew, happy birthday dear Sidney, happy birthday to yew."

Sid opened his eyes to find Dawn, Mae and Juke bursting through the doorway, singing and laughing. Mae held something in her hand, covered with lighted candles. The three of them seemed very pleased, happy with themselves. Sid looked more closely at the cake. It was too flat. More like a pie. Oh no! Sid saw the horrid little anchovies lying amongst the cheese and mush-rooms — there were hundreds of 'em! Sid felt his stomach begin to churn and the nausea start.

"For he's a jolly good fellowww, for he's a jolly good fellowww. . ." The chorus went on.

The exception

The normal delayed learning system requires many pairings of the response and results before those results gain control of the response. But there's one delayed result that might be fatal if more than one pairing was required — food poisoning — a result that's caused by the response of eating poison.

Getting sick from food poisoning rarely occurs right after eating — it's a delayed result. If the creature survives the ordeal it was due likely to dumb luck. But the next time, luck may not be with it. If only the creature could learn from just one exposure and thus one delayed result — then it would avoid eating the poisoned sub-stance in the future. Once again, evolution has ground away through millions of years — mutation, success and failure — until today, many creatures, we among them, have acquired the structure to achieve this one-trial, delayed-result learning. It's called the "bait-shy effect".

The term "bait-shy" comes from the fact that animals will no longer eat poisoned bait that humans hoped to kill them with.

After living through one expo-sure, the animals learn to avoid the bait in the future. It's clear that only one contact with the poisoned food does exert delayed control over their behavior. This is a worthwhile exception to both the Law of Immediate Results and the Law of Repeated Delayed Results.

Bait-shy effect: creatures tend to avoid eating a substance that tastes or smells like poisoned food previously eaten just once before.

Sid has had what looks to be a bait-shy response to anchovies — perhaps to pizza. This doesn't mean the pizza he had before was poisoned, spoiled, or anything like that. Other factors — food allergies, other drugs or foods that react to the new food — could account for Sid's sickness.

But now, Sid has a real bait-shy response — the exception to the Laws of Immediate and Repeated Delayed Results. The question is: How's Sid going to keep his stomach and his social conscience happy at the same time?

- ■26 How does the bait-shy effect violate the Laws of Immediate and Repeated Delayed Results?
- ■27 How did the bait-shy effect come about?
- ■28 Cite an instance of the bait-shy effect.

The party's over

"Boy, that Sid was down," Juke said. "Did you see how pale and out of it he looked when we first walked in?"

"He sure looked puny all right. I guess a few wedges of his most favorite pizza picked him up," Mae said. "Come to think of it, I don't think Sid ate much of it. I saw him pick up a piece — don't recall him takin' a bite, though."

"He must have — did you see how his spirits picked up after we were there a while?" Juke said.

"I still say he didn't eat any. But it does seem like he felt a lot better after it was all gone. Then's when he started laughing and cutting up."

"But if Sid didn't eat it, who did? I only had one piece," Juke said.

"I only had two myself." Mae and Juke looked over to Dawn. "How many'd you have Dawn?" Mae said.

Dawn didn't hear. She was tuned-in to signals from within — her bloated stomach screamed and moaned like a banshee. She was in for some wild dreams tonight.

CONCLUSIONS

In this chapter we've stayed with a simple theme — how results tend to select some responses and not others. We saw how the Laws of Immediate and Repeated Delayed Results apply to all creatures, while mediation, although present in some simple form in many creatures, is more the domain of humans — allowing us to learn many things other creatures couldn't. The bait-shy effect was offered as an exception, a unique product of evolution. In the two chapters that follow we'll discuss some complex learning principles that must be employed if we are to account for the gamut of responses that humans and other creatures learn.

CHAPTER 8
LEARNING:
FACTORS AFFECTING
LEARNING

SHAPING: THE METHOD OF SUCCESSIVE APPROXIMATION

The blond

When they were inside Chet and Carol's apartment, Chet took the blond in his arms. "Come here you gorgeous thing!" His hands fit neatly around the smooth, slim waist. His cheek gently touched the ash-yellow satin finish — it felt cool. Yes — it was a handsome guitar. Now all he had to do was learn how to play it. Once he'd mastered it, there'd be no problem — make a few contacts, get into a group, or maybe form his own. Two or three gigs a week and he could rack up twice as much money as he did pumping gas. Of course, Carol wouldn't see it that way. All she'd see would be the price tag. A fine woman, but no vision. Have to keep the guitar a secret for a while. He'd tell her later — in a day or two after he'd learned to play it.

Mae and Cecil

"You're a no good rat, Cecil, but I love you anyway," Mae said. Cecil sniffed, swished his long tail, and clutched onto Mae's blouse, all without a great deal of passion. As a rule, there were two students to a rat in the psych rat lab; Mae was the odd student with no partner, so it was she and Cecil one-on-one.

Mae took great care to handle Cecil as gently as she could, placing him inside the clear plastic rat chamber or Skinner box. Mae recalled the animal chambers Dr. Harper had shown her in his lab a few weeks back. The Skinner box she was using wasn't nearly as fancy as the ones he used in his research — still it worked much like them. A small lever faced inward on the side, just the right height and size for Cecil to press down with his front paws. When he pressed it, a counter mounted on the outside racked it up and displayed the number in a plastic window. There was a tiny hole below the lever where the floor and wall met. The hole was just the right size for Cecil's pink tongue.

A hinged metal rod with a minute dipper on the end could be swung upward from its resting place in a pan of water. Laden with water, the dipper slid neatly into the hole when Mae pushed down on the other end of the rod. Once the dipper was in the hole, it awaited Cecil. There was never need to worry about water being a reward. As with all rats in the lab projects, Cecil was deprived of water for the 23 hours just prior to the lab session.

As soon as Mae put Cecil in the box he made straight for the dipper hole. Of course it was empty, as it always was in the resting state, the dipper resting below in the water dish. Then Cecil reared back on his haunches and pressed down on the lever with his forepaws. The counter clicked and Mae swung the dipper up through the hole to make contact with Cecil's waiting tongue. Mae breathed a sigh of relief. "Why you cute little dickins! You didn't forget a thing, did you!"

Shaping Cecil's lever-press response

It all looked so easy now. But it had taken a while — a number of sessions — to get Cecil this far. When she'd first started with Cecil, time was spent in letting him mill around, getting used to the Skinner box. The next phase involved teaching him to drink from the dipper — dipper training, the lab book called it. It was soon after that the shaping procedure began. Mae found that rats aren't born into the world ready to press little stainless steel levers. Sure, they do it fine once they learn how. But you might wait forever before they did it on their own. The lab book explained how students were to use shaping, or the method of successive approximation, to teach their animals the lever-press response.

You started by rewarding your rat for doing something that only faintly resembled a bar press — at first for just coming close to the lever, then for touching it, and at last for getting it to press hard enough to push the lever all the way down, making the counter work.

Of course, there were a lot of steps between and sometimes you had to drop back to an earlier one, and then go on. It sounded pretty easy when it was explained in the lab book. But when it got down to cases, there were many times when Mae wanted to shout at Cecil, "Hey, dummy, press down on it! Not sideways! Not up! No! Don't try to eat it — press down!" Not that it would have done any good — Cecil wasn't controlled by pleas for mercy.

But shaping was all behind her now. Cecil had learned his lessons well. Mae watched him now with some pride, as time after time, he pressed the lever, scurried to the dipper, licked it dry, and then returned to the lever to repeat the cycle.

***

Reward results in learning when it follows a response. This means that the response has to first occur. But what if, in fact, it never does — or if it occurs so seldomly that old age could settle in before the great event takes place? A quite useful method developed in the animal lab gets around this problem. It's known as "shaping"; or more formally, as the "method of successive approximation". In this technique, the animal learns a series of responses, each one coming closer or approximating the one the trainer wanted in the first place. As a closer response appears, it's rewarded and the old one abandoned. This sifting through responses goes on through as many approximations as are needed.

Shaping seems to work on most creatures — and since it works on humans, it's a potent tool for the teacher, parent, or counselor. It's also a mainstay in behavior modification — a science where techniques like shaping are used to change human problem behavior. We will discuss behavior modification in a later chapter.

Shaping (method of successive approximation): procedure where a person or animal is taught to make a new response by reinforcing any responses that approximate or are part of the correct performance. This is done to increasingly narrow requirements until the desired behavior is attained.

At first a response most like the desired response, and one that currently takes place, is rewarded; it increases in frequency as do other responses similar to it, some of these being still more similar to the desired response. One of these new responses is therefore rewarded and the old one forsaken. It in turn leads to a response still closer to the desired one. At last, after many such successive approximations, the desired response occurs.

- 1 Define shaping. What's another name for it?
- 2 Why is shaping needed?
- 3 Name three types of people who might use shaping on humans.

EXTINCTION

Welcome to hard times

Cecil didn't know it, but the party was over — hard times were on the way. He was about to find himself in the throes of extinction which was the topic for the day's rat lab session. The principle of extinction was simple: once a response was learned, it could be unlearned — would stop occurring — if the reward it had always produced was withheld. The trick now was to stop rewarding Cecil when he made a lever press.

After allowing Cecil five minutes of rewarded lever presses, Mae stopped working the water dipper. Cecil pressed, ran to the dipper hole — but there was no water. He returned to press again; back to the dipper — still nothing. Soon Cecil's presses began to slow. He took more time between presses, sniffed around exploring the corners of the box. At last, he quit. The response had extinguished.

* * *

In the last chapter we saw that learning proceeds when actions are followed by reward. But this is hardly the end for rewards, their job has just begun — their importance in behavior far from over. If learned actions maintain, it's only because rewards must keep coming. The direct role of reward is thus twofold: rewards are crucial to the learning of new actions; and, once learned, actions will maintain only if they continue to produce rewards — without reward, actions slacken and stop.

When responses stop because they don't produce any more rewards, this result — the stopping of actions — is called "extinction".

Extinction process: a reduction in response frequency that occurs when the response no longer yields a reinforcer.

The definition above puts the focus on the result or outcome caused by the ending of rewards. Extinction can also be thought of as a "procedure" — that is, a way of making responses stop.

Extinction procedure: withholding the reinforcer that has followed a response.

Of course, the outcome of an extinction procedure is the extinction process. The response stops being maintained; its frequency is reduced. It will sooner or later stop cold unless rewards reappear.

- 4 Define extinction process.
- 5 Define extinction procedure.
- 6 What is the twofold direct function of reward?
- 7 What happens to actions when they stop producing rewards?

Rock and roll I gave you the best minutes of my life

Less than an hour after Chet started strumming the guitar, he looked in anguish at the sore and swollen tips of his fingers. Distinct grooves stood out where the strings had born deep into the flesh. *Maybe there was more to learning the guitar than he'd thought. Oh well, he'd get it — but right now he had to go to class.*

* * *

Chet practiced three more times that week — then a round of exams came. That was it. He forgot about the guitar. In the meantime, he'd arrived at a solemn truth: pop singers were shallow — all tinsel and glitter — no substance.

* * *

Extinction's more than a rat lab project — it's a fact of the world. Cecil's performance is a simple, clear-cut case of extinction. But, of course, that's the point of the rat lab in the first place — to allow the student to see the principles of behavior portrayed as clearly and cleanly as possible.

Chet gave up the guitar — lost interest in it so to speak — in much the same way Cecil lost interest in the lever. Can we say that Chet's responses extinguished? Quite likely we can, but to say only that would tend to mislead the reader.

We were there when Cecil learned the lever-press response; we know the reward he got and the exact place where it all happened. We hardly know anything about the mish-mash of futile motions Chet went through during his short-lived practice periods. Doubtless, they were never rewarded in the same direct way as Cecil's lever press.

What Chet had been rewarded for was "doing what others do" — this is called imitation — holding and strumming the guitar somewhat like he'd seen others do — but only somewhat. For if it had been the same, the results — the sounds — would have likewise been the same. Yes, it's certain that there were distinct imitative cues that helped control Chet's actions. The rat's actions were clearly under the control of the water reward.

The subject of reward presents still a new puzzle. Cecil's reward was water — a known biological reward when creatures have been deprived of it for a time. What was Chet's reward? It appears the only things his strumming produced were sounds that we can presume weren't too pleasing to human ears. As a class, sounds aren't biological reinforcers — they don't fill our stomachs or in any direct way keep body tissues alive. Deaf people grow and develop physically without sound. There's some reason to believe that sounds can function as unlearned biological rewards; babies perhaps shake rattles just to hear the sounds — we know that some non-human creatures are rewarded by certain sounds.

But it's unlikely that guitar sounds are ever innate rewards. They're learned rewards — we acquire the tendency to be rewarded by them because of their association with other unlearned rewards, or with other potent learned ones. We will discuss how learned rewards come about, and the process of imitation in later pages.

For the time being, though, let's say that Chet's actions did occur, and were at first rewarded — rewarded by the issue of sounds that were somewhat like sounds he'd heard and found rewarding when others played the guitar. Although his attempts didn't last long, they did maintain far longer than if they'd produced no sounds at all — or if the sounds were like those heard in freeway traffic or a steel mill in full swing. Chet's actions were at least mildly rewarded. And in the end his actions did extinguish — what he got simply wasn't worth what he had to do and put up with to get it.

In this regard, his performance is just like Cecil's. The lesson we should learn from this discussion is that the principles of behavior learned in the rat lab do apply to humans. Rarely, however, are they seen at work in such a simple and clear-cut fashion.

- 8 What is the purpose of rat labs in introductory psychology courses?
- 9 Would you say that guitar practice responses extinguished?
- 10 What kind of reward are guitar sounds likely to be?
- 11 Given the fact that you or someone else begins a self-taught guitar-playing course (no books or teachers are available), what cues are likely to produce your first responses?
- 12 What controls a rat's lever-press response; and how does that differ from the above?

Extinction and survival

It's good to learn — but it's also good to unlearn — to stop doing things that once were rewarded but aren't any longer. Things change. Acts that once got us food, chased foes away, or helped us find a mate, stop working. Survival depends on new responses — a new approach. But new actions can't come about if we're tied up making old ones. Extinction is a means whereby actions that stop doing the trick are dropped, leaving the way open for new, more effective responses, to be learned.

- 13 What is the value of extinction in survival?

EXTINCTION AND OTHER FACTORS

Gore makes a comeback

Gore spent the morning gnawing on the large sapling at the edge of the stream. By the time the sun was overhead, Gore's jaws were stiff and sore; muscles and bones weary. Gore stopped work, slipping into the cool water, sinking to the bottom as neatly as a hard-packed ball of clay. At last Gore surfaced, crawled out onto the grassy bank, turning over with underside facing skyward. For a time the warm sun took over Gore's body, rest seeping into tired muscles and bones. Short minutes later, Gore got up. The sapling beckoned. The doorway to the dam would be done once the sapling was felled, stripped and fitted. Rest over, Gore returned with renewed vigor to the task.

Cecil makes a comeback

The lab session following the extinction exercise was supposed to demonstrate a new learning principle called "spontaneous recovery". Mae did as the lab book said — she placed Cecil in the Skinner box.

But what's the point? Mae thought. *Cecil's bar press has already extinguished. All he's going to do is sniff around and then lay down on the job like he did at the end of yesterday's session.*

But that's not the way the script went — Cecil did nothing of the sort. He charged the lever and began to pound on it with a vengeance.

Mae didn't reward the bar presses — the instructions said she shouldn't — yet Cecil pressed on.

I don't get it — I thought an extinction procedure got rid of a response. Looks to me like all Cecil needed was a good night's rest. Maybe he got tired yesterday — worn out. But that means that extinction and fatigue are the same thing. If that's true, why do they use a fancy word like "extinction"? Why don't they call it what it is, just plain "tired"!

Fatigue

Mae's wise to recognize that fatigue and extinction have some common features.

Fatigue: a slowing down or complete stop in response frequency, often accompanied by reduction in general activity (rest) followed sometime thereafter by a return to the previous response and activity level.

Fatigue lowers response frequency, sometimes reducing it to zero. Then after a period of non-response (rest), the response returns at full strength. Such fatigue-rest cycles may go on day after day, week after week, all without any lasting reduction in response — or during which response frequency could even show a steady increase.

A response on extinction can look much like it's falling victim to fatigue. Both result in an initial lowered response frequency; and in both cases we may expect a new surge of responding at a later time. But the return of responding isn't certain in the case of extinction. Sometimes, response frequency never returns. Further, when and if responding does return, it's always less frequent and lasts a shorter period before stopping than it did before.

■14   Define, and cite an instance of fatigue.
■15   In what two ways are fatigue and extinction alike? In what two crucial ways do they differ?

Spontaneous recovery

Although Cecil started out like a house afire, his pressing started to slow after those first few bursts. The response seemed to extinguish all over again — only this time much faster than before. Mae could see now that it hadn't been fatigue. No — Cecil hadn't quit yesterday because of fatigue, nor was it fatigue now. It was extinction; extinction and fatigue were clearly two distinct things.

When a response that's been placed on extinction does stop and then, at a future time, reoccurs when the creature's placed in the same setting, it is called "spontaneous recovery".

Spontaneous recovery: event taking place during an extinction procedure — a temporary and somewhat fleeting return in responding after an initial stoppage.

We've discussed how extinction and fatigue are alike, and to some extent, how they differ. But thus far we've failed to mention the most crucial point of contrast: fatigue results in spite of the fact that the reward that maintains the response is always present. In extinction, both the reduction in response frequency and the increase seen in spontaneous recovery, occur in the absence of reward.

■16   Define spontaneous recovery.

Deprivation and satiation

This brings up a third instance where responding stops — only to return later; an instance where neither fatigue nor extinction are to blame. It is called "satiation". Satiation occurs after many instances of reward. And, as a result, and for a time at least, what was a reward stops working as one. It will no longer maintain responding — actions come to a screeching halt.

Satiation: a reduction in the power of a reinforcer as a result of repeated frequent exposure to it.

It's easy to see how satiation works with biological rewards such as food or drink. Once our stomachs are stuffed with food or filled to the gurgling point with fluids, a response that makes more food or drink appear will not be rewarded. But the effect isn't limited to things we consume. Recent heavy contact tends to make all rewards lose their power. After a period of time without them, these potential rewards regain their vigor. The interim period where there's no contact with a reward is called "deprivation".

Deprivation: period of time during which there is no contact with a reinforcer.

Animals used in Mae's rat lab had been deprived of water for 23 hours prior to the time she and her classmates worked with them. This period of deprivation insured that water would act as a potent reward — one that would support new learning and maintain old responses.

When we compare satiation, fatigue and extinction, we can see that satiation and fatigue are short-lived effects. Responses come back full and strong after a period of rest in the case of fatigue; after a period of time without reward in the case of satiation. Not so with extinction. As long as there's no more reward, a response is on its way out. Extinction kills. In some ways spontaneous recovery isn't a real return to responding. It's a ghost response — the shadow of a response that once lived and thrived.

- ■17 Define satiation.
- ■18 Define deprivation.
- ■19 What kinds of rewards will deprivation make potent?
- ■20 How are fatigue and satiation different from extinction?

STIMULUS CONTROL

The mark

Chet got the notice telling him his payment at Musicland was overdue. It was an utter shock; he'd not thought about the guitar in weeks. He'd have to do something and quick — before Carol found out. Lucky, he'd been the one to get the mail first that day. But what could he do? Take it back? No way, too late for that. Just then there was a knock on the door. Chet opened it.

"Chet," a voice said. Chet couldn't see who it was. The bright sun shone over the person's head like a halo — blinding Chet.

"Sid?" Chet said. "That you, Sid?"

"'Course it's me," Sid said. "Hey, why're you lookin' at me so funny?"

"Tell me something," Chet said. "Do you believe in omens?"

***

"Let's see," Juke read aloud but to himself, "if the area subtended by the acute angle . . ."

Twang!

"If the area subtended by the . . ."

Twang! Twang! Juke stared at Sid, hoping Sid would look up and see that he was put out by the racket. No such luck. Sid was transfixed.

"Hey little buddy."

Twang! Twang!

"Hey, Sid!" Juke yelled. Sid stopped, turning toward Juke, a puzzled look on his face.

"You say something, Juke?"

"Yeah, man. Look, if you insist on strummin' that thing, why don't you tune it first."

"Tune it?" Sid said. "Sounds find to me." Sid twanged it three or four times in a row just to show Juke.

"No man, off a country mile. Let me have it. I'll give it a try." Sid watched enthralled as Juke plucked the strings, tightened or loosened the tuning pegs, then struck the strings again — listening to the new pitch. "There," Juke said. He put his fingers on the fret board, and strummed through a half-dozen chord changes. "Not a bad soundin' guitar." Sid was agog.

"That's great! How did you do it?"

"It's nothing. Just foolin' around," Juke said.

"You think you can teach me that?"

"S'pose so," Juke said.

"Now?"

"Right now, man?"

"Come on, Juke — please."

* * *

"If the area subtended by the . . ."

Twang — twang — twang — twang — twungg. Juke shook his head.

"Like the man said — a little learnin's a dangerous thing!" Juke muttered.

Twang — twang — twung — twung.

"You say something?" Sid asked.

Basic stimulus control — revisited

Many stimuli neither reward nor harm us. Yet they can become a great factor in the control of our actions. A stop light controls braking action — when the light turns red, we'll do what we can to stop. A funeral service controls laughing — we're not likely to laugh when involved in that social setting. The tendency for stimuli that are neither rewards nor punishers to control actions should sound somewhat familiar. We talked about it before in a general way as basic stimulus control — "control exerted by a stimulus over the form or path of a response".

In dealing with basic stimulus control we mentioned zoo-plankton, simple creatures who survive by eating minute plants called algae. Algae grow in the light, and therefore are found only in that part of the ocean where there's ample sunshine. When zoo-plankton are running low on fuel, they move toward the light — a place where they're more likely to find algae. The light itself neither rewards nor harms the zoo-plankton — it does control their movement — a case of basic stimulus control, programmed by natural selection.

■21 Review: Define basic stimulus control.

■22 Cite an instance of basic stimulus control.

■23 How is basic stimulus control programmed?

Learned stimulus control

A young man alone with his guitar — Sid Fields tuning up. Before Juke showed him how, Sid fiddled around with the pegs that tightened and loosened the strings, but he didn't know what he was doing. Of course, twisting the pegs changed the pitch of the strings. At that time, one twang was about the same as the next to Sid. But not now. Juke's training has changed things. The sound the string makes when Sid strums it controls both the direction (clockwise or counter-clockwise) and the amount of twist Sid gives each peg. Thus the sounds control Sid's actions — stimulus control. But this instance of stimulus control is a far cry from zoo-plankton moving toward light. It is first of all stimulus control that arose through learning — learned stimulus control.

Learned stimulus control: control of the form, path, or rate of a response by stimuli that have no unlearned control. These stimuli gain control by being present when that response is reinforced.

How does learned stimulus control come about? Mae's ready to find this out for herself as Cecil's saga unwinds.

■24 Define learned stimulus control.

Cecil in the light — Cecil in the dark

Cecil and Mae had come a long way together: shaping, extinction, spontaneous recovery. Now it was time to move on. It was no problem at all to retrain Cecil on the lever press. After one or two rewards the response was as regular and frequent as it had ever been.

The new lab exercise dealt with stimulus control. The point was to get Cecil to press the lever under one stimulus condition and not to press it under a different condition. Both conditions were provided by a small light mounted inside the Skinner box on a side panel above the lever, where Mae could turn on the light, leave it on as long as she wanted, and then turn it off.

At first Mae switched the light on, then off, doing this a number of times — just to see what would happen. Nothing. It didn't seem to affect Cecil at all — he just kept on with his pressing business. Without doubt, the light had no basic stimulus control over Cecil's bar press.

But all of that would soon be changed. When the training was over, Cecil would press when the light was on, but wouldn't press when it was off — that's what the lab book said. Mae had her doubts, but she followed to the letter the method the book outlined. She placed Cecil in the box and turned on the light. It was left on for 30 seconds. During this time Cecil made many lever presses and was rewarded with a dipper of water for each one. Then she turned off the light. Cecil pressed, ran to the dipper opening; there was no dipper, no water, no reward. He pressed again and again. No reward. Cecil started to sniff around then, just like he had during extinction. But every few seconds he'd return to the lever and hit it a few whacks. Then, finding no reward, he'd wander off again. This happened many times. All the while Mae was keeping track of how long he went without making a bar press, one eye on Cecil and the other on the sweep second hand of her watch. *Ten seconds, thirteen, fifteen — now!* Mae quickly switched on the light and sighed in relief. *Now if the dummy will just press!* Mae didn't have to wait long. Cecil pressed and Mae pushed the dipper, giving Cecil a well-earned reward. He got many such rewards before the 30-second light-on period ended. Time to turn off the light and stop the reward.

Mae took Cecil through many such light-dark cycles. Rewards came during the 30-second light-on period; no rewards were given during light-off period. The light wouldn't go on until Cecil had gone a full 15 seconds without making a response.

By the end of the session the results of the training were clear cut. When the light came on Cecil rushed to the lever and started to work. When the light went off, he left the lever alone, roaming around the rat chamber, doing his rat things — licking, grooming, sniffing. Light-on was clearly a stimulus that controlled bar pressing; during light-off, pressing was rare. When it was time to end the session Mae took Cecil from the box and gave him a big hug. "Cecil, you sure are some kind of genius rat dude!"

Discriminative stimulus

The rat lab exercise demonstrates a case of simple learned stimulus control. A stimulus that precedes or is present when a response is rewarded gains control over that response. Such a stimulus is called a "discriminative stimulus".

Discriminative stimulus: a stimulus in whose presence a response is likely to yield reinforcement.

A far shorter term that means the same thing as discriminative stimulus is cue. Since it's shorter and easy to recall, we'll most often use cue rather than discriminative stimulus.

Cue (discriminative stimulus): a stimulus in whose presence a response is likely to yield reinforcement.

- ■25 Define discriminative stimulus.
- ■26 What is a shorter name for discriminative stimulus that we'll use throughout this book?
- ■27 Design an experiment where a tone would come to control a child's play behavior. (This was not given in the text, you'll have to wing it.)

Basic and learned stimulus control

Zoo-plankton moving toward the light — basic stimulus control — an unlearned event. The power of the light to control the zoo-plankton's response is unlearned, but also, the response itself — moving toward the light — occurs without learning.

In the learned stimulus control, both the power of the stimulus and the response it controls are almost always learned. Mae taught Cecil the lever-press response. Then, through the method just described, she taught Cecil to respond to the light — learned stimulus control.

Guitar tuning is also an example of learned stimulus control. It is a complex case — a far cry from the simple case with Cecil. Sounds produced when strings are plucked control the movement of the tuning pegs. Yet sounds control more than just peg movement; they also control the direction and the amount or extent to which each peg is twisted. Contrast this with Cecil and the light. When the light was on Cecil pressed the lever or he didn't. Of course he could have pushed it in many directions or with more or less force, but the light in no way controlled these aspects of the response.

Guitar tuning is a special form of stimulus control called feedback stimulus control — a type of stimulus control we spoke of in an earlier chapter. It's a case where the form or path of a response is controlled by stimuli resulting from a preceding response. The current response then controls the next, and so on down the line. The feedback stimulus control we spoke of earlier was unlearned. Some aspects of the behavior of both human and other creatures are controlled by unlearned feedback stimulus control.

Guitar tuning is feedback stimulus control, but it's acquired through learning. Further, it's only one example of this type of learned control. For humans, learned feedback stimulus control and other forms of complex stimulus control are quite common.

There's one other feature of the guitar-tuning sequence that makes it unlike simple learned stimulus control. Contrast it with what goes on at a stop light. The light turns green; you give the car the gas. Gunning the engine is controlled by the green light, but reward for stepping on the gas comes when we move out — get going. In tuning a guitar, tuning actions are both rewarded and controlled by the same event — the sound produced. Does this mean a cue or discriminative stimulus can also serve as a reward? Indeed it does. We'll have occasion to talk about this at some length in a later chapter.

■28 In the zoo-plankton's movement toward light, the control is (learned; unlearned). The response is (learned; unlearned).

■29 In simple learned stimulus control, the control is (learned; unlearned). The response is generally (learned; unlearned).

■30 Guitar tuning differs from the animal lab example because _____ and _____ of the response are controlled by the sound.

■31 Guitar tuning is an example of what kind of complex learned stimulus control?

■32 Review: Define feedback control.

■33 Can cues also be rewards? If so, can you cite an instance?

Warning stimuli

Gore ate the termites with zeal — whitish, winged creatures. Gore saw a fat juicy one, five or six times the size of the others. A fine morsel. When Gore approached, it made a strange buzzing sound — a sound Gore hadn't heard before. Gore thrust out its tongue, wrapping it deftly around the would-be victim. All at once there was a sharp jolt in Gore's mouth, an explosion of pain. Gore screamed, shook its head, ran in circles. It was some time before the throbbing calmed down. The next time Gore would be less likely to eat termites when they made a buzzing sound.

***

As we've seen in examples from both real life and the rat lab, stimuli control actions that lead to reward. Stimuli also serve a crucial control function where punishment rather than reward is the likely outcome of actions.

Moving away or making other responses that keep tissue from being harmed or from losing a cache of fuel, occurs as an unlearned pattern in most crea-tures — the human among them. But if it's worthwhile to move away once such things happen, it's even more worthwhile to do it before they happen. Stimulus control allows this. Stimuli that came just before or were present when punishment occurred in the past, work in the future to prevent actions that were punished.

Gore's run-in with the bumble-bee is such a case. You can bet Gore will be less likely to try another of those buzzing "ter-mites" — no matter how big and juicy. Stimuli that control actions in this way are called "warning stimuli".

Warning stimuli: stimuli in whose presence punishment is likely to occur.

The terms discriminative stimulus or cue apply when a stimulus controls a response that produces reward; warning stim-ulus is the term that's applied when the result is punishment. Warning stimuli get control of our acts in much the same way as cues — they're present when a response produces the unique result. You will recall how buzzing became a warning stimulus for Gore:

Gore was feasting on bugs. A buzzing sound was made by a very large one. Gore tried to eat it and received a harsh sting. 1) At first the buzzing sound was neu-tral. 2) Gore made a response in the presence of the buzzing sound and was punished. 3) In the future Gore will be less likely to make that response when it hears the buzz. The buzz is now a warning signal.

- 34 A stimulus that controls a response that has produced a punisher in the past is called a _____ _____.
- 35 Give the exact definition of the term asked for above.
- 36 What is the difference between a cue and a warning stimulus?
- 37 Briefly outline how a neutral stimulus becomes a cue.
- 38 Outline how a neutral stim-ulus becomes a warning stimulus.

INTERMITTENT REINFORCEMENT

Juke creates a Frankenstein monster

Poor Juke. Sid's twang-twang-twung's are driving him right up the wall. Why doesn't Juke just habituate to the sound, get used to the tinny and nasal creaks and groans coming from Sid and his guitar? Habituating takes time, and by then Juke could have flunked math. At first, there was hope that Sid, like Chet, would give up the guitar; get tired of it, find banging away on it wasn't a reward any more. Efforts would undergo extinction, and he'd stop. That could have happened, but it didn't. All because Juke taught Sid those few chords. It's Juke's fault that Sid's guitar playing doesn't extinguish — he has only himself to blame. He created the monster!

Cecil and intermittent reinforcement

The exercise for the day was titled "Intermittent Reinforcement". The point was to show that animals didn't have to get a reward each time they made a response for the response to maintain. If the correct method was used they could be trained to make dozens of responses for the same type and amount of reward they used to get for just one response. It didn't seem to make sense to Mae — and if it did work, she thought it was a dirty trick to play on poor old Cecil. But that's what the lab book called for, and that's what Mae did.

Once she got to it, it went so fast she scarcely believed it. She started with Cecil just like before — one lever press, one reward; then she jumped it to two — two presses, one reward. No problem. After a few rewards, she required three responses of Cecil — still no problem. By the end of the session Cecil was making five responses for each reward, and showed no signs of extinction. He pressed faster and worked harder.

After she'd stroked and petted Cecil for the good job he'd done and put him away, Mae thought about what had happened. *Were all animals like that? Could you con them into working harder for less — and was it true of humans? Yes, she was sure it was. But that was awful — or was it? Suppose there was some kind of animal that would keep working if only it got a reward for each response? How would that creature make out?*

***

Dodo ripped the side of the pod open with one swift tug of its beak. A green and yellow worm waved to and fro in the air, its snug house undone, walls ripped away. Dodo grabbed the worm — one swallow and it was gone. Dodo revived, for the first time in days, shrugging off the stupor of hunger, moving faster, alive with action. Dodo grasped a new pod, shucked it down with a dip of head and shoulders. The pod was exposed, bare, the hair-like silk tendrils waving in the breeze. But no worm. Nothing. One more dead end for Dodo. Dodo quit the stand of giant pod plants. There was food elsewhere. There must be. Back in the field of pod plants, many green and yellow worms were snug in their silken homes. They would live to see a new day — to lay eggs and feed. Dodo would not. Dodo had quit too soon. So it goes.

Speed of extinction and intermittent reinforcement

After reading the latest episode from the life of Dodo the loser, do you find yourself wanting to yell, "Hang in Dodo — go try a few more pods! Don't quit so soon!" Yes, most of us know that many important rewards don't come each and every time we respond. They occur far less frequently — sometimes we must make dozens of responses before at last one of them produces reward. It's a fact of the world that rewards are often less frequent than responses. This is called "intermittent reinforcement".

Intermittent reinforcement: occasional, rather than consistent reinforcement of a response.

It's a good thing we're not as quick to stop responding as Dodo, since intermittent reinforcement is the best we can expect from life in many cases. Yet how long will we keep responding before we quit? It depends on a number of factors — but most of all it depends on how many responses it took to get a reward in the past. Let's take a candy machine as an example. How many times have we had to pull the plunger in the past before candy came tumbling out? If it's always taken only one pull before that response was rewarded, we're likely to stop pulling the plunger (and perhaps resort to more aggressive acts) after a very few unrewarded plunger pulls. If, on the other hand, we're used to a machine that takes at least a dozen plunger pulls before it works, we'll make many more responses before we walk away or resort to violence. It can be said that the more responses that occur between rewards, the longer the response will keep occurring during extinction (non-reward) before it stops. This is so standard it can be stated in the form of a law.

Law of Intermittent Reinforcement and Speed of Extinction: the more intermittent the reinforcers that have maintained a response in the past, the more often it will occur without being reinforced before it extinguishes.

Pause just a moment to mull over this law. You'll see that it seems to run against common sense. What the law says is if you reward a response less frequently, it will last longer before it succumbs to extinction. This isn't like your car — where the more frequently you lubricate vital parts, the longer they will last and the longer your car will run. No, just the reverse.

But it was evolution and not Detroit that made the model to which behavior conforms. Dodo didn't conform to nature's model. Just one case of non-reward and Dodo stopped responding. If — as with other creatures — infrequent reward had made Dodo hang in all the longer, Dodos would be among us still.

- ■39 What is the term used to describe a situation where some but not all responses are rewarded?
- ■40 Define intermittent reinforcement.
- ■41 State the relationship between intermittency of reward and speed of extinction.
- ■42 What's the advantage of fast extinction? (This wasn't in the text — you're on your own.)
- ■43 What's the advantage of long extinction? Disadvantage? (You're on your own again.)

Sid's guitar playing and intermittent reinforcement

Sid's guitar strumming was on its way out, extinction was coming to Juke's rescue; then, not able to resist showing off a little, Juke blew it — he taught Sid a few chords. That did it. Not that this bit of knowledge made Sid's fingers any more nimble. He still made all kinds of mistakes, hit the wrong strings, wailed out sour notes — the ballads he sang may have sprung from deep in the heart, but they still came out through the adenoids.

But now and again Sid hit the strings just right, groaned the perfect groan — the golden chord, the silver note. This rare reward — even in the face of massive non-reward — was enough. Enough for Sid if not for Juke. It kept Sid going, made him try harder, longer. Louder, even. Yes, Juke, you could grow old waiting for extinction to save you. Sid's under the spell of a strong new force — intermittent reinforcement — it has long helped make humans the tough customers they are in the game of survival.

CONCLUSIONS

In this chapter we have looked at some of the conditions that support, and control learning. In general these conditions dictate whether learned acts will drop out or endure. It's easy to see how they relate to survival. Learning without extinction; extinction without spontaneous recovery; reward that must be constant and would not function on an intermittent basis; all these would penalize most species more than they could endure. But perhaps nothing would hamstring a creature more than the inability to come under the control of stimuli in the environment that in and of themselves have no biological impact. We are talking about stimulus control. In the next chapter we will discuss some of its more complex and intriguing aspects.

POSTSCRIPT

Juke lay awake that night. He had a problem, an urgent one. Across the room Sid was sound asleep. He had drifted off playing his guitar. You had to hand it to Sid, when he did something, he did it right. Straight-on, gung-ho, full-tilt — by the numbers, like a field marshall laying out a giant battle plan. That was a good thing — Juke liked that about Sid. But this guitar mania of Sid's; that was something else. It might be different if Sid had any talent. But as close as Juke could figure it, it'd take at least ten years before Sid'd be good enough to be "awful". No way he could tell Sid that. Not without killin' his gentle soul. Juke smiled. Somehow a plan had started to form — one that wouldn't force him to take the bull by the horns — one where he could slip neatly through them.

CHAPTER 9
LEARNING: LEARNED RESULTS AND GENERALIZATION

LEARNED RESULTS

Juke's gambit

It was a stroke of luck, finding Dawn alone in the dining hall; perfect, just right for Juke to make his move before Sid showed up.

"How's it goin'?"

"Oh hi, Juke. Okay, I guess — sit down won't you?" Juke sat down; then he got right to it.

"Somethin' I been meanin' to ask you, Dawn. Just a hunch I got about you. Somethin' I was curious about. I bet you've done some acting — or maybe dancing.

Singing, that's it! Yeah, a singer! You've done some singing in clubs — professional; right?"

"Well, I . . ."

"I thought so!" Juke slapped his knee. "Man, you can't fool me! Jus' had to be, way you carry yourself — poise. A born performer!"

"I never really . . ."

"It's written all over you. Know how I see it? You're there in some little nightspot, coffee house, that kind a thing; got

your hair down, sittin' on this stool playing your guitar, and singin' some a' them old English folk tunes, people all 'round listenin'; real quiet-like. That's it — that's you." Juke paused. "You do play the guitar, don't you?"

"No, I'm afraid I don't."

"Come on!"

"No, I . . ."

"Man, that's bad," Juke said, forlorn. "Too bad — that's your thing." Juke was quiet. He sighed.

"I've thought about learning how to play — many times. Really I have," Dawn said.

"Yeah?" Juke said perking up. "You're just sayin' that."

"Oh no. I mean it. Why, just the other day I saw one in a window downtown. I almost went in to see about it."

"Talk about a nice guitar — you should see Sid's. Boy, is his a beauty. Come to think of it, I believe he's tryin' to sell it. It's got this blond finish on it — say, it sure would suit you. Go great with your hair and eyes."

"How much does he want for it?"

Juke waved his hand as if to dismiss the topic of price as a factor. "You know Sid — easy come, easy go."

Just then Sid appeared in the doorway — right on cue.

"Hey, there's Sid now," Juke said. "Why don't you ask him about it?" Juke waved to Sid, motioned him over.

"Hi Sid," Dawn said as Sid approached.

"Say gang, I gotta split," Juke said getting to his feet. "I was just talkin' to Dawn. She's in the

market for a guitar. Told her she might talk you into sellin' yours." Sid was about to make a strong protest, but Dawn didn't give him a chance.

"Oh Sid! Juke told me all about it. Do you think — I mean, would you let me look at it?" Juke watched Sid melt. Things looked good.

"See ya!" Juke left. He looked back at Sid and Dawn as he got ready to go through the door. "Jackson, you are a rogue and a scoundrel," he said to himself.

What people work to get

Humans work for food, shelter, drink — these are potent rewards. They relate to tissue need and basic biology. But if we look at the things people do, only a small part of their time and effort is spent in pursuit of these rewards. For the most part, the rewards humans work hardest to get are at best only loosely tied to demands of either flesh or species.

In the same way, these things we try hardest to get away from, or that punish us most when we come in contact with them, don't relate to either tissue damage or loss of biological rewards. Sticks and stones do break bones — it's wise that we limit contact with them. But what about critical remarks —

being unloved, lack of respect, not being invited to join a club or serve on a committee? These events neither harm tissue nor result in the loss of fuels — why then, are they punishing?

As we watch our characters behave, biological or unlearned rewards play a very minor role in motivating their actions. For instance, why should the thought of an audience, raptly attending to Dawn Baker, have such a strong effect on her? Even if that were to come true, where's the reward?

By now we know when people behave there are rewards somewhere that support their actions. It just happens that for humans most results — rewards and punishers — that provide motive

force for actions aren't biological — they're acquired through learning. Mae and friend can perhaps show us most clearly how this learning occurs.

Learned results: reinforcers and punishers that begin as neutral stimuli, and gain their power through association with other reinforcers or punishers.

- 1 In terms of sheer frequency, what role do learned, as opposed to unlearned, results play in motivating human behavior?
- 2 Define learned results.
- 3 Name two unlearned rewards and two unlearned punishers.

HOW LEARNED REINFORCERS ARE ESTABLISHED

Cecil takes a music appreciation course

The rat lab project Mae was assigned to for the next few lab periods had to do with learned rewards. Its purpose was to show how neutral stimuli became rewards — learned rewards. Past sessions with Cecil proved he could learn most any response if it got him a few dippers of water. Now he was supposed to learn to pull a chain. And the reward? A sound, a simple tone coming from a battery-powered electric beeper. Now Mae was impressed with Cecil's talents, but she remained a skeptic. Cecil work for a tone? Not even for Roberta Flack. Still, Mae had to admit one thing: Cecil did have a great deal of natural rhythm.

The lab book explained that the exercise was based on a classic experiment done many years ago by a noted behavioral scientist. The first phase of the exercise was called the "pairing phase". Cecil pressed the lever as before with each press reinforced by a dipper of water. But something new was added. As the dipper journeyed from the water tray to the opening where Cecil hovered, Mae pushed the button that sounded the beeper. This meant the appearance of the water was preceded by, and then paired with, a soft tone that lasted about a half a second. These pairings — of tone and water — went on for an entire session.

The next session began as the last one had ended, with pairing of the tone and water. This brief period was just to get Cecil back into the swing of things, lasting only long enough for Cecil to earn three or four rewards. The phase that followed was the crucial one. The tone hadn't been a reward for Cecil before the pairing; now, after pairings, it should act as a reward. That's what the lab book said should happen, anyway. The test for this involved using the tone as though it were a reward, to teach a new response. Just like water or other biological reinforcers, it should work to shape and maintain a response Cecil had never made before. But only if it really was a reward. If not — well, not much would happen.

The new response was a chain pull. A small loop of stainless steel chain hung down from the top of the Skinner box. Cecil could reach it with his forepaws if he stood on his back haunches. The chain had been there all the time; Cecil had knocked into it a few times while roaming about. But, he'd never pulled it, or even acted like it was there. As with the lever, the chain also worked a switch that clicked a counter. Mae started the shaping procedure much as she had in training the lever press. But now there would be no water — just the tone. If Cecil's new response shaped up it meant the tone — and only the tone — was the reward.

Mae's doubts fell away once she got into it. She could tell right away it was going to work. In a quick series of approximations she shaped Cecil to approach the chain, make contact with it, and then pull down on it, working the switch and racking up a response on the counter. The whole thing took less than five minutes before Cecil had the chain-pull response down pat. The speed and regularity of response left no room for doubt. Cecil had learned it, and now the tone alone maintained the response. The tone was reward for Cecil. Cecil a music buff? Was there anything the little dude couldn't do?

The true test for a learned reinforcer

Neutral stimuli acquire rewarding value when they're paired with other rewards, as Mae has shown with Cecil. We know a neutral stimulus has become a learned reward when it can be used to shape and maintain a new response. In order to show this, let's suppose Mae's exercise had been a bit different. Suppose she'd started out the same — letting Cecil's lever press produce both tone and water for many pairings. But now to test the power of the tone as a learned reward, she kept the same response — the lever press — but let it produce only the tone. If Cecil kept pressing, receiving the tone alone, would this prove the tone is a learned reward? No indeed, it wouldn't. We know from the last chapter we would expect Cecil to keep pressing for a while anyway; it's a common occurrence during extinction, and would happen to some extent even if there were no tone at all. This is why using the tone to shape a new response, the chain pull, was a crucial part of the procedure.

- 4 Describe the first phase of the lab exercise that demonstrates how learned rewards are established.
- 5 What is the true proof that a neutral stimulus has become a learned reward?
- 6 Why couldn't the lever press be used to prove the tone's power as a learned reward?

Learned rewards and survival

As with other aspects of learning we've discussed, learned rewards enhance the chances for creatures to survive. Take Gore and Dodo for instance. Let's suppose that neither of them are born with a mechanism that makes approaching or coming near others of their species an unlearned reward. How would they make out?

* * *

Dodo was nursed, warmed, cared for by its mother. That was good, for at first Dodo was helpless — couldn't walk, fend for itself, make its own way. Dodo grew up, leaving the den without so much as a parting sniff at mother. Some time later when Dodo was mature and could breed, a creature like Dodo's mother came near. It stayed near Dodo for a while. But it soon left as Dodo paid it no notice. Dodo didn't follow. Since being near the creature wasn't a reward, Dodo died without mating.

* * *

Gore was also nursed and cared for by mother. Food, warmth, rewarding contact stimuli, all supplied by mother, her attention, her care. As Gore gained its legs it went where mother went, following, staying close behind. There was always something mother had — something mother could do, some way she could help Gore. Soon "nearness" itself became a reward, since nearness was always paired with such things as food, warmth, and safety. Later, Gore left the den after it grew and matured. One day a new creature a great deal like Gore's mother approached. Gore found that being near it, and later, contact, was a reward. They went off together. The next spring there were new little Gores in the wood.

* * *

It's simple enough to see how learned rewards helped Gore's species survive. Once nearness to others became a learned reward, it later made contact more certain and brought sex rewards into play. Gore mated. Without nearness as a learned reward, Dodo didn't spend time enough near others of the species. Contact was rare — so rare that sex rewards had almost no chance of being a force in molding Dodo's actions. Dodo didn't mate. So it goes — Dodos lose again.

Humans are like Gore and Dodo in that contact with others is a learned reward. Prolonged contact with other humans and mating might never occur if nearness didn't become a strong learned reward. The long helpless years of human infants and children, years where they must be cared for by adults, insure a more than ample chance for the many unique features of humans to be paired with food and other unlearned rewards. After years of such pairings, nearness — the words, sights, and sounds of other humans — emerges as the strongest of all rewards. The power of these social rewards will be the topic of later chapters.

- 7 How do learned rewards serve to propagate a species?
- 8 Why is nearness almost certain to become a learned reward for the human?
- 9 What is the strongest reward for most humans?

Music as a learned reward

This brings us back to Dawn. Why is she, or Sid, or Chet for that matter, turned on by the notion of learning to play the guitar? To begin with, hearing guitar or other music is a strong reward for most of us. Music is, as you might suspect, a learned reward. Mom sang songs to us while she held us on her knee. We've spent many hours having good times with friends, eating, drinking, talking — all the while the music played on. You see, music has not only been paired with food, it has also been paired with many other people who were at the time being very kind and nice to us. We shouldn't be surprised that music becomes a strong learned reward.

Does it strike you that our yen for music comes from the same source as Cecil the rat's? He's rewarded by the tone because, like our music, it's been paired with other strong rewards. One real difference is the wide number and type of rewards paired with our music. Cecil's music has been paired with only water. Further, people who study music plug into many other rewards.

But what's the payoff for the music-maker? Why bother when you can listen to others or play records? Making musical sounds is a double reward. When we make music we of course hear it, and so, many people like to play and sing when no one else is around, just to hear their own sounds. But this is not at all strange. Humans do many things that result in learned rewards; making music is only one of them.

Playing and singing gain new power as a reward when others take the time to listen. If it's the kind of music that rewards them, they'll say and do things that will reward the music-maker. This is quite a potent source of reward. The truth is, for most would-be guitar players at least, that the real reward comes when others listen, dig it, and say nice things.

It looks like Juke's gambit has worked. Dawn's making moves to get Sid's guitar. Dawn could get rewarded for playing the guitar, if she learns how, and if she's good enough. If so, just hearing herself could reward her. If others hear her and "go ape" (as Juke suggests they're bound to), then the whole guitar deal could be great for Dawn.

- ■10 How does music become a learned reward?
- ■11 How are music and the tone that the rat works for in the Skinner box alike? How are they different?
- ■12 In what sense is playing a guitar or other instrument a double reward?

LEARNED PUNISHERS

The short unhappy guitar playing career of Dawn Baker

It seemed at first that Sid didn't want to sell the guitar. That only made Dawn try all the harder. She wheedled, sighed a bit, pouted a touch, and then Sid gave in. Once he'd agreed, Sid seemed to be happy to be getting rid of it. He couldn't afford the payments, and didn't really have time to practice. Besides, he told Dawn, he'd thought — for just one fleeting moment at least — that Juke didn't like music. Dawn took over the payments. She also gave Sid ten dollars for the investment he'd made.

That night Dawn began her guitar playing career. She propped up the guitar book Sid had tossed into the deal. She tried to put her fingers where the book said. Then she strummed the strings. It sounded awful. It took a few more attempts before she found out what was wrong. The long nails on her left hand — those long, flawless nails she'd labored so long to perfect — wouldn't let her fingertips go down flush against the strings. She mashed harder. Bing, bing — two nails broke. "Oh no!" Dawn screamed. She ran to the bathroom to see if she could repair the damage. Thus ended the short, unhappy guitar playing career of Dawn Baker.

How learned punishers are established

Just as neutral stimuli paired with reward become learned rewards — neutral stimuli paired with harmful events become learned punishers. Harsh or mean words turn us off because they've often been paired with bad deeds. We have all been yelled at and called something other than "little dears" when we were spanked.

Neutral stimuli also become learned punishers when they're paired with the loss of rewards. Dawn's pretty fingernails are a source of reward for her. Losing them limits her chances to get praise and other social rewards. The guitar is to blame. Dawn's not pleased by the sounds she makes either. Sounds made on a guitar can vary greatly in their rewarding value. Some may be rewarding, or neutral. But some sounds offend us, creating such clamor that they're punishing. People who produce them won't only starve for social reward, they're likely to be run out of town. Dawn's career with the guitar was one big learned punisher, all the shorter because of it.

- ■13 How do learned punishers come about?
- ■14 Give at least two examples of learned punishers.

HOW LEARNED RESULTS LOSE THEIR POWER

Rat turns back on cheap thrills

Cecil pulled the chain again and again, responses occurring in bursts of five or six in a row at times. It was all Mae could do to keep up in sounding the tone when she should. The response rate trailed off, came back slightly, and then stopped. Cecil went to a corner and sniffed around. Mae waited. Nothing. It was near the end of the session, time for Mae to leave. Mae sounded the tone just to see what would happen, not that Cecil had even acted like he was about to respond. Mae thought the tone would perk him up.

Cecil did move a little — just a twitch, nothing more. Mae sounded the tone again, then a dozen times more. Pointless. Cecil had had it with cheap thrills. The tone had lost its power as a reward.

***

Learned rewards retain their power only if they are paired on occasion with other rewards. When pairing stops for good, it's only a matter of time before the power of learned rewards wanes. Soon they're done — bygone fancies. All learned rewards lose their strength if they're not backed up — occasionally paired with — other rewards. If pairing does occur — even though infrequent — learned rewards will maintain, perhaps keeping their robust vigor forever.

- ■15 Under what conditions do learned rewards lose their rewarding power?
- ■16 How could this loss of power be prevented?
- ■17 Thought question: How does the loss of power of learned rewards differ from extinction?

Loss of power of learned punishers

Learned punishers also lose their power if they aren't paired with other punishers. The rattle of sabers, threats, warning tickets given by traffic police, strange sounds in the night — all must sometimes occur along with a punisher if repeated exposure to them is going to affect us.

But there's one feature where learned rewards and punishers differ that's well worth a mention — something that makes the effects of learned rewards and learned punishers contrast sharply. Learned rewards support responses that bring people in contact with them. Like all rewards, people work to get them and thus contact is frequent. The more repeated the contact with learned rewards that aren't backed up, the more quickly their power fades.

Learned punishers are something else again. Being punishers, they make people do things that lessen contact with them. If people succeed at this, if contact is reduced or perhaps cut to zero, a strange thing may happen. Because contact frequency is low, it takes longer for the learned punishers to lose their power. As a result, learned punishers may remain at full strength for an entire lifetime. Some spend their time running away from them — running from punishers whose power would quickly ebb before even a few exposures were over. As you may suspect, many human problems result from the fact that learned punishers endure and retain their power. We will deal with these problems and discuss their treatment in later chapters.

- ■18 Provided we have repeated exposure to them, how may learned punishers retain their power? Are they different in this sense from learned rewards?
- ■19 How do learned rewards differ from learned punishers in terms of the likelihood of exposure to them, and why does this difference occur?
- ■20 Learned punishers tend to last for a longer period of time because _____. (Fill in the rest of the sentence.)
- ■21 What is the result of the enduring power of some learned punishers in terms of human problems?

UNLEARNED OR SIMPLE STIMULUS GENERALIZATION

A guitar goes from hand to hand

After the way she'd cajoled and eased Sid out of his guitar, Dawn didn't have the guts to try to get him to take it back. She was stuck with the guitar and out two fingernails. Besides that, there was the eleven-buck-a-month payment and the gnawing feeling that she'd been had — some talker that Juke. The upshot of the whole thing was that Dawn was forced to do what she could to make a few dollars, just to make the payment. Tonight, Carol LaPorte needed a baby-sitter for little Chet. Dawn liked Carol and little Chet, and of course, knew big Chet from the psych class they had together.

When Carol arrived, Dawn gathered up her books; at least sitting gave her some time to study. Carol noticed the guitar in the corner. It was love at first sight.

"What a lovely guitar!" Carol said. "Do you play?"

"No way," Dawn said. She turned to find Carol admiring the guitar.

"Can I pick it up?" Carol asked.

"Sure. But watch out — it eats fingernails."

Carol took the guitar gently in her hands. She plucked the strings — first one, then another, at last a tender strum.

"It's got a great sound!" Carol said. Dawn watched with some envy. Somehow Carol had tamed the savage brute with such ease.

"Do you play?" Dawn asked.

"The guitar? Oh no. Piano. I took for ages. Gave it up when we got married."

"Well, it seems to like you," Dawn said. Then she had a thought. "I been thinking about getting rid of it — how'd you like to buy it?"

"I'd love to, of course . . . I don't think we . . . how much do you want for it?"

"It's not paid for yet — the payments are eleven dollars a month. All I want's someone to get that monkey off my back."

"Eleven dollars. Not a lot of money I guess . . . but I just couldn't. I'd have to talk it over with Chet first."

"I'm tired of looking at the thing. Take it home and try it out. If you decide not to buy it, that's okay.

"I couldn't do that — what if it got broken?"

"I'll take my chances. I get so mad each time I see it, I feel like smashing it myself."

Are things ever alike?

Gore ate the first piece of fruit. It was red, smooth, shiny. The next
one was larger, the shape wasn't quite the same, but it was also red,
smooth and shiny. Gore gobbled it down. The biggest fruit had an
oblong shape. It was green and had crinkly skin. Gore sniffed it and
passed it by.

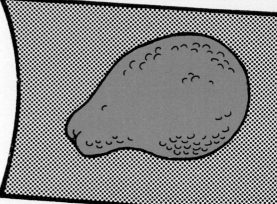

* * *

Can an apple, a person, a snowflake, a drop of water, an atom — be
the precise twin of another? Clearly the answer is "no". One apple is
rounder, redder, has a longer stem, and shines more than the other.
Yet, if both apples taste the same, fill our stomachs the same, and
nourish us the same, we were right to respond the same — to eat
both of them.

Lucky for humans and other creatures, there's a built-in feature of
our basic structure that makes it likely we'll respond the same to
objects and in settings that are somewhat the same but by no means
identical. Thus, we go from apple to apple, setting to setting,
problem to problem, making the same response and succeeding for
responding to the sameness of these situations. This is called
"stimulus generalization".

Stimulus generalization: a response that occurs in the presence of
one stimulus is also likely to occur in the presence of a stimulus
that is similar to the first.

Gore's actions show stimulus generalization. Slight changes in
color, texture, smell, etc. from fruit to fruit barely slow Gore down.
With a fruit that differs greatly from the others, Gore balks, passes
it by and looks elsewhere.

- ■22 Define stimulus generalization.
- ■23 Things are never precisely the same. Explain.
- ■24 The "proof of the apple is in the eating".
  Relate this to stimulus generalization.

Cecil and unlearned stimulus generalization

Looking back, it seemed long ago when Cecil had mastered the light-on, light-off, stimulus control exercise. The light had worked some kind of magic on Cecil. When it was on, Cecil worked at top speed, but when there was no light, there was no responding. The current exercise called for retraining Cecil on the same sequence. Mae soon found it was no problem at all to get Cecil's performance up to snuff. He was at his old standard or above before the first session was half over. The light controlled the lever press with near perfect precision; rarely was there a response in light-off.

It was time to test for stimulus generalization. A dial on the side of the Skinner box controlled the amount of current to the bulb, and therefore the brightness of the light inside the box that was used during the light-on phase. The dial was marked off in units that ranged from "1" to "10". One was the brightest, the place where the dimmer control was normally set and where Cecil had first been trained to respond in the light-on state. When the dial was at "10", the light was quite dim, about a quarter as bright as when on "1". The point was to change the brightness of the light and see what effect this had on Cecil's responding.

One thing about the procedure puzzled Mae. The lab book was quite clear in saying the test for stimulus generalization had to be done during extinction. That meant Cecil would go without reward. Mae paid him off all during the retraining period, but when it came time for the generalization test, there were no more dippers of water for Cecil.

"Sorry about that, fella," Mae said.

During the first light-on phase of the test, Mae set the light brightness dial at "3" as the lab book said. Cecil's response rate slowed little, if any. Still, it was easy for Mae to see that the light wasn't as bright as it had been.

Hmmm — I get the point, Mae thought. *A change in the stimulus that controls Cecil's response doesn't affect things much — he responds anyway. His response "generalizes" to a new stimulus that's not the same as the one he learned to respond to — and that's stimulus generalization.*

At about the same instant, Mae figured out why the test had to be conducted during extinction. It made good sense once she hit on the reason. If reward were present at all levels of brightness, it would be like training Cecil on all those levels. But the only way to see how a new value of a stimulus — brightness, for instance — controlled responding was to make sure Cecil never got rewards in its presence; and that's why the test had to proceed during extinction.

■25 Thought question: How would you design a lab exercise demonstrating stimulus generalization to tones, using human subjects?

■26 Why must the test for stimulus generalization occur during extinction?

Stimulus generalization gradient

Aside from the fact that the test for stimulus generalization had to take place during extinction, there was one more point the lab book stressed: the order or sequence that the levels of brightness were given mattered a lot. You couldn't just start at "1" — the level Cecil had been trained on — then go to "2", and so on down the line. Why? The book didn't say at that point. It just said what to do. Mae did it.

She went through all brightness levels in the mixed-up order the book specified. After each light-on period, she checked the counter reading and wrote down the number of responses Cecil had made. Then she reset the counter so that it was at zero at the start of the next light-on period. The test complete, she'd recorded lever presses for each of the ten light-on periods, each one differing from the other in terms of brightness. Here's the way her record looked:

When Mae took these data and plotted them on the graph her lab book provided, the whole thing came into sharp focus. The trend was clear from the data. The dimmer the light got — the more it differed from the bright "1" level that Cecil'd been trained on — the fewer responses the rat made. The lab book called this a "stimulus generalization gradient". It was a feature of all stimulus or cue

Order	Brightness Setting	Number of lever presses
1	3	8
2	7	18
3	10	2
4	5	10
5	1	25
6	2	22
7	9	3
8	4	15
9	6	10
10	8	3

control — the less a new stimulus was like one an animal had been trained on — received frequent rewards for responding in its presence — the less the new stimulus tended to control responses.

Stimulus generalization gradient: as a new stimulus differs from the one on which stimulus control was first established, its power to control a response is comparably lessened.

■27 What is a feature of all stimulus or cue control?
■28 Define stimulus generalization gradient.

LEARNED STIMULUS GENERALIZATION: CONCEPT FORMATION

Unlearned and learned stimulus generalization

Simple unlearned stimulus generalization begins on day one in the life of the human and most other creatures. It just happens — without training. And you're born with the structure that makes it happen.

For some creatures, simple stimulus generalization is plenty. But not for us. If we're going to make it, we've got to respond the same to objects and in settings that are alike in only one or two slight ways. It's one thing to respond the same to two apples — no big trick, requiring only simple, unlearned, stimulus generalization. But there's no way this simple unlearned mechanism would let you respond the same to a giant redwood tree and a cluster of algae, two objects that appear so vastly unlike and are the same only in that they share enough functions to both belong to that branch of biological entities called "plants". But that's the way it is in the human game — the slight and abstract likeness is often far more crucial than the gross difference.

Complex stimulus generalization takes training, unlike the simple unlearned talent of stimulus generalization most creatures inherit. We've got to learn to do it. It's therefore often called "learned stimulus generalization".

Learned (or complex) stimulus generalization: pattern of responding acquired through learning where a response occurs in the presence of stimuli that may differ in many gross features, but share at least one controlling feature.

It's really a double learning process. We learn to respond to the single feature that's crucial among the array of objects or stimuli, and at the same time, we learn not to respond to those features that differ. When this occurs it's because of learned stimulus generalization — complex stimulus generalization.

- ■29 Define learned stimulus generalization. What's another name for it?
- ■30 Why do humans and some other creatures need more than unlearned stimulus generalization?
- ■31 What is the double learning process that takes place in complex stimulus generalization?

Concepts and concept formation

When others observe learned stimulus generalization in action they may say that the person they're watching has acquired a concept. But this isn't strictly true. A concept isn't "in" people; it's not something they have, it's in the stimuli they respond to.

Concept: a class of stimuli that may differ in many features, but share at least one common feature.

There are many kinds of concepts — classes of stimuli that share at least one feature although they may have many features that aren't alike. "Roundness" is a concept. All things that have that kind of shape belong to the class of stimuli that comprise that concept. Colors, shapes, sizes, textures, tastes — any way that an array of stimuli can be alike — may be a concept. Learning to respond to the group of objects that have the like features, and, at the same time learning not to respond to those that don't have it, is called "concept formation".

Concept formation: learning to respond the same to a class of stimuli that form a concept, while not responding to others outside that class.

■32 Define concept.

■33 Define concept formation.

■34 Why is it not correct to say a person has a concept?

■35 We know concept formation has taken place when the person (does, doesn't) respond to objects in the concept class, but (does, doesn't) respond to objects outside that class.

Concepts are for the birds

The pigeon's name was Charldean. Mae didn't like Charldean at first; she'd grown used to Cecil and somehow it seemed fickle of her to forsake him for a mere bird. But the lab exercise was on concept formation. Dr. Harper assured Mae and others that concept formation could be shown much faster with pigeons than with rats.

The pigeon chamber was much like the Skinner box in principle. A small disc or key, as Dr. Harper called it, was indented into the side panel of the soundproof chamber; the key depressed slightly when Charldean pecked it. Yes, Mae was in the big time — she'd moved from rats to pigeons — from lever presses to key pecks. In the pigeon box key pecks were racked up on a counter like the one used with the rat chamber. The reward for Charldean — a tray or hopper full of pigeon feed — grain of some kind — swung up from the bottom of the chamber, giving the bird a few seconds of contact and a beakful of grain. What else should birds work for? Worms seemed a little unhandy.

One other feature of the response key was crucial to the concept formation study, aside from the fact that it was the response mechanism. It was slotted so that there was a thin space or groove beneath a piece of clear plastic that composed the outside surface. A small picture placed in the slot could be clearly seen from Charldean's vantage point. The picture was the cue for the pigeon to respond just as the light was a cue for Cecil. In Charldean's case, the picture and the response key were one. She would peck at the picture, her beak hitting the plastic that covered the picture and making the response key work. There were many pictures that could be placed in the viewer slot, pictures of designs and objects of all sorts, most of them having some basic geometrical form. But they differed quite a bit in other ways such as color and size.

The concept class Charldean was to learn was "roundness". The point was to get Charldean to respond to all the pictures whose designs were in some sense round, and not to respond to those that didn't have the round features.

Charldean knew quite well how to peck the response key when Mae first got her. She'd been used in past lab sections and the key peck was old stuff to her. When Mae first watched Charldean work, she was enthralled by the machine gun rat-ta-tat-tat of Charldean's responses. She pecked so fast that Mae had to hustle to keep up with her.

There were two stacks of picture cards for use in the exercise. The stacks had different pictures, but were alike in the number of round and unround cards each had. In both stacks half of the cards had some sort of round design or object — circles, eggs, balls, all sizes and colors, but all rounded. Pictures in the other half of the stacks varied in nature, many kinds of shapes and objects, but no round ones. One stack was used for

training — the other would be used later to test to see if Charldean really had formed the concept.

It was nearing the end of the session before Mae got around to starting the training phase of the study. She took the stack of training cards and shuffled them. This was standard practice — the order the cards were to be given Charldean should never be the same. This kept "order" from being a cue. If Charldean pecked when she should, it had to happen only because she was under the control of the "roundness" of the cue cards — and not a fixed order.

A card was placed in the viewing slot, and the bird was given access to it and the response key, for twenty seconds. If the picture design was round — part of the concept class — each tenth response was rewarded.

But no amount of pecking did Charldean any good if the card wasn't part of the concept. Mae had tried three cards before the session ended — two of them weren't part of the concept class, one was. Charldean responded away without regard for the design, pecking her fool staccato head off.

The next session started off the same way, but ended quite differently. She started to come under cue control as time passed. At first it was hard to tell — just a slight pause or two in pecking rate when the non-round cards were in the viewer. In time it grew more pronounced. Mae found herself holding her breath each time she put in a new card. There was a strict way this had to be done. After a twenty-second period was over with one card, Mae had to turn out the lights in the pigeon box,

leaving Charldean in the dark and not able to peck for three seconds. This gave Mae time to change cards and kept Charldean straight as well — no point in having her peck away when Mae wasn't on the job.

By the fifth session Charldean's pecking was under perfect cue control. She pecked at high speed when one of the round cards was in the viewer, and rarely pecked when one of the others was there. Mae was proud of Charldean, and just a bit proud of herself as well. She was the first in all the lab sections to get this far in the projects. But the concept formation problem wasn't in the bag yet. There remained the all crucial test.

Mae did the test during the next session. It was a test for learned stimulus generalization. The question was if Charldean's response patterns to the training pictures would generalize to a new set of stimuli — the test stack. These were pictures Charldean had never seen before — hadn't been trained on. The pictures were of new designs and objects, none identical to those in the training stack — still, they were like the training pictures in that half of them had designs that in some way were round.

As with all tests for stimulus generalization, there could be no reward. Charldean's response would be in extinction and she would get no grain — couldn't risk any new learning on the test cards; that would spoil the whole show. Mae put the first test card in. It was one of the round class. Charldean pecked at high speed for the full twenty seconds. Mae breathed a bit easier. That was good. But it proved nothing — not yet. The next card didn't have a round design. Charldean didn't make even one response. Mae could have kissed her. That's the way it went for the whole session. Charldean pecked only when the card had some feature of roundness, never when one of the non-round ones was in the viewer. She passed the test in grand fashion — concept formation. Her key-peck response was under the generalized control of the abstract stimulus feature of roundness.

■36 In the pigeon study, the stimulus cards that have a feature of roundness comprise a _____.

■37 The test was really a test for _____ _____ _____.

■38 How do we know concept formation had taken place?

Guitar playing and learned stimulus generalization

Carol had hidden the guitar from Chet. Why worry him before she tried it out? After all, it wasn't costing them a thing — not yet. She practiced each day after work before Chet came home. Carol wasn't spared these first painful sessions where fingertips rebel against the harsh pressure of the guitar strings. She suffered through it. At last she mastered the three chords diagrammed in the book Dawn loaned her along with the guitar. She seldom hit the wrong strings or muffled the sound by not pressing them down tightly and cleanly against the fretboard. Her past music training was of little help here, since this involved only the mechanics.

Learning to make each of the chords alone was just the start. The guitar book showed how these three basic chords would combine in sequences to fit the songs. Further, changes from one chord to the next had to be made quickly and with precision if they were to flow with the words and melody of the song. The book showed the sequence of changes for each song, and when — relative to the tune and lyrics — these changes should be made. Most new players have to keep their eyes glued to the book in order to follow the correct sequence of chord changes and to make them at the right time. But not Carol. She didn't need the book at all once she knew the words

and tune to the songs in the book. She knew — knew when to change and what sequence to follow. The concepts of chord progression and which chords sound right with a note, measure, or melody line were formed during her long years of piano study. These and many other concepts are common to all music of the western world — Carol's past training would have helped her much less, if at all, had the songs been of oriental or eastern vintage. The big surprise came soon after. Carol discovered she could play almost any song using these three chords — songs she'd heard as a child, had sung much of her life, songs she'd heard on the radio, new songs. As soon as she'd heard a song often enough to learn the lyrics and melody, she could play it with only a few minor mistakes. These concepts, and many others that had formed over the years of music lessons, gave Carol a great edge over Sid, as they would over anyone who had not had such training and had not yet come under the control of concepts common to music of our culture.

■39 Explain how concepts and learned stimulus generalization apply to music.

RESPONSE GENERALIZATION

Unlearned response generalization

No two things we run into in this world will ever be just the same. So, hooray for stimulus generalization! We'd be up the old creek without it. The other side of the story is that we are never the same either — not just from year to year — but second to second, instant to instant — moving, changing, always new. And, so it is with our actions. No matter how hard we try, we can't do the same thing twice. We come close, all right — it may look the same way, and feel the same. But sorry, it just isn't.

If you ponder it for a moment, you can see how this change in actions, that just happens, is a good thing. In a world that's always changing there has to be a way for new actions to appear — actions that could cope where old ones wouldn't. Yes, you guessed it. This variation in response features helps us survive — natural selection.

When a new response occurs in an old setting, it's called "response generalization". Some response generalization is un-learned — made possible by the structure that's part of the gift we got from our cousins in the dim past.

Unlearned response generalization: the tendency for new responses to occur spontaneously, even in a fairly fixed stimulus setting.

***

Gore lashed out with its left paw, claws bare, sharp and shining. The blow missed the wolverine's throat by a fraction of an inch. Too bad for Gore. The wolverine caught Gore off balance, biting deep, cutting clean through the tendon. Gore's left leg sagged, limp and flaccid. The wolverine edged in for the kill. Gore's right paw, razor claws, lashed out with cruel speed, deadly and certain. The thrust went deep, slicing the eyes of the wolverine. Blinded from the blood, Gore's foe made an unsteady retreat. Gore would live to fight other wolverines. Response generalization saved him.

***

One day when she had some extra time, Mae watched Cecil closely as he pressed the lever in the Skinner box. She'd never really paid much attention before to the exact movements he made. She found out something that was crucial to know about behavior. Cecil's lever responses were never the same — each lever press a bit unlike the one when he first learned to press the lever. The force of the press for instance — or sometimes he'd use both paws at once, at other times the right or left alone — new movements all the time. Mae hadn't taught him those many ways of pressing the lever when she shaped that response. They just happened without learning — unlearned response generalization.

- ■40 Define unlearned response generalization.
- ■41 Cite an instance of a creature surviving because of unlearned response generalization.

Unlearned response classes

Response generalization allows creatures to have an array of actions that could occur in a specific setting. Responses that differ slightly from each other tend to come under the same stimulus control — they're all likely to occur in some settings and not in others. These responses hang together as a unit or "response class". Thus, one response may be used instead of another, all of them alike yet not alike — involving bundles of muscles and neural units that differ to some extent As Gore showed us before, the right paw works well if the left paw's damaged. This way the job still gets done and the creature

survives. Right paw and left paw responses belong to the same unlearned response class.

Unlearned response class: group of responses that are alike in the sense that they tend to produce the same result, and are subject to unlearned response generalization.

***

Mae watched Cecil a bit longer. Yes, it was true, each lever press was somewhat unlike the next. They all shared one feature though — they all worked — they all managed to depress the lever far enough to click the switch. That meant reward

would be likely to result. All of Cecil's lever presses worked the lever, and Mae figured that meant they all belonged to the same response class. That's what the book called a group of responses that produced the same result. No, Mae hadn't trained Cecil to make all those many kinds of lever presses. Yet, they all seemed to hang together. It was because of the way Cecil was built — an unlearned response class. That was it.

- ▪42 Define unlearned response class.
- ▪43 What is the advantage of unlearned response classes?

Learned response generalization

Gore tried in vain to crack the nuts; its teeth were strong, but its jaw was weak and slack from days without food. A harsh famine was upon all the land. Gore struggled with the hard shell of the nut, growing fatigued from the effort. Still it would not crack. Gore rested, then tried once more. Jaws clamped in place, straining, tossing head and shoulders from side to side. By chance Gore's head struck the trunk of the nearby oak tree. The shell yielded, the nut cracked. The blow, though not harmful, had given Gore's jaws a needed boost in force. In days that came, Gore used the new way to crack nuts when needed — when it was faster or the nuts were hard, or when Gore was near the trunk of the tree.

***

Think for a moment about how you might measure the distance from your room to the kitchen or dining hall. You could pace it off, use a tape measure or maybe compute it by counting the number of tiles of known size that pave the way. All of these, and many other methods, would achieve the same result. We could use any or all of them in a given setting. They will generalize — response generalization.

But look at how the actions involved in each method differ. Could this happen as a result of unlearned response generalization? Hardly. This type of response generalization is a product of learning — "learned response generalization". Gore also displays learned response generalization. The creature stumbled on a new way to crack nuts. It worked, and now, when faced with that task again, the old way and the new way are both used from time to time — learned response generalization. What causes this? The answer should be clear: reward — the common reward that two or more responses can produce.

Learned response generalization: the tendency for responses that have little or no unlearned relationship to occur in the same setting because they have produced the same result there in the past.

Let's eavesdrop on Carol playing the guitar. She's a joy to watch, her fingers sliding across the fretboard without effort, moving up and down, actions that flow — smooth and fluid. Things have changed since the first few days when she played her three chords with cramped effort, her fingers always staying at the small end of the fretboard, never moving beyond the first two or three frets. Did she learn some fancy new chords? No, she still uses the same three. What she has learned — putting her past music training to good use — is that she can play the same chord at many places along the fretboard.

Each chord can be played a lot of ways — at other frets, other strings pushed down with the left hand, other strings plucked and strummed with the right. What Carol has learned is to use any of these responses when it suits, when it's easy, when one's better reached — learned response generalization again.

- ■44   Define learned response generalization.
- ■45   How and why does learned response generalization occur?
- ■46   Give two examples.
- ■47   Explain how playing the same chord in different ways is learned response generalization.

Learned response class

Mae was just goofing around with Cecil, killing a little time. He'd been pressing the lever for water, when he bumbled into the chain, pulling it down until the switch clicked. On impulse, Mae worked the dipper, giving Cecil a reward. It had a profound but not surprising effect on the rat. For the next few minutes, Cecil made many chain pulls — Mae kept the rewards coming. One time after drinking a dipper of water, Cecil being near the lever, pressed it. Mae rewarded that too. Then followed a string of lever presses. During the rest of the session Cecil sometimes pushed the lever and sometimes pulled the chain. Mae rewarded both. *That's response generalization,* Mae thought. *But it's learned response generalization. There's no way it could be unlearned — those two responses just differ too much, the movements aren't at all alike. The form of the chain pull is a far cry from the form of the lever press.* But as she pondered the subject further, Mae saw that in one sense the two responses were alike — precisely so. Mae'd made them so with the dipper. They were alike because they produced the same reward. *Well — that means they belong to the same response class. But can there be such a thing as a learned response class?*

* * *

Indeed there can, Mae. Gore's nut-cracking responses have acquired membership in the same response class; yielding a common result has bound them to each other.

Learned response class: a group of responses that may differ widely in form, but are likely to occur in the same setting because they have produced the same reinforcer under those conditions in the past.

Look at Carol's guitar playing too. The many finger placements and movements, each producing the same chord, belong to the same learned response class. Though movements are diverse, they all achieve the same result. Responses in a learned response class are glued into a unit through their common power in getting a reward. This takes place during a single creature's lifetime, and ends with its death unless it is taught to, or learned by, others. Responses in an unlearned response class gain membership in that class because of a creature's structure. An offspring becomes heir to these classes at conception — inheritance.

- ▪48 Define learned response class.
- ▪49 Cite three instances of learned response classes.
- ▪50 Responses in an (unlearned, learned) response class are inherited. They (are, are not) passed on to offspring. Responses in a (learned, unlearned) response class die with the creature.

Full circle

Carol waited for Chet to come home. She had to settle the guitar thing tonight, as a full month had passed since she took it on loan. Dawn would have to make a payment soon. If Chet was opposed to the guitar, better find it out now so she could give it back and let Dawn look for someone else to buy it. Carol heard the front door slam. It was Chet. *Here goes nothing!* she thought.

***

"Dawn? It's me — Carol. Listen, I wanted to let you know about the guitar. We're going to take it — isn't that great! Chet? Well, it was funny. When he first saw it he got all upset — not angry — just upset. Started to stammer and carry on. He calmed down then and got stubborn — at one point he just flat said we couldn't afford it. That's when the doorbell rang. Chet went to answer it. When he came back he was flustered. He'd changed his mind — said we could keep the guitar after all, but I shouldn't play it in front of other people until I got real good. Made me put it away right then. Boy, he got sweet all of a sudden. The visitor? Oh, Sid — Sid Fields.

CONCLUSIONS

There's been much meat in this chapter. The principles discussed apply to learning at many species levels, but some have their greatest import for the human. Learned results — rewards and punishers — are the prime motivators for human actions. They run a weak second place for all other creatures. Unlearned stimulus and response generalization apply to all creatures that learn. But when their learned counterparts — learned stimulus and response generalization — are at issue, it is again a topic that bears greatest on human actions. In the chapters that follow, we'll extend the principles studied here somewhat in the abstract, to new arenas of action — and in doing so demonstrate how they relate to the varied range of human behavior.

CHAPTER 10
SENSORY PROCESSES

THE SENSORY RESPONSE

Dodo, the amoeba, one of the simplest of moving creatures, bumbled blindly about — bumbling into food, but bumbling into harm as well. We've seen all this before: sometimes a Dodo bumped into enough food and missed enough harm to live to a ripe old age. But often a Dodo died young, either starving or running into trouble. Chance plays a life and death role when your actions aren't under stimulus control.

***

Now Dodo could only respond to a thing after making direct contact with that thing; and then it had only one way to respond: Dodo absorbed it if the object was the right size to produce the right distribution of mechanical force on its surface and if it was the right chemical composition. If not just right, the thing might be harmful, but it was often too late once Dodo had made contact. We call such a response to direct contact a "proximal sensory response".

Proximal sensory response: response to a stimulus in direct contact with a creature.

"Proximal" means "close" — "proximity". Creatures like poor Dodo have a hard time staying alive because they are limited to the control of only proximal stimuli. However, to survive they often need to respond to distal stimuli — stimuli at a distance.

Distal sensory response: response to a stimulus not in direct contact with a creature.

Creatures are much more likely to survive if they're under the control of distal stimuli. Then they can approach fuel in a more direct manner, and they can avoid harmful objects before making contact with them.

But distal sensory responses require more than a direct response to the biological value of the object — whether it is fuel or a harmful stimulus. Such responses require that the creatures react to other aspects of things as well, not just to their chemistry and size, but to aspects like their sight and sound.

And that's what this chapter is all about — the sensory process — our biophysical reactions to physical stimuli. We must be able to respond to many features of a stimulus if they are to exert adequate cue control over our actions. And we do need good cue control to survive.

So, as they have evolved, creatures have come to respond to more and more of these features of objects — features such as their sight and sound. And they've come to respond to more aspects of each feature; for instance, of light, not just its presence or absence, but to the intensity, pattern, and color. So, in other chapters we have seen, life has evolved more complex learned actions; and now in this chapter we will also see the complex and subtle stimulus details that control such learned actions. We will do this by looking at more and more complex sensory processes.

- 1 Define and cite an instance of proximal sensory response.
- 2 Do the same for distal sensory response.
- 3 Review: Define basic stimulus control.
- 4 How do distal sensory responses help a creature survive where a proximal sensory response might not?

VISION

Intensity

Remember Gore, the zoo-plankton? Though a fairly simple creature it did show some stimulus control — to stimulus intensity, which exerts the simplest kind of sense control. It responded to the intensity of light. Light consists of small packets of energy called photons — the intensity of light being the number of photons involved. The more photons, the more intense the light. Now when Gore was low on fuel it moved toward a fairly bright light — the land of many photons and a place that often contained algae — food for Gore. But Gore had to be built so that it could react to the photons bombarding it before this basic stimulus control could occur. Yet Gore didn't have eyes or any special organ that responded to the photons, instead most of its body absorbed the light units. And the only features of the light to which it did react were its intensity and direction. That's all Gore needed to get to the area where the algae grew.

Now some actions may be all or nothing — the creature responds if the stimulus intensity is above a minimal threshold value but it doesn't respond if the intensity is below that threshold value. And greater stimulus intensity above that absolute threshold value may have no further effect on the nature of that reaction.

Absolute threshold: the lowest intensity that will reliably produce a response.

But the stimulus intensity may have a more graded effect on other acts. The act may either grow or decrease in magnitude as a function of the intensity of the stimulus. For instance, our old friend the wood louse moves around at a higher speed as the humidity of the air decreases so it will be more likely to escape sooner from the dry air as that air gets more dangerous.

- 5 What is a photon?
- 6 What's the simplest form of sense control?
- 7 How does intensity of light relate to number of photons?
- 8 What is a fairly simple creature under such intensity control?
- 9 How would intensity control help the creature survive?
- 10 Define absolute threshold.

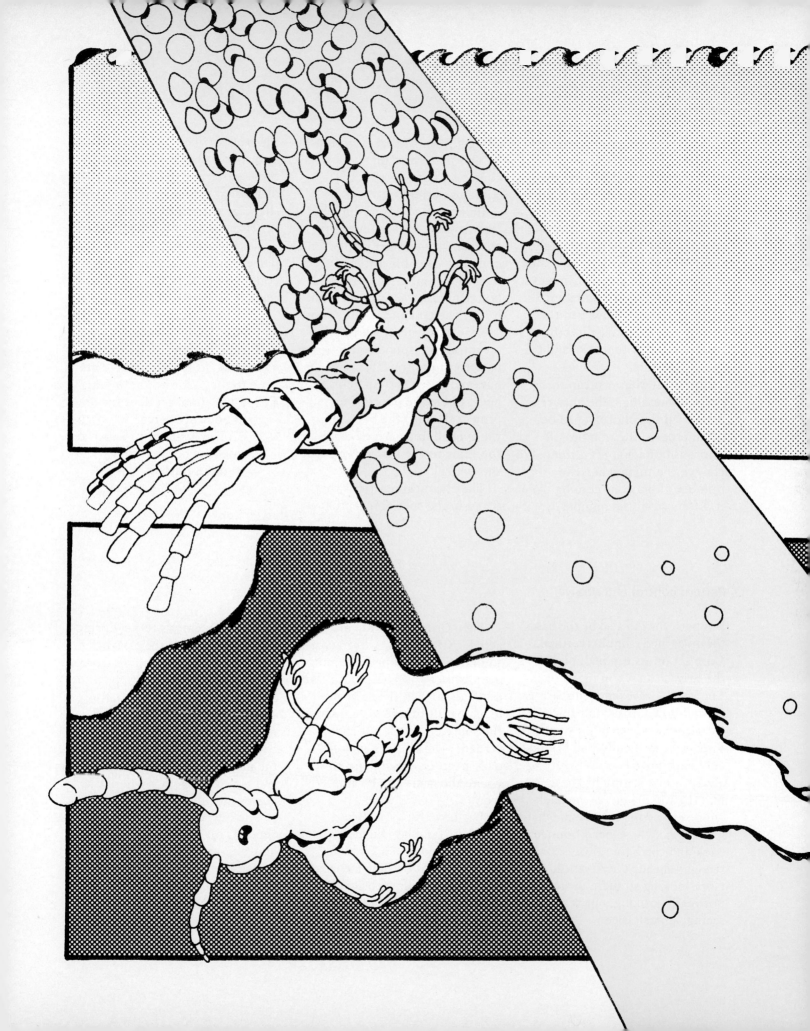

Pattern

Now larger and more complex creatures may have more complex sense control helping them survive. Most often, simple intensity control doesn't bring the creature to the precise spot where a bit of fuel is. It merely brings the creature into the same area, where the creature moves about "blindly" bumping into food by chance. However, the creature could move directly toward a bit of fuel if it could "see" that fuel.

But what does it mean to "see" something? The answer rests with the photon — to be more precise, the number of photons bouncing off a thing. We can see the thing when the number of photons coming from it differs from the number coming from all that surrounds it. This pattern of photons controls what we see — the stimulus pattern.

In a sense, this is nothing but a more precise type of intensity control. The number of photons bouncing off a bit of fuel differs from the number of those bouncing off whatever surrounds it. But the creature needs a more specialized structure, a light receptor, to respond to this pattern of photons. It needs an eye; and a lens system helps. The lens gathers the photons to project them to the back of the eyeball in a pattern corresponding to the stimulus outside the eyeball.

The chemical reactions that occur in the special receptors at the back of the eye, the retina, also follow that pattern. And these patterns can form the basis of learned stimulus control. The shape or pattern of a thing can function as an important part of a cue. In fact, right now the patterns we call letters and words control your actions — you're reading — a learned response.

■11 What's the drawback of simple intensity control?
■12 How do the photons relate to the pattern of a stimulus?
■13 What function does the lens in your eye serve?
■14 Cite an instance of a learned response controlled by stimulus pattern.

Pattern control and survival

But patterns can also be the basis for unlearned stimulus control. Gore sat on its lily pad, placid, the bright sun warming its back. The gentle waves moved its raft up and down, back and forth, Gore's head moved in the opposite directions as the lily pad bobbed about. It moved so that Gore always looked straight ahead, like the toy doggie in the back window of your car, the mechanical doggie whose head bounces back and forth but always looks straight ahead. There sat old Gore looking straight ahead, but not really looking, not really seeing, almost asleep.

Then Gore, the living machine, acted: "CROAK!" A huge croak, sound of an earthquake coming deep from a cavern's mouth, the croak of a magnificent living machine. But there sat old Gore, the source of it all, not concerned, placid, a frog on a lily pad, green on green, hard to see where the giant croak came from.

The little fly didn't see — flying its fatal last flight, buzzing into the field of Gore's blank stare. There it became a change in photons striking the back of Gore's eye — Gore's retina.

And that's where the action started — in Gore's retina during the last instant of the fly's brief life. These photons fell on Gore's light receptors, each bit of energy causing its own small chemical reaction. And these reactions produced brief electric bursts, bursts rushing up the nerves from the receptors, and coming together where the nerves meet, at the ganglia.

The output from these ganglia depends on the pattern of photons striking the receptors — on the number of strikings (intensity of pattern), on whether the neighbor receptors are also hit (shape of pattern), and even how long the receptors have been hit (motion of the pattern — the slower the fly, the longer it will cause photons to strike each part of Gore's retina as it moves across Gore's field of vision). That's the way the nervous system for Gorc's species evolved. It is a nervous system that's deadly for the poor fly.

The photons caused a moving pattern, bouncing off the fly and onto Gore's retina. That pattern in turn caused certain of the ganglia in Gore's eye to fire off electric nerve impulses — charges that ran up the optic nerves to special tissues in Gore's brain; there they produced more chemical reactions, causing still more electric charges. These charges worked with other electric action in the brain to shoot electric (another nerve impulse) current back down from the brain to Gore's tongue. And death's messenger, a white tongue from a green frog, met the black fly. Snared in mid-air.

Gore's pattern vision, its nervous system, its response system all evolved in a world full of small flying meals. This flying food was a part of nature selecting out Gore's pattern vision. And this vision system evolved over thousands of years to become a vision system that can deal with the patterns of flying morsels.

- ▪15 Define retina.
- ▪16 What are ganglia?
- ▪17 What are three features of pattern that determine the output of the ganglia in the frog's eye?
- ▪18 Cite an instance where pattern vision can help a lower creature to survive.

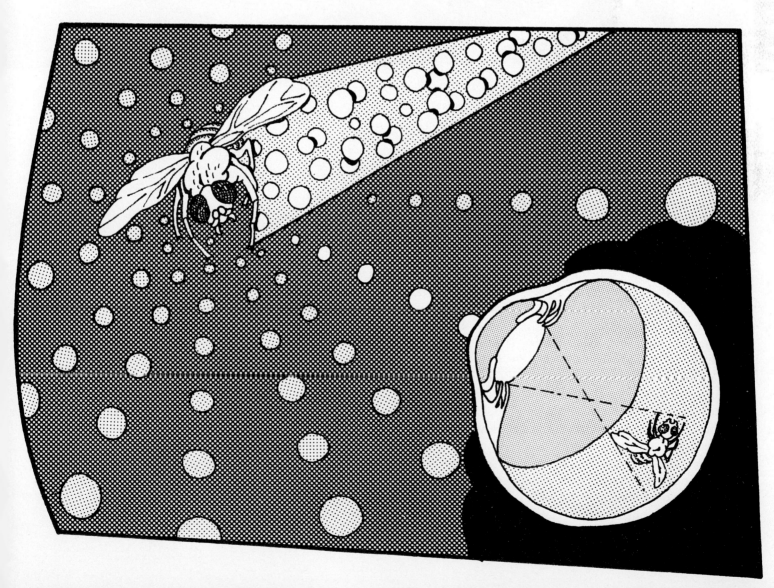

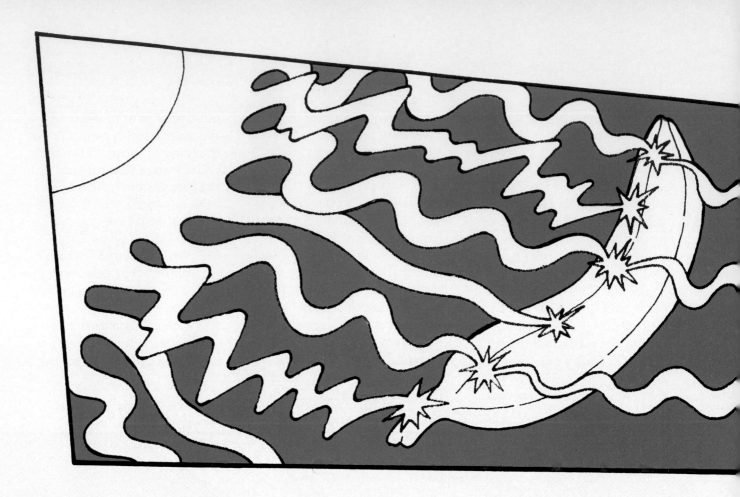

Color

Gore fluttered on the gentle wind, flopping its handsome butterfly wings in response to the breeze — and in response to the distant flower — the blue flower that contained its next meal — a meal of sweet nectar. Oh, the gentle life of the butterfly.

***

Dodo fluttered on the same breeze moving toward its next meal — toward the flower standing majestic in the distance. But on arrival poor Dodo found nothing it could eat. Not the first time Dodo had flown in vain, its strength ebbed away as one failure followed another. Dodo could not take many more such flights. Now seeing many flowers, it flew from one to the next,

always to the closest one, but still to no avail.

***

After eating from its blue flower, Gore hovered in the air above it and all the other flowers, not only the blue ones but the red and white ones as well.

But Gore didn't go to the red or white ones, not because some other butterfly seemed always to be there but because it just never flew toward red or white flowers. Gore's species evolved in a world where blue and yellow flowers held a treasure of food, though flowers of other colors held no worthwhile foods. And some of Gore's species survived — those controlled by the color of the flowers — creatures that had inherited color vision. But others,

like Dodo, died without offspring, nature's flops, creatures that responded the same way to all colors. So it goes.

***

Most sources of light, like the sun, send off photons that contain differing amounts of energy. And the amount of energy is the basis of color. Here's how it works: Most things the photons strike absorb some of those photons. But some things absorb high-energy photons and others absorb low-energy photons. The photons that don't get absorbed bounce off. Some of those photons will bounce off and into a creature's eyes, if it happens to be nearby.

The kind of chemical changes taking place in the retina of the

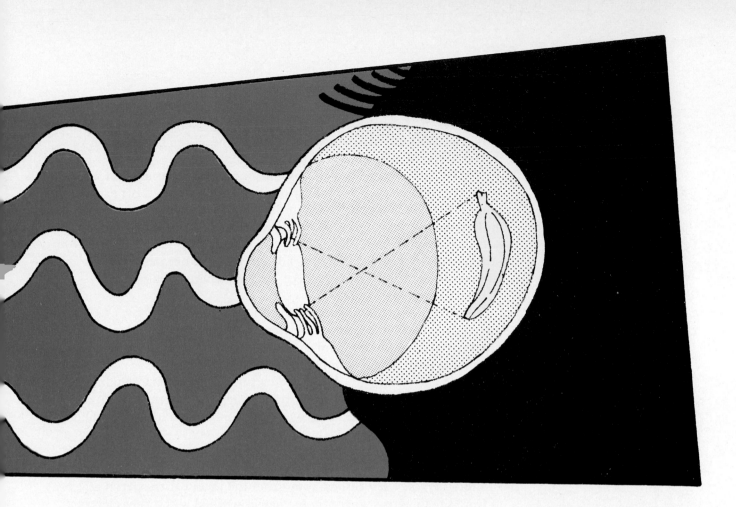

eye depend on the energy of the photons. Three different chemicals are involved: One reacts most when struck with low-energy photons; another reacts most to medium-energy photons; the third reacts most to high-energy photons. And how we react to these photons — what color we see — depends on the strength of the three types of chemical changes. We call the colors red if the low-energy-photon chemical is the most active; medium energy causes yellow-green colors; and high energy causes the blue colors. If all three chemicals react roughly the same we call the color white. White light contains photons of all energies at roughly equal strengths. Other patterns of action of the three chemical

changes cause other colors.

Color is a feature of most things — fuels, harmful stimuli, and sources of sexual reinforcers. So color seems to play a major role in much stimulus control. For instance, the color of other creatures of the same species affects the mating and aggression actions of some birds and fish. And, of course, color is helpful to us in much learned stimulus control; in responding to a stop light for instance. But many creatures (dogs and rats, for instance) can't respond to the differing energies of the photons as they don't have the needed receptors in their retina; so they don't see color, but must rely on other stimuli as cues. So color helps those things exert stimulus control over the actions of

creatures with color vision. And the more features of a stimulus that exert stimulus control over a creature, the more exact the reaction of that creature can be.

- ▪19 Cite an instance where color vision helps a lower creature survive.
- ▪20 What is it about an object that causes us to see a particular color?
- ▪21 What is it about photons that causes us to see different colors?
- ▪22 How do photons affect the retina to cause us to respond differently to different colors?
- ▪23 When do we see white light?
- ▪24 Cite an instance where color vision might help a human survive.

HEARING

SNAP! The noise cut through the late evening's silence like a rifle shot. The sudden noise of a twig breaking. And in the brief instant of its breaking, the twig vibrated at a high rate.

SNAP! The vibrating twig shook the air molecules around it for that same brief instant. And the molecules of air bounced off each other forming a sphere of waves in the air, tidal waves of sound, moving out away from the broken twig — the cause of it all.

SNAP! The waves of air splashed against Gore like the ocean's surf beating a rocky coast — but with a difference: the ocean's waves altered the coast only after years of beating, where the air waves changed Gore in an instant.

SNAP! The thin membranes, like drum heads stretched over Gore's ears, moved back and forth as the air waves beat against them, a drummer playing the tympani. And the tympanic membranes vibrated against the small bones in Gore's middle ears.

SNAP! The vibrating bones pushed a smaller membrane, sending waves of fluid rushing back and forth through the inner ear. Back and forth across tiny hair cells, causing them to move with the waves like seaweed in the ocean.

SNAP! The vibrating hair cells triggered a chain of electro-chemical reactions resulting in bursts of electric charges that rushed along the auditory nerves. They rushed away from the inner ear to special areas in Gore's brain, areas where those charges worked with other electric charges. And yet other electric charges went back from the brain to the muscles in Gore's body.

SNAP! And Gore, gentle and relaxed, sprang into action, heart pounding, hormones flowing, muscles tense, ready to defend its nest.

***

Sound transmission, a simple mechanical system: object vibrates air molecules, air vibrates ear drum, ear drum vibrates middle ear bones, bones vibrate oval window membrane, membrane vibrates fluid, fluid vibrates hair cells, hair cells set off electric charges, and the mechanical system stops. So simple but so finely tuned — sensitive. Any more sensitive and we'd hear the random motion of the air molecules as they beat against our ear drums.

Of course, these finely tuned hearing machines evolved through hundreds of thousands of years, shaped by what helps the species survive in nature, shaped by nature, the harsh but patient craftsman.

***

SNAP! The faint noise broke the late evening's silence like a rifle shot. Gore sprang up with a start, whirling toward the sound; there it was — the cat creeping toward their nest — stealthy, but not stealthy enough. Gore flew screaming at the killer — striking as she passed over its head. Diving for a second attack, hitting the cat's head, the defender rose for its third attack, circling short and streaking back down. But victory was already Gore's, as the startled cat lost its hold on the branch and crashed to the ground.

Picking itself up, it limped off, perhaps to find easier prey. But Gore's baby birds would live at least one more day in their harsh struggle to survive.

■25 Cite an instance of hearing helping a species survive.
■26 What are the steps of the mechanical process of sound transmission?
■27 What effect do the hair cells in the inner ear have?

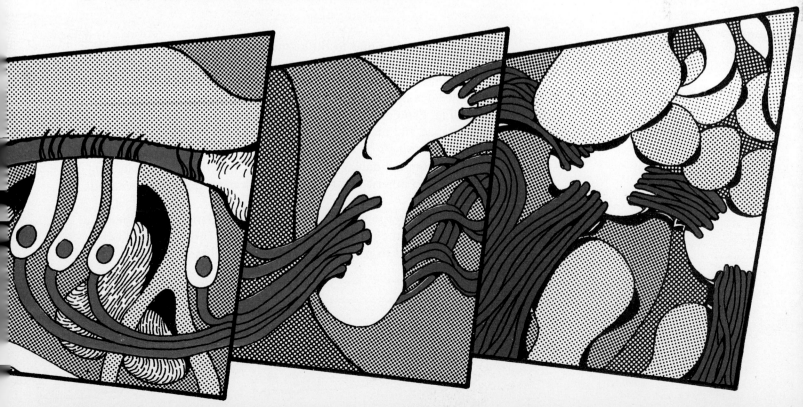

TISSUE DAMAGE

The two young wolves almost caught the clumsy mountain goat, as they ran side by side across the valley, panting yet gaining ground with each swift stride. But soon the goat was out of the valley scrambling up the steep, rock-strewn mountainside, its hooves treading the sharp stones with no trouble. Gore and Dodo also sprang up the slope. But now they were out of their turf — now they were the clumsy ones, stumbling and scraping their shins, stepping on the sharp rocks cutting their tender paws.

Gore yelped with each fall, each bruise, each scrape and cut. The young wolf slowed down to lick its wounds, at last stopping its pursuit altogether.

But not Dodo. Dodo kept after its prey, bruised, scraped, cut, stumbling, falling but never stopping, never yelping.

At last Dodo had the goat cornered — bleating, backing, head down, ready for the wolf's attack. Dodo stalked around its victim at first. Then it rushed the goat, its injured paws and limbs leaving a trail of red as it ran. The goat in turn charged, striking the wolf, with lowered head, and pitching it in the air. Dodo picked itself up, blood rushing from its side, but no yelping, no whimpering, and no stopping the wild creature. Snarling, Dodo lunged for the goat's neck when the luckless victim raised up on its hind feet. There the goat made one last, shrill bleat as Dodo crunched down on its throat. Dodo even bit its own ankle as it wrenched a piece of flesh from the goat's neck. But the young wolf ate its fill.

Dodo would never starve to death. But it did bleed to death on its way home. It died alone without a yelp, without a whimper, without the strength to return Gore's plaintive wolf's howl that rang throughout the night.

* * *

Dodo did not respond to the tissue damage — a cut, a scrape, a bruise got no response from this strange creature. Tissue injury wasn't a stimulus for any of Dodo's behavior, acting neither as a cue nor a punisher. So Dodo kept doing wrong things — things that damaged its tissue. It stepped on sharp rocks, didn't favor its injured paws, scraped and bruised its limbs, attacked in spite of an injured side, and even bit its own ankle — all because it was not controlled by stimuli from the damaged tissue. And Dodo died young, leaving no offspring to inherit this trait — the lack of response to damaged tissue.

But Gore did respond to the damage, as the damage punished the harmful acts. So the punishing stimuli stopped those harmful acts; and Gore survived to produce more wolves like itself, wolves controlled by pain. Thus a helpful trait becomes common in a species.

And what about the Dodos — those rare mutants that don't respond to the stimuli from tissue damage? They die off before that feature has a chance to be spread throughout the species. Like an automatic process, the world of nature prevents such harmful traits from spreading, just as it causes useful traits to increase — nature, the quality control inspector, the rejector of faulty items.

***

Some stimuli harm us when we make direct contact with them. We might avoid that direct contact if we could make a sensory response to that harmful feature — a response such as seeing, hearing, or smelling that harmful aspect. But sometimes harmful stimuli give no cues to warn us. For instance, we eat all sorts of foods that harm us, yet some give no warning cues to cause us to escape them. But most often we're in fairly good shape. We do, in fact, detect many harmful stimuli — those active in our world as we evolved. For instance, we can detect the odor of spoiled food. And, of course, this helps all creatures survive.

High intensities of most stimuli harm us. And, of course, the intensity often exerts sensory control when it reaches that harmful level. As we saw, for instance, with Gore, harmful stimuli may act as a punisher. These intensities may also exert unlearned stimulus control. The amoeba backs away from harmful stimuli it bangs into — an unlearned action. Or they may serve as a learned cue; for instance, extreme pressure on your foot can act as part of the cue for the learned response, "I believe you're standing on my foot; how about getting off it?"

■28 Cite an instance where being controlled by stimuli from tissue damage helps a creature survive. Show how a creature might inflict self-injury if it doesn't respond to tissue damage.

■29 Why aren't there species with many members that don't respond to tissue damage?

■30 Cite an instance of a harmful stimulus that may not exert control over our actions.

■31 Cite an instance of unlearned stimulus control by tissue damage.

■32 Cite an instance of learning controlled by tissue damage as a punisher.

■33 Cite an instance of learned stimulus control by tissue damage as a cue for an escape response.

■34 How do we respond to high levels of stimulus intensity?

EVOLUTION

The rate of natural and social evolution

But not all things control our actions, not even things crucial to our survival. Why not?

How could we survive in the past without being controlled by such stimuli? Has that patient craftsman become sloppy? No. But our world changes; and our senses evolved in ways that helped us survive in the old world, not the new world. Our new world has new sources of harm, stimuli that were much more rare in the old days, stimuli like the deadly x-ray that weren't around enough to affect how we evolved. But natural evolution proceeds slowly generation after generation, marking time from one rare mutant to the next. But that time may not exist, if our species is to survive in a world of sudden change, a world where each new threat might wipe us out. Something else is needed.

And sure enough that something else has evolved, at least with the human species. That something else is based on our skills at learning complex patterns of action, actions controlled by complex patterns of cues: actions like reading, writing, thinking, inventing, and cues like words, logic, problems, cause-effect patterns. These are complex cues and complex acts with complex ends.

And that something else we'll call "social evolution". It's based on natural evolution but it goes a step beyond it, giving us a chance to keep up with our world of sudden change — changes of which we may be both the cause and the victim. Social evolution is a change in the way we and our world affect each other — but a change that results from human actions, not from the evolution of our biophysical structure.

Social evolution — writing, printing, science, law, marriage, books, guns, TV, cars — results from direct human action, not from nature's slow process of biological evolution. And these results may help us survive.

What does this have to do with our senses? Well, social evolution has also affected our senses by increasing their scope, by allowing us to respond to energy hidden from us before, yet those stimuli are often crucial to whether we survive.

■35 Cite one more instance of a harmful stimulus that we can't detect with our normal senses.

■36 Why didn't we evolve in nature so as to detect such stimuli?

■37 What's the danger when we rely on evolution by nature?

■38 What is social evolution and what are some instances?

■39 How does social evolution go a step beyond natural evolution?

Social evolution of the senses

People working around x-rays often wear a device that detects those rays. This device gives out a warning cue before the person is exposed to too much radiation. It gives out a cue we can see. Humans who wear and respond to such a device are more likely to survive. And cultures that have evolved such a device are also more likely to survive.

Social evolution has produced a seemingly endless number of devices: telescopes, microscopes, stethoscopes, x-ray machines, infrared photos, radios, sonar, litmus paper, and on and on. So now we are able to react to small numbers of photons, airwaves, x-rays, radio waves, chemicals, etc. — stimuli that had no sense control over us before. We built these special sensors to respond to stimuli to which we can respond only with their aid. To energy forms that can't act as overt cues though they do affect our well-being.

And these devices serve a special function; they provide cues that fall within the range of our current senses; they allow us to respond to crucial energy forms, albeit in a round-about way. They allow us to go beyond natural evolution, freed from its limits. And arrogant though this may seem, perhaps we no longer need to evolve other special senses through nature's slow process of evolution; we may be no more likely to survive in the raw world of nature; but at least we may now be more likely to survive our own problems, problems found in the world of our own creation.

■40 How has social evolution affected our sense responses? Cite an instance.

■41 Why is it that we might not need natural evolution to improve our senses in the future?

CONCLUSIONS

As we evolved, our actions came more and more under the control of our world. And this control helps us cope with that world. It helps us get fuel and avoid harm. It helps us survive. The many features of our world control our actions by acting as unconditioned and conditioned stimuli, discriminative stimuli, reinforcers, and punishers. But we must be able to sense our world, react to it, for it to control us in that way. So we evolved to sense more and more of its features: its sights, the photons bouncing off it; its sounds, the molecules vibrating in it; but not just its gross features, also its detail — its intensity, its pattern, its color, and even its harmful events. We become more and more able to cope with the world as we respond to more and more of the great richness of detail of that world.

But now social evolution has moved into our world, perhaps even replacing the natural evolution of our senses. The quicker process itself wins out in our new world of rapid, human-produced change.

CHAPTER 11
PERCEPTION

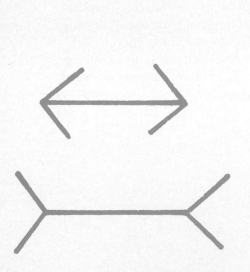

INTRODUCTION

In this chapter, we will deal with the topic of perception. We will look at perception as a type of stimulus control exerted by a special type of complex stimulus. In perception, the exact relation between the stimulus and the response often surprises us, as it is often rather strange. Let's glance at three standard problems in perception to see what this means: the Muller-Lyer illusion, the brightness-contrast effect, and size constancy.

The Muller-Lyer illusion deals with the apparent length of lines. You have a complex stimulus when you add a pair of arrowheads to the ends of a simple straight line. These arrowheads affect people's responses to the straight line. They cause people to say the same straight line looks longer under one condition than another. When the arrowheads point inward the line looks longer than when they point outward or when there are no arrowheads at all. In other words, you have a strange and surprising relation between that complex stimulus and the response it controls.

Or, take the brightness-contrast effect: You have a complex stimulus when you add a bright background to a simple grey spot. This affects people's responses to that grey spot. They say the same grey spot looks darker when you add the bright background, when in fact, the spot remains unchanged.

On the other hand, sometimes you have to think awhile about the relation between the stimulus and response before it seems strange. This is the case with size constancy. Compare a distant object with the same one up close. How do we respond? Our repsonse is to say the objects are the same size. Simple stimulus? Obvious response? Not if you think about it. The stimulus is complex since far and near objects differ in two respects: their distance from you and the size of their images on your retina. And this difference causes the mystery. The near object projects a larger image on your retina — an image that should cause you to say it looks larger. Yet you don't; you say they're the same size, of course. Why, since their images aren't the same size on your retina?

These are not the simpler stimulus-response functions we saw in the Sensory Processes chapter. Instead we have a complex set of functions that have amazed, puzzled, and confused psychologists for years. In this chapter we will try to study these complex functions, in basic terms we've found helpful before — in terms of stimulus control.

We do this because of the concept of "parsimony," a crucial concept in creating any scientific theory. This concept has governed much of what we have done in trying to understand the concepts and data of psychology for this book.

Parsimony: this guideline states that scientists should always look for the simplest way to explain data; they should invent new concepts only when existing concepts clearly can not account for all the data.

Scientists try to be parsimonious because we would soon have more invented causes than facts to explain if we did otherwise. And indeed, this may be a problem with much of psychology — we psychologists are all too often ready to invent a new inner process to account for our data, our facts. But in this book we have tried to keep the number of inventive inner processes very small in order to be in line with good scientific theory building, with parsimony.

- 1 Which is best thought of as a strange relation between a response and a complex cue — sensory processes or perception?
- 2 This chapter is aimed at showing which of the following — a) that perception can be understood in terms of the concepts we've already found useful, or b) that the complex data of perception require us to infer more complex inner concepts to explain them?
- 3 Define parsimony.

THE VIEW OVER THE CLIFF

The sun broke through the trees, bringing the woods alive with the action of bustling creatures, with the sounds of the singing birds. Young Gore struggled to its feet, stretching, wide awake, though its parents slept on — everything grey and still where they lay. But beyond, Gore could see other creatures flying and running about in the shining sun. And you can bet which sight was a stronger reward: the one with all the action, of course. So Gore started walking toward the bright colors and the motion, out alone for the first time.

Many fine new sights kept rewarding Gore's walking — when all of a sudden — what was that? Something Gore had never seen before — an awful sight. Gore stood there, shaking, its heart racing, before jumping back, turning and running to the safety of its home. Gore had just peered over the cliff and into the valley for the first time; and it suffered the awful effects of looking over the cliff — a heavy punisher.

* * *

At first, Gore's reaction may puzzle you, though you've most likely done the same thing yourself. Haven't you ever looked off the top of a tall building, or perhaps off the same cliff Gore dealt with? And didn't you feel just a bit queazy? Well scientists are finding evidence that such reactions are quite common. In fact, sights of this sort are unlearned punishers for many creatures. But why? To get an answer, let's look at a mythical creature less fortunate than Gore. Dodo, our ever present scapegoat for faulty mutation.

* * *

Dodo was up and out, running through the woods long before its parents even stirred. Many rewarding sights. But what's this? So beautiful — so breathtaking — such grandeur. Dodo had never seen anything like it before. The young creature rushed off toward this new experience, because moving toward rewarding sights had often been reinforced in the past. And indeed Dodo did have a new experience — it ran off the edge of the cliff. So it does go.

* * *

Dodo's fate shows why the sight over the cliff should be an unlearned punisher. Dodo didn't get a second chance. You don't get many second chances to fall off a cliff. If you did, then it might make more sense for the view over the cliff to become a learned punisher. On the other hand, Gore survived, since looking over the cliff was an unlearned punisher for that young creature. Let's see why.

* * *

Is such a sight a punisher for all kinds of creatures that have survived? Are there conditions in which some creatures might have evolved without the danger of falling off of cliffs? If so, the sight over a cliff might not be an unlearned punisher for them. Let's look at the sea turtle.

First of all, where does its mother lay her eggs? Near the beach, not near a cliff. Second, where does the newly-hatched turtle go? Straight for the sea — not for an aimless stroll, chancing a fall off some cliff. And where does it spend the rest of its life? In the safety of the ocean's depths — not in the peril of the mountain's heights. And, sure enough, the sight of the ledge isn't a punisher for the sea turtle — a fact that might not surprise you by this point.

But what about the land turtle, you ask? It would end up as dead as Dodo if it were like its swimming cousin. And, sure enough, it's not like the sea turtle. The sight over the cliff does punish it — thereby helping the land turtle survive.

- 4 Stimuli that result from looking over a cliff are punishers, though we haven't yet seen why. How does this help some creatures survive? Why should we inherit rather than learn that punisher?
- 5 How does the contrast between the sea and land turtle show that these stimuli may have gotten their punishing powers through natural selection?

ANALYSIS OF THE VIEW

Binocular convergence

Now, just what is it about looking over the cliff that's so punishing? What features of that stimulus cause us to back away? We will examine a few possible answers, though no clear answer has yet been found. First we will consider a reaction called binocular convergence. To see how this works, do the following exercise: Hold the index finger of your right hand about eight inches in front of your eyes. Look at it. How many fingers did you see? One. Now, hold this book with your left hand, as far in front of you as you can. But still keep your right index finger out there. Now look at the book. How many fingers did you see this time? Careful, don't look at the finger on your right hand, look at the book; just notice how many right index fingers you see while looking at the book in your left hand. How many? Two? Good.

Why is that? Well, when you look right at a thing, it's lined up with the center of your eye. It's fixated. "Fixating" the thing that way causes it to fall on the same parts of the two retinas. This gives you a single image. So the image of your finger must fall on the same parts of the two retinas, if you are to see one finger and not two. Otherwise, you get a double image. If the spots on two retinas are far enough apart, you see two distinct fingers. A double image results from failing to fixate on an object.

Fixation (visual): lining up an object with the center of the retina.

Now your eyes must "converge" or turn toward that thing to fixate it. This is called "binocular convergence". Our eyes must converge greatly to fixate on near objects like our index finger, but they need converge only slightly to fixate on distant objects like the sight over the cliff.

Binocular convergence: two eyes converge or turn in on a thing to fixate on it.

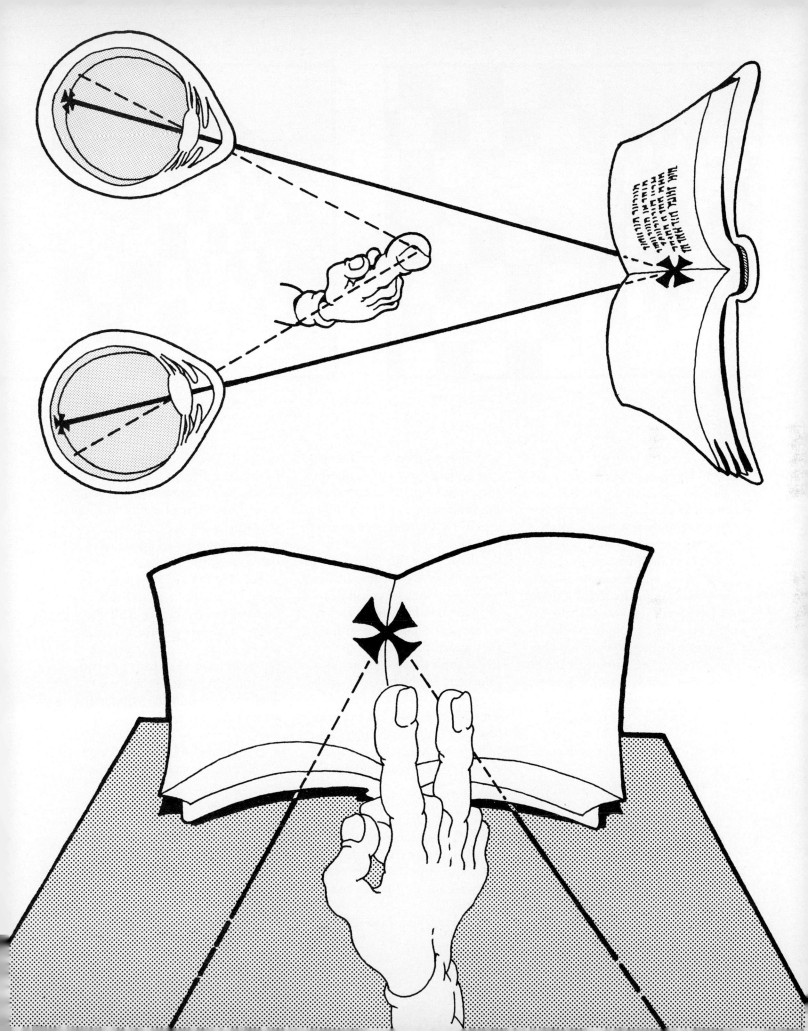

To control how our eyes converge, we control the muscles connected to them. Now those muscles produce certain feedback stimuli — stimuli called proprioceptive stimuli, the same sort of stimuli we saw in the Evolution and Behavior chapter.

What about the slight amount of convergence you need to fixate a distant object at the bottom of the cliff? Could the proprioceptive stimuli from the muscles in that position be a punisher? Sounded like a good guess, so scientists tested the notion by getting rid of the chance for binocular convergence to be involved.

They used a piece of equipment called the "visual cliff": a sheet of heavy glass or plastic which extends well beyond the edge of a "table". This gives the visual appearance of a cliff but gets around the danger of the infant or animal hurting itself by falling over the ledge. These

scientists studied an infant who had only one eye. In doing this, they ruled out the occurrence of punishing proprioceptive stimuli due to the convergence of two eyes since only one eye was involved. Now this infant fixates on an object by turning its head, since only one eye could be involved. It didn't need to converge its eye to a position that would produce proprioceptive stimuli that might act as a punisher. So the use of a single eye got rid of one source of stimulus control — the proprioceptive stimuli resulting when two eyes converge at a distance such stimuli could have no effect.

What happened? Did the infant now gaze at the view over the cliff tranquil, serene, at peace with its world? Or did the sight still make it beat a hasty retreat, escaping amidst fussing and howling?

Answer: the infant still

escaped. The view still acted as a punisher, even though the infant looked with only one eye; even though it did not have to put that one eye in a punishing position in order to fixate over the visual cliff.

So we must keep up our search since we've found that binocular convergence isn't the cause. At least it doesn't do the job by itself. We must keep up our search for the answer to our question: Why does the view over the cliff punish? What other stimuli are involved?

- 6 Explain how the finger-and-book trick works in terms of convergence of the eyes.
- 7 Define fixation.
- 8 Define binocular convergence.
- 9 What test or experiment ruled out binocular convergence as a factor in the visual cliff puzzle?

Focus

Now let's look at another factor that might be involved with the mystery of the cliff — the reaction of focusing. What happens when we look at faraway things? We must change the shape of the lenses of our eyes. When we do, we can focus the path of photons so they form a sharp image on the retinas at the back of our eyeballs.

Focus: adjustment of the lens to form a clear image on the retina.

Muscles attached to the lenses control their shape. And those muscles also produce proprioceptive stimuli. Perhaps the proprioceptive stimuli caused by the position of the muscles are a punisher. But that's not likely since it isn't a punisher when we focus on a distant object on the horizon or in the sky; so why should it be a punisher when we look over a cliff?

- ■10 Define focus.
- ■11 Why can't we explain the cliff puzzle solely in terms of the stimuli from focusing?

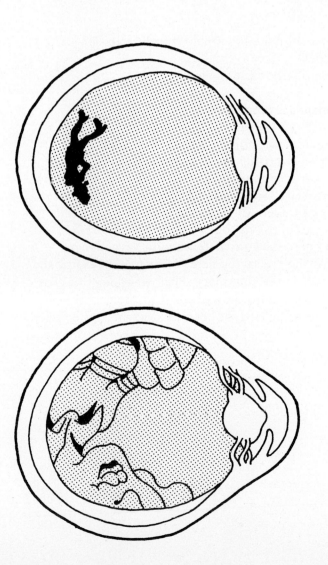

Other possible sources of punishers

There are many other possible punishers for looking over the cliff, but they all have the same drawback that focus has — all those other stimuli also being present when we're looking off into the horizon or the sky. So such stimuli must not be punishers since we don't escape those views.

Well then, what's so unique about looking over a cliff? Maybe this: your head's tilted down, causing fluid shifts within your inner ear. Maybe that's the punisher we're searching for. But not quite since your head's in that same position when you are lying on your stomach in bed. So perhaps it's the combined stimuli. Maybe one or more of the distant visual stimuli (like those present when we focus or converge) are punishers only in the presence of other stimuli — the internal stimuli that result from having our head tilted down. Perhaps that accounts for it. Perhaps distance cues combine with head-position stimuli to form a punisher. As people so often say after talking about unsolved scientific problems, only further research will give the answer.

- ■12 What stimuli might combine to explain the cliff puzzle?
- ■13 What is a visual cliff?
- ■14 What is the standard response to a visual cliff?

The objective vs. the standard approach

Dawn began to pick up her text, hoping to rush through the rest of this chapter before her eight o'clock date; but Mae wasn't through talking. Showing little concern for Dawn's frivolous social life, or her attempts to study, she asked, "You know there's something about the way these guys treat the problem of the visual cliff. It's not like I recall it from my high school psych course. In high school they talked like the creature perceived a real depth with a real danger."

"Well, isn't that what they're saying here?" Dawn asked, sorry she had started the discussion in the first place. She had hoped this chat would last only a brief minute. But now she had to choose between finishing the chapter and being late for her date. Yet she also enjoyed the discussion, perhaps almost as much as her date, she was surprised to admit.

Mae went on, "No, they keep it much simpler, by just saying that some stimuli combine to act as a punisher. They're saying creatures are born to respond to an unlearned punisher like the combined stimuli associated with depth. But those creatures are not born with an unlearned or innate concept of depth. They don't talk about what the creature perceives, like depth, since no one knows what it perceives, and since depth is a sort of abstract concept, one that requires human language to construct. They don't guess about what's going on inside the creature's head, since those guesses don't help anyway. And we don't need those guesses because we can see what's going on just by talking about stimuli that combine to act as a punisher. We can stay objective and deal only with what we see, whether it is inside or outside the creature. We don't have to deal with what we think is going on inside."

"But," Dawn argued, "I don't see what's so great about being objective, since it seems like your standard approach from high school is just good common sense. Like, of course the creature is afraid; who wouldn't be if they thought they might fall off a cliff? That standard approach just seems like the natural way of looking at things. What's wrong with it?"

"Seems to me, the standard approach kind of misleads you." Mae said. "Just because it's common sense doesn't mean it's the right sense. And there's no sense inventing things going on in the head of some little creature, just because that happens to be the way most people talk about things. Like the authors are on a parsimony trip. That's where their heads are at. They want to deal with things the simplest way they can, as long as they can account for all the data that way. And . . ." A rude pounding on the door interrupted Mae; Dawn's date, eager to whisk her away.

■15 Describe the standard approach to the study of the visual cliff. What are the problems with this approach?
■16 Describe the objective approach.
■17 Which approach is stressed in this book?

OTHER PERCEPTUAL EFFECTS

Size constancy

Let's look at a few more topics in the area of perception, a few more cases where the relation between the stimulus and response may seem a little strange. The first is size constancy. The problem: look at a six-foot-tall person who's 50 feet away; that person causes the same size image on your retina as a person three feet tall, who's 25 feet away. How does the person's height exert proper stimulus control over us? In other words, how can we tell the person's correct height? Answer: the size of the image on the retina combines with other distance cues — cues like proprioceptive stimuli coming from focusing and convergence, and like setting cues such as the size of known objects near the two people. This combined set of cues works to produce proper stimulus control. It works so people don't seem to grow taller as they walk toward us. This is called ''size constancy''.

Size constancy: the size of an object tends to have proper stimulus control over our actions whatever the distance of the object.

The basis for size constancy is that the size of the image on the retina combines with other distance stimuli to produce proper cue control. We learn to respond the same way concerning the person's height regardless of the absolute size of the person's image on our retina. We learn to respond to that combined set of stimulus features.

- ■18 Define size constancy.
- ■19 Thought question: Give a couple of examples of what it would be like without size constancy.
- ■20 State the basis for size constancy.

Brightness constancy

We've looked at size constancy, where our response to the size of an object is affected by the distance of that object. Now we'll look at brightness constancy, where our response to the brightness of an object is affected by the amount of light from the background surrounding that object. On the one hand, the object's distance causes us to respond as if it is the same size, no matter what its distance from us. On the other hand, the object's background causes us to respond as if it is the same brightness, no matter what its overall illumination.

For instance, what do you see when you look at this white page in the bright sunlight? A white page, of course. And in the evening's dusk? You see the same white page. Not a grey one. So where's the puzzle? Well, it's like the size constancy problem. What you see ain't what you get. What hits your retina and what you see are not the same.

First, let's look at what hits your retina. To do this, you must recall the cause of light intensity. It's the rate that photons come from a thing. The more photons, the more intense the light. But two factors control the number of photons bouncing off an object: 1) the percentage of photons the object reflects (as we've seen) and 2) the number of photons hitting the object in the first place. So the white page reflects more photons in the bright sunlight than at dusk. Therefore, the light it reflects is more intense in the daytime than in the evening.

Now let's look at what you see. You react to the page as if it were the same brightness, though it bounces differing numbers of photons into your retina when the overall illumination differs. So why is the page's brightness constant?

The answer has to do with the amount of light the background reflects, the amount of light bouncing off the desk this book is lying on. That amount is greater when the midday sun is streaming through your window than when there's nothing left but its last gasps of evening. Your response depends on both the amount of light the page reflects and the amount the desk reflects. You'll say the page is white under each of these states of affairs: 1) when the page and the desk both reflect a lot of light — at midday; and 2) when they both reflect less light — in the evening. You might not even notice how the two states differ, since both times your page will look white to you.

So you don't just tune-in to the absolute amount of light. That means you don't respond just to the page, you respond to your total visual world. For you to say your page is white it must reflect a lot of light when the rest of your world also reflects a lot of light. You'll say it's grey only if the relative amount of light your page reflects is less. Your response to the page depends on the amount of light it reflects relative to the amount of light your desk reflects. A low intensity background raises the apparent brightness of an object, while a high intensity background lowers that object's brightness.

So why does this white page look just as white in a dim light as in an intense light? It looks the same since the relative amount of light it reflects is still about the same when compared to the desk and the rest of the background. And that accounts for "brightness constancy".

Brightness constancy: an object is the same brightness even though the overall level of light may change, causing it to reflect less light.

By the way, experience with the

backgrounds involved will no doubt affect your response to the book. In other words, whether you've seen your desk before in various levels of light most likely affects your response. But lab research has shown there's more to it than that. The relation between the object and the background also affects your response, even when you've never before seen either the object or the background.

And this brightness constancy does help us survive. It's important that things look the same when they are the same, even though the amount of light striking them differs. We respond according to brightness constancy because we inherited a visual system that responds that way.

■21 Define brightness constancy.
■22 Describe brightness constancy for the same object under two different levels of light.

■23 Thought question: Describe brightness constancy in terms of two objects reflecting the same amounts of light though not in the same levels of light. Then relate this to brightness contrast described in the Introduction section.

■24 Why should we have brightness constancy?

Color contrast

We've studied size constancy, where the apparent size of an object is affected by its distance. And we've studied brightness constancy, where the apparent brightness of an object is affected by the intensity of its background. Now let's look at one final problem of perception: one more problem where our response to one feature of a stimulus is affected by another feature of that stimulus, where the relation between the stimulus and the response seems rather strange. Let's look at color contrast, where the apparent color of an object is affected by the color of its background.

Color contrast is an effect much like brightness constancy since it involves the effects of background on our response to an object. But this time it's the effect of the color of the background on our response to the color of the object, rather than the effect of the intensity of the background on our response to the intensity of that object.

It helps us predict the direction of this effect if we know a little about the physics of colored light itself. Recall that the color of light depends on the energy of its photons. Blue, green, and red lights are high, medium, and low energy photons. In fact, color forms a spectrum running from red to violet. It's just like the spectrum in the colors of the rainbow.

The background color causes us to see the object color as slightly changed in a direction that contrasts with that background color. The apparent color of the object shifts away from the place of the background color on the spectrum. In fact, the apparent color shifts toward what is called the complementary of the background color. The complementary of a color is the color it can be mixed with to produce white. And it turns out most colors do have a complementary color. For instance, you will get white if you project a blue-green light and a red light on a movie screen. Therefore, the blue-green light and the red light complement each other. So what would happen if you had a green spot on a red background? It would appear more blue-green. And what would happen if you had a green spot on a blue background? It would appear yellow-green.

A low energy background shifts the apparent color of an object toward the high energy end of the spectrum. And a high energy background causes a shift in the opposite direction. (It's like brightness constancy: a low intensity background shifts the apparent brightness of an object toward a higher brightness, while a high intensity background causes a shift in the opposite direction.) So a yellow object on a red background appears more greenish than it is. And that same yellow object appears more reddish than it is when on a green background. For any pair of colors we can predict the direction of the shift from the color spectrum.

Color contrast: a shift in the apparent color of an object away from the color of the background.

This color contrast effect is also a good example of an illusion, as it can make something appear other than it really is. We'll look at a more precise definition of illusion in the next section.

- ■25 Define color contrast and cite an example.
- ■26 How does color contrast relate to the color spectrum?
- ■27 Thought question: We may have evolved with brightness contrast partially as a result of the survival value of brightness constancy. What about color constancy? Do you think there is such a thing? How would it relate to color contrast? Hints: Under what conditions does the color of our overall illumination change? (Keep your eyes open for a couple of days and nights — dusks and dawns — indoors and out-of-doors.) Which of those conditions were present when our color vision evolved?

SENSORY AND PERCEPTUAL STIMULUS CONTROL

Eight:ten and there sat Dawn's date, champing at the bit, ready to boogie all night long. There sat Dawn's date on the unmade bed, clearing his throat, a discreet cough now and then, scraping his feet, tapping his foot — impatient, dejected, ignored, mad as hell.

"Hey, Mae, I feel like I'm up in the air on this sensation-perception thing; like, what is it? Seems like they've talked all around it without talking about it. What's a sensation? What's a perception?"

"That's the wrong question, since they're not really things," Mae replied. "There's no such thing as a sensation, or a perception either. They're types of stimulus control. Like we've just been reading about a kind of perceptual control — size constancy."

"What's that mean, 'perceptual control'?" Dawn asked, no clearer than before.

"Well, perceptual control is based on complex stimuli, like those involved with size constancy."

"What's complex about 'em?"

"Well, they involve more than just one feature of a stimulus — they involve both the size of the image on your retina and its distance from you. So two things are needed for you to say how tall a person is — two things must work together to produce their effect. The photons that bounce off the person and onto your retina make an image of some size or other. But that's not enough since the person's also some distance or other from you. Those two features, size of the image and distance of the person, combine to control your response of saying how tall the person is."

"And sensory stimulus control only involves one feature of a stimulus," Dawn added.

"Right."

"But that doesn't make sense," Dawn complained. "Everything you look at's got more than one feature; like what color a person . . . I mean, like that wall there's a putrid green; but it's also some distance from me, about three feet, I'd say. And its ugly little photons form an image of some size or other on my retina. So that all makes it look to me like color exerts a perceptual stimulus control, since it has three features — color, distance, and size. But I don't think the authors see it that way, since color was mainly covered in the sensory chapter."

Mae replied, "You got to listen close to get the message. It's a difference between how many features just happen to be there and how many features must be there to get proper stimulus control. Like, when you're looking at the color, the color's what's happening, not the other things. Not how far the wall is from you, and not how big the image is on your retina — they don't matter. You'll still call it putrid green, even if it's a smaller wall a long way off. What color you call it only depends on one thing, the energy of the photons hitting your retina, not those other things. And that's just simple sensory control, where a single feature of the stimulus controls your response. But how tall you say someone is depends on at least two things — the person's distance from you and the size of their image on your retina; that's perceptual control: at least two features of the stimulus combine to control your response."

"Okay, I got it," Dawn said. "But how does that jell with what we read in the last section, on color contrast? Remember: the color a thing appears to be depends on the color around it. Something green looks a little bluish when it's on a red background, but it looks a little reddish on a blue background.

"Yet," Dawn continued, "you

said the color we call an object depends on only one thing — it depends on the energy of the photons from that object, nothing else; but color contrast says it also depends on the energy of the photons from its background — the background color."

"That's okay," Mae replied. "I mean some features don't affect the way we see color — features like size and distance; so color does exert simple sensory control as far as size and distance are concerned. But other features do affect the way we see color — other features like the color of the background. So the color of an object **does** exert complex perceptual control when it combines with some other feature like color of the background."

Dawn nodded. "Then we're looking at stimulus control in both cases: Sensory processes involve control by a single stimulus feature independent of how other features might affect its control. And perception involves how control by one feature is affected by other features. Seems tight enough; I can get next to that."

Perception: stimulus control by two or more interacting stimulus features, where the value of one stimulus feature affects the nature of our reaction to another feature.

Sensory process: stimulus control by one stimulus feature in relation to other features that do not affect our reactions to that controlling feature.

"On the one hand, we say we're under **sensory** control when we look at the colors of objects at different distances. It's sensory, since changing the distance does not change the nature of our reaction to the color. On the other hand, we're under **perceptual** control when we look at the colors of objects against different colored backgrounds. That's perceptual effect since changing the color of the background does change the nature of our reaction to the color of the object," Mae added.

"And, I can see where they're coming from on that illusion thing too," Dawn kept on. "We call something an illusion when our response to one feature of a stimulus is affected by some other feature as well. Of course, that seems to define the whole field of perception, since perception always involves the way two or more features

interact. And sometimes the two features combine to cause us to respond to things right — like with brightness constancy. But sometimes two features combine to cause us to respond wrong — like color contrast; and we say that the perception control causes an illusion when it causes us to make that mistake."

Illusion: stimulus control when two or more features interact causing us to make an error in our response to a stimulus.

Done with her studies and her talking, Dawn got up to go out with her man of the evening. "You know, Mae, this was kind of fun. I guess I really do enjoy trying to figure out complex things like this from time to time. But not all the time. See you later."

■28 According to this book, are there such **things** as sensations and perceptions?
■29 Cite an instance where color is involved in sensory control. Cite one where it is involved in perceptual control. What's the difference in those two instances?
■30 Define perception and sensory process.
■31 Define illusion and cite an instance.

CONCLUSIONS

As we've seen, perception deals with topics where the relation between the stimulus and the response is often somewhat complex and strange. So following the standard approach, psychologists invent unobservable concepts to deal with these complex relations between stimulus and response since the data themselves are so complex. That might seem like a simple way to handle the problem — like our basic concepts must be at least as complex as the data they explain. Thus the standard approach invents concepts like "perceptions". When asked why we respond as we do to complex stimuli, the standard answer is, "because our inner self perceives the world in a complex way, causing us to act as we do."

But there are at least two problems with that approach: First, it just pushes the question back one stage further, when it tries to explain our actions in terms of assumed perceptions. Such an approach gives a false feeling that we've solved the problem. Yet the problem still exists, since we must now ask, "Why do our perceptions act as they do? What controls them?"

Second, the standard approach is not parsimonious. It's too easy a cop-out to invent a perception and the way it acts, in an effort to deal with each new bit of perceptual data we encounter. Such an approach tends to burden us with unneeded concepts. Science has made much more progress by being parsimonious, by using the smallest number of concepts possible to account for the data.

So, in this book we try to account for the data of psychology in terms of a small number of basic concepts, mainly stimuli, responses, and results. This approach makes little use of assumed concepts that can't be directly observed (though later we will project from the observed instances of these concepts to instances less easy to observe).

We have tried to follow this general approach in dealing with some of the topics of perception. This helps us dispel a bit of the mystery surrounding the field. But the task is not a simple one, even though our basic concepts are. We look at perception in terms of straight-forward events and the relations among those events. We believe there is no such thing as "perception". Instead, perception refers to a relation. Perception is a complex form of stimulus control, with two or more stimulus features combining to control the response. This approach provides a way of looking at many perception problems: the visual cliff with its possible combined inner-ear (blood-pressure) changes and distance stimuli; size constancy with its combined retinal image and distance stimuli; brightness constancy with its combined object and background intensity; and color contrast, an illusion, with its combined object and background color.

We have tried to reduce perception to its basic elements. Science and human knowledge progress in that way — but it's not an easy job.

BIOSOCIAL BASES

We've looked at the biophysical bases of our behavior — how our physical world affects us as biological creatures causing us to act as we do. Now we'll look at the biosocial bases of our behavior — how our social world affects our actions.

To become more human is to become more social. We human beings start as infants mainly under the same biophysical control as other creatures. But our actions soon become more and more controlled by the actions of others around us, until, as adults, there is little we do that isn't greatly influenced by social factors.

Almost all of our uniquely human actions result from the influence other human beings have upon us. Our human biology has given us the ability to learn and the physical structure needed to acquire complex language skills. And in turn, these language skills affect nearly everything else that we do. If we didn't have language, the present section of this book would be short indeed. But with our language, we can act in an intelligent manner: we can think; and we can have social values, attitudes, roles, moral and rational control, consciousness, and feelings of emotion. These learning and language-based factors all combine to make us the complex, fascinating, and vexing creatures we have evolved into.

CHAPTER 12 DEVELOPMENT OF BASIC RESPONSES

INTRODUCTION

In this chapter, we will look at how children develop basic responses — responses like nursing, focusing, and walking. We will see how children's learning environments interact with their inherited biological capacities to produce those responses.

In addition, we will study two approaches to child rearing. The first, the natural approach, says we should not interfere with the way the child develops in any planned manner. The second, the helping approach, says we should use all our knowledge to help the child develop in worthwhile ways.

PHYLOGENETIC AND ONTOGENETIC DEVELOPMENT

In the first chapters of this book, we saw how the species develops — this is called "phylogenetic development". Now we will see how the single creature develops — "ontogenetic development".

Phylogenetic development: the development of a species from an earlier form, through evolution. Often it develops into more complex structures and functions.

Ontogenetic development: the development of a single creature during its lifetime. Often the creature becomes more complex as it develops.

The world controls the way both the species and the single creature develop. That world causes phylogenetic development by selecting members of the species. It does this by selecting those members that have evolved response patterns that help them survive. The same world also causes ontogenetic development, this time by selecting response patterns that help the single creature survive. It does this by reinforcing or punishing those response patterns.

But the world shapes the ontogenetic development of the creature in more ways than through learning. For instance, the creature's sensory and response capabilities increase as the embryo matures from egg to newborn infant. This is greatly controlled by its inherited structure. (The inherited structure affects ontogenetic development, though that structure itself resulted from phylogenetic development.) And, of course, people's environments also affect how they develop, with children's development controlled by diet, exercise, level of stimulation, etc.

Thus three features combine to determine how the child develops: 1) the way the world causes the child to learn certain acts, 2) the biophysical structures the child inherits, and 3) the physical features of the world that impinge upon the child.

Now a young child's social world, mainly parents and siblings, controls much of what that child learns. This is because we humans are among the most social of all animals. Our social nature results from depending on our parents to help us survive for so long; thus we acquire many of our response patterns through social contact with other human creatures. And these response patterns are fairly common. They include such things as locomotor acts, sense-organ adjustment acts — like focusing and convergence — and protective acts. Such patterns

occur among people in different social settings, as well as among people in the same social setting. People have similar actions to the extent that similar social groups rear them. And most social groups are fairly similar, since we all live in much the same physical world with its gravity, temperature and seasonal changes, day-night cycles, needed fuels, harmful conditions . . . That world provides us all with much the same biophysical bases for our cultures.

- 1 Define phylogenetic development.
- 2 Define ontogenetic development.
- 3 What three factors combine to determine how the child develops?
- 4 Why do we share many common response patterns, even though those response patterns may have been acquired through various social contacts?
- 5 Thought question: Based on your knowledge of different cultures and different physical environments, can you think of examples that support, and examples that contradict, the notion that many of our socially learned acts are fairly common within and among cultures?

PRENATAL DEVELOPMENT

Carol and Chet had been married three years, married not so much from choice as from "need". Carol had become pregnant during her third year at BSU. Chet did what he felt was his duty. However, he remained reluctant and pouting, showing Carol the burden he took on. On the other hand, she had to drop out of school to get a job. They needed her income because her parents no longer saw fit to support a married daughter . . . "If she's old enough to get married then she's damned well old enough to support herself." . . . That view also helped her parents out of a financial bind.

So Chet Jr. grew and developed inside Carol — a tiny fetus floating in his amniotic sac — while his mother worked at the Mental Health Clinic, waiting for the baby to be born. During this time, the fetus developed a body and a set of basic actions. Each day he took on more and more of the acts he would exhibit at birth, becoming a little, human, biophysical system.

Prenatal period: the period from conception to the birth of the creature.

Amniotic sac: the sac filled with protective fluid which holds the fetus.

Fetus: a prenatal creature in its more advanced stages of development: the prenatal human after the sixth to eighth week of pregnancy.

Fetal Chetty had plenty of chance for action inside his mother as she went about her work at the clinic. A little pressure here when she bent over to pick up a pencil; a nudge there as she leaned against a file cabinet. It wasn't the quiet, sleepy world we might think, but one filled with action, action that might help him develop those reactions he would display soon after birth.

Carol commented about how much Chet Jr. moved around during the last months of her pregnancy, but from the fetal view there was a lot going on outside his amniotic sac as such things affected him more and more. Thus the little human biophysical system also began to respond more and more: Pressure on the cheek caused a head-turning response; a touch on the lips caused a slight sucking response; a touch on the hand caused a grasping response; and a touch on the feet caused a retraction response. Researchers have noted such reactions while watching fetuses, after being delivered prematurely through Cesarian Section.

Was Chet Jr. maturing in a passive manner, showing his new responses as the time arose? Or was each stimulus also a chance for that response to develop further? Could Chet Jr. have really been learning those actions because of the effects of the tactual stimuli? We don't know if he was, but we do know that Chet Jr. was able to learn even before he was born.

A scientist discovered fetal learning in the late 1940's. This researcher used a respondent conditioning procedure with seven-month fetuses. The unconditioned stimulus (the loud noise from a large oak clapper) elicited the unconditioned "startle" response (a leg kick from the fetus). The stimulus to be conditioned was a slight touch to the mother's abdomen. The experimenter recorded the conditioned kick response in two ways: 1) the mother pushed a button to indicate when she felt a kick by the fetal infant; and 2) a pressure-measuring device recorded pressure on the mother's abdomen produced by such a kick. The conditioned stimulus (the touch to the mother's abdomen) did not produce a kick by itself. But the clapper noise always did. (Very few mothers showed any startle response to the clapper sound as they were warned of its occurrence in advance.) All three fetuses tested in this experiment acquired the conditioned kicking response to the conditioned, touch stimulus.

Tactual stimulus: stimulus having to do with touch.

- 6 Define fetus, amniotic sac, and prenatal.
- 7 Describe the behavior of the fetus.
- 8 Can the fetus learn?
- 9 Define tactual stimulus.

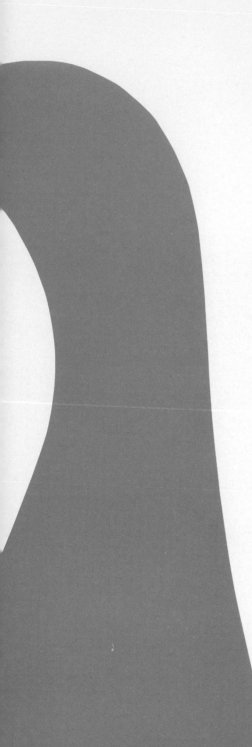

MATURATION VS. LEARNING

As we just saw, active learning as well as passive maturing can affect how children develop — even in the prenatal state. The question of the relative roles of learning and maturation becomes even more crucial after the child's birth.

Throughout this chapter we will deal with issues that can be looked at from either the maturation or the learning views.

Maturation view: development of responses follows a biologically predetermined sequence.

Learning view: development of responses results from learning.

Both views try to account for the facts of how the child develops — the facts that the child's actions become broader in scope and more complex as the child grows older. On the one hand, the maturation view stresses this notion: the child's behavior becomes more complex simply because it matures, a normal biological process that takes place over time. This would happen much as the growth of the child's body results from biological processes while the child grows older. Such processes would function in a normal world with good sources of fuel and only small amounts of contact with harmful states.

This may seem like a sound view since the child does indeed grow older, the clearest fact about the child as it develops. So it seems normal that the child's behavior should grow just as its body does.

On the other hand, the learning view stresses this notion: the child's behavior becomes more complex simply because the child learns as a result of rewards and punishers. Such changes need not result from maturation.

Of course, each view notes that both sets of causal factors may be involved. The maturation view does acknowledge that learning occurs, while many people who support the learning view feel biological maturation may play some role in the child's behavior. But both views tend to stress one set of causal factors as being more crucial than the other, either the maturation factors or the learning factors.

But it is meaningful to ask whether maturation or learning plays a specific role in the way a specific response develops, though both may play a role in the way the child develops overall. Consider how typing skills develop. Clearly the person must develop the needed muscles, skeletal structure, etc. to support those responses. But it is also clear that nothing about having that musculature will cause a person to develop those skills. The maturational factors simply allow the person to develop such skills. The person learns how to type. So it is meaningful to ask whether some specific set of responses develop due to learning or maturation.

In the next sections we will see how these views apply to certain
areas of child development.

- 10 Define the maturation and learning views of child development.
- 11 To what extent do these two views acknowledge each other?
- 12 When is it meaningful to ask whether maturation or learning
  plays a key role?

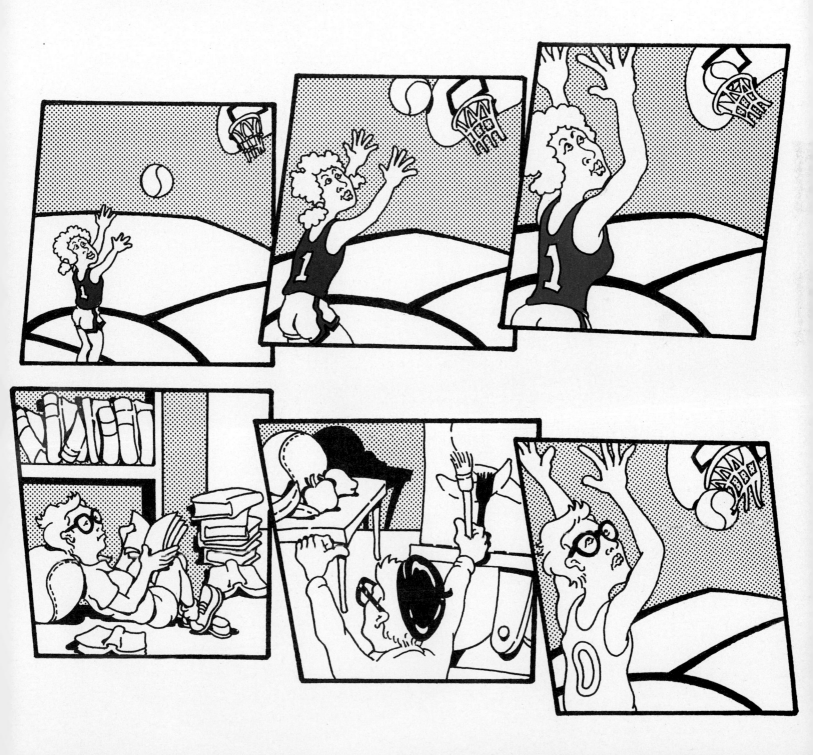

INGESTION

Carol's wish had come true — she had been able to work almost to the day she gave birth to little Chet. And big Chet's wish had also come true — Carol had delivered unto him a man child — healthy, handsome, and howling.

* * *

A few days after her son's birth, Carol was home and into the thick of it once again. Big Chet shouted as he ran out the door, late for class, "Remember, I'll be home for supper about 6:00." Carol nodded, too involved with feeding little Chet to answer. Not that it was any more easy to feed the son than to feed the father; Carol was hurt that little Chet didn't seem to like her milk, any better than big Chet liked her cooking.

* * *

The mountain came to Mohammed. The white object approached little Chet as he lay there. The photons bounced into his eyes. The three types of receptors in his retina fired. But they fired less and less as the white object moved closer to his face. Then the receptors in his skin started firing rapid pulses up through his central nervous system, as the object touched his nose and mouth. Shortly after that, the object stopped his breathing, when it covered his nostrils and little mouth.

He jerked his head away — jerking violently and twisting until he could breathe again — a valiant escape response — perhaps unlearned, perhaps learned during the first few contacts of that sort. In any case his response helped him survive. But the act concerned Carol; for with every violent twist he seemed to reject her breast, to reject her as a mother. She had looked forward to breast-feeding. She had been told it was a warm, intimate, rewarding way for a mother and child to relate; but she was having as much trouble being accepted by little Chet as by his father.

Am I a failure as a wife and mother? She was worried. So she called her boss at the clinic, Dr. Stein, a woman she could talk to, a woman with wisdom and compassion. Dr. Stein had already helped Carol get through the first few months of her new life as a wife. Perhaps she would also help now.

"Don't worry, Carol, it's just a little problem of technique, nothing more. Your baby doesn't reject you. You need a little more structured feedback on your feeding technique, that's all. Most likely you're covering his mouth and nose at the same time you're trying to nurse him. It's a fairly common mistake. Mothers often fail to notice, but infants never fail to — a good thing for them.

"Just be careful how you hold his head and your breast, when you're feeding him. Better give your doctor a ring if you still have problems, but I think you'll be okay."

Carol went back to little Chet, more certain of herself, but still concerned. At first he was reserved, to say the least, balking and squirming. The stimuli paired with her breast had become learned punishers or warning signals since they had been paired a few times with his impaired breathing. Still Carol didn't give up; and she and her baby were both rewarded for her efforts. The learned punishers lost their effect since they were no longer being paired with the unlearned punisher of not being able to breathe. Little Chet made fewer and fewer escape responses and more rewarding nursing responses. Soon he was nursing with vigor, causing Carol to feel much more secure.

***

The nursing response provokes a lot of interest, because it's often at the center of the heredity and maturation vs. learning debate. For one thing, infants inherit the ability to be rewarded by milk. This causes them to learn quickly any easy response producing this reward. (By the way, research has shown that the nature of the milk effects its reward value, sweeter milk being a bigger reward.)

There is another result of the infant's nursing response. This result may also act as a reward or punisher causing that response to be learned or dropped out. The result is the sensory stimuli coming from the nursing response. Researchers compared the flexible rubber nipple of a baby bottle with a less flexible rounded tube. The baby's nursing response was rewarded more by the stimuli from the flexible nipple. In the same way, the tactual stimuli from the mother's own nipple also affect the reward value of nursing, as nipples differ from each other in shape and texture.

Furthermore, we all evolved with many tactual receptors in our lips. So, some kinds of touching of our lips are very rewarding; for instance, when the infant's mouth touches its mother's breast.

But there are also learning factors. Sometimes a newborn infant needs guidance from its mother before it can nurse. That mother must teach this "natural" response to her baby by adjusting the infant's mouth until it learns to latch on to the nipple. And the fetus may also be learning as it gets tactual stimuli from sucking while still in its amniotic sac.

Nursing is rewarding for the mother as well as the child. Again, tactual receptors play a role as there are many in her breasts. There are also instinctive rewards, events made rewarding by biochemical changes, namely the rewards resulting from the nursing of her post-natal, swollen breasts. So these factors all combine to bring together the hungry infant and the nursing mother. They make it likely the infant will soon learn or make the response that gets it food. And they also make it likely the mother will soon learn the response that gets her both the tactual rewards and the decrease in discomfort.

That alone is enough for most creatures in the wild state; but a heavy cultural program also strengthens child care for many human parents. Many human females are exposed to this program for years; they receive much schooling in both the delights and duties of caring for and nursing their offspring.

For most of us, the crucial point is that we do start nursing soon after birth. We may be born with a nursing response, one that's built-in; or we may be born with a set of unlearned rewards ready to help us quickly learn that response before we starve to death. Or we may be born with a response that is more or less ready to go even though it is also shaped by unlearned rewards; for instance, the sucking component of the nursing response occurs in the fetus. In any case, we do survive.

▪13 What common mistake do some nursing mothers make? Analyze the infant's reaction in terms of rewards, punishers, etc.

▪14 What are the rewards for the nursing infant?

▪15 What are the rewards for the nursing mother?

▪16 What are some factors affecting the reward value of the results of nursing for the human infant?

▪17 Thought question: What programs are human males exposed to in our culture concerning the "delights and duties of child care"? Should men or women be exposed to **any** sort of programs? If so, what do you think they should be like? If not, why not?

IRRITANTS — HARMFUL STATES

The infant, animal or human, is born with the responses it needs to deal with most harmful events it contacts, even shortly after birth.

The Moro reflex

Carol was trying to do it just the right way as she nursed baby Chet, taking care to hold him as the nurse had taught her. But, once she did let go of little Chet's head when she was distracted by big Chet as he entered her room. Within an instant, however, her concern shifted back to her son, who was fending for himself with all his might, clutching her breast. The infant had displayed the Moro reflex.

Moro reflex: the newborn infant makes a clutching response when its head loses support and falls backward. This response consists of stretching out its arms and bringing them together over its chest.

Reflex: a stimulus response relation. It refers to the idea that a stimulus elicits a response. It can be either an unconditioned reflex (an unconditioned stimulus and response) or a conditioned reflex (a conditioned stimulus and response).

The Moro reflex must have helped our ancestors survive. It's still of some slight value, even with as concerned a mother as Carol. It must have been even more worthwhile at the time it evolved in lower species whose mothers were not so well-trained in the care of their infants.

- ▪18 Define the Moro reflex.
- ▪19 Define reflex.
- ▪20 Thought question: What species still **need** the Moro reflex to survive?

Other reflexes

Other reflexes protect the eye of the infant, just as the Moro reflex protects its head and body. The infant will close its eyes tightly when the cornea of the eye or even the bridge of its nose is tapped. This might have evolved because it helps keep the infant's visual system intact despite being hit by harmful objects.

In fact, the infant protects its eyes from objects even before they make direct contact with the child. Infants place their hands in front of their face if an object moves rapidly toward them. They do this even when they are only a few days old. An optical expansion pattern seems to control this response. That pattern consists of a rapid increase in the size of the image on the infant's retina as the object comes nearer. Careful research has shown the crucial role of the optical expansion pattern in this reflex by ruling out other stimulus features such as the size of the projection of the image on the retina, the motion of air against the face, binocular convergence, and focusing.

On the one hand, the optical expansion pattern might be an unconditioned stimulus, one that elicits the reflex of bringing the hands over the face. On the other hand, the sight of the expansion

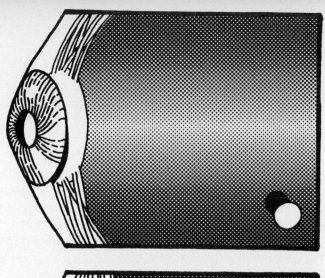

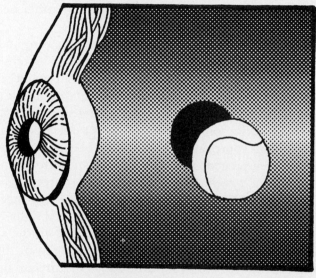

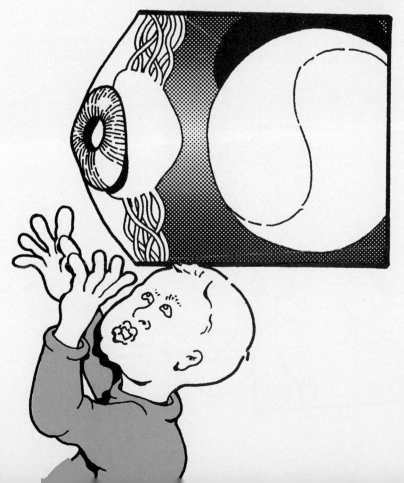

pattern might be a punisher, one escaped by the hands-over-the-face response.

But why would the infant learn that hand movement as a response that escapes the punishing sight? Instead, it could learn the simpler eyelid-closure response, since that response would also get rid of the sight of the optical expansion pattern. Well, simply closing the eyes would often not protect them enough from approaching objects. Whereas, a child's hands in front of its face might. But the child might learn eye-closure, the least effective response, if it were just a learned response, escaping the sight of the expansion pattern. Yet, it seems the species would better survive if it evolved so that the optical expansion pattern acted as an unconditioned stimulus eliciting the hand movements, a reaction that would better protect the eyes. So we might conclude that the face-covering response is most likely an unconditioned reflex — not a learned escape response.

■21 What are two responses the infant makes that protect its eyes?
■22 Is the hand-movement response most likely a learned escape response or an unlearned reflex?

SENSORY-MOTOR RESPONSES

Sensory processes

Little Chet was born with his sensory systems complete and intact, though some of them still needed a little fine tuning, as with all human infants. For instance, he was neither able to focus nor cause his eyes to converge during the first weeks after his birth. So visual stimuli were not too clear to him. But human infants don't need to be under such precise control of visual stimuli at that time, since they aren't mobile anyhow. Instead they rely on other people to bring food and keep harm away.

A maturational view might assume acts like focusing and converging improve because the infant's muscles and nervous system mature over time. But a learning view suggests the infant might simply need time to learn those actions. If that's the case, we can ask what stimuli might reward focusing and binocular convergence. Two sources of reward seem to exist: one learned, the other unlearned.

The sight of an approaching parent might become a learned reward. Such sights often precede biological rewards, like food and comfort, or the removal of wet diapers and other mild sources of harm.

But, why wouldn't that fuzzy, double-imaged sight become just as strong a learned reward as the sharp, single-imaged sight? In fact, why wouldn't the infant try to maintain its poor vision, since that poor vision might have become a strong learned reward first? Such a reward could cause it to avoid the strange but precise image when the infant focused or converged its eyes.

Well, here's one possible reason the infant might prefer better vision. When it looked at a clear image the infant could discriminate better between those stimuli paired with other rewards than those

stimuli not so paired. Then the sharp images would themselves become learned rewards sooner than would their fuzzy double-imaged counterparts, since they would be more consistent in their pairing with other rewards.

But we can't be confident in relying on the learned-reward value of the visual stimulus to account for the infant's rapid learning of how to focus and converge. Especially since the infant might never learn those acts, if the blurred double image has the greater learned reward value. So we should search for another source of reward.

What about the unlearned reward value of the visual stimulus? Perhaps a well-focused, single, sharp image is a stronger unlearned reward than is the blurred, double image, for the newborn infant. We may have evolved that way because it ensured that we would learn how to focus and converge. That way the development of those responses would not depend upon the somewhat chancy acquisition of learned rewards. And perhaps that unlearned reward alone causes the infant to learn the correct muscle responses needed to focus and converge its eyes. But whatever the causes, most of us have evolved so that we have those receptor-adjustment responses we need by the time we require them.

■23 At birth, the infant is not able to make two responses needed for precise visual control. What are those responses?
■24 Give two accounts that might explain how the infant comes to be able to make those responses.
■25 What are two sources of reward that might be involved?

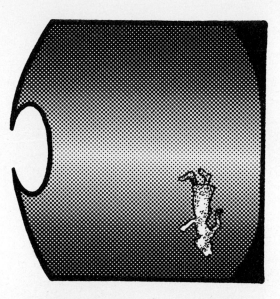

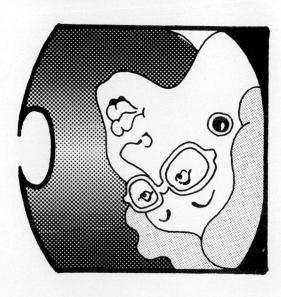

The helping approach and motor skills

It's important to decide which view to adopt — the learning or the maturation view. They can greatly affect the way we rear our children. The learning view suggests we can insure that our children have the chance to learn worthwhile skills. We can do this by rewarding early actions that look somewhat like correct acts. We can shape those acts that will be of value to our children now and later on. One area of skills to which the learning view addresses itself is the area of motor skills.

Motor skills: skills of muscular movement.

* * *

Because of her learning view, Carol used the helping approach in raising Chet. She hoped to provide a world that would be responsive enough to reward his actions, so he would learn to behave in worthwhile ways. She hung small toys from his crib, so his slightest motion would start lightweight mobiles spinning around, making a delightful tinkling sound and whirling sight, rewarding his movements.

She also played games with him, including peek-a-boo. She'd hide behind a blanket draped over the end of Chet's crib, then she'd poke her head out singing, "peek-a-boo", whenever he babbled or made a pleasant cooing sound. Sure enough, Carol's peek-a-boo must have been a reward, since little Chet soon began babbling and cooing at a much higher rate whenever they played the game.

* * *

A few months after his son was born, Chet noticed Carol and little Chet playing a new game: Carol placed a brightly colored rattle a few inches beyond little Chet's reach; then she gave him a big hug with a loving shout of joy, each time he was able to grasp the noise-making toy. The baby's actions got two types of rewards: First, there were the rewards that had a natural relation to the response — the audio-visual-tactual rewards resulting from grasping the object. And second, there were the personal rewards, a less normal result of our effect on the physical world — the hug and loving shout of joy, perhaps mixed in with a kiss, a smile, or a laugh.

Big Chet also noticed Carol was placing the toy farther and farther away from the baby as he became more and more skilled at reaching it. (Before too long, little Chet would be able to crawl halfway across their small living room floor.)

■26 In what practical way does it matter whether we follow the maturation or the learning approach?

■27 Define motor skills.

■28 How can you help your child learn motor skills?

THE DEVELOPMENTAL SEQUENCE

The helping approach and the developmental sequence

"Hi, Chet," Carol greeted her husband from the floor. "Would you mind giving me a hand with Chetty? I've been playing a little game with him. I think it'll help him learn some useful skills."

"What are you tryin' to do, make a marathon crawler out of the kid?" Chet asked in a tone that said he wasn't too excited by his son's becoming a renowned crawler. "I don't get it. What for? Kids learn to crawl without some silly mother trying to teach 'em."

"Sure they do. I just want to help him a little bit, that's all."

"Well, it's not normal. Kid's crawl just because they want to crawl, that's all. Why make such a big deal out of it?"

"The way I look at it, they crawl because crawling gets rewarded. Maybe something about the act is a reward itself; but it also gets them places where there are other rewards," Carol replied.

"So let him alone and he'll get there by himself," Chet argued.

"All I'm tryin' to do is just add a few more rewards — just give Chetty a little extra attention when he starts moving around. I'm just tryin' to make his world a little more rewarding; and I'm just tryin' to put those rewards where they'll do the most good in helping him learn."

"Well, he'll learn all he needs to know soon enough," Chet said.

Carol answered, "Maybe, but it seems to me he'll cope with life a lot better if he gets in there and deals with it; he'll get more rewards from life the sooner he learns to crawl and to walk — in fact, he'll get and give more rewards, the sooner he learns all the skills we use in dealing with our world. And he'll be able to learn much more about the world the sooner he can get up and move around in it. He'll learn about the world by dealing with it. And he'll act in a more intelligent manner, if he's learned more about what's going on. The longer he sits in his crib, the less he'll have a chance to learn. We don't have to stand by, passive, while the rewards that just happen to be around at the moment may or may not help him learn worthwhile skills." Carol stopped, knowing she had come on much stronger than Chet liked.

"I don't know why you can't leave off buggin' that poor kid half to death. You should have supper ready by now anyhow. Besides, all kids develop at pretty much the same rate — and in pretty much the same way; the kid'll crawl when he's ready to crawl. And he'll walk when he's ready to walk. Leave him alone. It's crazy to expect a young baby to be able to stand up and run around the house no matter how many of those damned rewards you give him. He just don't have the muscles and bone structure yet."

"You're right about that," Carol replied. "Chetty's muscles must develop well enough to support him and his actions. And that is a normal result of biological growth and exercise. But we're not guaranteed Chetty will learn how to use his muscles to reach and grasp, and crawl and walk if we simply let him mature. His acts must get rewards if he's going to learn. Of course he naturally gets some rewards for moving about. But we can give him more."

"Well, there's no guarantee your rewards are going to help either," Chet replied. "So just leave him alone and let nature take care of it."

Carol had a brief urge to let nature take care of big Chet's meal though she said nothing.

■29 Why might someone go out of their way to help a normal child learn to walk?

Learning, maturation, and the developmental sequence

Carol and Chet's debate on maturation vs. learning keeps cropping up since it is a common one in the field of child development: Little Chet's actions become more and more complex as he grows older. They allow him to deal with greater and greater portions of his world.

Chet's actions become more and more complex as he grows older. They allow him to deal with greater and greater portions of his world.

Did he inherit a biological structure that affects the rate and path of his progress with only a little help from his normal environment? Is his development mainly the result of maturation? Or is the environment the main cause for the way he develops, as long as he has the more or less normal biological equipment needed to respond? Is his development mainly based on learning? Those are the maturation and the learning points of view. And they both deal with the "developmental sequence".

Developmental sequence: the normal order in which behavior develops for a given species.

The maturation view states that there must be some sort of biological predetermined sequence of human development, since most children do develop in much the same sequence and at much the same rate. The learning view states that this developmental sequence may be due to the fact that we all live in the same physical world, with its gravity, its bumps and bruises, its good tastes and its bad tastes. And those things affect us all in much the same way — causing us all to develop in much the same way.

Here's one of the problems with the maturation view. Those motor skills were most likely learned through operant conditioning since they are now clearly controlled by their results. You don't walk someplace unless that act has been reinforced in the past; and you don't pick up something unless that act has been reinforced in the past. So it doesn't seem consistent to say those complex, operant acts are merely products of maturation, not based on learning through rewards and punishers. It's almost like saying people will be able to drive a car if they simply sit around waiting until they mature. Those skills don't differ much from motor skills like walking. It's just that the role of learning is much clearer with driving. But the theory of maturation makes no more sense in one instance than in the other.

Chet is right: most children do progress at much the same rate and in much the same sequence. But that doesn't mean they inherit some sort of blueprint for development. Maybe all children seem to develop in the same way because their worlds are all much the same: they have to crawl before they can walk, they have to stand before they can walk, they have to stand before they can reach things on the coffee table, and they bang their heads when they stand up under that table. Their physical world is much the same, no matter where the child grows up, no matter who the parents are; and that physical world provides many of the rewards and punishers that shape the sequence of skills the child learns.

***

Carol couldn't help going on with her debate with Chet, though only to herself, as she fixed dinner. *What I'm doing is just adding some rewards to make it easier and better for Chetty, that's all.*

Besides, I feel real good about being able to help Chetty. I just felt like a passive by-stander at first, but now I see I can play an active role in helping him learn and grow.

I suppose I shouldn't feel this way, but just being like most mothers gets a little boring; I have so much more fun when I feel like I'm really doing something, when I feel like I'm really helping Chetty. I guess I should be happy just to have Chet and Chetty, but I really like it when I feel like I'm playing a special role in Chetty's growth as a human being.

"Come on, Carol, let's get a little food on the table, will ya?"

- 30 Define developmental sequence.
- 31 Most children progress at much the same rate in much the same sequence. Explain this from a learning view.
- 32 Thought question: What sort of program of rewards and punishers prior to their marriage do you suppose set up Chet and Carol to act the way they do toward each other now? What sort of program of current rewards and punishers keeps them acting that way? What's wrong with it? How could they change this?

THE NATURAL AND THE HELPING APPROACHES

The natural and helping approaches compared

Carol and Chet's debate also involves another common question: whether or not we should try to affect the standard way our children develop, the way that seems so natural to us.

The helping approach: we should go out of our way in a planned, careful, and thoughtful manner to influence the development of our children along worthwhile paths.

The natural approach: any planned intervention on our part is either not needed, fruitless, or a source of problems.

The "natural approach" suggests we may be heading for real trouble, if we try to change this relation between ourselves and our world, if we try to affect the way we develop. Our biophysical structure evolved allowing us to succeed in dealing with our world — allowing us to survive long enough to produce offspring — thereby keeping our species alive. So we should let well enough alone. We may end up creating more problems than we solve.

We can find support for this natural approach by looking at many of our attempts to make our lives better when we may really end up making them worse. Factories produce pollution as well as needed goods. Cars produce pollution as well as a ride to where we need to go. Insect sprays produce poison for us as well as for insects.

Thus, it might seem, we should stay away from any attempts to change the status quo between us and our world. But the status quo has already changed, whether we like it or not. Now we live in a world that differs a great deal from the one in which our species evolved. So now we must deal with the results of a change we had no vote in. We need to brush and floss our teeth, since our culture has programmed us to consume foods that weren't around when we evolved. We need to jog or ride our bicycle, since our culture has programmed us to lead a life that requires much less effort to get our needed fuels. We can attempt to get back to that good old life, the life where the chances were much higher that we'd die of starvation, yet much lower that we'd die of a heart attack or lose all of our teeth. But in the meantime we must deal with the fact that we do live in a changed world.

Now others say we shouldn't try to aid nature as our children develop; we shouldn't add rewards to help them learn. Instead, we should leave the job to the physical world of nature and the rewards it provides. In fact, we all aid nature as our children develop their learned actions. We do this by adding personal rewards, though we may not intend to.

The first time our child toddles across the floor, for instance, we beam with pride at our great feat. After all, we created the child, an infant clever enough to learn how to walk all by itself. We shout with joy at each milestone passed as our children develop. And this beaming and shouting are not without their effects as rewards. Most parents will attest to that, though they may not always be too tuned-in to the effects of their acts. So it's hard for us parents not to be involved as our children develop motor skills, whether or not we think nature is just taking its course. The helping approach merely suggests we be more thorough, more planned, and thereby, more effective.

Still, many argue that our current ways of rearing our children are right and natural, just as they might argue that stuffing those little children with sweet-tasting but unhealthy foods is right, a position many parents, in fact, take. But it's foolish to argue that our current methods are natural, even though they may seem natural. We can't argue for these methods, since we don't know how our ancestors raised their children at the time our species evolved.

But, we do know how rewards help our children learn new skills. And we do have data about what some of those skills are that will help our children deal with their world. Therefore, as parents, perhaps we have a duty to arrange our children's world so they learn as many useful skills as possible, as early as they can.

In our culture, most parents subscribe to both views, at least to some extent. On the one hand, we tend to justify what we happen to be doing. We say it's "nature's way", our children will mature any-how. On the other hand, we also buy educational toys for them, we have them watch *Sesame Street*, and we send them to pre-schools. We parents can have a profound and positive effect on how our children's actions develop even without the aid of those fine helping tools. We can do this by using a planned, careful, thoughtful helping approach to child rearing. We can do it ourselves.

Of course, we should always watch out for any problems arising from our new learning-based helping approach to child rearing. For instance, suppose we teach our children intellectual and academic skills, as the next chapters will suggest. Then we should try to make sure those behaviors don't extinguish if our child is enrolled in a standard grade-school classroom. We must take care that our child does not become bored through lack of rewarding challenges.

But we should also avoid a much more common pitfall if we use the helping approach. We must beware of becoming boorish parents, bragging about the great feats our children accomplish. In any case, we must use a grain of salt in dealing with arguments that say we should not try anything our grandparents didn't do.

■33 Define the "natural" approach to child rearing. What is the argument in support of it?

■34 Define the "helping" approach. And what's the argument for it?

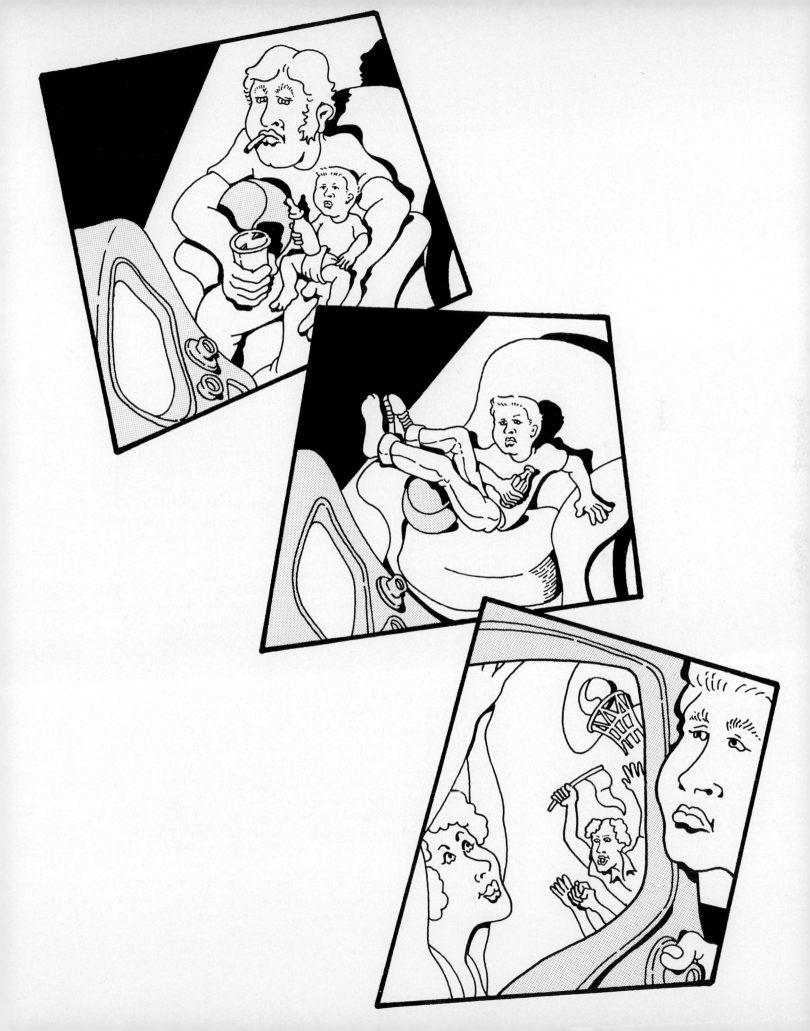

The natural and helping approaches related to the maturation and learning views

The natural approach tends to result from the maturation view — while the helping approach tends to result from the learning view. However, each approach can find some support in the other view. For instance, some people who stress heredity advocate one form of the "helping" approach — the "eugenics approach". This suggests that selective breeding will improve the human condition. It suggests that people should not breed if they are poorly fitted to their world. Many who hold this view extend their suggestions from clear biological problems to much less clear behavioral problems.

On the other hand, some people support the natural approach though they believe in the crucial role learning plays in the way the child develops. They agree that crawling, walking, etc., are learned acts resulting from rewards and punishers in the child's natural world; they agree that those acts don't result from simple biological maturation of the infant, but they still argue for the natural approach rather than the helping approach. They say that adding a few extra rewards for crawling, as Carol did, surely couldn't help much, since so many things in the child's natural world reward those acts.

Their objection to the helping approach is valid unless the helper adds those extra rewards with great care. The point is not simply to add more rewards but rather to add them wisely, to make sure those extra rewards occur at the precise time when the child needs them most. The secret is in the use of the method of successive approximation or shaping.

Often the world of nature is not nearly as good as is a careful human being when it comes to teaching or shaping new skills. The human being is more able to react to the slightest step forward as the child acquires skills whether those skills be reaching, grasping, crawling, or walking; whereas, the world of nature is more-or-less fixed.

Reaching, grasping, crawling, or toddling a foot or two will not get a reward if the reward is ten feet away from the infant. The child needs a good helper to bridge the gap by shaping better movements until it can get nature's own rewards. So careful, helpful shaping can greatly boost the learning of complex skills even in settings containing many natural rewards.

Furthermore, we do not rule out the helping approach, just because some behavior deficits have biological causes. A learning-based helping approach is one of the most effective ways of working with the mentally retarded, even though some retardation results mainly from biological factors, as we will see in a later chapter.

■35 Which approach, natural or helping, most often results from which view, learning or maturation?

■36 State an exception to each of the above cases.

CONCLUSIONS

Our study of psychology has passed from phylogenetic development to ontogenetic development, from change through the evolution of the species to change through the life of each creature. And throughout our study of the growth of the child a major question persists: What affects the way the child develops? What does the child inherit? And what role do his current surroundings play?

Those questions are crucial because their answers affect how we raise our children. They tend to tell us how concerned we should be with the details of our child's world. Should we try to arrange a world of rewards — one designed to aid our children in learning useful skills, helping them get the most out of their world and helping them give the most to their world? Or should we be more concerned with the genetic background of our children? Do our children inherit a structure that controls the nature of their actions? If so, should we just sit back and not contribute anything, feeling that we won't have much impact on our children's development by trying to arrange a rewarding world?

The questions of environment and heredity persist as we look at the details of how the child develops. It is often hard to tell whether an effect is due to heredity or environment. We can not even rule out the role of the child's environment in affecting those actions it performs shortly after birth. Such acts could be a result of the prenatal, biochemical world or even a result of prenatal learning. But, whatever the cause, most children soon get the set of actions they need to deal with the world they're likely to meet shortly after their birth. This is true whether those are unlearned acts, acts the child learns while still in the prenatal stage, or acts it learns with great speed after its birth.

We are well-suited to our world, at least the world in which we evolved, since our species is a product of evolution by natural selection. So we inherit useful biophysical structures causing us to respond in ways that help us survive. These may be structures that insure that we will learn needed acts, or they may be structures that produce the acts directly themselves.

These issues of maturation and learning will stay with us, as we look at the next chapters. They will raise further questions about the major causes of our differing language skills, intelligent behavior, and cognitive, or thinking, skills.

CHAPTER 13
DEVELOPMENT OF LANGUAGE

INTRODUCTION

In the last chapter, we looked at the debate between maturation and learning views of child development: do we acquire our complex adult response patterns as a result of the passive growth of the child; or do we acquire them as a result of active learning through contact with our physical and social world? In this chapter, that maturation-learning debate is less crucial. Most people agree that language is a result of active learning rather than passive maturation.

However, some still do argue that our biological structure affects the laws of grammar of all human languages. And of course, we all agree we must have the correct biological structure to even have language. Therefore, we will look in some detail at language as a complex pattern of learned stimulus-response chains children acquire through their day-to-day contact with their world. And we will discuss ways to improve such contact, helping children who are not learning language skills well and improving the learning of those children who are at or above average in their use of language.

- 1 Does the social and physical world play much of a role in the development of the child's language?

UNDERSTANDING SPEECH

Normal learning

Like all children, little Chet seemed to understand some of what his parents said to him before he learned to say things in return. He would often do the right things when they asked him to. For Chet, this started during his sixth month.

"Now Chetty, open your mouth; this will taste good. You'll like it."

And a little later:

"Hold still while I put this shoe on you."

"Lift up your arms so Mommy can help you put your sweater on."

Yet little Chet could not even begin to ask his parents to open their mouths, as the infant had not yet learned those needed language skills.

How does this happen? How can little Chet understand language before he can speak it? Does he inherit his knowledge from his parents? Few would suggest that, not even the most extreme of those who argue for

maturation. So he must have learned to understand language from the people around him — learned to understand much of it as a part of his daily life. To some extent this was because Chet and Carol acted like most parents. Parents tend to talk to their children as if those infants understand what they're saying. They do this much like we talk to our pet dog, our gold fish, or even our car when it's not working. In other words, they generalize from people who understand language to animals, things, and infants who don't.

But what does little Chet learn when he learns how to understand language? He learns to respond to a set of very complex discriminative stimuli, a set of cues that some acts will get rewards, some will get punished, and some will get nothing.

At first these cues come to exert stimulus control over his actions, just as the light cue in

the Skinner box controls the pigeon's key-peck response. Specific sounds from his parents work as cues for specific acts from Chet — really a pre-language stage much like your pet dog coming to you when you whistle. So the sounds of Carol's voice act as cues for the correct responses, as she says, "Open your mouth," and little Chet does so.

Pre-language control: simple stimulus control where specific stimuli are discriminative stimuli for specific acts.

But at first there are also other cues, visual cues such as his high chair and baby spoon. Little Chet often sits in his high chair with Carol holding his spoon in front of him while she presents her vocal cue. Over time these vocal cues come to exert more and more control than the visual cues, because they remain a constant factor in a changing set

of visual cues. And those visual cues change, since little Chet is not always in his high chair, and the spoon is not always there. For instance, Carol might hold him on her lap while feeding him a bit of food with her hand. Thus after a while the vocal cue, the only common element, comes to exert stimulus control over little Chet's opening his mouth. The reward, of course, a bit of tasty food.

There is also another reward — escape from an irritant: Mom will pester poor little Chet until he does open his mouth, even if it's spinach she's forcing down the poor lad. Control by escape from an irritant is also clear in the "raise-your-arms-kid-so's-I-can-put-this-sweater-on-you" cue. And we don't mean the child escapes the cold nursery-room air. No, once again, little Chet escapes a pest of a parent, one who just won't let the child alone until he puts on his sweater, or shoes, or pants, or whatever.

So, in general, two types of reinforcers may cause the child to learn certain responses to certain sounds. One is the natural reinforcer like food in the mouth, or the comfort of a warm sweater. The other is escape from the nagging parent who keeps insisting that the child open his mouth or raise up his arms, or whatever.

After a while, Chet's parents' vocal sounds exert somewhat more complex control over his actions. The sounds start to function as words, combining with other words to form sentences. And each new sentence controls a response that differs somewhat from the others, as the words and patterns of words begin to work as meaningful units. The sounds are working as true language! These sounds are never more than stimuli acting as cues for actions, though now they are much more complex cues than the simple light in the pigeon's Skinner box. This is no

longer pre-language, but now real language control, language acquired through the normal process of being raised by vocal parents.

Language control: complex stimulus control where the arrangements of various stimuli (like words) function as discriminative stimuli for various acts and combinations of acts.

- 2 Do children understand language first or do they speak it first?
- 3 What do children learn when learning how to understand language?
- 4 Define language and pre-language control. How do they differ?
- 5 Describe two kinds of reinforcers that might be working as a child learns to open its mouth when asked to do so.

The helping approach to understanding language

Carol didn't want to rely on chance rewards and punishers to teach her son to understand language. She went out of her way to help little Chet learn language as soon as she could. She did this because she felt good language skills formed the basis for good intellectual behavior. And she wanted to give her child every chance she could to lead as worthwhile a life as he could attain. So she arranged to teach him to discriminate among the language cues and to make the proper responses, much as she helped him learn his motor skills.

She arranged his world so that it would reward correct acts in the presence of various language cues. She took care to present him with cues he could discriminate with the most ease. At first she used simple cues, making them more and more complex only as he mastered the easy ones. Young Chet was learning language at the same time he was learning motor skills.

When Chet was nine months old, Carol used the reward of a hug and a smile each time he crawled over to her when she said, "Come to Mommy." At first she needed to use the visual cue of beckoning with her hand. Then she faded out that cue, making less and less of a motion, as the child's actions came more under the control of the audio cues and less under the control of the visual cues. This fading of the visual cue then caused the response to be under greater and greater control of the audio cue.

Of course, feeding time was also great for learning because it involved food, a very strong reward for a hungry infant. So Carol sat with great patience waiting for Chet to open his mouth at her request. She also went out of her way to stress her vocal cues by fading out the visual prompts of the high chair and the spoon. She did this as he began to open his mouth with greater speed and precision following her requests. Again this fading caused the process to progress even more quickly.

They also played another little game — the trickster game. She would give wrong cues, like, "Stand on your head," to see if he would be fooled and open his mouth. And, of course, he did open his mouth at first. But he learned not to make that response, as there was never any food for that act when the wrong cue was present. Besides, Carol would reward his closed mouth with a smile and a kiss when he managed to restrain himself. Little Chet learned to respond to what Carol said, not whatever she said.

Carol and her son progressed little by little as they worked together, changing a simple creature into one with a great command of language, our most important tool — changing a creature who functioned only at an animal level into a complex, intelligent-acting human being. And as time went by the mother and son grew closer, becoming stronger learned rewards for each other. The mother was paired

with each discrete bit of food, with each hug, each kiss, each shout of glee and joy; so she became a strong reward. The son was paired with progress (a strong learned reward for Carol). He was paired with the feeling of doing something worthwhile, something of real value for another human being, the feeling of building something that wouldn't be there if she weren't helping. And little Chet became a strong reward. As a result, Carol started feeling like she too was a worthwhile human being — more than a burden, a downer for her husband.

But this feeling had its price — another feeling — guilt. She had to sneak her helping time with little Chet, because big Chet didn't approve of her efforts. He held tightly to the notion that it wasn't right for Carol to interfere with the normal way his son matured. After all, his mother didn't use any of that psych stuff on him. And he'd turned out pretty good, even if he did have to say so himself. But Carol was not overwhelmed by the logic of his argument. She was even beginning to get a little resentful that her husband was causing her to feel that way.

- 6 Cite an instance where the helping approach can be used in teaching a child to understand language. What rewards can be used for the child? What rewards might there be for the helper?

BEFORE LANGUAGE

Direct, biophysical reinforcers for vocal acts

What causes a child to make its first vocal responses — to coo and babble during the first few months of its life? These responses may be unconditioned responses elicited by some unconditioned stimuli. Or those acts may be learned through operant conditioning. The rewards involved in learning such acts might be direct biophysical stimuli — those stimuli produced by the movement of muscles, the muscles involved in making sounds, for instance. Either is possible, because even deaf children emit such sounds. However, we do not yet have enough data to determine whether those responses are unconditioned responses or learned through operant conditioning.

What about that other common vocal response — crying? What causes it? Some crying may be a reflex, such as the crying that occurs just after birth, or when the doctor smacks the baby on the rear-end. But much crying may also be an easy response to learn — like the other acts (aggression, for instance) that are learned because results become rewarding when the creature is without food or in a harmful state. This seems likely, since babies most often cry under those two conditions. And the sound of their crying depends to a large degree on whether a diaper is wet, or whether some time has passed since the last feeding. So we may inherit the capacity to be reinforced by our own crying itself (or more precisely, the direct biophysical stimuli from crying) when we are without food or when we are in a harmful state.

- ■ 7 What are some possible causes for the infant's first cooing and babbling?
- ■ 8 Under what two conditions do newborn infants most often cry? What might be the initial rewards for such crying?

Reinforcers given by others for crying

Other rewards soon come to control crying — rewards having a more direct effect on the child's chances to survive — results such as the child having its troubles tended to or being fed quickly. These rewards are all given by another person. It seems likely that such rewards take control since children in institutions with little adult care don't cry very much — most likely because that vocal response doesn't receive much outside reward in the form of help from the attendants. Therefore, if the child inherits an ability to be rewarded by those direct biophysical events, the reward value must not be too strong — not strong enough to maintain the act of crying for any great period of time. That act must also be backed up with other rewards, rewards dealing in a more direct manner with the problems of pain and lack of food.

So, in a sense, the child's crying becomes a pre-language vocal response. The crying serves much the same function as the more complex responses, "food" and "hurt", once that act gets beyond the stage where its sole reinforcers are biological stimuli resulting directly from that act, stimuli like the direct biophysical stimuli. Their effects on the outside world control both sets of actions. The pre-language cry and the older child's words both cause the parent (the outside world) to bring food or change a diaper.

■ 9 What rewards given by other people support crying?

The function of direct biophysical rewards for crying

But why might children inherit the capacity to be rewarded by the direct biophysical results of crying? Because that capacity to be so rewarded must have helped our ancestors survive. How would that work? The crying would cause their parents to take care of them when they needed help. In that way infants so rewarded cried more when they needed help, got more help, survived to produce more such infants themselves, and on and on until here we are, a species that is rewarded by the direct biophysical results of crying under certain conditions.

Yet why do infants need a direct biophysical reward for crying? By now you should be able to answer that question yourself. Your best guess should be that this direct biophysical reward must have helped the species survive. But how? You should look at a case that's comparable to this one for a hint about the sort of thing that might be going on.

What case is that? Aggression of course. And what happens in that case? Look at the direct biophysical rewards for those aggressive acts. Recall we said those rewards might become effective only when the creature was in a harmful or frustrated state. Those rewards could be stimuli resulting from the pressure of the teeth when a biting response is made, or the pressure of the claws when a clawing response is made. But what function do such aggressive reinforcers serve? They help creatures quickly learn how to aggress: Creatures might not so quickly learn to aggress if they were to rely on the results of escaping from harm as the only effective rewards.

So what about crying?

"Well," you answer, "the direct biophysical rewards for crying insure that infants will also quickly learn this response, when they are in a harmful state, or when they have been without food for some time. The crying response then controls the actions of the parents, causing the parents to help the infant. The infants might not so quickly learn to cry if they were to rely on the help from their parents as the only effective reward. But such help from the parents does also act as a reward, strengthening and maintaining the crying response once the infant has learned it as a result of the direct biophysical rewards."

■10 How might it be that our ancestors have survived better because of a capacity to be rewarded by the direct biophysical results of crying?

■11 Compare the role of the direct biophysical rewards for crying with those for aggressive acts.

Learning word sounds

Big Chet neither talked very much to his son nor was he much of a source of reward for the infant. But Carol was always talking to little Chet as she attended to his needs. So her voice and the words she said became strong learned rewards for the little boy. This was due to the fact that those sounds were so often paired with the food and comfort she gave. Thus little by little his babbling came to sound more and more like his mother's English sounds. Why? Because a sound that happened to be a little more like one of his mother's words would have extra, learned-reward value for little Chet. So he would be more likely to repeat such sounds later on.

Natural shaping is at work. As Chet Jr. babbles on, a new form of his response is more likely to occur — a form even closer to his mother's English sounds. Therefore that sound is an even greater reward. That newest form of the response slips into young Chet's set of vocal responses. And this process keeps going on as each new response form comes closer and closer to his mother's. And each new form brings with it slight variations, some being even closer to the sounds his mother makes. Thus little Chet made sounds that were like English syllables within only a few months. Even before he was eight months old, he could say the syllables together in little, vocal, stimulus-response chains that sounded like words, though they weren't really words.

Now there was another outside source of reward moving little Chet's vocal sounds closer and closer to English — the effect it had on his parents in causing them to reward him. For instance, one day little Chet sprang a new one on them when he said, "bee-bee." This even got to his father — what father is above being proud of the fine set of genes his son inherits from him?

Chet started, "Huh, wha'd he say? Did he say 'baby'? Do you want your baby? Here's your baby." Chet had mixed feelings as he handed the Raggedy Andy to his son. He didn't want his son to grow up being a sissy. He wished Carol had bought him one of those little, plastic GI-Jimmie Killer dolls. But at least it wasn't a Raggedy Ann. And at least the kid was talking.

So little Chet's first English word got a reward. Not that he was trying to get the doll — he was just making the right sounds, learned rewards. But getting the doll was a bonus reward — one that had its effect in shaping the young talker.

■12 What are the two sources of reward causing a child's vocal responses to sound more and more like its parents' language?

LEARNING COMPLEX SPEECH

Using imitation in teaching word sounds

Children learn to imitate through the rewards such actions get from their normal world. And good skills at imitation can be an even greater asset in learning complex speech patterns. So Carol taught Chet how to imitate speech sounds as one of the first skills he acquired.

Imitation: a type of stimulus control in which the form of the response matches the form of the discriminative stimulus.

Early in their program, she and little Chet started off with a sound imitation game. She chose a response little Chet could already make — "pa" — (always a good way to start shaping).

"Say 'pa'?" she asked.

Nothing.

"Come on, say 'pa'."

"wa."

"Oh that's great," she beamed, as she petted the eloquent youth. She reinforced any response just to raise his rate of babbling when she asked him to. That way, her request came to act as a cue for his babbling. Babble now and talk will come later.

"Okay, now say 'pa'."

A few minutes of this game every day added up to several hours over the next weeks. And Carol's vocal request to imitate came to function as a cue — at least as a cue for those sounds little Chet already made anyway. But now he could make those sounds under the cue control he had learned in the imitation game.

Next Carol tried getting little Chet to combine those old sounds into new patterns — something they hadn't done before.

"Say 'pa-pa', Chetty."

"pa," he replied.

"No, Chetty, say 'pa-pa'?" she kept asking.

"pa . . . pa."

"Good boy, Chetty. That was really good. Let's do it again. Say 'pa-pa'."

"pa."

And on it went, as the child learned, with greater and greater speed, to imitate simple sounds combined into words.

Then one day, little Chet happened to say "pa-pa" as big Papa himself walked through the door.

"Did you hear that, Carol, he called me Papa. He called me Papa. The kid knows. That's my kid. See, you don't have to do all that psych stuff. He just knows, that's all. And he hasn't called you Mama yet, has he?" While shouting, Chet had picked up his son, horsing around with him — great fun for father and son alike. You don't suppose Chet's horsing around acted as a reward for the little "pa-pa" response, do you?

Carol continued to set the table, thinking about her deceit and finding it a mild reward, in turn making her feel guilty again.

■13 Define imitation.
■14 How can we use imitation to teach speech sounds?

The helping approach to functional speech

Carol wanted little Chet to really use his speech, not just make mere speech sounds, so she went further out of her way to help him learn to use English as a helpful tool. At first she gave him a drink of water each time he happened to say "wah-wah". But then she shaped a more correct response as Chet learned the first form of the response well enough to say it at a fairly high rate. After that, she raised her standards slightly, when he said "wah-wah," by asking, "Can you say "wah-dah'?"

Using this imitation procedure, she again took care not to ask for too much. She asked for the speech sound "dah" — one that she had heard him make before. Then she waited for little Chet to learn the "wah-dah" response before moving on to the more advanced "water". (This occurred during his ninth month, a few months earlier than would have been the case without Carol's help.)

▪15 How can a parent help a child learn more precise and useful speech?

A natural factor helping the learning of precise speech

Carol used shaping to help Chet learn more precise and useful speech. Another factor also moved his speech along the same path. His sounds were more likely to get rewards from the outside world, or at least they would get rewards sooner and with less effort (the closer they were to English words). For instance, Carol's parents often baby-sat half days, when Carol went back to work. And Grandmother had some trouble with little Chet's half-English.

"Wha'd you say?"
"wah-wah, ma-maw."
"Wah-wah?"
"wah-wah!"
"What do you want? Do you want Ma-maw to bring you some water? Is that it? Well here it is . . . Look at that kid drink. I reckon he did want some water after all."

Little Chet would have gotten his water sooner if he had spoken more clearly. Thus Grandmother provides a natural source of shaping.

▪16 When does children's talking cause infrequently contacted adults to "naturally" help them learn more precise speech?

A natural factor retarding the learning of precise speech

But there was a factor acting to keep little Chet's speech at its simple, half-English level — namely, big Chet. He had been around his son enough to learn the infant's half-English. So, without meaning to, he tended to keep his son's language at its early level, by responding to it without trying to shape more precise speech. If big Chet would respond at all, he would bring his son a glass of water right away, whenever the boy said "wah-wah." He wouldn't wait for a clearer response. This took place on those occasions when he had to baby-sit.

Carol noticed Chet rewarded his son's sloppy speech, even after she had taught the child to speak much more clearly. Of course, big Chet had a ready answer for her when she raised the issue:

"Now listen, Carol, we don't have to teach kids how to talk. They discover it. They find it out for themselves. That's what their minds are for. Just let the kid mature; that'll take care of it. Besides, I don't have time to be a nurse maid to no kid. I got more important things to do. I can't stand around waitin' for him to start talking like some TV announcer."

Chet would also get things for his son, if the child simply pointed and whined. Chet did this even though the child could make a response closer to the proper English word. But Carol's special efforts more than made up for her husband's lack of effort. Still, the child continued to discriminate between his two parents, regressing to more primitive ways of getting help and attention when around his father.

■17 How can a lazy parent retard the child's learning precise speech forms?

■18 What is an argument for not trying to help the child **learn** more precise speech?

Teaching nouns

So Carol and little Chet kept up their language games, month after month, progressing to the name game. "What's that?" Carol inquired, pointing to a creature in the front yard.

"kit-ty," the young, clear-sighted observer was quick to reply.

Carol laughed. "No, that's a doggie. Say 'dog-gie'."

On it went as Chet learned to discriminate between classes of stimuli and to generalize only within those classes. His behavior was coming under the stimulus control of those concepts. But his parents had a few laughs in the process. He misnamed things in cute ways due to his generalization between concepts.

"That's not Daddy, that's the postman," Carol replied with a smile.

Big Chet didn't smile at that one.

■19 How can we teach nouns?

Teaching verbs and original sentences

It took some time before little Chet acquired the skills of imitation, attending to the stimuli Carol pointed out, and naming them. But when he did, he was ready to learn verbs.

* * *

Carol pointed out the window. "Look, Chetty, see the doggie. The doggie's running. Say 'doggie runs'."

"doggie."

"Say 'doggie runs'."

"doggie."

"No, Chetty, say 'doggie runs'."

"run."

"Oh, that's good, Chetty. Now say 'doggie runs'."

And so on until the little toddling talker was saying simple sentences with verbs as well as nouns. His language was controlled by action stimuli such as running, barking, laughing, and crying as well as object stimuli such as doggie, kitty, Ma-ma, and Pa-pa. And after a while, his speech was controlled by complex but novel stimuli. This happened when the parts of old stimuli combined to exert new cue control over his speech.

For instance, he had learned to say "doggie run". He had also learned to say "kitty", at the correct times. And then he made a new response — his first original statement about the world. On his way to being a creative person. He said, "Kitty run!!!" The abstract property of running exerted cue control over his speech at the same time the more concrete cue, cat, maintained its well-learned cue control. So he said a new sentence — one he had never said before. Notice Chet did not say, "run, kitty," he said, "kitty run." In saying a proper sentence, little Chet was also coming under the stimulus control of the grammar of the English language.

Now, the words and word order in our sentences are a crucial feature of their stimulus control. The word order can change the meaning of the sentence, thereby changing how we respond to that sentence; or the word order can make the sentence meaningless, so that we can't respond in any proper way to the sentence. Chet was forming the abstract concept of subject of a sentence as a stimulus class. Doggie and kitty were members of that concept or stimulus class. Therefore, the placement of the word "kitty" at the beginning of the sentence was under the multiple control of both the sight of the kitty and its membership in the concept of subject of sentence.

That is how language comes to have its most useful impact on our lives — how it helps us to deal with novel events — to make original statements. This involves multiple cues combining to exert complex control over what we say. Thus we can deal with our world in more precise ways.

Grammar (syntax): the ordering of words in sentences to form larger units of stimulus control.

We can see creative behavior in the statement of original sentences under the proper stimulus control of the setting and of grammar. Creative acts occur when old events combine in new ways to cause us to make a novel response — a response combined in a new way, out of old components. Language-speaking Chet is on his way to becoming a creative human being.

Creative behavior: a new response or set of responses that is in some sense appropriate to the setting in which it occurs. These responses should be new to the person though not necessarily new to others.

The problem of determining whether behavior is appropriate or not is not always an easy one, as it does include an implicit value judgement. But it is a distinction that needs to be made, as some novel behavior will be so inappropriate as to cause the person to be committed to an institution. The concept of creativity does include an implicit value judgement.

■20 How can we teach verb usage?
■21 Define grammar.
■22 Define creative behavior.

The creative chimp

For some time, psychologists have tried to find out if lower animals could learn a language. The real test of language learning is the creative use of language. Can an animal correctly produce or respond to a novel sentence, symbols combined in a novel manner? Animals in their normal world don't seem to do this. Their vocal sounds seem to be unconditioned reflexes rather than learned acts. They seem to be unconditioned responses caused by unconditioned stimuli. The effects or results of those unconditioned responses do not act as rewards to cause those responses to be learned, even though their sounds do affect the actions of other members of their species. However, those effects on the actions of others most likely do account for why the species evolved to have such vocal reactions.

But what about birds such as the myna and the parrot? Well, their vocal responses also fail to meet the criteria of language. They are simple stimulus-response chains, without meaning. They are not under the control of cues, that is they do not combine those sounds in new and correct ways when they see or hear a new arrangement of cues; they don't respond like little Chet did with his "kitty run".

At last, however, we seem to be getting evidence that some animals can learn to understand and produce language in much the same manner as we do. Scientists have now taught chimpanzees to speak using the finger and hand motions and positions of the American Sign Language used by the deaf. Chimps have also learned to write by placing plastic symbols in the proper order on a table. The symbols are of two types: some stand for nouns such as "tree" and "house", while others stand for relations such as "on" and "at the side of".

Other chimps have learned how to read and write by touching keys with the symbols on them, much as a typist touches the keys of a typewriter. These chimps have all learned to understand and produce language. They have also shown creative uses of their languages in two ways: 1) by responding in the proper way when scientists combine the symbols in novel ways; and 2) by themselves combining their symbols in novel ways when the occasion warrants.

We can see this clearly in the following report* of a discussion between Lana, the chimp, and Tim, the scientist. We have the exact transcript of their talk since they spoke to each other by means of a chimp typewriter — a device which functions somewhat like a typewriter though it doesn't look like one.

*Duane M. Rumbaugh and Timothy V. Gill, "Language, Apes, and the Apple Which-is Orange, Please," presented at the Fifth International Congress of Primatology, Nagoya, Japan, 1974.

On April 29 Lana was very disinclined to work. Consequently, her evening ration of food was restricted so as to elevate her motivation for the following morning's work session. On the morning of April 30, Tim Gill entered the anteroom, in full view of Lana, carrying a large pitcher of cold milk in one hand and his coffee cup in the other. The following exchange transpired:

Lana: Milk name-of this. *8:54 a.m.*

Tim: Yes.

Lana: Milk name-of this. *8:55 a.m.*

Tim: Yes.

Lana: Milk this. *8:56 a.m.*

Lana: ?Tim give Lana coffee. *(She relishes black coffee!) 8:57 a.m.*

Tim: No.

Lana: ?Tim move milk coffee. *(The first suggestion that she wanted both the milk and coffee moved to and deposited in her vending devices so that she could ask the machine for them.) 8:58 a.m.*

Tim: *(no response)*

Lana: ?Tim move behind room. *(Which would serve to bring Tim to the general area of the vending devices, a requisite for loading them.) 8:58 a.m.*

Tim: Yes. *(Tim moved behind the room to the general area of the vending devices,* but *he intentionally left the pitcher of milk in the anteroom. Lana's response was to hoot with apparent disturbance, as suggested by her frowned expression. In a few seconds, Tim returned to the anteroom, picked up the milk, and the following exchange ensued.)*

Lana: Milk of this coffee. *8:59 a.m.*

Lana: ?Tim give milk name-of. *9:00 a.m.*

Lana: ?Tim move milk behind — *(sentence not completed.) 9:00 a.m.*

Tim: ?Behind what.

Lana: ?Tim move milk behind room. *9:01 a.m.*

Tim: Yes. *(And he loaded the vending device with milk, and Lana commenced to work for it by asking* Please machine give milk.*)*

Lana: Please machine give milk. *9:02 a.m.*

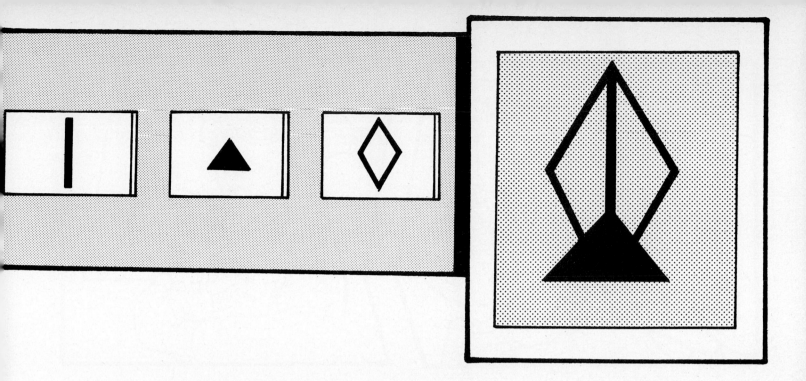

The significance of this conversation is that, first, Lana spontaneously named the desired incentives (as she had done on earlier occasions with other incentives). Second, Tim was asked to "move behind the room" (as she had done on earlier occasions of equipment malfunction). Third, and most significantly, Tim was asked to move the desired incentive behind the room. Lana had never been trained to ask that something be moved from one point to another in space, and the technicians had never announced to her that they were going to move "something" from one point to another in space except *their own bodies. To clarify this last point, when Lana asks, "?Tim/Shelley/Bev move into room," they usually respond, "Yes, Tim/Shelley/Bev move into room." Lana also can and does ask, "?Lana move out-of room" or "?Tim/Shelley/Bev carry Lana out-of room" in order to be taken out-of-doors for play and exercise. Lana extrapolated, apparently, that she could request that materials, as well as animates, be moved in space. This type of conversation was repeated in essence on May 1, 2, and 7, and several subsequent occasions. She uses again and again linguistic innovations which result in success when first devised and used.*

- ▪23 Do animals have language in their normal settings?
- ▪24 Are most natural animal sounds learned acts or reflexes?
- ▪25 What are three forms of animal language devised in the laboratory?
- ▪26 Can animals produce novel language sequences in the laboratory?
- ▪27 Thought question: In what way does the behavior of Lana fit, or fail to fit, our definition of creative behavior?

THE FUNCTIONS OF LANGUAGE

Language is both a response and a stimulus — a response when we talk or write — a stimulus when we listen or read. We were looking at language as a stimulus when we discussed factors that affect how we understand speech. We were looking at language as a response when we discussed factors that affect how we learn to talk. So a given utterance can function both as a stimulus and as a response at the same time. The speaker says it. It is a response for the speaker or at least a product of a response. The listener hears it. It is a stimulus for some other response on the part of the listener. The same instance of speech almost always plays both roles at the same time — the response for the speaker, and the stimulus for the listener.

Language as a response

Talking is a learned act, as we've seen; an act rewarded by its results. And we need those results to maintain our speaking even after we've learned how to talk.

Speaking is often a social act rewarded by others, with either of two types of rewards: one a direct reward for the act of speaking and the other, a reward named by the act. Here are some instances where speech receives a direct reward simply for its own sake: Carol says, "That's very good, Chetty. You said it right." Or someone says to you: "That's a great story you just told." "That's the funniest thing I've heard all day." "You're really right about that." All of these forms of approval act as learned rewards given directly for our speaking.

Often this form of response and reward takes the simple form of the speaker describing something with the listener providing a rewarding, "thank you". For instance: "This building's on fire."

"Thank you for letting us know."

But much of our language is maintained by the second type of reward — rewards we ask for in the very statement itself — rewards we indicate in our requests.

"Where's the nearest fire exit?"

"Over there."

"Thanks."

The request for directions to the door is reinforced by the receipt of those directions. Giving those directions is reinforced by the hurried "thank you".

Little Chet says, "Milk, please." And his request is reinforced when Carol hands him a glass of milk.

Thus much of our speech is reinforced through the control it exerts over the actions of others. Our speech may cause others to say, "Thank you" — one type of reward for the speech. Or it may cause them to give us something we request — another type of reward for our speech. In either case, our speaking is caused by the fact that it gets rewards. Which explains speech as a response.

■28 In what sense is language both a stimulus and a response?

■29 What are the two types of reward for speech as a social act? Cite an instance of each.

Language as a stimulus — rule control of our actions by others

We've seen how language functions as a response for the speaker; now let's look at its function as a stimulus for the listener's future actions. How does it control those actions? It functions as a cue, helping the person to act in a way that will get reinforced, and avoid acting in a way that will get punished. For instance:

"Milk, please."

And Carol complied with her son's request.

"Thank you, Ma-ma."

The request, "Milk, please," was Chet's response. He was the speaker. On the other hand, it functioned as a stimulus for Carol's next response. It was her cue. Following his request, her response would not get a reward — a "thank you" — if Carol had handed him a teaspoon of cod-liver oil instead.

Or, at a later age: "Chetty, bring me the evening paper," — a cue from big Chet for little Chet's response that will avoid the punishment of being shouted at.

Or: "But that door is locked, so you'd better use the second window on the left to get to the fire escape."

You may have noticed that this last statement differs from the others — it doesn't involve the same source of reward as the other statements do. Here the verbal cue controls the responses of getting to the fire escape, but that control does not involve any punishment or reward coming from the speaker. Instead the rewards or punishers come from features of the listener's world other than the speaker. For instance — the fire.

In the above cases, words function as instructions or rules for how to get rewards and avoid punishers. Sometimes these rules can be very complex sets of cues. For instance, you might consider these four chapters on development a set of rules or guidelines for the use of a helping approach in raising your children. The chapters are a complex set of verbal cues for a complex set of actions. The rewards may be your children coming a little closer to achieving their potential as human beings.

■30 Cite an instance of rule control where the rewards or punishers for the listener come from the speaker of the rule.

■31 Cite an instance where those results come from somewhere other than the speaker.

Rule control of our actions by ourselves

We've looked at language as a response from one person serving as a stimulus for the actions of another person. However, the speaker and the listener can be the same person. You might talk to yourself, giving yourself instructions you would then follow. For instance, you might memorize a complex set of procedures which you would then say back to yourself, rather than read them from the instruction book, as you went through the sequence of actions.

* * *

Little Chet's language skills progressed. Soon not only could he follow rule-governed cue control but he could also state the rules to himself. "Put green thing on log things . . . Mama, see house." And little Chet pointed to the toy log-cabin he had just finished with the help of a little rule-governed cue control: roofs go on houses.

* * *

Let's see, now. I gotta get an egg first. And so you do.
Now I gotta drop the yolk in that bowl, and dump the white in the blender. Let the white beat until it's stiff.
Now, I toss in the yolk; add a tablespoon of honey, a dash of vanilla, and, oh yes, gotta get a cup of skimmed milk.
You say each component of the recipe to yourself, producing a cue for the next response in this stimulus-response chain. The final reward at the end of the sequence will be a great eggnog.

So indeed, rules allow us to control our own actions whether we've read a complex set of instructions (from a cookbook for instance) or simply repeat them to ourselves, once we've memorized them.

Rule: a statement that 1) describes the nature of the response; 2) describes the relevant setting or stimulus conditions; and 3) describes the results of the response in that setting.

Rule control: stimulus control in which rules function as discriminative stimuli.

- ■32 Define rule.
- ■33 Define rule control. Cite an instance where the speaker of the rule and the follower of the rule are the same person.

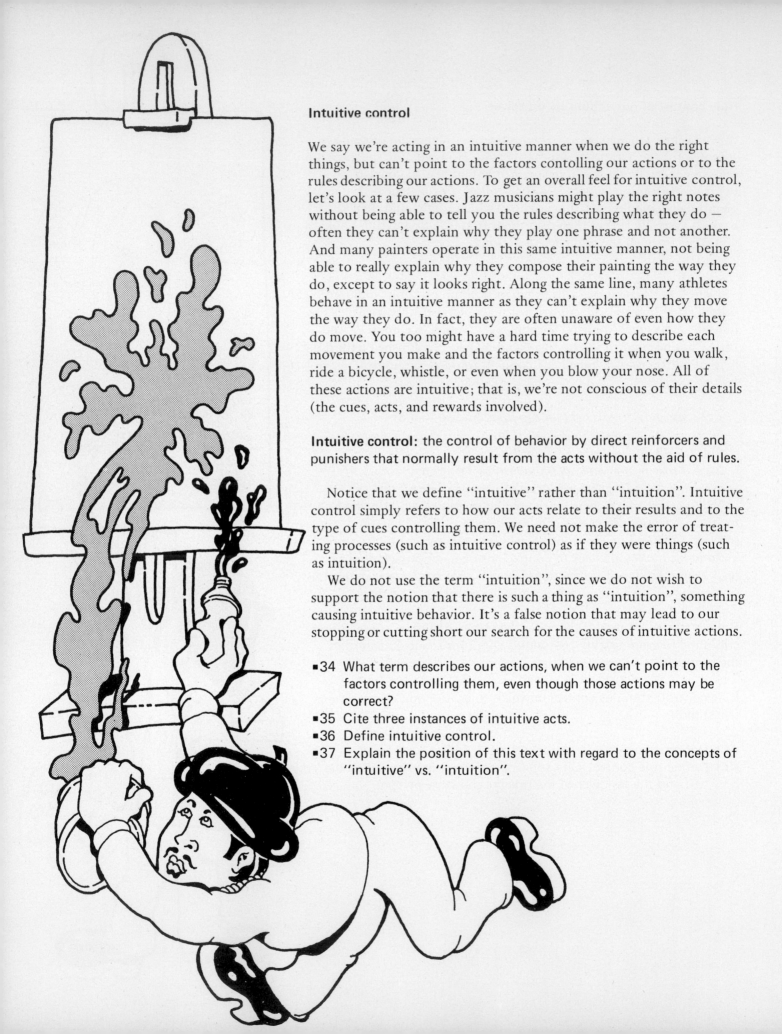

Intuitive control

We say we're acting in an intuitive manner when we do the right things, but can't point to the factors contolling our actions or to the rules describing our actions. To get an overall feel for intuitive control, let's look at a few cases. Jazz musicians might play the right notes without being able to tell you the rules describing what they do — often they can't explain why they play one phrase and not another. And many painters operate in this same intuitive manner, not being able to really explain why they compose their painting the way they do, except to say it looks right. Along the same line, many athletes behave in an intuitive manner as they can't explain why they move the way they do. In fact, they are often unaware of even how they do move. You too might have a hard time trying to describe each movement you make and the factors controlling it when you walk, ride a bicycle, whistle, or even when you blow your nose. All of these actions are intuitive; that is, we're not conscious of their details (the cues, acts, and rewards involved).

Intuitive control: the control of behavior by direct reinforcers and punishers that normally result from the acts without the aid of rules.

Notice that we define "intuitive" rather than "intuition". Intuitive control simply refers to how our acts relate to their results and to the type of cues controlling them. We need not make the error of treating processes (such as intuitive control) as if they were things (such as intuition).

We do not use the term "intuition", since we do not wish to support the notion that there is such a thing as "intuition", something causing intuitive behavior. It's a false notion that may lead to our stopping or cutting short our search for the causes of intuitive actions.

- ■34 What term describes our actions, when we can't point to the factors controlling them, even though those actions may be correct?
- ■35 Cite three instances of intuitive acts.
- ■36 Define intuitive control.
- ■37 Explain the position of this text with regard to the concepts of "intuitive" vs. "intuition".

Grammar and intuitive control

Most of our grammar is intuitive, at least until we go to school to learn the rules that describe what we had been doing all along, more or less the right way. We say, "Spot runs," and "Puff and Spot run," because they sound right that way. They sound right since we've heard our parents and others use those words in that manner.

Of course, there's also some generalization so we don't need to have heard the specific words in order to respond correctly. We may not need to have heard "Spot runs," and "Puff and Spot run," since we may have heard "Dick runs," and "Dick and Jane run."

On the other hand, stimulus generalization can get the novice speaker into trouble with irregular verbs. For instance, the child might hear someone say, "Dick kicked Jane." And our young linguist may over-generalize, from a standard form to the irregular verb, saying, "I bet Dick runned away after he kicked Jane." But most often generalizing to "ed" forms of the past tense will be okay.

■38 Cite an instance of intuitive control of correct and incorrect forms of grammar.

Words and intuitive control

Much of our word usage is also intuitive because the world rewards correct usage. And we learn to understand words because the world rewards responding in a correct way to those words. We learn much, if not most, of our vocabulary through these direct rewards — rewards for a correct response to words and rewards for our correct use of words. Often we might not be able to define these words under intuitive control even though we use them in the proper manner. "I know what that word means, but I'm afraid I can't define it for you."

Of course, some of our word usage is rule-governed. For instance, we say, "What does 'blah-blah-blah' mean?" And our parents reply, "Why that means 'bleep, bleeb'." When they define the term, it's the same as stating a rule — a rule that acts as a cue for our dealing in a correct way with the word "blah-blah-blah".

Children's language skills improve as they have more contact with language. At the same time, the actions and concepts they learn more and more often start out as rule-governed rather than intuitive. Yet we still learn many words in an intuitive manner even after we've become skilled in language.

■39 How do we acquire intuitive word usage?

Rule control vs. intuitive control

Guidelines or rules move our species a great step forward in our efforts to survive. These rules contain much of the hard-won knowledge of our culture. And this knowledge can help us succeed without having to go through as long a learning period. In fact, without those rules, we might never learn the skills we need to succeed. There are normal rewards for doing our task well, but they might not cause us to learn how to do that task. Those normal rewards might be too distant, or we might not make the correct, complex sequence of responses. For instance, it's not likely that any of us would stumble across the correct way of doing long division, without a good deal of help from our friends, the rules of math.

Thus the normal rewards are often not enough to insure our doing complex tasks the right way; therefore, rule control is a great asset in learning complex tasks. It allows us to acquire complex response patterns even before we make direct contact with the normal rewards for such actions. So rules govern most of our complex response patterns when we first learn those patterns.

■40 Compare the advantages of actions under the control of rules and actions under the direct control of their normal results.

From rule to intuitive control

We learn many complex response patterns through rule control. Then such response patterns may come to be under intuitive control, if those patterns are practiced often — often enough that their normal cues and results have a chance to make direct contact with the response patterns.

* * *

At first, rules governed some of the newer skills Juke was learning at football practice. Those rules resulted from his coach's advice. His actions stopped being controlled by rules and started being controlled by the normal rewards for performing well, only after much hard practice.

Such actions are often smooth and unified when under the control of normal cues and results, but they are often awkward and disjointed when under the control of rules. It's hard to be smooth when you're saying each step of the sequence to yourself as a cue for the next act. Juke's performance as a football player would never have gotten him a scholarship to BSU if he had to stop and think what to do next before each move.

* * *

Here's one more instance where rule control gives way to intuitive control.

Chet put his complaint to Carol in the form of a question, "Did you have to memorize all these terms when you took psych?"

"Sure," Carol replied.

"This is just busy work. Why don't they test us on the basic issues? Why don't they test us on how much we really know, not just how many terms we can define?"

Carol answered him, knowing he didn't really want an answer. "I used to think that at first too; but I changed my mind, as I got further into psych. I found I made a lot of use of the definitions when I was trying to figure things out. For instance, when I was just getting started I almost had to have the definition of "reinforcer" right in front of me to act as a rule in helping me discriminate whether some tricky case involved an instance of a reinforcer."

"Yeah, but it seems like you wouldn't need to memorize the terms if you really knew that stuff. Not if you've really got it down as a concept. Seems like that's what they should be teaching us."

"I suppose you're right," she fibbed, "but I've talked to quite a few really good students and they all say the same thing. They say at first it helps to memorize the terms and how they are defined. That way you can compare the instance directly with the definition. It's really a form of rule-governed, concept formation. You know, 'Is this a reinforcer?' 'Well does it follow the response?' 'And does it make the response more likely?'"

"But that's a drag, if you always have to recite your definitions before you can use the concepts you've learned. It seems so mechanical."

"You're right." And this time she meant it. "After a while you don't have to anymore. After a while, it becomes second nature, intuitive."

"You're worse than Harper, the way you talk," Chet retorted.

* * *

Many good students are like Carol. They find learning psychology and other subjects works best if they first rote memorize the definitions. Then the concepts start shifting away from rule control and toward intuitive control as the correct responses get more rewards. So our language moves from intuitive control as children to rule-governed control as students and then back to intuitive control as practiced users.

In fact, it often helps to start out with our use of some terms first being under rule control. This is true with many technical terms, new terms, or terms used in a precise manner that differs somewhat from their everyday

use. We can move into the more handy intuitive control only after many correct instances of the use of the rule.

So thinking and language behavior work much the same way as physical movement. When we're young, we learn all behaviors through direct reward control — intuitive control. But rule-governed control takes over when we receive formal instruction in motor skills like football, and thinking skills like psychological analyses. In turn, both sets of actions come under intuitive control after repeated rewards. And it often helps to shift back to rule-governed control even after a skill or concept has gotten intuitive control over our actions. This is the case when things are hard to do, when we're trying to make the right moves with a tough job or when we're trying to think about a tricky problem. Then it may be helpful to state those rules so they can control our actions and see us through those rough times. Of course, another time rules prove helpful is when the hard-won knowledge of our culture needs to be passed on.

* * *

Note that rule control seems

to apply to three conditions: 1) The simplest is where the rule states a result that will follow right after the response. For instance, "Exit through that door to escape the burning building." 2) Another is where the rule states a result that affects the responses only after a complex response pattern has been practiced many times. For instance, Juke gets the direct rewards for his skilled moves on the football field only after much practice. 3) Some rules state results that are always going to be too delayed to have a direct effect on the response. So some sort of added reward must mediate those results. For instance, "Floss your teeth every day to keep them from falling out of your head when you grow old. And in the mean time, we'll give you a Johnny Flosserfaster badge."

■41 Cite two cases where rule control is replaced by the intuitive control of normal results.

■42 When is it helpful to shift from intuitive control back to rule control?

■43 What are the three conditions to which rule control applies?

Thinking

What is thinking? Thinking is behavior. The most clear case is talking to yourself. As little children first acquire language their thinking is almost all out loud. After a while they learn to whisper to themselves. Then they learn they can talk to themselves just as well without speaking out loud. We talk to ourselves in about the same way we talk to others. In fact, when no one is around we may have an imagined chat with a friend or an enemy: *Here's what I should have said to that smart aleck. . .*

Sometimes we may talk or think to ourselves out loud when we're alone. Also we may talk to ourselves or think out loud if we're having trouble thinking because of the hard nature of the task, or because of noises that distract us, perhaps when we're doing mental arithmetic or counting. Our speaking out loud generates auditory stimuli — stimuli with stronger cue control over our subsequent speech than when we don't talk out loud. Then we have less of that "let's see now, ah, where was I", because we clearly have just heard where we were.

But at other times it may be hard to maintain a good conversation with ourselves. Maybe we're trying to think through a boring problem. It's not as rewarding as thinking about our sex life or whatever our sex life should be. So we end up thinking about the more rewarding topic.

Many of us are social thinkers — we stay on the subject much better when others are listening. Often we may wish to talk to someone in order to hear what we have to say. Then we become mildly irritated when listeners keep disrupting our talk with their own opinions.

Sometimes we may be having a very rewarding talk with ourselves when we're driving on the highway. At such times, we're not likely to pick up any hitchhikers. Most likely they will not have anything to say to us as interesting as what we have to say to ourselves.

- ▪44 What is thinking?
- ▪45 When do we talk or think to ourselves out loud?

Language and the future

Language also functions as a crucial tool in helping us prepare for our future, much as instinctive rewards help other creatures prepare for their futures. Both control actions at the moment, causing us, and the creatures, to act in ways now that will often have value later on. Language provides current cues for correct action at the present moment, even though the real value of the act may lie beyond this present moment. Language also sets up learned rewards for those correct acts, and learned punishers for incorrect acts.

* * *

Dr. Harper had said, "At the start of each class, we're going to have a quiz over two of your texts, *Psychology* and *Concepts of Psychology.* This will help you stay up-to-date with the work in this course. However, we won't do it that way for the third book, *Science of Psychology.* We'll just cover that one on the mid-term and final. But we'll give you the daily reading assignments for that book to help you stay up-to-date there as well. And you really shouldn't get behind on any of the books, since you'd have a hard time getting it together at the last minute before the exam."

* * *

Dr. Harper gave instructions — words spoken in class and written in the reading assignments. And his words served as a cue for what the students should do now. That way they will be able to do well in the future when mid-terms and finals roll around. But those results are a long way off, leaving the current actions without much support. Not much support in the form of rewards and punishers, even if the correct cues are present. Therefore, another function of language comes into play in giving us current rewards and punishers, something to help bridge the gap between the now and the future — something that helps deal with delayed reinforcement.

* * *

The night before his second psych class, Sid was preparing to go down to the lounge to watch a little TV. He had just finished his first reading in *Psychology* and *Concepts of Psychology.* But he glanced over the assignment sheet one more time. And what he saw made him wish he hadn't given the sheet a final check.

Damn, I'm supposed to read a chapter in the Science *book too. And I know Harper's right — I've got to be careful not to fall behind on my reading or I'll never catch up. I learned that one last year when I was a freshman. Still, I'm tired of working; I'd like to cool it awhile by the tube. But I'll just sit down there feelin' guilty if I don't finish my work first.*

An hour later, Sid put the *Science* book down, having finished the first chapter. *I do feel better now that I've put in a good day's work. And I sort of get off on reading that stuff too. I guess it's like swimming, the water's fine once you get in. I'm not like all those noisy freshmen, who don't know where it's at. So now I can go down and catch a little tube action. Naw, to hell with it; I'd better go to bed and catch a few z's instead. I need all the sleep I can get now that I've got that job in the dining hall.*

* * *

First of all, Sid's own words acted as a warning cue: Sid, the speaker, said he would sit there in front of the tube feeling guilty, worrying about his studies, if he goofed off before finishing his work. Second, his words acted as a punisher for Sid, the listener: Feeling guilty and worrying take the form of things he says to himself — things about what a lazy slob he is, and how he's headed down the old flunk-out path — words that act as strong punishers for goofing off. Third, his words also acted as a reward for sticking to his job until it's done: he pointed out to himself what a super-human scholar he was to have his act down so tight.

It also helped to tell himself how he pitied all this campus lowlife that called themselves freshmen. Such self-praise often works; gross and crass as it is, overstated and overblown as it is, self-serving as it is, it can work. Such rewards help him hang in as they improve his self-image with their grain of truth. Not that he can't swing to the other extreme when he screws up something, or gets into trouble by goofing off. Then he fills himself with punishing self-hatred as he chastises himself for being lower than the lowest freshman — a position he does not find rewarding.

In any event, Sid did manage to keep his actions headed in pretty much the right direction. And he did that by using language to give himself rewards and punishers at the right time. However, he didn't reward and punish himself on purpose. In fact, he was only barely aware he did it at all. Like Sid, we all deal with the future with varying degrees of success, and our success depends largely on two general language functions: 1) how well we manage to respond to language cues — cues that point out what we should do now to obtain good results in the future; and 2) how well we manage to use language to reward and punish our actions as they warrant it. How well we manage these things depends on the extent to which these activities have been rewarded in the past.

■46 What two general functions does language serve in helping us deal with the future? Cite an instance of each.

■47 Thought question: How can we teach ourselves and others to respond well to language cues, and to use language well for self-reward and self-punishment?

Language and planning

In the last section, we saw two ways language can help us deal with the future. It can give us cues for current actions that will pay off in the future. And it can allow us to give ourselves learned rewards and punishers now for our current actions. In this section, we'll see another way language can help us deal with the future — through planning. Using language, we can plan for the future, we can imagine various alternative courses of action and their results, with one of those imagined courses of action coming to serve as a cue for our real actions.

In planning, we can test out options without really carrying them out. We talk to ourselves and others, going through a verbal sequence of sentences. "Now it will take an hour if I do this. And then it will take two hours when I go there. So I'd be a half-hour late for the big one, the main event, or whatever. I don't want to be late so I need to try some other sequence." After a while, we hit on a sequence that gets us there on time and still lets us do several other things on the way there. That verbal sequence then serves as a set of cues for our later actions. We may even make a list of the various acts that make up our plan. We can then mark them off as we complete them.

Let's distinguish between planning for action and fantasizing about the future. It is usually much more rewarding to fantasize than to plan. We do spend some time planning our vacations, for instance. But a large part of that is maintained by looking at the bright colors of the rewarding travel brochures, etc. We spend less time planning the less rewarding aspects of our vacations — getting passports, vaccinations, and the money for the trip.

Rarely do people succeed at anything that's very complex, without detailed planning. However, there is not enough immediate reward for planning. Furthermore, the results for failure are too delayed too far in the future. We want to get on with it. Play it by ear. The details will take care of themselves. We need to build in more prompt rewards for our planning behavior. Then we would avoid many of our human *faux pas* through good planning.

- ■48 What role does language play in planning?
- ■49 Why do we need to build in more prompt rewards for our planning behavior?

CONCLUSIONS

In this chapter, we've looked at how our language develops and functions — how we learn it and how we use it. We've seen how language begins to exert stimulus control over actions of infants even before they themselves are able to speak; and how most children learn this stimulus control through the rewards and punishers from their normal world. We've seen how children may do even better, with the help of planned rewards from their parents; and how, in any case, the parents play a crucial role in how the child's language develops.

We've also seen how the process of imitation affects the way a child's language develops — imitation functioning both in natural settings and in a parent's planned approach.

We've looked at the normal rewards for using language, some coming from our dealing in better ways with our world, through the use of rule-governed cue control; others coming from our listeners in the form of their approval or in the form of their helping us get some other rewards.

We agree with an old notion — the notion that our language is a major factor causing us to differ from other animals. And in the next chapter, we'll extend that notion further. We'll suggest that the skill with which we use our language is also a major factor causing us to differ from each other. We'll see how that skill affects the level of our intelligent behavior.

Language is indeed the major feature of our civilization. We owe our humanness to it.

CHAPTER 14
DEVELOPMENT OF INTELLIGENCE

INTRODUCTION

In this chapter, we'll look further at how children develop useful response patterns. Thus far we've seen how they acquire many basic responses, actions so basic it looks almost like they inherit them, so basic we often share them with lower animals. We've also seen how children become more and more "human" as they acquire the skills they need to produce language and to respond to it. In this chapter we'll see how some of these language skills combine to create human creatures who behave in an intelligent manner.

As you may note, we talk about intelligent acts rather than intelligence itself. We'll discuss the notion that people behave in intelligent ways, but they don't have something called "intelligence". We'll look at a set of basic skills people must learn in order to behave in an intelligent manner and in order to learn more advanced skills for intelligent acts. Then we'll look at the crucial role language plays in intelligent behavior. Throughout, we'll see how we can use the helping approach to aid children in learning these basic skills and language skills, allowing them to function in a more intelligent manner for the rest of their lives. With such skills, they can come nearer to achieving their maximum potential in areas depending on intelligent action.

- 1 What is the authors' position on intelligent acts vs. intelligence?

BASIC SKILLS

Natural control of orienting responses

If we're going to act in an intelligent manner, we must learn to orient ourselves, so we can attend to important cues like our parents' voices. And in fact, most infants do soon learn to orient or turn their heads in the direction of their parents' voices.

Orienting response: a response to a stimulus that changes the position of the creature's body relative to that stimulus, often putting the creature's receptors in a better position to sense that stimulus.

Let's look at little Chet to see how children might acquire this act of orienting. Infant Chet lay in his crib, moving only slightly, when he heard the sound of his mother's voice — dim but clearly Mother. Her voice was rewarding for Chet because of its pairing with other rewards such as food and comfort, as we've seen. But that sound is more rewarding the nearer it is, because when it's closer, Mother is usually providing the direct unlearned rewards which form the basis of the learned reward of the sound. This is a type of stimulus generalization — a different stimulus will be more rewarding the more similar it is to the original learned reward (the one paired with the other rewards).

Mother's distant voice is the different stimulus. Her voice when it was up close to Chet was the original learned reward. It was there that her voice was being paired with food and comfort. Now the close voice (the learned reward) will often be fairly loud, at least not faint. Therefore the louder the distant voice (different stimulus), the more similar it will sound to the original learned reward. So the louder it is (up to a point), the more rewarding it'll be.

The voice becomes even dimmer when he happens to turn his head away from her; but it becomes slightly more intense when he chances to turn his head back again, turning those soundwave scoops, his ears, toward the source of that rewarding sound — Mother's voice. Thus Chet soon learns to move his head until his ears orient in the direction of the sound, getting a more rewarding sound and thereby getting a reward for the orienting act itself. So the sound of a parent's voice acts as a cue for the child to orient to. That act will be reinforced when the voice becomes nearer the loudness of the voice when it was being paired with other rewards.

The sound of the voice is also a cue for other rewards — like the sight of the speaker. Turning toward the sound will often produce the sight of the mother or father — rewarding, because it too has been paired with food and comfort, just as the sound itself has been. As we've noted before, the visual, orienting-response pattern includes more than just head turning. It includes such acts as focusing and fixating — acts that also help produce the reward — the sight. But we

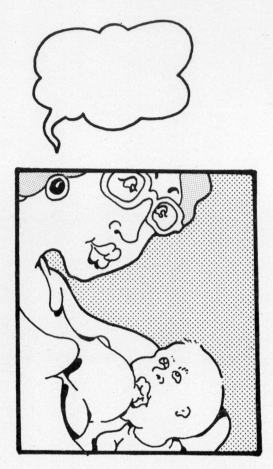

often overlook the cue-response-reward relation present in almost everybody's world.

Let's think about a state of affairs not likely to occur, but one that will help show the effects of our normal world. It will help us see the way the world teaches us how to orient. Think about a world where little Chet might not learn how to orient in the right manner. Instead he'd learn a response that wouldn't work so well in the normal world. For instance, suppose he always lay in his crib so the entrance to his nursery was on his left. He'd learn to turn to the left every time Carol or big Chet came into his room. Now suppose his parents turned his crib around? He might be in some trouble at first. His head would now face the other way with the entrance now on his right. What would he do when he heard a voice this time? He'd turn to his left on hearing the sound, thereby missing the great sight of Mom or Dad. He'd learned only to turn to the left at the voice cue, while he should have learned to turn in the direction of the sound.

But Chet, like most other children, didn't really have this problem, since he didn't always lie in his crib. He changed and his world changed around him quite often — often enough to prevent him from learning the wrong set of actions to those audio clues.

- **■ 2** Define orienting response.
- **■ 3** Describe an instance where natural rewards shape the orienting response and analyze that instance.
- **■ 4** What is meant by the stimulus generalization of **rewards**? Cite an instance.
- **■ 5** How could a child learn the wrong head-turning orienting responses to auditory cues?

Symbolic control of orienting responses

Big Chet pointed to the window. "Lookie there, Chetty. Look at that doggie out there in the yard." But his infant son kept looking at Daddy, while Daddy kept talking and thrusting his arm back and forth, making a very rewarding visual stimulus for the young child.

Frustrated, Chet grew louder, not quite shouting, waving his arm wildly about as he pointed to the window. *The kid must be blind not to see I want him to look out the window. Blind or stubborn.* "Kid, look out the window when I tell ya to!"

Little Chet was more than content to keep looking at funny Father shouting and jabbing his arm wildly in the air. Thus ended one of big Chet's few attempts to apply the helping approach to child development — ruined becasue he assumed children inherit a knowledge of how to respond to symbolic gestures such as pointing.

On the other hand, Carol did help her son learn those visual cues for orienting actions. She did this because she felt such cue control would greatly help him learn other things in the future. For instance, she'd be able to point to things and play the name game with him, once he could orient under the control of such symbolic cues.

Now how would you go about teaching a child to look when you pointed at things? What would be the first thing you'd need? A reward. Of course, there are many you can use from the simple but hardy, "Good boy, Chetty, that's great," to a hug and a kiss, or a little taste of the child's favorite food. Sometimes the sight of the thing you point to may also be a reward: "Look at that nice spoon of pablum, Chetty." "Oh, look out the window, here comes Daddy." "Look at the TV. See the pretty picture."

What about the concept of shaping? Would it apply here? Yes, you should almost always shape new actions rather than wait for them to occur. This is even more true if the responses arc very complex or occur at a low rate. So how would you shape the response of Chet's looking where you were pointing? Well, you'd start by shaping the direction of the looking response, by rewarding that response as the child orients more and more closely in the direction you're pointing. How? First you'd reward the response if it involved even the slightest head movement in any direction, when you say, "look at this," and point toward something. Next, reward any response that's just a little bit more in the right direction. As you keep shaping, the child will learn to look at the very thing you're pointing toward, perhaps touching it if you require it as part of the response sequence.

Of course, you'll point in many directions, setting up cue control with those different pointing responses. You must do this since each sight of you pointing one way or another is a new stimulus, and Chet must learn the looking response to many such sights if those sights are to function as cues.

So we've seen that orienting to symbolic stimuli is a learned response — one that can be improved through the use of the helping approach. Most often children acquire this response over a long period of time, with the sole reward value being the thing pointed out. This normal process is much slower than the helping approach since it doesn't involve shaping. In other words, normal rewards occur only when the child chances to look directly at the thing being pointed to. We've also mentioned that children can more quickly learn other things, if they orient under the control of the pointing cue. So you can see why it's really worthwhile to use the helping approach in teaching orienting.

- 6 Cite an instance of the symbolic control of an orienting response.
- 7 How would you use the helping approach to teach this response (mention shaping and two general sources of rewards)?
- 8 How would it help a child to orient under symbolic control at an early age?

Orienting and attention

After you've oriented toward something, you still might not be attending to that thing. We may not attend to a stimulus just because our receptors are in a good position to receive those stimuli and produce sensory responses.

Attending: a person attends to a stimulus when that stimulus exerts some form of stimulus control over the person's actions.

We don't know that the person is attending to the stimulus simply because there is a sensory response (receptor response). That stimulus still may not exert cue control or stimulus control over the person's actions. However, the sensory response does suggest that the person is at least orienting more or less toward that stimulus. Attending is often a component of orienting — even more so when Carol succeeds in cuing attending by saying not only, "Look out the window," but also, "Look at Daddy, while you're at it." Carol's setting up the occasion for little Chet to attend to Daddy — the sight of Daddy may exert cue control.

- 9 Define attending. How does it differ from orienting?

Control of orienting and attending through language

Language cues came to control little Chet's looking, as had gestures such as pointing. These language stimuli controlled his orienting and attending because of two sets of factors. The first set were the same as those common factors most often helping other children learn to attend when directed by language stimuli. The second set were those more unique factors resulting from Carol's helping approach.

The common factors were due to the fact that, like many parents, Carol always talked to Chet at the same time she pointed, "Look out the window." "Look at the TV." "Look at the table." "Look at me." And little by little, the language cues began to control Chet's looking — he was learning the meaning of the words. It also helped that Carol and big Chet often told him to look at something without pointing toward it. But those words wouldn't have acquired cue control if the controlled response hadn't produced a rewarding sight now and then: "Look in my hand. See what Daddy brought you." An M & M — far out! What would happen, though, if Daddy's hand was always empty? Or if there was never some sort of reward? Soon the looking response to that language cue would extinguish.

But life was not so cruel for little Chet. In fact it was rich with other factors helping his orienting and attending to come under the control of language cues. His mother often played the looking game with him. How would that go? Right — she'd present the language cue, wait for something that seemed vaguely like he was orienting in the right direction, and then give the reward. She'd also shape the response, asking that he orient in a more and more precise manner, before giving a reward.

At first, she used the pointing stimulus, fading it out as her words came to exert cue control: "Look at the flower, Chetty," Carol said, pointing to the plant. "Good boy, you're so bright and clever," she added. Chetty smiled as she caressed his cheek. "Now look at the flower again," this time making only a slight gesture with her hand rather than using her extended arm as before. And after a while she was able to fade out using gestures altogether, except when teaching Chet a new word.

- ▪10 Describe how children most often learn to attend when directed by language stimuli.
- ▪11 How would you use the looking game to teach language control of orienting?

Attending, orienting, and the importance of good cue control

Cues for attending and orienting are sort of higher order cues — they're cues for cues — a cue telling you what the next cue is that will indicate the response to be rewarded. For instance, the baseball coach may cough to get the batter to orient toward her before giving signals to make a certain type of hit.

Why must our orienting or attending be under good cue control? We'll be more likely to attend to the crucial features of our world if our attention is under good cue control. Those features will, in turn, control our actions so we will be able to deal best with that world. For instance: "Hey, Carol, where's that Sound-o-Rama stereo repair shop?" Chet asked, heading toward the door with their ailing stereo in hand.

"Go down Main 'til you get to Rose Street; then hang a left. It's about two blocks down on the right. You'll have to look close though, 'cause it's just a little store crowded between a couple others."

Later, as Chet was heading down Main Street, *Which way was I supposed to turn on Rose? She told me to turn on Rose, but she didn't say which way. I think I should turn right.*

Two miles later, *Now here I am at the end of South Rose and there's no Sound-o-Rama. I wish Carol'd give better directions next time. I'll just have to turn around and go down Rose the other way 'til I get on the other side of Main.*

But when Chet did get to Sound-o-Rama, he drove right on by, as he was busy adjusting the AM dial on his radio where "Slimus in the afternoon, the DJ with the big sound, that goes round and round the greater metropolitan area to bring all you dudes and dudettes the latest boss sounds", was saying, "Be sure to stop at Sound-o-Rama, 315 North Rose, just three blocks off the square. Yes it's Sound-o-Rama, the world's greatest stereo center with a great bunch of . . . szapp, bzzz." But Chet wasn't even attending to the directions given by Slimus while he tuned in the radio. *That static. Now here I am at the end of North Rose and still no Sound-o-Rama. And I'm late for work. Guess I just won't get it done today.*

***

What was Chet's problem? His attending wasn't under good cue control. For instance, Carol gave him spoken cues for what stimuli to attend to: "Look for Rose Street." The fact that he asked Carol a question should have been a strong cue to him to attend to her answer. But, in fact, her words "hang a left" weren't a cue for his actions. It's almost as if Carol should have said, "Yes, Chet, this is my answer. Now listen carefully to it." Then he might have attended to her answer. Then again, it might not have done much good for her to tell him to pay attention. He wasn't even able to attend to the store signs as he drove down Rose Street. He couldn't attend, even though she had tried to cue his attending by saying, "Look carefully . . . two blocks down on the right . . . look carefully . . ." He missed Sound-o-Rama once he got on Rose Street, because he failed to look on the right as she had said. Chet's actions weren't under good cue control, not because he didn't know the words Carol had spoken, but because he hadn't had good enough training in following spoken directions.

- ■12 In what sense may we think of cues for attending and orienting as being higher order cues?
- ■13 Cite an instance of poor attending by an adult (to both audio and visual cues).
- ■14 Why is it important for our orienting or attending to be under good cue control?

Teaching good cue control

One of the reasons for Chet's poor attending was that he had never been taught to attend. He often missed the problems that should have resulted from his failure to follow the right cues. In other words his failures were rarely punished. His watchful parents were always at hand to intervene. They made sure he got all the rewards he would have if he had been under good cue control. And they made sure he didn't get many of the punishers he would have for being under poor cue control. His parents did his attending for him. So, the lack of good cue control over his attending was a side effect of his being a spoiled child.

Chet often had trouble attending to cues the setting indicated were relevant. In the classroom, he found he had a hard time listening to the teacher lecture, finding it more rewarding to attend to his own daydreams. The results of the test were too far removed to exert much control.

In the same way, he found himself attending to his daydreams more than to the textbooks he was reading — dare we suggest even his psych text? Daydreaming was almost always more rewarding than attending to these texts. The words do exert good cue control over part of his actions, the parroting part. However, they don't control other parts of his actions, those parts involved in understanding what he's reading. So he's only partly attending to the words. We might say he's not attending to those features of the words that exert meaning-type, cue control.

And worse, he's not aware of his problem. He'll say he knows what he's read, but you shouldn't be so rude as to press him too hard on that point. Even his failure, itself, doesn't exert good cue control.

Chet's had trouble attending to the proper cues for school work since he was a child, whether someone asked him to do so, or whether the setting implied the instructions. For instance, his first-grade teacher told Chet, "I want you to sit still and look this way young man. Act like you're listening to me when I'm talking to the class." But the teacher's demand that Chet attend to what was said didn't serve as a very good cue. He failed to attend so the rest of the teacher's words could not act as cues for later actions; therefore, he didn't learn very much.

He runs into the same problem in college, where the cues for him to attend are a little more subtle, but nonetheless present. Dr. Harper doesn't instruct Chet to sit still and listen. He assumes Chet's paying attention, just because Chet, the student, is in the classroom, and he, the teacher, is in front of the class teaching. But Dr. Harper shouldn't assume that, if he wants Chet to learn. The classroom setting exerts little cue control over Chet's attending, even less than the first-grade teacher's spoken demand.

Carol's aware of her husband's problem, and of the learning problems that result. She wants to help her son avoid this. She wants to help him learn to attend to the right features of his world. This requires that the right cues control his orienting.

And how does she do that? By playing the attending game, how else? The same as the looking game, really. But we attend in more ways than just looking — for instance, we also listen. And we need to be able to attend to complex cues. So she helped her son learn to attend to such cues when he had mastered the simpler ones. In fact, she did this as part of the looking game. "Show me the wagon, Chetty. Point to it. Good." "Now show me the big wagon. No the big one. Good boy." "Now show me the front end of the little, red wagon. Good, that's right." Thus she got him to attend to the details of her verbal cues as well as to the details of the objects he looked at. Little Chet was on his way to behaving like a very intelligent young man. He was learning to attend to his world — a needed skill if he was to learn from that world and survive in it.

- ■15 How might we account for poor attending by an adult in terms of the child-rearing practices of the parents?
- ■16 How can poor attending to the proper stimuli affect the student in grade school and in college?
- ■17 How could you teach a child the good cue control of attending?

PREREQUISITES

Test taking

Little Chet must learn to attend to the crucial features of his world, if he is to deal with it. And one small but important part of the world of many people is the intelligence test. Scores on such tests often predict our success later in life. They may also affect our chance to obtain certain rewards later in life.

Now little Chet was an intelligence test ace, even at the age of two. Sue, a psych major and former classmate of Carol's, practiced her test-giving on the young lad. For instance she'd say: "Watch what I do," or "Show me the dolly's hair," or "What's this?" On and on, giving a test requiring that little Chet understand her words, and attend to both those words and the test items. Easy tasks for the old pro, fresh from the how-to-attend games he and his mother played.

And just for the fun of it, Sue came back when Chet was three-and-a-half years old, with the intelligence test for that age level. "Which stick is longer?" she asked, requiring Chet to look back and forth at the two sticks. The relation between the two sticks had to control his pointing response. But he had no trouble since Carol had already taught him such complex and detailed discriminations.

At the age of four, he might be asked to select a circle from among ten figures — a circle that looked like the circle the tester pointed to — a very complex, matching discrimination requiring Chet to attend to complex verbal instructions as well as to the details of all the figures.

Little Chet wouldn't have done nearly as well at the intelligence test if he hadn't learned to attend to the details of things pointed out to him. But of course most children don't have the chance to learn those attending skills in as well-planned a manner as he did. Most children must learn such skills catch-as-catch-can, some learning them fairly well and some not so well. This in turn causes some to score well on intelligence tests and others to score poorly.

■18 Cite three instances where we need cue control to do well on intelligence tests.

Test taking and language

Chet must be able to speak as well as understand language for him to do well on most intelligence tests. This becomes even more true because the tests require him to speak more often as they advance. And Sue listened with care to anything two-year-old Chet might happen to say, giving him a higher score on his test if he tied words together in his talk: "Pretty cat," "Bad boy."

Even the sentence structure he uses will affect his intelligence-test score, by the time he reaches the age of four. The tester will ask, "Why do we have houses?" And Chet's score will depend on the word sequences he's learned with respect to houses.

Large parts of intelligence tests really seem to be tests of word knowledge when the child is older. So clearly, good vocal and written language skills are needed if a person is to do well on such tests.

■19 Besides being able to understand language, what skills are needed for a person to do well on intelligence tests?

PSYCHOLOGICAL TESTS

Achievement tests

Let's look a little closer at the nature of tests, noting that a psychological test is a sample of behavior taken under standard conditions (often used to predict future actions). You've no doubt taken quite a few such tests since starting school — most often, achievement tests. How much have you achieved? How much have you done? How much have you learned?

Achievement test: a psychological test based on samples of behavior that relate in a direct way to past occasions for learning.

For instance, you may take a final exam in this course at the end of the term. Perhaps you're supposed to learn the correct answers to several hundred questions. But your teacher won't be able to test you on each question since the exam lasts only fifty minutes. Therefore the teacher will use a sample of the questions, perhaps only fifty, and will assume the sample is a fair test of all you've acquired in the course.

You may ask, "Why does the world keep pestering me with such tests?" Because it wants to predict what you'll do in the future. It can do this in two ways, using achievement tests. First, the world can predict future actions by looking at how much you've learned that will be of use in the future — that you can apply in the future. For instance, how well you do on a French language test may predict how well you'll do as an interpreter at the U.N.

And second, achievement tests can predict other future actions if the future setting is much the same as the setting related to that achievement test. For instance, how well you do on that same French language test may predict how well you'll do when you start to study German. That's because people act in the future like they've acted in the past, if the conditions remain fairly constant. How can we predict what you'll achieve next term? We can look at how much you achieved this term. Your final exam scores this term will do a fairly good job of predicting your exam scores for next term, as long as you study under the same conditions.

Note: Don't despair if you don't like the grades you've gotten this term or last term. You can change things. But you will not do the trick by simply saying, "I'm going to do better next time." In fact you'll need to change your personal world so it will support a large amount of good study behavior. How much you achieved in each course results from many things: your general attending skills; your reading skills; your study skills; and, perhaps most important of all, how much time you study. The amount of time you study is determined by the rewards and punishers for studying vs. the rewards and punishers for doing other things. So your best approach may be to try to change the balance of your rewards and punishers. In the Behavior Modification chapter we'll look at how we can deal with this sort of thing.

- ■20 Define achievement tests.
- ■21 What are two ways achievement tests help predict future actions?

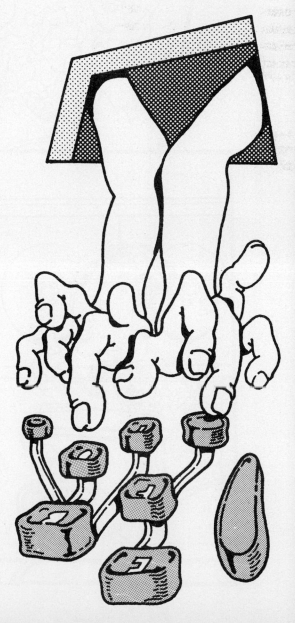

Intelligence tests

What are intelligence tests? In a sense, intelligence tests are like achievement tests. They both measure what we've achieved, though at first glance, it's often less clear where and how we learned those acts sampled by intelligence tests. However, if we look further, we can see that intelligence tests do sample the behavior you've acquired in school and elsewhere. They often sample your reading behavior, mathematics behavior, vocabulary behavior, reasoning behavior, etc. They sample skills you've achieved.

Intelligence test: a psychological test designed to sample behaviors that relate in an **indirect** way to past occasions for learning. The sampled behaviors are useful in many settings, but those samples do not often include physical or social skills.

For instance, the intelligence test samples behaviors that are useful in the school setting. As we've seen, you must learn how to attend to the right cues in order to do well in school and to do well on intelligence tests. Your attending must be under the cue control of written instructions. You must be able to attend to the subtle details of complex visual cues in order to discriminate among them. You won't do well in school or on intelligence tests without those skills. So the intelligence test samples useful skills you've learned in order to predict how well you'll do in school in the future.

Also, you must find it rewarding to do well on tests, since taking tests requires a certain amount of work — work that has to be rewarded. Most likely, you won't happen to find it rewarding to do well on achievement tests in school if you don't also happen to find it rewarding to do well on intelligence tests. Therefore you won't be surprised to learn that children raise their intelligence test scores a great deal when they receive special rewards for doing well on those tests.

Intelligence tests sample what we've achieved in the classroom. And we need some of the same basic skills and rewards to do well in school and on intelligence tests. So people who do well on intelligence tests also tend to do well in school. So we say intelligence tests are valid if they predict something like school performance.

Test validity: a test is valid if it predicts the behavior it was designed to predict.

- ■22 Define intelligence test.
- ■23 How do achievement and intelligence tests differ?
- ■24 How are achievement and intelligence tests alike?
- ■25 Define test validity.

WHAT IS INTELLIGENCE?

There's no such thing as intelligence. We say a person is intelligent, but we mean the person acts intelligently. There is one correct way to use the word "intelligent" — as an adverb describing how people act. We shouldn't say people have a high intelligence inside them causing them to act in an intelligent manner.

Let's look at a similar case that may be a little clearer: We say people have "a good sense of humor" when they laugh at the right times and say funny things. How do we know they have a good sense of humor? Because they act in that humorous manner. Why do they act in a humorous manner? Because they have a good sense of humor. How do we know they have a good sense of humor? . . . Does the argument seem to be running in a circle? Of course. That's because it tries to prove a "sense of humor" exists by pointing to the actions this sense is meant to account for. There is no independent proof that "sense of humor" exists.

The concept of "sense of humor" shows how we often mislead ourselves by the way we use words in our everyday language. This isn't as tragic in the case of "sense of humor", because people in our culture aren't that concerned about humor. But suppose being a comic was a major profession. Suppose the school with the most prestige in the country was the Lenny Bruce Memorial College of Laugh-a-Minute Rou-tines, Peppy Patter, Snappy Clichés, and Sardonic Social Satire. Then things might not be the same. Then we'd be hurt much more by the poor thinking resulting from that sort of language use.

It's too bad the same problem exists in the much more crucial area of intelligent actions. We say people have intelligence just as we say they have a sense of humor. We say people act as they do because of that intelligence. The circular reasoning here can do much more harm since we're dealing with a much more serious area.

People often make the mistake of pointing to the intelligence of the person's parents as proof of the genetic nature of intelligence. Yet geneticists and anatomists have not had much luck in getting at the biological roots of intelligence — not much more luck than they've had in getting at those same roots of a sense of humor. We do, in fact, use the word "intelligence" as if it were a thing, but that doesn't make it so. That word can cause serious problems since it leads us astray in our search for the causes of human behavior and in our attempts to improve the human condition.

Intelligence tests do not measure a thing called "intelligence". They simply provide a chance to see how we act in the test setting. But how we act there may be fairly close to the way we will act elsewhere, if elsewhere is enough like the test setting. Then we can predict from such tests what kind of acts we can expect in other places — with which we're more concerned. So tests of intelligent acts can be useful tools, even though there's no such thing as intelligence.

Intelligent acts are a set of learned acts. They involve good attending skills, language responses, etc. But for most of us, there's no clear proof that any biological factors affect how we normally differ in the quality of our intelligent actions. There isn't even proof that biological factors are a direct cause of the behavior problems in over eighty percent of the people we classify as mentally retarded. However, there are some clear cases of brain damage, either inherited or from injury. And brain damage can make it harder for a person to learn behaviors that are complex or need to be under good cue control. But, for the most part, it's not clear that there is any biological basis for how people differ in their intelligent actions.

Perhaps, some time in the future, we'll find biological factors that do affect the way normal people learn. Perhaps normal people vary in the amount of behavior change resulting from the delivery of a single reward. Perhaps they vary in the speed with which they learn complex actions. Perhaps they vary in the number of complex sets of stimulus-response sequences they can maintain. Perhaps, but we have no direct proof.

Yet we do know this: people won't learn to act intelligently if they don't have a chance to learn to do so; and the chances to learn vary from person to person. Maybe we'd all act in an equally intelligent manner if we all had equal chances to learn. We'll have a hard time providing these equal chances — but we must, if our culture and the people are to achieve their greatest potential.

■26 What is intelligence? (Watch out, that's a trick question.)

■27 Compare the nature of the concepts of intelligence and sense of humor.

■28 Discuss the notion that intelligence tests do not measure "intelligence".

■29 What role does brain damage play in affecting intelligent behavior?

■30 In what way **might** biological factors affect the way normal people learn?

■31 People differ in the amount of intelligent behavior they exhibit. Explain this in terms of chances for learning.

CONCLUSIONS

We must act in an intelligent manner, if our society and the people within it are to get the most out of life and give the most to life — perhaps if we're even to survive. But we must know how people learn intelligent actions, if we're to insure that we all have a chance to move closer to our greatest potential for such action.

As we've seen, intelligent acts are not caused by some inner-structure called "intelligence" — a structure we invented. Instead intelligent acts are learned acts. That means we can have no intelligent acts without a chance to learn them. Still, inherited, biophysical factors might play a role too, as they could affect the quality of our intelligent actions through their effect on the quality of our learning. But there have been decades of debate, without any direct proof as to whether our inherited, bio-physical structures do affect the extent that our intelligent behavior differs in quantity or quality among people, social groups, and races. On the other hand, we do know we all have differing chances to learn intelligent actions; so that may account for the ways people, social groups, and races differ in the level of their intelligent actions.

What are some of the components of these intelligent actions we should help people learn? First, almost all of our intelligent acts involve language, either in our reading, speaking, or thinking. So we should help people learn good language skills. We need those skills to do well on intelligence tests, but what's more crucial, we also need such skills to act in an intelligent manner in other settings.

Second, we need to be able to observe closely the main features of our world if we are to learn those language skills and the knowledge they may represent. We need to respond to the right orienting and attention cues — natural cues, symbolic cues, and language cues.

Children learn the basic skills needed for intelligent action, with their rate of progress depending largely on how their parents interact with them. Thus, parents can enhance their children's progress by using a helping approach — one based on a knowledge of the components of intelligent actions and a knowledge of how to teach those components. This helping approach involves rewarding correct responses to stimulus cues and building complex stimulus-response patterns through the use of more and more complex cues and actions. Though you may present this approach to your child in the form of a game, it is, in fact, no mere game. Instead, it's a tool for social revolution — a revolution aimed at building a just society — one where we're not held back because of a lack of intellectual skills — where we all have a chance to do our share for society and to get our share from society. Such "games" may move our social system one step closer to our goal of a just and equal society.

CHAPTER 15
JEAN PIAGET AND THE DEVELOPMENT OF COGNITIVE BEHAVIOR

INTRODUCTION

Jean Piaget, the Swiss psychologist, has had great impact on the way many psychologists throughout the world look at the development of cognition, or thinking, in children. He's a cognitive theorist — one who stresses the crucial role of thought in the life of humans. He says, to understand why people act as they do, we must find out what they think, what they expect, what they know.

Piaget uses two methods to find out what people think: one is simply to ask them what they were thinking; the second is to ask them to solve problems. The first approach assumes people are good observers of their private thoughts — that they really know "why" they have acted in a certain way. Sometimes this may be the case; but in later chapters, we'll see that we can often be fooled by what we tell ourselves

are the reasons for our actions.

In his second approach, Piaget performs complex studies where he asks children of various ages to solve problems. He then notes the way they do this, observing that children can solve more and more complex problems as they grow older. He also notes that all the children in his studies seem to develop these cognitive, or problem-solving skills in much the same order. From this he concludes that there is a strict sequence of stages of cognitive development through which all children must pass if they are to reach higher stages — each stage consisting of a set of complex cognitive skills.

Like most other cognitive theorists, Piaget also assumes cognitive events are unique, not really behavior of the type we observe when looking at people's movements. He doesn't deal with

cognitive processes as learned acts under the control of cues, rewards, and punishers, as we who take the learning view do.

We agree with the cognitive theorists — it's worthwhile to study how children develop complex cognitive skills. We also agree that cognitive events may greatly affect our observed actions. But we'll look at these cognitive events from a learning view, in much the same manner as we've done with other issues — we wish to be parsimonious. Furthermore, we hope these two great approaches, cognitive and learning, can combine to help us look at our field in a way neither approach has done by itself.

- 1 Who is Jean Piaget?
- 2 How does Piaget's approach to cognitive events differ from the learning approach?

SENSORY-MOTOR PERIOD

The problem of object constancy

Big Chet was just beginning to worry about how smart his son was. This started when they were playing a game, a game just for fun, as you will see, not quite like Carol's helping game. In his game, Chet played with the baby's rattle, teasing him, much to the delight of both father and son. He brought the rattle toward the youngster, only to pull it back as the child reached for the toy. Much to big Chet's dismay, his son lost all interest in the game when the rattle went out of sight, behind the father's back.

"Hey, Carol, look at this. The dumb kid doesn't even know the toy's there when I hide it from him. You'd think he'd care about what's behind my back, but he doesn't. He doesn't act normal."

In vain, Carol tried to calm her distressed husband. "He's okay. Just needs a little time to learn what's going on — that's all."

"Learn! What do you mean learn? It's normal he should know the toy's there, even when it's behind me! No one taught me those things!"

* * *

It's easy to see how Chet feels. It seems hard to conceive of children failing to know something's behind a person's back when they saw the person put it there. Yet all infants act that way no matter how smart they are.

The problem is called "object constancy". In cognitive terms, it means people know an object is still there (is constant or exists) even when they can't see it. But we'll offer a more behavioral definition, since we find the term "knows" too often leads to confusion.

Object constancy: responding in a manner appropriate to an object, even though that object is out of sight.

- 3 What does object constancy mean in cognitive terms?
- 4 Define object constancy and cite an instance.

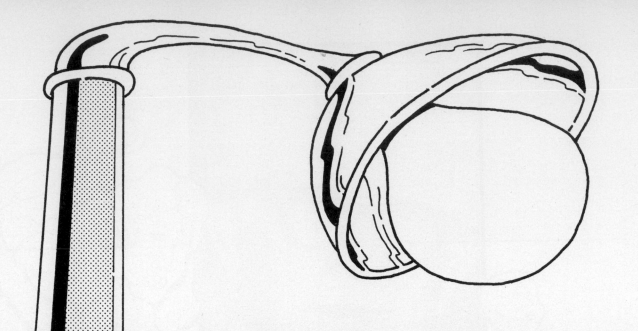

Learning object constancy

How will little Chet learn to respond according to object constancy? First we must decide how he will act when he does respond the right way. What will we see him do? We'll see him look or orient toward the rattle. And, we'll see him approach the rattle, reaching out or even crawling toward it, even though it's out of his sight.

What rewards may result if he orients and approaches in this way? Sometimes he gets to touch and shake the rattle — a fantastic reward. What cues the response? The sight and sound of the rattle of course. That all makes sense. In fact, it looks like the real question is, "How can anyone be controlled by a cue that's not there?"

Why would we expect little Chet, or anyone else, to orient toward a stimulus if he can't see or hear it? The answer is that more complex cue control comes into play, over time, as the child sees more and more things vanish and then come back.

Think about the sight of Carol's face as a reward for her son. His orienting response is rewarded by the sight of that face when he turns toward her voice. But what happens when Carol turns around? The face will vanish. And what happens if Chet keeps looking toward his mother for a second or two? At least once in a while, that maintained orienting will get a reward — the sight of Mom as she turns back around.

Or perhaps little Chet orients toward the sound of the TV, a response that gets very strong rewards — bright, moving, changing pictures. Then, all of a sudden, an awful thing happens. A huge form takes the place of the TV, as big Chet walks in front of the tube on his way to get a beer from the kitchen. Then the TV appears again, before little Chet can orient to a better visual reward than that huge form. So the child's orienting response was reinforced for hanging in there for a fraction of a second, even when the sight of the TV had gone away.

How do these two episodes relate to the issue of why we expect people to orient toward stimuli that aren't there? Well, both cases show how the orienting response got a reward when it endured for a brief period of time in the absence of the stimulus itself. Fine, but how does the child learn to persist for longer periods of time? Well, with most children, this is a chancy affair. The child keeps looking for a fraction of a second at where the object had been. Sometimes that looking gets its reward. And sometimes the child keeps looking longer than a fraction of a second, since how long a child looks varies from time to time. And sometimes that longer response also gets its reward, making it more likely the child will again orient a little longer.

The child will orient even longer, as those longer responses start getting more rewards. On it goes, as the length of time the child will orient increases.

At first glance it may almost look like this happens just because the child matures while growing older. But, as we can see, the change in the orienting response results more likely from chances to learn due to events taking place in the normal world of most infants.

■ 5 How would a child learn object constancy for a "stationary" object? Cite a couple of instances where the child would have a chance to learn such object constancy.

Learning constancy of moving objects

Object-constancy cue control becomes more complex, even while the child is still an infant. For instance, little Chet soon learned to follow moving stimuli with his eyes. He would turn his head as his mother walked across the room. Mom, the moving stimulus, became a part of a complex cue — two cues combining to control moving his head. The combined cues were that he was looking at something, and that the thing was moving across his field of vision.

But that's not all; sometimes moving objects also vanish. Suppose little Chet watched a dog as it strolled through the front yard. What happened when the dog walked behind a tree? Did Chet look at the side of the tree where he last saw the dog? Yes, at first he did. But his following response came under more complex cue control, as he learned the correct actions: keep moving your eyes along the same path, if you were following something with your eyes and that thing went out of sight. You can think of this as "constancy of moving objects".

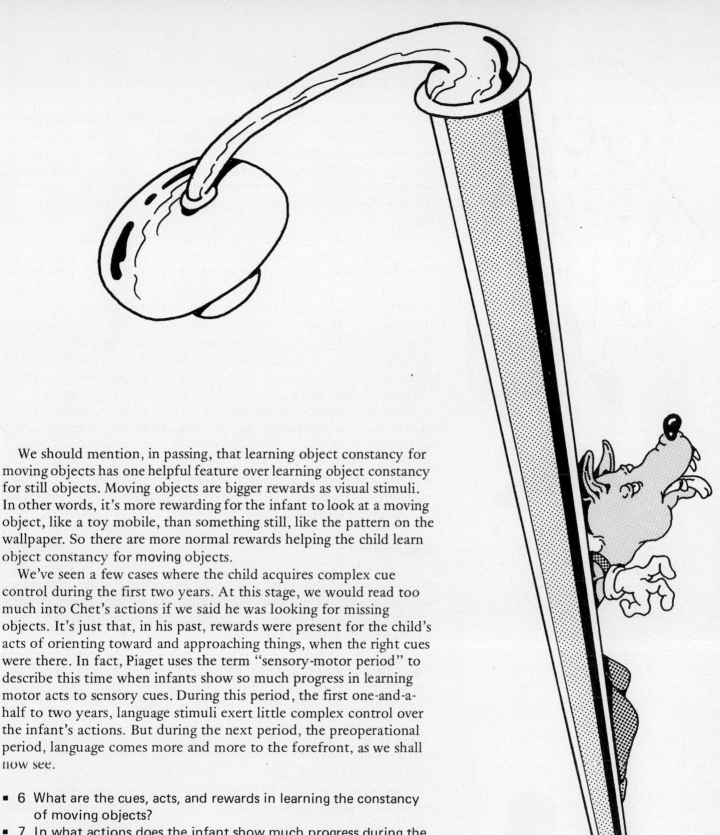

We should mention, in passing, that learning object constancy for moving objects has one helpful feature over learning object constancy for still objects. Moving objects are bigger rewards as visual stimuli. In other words, it's more rewarding for the infant to look at a moving object, like a toy mobile, than something still, like the pattern on the wallpaper. So there are more normal rewards helping the child learn object constancy for moving objects.

We've seen a few cases where the child acquires complex cue control during the first two years. At this stage, we would read too much into Chet's actions if we said he was looking for missing objects. It's just that, in his past, rewards were present for the child's acts of orienting toward and approaching things, when the right cues were there. In fact, Piaget uses the term "sensory-motor period" to describe this time when infants show so much progress in learning motor acts to sensory cues. During this period, the first one-and-a-half to two years, language stimuli exert little complex control over the infant's actions. But during the next period, the preoperational period, language comes more and more to the forefront, as we shall now see.

- 6 What are the cues, acts, and rewards in learning the constancy of moving objects?
- 7 In what actions does the infant show much progress during the sensory-motor period?
- 8 Thought question: How could Carol use the helping approach to teach little Chet the two types of object constancy we've looked at?

PREOPERATIONAL PERIOD

What Piaget calls the "preoperational period" often lasts from about the child's second to its seventh year. During this period, the child's actions keep coming under ever greater complex cue control. For instance, in the case of object constancy, we saw control by a cue based on events that had happened in the past. Part of the complex cue was the result of an event that had happened a few seconds before.

This sort of delayed cue control becomes even more complex during the preoperational period. For instance, children learn delayed imitative control; they learn to imitate the actions others have made some time before. This imitative cue control is more complex in two ways: 1) the cue and the act themselves may be more complex; and 2) the time delay between the cue and the response can be much greater than a few seconds. During this period, the child also makes the most clear-cut progress in learning language. As we've seen, this is a skill of great value in thinking and dealing with complex, delayed problems.

However, the child's cue control has a long way to go before reaching the complex level of the cue control of most adults. We'll look at some of the limits of preoperational cue control in the next sections.

- ■ 9 Preoperational period often covers what age range?
- ■10 What is a type of cue control in this period that's more complex than in the sensory-motor period?

Egocentrism

Preoperational children are egocentric. In cognitive terms, this means children always look at things from their own points of view rather than from the points of view of others. Here's a definition in somewhat more behavioral terms:

Egocentric behavior: behavior controlled by stimuli from the immediate point of view of the person behaving rather than from the point of view of others, even when the latter is called for.

Piaget developed a research setting to study this egocentrism. He showed children views from opposite sides of a three-foot toy mountain. He then stood on one side of the toy mountain while the child stood on the other. He gave the child two pictures of the mountain — one from the child's point of view (from where the child was standing), the other from Piaget's point of view (from where he was standing). He asked the child to point to the picture of the view that he, Piaget, saw. Preoperational children weren't able to select the picture of Piaget's view of the mountain. Instead they picked a picture of their view. Egocentrism.

This is also a problem of complex cue control — a problem of stimulus matching much like delayed imitation. Let's look at how children might learn to respond to another person's point of view in a lab setting, before we look at how this would happen in a normal setting. It might work like this: the children first look at a stimulus (the side of the mountain opposite where they will stand during the reward phase to come). Then the teacher shows them two stimuli — a picture of that opposite side of the mountain, and one of their side. During the next phase, the teacher rewards the children if they select the picture matching the opposite side of the mountain when asked to do so. Normal young children should have little trouble learning this sort of cue control since other creatures, such as pigeons, have learned it in lab settings. This is called a "stimulus matching procedure" because the response is rewarded if the observer picks a comparable stimulus that matches a sample stimulus (the pictures matching Piaget's view). It's called "delayed stimulus matching" because of the time delay between seeing the sample stimulus (Piaget's view) and the comparison stimuli (the pictures).

Stimulus matching procedure (matching-to-sample): a sample stimulus is presented along with a set of comparison stimuli. A reinforcer is given for the response of selecting the comparison stimulus that matches or is the same as the sample stimulus.

Delayed stimulus matching: the presentation of the sample and then its removal, with a delay period before the comparison stimuli are presented.

We don't mean to imply that egocentrism is just a memory problem, by treating it as a problem of delayed stimulus matching or delayed imitation. We're simply saying it's a matching problem. When Piaget asks them to select the view matching his, the children should match the pictures to Piaget's view rather than to their own view. That preceding language cue (Piaget's request) selects which view the child is to match — namely Piaget's view. We shouldn't be too surprised if it takes quite a while before a set of cues this complex gets control of the child's actions. In the normal world of children, much the same thing takes place.

At one point children see the same view other people have. Then from time to time, they're asked to respond according to those other views. Rewards or punishers may follow in keeping with their responses.

When, in everyday life, might children learn to respond to another person's point of view? Perhaps when they're trying to explain something to, or to instruct, someone. Suppose they're telling another child to put a ball in a bucket. After a while, they'll learn that the other child won't be able to make the correct response unless that child can also see the ball and the bucket. Events in formal grade-school classrooms may also reduce egocentrism. No doubt children need rewards in many settings with many cues, if such complex cue control is to apply to those other settings and cues. And children must learn in many conditions if they are to be able to respond to questions about what someone else sees, or hears, or feels. So we shouldn't be too surprised if a seven-year-old child is still egocentric. In fact, we shouldn't be too surprised if adults are also still a little egocentric. Ever try to teach someone to tie his necktie or her shoelaces? Most of us haven't had enough rewards for dealing with those settings to lose our egocentrism there.

- ■11 What is egocentrism, in cognitive terms?
- ■12 Define egocentric behavior.
- ■13 Describe Piaget's mountain study.
- ■14 Define stimulus matching procedure.
- ■15 Define delayed stimulus matching.
- ■16 How would you teach a child to respond to other people's views using a delayed stimulus-matching procedure?

Weak language control

Preoperational children also have other limits to their cue control, such as the extent to which a long series of words can combine to control their later speech. For instance, in talking, a child might ramble on, each word acting as a cue for the next; but all of the words that went before might not combine to form a single cue for the rest of the child's speech. The child might say something like this, "The coke truck runned over my dolly. Give me some coke." The words in the first sentence didn't combine to control the second sentence. Instead, the word "coke" was the sole cue for that second sentence.

This weakness in cue control limits the level of the child's thinking, since thinking is so much a function of what people can say to themselves. You can't think anything through that's very complex if each thought is controlled by only single words of the thought that went just before. Again, the child needs a good deal of training with language before a long language sequence exerts much cue control.

■17 Describe the weak language control of the preoperational child. Cite an instance.

Anthropomorphism

A two-year-old boy described a cup as "tired", when he saw it lying on its side. A child said a towel hook was "cruel", perhaps after bumping into the hook. A four-year-old said a tall and erect tripod was "proud". These cases show "anthropomorphism".

Anthropomorphism: describing animals and objects in human terms.

We look at these anthropomorphic acts as a result of stimulus generalization. The response of saying, "that person is tired", has gotten rewards in the presence of cues — stimuli like people lying on their side. So those stimuli may generalize too far — to anything lying on its side in a non-working pose. But the child's speech will come under proper cue control because only the correct response will get rewards. In fact, there may even be mild punishment of that response, when the parent says, "No, that's not right! Don't be silly — the cup's not tired." In a sense, children's language becomes more precise as they generalize less, due to extinction and punishment of too much generalizing. But that takes time.

■18 Define anthropomorphism. Cite an instance.
■19 Analyze an instance of anthropomorphism in terms of too much stimulus generalization.

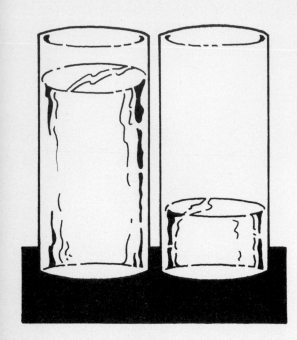

Learning two-dimensional concepts

The concept of stimulus dimension plays a crucial role in the way we look at Piaget's work on the cognitive development of children. We feel we can best understand the child's increase in cognitive skills, in terms of the control of more complex stimuli. And we look at these complex stimuli in terms of the number of stimulus dimensions involved. A stimulus dimension is a feature of that stimulus such as color, brightness, height, width, or volume. So, from our view, the actions of advanced children may be controlled by concepts made up of two or more such stimulus dimensions.

Before learning two-dimensional concepts, children may learn one-dimensional concepts. And before learning one-dimensional concepts, they may learn simple discriminations. Let's look at such a discrimination: In playing with his log-cabin blocks, little Chet learned to discriminate between the long logs and the medium ones. No reward occurred when he picked up a medium log and placed it on the wall of his log cabin where a long log should have gone. But, getting the correct log was reinforced by the proper fit of the log on the wall.

These simple discriminations may combine to form a concept: "longer than", in other words, the concept of length. Over time, the child learns to discriminate between many pairs of logs — not just long and medium logs, but also medium and short logs, and long and short logs. This, in turn, generalizes to other areas: Chet learned to discriminate between the different lengths of other objects like tinker toys, and then to novel lengths he had not worked with. Soon he'll be able to tell which of a set of lines is the longest. This is a single-dimensional concept.

* * *

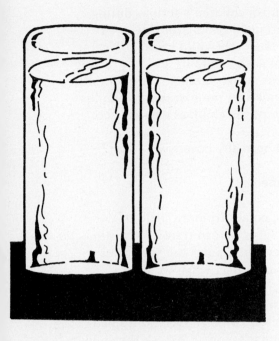

Let's look at one more single-dimensional concept. We show a child two glasses of water that are the same in width but filled to different heights. The preoperational child can tell us which glass has the higher water level. Now the two stimuli (the glasses) differ in only one dimension — the height of the water — since the other dimension, the width, is the same for both glasses.

However, more complex concepts also begin to control the actions of preoperational children; these concepts involve two stimulus dimensions. Let's look at an example of such a concept. First we show the child two identical glasses filled to the brim. Then we show two more glasses, a narrow one and a wide one. We ask which glass would have the higher level of water, the narrow or the wide one, if we were to pour into them the water from the medium glasses. The child's answer must now be controlled by two stimulus dimensions: not just the height of the water in the two glasses, but also the width of the glasses — two dimensions. So the child's actions are controlled by a two-dimensional concept.

■20 Cite an instance of a two-dimensional concept most preoperational children have learned.

CONCRETE-OPERATIONAL PERIOD

Even more complex cues come to control children's actions during what Piaget calls the "concrete-operational period", roughly their seventh to twelfth years. During this phase, the child learns to deal with concrete operations — operations such as adding and subtracting with concrete objects — objects present at that moment. And during these concrete operations, concepts based on three or more stimulus dimensions often control the behavior of the child, as we shall see.

■21 The concrete-operational period normally covers what ages?

The problem of conservation of volume

The notion of conservation of volume comes from the field of physics. It states that there are many ways we can transform a substance while its volume is conserved, or remains the same. For instance, the volume of fluid remains the same, when we pour it from one glass into the other.

Let's get out our water glasses again, this time with the concrete-operational child. Now we have two short, wide glasses, both filled with water, and one tall, narrow glass that's empty. We ask the child which of the two wide glasses has the most water, and the child says they're the same. Then we pour the water from one of the short, wide glasses into the tall, narrow glass. We ask the child which glass holds the most water — the remaining short, wide one, or the tall, narrow one.

It's clear to us that the two glasses hold the same amount of water, since we just saw an equal amount of water being poured from the matching glass into the tall, narrow one. So we're not surprised when the concrete-operational child gives the correct answer. But we might be surprised to know that the younger, preoperational children can't deal with that problem; they will not say the amount of water is still the same. Preoperational children will most likely say the tall, narrow glass holds the most water.

Once again, it almost seems like this knowledge results from our passive maturation since people didn't go out of their way to teach it to us. And that may be why most children take some years to learn many things that seem so clear to us as adults.

■22 Describe the problem of the conservation of volume of fluid.

Learning conservation of volume

What do concrete-operational children learn that helps them give the correct answer? We saw that the preoperational child can say which level of water will be higher; that act is under good cue control of the two stimulus dimensions — width of the glass and height of the fluid. So perhaps a third dimension, volume of fluid, is involved in this conservation problem solved by the concrete-operational child. This child's response must be controlled by a three-dimensional concept — volume of the fluid as a function of height of the fluid and width of the glass. Note that a short, wide glass can contain the same volume as a tall, narrow one.

But it's hard for the concept of volume independent of shape to gain control over children's actions. This may be a problem for two reasons: 1) the concept involves three stimulus dimensions; and 2) most children have only a small number of chances to get rewards for a correct response to that complex three-dimensional cue. It may not be enough to merely expose children to the reversible operation of pouring one volume of fluid back and forth between two glasses. That may not cause them to master the concept of conservation of volume when the shapes of the glasses are transformed.

Preoperational children may spend a good deal of time pouring fluids from one container into another and back again, while hovering over the kitchen sink, the bathtub, the wading pool, etc.; but their play doesn't depend upon the fact that the volume is conserved through this transformation. Therefore, conservation may not exert much cue control over their actions. The children may not attend to those dimensions of the complex stimulus. But those dimensions of the stimulus might exert much more accurate control over the children's behavior if the rewards in their play were based on a correct response to the volume once it had been transformed.

We should also suspect that children, and even adults, would not often acquire a generalized concept of conservation without some chances to learn along more stimulus dimensions. Our actions might be controlled by the concept that volume is conserved through the transformation of pouring from one glass into another. But most likely that concept would not generalize in a direct way to the concept that weight is also conserved in such a transformation. We might also have a problem with the concept that weight is conserved, though volume is not, when a block of ice melts into a puddle of water.

***

During the concrete-operational period, the child's actions also come under the cue control of the language involved with such concepts as conservation. This is another crucial feature of this period of cognitive development. You don't have to show the child the glasses and pour the fluid from one glass into the other. You can get the correct answer if you simply describe the operation to such a child before asking your question about whether the fluid is conserved. A very complex cue, your question, and the physical stimuli described by your question become a cue for the proper language response.

- ■23 At what level of cognitive development can the child first solve this problem?
- ■24 Analyze this conservation of volume problem in terms of multi-dimensional stimulus control.
- ■25 How would you find out if a child is under the control of the language associated with the concept of conservation?

The problem of classification

The preoperational and concrete-operational child also differ in other ways. The advanced preoperational child is able to divide concepts into subconcepts (classes into subclasses). For instance, preoperational children might be able to divide a set of toy animals (the class) into subclasses of poodles, terriers, and cats. And they can answer simple questions where they **compare two subclasses.** For instance, "Are there more poodles or terriers?"

But only **concrete-operational** children can answer complex questions where they must compare a class (dogs) with its subclasses (poodles and terriers).

Only the concrete-operational child can answer tricky questions like: "Are there more poodles (subclass), or dogs (class)?" or "Are there more dogs (subclass) or more animals (class)?"

Such questions may exert good cue control over the answers of concrete-operational children because they have many chances to compare classes and subclasses. Such children may have dealt with problems of this sort: "There are five of us here, and we've got four peaches and two pears. Have we got enough peaches or pears to go around?" "We don't? Well have we got enough fruit to go around?"

Such problems might teach the concrete-operational child how to compare classes with subclasses. But the preoperational child has not yet been involved in enough occasions where such learning will occur.

* * *

Let's look at another problem dealing with classes and subclasses — one showing clearly that concrete-operational children need to come under multidimensional stimulus control before they can answer some types of questions. This problem requires children to multiply classes. Suppose we give a child a

pile of forms composed of the letters "A", "B", and "C", with samples of each letter colored red, green, or blue. This involves two dimensions — form (the letter) and color — with three values of each dimension — the three letter forms and the three colors. So there are a total of nine (three multiplied by three) color-form pairs. Concrete-operational children can arrange the forms into the correct nine piles when asked to put together only those that are exactly alike. But preoperational children can't do this, since they make the mistake of combining some of the subclasses. For instance, such

a child might combine the red "As" and the red "Bs" into one subclass.

This problem where the child must multiply classes is a little more complex. It isn't just stimulus matching involving two-dimensional stimuli. Here's what such matching would look like: You'd set up the nine subclasses of colored forms with a sample from each subclass. Then you'd give the preoperational child the class of the nine forms all mixed together. You'd ask the child to take each of those single, colored forms and place it in the proper subclass next to the one of the nine samples it looked like.

Preoperational children might well be able to do this sort of matching. But again that's not quite like having the child multiply classes as described above.

- 26 Describe the toy animal classification problem where the child must compare a class with a subclass. How do preoperational and concrete-operational children do on such problems?
- 27 Describe the color-form classification problem. How do preoperational and concrete-operational children do on such problems?

Learning to multiply subclasses

When we ask children to put those colored forms that match in the same pile we're asking them to construct the subclasses themselves, without samples. A more complex task. But in what way? Perhaps our language still doesn't control the child's actions well enough. We say, "Put together all the things that are exactly alike." Perhaps few such acts have produced rewards in their young lives; yet we might be able to train these children in what we mean by "exactly alike". Then each object would act as a cue for a distinct response, that is, a response of putting each object in a different pile if the two objects differed in the slightest way. The child would thereby create exact subclasses or stacks for each distinct class of objects — red "As", red "Bs", etc.

Here's how we could do this: We could train children using three colors: red, green, and blue, and three forms: the letters, "A", "B", and "C". We would reward each response when a child made a correct new subclass — when the child started a new stack with a new object — red "A", green "B", etc. And we would mildly punish each error by asking the child to try again. Then we would give the children a new set of color-form objects, after they'd learned to create correct subclasses with the first set of objects. The new set might consist of the colors, orange, yellow, and violet with the letters "D", "E", and "F" as the forms.

We'd expect the children to learn more quickly, with fewer errors, to create this new set of subclasses: orange "Ds", yellow "Es", violet "Fs", etc. In fact, after training with a few such sets of objects, they should be able to create, with no errors, a set of nine subclasses of new color-form objects — pink "Xs", chartreuse "Ys", etc. We could help that training to generalize to more novel shapes as well by giving more training. The added training could involve other dimensions of the stimuli such as their size, weight, and texture.

In summary, what do children or adults need, to create subclasses with proper detail? We suspect they need training with the stimulus dimensions along which they construct the subclasses, though they may not need prior contact with the exact values of those stimulus dimensions. For instance, training might generalize from the red, green, and blue ABC's to black, white, and brown circles, squares, and triangles.

Their normal world provides most children with rewards for discriminating among proper stimulus classes, though often the rewards come in an unplanned, chancy, and therefore, obscure and slower way. Thus children have had enough rewards to learn to create many such correct subclasses by the time they reach the age of twelve, the end of the concrete-operational period.

■28 How might you teach children to multiply classes?

FORMAL-OPERATIONAL PERIOD

During what Piaget calls the "formal-operational period" (starting around the twelfth year), children learn to perform operations in a formal manner; that is, they learn to deal on a symbolic level with events and objects not present at the moment.

Their actions also come under the proper control of even more complex concepts at this time. Think about working the seesaw as a problem of complex, concept control. The well-balanced seesaw is a multi-dimensional concept with balance (distance of the end of the board from the ground) a function of four other dimensions: the weight on each side are two of the dimensions; and the distance of the weights on each side from the fulcrum (pivot) are the other two. We expect these dimensions to come gradually and individually to exert cue control. We also expect this multi-dimensional concept to control scooting and leaning back and forth as well as the response of getting someone else to sit on your side or the other side, if you're too light or too heavy. The dimensions of this concept will control those actions if the proper results have followed such acts. Those acts must have been rewarded or punished in the presence of many values of those dimensions.

The seesaw cue control becomes more complex as the child moves from late preoperational, through the concrete-operational, and into the formal-operational period. During the **preoperational** period, children scoot forward or backward on the seesaw solely as a function of the stimuli arising from balance. During the **concrete-operational** period, they can respond to one other single dimension: either 1) the weight on each side of the fulcrum, when both children are the same distance from the fulcrum; or 2) the distance from the fulcrum, when both children are the same weight. In other words, they can predict which end will go up: 1) when two unequal weights are at the same distance from the fulcrum; or 2) when two equal weights differ in their distance from the fulcrum.

But children can respond to both those dimensions **at the same time** only after they've entered the **formal-operational** period. To some extent they can then predict which end will go up, even with two unequal weights that **also** differ in their distance from the fulcrum. They can look at two people on a seesaw — a large child and a small child the same distance from the fulcrum. And they can instruct the small child to scoot further back away from the fulcrum. Only the formal-operational child can solve the problem without being involved in it — dealing with it only on a language or symbolic level.

∎29 What are the stimulus dimensions of the seesaw problem?
∎30 Describe the stimulus control of the seesaw for three cognitive periods.
∎31 At what age does the formal-operational period begin?

THE COGNITIVE-BEHAVIORAL APPROACH

Piaget is a cognitivist. He's mainly concerned with cognitive events, stressing how these events, like thinking, affect what we do — our behavior. Yet he believes such events are not the same as behavior — they are somehow unique. So he believes the main concepts we deal with (cues, acts, and rewards) play only a minor role, if any, in the development of children's thinking and reasoning. He agrees that children must contact things taking place in the normal world if those cognitive processes are to develop. But he implies that the children only need a chance to see these events for them to come to think about the events in a logical manner. He seems to discount the fact that the same normal world also rewards the child's acts of dealing in a logical manner with those events, so those rewards must also affect the child's logical thinking. He stresses biological maturation much more than learning, though he does not point to any biological structures involved in this maturation.

Piaget seems to oppose planning children's worlds to help them acquire logical thinking more quickly. It's as if this goes against nature and thereby might warp their skills as clear thinkers. In short, he opposes the sort of helping approach we suggest. He also believes all children develop by going through normal cognitive stages. He implies that these stages are caused more by biology than by the nature of logic and the nature of the physical world. On the other hand, he stresses crucial issues in dealing with the way cognition develops. We've covered some of the issues in this chapter, though they're not often discussed by psychologists with a behavioral view. Yet these issues are of great import if we are to know and help the whole person.

We've made a step toward looking at cognition as complex stimulus control. This doesn't reduce the value of Piaget's efforts as a scientist. Instead, it may add to the value of those efforts by putting them within the context of a behavioral approach — an approach that's been helpful in dealing with many other topics. We might call the result a cognitive-behavioral approach — a combined approach that sees that people's thoughts affect some of their outside acts. And an approach that also sees that the inner acts of thinking are of the same sort as those outside acts like walking and talking. The same laws that govern the outside acts must also govern the private inner acts of thinking and reasoning.

■32 What area of psychology is of chief concern to Piaget?
■33 In looking at cognitive development and stages of development, what does Piaget think of behavior, rewards, events of the normal world, maturation, and a learning-based helping approach?
■34 This book looks at cognition as complex _____ _____.
■35 Describe the cognitive-behavioral approach.

CONCLUSIONS

Jean Piaget, the famous Swiss psychologist, may be the most well-known person in the area of cognitive development. We've used a behavioral approach to look at some of his work.

We've looked at Piaget's proposed periods of development: the sensory-motor period with its object-constancy; the preoperational period with its limits (egocentrism, weak language control, and anthropomorphism), and its two-dimensional concepts; the concrete-operational period with its multi-dimensional cue control and the concept of conservation, levels of classifying, and multiplying of class; the formal-operational period with its treatment of multi-dimensional problems on a language or symbolic level.

We've stressed stimulus control in our analysis of these cognitive processes as we did in the two chapters just before this one. In all three cases, we've looked at language behavior, intelligent behavior, and cognitive behavior, in terms of stimulus control by complex concepts. These concepts are often based on language stimuli and rule-governed stimulus control.

We've also looked at Piaget's common sequence of cognitive development from a learning view. Here are three factors that may be involved: 1) Children learn some concepts sooner because they have more contact with instances of those concepts. But, 2) mere contact is not enough — their proper actions need to be reinforced many times in the presence of complex stimulus conditions before high-level concept control takes over. And, 3) some concepts logically go before others. So perhaps those factors help account for the common finding that many children seem to acquire complex concepts in much the same order — in other words, they all go through Piaget's periods or stages in the same order, though not at the same rate.

We've compared Piaget's cognitive approach with a standard behavioral approach, suggesting that a combined cognitive-behavioral approach might work best. Such an approach states: 1) the laws of learning control our cognitive acts (our thoughts and our reasoning); and 2) these language-based cognitive acts, in turn, control many of our external and more directly observed actions. Perhaps this cognitive-behavioral approach will allow us to deal with more of the topics of psychology than will either approach by itself. This approach may be one further step toward understanding and helping the whole person.

CHAPTER 16
SOCIAL REINFORCEMENT

INTRODUCTION

Many people hold unlearned rewards for us; and many of our unlearned rewards are given to us by other people. But those people holding the rewards must be aware of us, they must be paying attention to us, often they must approve of us before they will give us those rewards.

So their attention and approval often precede their giving us the unlearned reward. Thus the frequent pairing of attention and approval with unlearned rewards causes both attention and approval to become strong learned rewards. Therefore, we find ourselves often doing things that are rewarded by the attention and approval they produce.

We call such learned rewards social rewards since they involve other people; for instance, when someone says, "Thank you," or smiles at you.

Social reinforcer: a reinforcer that involves another person's actions.

Social rewards make our world go around, affecting most of what we do. They alone cause us to tell funny stories or sad stories, work hard or play hard, be nice or nasty. On the other hand, they often work along with other rewards; for instance, social factors and better studying both reward going on study dates, though often we aren't even aware that those social rewards are involved.

Let's look at Dawn in her last year at Central High. Social rewards were flying all over the place, hitting some bizzare acts, no one even knew. Take care, as things are not as they seem.

- 1 Review: Define an unlearned reinforcer.
- 2 Review: Define a learned reinforcer.
- 3 Review: How does a neutral stimulus become a learned reward?
- 4 Define a social reinforcer.
- 5 Give an example where a social reward works by itself.
- 6 Give an example where a social reward works with other reinforcers.

TYPES OF SOCIAL REINFORCEMENT

Dawn's high school decision

Everyone in her high school liked Dawn. The teachers liked her. And so did the kids, loving to chant with her while she led the cheering section at the football games, and choosing her queen of the senior prom . . . But soon Dawn would leave good old Central High. What then? Let's visit Mr. Jones, her high school counselor, to try to find out.

***

With your fine grades, what're you going to do when you graduate?"

"Well, Mr. Jones, I think I'll be an airline stewardess . . ."

"Dawn, with your talent, you should go to Big State U."

She smiled with a slight, modest smile, "I could go to college first and then get an airline job."

"Not a bad idea."

***

"Johnny, you're upset. What's the problem?" Dawn asked.

"We've been going steady for two years. Now we'll have to break up. You know I can't afford Big State."

"Well maybe I could stay here and go to Local College with you."

"That'd make me real happy."

***

And Barbie Green said, "Forget about John. You'll meet BSU dudes who'll turn your head around."

***

"Mom, I still don't know what I'm gonna do next year."

"I'd worry myself sick if you went all the way down to Big State. Besides, you can learn a lot right here. Then in a couple of years you might go to Big State."

"Maybe you're right, Mama. Why don't I stay here — at least for next year."

***

"Dawn, I'm afraid Mother and I don't see eye-to-eye on this school business. Daddy wants the very best for his little girl, and he can pay for it. If Martin Green can afford to send Barbie to Big State, I sure-as-hell can . . ."

"But, Daddy, I want to stay here with you and Mama," Dawn insisted as she touched her father's arm.

"And we want you to. But if that Green girl goes to BSU, so do you. You need to spend less time with Johnny Miller anyway. Then you can get a job to earn your keep if, God forbid, you should ever have to."

"You must be right, Daddy, you always are."

"I didn't get where I am today by being wrong."

***

That ended round one. Dawn ran through her cycle of friends and family several more times. Then, at the last minute, she announced her plans to go to Big State.

Attractiveness

Now what caused all that action? Let's look at Mr. Jones. Just doing his job?

Yes, but some people got a lot more help than others. Everyone was equal in the eyes of Mr. Jones, but some were more equal. Data show that attractive therapists and attractive patients spend more time with each other in therapy than do less attractive pairs. This may be true of much school counseling as well.

Seeing Dawn's good looks rewarded Mr. Jones' spending time with her, at least it seems that way; they had five sessions that term.

Of course, we're not just saying this works for therapists, patients, and counselors, as we suspect it works for all of us. We all come from the same culture, a culture that pairs physical beauty with other rewards, thus making physical beauty a learned reward for us all. So we all may tend to spend a little more time with attractive people than with plain people.

But there were more rewards for Mr. Jones' spending time with Dawn; rewards such as her pleasant voice, her great respect for his advice, and still others that we will look at in the next sections.

■ 7 Cite evidence that a person's physical attractiveness can be a reward.

Attention

Why do people give advice? What's the reward for advice giving?

"Being able to help people."

Well, do advice givers really help people?

"Don't they?"

Who knows.

"They know."

Don't be too sure. There aren't much data to show advising helps.

"Even for school counselors?"

One of many sad facts of life.

"Then why do they counsel?"

You mean what's the reward?

"Okay."

People listening is a reward for advice giving. People listening rewards talking. Just holding their attention is a big social reward. When they stop listening, we stop talking. Advice giving is one form of talking — it's one that most people listen to. And so advice giving gets that social reward.

"Why is attention such a big deal?"

Attention is such a big learned reward because it's so often paired with other rewards. People are always helping us get our learned and unlearned rewards from the day the doctor spanks us on the fanny 'til the last day she adjusts our pace-maker. And those people must attend to us before they can help, so attention is often paired with other rewards, and that's why it's one of the most important learned rewards for human beings.

- 8 What rewards advice giving?
- 9 Why is attention a reward?

Control

"But attention can't be the only reward for giving advice."

Right, sometimes, the advised follow the advice of the advisor. Think what it'd be like if no one followed the counselor's advice.

"They couldn't stand it. They'd quit their job."

Without the reward of at least some people following well-meant advice, they might indeed quit. And everyone else would stop giving their free advice too.

"But that's because they want to help people."

Sure they do. But we said there's no evidence that counseling helps. Yet we can all see one result of our advice: whether it controls the actions of the advised. And that's another strong reward — control over our world — particularly the social world of people. What would our world be like if we couldn't control each other's actions? For example, "Driver, let me off at . . ." —

"I'll let you off where I damned well please."

"That'll be $5.98." —

"That'll be nothing, you money-grubbing pig."

"Waiter, may I have a piece of bread?" —

"You get's no bread with one meatball."

In a social world, we must control each other's actions to get many of our rewards, since we help each other get those rewards. So being able to control the actions of others is also a strong social reward.

- ■10 How is control involved in the reinforcement of advice giving?
- ■11 Why is control of the behavior of others a reward?

The important person

"Okay, attention and control reward advice giving. But I thought you had some extra little surprise for me — some extra reward that caused people to spend so much time with Dawn."

Right you are. Attention and control do reward but they are even stronger when they involve someone who's important — a high school superstar like Dawn.

"Why?"

A guess: Important people often control many rewards. The most important people are the people who control the cookie jar. Mommy and Daddy control the cookie jar. So you'll do all sorts of things to get their attention and control their cookie giving.

On the other hand, little brother doesn't control anything. Having him pay attention to you isn't much of a reward; in fact, he may just be a nuisance hanging around all the time.

So why's it worthwhile to control the attention and action of important people?

"Those people have the rewards. Control them, and you may end up with some of those rewards. The more important they are, the more rewards you may get. So control of important people is paired with more or bigger rewards; and that control becomes a very big, learned, social reward."

- ■12 What effect does the importance of a person have on the person's social reinforcing value?
- ■13 How does the importance of a person come to affect his or her value as a social reward?

Imitation

Another kind of reward also controls much counseling: Mr. Jones leaned across his desk, looked Dawn straight in the eye and said, "Did you ever think about becoming a high school guidance counselor?"

Dawn was flattered. "It must be awfully hard."

Mr. Jones smiled; he understood, "Yes, my dear, it is hard. But if you want to help people, this is the career for you."

It's very rewarding for people to imitate you — to use you as a model.

"That may be true of Jones, and it may be true of you, but it's not true of me. Us kids today aren't into that stuff. We want people to be free to do their thing. At least I think we do."

Maybe you're that unusual — but don't give me that "us kids today" stuff. Students find it very rewarding for other students to be into the same things they are. You are always pushing your rewards on each other.

***

Barbie glanced at Dawn. "Why don't you do what I'm gonna do — go to BSU."

- ■14 How does imitation play a role in the reinforcement of advice giving?

Approval

It's a big reward for someone to imitate you, and that brings in another heavy social reward — approval. You had a heck of a time getting at those cookies when Mom and Dad didn't approve of what you'd been doing. So approval gets to be a big social reward itself, since approval and other rewards often go together.

"But what's that have to do with imitation?"

Ah, it has oft' times been said, "Imitation is the sincerest form of approval."

"I never heard it said like that."

Well it should have been. If I do what you do I must surely approve, and that's a big reward. So telling future college students to go to college is a response that may be reinforced by approving imitation since Jones himself went to college, in fact, to BSU. But Mr. Jones spends less time with vocational ed students. There's much less reward for him there, since he can't advise them to go to BSU.

- ■15 How does approval become a learned reward?
- ■16 How does being imitated acquire its rewarding value through approval?

CONCERNS ABOUT SOCIAL REINFORCEMENT

Awareness

"Mr. Jones was using his job for his own pleasure, not to help students."

No. He thought a lot of his job, being a sincere man. And he'd have denied spending extra time with good-looking students as he wasn't aware of the rewards controlling his actions or even of what actions were being controlled. And if he admitted spending more time with college-bound kids than vocational kids, he'd have an excuse: "College students need more help." In short, he'd be even more shocked than you to find out how he was being controlled by those diverse social rewards.

"You don't know what's happening, do you, Mr. Jones?"

No, Mr. Jones didn't know what was controlling him, nor did anyone else. Recall that Dawn went through this advice seeking with her friends and parents many times. She was a big reward for Johnny Miller and he'd do a lot to keep that reward at home for next year. And besides, the act of giving Dawn advice was just as rewarding for Johnny as for Mr. Jones — and for the same reasons, the same quick social rewards. And Johnny was not aware either that those little social rewards controlled him.

This also holds true for Barbie Green — and Dawn's parents — since giving advice to Dawn got social rewards for them all. But no one knew this constant advice giving was being caused by all those social rewards.

And Dawn's point of view? These nice people talked with her so often. "They all care so much about me."

What a social reward!

Dawn was honest: "I like to talk. But I really like to talk about ME."

And so do you; come on now, look deep into your own soul. Notice how you too pick up when you become the topic of discussion.

- ▪17 Are people usually aware of the way social rewards affect what they do?
- ▪18 What is most people's favorite topic of conversation?
- ▪19 Can a person be a big social reward without meaning to?
- ▪20 Can a person exert control over someone else without meaning to?
- ▪21 What's the role played by immediate and long-range results in making important decisions?

Are we all like that?

"I don't like what you're saying about us human beings. It's unkind, makes us seem silly and shallow. Bad enough that our actions are controlled, but it's even worse that we're controlled by such crummy social rewards. In fact, I don't believe it's true. Maybe it's true of some fools. And maybe most of us are fools. But not all of us."

Sure, people aren't all the same. Yet when you look closely, we're more alike than not alike since many of the same things happened to all of us, and since we are products of what's happened to us. For instance, we can't escape the fact that we're social animals. In raising us, our parents gave us many rewards so their acts became learned social rewards and because they generalized to others, the acts of those humans are also learned social rewards for us. So we're all alike in that

we're all greatly controlled by most social rewards.

But the process can get a little more complex than that, with approval from some being more rewarding than from others. For instance, people who are winners may be better than losers at calling the shots — at predicting success; so their approval is more rewarding, as it may be more often paired with success. Yet each of us responds to that complex process in much the same way. Though we may differ in detail, and chance circumstance may differ, we're all cut from much the same cloth, in terms of both the biophysical and biosocial bases of our behavior.

Sometimes we may see that these social rewards are causing us to act in ways that may have bad results in the future, like dropping out of school when we shouldn't. Then we should try to

change our lives so that those social rewards no longer cause us to do the wrong things.

Most people have about the same rewards, but they don't have the same friends, family, teachers, etc. So the same acts don't get the same rewards. Those same rewards can shape up foolish acts as well as wise ones, depending on what acts those rewards are going to.

▪22 Are some people immune to social rewards?

▪23 Are some people bigger rewards to us than others? Give an example.

▪24 Do most people have many of the same rewards?

▪25 Then why do people differ?

▪26 Do social rewards always cause us to act in ways we end up regretting?

RATIONALITY AND SOCIAL REINFORCEMENT

Mr. Rational in high school

Sid, one of the brightest kids in his high school class, a hard worker, a planner — rational man.

"Let's see, Mr. Sidney Fields? You've got very good grades and exam scores. What do you plan to do with all that talent?"

"Well, I read a lot of psych books and I . . ."

"I've heard about a good psych program in the Midwest."

"Not out there. The cowboys and Indians are still bugging each other aren't they?"

"Suppose one of the best psych programs in the country is hidden out in that great unwashed Midwest? Would you agree to go?"

"But I can't afford college unless I live at home and pay state tuition."

"Listen, Sid, you'd better put these next four years in where they'll do you the most good. Don't let any hurdle stand in the way; go where you can learn the most."

Sid squirmed, nervous, "For sure, if I come up with the cash."

"By the way, the name of that school is Big State University."

"Never heard of it."

***

"Sid, your mother and I want the best for you. But why the Midwest?"

"Dad, I listed the pros and cons of staying here in Long Island with you and Mother, and also of going to BSU. I want to stay here, but the Midwest wins."

Now it was Mrs. Fields' turn, "I'm glad you thought it all out, but does BSU really win? Have you made a list of how much it's gonna cost and who's gonna pay for it?"

Sid began to get angry — a response that was getting more and more common under his parent's subtle but frequent put downs. "Matter of fact, I do have those lists — one for expenses and one for sources of support."

"That I've got to see."

Sid handed his mother the lists as if he were giving her a challenge. "Not bad, not bad. But your books don't quite balance; you're short 340 bucks. What're you gonna do about that?"

Sid, upset because his list wasn't perfect, and angry because his parents could still upset him, "I'm still working on that one."

Mrs. Fields, in a mild effort to make up, "Morey, I'll admit Sid's done a fair job planning this out. You don't think we could get some help from Uncle Jason?"

"It won't hurt to find out. If the kid's got it all worked out, the least we can do is try ta help him."

How to program your daughter to be a silly ninny

Dawn smiled, "You know, I've thought about it, Daddy. I want to be an airline stewardess. So it's not logical for me to go to BSU. But I do want to go anyway."

"That's Daddy's little girl. Thinks just like a woman, and I love her for it."

***

Dawn was a clear enough thinker to see that what she should do wasn't what she wanted to do, though her thinking didn't exert much control over her doing. But her father caused the most problems, giving rewards for responses in keeping with his own notions. It'd take a lot of rewards from other sources to wipe out her father's program. Her roommate, Mae, was good at both clear thinking and reasoned action. Perhaps she'd be a source of some of those counter-rewards.

Analysis

Dawn thinks just as clearly as Sid, solving any problem as well as he, as she learned the same skills of clear thinking with almost the same background of social rewards shaping their thinking skills. But the sameness stopped there. Sid's careful thinking produced cues, with his family, teachers, and friends rewarding acting in the ways pointed out by those cues. If the smart thing is to go to the school in the Midwest, then that behavior is rewarded, and anything else is punished. "Don't be dumb; don't be silly, flighty, stupid."

Too bad for Dawn. Her parents' rewards failed to support reasoned action — supporting only clear thinking.

The results of clear thinking provide cues for acting in ways to increase the amount of rewards, including the distant ones, though often at some present cost. Now Dawn learned how to be cute, and charming, and cajoling in order to cop out — to avoid the present cost. What did she do when clear thinking produced cues for some action that was a little awkward at the moment? She cuteseyed her way out of it. She girly-girlied her way out. Daddy didn't want his little girl to do anything she didn't like. Nor did anyone else. In fact, she was so charming people even gave rewards for this copping out.

So Dawn's actions are mainly controlled by the moment-to-moment results, always being easier for her to cajole others into letting her cop out. But for Sid, who never learned to be charming and cute, how to cop out, only reasoned behavior got rewards. If rational cues pointed the way, he had no choice but to follow.

The same rewards are working for Sid as for Dawn, social rewards are controlling both of them. But those rewards are not given for the same responses.

Clear thinking and reasoned action may also get unlearned rewards. Suppose you're working on a live 110-volt circuit. An unlearned punisher, a 110-volt shock, should control your clear thinking right away by causing you to think and plan, before working with live current.

- ■27 How can two people be clear thinkers and yet one person act irrationally while the other acts rationally?
- ■28 Give an example of natural, or non-social rewards, for clear thinking and reasoned responses.

CONCLUSIONS

We've looked at social reinforcers, learned rewards that involved the actions of others, rewards we're often not aware of, as they take many subtle forms: control, attractiveness, attention, a person's importance, imitation, and approval. Nonetheless, these are rewards that affect every one of us. They cause us to be the kinds of people we are — rational or silly, pleasant or grouchy, steady or flighty. They cause us to go where we go and do what we do. They even affect our values as we shall see in the next chapter.

As we study social rewards and their effects, it begins to look almost as if our main function in life is to get and to give those social rewards. But at least, knowing their power, we are better able to deal with ourselves and our world.

CHAPTER 17
SOCIAL VALUES

INTRODUCTION

Know a person's values and you know that person, or at least you know a lot about that person and his or her actions, since by "positive and negative values" we mean reinforcers and punishers. But you may not have thought that way before about values as rewards and punishers, so let's take a moment to think about it now.

You're saying something's a reward whenever you say you value it or it has positive value for you. And you're saying something's a punisher whenever you say it has negative value for you. In other words, you can always exchange the word "reward" or "punisher" for the word "value". Okay, so what's the use of this little word game? Well the word "reward" makes clearer the way values can affect you. Your values control your actions, just as your rewards do. So you know people when you know their values — their rewards. You know them, since you can then predict their response to various rewards.

In this chapter, we'll look at social factors that cause a person to have certain values — certain rewards and punishers. We'll see that the social factors operate on all of us, causing us to value the things we do and therefore act as we do. And we'll see that our values are shaped by those basic concepts that pervade all we do: stimulus, response, and results.

- 1 What do we mean by "know a person's values and you know that person"?

IMITATION

Imitating the rewards keeper

Sid scooted the chair back, putting his feet up on the desk, trying for the third time to light his new pipe. Be extra cool — Juke watching, a look of wry scorn forming on his face, "What you got there, Sid?"

"A pipe," Sid answered.

"I can see you got a pipe. 'Course you got a pipe. Question is, what you got in your pipe?"

"Don't get stirred up; it's just tobacco."

"Just tobacco. Biggest news to hit campus this year: BOY SMOKES PIPE WITH STRAIGHT TOBACCO!"

"Cut it out, will ya'?" Sid complained, picking up a pipe cleaner to work on the stem of the defiant pipe. "I really like smoking a pipe; I'd been meaning to for years — just never got around to it. Besides, Professor Harper smokes a pipe all the time."

"Harper? Our psych prof! That's taking this psych stuff too far."

"Naw, that's not why I'm smoking a pipe. Just thought I'd give it a try," replied Sid, a little upset at his roommate's insight.

* * *

And Sid wasn't lying, as he almost believed what he said. But he was wrong. If Professor Harper smoked cigars, Sid wouldn't be hassling that pipe — no doubt he'd be coughing his way through his first cigar. We imitate important people — people who get rewards and people who give rewards, though often we're not aware we're imitating. And like so many things, it all started when we were toddlers.

Children imitating adults

When daddy crossed the street, you crossed the street. You could toddle ahead out into the street; or you could stand there watching the street light change while he was halfway down the next block. In either case, a punisher — a harsh word or two from dad — would soon be on its way. But if you did what daddy did, everything was cool — at least most of the time:

A man comes into the living room. Dad looks up from his newspaper, "Hello, John."

You look up from your toys, "Hello, John."

"No, that's Uncle John to you."

Well, almost everything will be okay. From then on, the grownups always call John, "Uncle John" when you're around.

After awhile you imitate those actions you should — but not those you shouldn't. Your parents laugh when you imitate them by taking a drink of their beer so you might keep this routine going every time they open a beer, in spite of the nasty taste. But they get strangely uptight when you start messing with their lighted cigarettes. So you don't imitate their smoking.

Yes, you learn what to imitate and what not to imitate. For instance, you'll be more likely to pick up rewards and avoid punishers when you imitate mom if you're a little girl, or dad if you're a little boy. Sex roles are most often handed down from father to son, mother to daughter. But by and large, you get a reward when you imitate the actions of any adult.

- 2 Review: Define imitation.
- 3 What are two features of adults that influence our imitation of them?
- 4 Why do children imitate adults?
- 5 What is the relation between sex roles and imitation?
- 6 Cite an instance of reinforcement for a child imitating an adult.
- 7 Cite an instance where a child shouldn't imitate an adult.

Imitating other children

Imitating the actions of other kids will also get rewards. But you'd better be careful.

Don't look just at their acts; look at the results of those acts as well, even if you're only a little child. For instance, Jane tells a dirty joke: "A little boy fell in the mud." Mother laughs. Father laughs.

But watch out Dick. Take care! Jane tells one more dirty joke: "Mickey Mouse ran out of this wheat field, see. And he's real mad, see. And he says 'Help, help! I been reaped.'"

Wham!

"Don't hit me again, daddy."

Do you think Dick will tell the story of Poor Mickey? Fat chance.

This shows that children's acts themselves are not always a good cue for what response other children should imitate — for what response will be rewarded. Rather, the act and its result (whether natural or social) combine to form a better cue for children who imitate other children. This allows them to imitate reinforced acts and avoid punished acts.

Most people think we're born to imitate — it seems so normal, since no one tried to teach us to imitate. But that does not mean we didn't have to learn to imitate. We have learned it. Both the natural world and other people give rewards when we imitate, even though we may not be

aware of it. And we don't need to be aware that an action is getting a reward to learn that action. So the acts of others and their results combine to form cues — cues that control much of what we do — cues for us to imitate.

- 8 Why do children imitate other children? What two features combine to form cues?
- 9 Cite an instance of reinforcement for a child imitating another child.
- 10 Cite an instance where one child's imitating another child will not be reinforced.

INTERPERSONAL ATTRACTION AND THE CULTURAL PROGRAM

Juke stopped reading his psych book — because he couldn't help but listen to Sid's side of a phone call.

"Hi, Dawn, this is Sid."

. . .

"Remember the date we had at the fall fling?"

. . .

"Yeah, that's right, when I spilled hot coffee down my front."

. . .

"No, I'm okay now."

. . .

"Well, the reason I called was, ah . . . , I thought if, ah . . . what're you doing Saturday night?"

. . .

"Sunday?"

. . .

"No, that's all right. Really."

. . .

"Yeah, I'll give you a ring again sometime."

                                        * * *

Sure I'll call her again. Why'd I call her in the first place? Last thing I need is a Susie sorority shiksa. What a bummer! I'm acting like every red-blooded Amerikan clod; no New York Jew should do that. She's blond, beautiful, blue eyes, soft voice. What's the matter with me? I know what's the matter: I've seen the same movies every red-blooded Amerikan boy has. I've been programmed just like them. The Madison-Avenue-Hollywood Jews have done it — conspired to program every little Jewish boy in America to fall in love with big-breasted blond goyim.

Yeah, but that little bit of kissing was nice too. She was soft and nice. What'm I saying? Am I going to let Playboy *run my life?*

* * *

Sid liked Dawn's looks and her way of doing things — rewards that attracted him — prompted him to call her — to want to be around her. Are her looks a learned or unlearned reward? Most likely a learned reward, since you've almost always got a learned reward when two people don't agree on the value of the reward. Standards of beauty do vary widely — what turns on kids may turn off adults; what one culture likes, another may hate.

But how does a style acquire its reward value? What about dating a big-breasted blond? Is that date more likely to involve some greater reward than dating a small-breasted brunette? How do these visual stimuli become such strong rewards? And what role do the movie moguls play in all this?

■11 Are our standards of beauty unlearned or learned rewards? What evidence indicates this?

ESTABLISHING VALUES

At first we act as if things are of value just because we're told they are. "It must be a reward for me, since it's a reward for Mom and Dad. Later: "All them other folks are into it, so I'd better give it a try." Why is this?

Well, we've seen why we imitate: the model's actions form a cue that the same actions by us may get a reward. It also works that way with values: after licking his ice-cream cone Dad smacked his lips and cried, "Far out!" In essence, Dad was saying, "Ice-cream is a reward." And Dad's words were a valid cue — you took a bite and sure enough, ice cream tasted very good. The words of most "experts", and just plain folks work since when our culture tells us something's a reward, it often turns out to be one.

And what's the effect of this fact that our culture is fairly good at telling us what will be a reward? Such statements act as cues for a general set or class of responses — the response class of approaching or going toward things — to be more precise, the response class of approaching the things we've been told are rewards. So in the future what happens when we're told something is good? We're likely to approach it — to try to get it.

We act as if that thing does have reward value. But we've not yet received it, so it might or might not really reward our approach.

■12 The statement that such and such is a reward, acts as a cue for what response?

■13 Suppose something takes on reward value because it's been set up as a cue by our culture. How would we know that it does have reward value — that it will function as a reward?

■14 Cite an instance of a) a stimulus or event that is set up as a potential reward by the action of someone else. What is the event and the behavior of the other person? b) Show how we can tell if that stimulus or event is, in fact, also a reward.

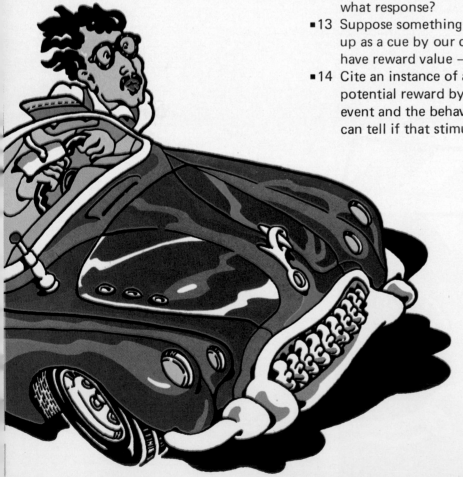

Outside social influences on values

"Hey, Dawn, who's that creep I saw you with last night?"

"That was no creep, that was Sidney Fields."

"Oh, Jewish, huh; he didn't look that cool to me."

* * *

Some things get paired with social punishers from our friends. This will happen when those things don't conform to what our friends tell us are the right values. This hurt Sid's value for Dawn. And that's how much racial and religious prejudice is set up, not through direct contact, but through outside social influences on the reward and punisher value of other groups.

On the other hand:

"Hey, Sid, who was the fine looking lady I saw you with last night?"

"That was no lady, that was my date, Dawn."

"She sure looked foxy to me."

■15 Cite an instance of how the reward value may be increased by outside social events. Also cite an instance of how it may be decreased. What does this say about racism?

The values trap

"Sid's okay; but Johnny's so cute. We've been goin' steady since we were freshmen. I never looked at any other boy. Johnny has dimples and sandy-blond hair just like John Davidson. And he's so strong. And he's so much fun."

Our culture has an ideal of what's handsome — an ideal value that programmed Dawn right toward Johnny. And sure enough, he was rewarding. So all of those unlearned and learned rewards involved with dating were paired with his ideal looks — a pairing that strengthened the reward value of this ideal. So Dawn never

went with other boys — boys who might not look like John. So the reward value of John's ideal looks got stronger and stronger compared to other looks.

Our culture's values are self-fulfilling prophecies, telling us something will be a good reward, causing us to go after that thing, causing us to pick up on those rewards. And since, in fact, it is a reward, we might not contact other potential rewards. So that thing goes on being paired with its unlearned and learned rewards becoming such a strong reward that we stay locked right in there with it.

■16 What is meant by the social values trap? Cite an instance.

■17 What does it mean when we say that our culture's values are self-fulfilling prophecies?

Values and discriminative stimuli

Could it ever work like this? Maybe just being told something's a reward is all we need, though, of course, we might have to be reminded of it from time to time. For instance, think about the young girl who's not like Dawn, who doesn't have the opportunity to date Mr. All-American-dimples-white-teeth-no-bad-breath-no-underarms-at-all. But wherever she turns, her world tells her that Mr. American Pie is IT.

Movies, TV, magazines, friends, parents, they all say the same thing — maybe not in so many words, but they say it. If everyone says it often enough and long enough, does that make it true? Can any old thing become a reward simply through pairing with people saying, "Try it, you'll like it", even when we never get a chance to try it? Most likely not, being told something's a reward doesn't make it one but we may approach that thing a few times, because our being told so acts as a cue — a cue to approach that thing. Still being told it's a reward is not enough if that thing was at first a neutral object. It will really function as a reward only if it is paired with some other rewards once in awhile; as described in the sections we just looked at.

■18 Can a value be maintained solely by association with cues? Explain.

OTHER CAUSES OF INTERPERSONAL ATTRACTION

No, it's not because he's Jewish! But he is rather poor.

"I still can't see why you don't want to go out with Sid? When I fixed you two up for the fall fling, I thought you'd really like him."

"Mae, he's real bright, but . . ."

"Yeah, and he wants to do something with his mind besides rip people off. He wants to help people, not exploit them."

"But there's nothing wrong with a little money. And maybe even a car. And he doesn't seem to know anybody. If you don't have some heavy friends by the time you've been here a year, you must be some kind of creep. And I'm not into those poverty-style Levis all the time."

"It's not because he's Jewish is it?"

"N — O spells no. I am not a bigot. I like you don't I? Some of my best fri . . ."

"Don't say it, please; I was just kidding."

Mae turned from Dawn and stared out the window — thoughtful. "My first response was to put you down 'cause you're so into material things. But maybe we all are a little bit. I remember when I was fifteen, I had a friend with a car. I liked my friend. Then I became old enough to drive the family car. An' I just didn't have much time for my old friend. I didn't mean it to be that way; yet that's the way it worked out. When I figured out what was goin' on, I felt ashamed but that didn't change anything."

"I don't know, maybe I should go out with him if he calls me again."

"Why don't ya'."

Analysis

Dawn's always ready to agree. She can never hold out when given clear cues on how to get some social rewards. But she is right in her guess about some of the things that make us attractive to each other. Money, cars, pleasing friends, prestige, and, of course, looks (e.g., nice clothes) are strong rewards for many of us.

But you may object, "No, I love a person for what that person is."

Okay, let's put it this way: how *interpersonally attractive* someone is means how much attraction there is between two people or how much people reward each other for being together. Now how can people reward your being with them? They can buy things and activities for you with money. That doesn't mean you're so crass as to go looking for Daddy War$. But money does help you have a good time. So does a car. "Seems like anything worth doing is on the other side of town and I always need a car to get there." And you always have more fun with someone who has clever friends.

"But what about the person as a person?" you persist.

Well, we've already talked about appearance as a reward; a nice pleasant voice might also be a factor. And Sid mentioned Dawn as a source of tactual-sexual reward. And, don't kid yourself, all these things affect how we respond to each other.

But the biggest factor can be how many social rewards the person gives directly to us. This is Dawn's strongest suit. And this may be Sid's weakest area. Without meaning to, Dawn always says the right thing, the thing that makes others feel good; she laughs a lot and at the right time; she nods her head in agreement; and she never puts anyone down. What about Sid? He's a great talker, but sometimes Dawn would like to do some of the talking. Too bad. She's rewarded Sid's talking so much that he never stops. And Sid's not much for showing his approval of anything — even the person he's with.

- ▪19 List seven factors that may affect interpersonal attractiveness.
- ▪20 What do we mean when we say a person is attractive to us?
- ▪21 What is suggested as the most important factor in determining interpersonal attractiveness?

GREGARIOUSNESS AND THE GROUP

Not another party

At last Sid scored a second date with Dawn — a date for the Halloween party at the Alpha Cholera frat. By the time they arrived, the Ripple-guzzling contest was well underway, the house crowded, loud, and hot, a lot of boogying going down. Dawn saw a dozen friends as soon as she entered the door. Sid saw a classmate, hardly a friend; in fact, the guy bugged him, but he waved anyhow. The snob wouldn't even nod. But Dawn didn't ignore Sid; she introduced him to all her friends. "Sid, this is Ralph. Ralph, Sid."

"Hi."

Sid nodded, "Pleased t' meet ya'."

"You two ought to hit it off; you're both flunking phys ed." Dawn laughed.

"Are you taking Swimming II?" Ralph asked.

"Yeah," Sid replied.

"What a drag. I shoulda' taken Swimming I."

"Yeah."

"They want me to swim all the way across that damned pool."

The talk faltered. Dawn was off with other friends. Ralph tried a new topic, but Sid couldn't make it with much more than a "Yeah" and a nod — he couldn't think of a single thing to say — not clever, witty, bright, or even standard. Ralph looked around the room until he saw his date.

"'Scuse me, Sid; was real nice, but I gotta get over to my woman. See ya' at the Gym."

"I doubt it." As soon as he said it, Sid wished he'd not been so rude.

Dawn tried to help Sid, rescuing him from one small social failure after another. And Sid tried to act like he was into the scene, walking around the room as if he wanted to look at the hip wall posters plastered about, touring the poster collection three times before giving up.

Analysis

"Gregarious" means "fond of being with a group". And that's Dawn; she found groups of people rewarding. But not Sid; he even found groups punishing. Why? Is it merely the fact of having people around that's rewarding or punishing? No. The people give the social rewards and punishers. Dawn was a hit at parties — everyone talked to her — no wonder since she herself was very rewarding to talk to. Sid was not, as he had not learned how to make pleasant small talk at parties, though at other times he might even talk too much. His failure at small talk punished his being at parties. These punishers sometimes caused him to aggress with snide remarks. His lack of social skills, his obvious pain, and his sarcasm did not help Sid's reward value at parties. Sid was no hit. He was even avoided — within the limits of good taste, of course.

Once again: how did Dawn and Sid differ?

"They don't have the same rewards. Dawn likes parties and Sid doesn't."

Not that simple. Their basic rewards are about the same; like all of us, social rewards and social punishers control much of what they do. If Sid were less controlled by those rewards and punishers he wouldn't find parties that bad. It's his failure to get the rewards as well as getting the punishers that bugs him so; he wouldn't mind so much if those social rewards were of no value to him.

"Got it: the difference isn't their values; it's their skills. Dawn learned how to make small talk and Sid didn't. So Dawn gets rewards at parties, and Sid doesn't."

If Sid learned how to handle himself at parties, he'd be just as gregarious as Dawn. But he'll always maintain his aloof shyness unless he sets up some program to learn how to make casual talk.

Now Sid and Dawn might just get married. What happens then?

"They'd be able to work out their problem if they were really in love."

Wrong. Often husbands and wives have not learned the same ways of getting their rewards. And their different ways provide fertile grounds for married strife: she wants to watch football and he wants to go to the opera; she wants to go to a party and he wants to read a good book; she's better at getting social rewards from groups of people than he is — a problem for many couples.

■22 Suppose a person doesn't like parties; does that mean he or she doesn't like social rewards? Please explain.

ASSOCIATION AND INTERPERSONAL ATTRACTION

Sid to Dawn, "By the way, I'm switching into your psych lab. And you said you're having trouble training your lab rat to press the lever since your lab partner dropped the course. So . . . ah, I thought we might . . . ah, work together on it."

***

What do we mean when we say we find a person "attractive"? We mean that person is a reward. For instance, Sid even changed classes to be with Dawn, since her presence was such a reward.

But it works the other way too: people become more of a reward for us, if they're around when we're getting other rewards; so they're more likely to become a reward if we're around them a good amount of time. And sure enough, Sid's value as a reward for Dawn increased due to his being with her when she got other rewards.

***

A few weeks later, Dawn agreed with Mae, "I'm starting to see what you mean about Sid. He's not really so bad. Sure glad he's helping me with that dumb rat, too. He also helped me on the mid-term."

But it wasn't just Sid's help that increased his reward value;

he was a good talker, and his heart was really in the right place — he was a nice boy. And after class, they'd have a beer in the union. So as time passed Sid became paired with many rewards, causing him to become a stronger reward himself.

But what about handsome, hometown Johnny? He's out of luck. And so's that old high-school gang — the one Dawn was so sad to leave just a few short months ago. They're all losing out, fading into the past. But why? Why is it so hard to get wrapped up in school and keep things going at home at the same time? Well, here are a few guesses.

First, you'll find you spend less and less time with the old gang, as the reward value of your new friends grows. Because it's harder to get back home to the old gang than to visit a friend living across the hall in your dorm; you're more likely to travel 100 feet than 100 miles, as the reward value of your college friends grows. That doesn't decrease the value of your old friendships, but it does make it a lot easier for the new friendships to compete.

Second, you'll learn new values and new ways of thinking, talking, and doing, with those new ways getting many fewer

social rewards back home than at school. For instance, you might get turned on to the point of view of this book, a way of looking at the world that will, most likely, be met with yawns (extinction) or outright hostile remarks (punishment), when you return to that old hometown soda fountain. And this will decrease the reward value of that whole scene.

And third, the other members of that old gang may be learning new values and ways of thinking, talking, and doing — ways you don't find so rewarding to be around. The result is that the scene becomes even less rewarding.

So, to the extent that college affects you, it makes you a new person, and most likely, one who will find it harder and harder to look homeward.

- ■23 Why does association affect interpersonal attraction?
- ■24 What is likely to happen to the reward value of an old but absent friend as we get new friends? Cite the factors causing this.

CONCLUSIONS

We are what we've learned to be. Social rewards mold us into unique
human beings. Other unique human beings give us those social
rewards. What those unique human beings reward results from what
they learned to reward and what they are now reinforced for
rewarding. This big net of social rewards contains us all — we
reinforce and are reinforced in turn; and that's the essence of social
psychology as we view it.

CHAPTER 18
ATTITUDE CHANGE

ATTITUDE AND ITS COMPONENTS

Women's liberation — sowing the seeds

Mae and Dawn scraped their food trays clean and slid them through the window. "I don't care what they say, dorm food ain't like down home cookin'," Mae shook her head. "Say, what you doin' tonight? Want to go with me? NOW's having a meeting at 7:00."

"NOW? What's that; a color . . . a black group?"

"No. NOW's National Organization of Women. And it isn't black. That's why I'm going. We got to get more of my sisters into the women's activist bag. It's not enough my people be free; my sisters have to be free. We all slaves now — black and white."

Dawn had heard some of this before — and didn't like it. No one likes hearing she's not free. *I'm free. Free not to waste tonight listening to a bunch of silly talk. I'll play bridge with the girls in the lounge.* "No thanks. Not tonight, Mae — I've got to study."

That night, as they were getting ready for bed, Dawn said, "I just don't see what all the fuss is about. Women are free. I'm free."

"To do what?"

"What I want."

"And what do you want?"

"Go to college, be a stewardess, get married, and have two kids, and I want to be happy and have a good time."

"Suppose you didn't want to be a flight attendant. Suppose you wanted to be a pilot. Are you free to do that?"

"But I don't want to be a pilot. That's silly."

"It's not silly. Some women want to, but they're not free to."

"But I wouldn't even want to fly in a plane with a woman pilot. Women are bad drivers."

"Just an old husband's tale," Mae had to smile at her own little joke; but to restore the mood, she added, "You're not free. You've been taught to want the old-fashioned woman's role — but you're too good for that, damn it. You're bright, and you work hard, and you get along well with people; yet all you want to do is end up being a housewife." Sometimes when she did get serious, she lost her ghetto accent.

"What's wrong with that? My mother's a housewife," beginning to get angry.

"Do you want to be like your mother?"

"No."

"Don't you see; that's what you're being programmed to be — a copy of your mother. We're taught to want only certain roles — we're restricted from other roles — many worthwhile ones."

"Don't care, long as I'm happy."

"But there's more to life than just being happy. There's being of service to others — helping people."

"I'll help people as a stewardess."

"You can do more than serve drinks to a bunch of businessmen."

"I'll be a wife and mother."

"That's not the way to spend your life — taking care of one man and two brats."

"But my kids won't be brats."

"Damn it, Dawn, you're selling yourself short. You can do more. More than just help one man and two kids. You can get a job helping a lot of people — people who really need you."

"I'll admit that mother's sort of sad now she doesn't have me to worry about. She even talked about getting a part-time job and that surprised me 'cause Dad said we don't need the money. As a matter of fact, he got real mad about it. He said 'no wife of his was ever going to have an outside job'."

Values

Dawn and Mae don't have the same attitudes about woman's role. But what do we mean by "attitude"? The concept of attitude can be divided into three parts: value, belief, and actions; and looked at in terms of discriminative stimulus, response, reinforcer, and punisher.

As we have seen, "value" means "value of the reward". So both Dawn and Mae hold strong though different values about the woman's role: Helping many people has high reward value for Mae, while helping her future husband and children has high reward value for Dawn; either performing their preferred role or seeing someone else in that role is rewarding. But of course, we can also have negative values, where certain things can punish. For instance, hearing Dawn talk about living the housewife role is punishing for Mae, while Mae's criticism of that role is punishing for Dawn.

- ■ 1 What are the three components of attitude?
- ■ 2 Define value. Give an example of a positive and a negative value.

Beliefs

When we study attitudes, we often speak of the role of thinking covered by the concept of "belief". Mae has two beliefs of concern here: one that Dawn is bright, hard-working, and well-liked; and the other that Dawn could help many people. So those belief statements work as cues causing Mae to act in accord with those beliefs, by trying to get Dawn to change her attitude about the woman's role. Mae wants her to adopt a new set of values and beliefs; thereby, acting in accord with the role of the liberated woman.

- ■ 3 Define belief.
- ■ 4 Cite an instance.

Actions

How does "attitude" relate to "action"? Well, action (or response) is the link between belief and value — between cue and reward. And verbal cue, response, and reward combine to be called "attitude".

Attitude: the combined efforts of beliefs (verbal discriminative stimuli), actions (responses), and values (reinforcers).

- ■ 5 Define attitude.

Values: people's values are their reinforcers and punishers, and the strengths of those reinforcers and punishers.

Belief: a verbal statement that functions as a discriminative stimulus, pointing the way to those actions that get valued results.

Action: an action is equivalent to a response. Sometimes it implies a sequence of complex acts or responses.

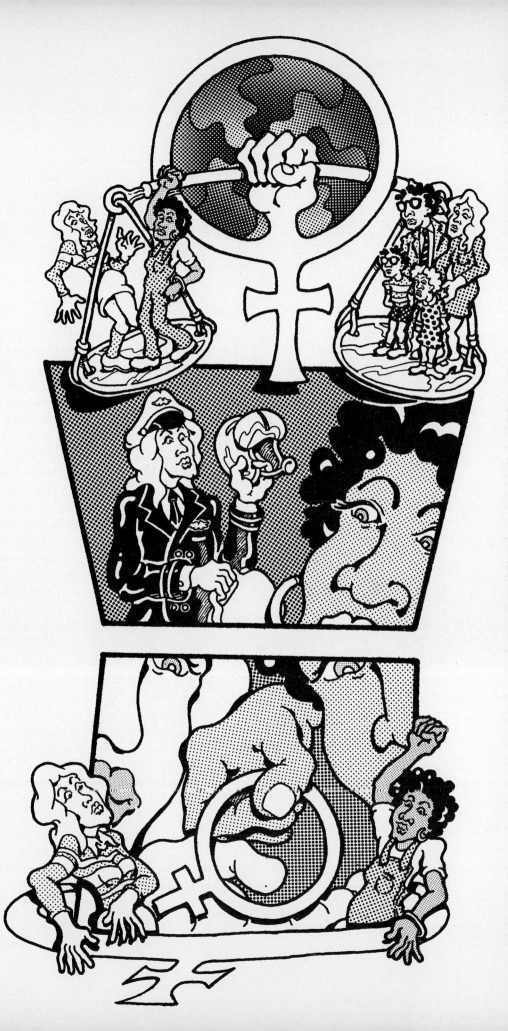

ATTITUDE CHANGE

Compliance

Now people can act in a way that makes us say they have some attitude. They can state a belief, or they might approach one thing or avoid another, causing us to guess the value that thing has for them. But sometimes we're fooled. Sometimes things they say or do are controlled by something else — something we don't even know about.

Dawn said, "Maybe I'll go with you to the next NOW meeting." And Mae was happy, since it looked like Dawn might believe in the women's movement — that their values and methods were good. Did the new woman's role take on a higher reward value for Dawn? No. There was really another reward that controlled her going to the NOW meetings — the fact that Mae approved of that response. And Dawn often did whatever was needed to get others' approval and to avoid their scorn. She went along with their requests, though she didn't always believe in them. We call that "compliance".

Compliance: when an outside reinforcer controls an action, and neither the value of the direct results of that action nor belief statements about that action exert control.

Compliance does not involve attitude control, though it may be the first step in a changing attitude. This concept of compliance deals with the notion that our actions aren't always controlled by our beliefs. For instance, the first few times Dawn went to NOW, what was the reward? The fact that Mae approved. But didn't Dawn believe she'd get social rewards from Mae? No. She didn't even think about it, as she wasn't aware of the rewards that really controlled her actions. She thought she believed in NOW, though her action wasn't really under the control of the belief statement, since she would have stopped going if Mae had.

Sometimes beliefs are cues for our actions, and sometimes they're not. Many factors controlled Mae's efforts to involve Dawn in NOW; but one factor was a belief — the belief that Dawn could do more for the world if she changed her attitudes about women. That belief was a cue for Mae's efforts.

Though compliance doesn't involve attitude control itself, it may still be the first step in a changing attitude, as we will see in the next section.

- 6 Define compliance. Give an example.
- 7 What's the relation between belief and public behavior?
- 8 Give an example of how a belief can be a cue for public behavior.
- 9 Give an example of how a belief may only appear to be a cue for public behavior.

Identification

Dawn did start going with Mae to a few NOW meetings. At first the meetings upset her. Some of the things that women said hurt her and some of the women put her down. But that soon dropped out when she learned what to say and what not to say, her talk being shaped by the social rewards and punishers of the NOW women; she was complying with NOW. But she began saying more and more things in keeping with NOW's values; and little by little such belief statements themselves became rewards for her.

And that wasn't all: The few times Dawn picked up a copy of *Women* really pleased Mae. And the first time Dawn didn't wait for Sid to open the door for her was awkward, with Sid, the gen-

tleman, being flustered. He started to put her down (pain-produced aggression), but Sid, the modern man, let it go with a combined reward-punisher, "About time you got up to date."

Sid never got much closer to giving Dawn a social reward, so it did act as a reward for her, causing her to open the door herself from then on. Over time the effects of these rewards spread to other actions in keeping with the movement values, causing Dawn to learn to light her own cigarette, to seat herself at a table, and to put on her own coat without Sid's help. After all, that's the way Mae was; and Sid liked it better too; and it really did seem better.

These acts are paired with

many social rewards: taking part in NOW meetings, reading the right things, doing the right things. And because of the reward pairing, such notions also become learned rewards themselves; so that doing those actions or seeing others do them is a learned reward.

Now, from time to time, learned rewards must be paired with other rewards; if not, they lose their reward value — they extinguish. Suppose Dawn quit school and went back home with Mom, Dad, and John. What then? Right, her liberated acts would lose their reward value — extinguish. They'd be punished too, causing her to soon return to her sexist attitudes. Now she wasn't a phoney, since she really

believed in the women's values. But those beliefs could be easily changed. In fact, whoever was around had very tight control over her "women's" actions, since sometimes she behaved in a much less modern way — mainly at home.

First of all, such acts had never gotten rewards back home, so their strength was very low there, only a slight amount of stimulus generalization from college to home. (In other words the cues of home differed enough from school that actions learned in the one setting were not too likely to occur in the other.) And second, those actions got extinguished or punished, on the rare times when they did occur at home.

So Dawn's attitudes were real, but fragile. What would happen if she lost the support of her new friends with their social rewards? Her new attitudes would fall apart fast. This type of attitude control is called "identification".

Identification: the learning and keeping of an attitude due to social reinforcers, with the values of that attitude becoming learned reinforcers.

Note that identification does involve all three components of attitude — belief, values, and actions — beliefs about the value of the direct results of those actions. On the other hand, compliance involves only actions, with beliefs and the value of the

direct results of the actions exerting little control. Of course, social rewards play a role in both cases; but the direct rewards of the action itself play a role only in the case of identification, where those direct results have become a learned reward. But now let's see what happens when Dawn and Mae do go back to visit Dawn's home.

- ■10 Define identification and cite an instance.
- ■11 What happens when someone in the identification phase loses contact with the support group? An instance?

Dear Dawn,

   It was sweet of you to bring that
little colored girl home with you.
I guess it was a mistake, though. Your
Daddy is very upset about the way she
talked back to him. She should have more
respect for grown-ups — and, to be frank,
for white people. Your father is held in very
high esteem in our town; so she should
have shown him more respect. And you tell her
that.
We didn't know you were seeing that Jewish
boy either. We are glad you assured us
you were not really dating him.
   You should try to get someone else for a
roommate next term.

                    Love,

                    Mother

Internalization

They felt awkward for awhile, driving back to school. Finally, Mae broke the ice, "Your daddy's something else. He really believes all that jazz: like he really blew his cool when I said you should be your own boss, and when I said if you couldn't find a man was into that, you just shouldn't get married."

"Gosh, Mae, I'm sorry about the awful way Daddy acted. He's okay. Just sometimes he's kind 'a funny. I had no idea he was so old-fashioned though."

(When students go to college they may get new values. But they often assume their parents hold those same new values. Don't make that mistake — it means trouble.)

Now Mae's not like Dawn, as what she does and says is not so controlled by the social approval of whoever happens to be there at the moment. Her actions are more part of her long-standing attitudes. But why do Mae's attitudes exert such strong control over her? Because her women's attitudes agree with other strong attitudes, those that provide support. For instance, most of us had a lot of childhood religious training, training that set up values: do unto others . . . , justice, fair play, etc. We also learned the same thing in school. And our culture rewards saying things in keeping with those values, causing them to become strong rewards themselves, rewards that are well-maintained. We also learn the value of "freedom" from our religious training, and culture, with "good people" striving for religious or private freedom, and "bad people" standing in their way.

And we've also had rewards for clear thinking or more likely, punishers for unclear thinking. Say two things that don't agree with each other, and if someone catches it, they'll punish it, "No, stupid. You just said something else two minutes ago." And though we repeat the misquote, "Consistency is the hobgoblin of small minds," the fact remains — we were stupid.

Now Mae had the religious and freedom-loving values of our culture, and the Black civil-rights beliefs of her parents. She's also had a lot of training in tying those two sets together. She believed that Blacks were being deprived of their freedoms, they weren't getting fair play. And this controlled her actions — what she did, said, and read, her attitude in support of the Black movement.

Her parents placed a high value on school work and clear thinking giving her many rewards for finding subtle errors in thinking, and some mild punishers for failing to do so. So she was good at building one set of attitudes on other sets, by showing how two attitudes agreed or differed.

Mae first made contact with notions of the women's movement while reading *Ms.*, where she soon saw that the women's movement was like the Black civil-rights movement with the same basic religious and freedom values that applied to both. Thus, many of the same beliefs should also apply to both — with the actions that were right for the black movement also being right for the women's movement. And these beliefs had much cue control over her actions. So she did more reading, talking, and thinking, soon giving her a set of clear belief statements in support of the women's movement, her women's attitudes being strengthened by her other attitudes.

"Does that mean women's values were more than learned rewards for Mae? Does it mean they no longer had to be paired with other rewards to keep their value?" you may ask.

No. The women's movement values are still best thought of as learned rewards, even for Mae.

"What kept them going then?"

They were kept up by the way they agreed with her other values. In other words, stating women's beliefs was strengthened by being in line with her other beliefs, while stating anti-women's beliefs was out of step with the others. And that's how the women's attitudes were acquired and held by Mae, by being strengthened by their closeness to other strongly held beliefs.

This type of attitude control is called "internalization".

Internalization: the learning and keeping of an attitude due to its closeness to other attitudes — with close attitudes that agree being reinforcing and close attitudes that disagree being punishing.

"Does all this mean there were no social rewards?"

No. Some social rewards also helped. For instance, Mae spent time with others in the women's movement, others who gave social rewards for statements and actions in keeping with movement attitudes. She said she went to the NOW meeting to help black women get into the movement. True; but that also put her with women who gave social rewards and not punishers for her actions — actions that already occurred at a high rate, due to their pairing with other values. So she had several sources of control of her women's attitudes. And those sources strengthened each other in ways that spiraled: The women's values became stronger rewards; so she acted more in keeping with those values. Other movement women gave reinforcers for those acts; so she spent more time with such women. Time with the women made the women's values stronger rewards; so more liberated actions; so more time with the movement; so stronger women's values. So . . . ; so . . . ; so . . . . The spiral.

- ■12 Define internalization and cite an instance.
- ■13 How does clear thinking relate to internalization?
- ■14 What maintains internalized values? Cite an instance.
- ■15 Show how social rewards can support internalized values.

INCONSISTENT ATTITUDES AND RATIONALIZATION

"You said Mae worked with the Black civil-rights movement and that helped her get into the women's movement."

Yes. She had acquired the skills of tying the Black movement values to more basic values; so she had no trouble tying the women's movement values to those more basic values also, since the two movements had much in common.

"That doesn't agree with what I've seen, since some of the biggest sexists I know are heavily into other movements."

Here's what we said: Being in one liberation movement helps us adopt the attitudes of other movements of the same sort. But it doesn't insure it. This is true for several reasons. First of all, some people hold the attitudes of their movements lightly — at a compliance or identification level — not internalized. Second, even if they are internalized, there may still be a problem: most people don't have Mae's thinking skills. She's good at finding ideas that don't agree with each other. It is often more rewarding if those inconsistencies are not noticed. For instance, many men and even women, prefer to keep the "old lady" in the role of servant. Then the men wouldn't have to take part in tasks that aren't big rewards for them. And some women don't know what they'd do if freed of their standard roles. And finally, it's punishing to find that two attitudes don't agree — or that our actions don't agree with our "attitudes". So we may make an error in thinking — an error that will hide the problem. Then we won't have to straighten things up.

We make these errors in thinking about why we do things and about what things we do — but we err without knowing it. And those errors cover up any awkward places where our actions and attitudes don't agree. We call that "rationalization".

Rationalization: faulty thinking so that the truth about our actions can not serve as a discriminative stimulus for punishment of those actions.

"Well, yes, black men should be free; but I won't have anything to do with a woman who don't know her place. They're just not able to do men's work. Besides, they're really more happy at home." When you solve a moral problem so that it's easy for you, be careful — it may just be a rationalizing cop-out.

- ■16 What are the causes for inconsistent values? Cite an instance of each.
- ■17 Define rationalization. Cite an instance.

CONCLUSIONS

We've looked at women's liberation in order to learn about "attitude", while at the same time learning something of women's liberation, things causing people to get into the movement, and its impact on their lives. And we've seen attitude control involves values, beliefs, and actions, with the three types of control being compliance, identification, and internalization. We've also seen how these three types of control can affect attitudes about the women's movement.

This chapter also shows how important clear thinking is if we are to achieve internalized attitude control — a worthwhile goal. In the next chapter, we'll study the problem of making moral choices, an act that also demands clear thinking.

CHAPTER 19
MORALITY

FORMS OF CONTROL

Simple forms of behavior control often suffice to help us survive the wide, wild world of nature — simple forms like the sort of response-reward controls we're born with. But complex social control is needed, as cultures develop, if those cultures are to survive. We'll glance at a few of these forms of control before dealing with moral control, the main topic of this chapter.

Natural

The pressure built up inside baby Sid, causing him to make the proper response to stop that pressure — he pottied. Instant escape — nature's reward. Now no one had to teach baby Sid to pottie. Nature built in the rewards for such acts, causing all creatures to evolve so those natural acts get their rewards. We've evolved so that the right acts get rewards, but this only works well as long as we stay in much the same world where our evolution occurred.

Natural control: control over a creature's actions due to the normal results of those actions.

But those natural controls often fail us when we change our world, creating a need for social control to help us survive in that new world.

Social

For instance, we're under social control when people ask us to give them a hand with their work; they are giving us a cue and may follow through with a reward, like a thank you if we do help them.

Social control: control over a person's actions through the efforts of others.

Guidelines

Juke came bursting into their room, to Sid's dismay. "Hey, Sid, my man, what ya got there?"

Sid blushed, "Oh, nothing. Just prune juice."

"That's cool, what's the hang-up?" Though Juke knew what the hang-up was.

"You know what they use prune juice for."

"No, man," said Juke, both enjoying and feeling guilty about the game he was forcing Sid to play.

"Well, ah, my mama always told me that if I couldn't ah . . . ah . . ."

Sid's pain won out as Juke helped his friend, "I know, man; you take prune juice so you can go to the john. That's cool."

"See I haven't hardly been able to go to the bathroom since I came back to school, and I thought, well you know."

* * *

What he-man can admit he can't go to the bathroom? Baby Sid, the child of nature, had no problems. But big Sid has a rough time, the product of our social world. So his actions come under the control of a guideline — one from the same social world that caused the problem in the first place.

Guideline control: control by a statement of the discriminative stimulus, the response, and the natural results.

When you can't go to the bathroom (cue), drink prune juice (response), and you may be able to (natural results). Guidelines are one of our simplest forms of social control, as they merely state the rule, relying on the normal results to control the response. So simple guidelines are just a clear statement of the normal cue-response-results relation, stated with the notion that their cue value plus the normal results will suffice to control the response.

But guidelines aren't enough when the normal, natural results of the act itself are too weak, when the immediate results for following the guidelines are too punishing, or when the immediate results for not following them are not too rewarding; then some outside results are needed to bolster the control of the guideline.

Legal

Grade school Sid trotted through the showers, heading for the Y swimming pool, when he noticed this sign: "Help us keep our swimming pool clean. Anyone caught going to the bathroom in this pool will be asked to leave." Imagine, expelled from this child's wonderworld for going to the bathroom in the pool — a clear example of legal control.

Legal control: control by a statement of the discriminative stimulus, the response, and the added physical results.

When in the pool (cue), don't go to the bathroom (response), or you'll be kicked out (added physical results) — results not normal to the act itself. No doubt the pool director had found that a simple guideline didn't exert enough control; the normal results of having a dirty pool didn't exert enough control over the children's actions.

Now the pool director may have been faking it just a bit by hinting that he could detect an instance of law violation and thereby deliver swift justice to the scoff-laws; but many other times the source of social control must admit not having any adequate means of seeing rule violation, and that's where moral control really comes into play.

Moral

High school Sid jogged through the showers, heading for the lake when he noticed this sign: "Don't do it in the lake — be a caring person. — Signed the Earth People's Ecology Movement." Sid knew none of the Earth People would be watching; no one would be watching, except maybe God though she rarely dealt with issues so trite; so Sid could safely sin; but then he would be letting down all his brothers and sisters — the Earth People. And Sid wanted to think of himself as a caring person — not one of those earth spoilers he hated so much.

Moral control: control by a statement of the discriminative stimulus, the response, and the added verbal, social, or supernatural results.

Sid was under moral control: when in the lake (cue), don't do it (response), or you're not a caring person (added result — but not a physical one).

* * *

Note that legal and moral control differ mainly in the results they use. Law violation causes a physical result, like being cast from the pool, and moral violation causes verbal, social, or perhaps supernatural results like, I think I'm a slob for doing it in the lake, we all agree I'm a slob, and we bet God doesn't think too much of me either.

But now it's time to look at some of the details of moral control — now that we've seen how it fits into the bigger scheme of natural and social control systems.

- 1 Please define and give an example of natural control.
- 2 Do the same for social control.
- 3 And guideline control.
- 4 And legal control.
- 5 And finally, moral control.
- 6 What is the crucial difference between natural and social control?
- 7 Between guideline control on the one hand, and legal and moral control on the other hand?
- 8 Between legal and moral control?

Why moral control?

A wise man once asked, "Why are our rewards either immoral, illegal, or fattening?" Here's why: Our bodies haven't evolved in ways to help us deal with these new rewards, because they were not found in the world where we evolved from lower life forms, as we humans invented many of them only in recent times. And most of these invented rewards act right away, since our actions are controlled by what they get us right away, and were invented with little regard for their long-range results, either for us or for others. For instance, booze and other drugs, or fast cars, or booze, drugs, and fast cars combined. (Oh what fun. Whee! Ooops. Splat!)

We must learn to take care of ourselves since nature didn't prepare us to deal with our dangerous, new rewards. So we humans have invented moral control, rules telling us how to act.

And when do we need these moral rules? When the present results, those nearest our actions, cause us to act in the wrong way — ways having bad results either for us or for others in the present or the future. It's not moral to smoke, steal, gossip, slander, blaspheme, kill, commit adultery, covet other people's spouses or their goods, etc.

When don't we need moral codes to control our actions? When the present results and the future results agree. We don't need to say, "Be sure to keep your hand out of the fire," since the present results (pain) are in line with the long-range results (tissue damage).

- 9 Why do human beings need moral control when lower animals don't? Example?
- 10 When do we need moral control? Example?
- 11 When don't we need moral control? Example?

PRE-MORAL CONTROL

The Devil and St. Chet

Chet sat in the lower level of the student union building, sipping coffee and waiting for Carol. She would stop by from work to pick him up. Sitting there he noticed a handsome man, in his mid-thirties, well-dressed, gray-striped suit, briefcase, with the air of a busy man on his way to the top. Or maybe just on his way to Chet's table. On reaching the table, he stopped and addressed Chet, "Do you mind if I join you, Sir?"

This surprised Chet, since there were plenty of empty tables all around. But, "Sure. Have a seat," Chet said nodding toward a chair. *What was this man doing in the lower level of the union — the student jungle — not even the faculty dared come down here,* Chet wondered. And he couldn't help staring at him; his ears slightly pointed, and his nostrils exhaling smoke, though he was smoking no cigarette, cigar, nor pipe of this world.

"I couldn't help but notice; you seem worried about something," the stranger observed. "How are your studies going?"

This shocked Chet as he thought he always hid his feelings, since he figured you had to to make it to the top. So how'd this stranger know his feelings? "Yeah, matter a' fact, I am worried. Got a psych exam, and I bombed the last one."

The man smiled — he knew how it was, "What a break. That's Psych 100 is it?"

Chet was sure the man already knew the answer even before his reply: "Yeah, it's Psych 100. So what's the break?"

"I happen to have a few copies of that exam."

"How'd you get 'em?"

"Friends. Want a copy?" He reached for his briefcase.

"Like to, but I'd better not."

"Why not? What can you lose?"

"The whole thing. I'm a senior; can't afford to blow it now."

"Right. That's why I'm giving you this sure-fire way to ace the test."

"No, no. You don't know the trouble I'm in." But Chet thought the stranger really did. "I'm on probation 'cause I was caught cheating last term."

"You won't get caught this time."

"Yeah, that's what I thought last time. But if they catch me again it's my neck, they'll kick me out a' school."

As the man arose he said, "Of course, of course. I know. But take this number . . . in case you change your mind." He handed Chet a name card with no name — just a phone number — a pay phone in the Greyhound bus station.

Defined

Chet's cheating was harshly punished — probation. And the dean gave him a verbal cue: the next act of cheating will get an even harsher punisher — the ax — kicked out. This cue for a direct punisher controlled Chet's cheating. We call such control "pre-moral" control.

Pre-moral control: social control where the act is controlled solely by the direct (perhaps physical) results to the person; similar to legal control — not really moral control, but rather pre-moral control.

■12 What's pre-moral control? Cite an instance.

Acquisition

Pre-moral control is often the first step to more advanced moral control. And a direct punisher often lies behind it, "Act properly, or else."

* * *

Carol frowned at her 18-month-old son. "Now Chetty eat your lunch and stop fooling with the food. I'll be late for work. Chetty, stop throwing your food around . . . Now look what you've done." Carol firmly shook young Chet a few times — a direct punisher, as his actions were scarcely controlled by the trouble he might be causing others, others like his mother. Then picking his plate off the floor she put it back on his highchair. Late for work again.

* * *

The sights and sound reinforced little Chet's throwing food and plate on the floor — but that response got punished since it was the wrong thing to do. We've learned our lesson well thanks to our punishments; now it's hard for us to get turned on by throwing our food — except, of course, when it's a custard pie in someone's face. We can't really enjoy a good mess since we're so concerned about the poor person who must clean it up — even if that poor person is someone other than us.

* * *

Now Carol was a rare mother, as she went out of her way to use rewards not relying solely on punishers. She used rewards as often as she could: "Chetty, you're such a good boy. You ate your whole meal and didn't drop a bit."

Carol had to work hard not to forget to give a reward to her son for his good deeds at first. But she got used to it after awhile. She was using almost all rewards with only a rare punisher by the time little Chetty was two years old, even though big Chet was still heavily into punishment.

Little Chet got a big bowl full of great gold fish for his second birthday, the best present of all, such fun to watch, swimming up and down, golden glitter. But little Chet really liked watching them flopping and splashing around as Mommy netted them and transferred them into another pan while she cleaned the fishbowl.

Little Chet ambled over to the coffee table, struggled up onto it, and crawled toward the big, bright, shiny bowl with the glittering gold. His hand was in the bowl when — "Don't touch that!" Chet cried. Smack! "I warned you!" Bright shiny objects that glitter also reward. And it required the lives of at least three of the helpless goldfish for Chet to set up pre-moral control over his son's response of grabbing them and putting them on the table to watch them flop.

* * *

Big Chet saw no point in spoiling the kid. (Could his lack of insight here be due to the poor job he was doing in psych class?) He just shouted at him or boxed his ears when his son made a wrong move. Standard parent. Even his requests were based on punishment: "Why? I'll tell ya' why. 'Cause I'll beat the hell out a' ya if you don't." Chet did refrain from some of the threats that produced his own pre-moral control: "Tell one more lie, and you'll grow a long nose." Or, "God'll strike you dead with a lightning bolt." Or, "You'll roast in Hell." Or, "You make an ugly face like that, and it'll freeze and always stay that way."

But most of us were first exposed to pre-moral control, control by the direct results of our acts, prior to more advanced forms of moral control, even though the details of our parent's child-rearing practices might differ greatly.

■13 Most children are first exposed to what form of moral control? Give an example.

GUILT — A FORM OF INTERNAL, PRE-MORAL CONTROL

Acqusition

Most children acquire pre-moral control from punishment by others before getting pre-moral control based on punishment from themselves. Little Chet moved toward the fish. "Don't touch, Chetty. No-no," Carol warned.

"NO!" big Chet shouted. Whack! That punisher backed up Mother's warning; so her warning will have more cue control next time. And that same punisher — the smack — backed up Chet's one word, "NO!"; so his "NO!" will also be a strong punisher next time, though not as strong as the smack.

Later, alone with that tempting fishbowl, little Chet will imitate his parents as he moves toward it. His action would be a cue for Mother to say, "Don't touch. That's a no-no"; so he imitated what she had done before. As he moved toward the bowl he said, "Don't touch, no-no", and his own words also failed to exert cue control. But just as his little arm was in the bowl up to his elbow, big Chet, the avenger, returned. "I said NO!" Smack!

Next day, alone again with the fish, moving toward them, little Chet said to himself, "Don't touch, no-no." But soon he was up to his elbow in trouble again, and now he also imitated his father, saying "NO!" and jerking his hand out of the bowl. Little Chet was learning guilt control.

Shouting "NO!" to himself was a strong punisher for little Chet — stopping him in his tracks. But his saying, "Don't touch, no-no," had not been a cue that the punisher would be on its way.

Next day. Little Chet said, "Don't touch," and he didn't.

Guilt control: self-punishment of acts similar to those that have been or would be punished by others.

And here's why guilt control is so worthwhile: A well-trained conscience follows you wherever you go, always there to punish wrong deeds.

- ■14 Define guilt control.
- ■15 Describe the stages of the acquisition of guilt control and cite an instance.
- ■16 Why is guilt control worthwhile?

Bad side effects

Guilt control sometimes causes problems due to its being based on punishment, a basis many people object to, since we would all like to see a world based solely on rewards, though most likely such a world couldn't be achieved. But the bad side effects of guilt control are not due just to the use of punishment; instead they are due to punishment's failure to always work — to always prevent immoral acts, leaving many people in our culture tortured by their conscience — their guilt control — their self-punishment.

For instance, some people have been taught that sex before marriage is a sin. But the tactual rewards from sexual contact often shape the person's actions into sex prior to marriage, since those rewards are so strong.

And this sex act may have two results — strong sexual rewards and weaker guilt-produced punishers — weaker than the sexual rewards. What then? The person may continue with sex and also continue to self-punish, since the guilt punishers aren't strong enough to win the battle with the sex rewards, though those punishers still hurt — they still make the person suffer.

Stronger punishers would prevent the sex act; leaving the person free from suffering. Weaker punishers would allow the person to indulge in the sex act but also with little suffering. Punishers in the middle cause the trouble.

■17 When do you get bad side effects from guilt control? Cite an instance.

A problem with guilt control as self-control

Guilt control as self-punishment is often hard to maintain, since you punish the act of self-punishment at the same time you're punishing the sinful act. For instance, little Chet says "NO!" after putting his hand in the goldfish bowl, punishing the very act of saying "NO!", as well as the sinful act of perhaps harming the goldfish. So the words he says punish the very act of saying "NO!" or telling himself he's a bad person.

Now punishment works better when the act is closer in time to the punisher. So saying "NO!" is more strongly punished than putting the hand in the bowl,

since saying "NO!" occurs closer to the punisher than the act of putting the hand in the bowl.

So little Chet might stop the self-punishment if it doesn't stop the sinful act fairly soon, since the self-punishment act is getting more punishment than is the sin, leaving him to just keep sinning in comfort.

Most often starting and stopping self-punishment isn't done on purpose with your saying to yourself, "I have sinned; therefore I shall punish myself," or "Punishing myself hurts; therefore I shall stop." These events may take place without our even being aware of them.

Guilt control has the best chance when you've only sinned a few times, since your verbal cues may get good control, stopping the sinning before you stop punishing yourself. There are many flaws in the system of guilt control, as you've seen; but it's the best we've got — being the basis of most of our advanced moral behavior. Flawed though it is, it keeps us out of the jungle — at least some of the time.

■18 How can guilt control lose its effectiveness?

RULE-GOVERNED MORAL CONTROL

Acquisition

Other punishers control the child's first "moral" act through direct punishment — pre-moral control. After awhile, the child comes to control his own "moral" acts through that same direct punishment of the act — guilt-based pre-moral control. And at the same time, the child may learn rule-governed moral control.

"Chetty, leave the kitty alone. You have to be careful not to hurt little creatures." At this stage we're not just dealing with single things — goldfish; we've got a rule — be careful not to hurt little things. The rule is based on two concepts — "hurt" and "little creatures". This is a very useful form of moral control since then the rule can exert a generalized control after the child learns the concepts "hurt"

and "little creatures". Little Chet no longer needs to have a cue and punisher for not touching each little creature. Once the concepts are learned, he is under good rule-governed control; now he can avoid the dangers of touching anything he might hurt.

"Mama, what is that?"

"That's a little birdie." Watch out!

This stage of moral control is often called the "law and order" stage because the main source of control that supports the law is direct punishment — either from someone else or the person himself (guilt control). No appeal is made to more basic moral rules.

"Why can't I touch little things?"

"'Cause it's not nice to hurt them."

Rule-governed moral control: moral control where a rule covering many different actions serves as a discriminative stimulus. The results that control that act are punishers or reinforcers given directly by that person or by someone else.

This rule-governed moral control is more useful than simple pre-moral control since the person does not require punishment training with each specific instance, as training with a few instances of the rule will generalize to novel instances.

- ∎19 What is rule-governed moral control?
- ∎20 What is the law and order stage?

The temptation of St. Juke

What was that? Out of the shadows stepped a strange figure — not strange to Juke, but strange to this campus. Superfly! Superfly strolled on up to Juke loose — super-cool — laid to the max. "Hey, brotha'. Wha's the rap, my man?"

"Later." Juke didn't even look his way — ignoring him as best he could.

"No, you my main man. An' I know you worried 'bout that psych test. It gonna be a bitch!"

"I can get a 'B' easy."

"Any nigger can get a 'B'. You

wan' a 'A', brother. An' I got a copy of the test to lay right on you."

"Any nigger can get a 'A' by cheatin' too. Don' worry. I'll get my 'A' an' I'll do it the right way."

"'Case you change yer mine, here's my phone number." Juke took the business card, folded it into a small wad, and threw it on the ground; he'd have no need to call a bus station pay phone.

***

Juke's moral actions were

mainly rule-governed. They were also under the control of punishers he gave himself more than outside punishers. You don't cheat — not even when you can get away with it. If you do cheat, you'll know it — you'll know you didn't really earn your reward. Anyone can cheat. Cheaters are bums. Juke needed no further reason for his moral action; he was a law and order man.

- ∎21 Cite an instance of rule-governed moral control.

RATIONAL MORAL CONTROL

Ladies and gentlemen — St. Sid

Chet walked toward the dorm to study with Sid before the big test. He pulled the stranger's phone number from his pocket, shaking his head, as he started to crumple up the card, then slowly smoothing it out, and putting it back in his pocket. In Sid's room at last — now someone else could help with his pre-moral problem.

Before he even put his books down, Chet blurted out, "Hey, Sid I can get a copy of the test. You think I need it?"

Sid just sat there, shocked.

"I guess I don't need it, do I, Sid?" Chet asked, not knowing what to make of Sid's silence. *Why doesn't he get me off the hook? Why's he just sittin' there?*

Sid was thinking — not about whether Chet needed to cheat, but did "A-student" Sidney Fields need to cheat. He'd probably get an

"A" without cheating but he was always scared half to death that he might get a "B". Sid was like many "A" students; in spite of constant success, he kept on busting his tail, since next time might be a loser.

But then, years of strict moral training took control, causing Sid to reply in slow, measured words, "It's not a question of need to do. It's a question of should do. And you should not cheat on this exam." Sid didn't share his secret shame — that he too thought about using the advanced copy to cheat on the test. *Why am I such a phoney?* Sid asked himself. But before he could answer his own question, Chet started talking.

"Yeah, I was afraid I'd get caught too."

Sid shook his head — sad. *What a clod; do I have to explain everything to him?* "It's not a matter of getting caught. Even if you don't get caught, it's still a pimp job."

"How's that?" asked Chet, nervous.

"You're pimping the people. You're cheating the taxpayers; they're paying a lot of the bill here. You took their help, so you're obliged to learn as much as you can. Grades are supposed to mean something. When they look you over for a job, an 'A' in psych means you mastered the course — not that you cheated."

Chet was relieved, "Thought for a minute you meant it was me that was getting pimped."

"You are. You're getting screwed out of your tuition and the time you put in school."

"You mean if I get kicked out."

"If you don't get kicked out. Sounds corny, but you're here to learn. Cheat your way through college, and you won't learn. Don't learn, and you won't be a success on your job. You won't move up as fast; you won't get as many raises. You're gonna get paid for what you do, and that depends on what you learned. Cop out — cheat — and you won't learn."

Chet knew all he needed to know about those things and didn't want to keep up the debate. He always lost with Sid. Besides he was here so Sid could help him pass this course — not get him into heaven. "Let's get down to work."

Defined

Sid provides an instance of a final type of moral control — rational moral control. It's a form of rule-governed control — just more complex, with the rules covering more ground.

"Do unto others . . ." is a general rule since you can derive more special rules from it, rules like most of the Ten Commandments.

Or, the categorical imperative: Think about how others should act if they were in your shoes; then act that way yourself.

Or, do what will get the most rewards for the most people; do what will get the least punishers for the fewest people — people today and people yet to be born. That's Sid's moral rule — the one he hopes will exert cue control over him, using it to decide what he should do, trying to weigh the present and future, both good and bad, for all concerned, thinking it through, deriving special rules for new problems — Thou shalt not cheat on thy psych test.

But clear thinking is hard to do. And most people are not too good at it since it takes a good deal of training to acquire the skills of clear thinking.

And we must not only learn how to think clearly, but we must keep on doing it as well. So we must get rewards for doing it, and, just as important, we must get punishers for failing to do it; and we must keep getting those rewards and punishers even when we leave our moral trainers. We learn the clear thinking skills used in rational moral control; we derive the moral rule for a specific act from our moral code; then we must get a reward if we follow that or a punisher if we break the rule. And here guilt control rears its helpful little head. Break the specific rule, and we've gone against our moral code, which is what the rule was based on. That means we're bad, evil, not moral. So guilt helps us stay with our larger moral code.

Rational moral control: moral control where rules acting as discriminative stimuli for specific acts are derived from a larger moral code; punishers and reinforcers for following the specific rules have their effect because they are stated in terms of the larger moral code.

But that's a lot of work — getting a special rule from the larger rule or moral code. There are too many things to think about. Why not just bag it; do what we wanted in the first place. We don't do what we wanted in the first place because we know we'd cop out, doing the easy thing, not the moral thing. So guilt control goes to work again, giving a punisher when we fail to think things through. But how does it work when we're under rational moral control? We think things through because we will punish ourselves otherwise — guilt control. We follow the special cues we thought up for the same reasons — we will punish ourselves otherwise — guilt control again.

But rational moral control is fragile — easy to lead astray. Few of us are under good rational moral control since there are so many things to weigh, so many places to fool ourselves, so many places to cop out. Some of the world's worst acts come from rational moral control gone astray. But perhaps some of the world's best acts come from rational moral control that was right on.

- ▪22　What is rational moral control? Cite an instance.
- ▪23　Cite two ways in which guilt control supports rational moral control.

CONCLUSIONS

We're not like lower animals — we need moral control to survive — they don't. That's the price of civilization. Instinct will not protect the human species — moral control may. And the more advanced our moral control, the more likely we will be to survive. As parents, we must take on the job of helping our children learn advanced moral control. As people, we must help ourselves make this advance.

CHAPTER 20
SOCIAL ROLES

ROLES

Going home with roommate

Ever go to your roommate's home? Roommate's not the same person at home with mom and dad. In the dorm, roommate's a loud, radical, foul-mouthed, put-down expert. At home — soft-spoken, respects mom and dad, conservative (at least not radical), non-commital, and never a foul word passes the lips.

"You're like someone else when you're with your folks."

"Never noticed. Seems like I'm just myself wherever I go. Well, I mean they are my folks; but I mean gee, I have to treat 'em like my parents, but I mean seems to me like I'm myself wherever I go; I mean I'm not a phoney, am I?"

Analysis

Two different roles — student and offspring. How do they work? Let's look at role playing in terms of our basic concepts: discriminative stimulus, response, reinforcer, and punisher. Now one role gets rewards in the dorm and another at home. We all have many roles: student, son or daughter, parent, lover, worker, punk kid, rebel, athlete. Sometimes it's like two distinct people — Saturday night vs. Sunday morning. It's just that we have more than one set of actions, with each set controlled by its own cue, Saturday night party, or Sunday morning church. We may not even be aware we perform all these roles — rude and boorish to our parents or polite and thoughtful to our friends. And we think we treat everyone the same. We're not being phony; it's just that old cue-response-reinforcer at work, causing us to act out some role or other.

"Role" is a useful concept in social psych. We've used the term a few times, so now let's define it.

Role: a consistent way of acting under the control of a specific set of discriminative stimuli.

- 1 Cite an instance of different roles.
- 2 Discuss our awareness of our own roles.
- 3 Analyze role playing in terms of cues, responses, and results.
- 4 Now define role.

Psychology and religion

In the psych class, Mae raised her hand causing Dr. Harper to nod, pleased to see a student take part for a change.

"Dr. Harper, I agree with most of what you've said this term; and I agree with the text. But it seems 'like something's missing — like we're not gettin' the whole story."

Dr. Harper puzzled, "What're you getting at, Mae?"

"Well, all you talk about is stimuli and responses, but there must be more to it than that. What about the human spirit — the soul?"

Dawn was surprised at this, as she'd never heard her roommate talk about "spirit" and "soul", even though her father was a preacher.

Dr. Harper was surprised, too, "I don't know if there is such a thing as 'human spirit' or 'soul', at least we'll need more proof than we've got now. And, in fact, I don't think there are any human data we can't explain in terms of the concepts of this course."

"You may be right, but I've got this feeling there's got to be more to me than responses and rewards. I feel like I have a soul." Mae, the student of religion was puzzled.

Dr. Harper forced a nod to show he shared her concern. "I don't deny your feelings. They exist, though I also don't admit those feelings are proof that you have a soul. In the old days, people used to have strong feelings that an evil spirit or the devil was inside them. But we doubt that nowadays, since having those feelings doesn't prove such a thing is inside you. Of course, you have your feelings because of the kind of verbal responses, and thinking responses, and imitation responses that got rewards in your past; you feel you have a soul since talking and thinking about a 'soul' has been rewarded, and you've listened to others talking about their soul. You wouldn't have the same feelings if other responses had gotten those rewards."

The bell rang. Class was over.

***

Another role: Mae the psych student. Where? Religion class, where else? Hand in air. Teacher nods, pleased.

"Dr. Salk, you ever think about looking at religion as a branch of psych, like trying to think of all religious acts and feelings as responses controlled by cues, rewards, and punishers?"

"No, I don't see how you could. You psych students are all the same — always trying to reduce everything to stimuli and responses.

***

Mae learned how to get a response from people. Say something they don't believe in and they'll have to attend to you — a big reward. So in psych Mae played the role of the searching religious student; and in religion, the psych student. Many students do this. (Result: Psych prof thinks campus full of religion nuts; and Religion prof sure psych has brainwashed the whole campus.) But the role Mae plays is a result of the cues for the rewards she might get in each class.

- 5   Incidental information (but of value): What is a typical psychologist's response to the concept of "soul"? And to the feelings that you have a soul?
- 6   What's the reward for playing the role of debater with your teachers?

PEER CONTROL

Analysis

At first we play the roles our parents reward, since most of our unlearned rewards come from our parents and other adults. And the mere sight of these adult givers of unlearned rewards becomes a learned reward itself. Then the reward value of the sight of adults generalizes to other children. Thus, a three-year-old child plays close to other children though they may not play together; the mere closeness of other kids being a slight reward in itself. This is called "parallel play" — playing near each other but not together.

But children start really playing with each other as they get older, giving more social rewards to each other. So playing with others, itself, becomes a reward, one that children can control. But the child must play the proper role of kid-playing-with-other-kids, learning to cooperate, to get those social rewards — since the others won't play with the child if the child is selfish or doesn't conform.

So the control of our rewards shifts more and more from adults to our peers (people of our own status) as we grow from infancy into our teenage years, peers controlling more of the roles we play.

- 7 Define peer and cite an instance.
- 8 Define parallel play. Why does it occur?
- 9 Describe and explain the shift in the control your peers exert over you throughout the years.

The battle between roles — teenager vs. model child

One day on visiting her parents, Carol found her mother crying in the kitchen. "What's the matter, Mom?"

"It's your brother, Bob. Seems like he's just been awful, ever since he got into high school. Used to be a nice boy, but now he's gettin' worse and worse, runnin' 'round with a bunch of bums, and him the worst of the lot. Looks like a bum — look at his hair. Dresses like a bum — keeps putting patches on those same old blue jeans. And all he's got for us is smart remarks. But that's not the worst since he's become a thief now, shoplifting a record album; won't admit it, but I know he did."

* * *

And the roles collide — Bob, the model son meets Bob, the model teenage boy, the delinquent. And the contest is under way, with the ones who control most of the rewards winning. And the peers do win since they exert active control over most of the rewards. Now Bob's parents still provide many of his basic rewards — food, new clothes whenever he wants some, spending money, and shelter. But those rewards are free-flowing, with everyone seeing them as Bob's right no matter how Bob acts. But not the peers: they only give rewards if Bob does the right things — plays the right roles; so they win, hands down.

But how can we say Bob's still playing a role, if his actions are now pretty much the same, whether he's with his family or his friends? At what point do we say the punk-kid routine has stopped being a mere role, now becoming the way he really is, his personality?

Well, it helps to look again at how this role conflict progressed. No doubt the roles started out under fairly strict audience control, with the punk-kid act reserved for the peers, the model son playing an exclusive performance for the family. But it gets a little hard to always change costumes from one show to the next, coming home with the punk-kid clothes on, the punk-kid hair, and the punk-kid act needing more and more time, as any punk kid must be able to stay out as late as the next kid.

Bob would have kept the two roles separate if he could, most likely not even knowing he was doing so. But he can't. The punk-kid role comes to encroach on the family turf, leaving no choice but open warfare, victory going to the side that reserves its rewards only for those who really play their role all the way. But is the punk-kid act still just a role or has it now become the real Robert?

Most likely we would still be ahead to look at it as a mere role, not being fooled by its present consistency — as Bob's roles will no doubt change, when his peers change, coming under the control of other sets of outside rewards, like the job, college, marriage, the adult world he and his peers will become an active part of. Even Bob won't be a 40-year-old punk kid — at least let's hope not.

■10 Give an example of control by teenage peers vs. control by parents. Who really holds most of the needed rewards? Why do the peers so often win the battle?

■11 Why should we still think of teenage behavior as role playing rather than personality change?

CONFORMITY

What does it mean to conform? It means to fit in, playing the roles others give us rewards for or hold off punishers for: conforming to traffic laws (the safe-driver role), conforming to the social customs of our peers (the young rebel role). Often conforming to laws is rule-governed, with social customs being contingency-controlled, no one ever spelling out the customs for us, just giving direct and indirect rewards (through modeling) causing us to conform. Once again we conform because those acts get rewards and non-conformity may get punishers. But those same rewards and punishers can also sometimes combine to produce the non-conformist, as we shall see.

■12 Why do we conform? Give an example.
■13 What is a difference in the kind of control of conformity to roles proscribed by laws and by social customs?

What's a nice colored girl like you doing in a course like this? — The racial-sexual stereotype

The counselor smiled, "Let's see, your name is . . ."

"Mae Robinson."

"Oh yeah, here's your class list for next term. Seems okay, except maybe that electronics course. Do you need it?"

"Don't have to take it, but some of the other students say it's a good idea for psych majors."

"Well, frankly that's not a woman's course."

Mae felt herself get tense, "What do you mean?" she asked — precise — no black accent.

He was sorry for his frankness, having to pursue the issue now. "Well, girls just don't do too well in these courses. Maybe I shouldn't say this, but Negroes don't do too well there either. If you want something from the Applied Arts, why don't you take a home ec course?"

Mae sat there rigid. Waiting to get her voice under control. *Why doesn't he just come out and tell me to take House Nigger 101? I'll tell that honky facist . . . No, why bother? To hell with him.*

"I'll take the electronics course."

Group pride

Not meaning to, the counselor had increased the reward value of success in Electronics 200, a course Mae had not really cared about until now. Why does it work that way?

Words function as cues, rewards, and punishers. (His words were a punisher for Mae's response of seeking advice from him.) But it's the cue function we're concerned with here. His words were a cue that good work in Electronics 200 will get a bonus. Doing a good job in that course will open the doors for more members of her group — black women — giving them more options, more choices. She'll help the movement by also helping herself. And, women in the movement are a big source of social reward for her; they'll give plenty of rewards now — rewards for her trying and winning at this white man's task: Black pride, women's pride, in action.

But in a way the man was right. She'd been taught the women's role — dolls, play house, etc., never having an erector set, never working on a car, never repairing a light switch. *Be ahead of those honkies by the time the course is started if I do a little reading between terms.*

***

The counselor had tried to impose a role on Mae, the role he thought correct for women, for black women. But she had little trouble not conforming to that stereotype, since the movement controlled more of her rewards than this man did. She was playing another role, no doubt, but not the one the culture at large was trying to force on her. Praise the Lord for little counter-control groups here and there. But Mae had other sources of reward for not conforming, as we will soon see.

■14 Give an example of how group pride can increase the reward value of success. Analyze it.

Programming a non-conformist

Mae was unique, growing up in a small town down south, but not growing up like the others, not conforming, and so not fitting in too well with the other kids, the kids who were black, but not proud, who didn't care about the problems of their own people, the kids she liked and even tried to love, but couldn't relate to. She wanted to help them, though they didn't think they needed her help.

It looks like the world's set up to make everyone conform; so how did Mae slip through the net? Was she immune to the laws of behavior — to social rewards? No. She was programmed by her world like everyone else was. But her world was a little different.

First of all her parents weren't like the parents of most of the other kids, her papa being the preacher, whose values and attitudes differed from those of the others. Though they didn't agree, still they didn't put Mae down for her strange ideas since they saw where she was coming from, from good basic Christian moral values.

A second big part of Mae's world was the public library, since long ago her parents had gotten her hooked on words, books, and reading. She read Malcolm X, *Muhammad Speaks*, about the slaughter at Jackson State, about Fred Hampton and Mark Clark, about the Soledad brothers, about Angela, about Huey, wanting to do something, wanting to help, having to help. Watch out for Andrew Carnegie and his little public libraries full of words. They may be one of the biggest causes of non-conformity in our country. No matter where — Anytown-Silent-Majority, USA — that humble little building, the library, contains the seeds of non-conformity — the words of the world's greatest thinkers. And those words form the basis for moving way out.

Mae was not completely alone, having her parents, her reading, and also a third source of support, a friend, Emmy, two years older. And Emmy always had new notions or books to put on her — that was really true after she went away to college, coming back with all sorts of great new things. Mae learned to talk Black from her, not on purpose, just a little unconscious imitation. Emmy always talked to her about what she'd been reading or thinking — a big reward for her — a deep young woman.

Now Mae also had other sources of reward for doing things that didn't conform, as we saw in her psych and religion classes, playing one role in religion and another in psych. But each of those sub-roles was a part of the super-role: woman who does not conform, woman who plays whatever role is not being played by most of the others.

Conforming and not conforming are both roles, consistent ways of acting maintained by their results. And once again the basic concepts are the same for each role: cue, response, and reward, with the rewards also being much the same — they differ only in the response that happens to get rewarded. It's just that the world happens to reward conforming for some people and non-conforming for others.

For instance, Mae's older brother conformed — in fact he could play football, laugh, and sing; a lot of fun. His world happened to get him going in that direction, while Mae's world, almost but not quite the same, got her going in another direction. As one role became better learned, it was harder and harder to acquire the skills needed for the other role — easier and easier to get their rewards with their tried and true roles. These roles became so ever-present they became their personalities, as we will see in the next chapter.

Now you might ask just what does all of Mae's non-conforming have to do with role playing? It shows two major causes of not playing the standard roles most people play. First, Mae sometimes got more social rewards from those around her by not playing the standard role, e.g., playing the spiritual soul for Dr. Harper, the psych prof. And second, her actions may be more under the control of rewards from sources other than those around her at the moment, sources like her parents, her books, her college friend, and the movement people. Our point here is not that roles are bad and something we should escape, but rather that

the same basic principles of psychology operate whether we're playing the standard roles or not; though we may escape human-made laws, we never escape the laws of human behavior.

■15 List several factors that support non-conformity.

■16 How can these various factors support non-conformity (give examples): parents, poorly acquired conforming roles, the library, a non-conforming friend, people's reactions to non-conformity, arguing skills.

CONCLUSIONS

We've looked at role playing — a basic concept in social psych. Like so many psych concepts, we can study it, too, in terms of the three notions: cue, response, and results. "Role playing" brings out two important features of our actions. First, we tend to always act the same way when the same cues are present. And, second, we may change the way we act when the cues change. Thus there is no cause for alarm when we note that someone's actions change from one group to the next.

But, on the other hand, we shouldn't be surprised when someone doesn't play the standard role for some group. That person's actions are still being controlled by their results, though the source of those controlling rewards and punishers may be more obscure.

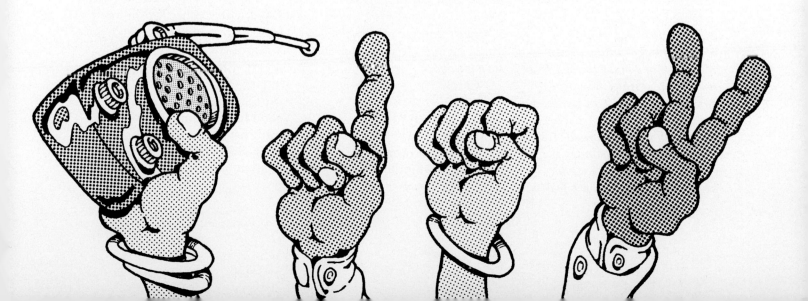

CHAPTER 21
SIGMUND FREUD
AND PERSONALITY

INTRODUCTION

In search of the orgasm

Carol and Chet lay in bed. Little Chet still asleep in his own bed. Sunday morning, with no work, no school, just time to relax, to make love. Nice, warm love. Carol loved Chet so much. She was getting aroused. Very aroused: *I love Chet. Hhummm, thought that was Chet moaning, it's me. My God, I'm moving back and forth — didn't even realize it. Chet must think I'm an animal; I'm acting like one. That's awful — am I so crude? I just keep groaning and pushing against him like an animal. Got to control myself. Wonder if I made so much noise I woke Chetty up? Funny, don't feel* turned on anymore. Always happens.

Humm. Wonder why Carol's slowed down. Always does that. She shouldn't. It feels so good. I can't last much longer. Guess I should slow down too; try to help Carol. Can't. This feels too good.

Chet's doing it. I think he did. Yeah, he did. He's quiet now. I love him so.

"Carol?"

"Yeah?"

". . . Did ya?"

"Don't know."

Chet rolled over on his side, raised up on his elbow, and looked at Carol — annoyed. "You have to know. Why don't you know? I know I did."

"Well, maybe I . . .", Carol knew what Chet wanted but she couldn't lie for him; "No, I don't think I had an orgasm."

"How d' ya' think I feel with a frigid wife?" Chet lay on his back and stared at the ceiling.

Carol tried to keep from crying. "I'm not frigid Chet. I like to give you pleasure. And I get pleasure from you. You're a good lover. I don't know why I can't have an orgasm. But it's not your fault." And that was what really worried him.

Freud

Chet and Carol can thank Dr. Sigmund Freud for their concern over her orgasm. It's not Freud's fault that Carol didn't have one. But it's because of him they think she should — that they see it as a problem. No one questioned the sex role of women in our culture before Freud's impact, 50 to 75 years ago, as it seemed clear women were to bear children and perhaps provide reinforcing sex contact for their husbands; but surely, it was thought, no real lady should find sex a reward for herself. Freud changed that by saying, in effect, sex is the big reward for all of us — men and women alike. In only a few decades, women lost their fear that sex was too big a reward and gained the fear that is wasn't big enough for them. And men began to worry too: were they really good sex partners if their women didn't achieve climax?

Freud was a product of the nineteenth century, feeling women should serve husband and child; a product of the nineteenth century, feeling it was too bad sex was such a strong reward

for them. But his nineteenth century training didn't stop Freud, the scientist, from noting that sex rewards were indeed behind many of the actions of women as well as men. Freud, the scientist, won out over Freud, the nineteenth century gentleman, in at least that instance. And Freud's equality of sexual rewards may well have been a first step toward other forms of equality for which modern women are now striving. But how did all of this come about?

Freud saw many troubled patients while a doctor in Vienna. And in studying their problems, he developed a notion that shocked him — most of their troubles involved sex. After awhile Freud's reports of what he saw and guessed came to greatly affect the way our whole culture looked at people, for better and for worse. And years later we still believe he cited many valid facts about human actions as well as many valid causes for those actions, though he may have talked about those facts and their causes in ways that misled. So in this chapter,

we will try to show some of his valid insights but within the context of this text — a point of view we find to be simpler, more straightforward, and more general, in that it relates to more areas of behavior than Freud studied.

Now Freud talked about three factors of personality that controlled us, calling them id, ego, and superego. He said these factors were in conflict for that control, and that this conflict caused personality problems. In the next sections, we will restate these basic notions of Freud's in behavioral terms and briefly examine each one, hopefully still doing justice to those basic notions of Freud's.

- 1 Before Freud, what was woman's role? How was she to respond to sexual reinforcers?
- 2 What did Freud see as the cause of most of his patients' problems?
- 3 How might Freud have inadvertently contributed to the women's movement?

CONTROL PROCESSES

Id

Two unlearned rewards controlled Chet's high rate of sexual movements — the instant rewards of touch and orgasm. He might slow down, allowing Carol a chance for her orgasm and getting him a social reward, but this reward would have been a bit more delayed and so it didn't happen. The immediate reinforcer — orgasm — won out over the delayed reinforcers — Carol's appreciation and the confirmation of Chet's manhood. So he called himself a "poor lover", yet even that self-punishment didn't slow him down either. This is id control.

Id control: prompt, unlearned reinforcers and punishers exert greater control over us than delayed social reinforcers and punishers.

This is based on Freud's notion of the Pleasure Principle.

Pleasure Principle: reinforcers and punishers control all that we do.

Now, the Pleasure Principle is old news for you, as you've read that sort of thing many times. But imagine how your grandparents felt when Freud told them such

base biological forces as sex caused so much of what they did.

"But," you might say, "what about Carol? No id control there. Her love for Chet controlled everything she did."

Not quite. At first, sexual touch controlled her high rate of motion — and that's pure id control, but then the superego control came into action, as we will see.

- 4 What are two unlearned rewards for the sex act?
- 5 Define id control. Cite an instance.
- 6 State the Pleasure Principle.

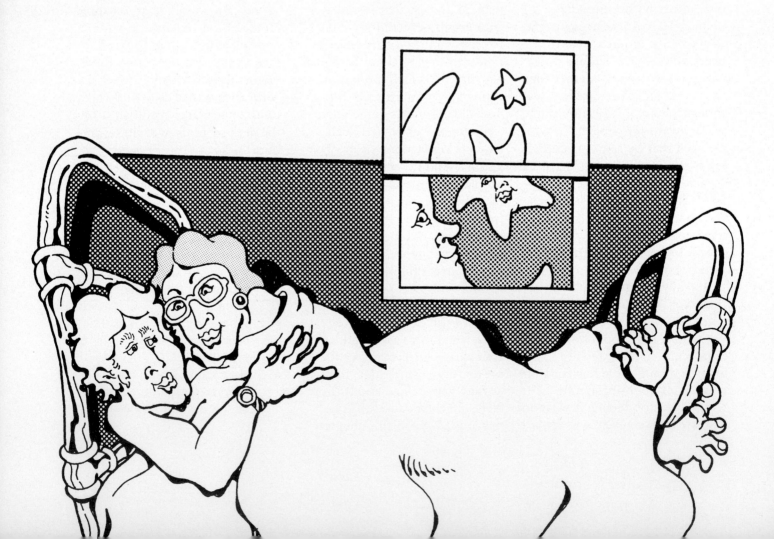

Superego

Chet got up and went into the bathroom, while Carol lay there thinking. *I feel guilty about Chet. I'm a failure as a woman. I don't have orgasms and that hurts Chet. I should just let myself go. But then I feel like a dog in heat — it's awful. But I shouldn't make Chet feel bad.*

Chet thought for an instant as he washed his hands. *Maybe I should try to hold off a little longer; then Carol might have a shot at it. Maybe I'm selfish; but she said she was happy. She'd tell me if she wasn't — wouldn't she?*

* * *

Carol said to herself she should avoid hurting Chet; Chet even hinted to himself maybe he was being slightly selfish. This is superego control.

Superego control: social reinforcer and punisher control by the culture's values — usually through guilt control.

This may be either conscious or unconscious control.

Superego control also played another role in Carol's sex life, through a value of her culture: it's bad to be sensuous — to be greedy. Too much sexual motion seemed in poor taste to Carol. And telling that to herself punished the sex response. So these social punishers suppressed that response even more than the unlearned sex rewards strengthened it. Thus, the sex responses were punished, and stopped, removing the chance for the other sexual reward — the orgasm. For Carol superego control was winning out over id control. Carol's problem is far from unique, even among young women today, though it was much more common during Freud's time.

- ■ 7 Define superego control and cite an instance.
- ■ 8 How can superego control interfere with the sex act?

Ego

I can have kids, why not orgasms? Is it me or Chet? Maybe both. But it's not that big a deal, since I like sex and so does Chet. But we'd have more fun — less of a hassle, too, if we could solve this problem. We need help. Problems can be solved. So we've got to find someone who can solve it, then we'd like our whole marriage more. But I'd feel silly asking for help. But we'd be better off in the long run though.

***

Maybe Carol would have a chance to have an orgasm if I could hold off. But it's her own fault. I wouldn't get so excited, if she'd lie still. But when we're makin' love I could think about somethin' else — that might slow things down. But I've tried to — can't do it. Feel more like a man if I could turn her on though.

***

Both Carol and Chet were trying to solve a problem, the orgasm problem, by weighing the results of this and that approach: trying to decide whether to ask for help or not? Whether to feel silly but have a better marriage? To slow things down or not? To have a quicker orgasm or a better marriage? Ego control had arrived.

Ego control: rule-governed control, based on reason and logic — a conscious weighing of the results of our acts, both present and future, good and bad.

The ego or reasoned control sets up cues for our actions. And once the cues are there, ego control ends. Then we give ourselves mild, learned rewards when we follow those cues. And learned punishers when we fail to follow them. Our culture's values of right and wrong control most of those rewards and punishers we give ourselves through superego "self-control". But many times, these gentle, learned (superego) results lose out, beaten by the stronger, unlearned (id) results, with id control winning out over superego control, many times but not always.

- ■ 9 Define ego control. How does it work in terms of cues?
- ■ 10 How does superego control interact with ego control?

Reification

Once again Chet was studying in Sid's room, but this time it was "Sigmund Freud and Personality Theory". And now he was ready to review the first sections.

"Here's the way I see it: there's these three little guys in your head, see. They're the id, the ego, and the superego. And they decide what you're gonna do, see. Now the id's a selfish little devil, and he wants to get his unlearned rewards and right now. But the superego is a little angel, and he wants to do what's right for everybody. And the ego, he tries to be the wise old judge, weighing what the id wants and what the superego says you should do. So this ego has the final word on what you're gonna do."

Sid shakes his head, "Well, that is pretty much the way everyone looks at it. Even Freud. But . . ."

"It was Freud's theory, so I've got ta be right."

"Well, that's the main problem with Freud's theory. See, there aren't any little people in your head. It's . . ."

"No, I don't mean they're really in your head. I mean it's sort of like they were in your head. It just makes it easier for me to think about things that way."

"Well Malott and Whaley would say that's risky. You invent those little guys to help you think about people, but you gotta be real careful. There isn't really any such thing as an id, or

an ego, or a superego. Those words aren't things. They show how cues, and actions, and results relate to each other. They show us ways the world controls us. But they're not real things."

"What did Malott and Whaley say that's called?"

"Reification."

Reify: to invent things that help to explain how real things relate. Reification is the turning of a relation between real things into a thing itself.

"And what's wrong with reifying things?"

"You end up more concerned about what you invented than about what people are really doing. They take you away from the real world."

***

You may have noticed we prefer to speak in terms of id control, superego control, and ego control, even though Freud himself spoke in terms of the id, the ego, and the superego. We do this to help us keep in mind the notion that we're dealing with relations among events — cues, acts, and results — we're dealing with processes and not with concrete things.

- ■11 How do most people look at the id, ego, and superego?
- ■12 Define reify. Cite an instance.
- ■13 What's wrong with reifying things?

PSYCHIC NEEDS AND MENTAL HEALTH

Chet walked into the kitchen, grabbed a handful of cereal and then Carol. "Honey, I'm horny again. Let's go back to bed."

"I'm feeding Chetty."

"You are frigid."

"Don't be so grouchy."

"Don't be so grouchy. I got a right to be grouchy." Chet slammed the cupboard door. "It's not good for a guy to be horny. It's not healthy."

"Oh Chet."

"Naw, it's really bad. It can drive ya crazy." Chet stormed out of the room. Who knows what crazy things this poor, frustrated boy will be forced to do?

Crying, Carol followed him into the bedroom, "Don't be so mean to me," she pleaded.

"That's the way I feel, and I got ta say it. It's bad for me to keep all my feelings inside me."

Carol sat down on the bed next to Chet, hugging him. "Honey, I'm sorry. You know I am. We can make love now."

***

"Psychic" means "of the mind" or "mental". So "psychic power" meant "the power that runs the mind". Freud thought this force or power stored inside us must be let out in the form of sex or aggression or we would explode with psychic problems. "Letting off steam" gets at the notion.

But we're not like steam engines driven by psychic pressures. We have no forces that must be let off in the form of sex or aggression.

Instead, rewards and punishers control our actions. We do something that leads to a reward like sex or aggression, and what happens the next time the cues are there? We'll do that same thing again.

True, deprive us of sex, and sex becomes a stronger reward; harm or frustrate us and aggression becomes a stronger reward. But there's still no pressure that needs to be let off. In sum, this notion confuses needs with reinforcers — just because something is a reward doesn't mean it's needed.

We're all hurt by this notion that sex and aggression are needed for good mental health — a notion without any scientific support, as far as we know — a notion that causes us to approve a lot of crummy behavior like bullying and temper tantrums.

Chet has no sexual pressure pent up inside him that must be let out. And his mental health won't suffer if he holds back his verbal abuse of Carol, but he acts like it will. And this false psychic pressure notion influences Carol too. She doesn't want poor Chet to fall apart, or burst out in psychic boils; so she lets him abuse her and bully her into more sex. She reinforces his tantrums; so, of course he will be even more likely to throw a temper tantrum the next time he runs into even the slightest frustration since Carol reinforced that kind of behavior the last time.

- ■14 Cite an instance of how the notion of psychic energy sources can result in reinforcing a tantrum.
- ■15 Discuss Freud's theory in terms of letting off energy. What are its shortcomings?

DISPLACEMENT

Now we'll take a detailed look at the concept of displacement — an important concept to general psychology as well as to Freud. We will see how it applies to both sex and aggression, showing both a standard and a new way of looking at when and why it occurs and what it is.

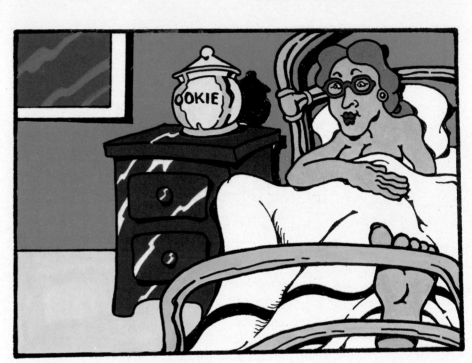

I love my wife, but oh you kid

Monday afternoon. Chet arrived for psych a few minutes early, giving
him time to review the study objectives before the quiz. He gave the
room a quick scan as he entered. *There's Dawn. Thought she always
got here early. Sit next to her. Why not? Nothing wrong with that.*
Chet smiled at her as he sat down. "How's it goin', Dawn?"

"Oh, hi, Chet. How's it with you?"

"Not bad. Not bad. Been workin' real hard with Sid. Gettin' this
stuff down cold."

Sex

Why did Chet go to class early?

"To review," you say.

No, to sit next to Dawn. In fact, he talked to her until class started,
failing to get around to the review. Why'd he sit next to Dawn?

"To talk about psych."

No, to get closer to a sexual reinforcer.

"Oh. He was hustling her?"

Not really. Since married Chet might get too much social punishment for such an act. He's not going for direct sexual rewards —
just the rewards of being next to a pretty woman.

Next question: Why'd Chet study with Sid?

"So he could learn more."

Perhaps, but also so he could brag to Dawn and get other social
rewards as well. At least those are some of the rewards. What does
this show? Mild, learned, sexual rewards control Chet, even where
we might not expect it, like in the classroom. Freud called this
displacement. And by "displacement" he meant the notion that
some of our acts don't seem really to deal with the issue at hand.

Chet wants to have sex but can't, so he sits next to Dawn instead;
less rewarding, but at least something. This is one form of displacement — sexual displacement.

"Chet acted childish. Adults don't plan their lives that way," you
might object.

But Chet doesn't think he planned his life that way either. Even to
himself, he'd deny those displaced rewards had any effect on him.
But they did. Chet rationalized, a concept Freud himself introduced.
It would never do for married Chet to admit why he sat next to
Dawn or why he studied so hard since he can't admit those sexual
rewards. Chet must rationalize — but not lie; as he believes what he
says.

■16 Cite an instance of displaced sex.
■17 Relate rationalization to displaced sex and cite an instance.

Aggression

Another common form of displacement is displaced aggression. In this case a person or animal aggresses toward someone or something other than the source of the original harm, other than the cause of the aggression; and so displaced aggression does not really stop that source of harm.

For instance, Chet might fail one of his psych tests, in spite of his belief that he has "this stuff down cold". And perhaps he can't get his grade changed; so then he's nasty to Carol at dinner, like many of us who aggress against someone or something other than the source of harm.

▪18 Cite an instance of displaced sex and displaced aggression.

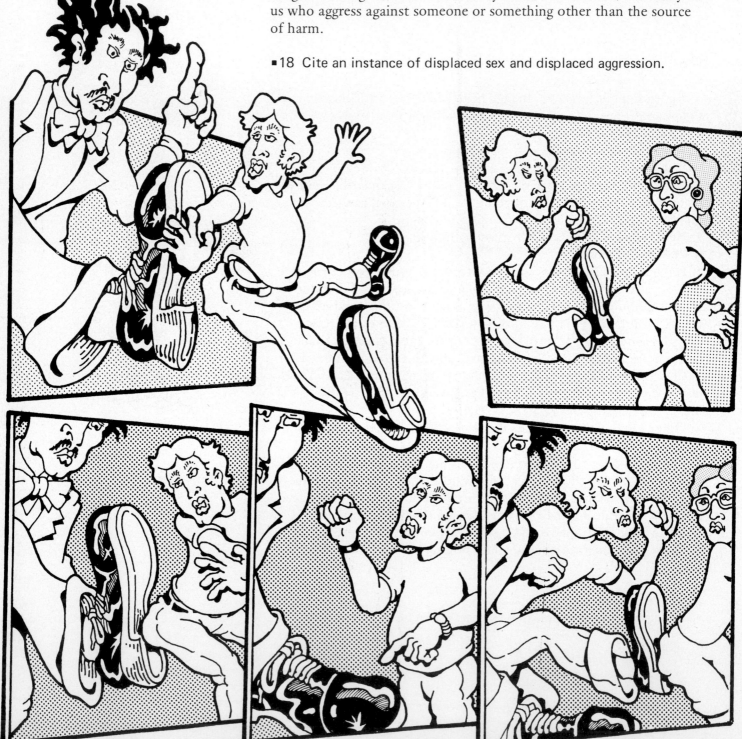

When

But when do displaced acts occur? They occur when we're deprived of sex or hurt, and when we're not able to achieve our unlearned sex rewards or when we're not able to stop the harmful condition. So our notion differs from the standard notion about when displacement occurs. The standard notion says displacement occurs when a direct response is blocked. For instance, that notion would say that Chet, the failure, shows displaced aggression toward Carol when he's afraid to aggress against Dr. Harper, the source of his problems. But we believe aggression may occur as long as the harmful state still persists, even when direct aggression has occurred. For instance, failing Chet would most likely show displaced aggression against Carol even if he had already given Dr. Harper a piece of his mind, but had failed to get him to change the grade.

On the other hand, displaced aggression will not occur, regardless of whether direct aggression has occurred, if the harmful state of affairs has been stopped. For instance, failing Chet would not displace aggression against Carol, even if he had not aggressed against Harper, as long as he had gotten his grade changed, perhaps due to the well-reasoned, charming way he had pleaded his case with the teacher.

We believe people thought the lack of direct aggression was the cause of displaced aggression, because the harmful state of affairs often does persist unless it is stopped by direct aggression; but displaced aggression is caused by the harmful state itself, not by the lack of direct aggression.

We should add that Freud was mainly concerned with those displaced acts occurring when sex or aggression is blocked by the threat of punishment, most often some form of social punishment. And we agree with him: Social punishment is often the cause of our failure to get direct sexual rewards and our failure to stop harm by means of aggression.

- ■19 When do displaced acts occur according to the standard notion? According to the authors?
- ■20 What form of control often blocks direct action resulting in displacement?

Why

So we've seen when displaced acts occur, but now we should ask why they occur. We believe the rewards for displaced sex differ somewhat from those for displaced aggression. In the case of sex, the learned rewards, like the sight of a good-looking person, maintain the displaced act for two reasons. First, learned as well as unlearned sex rewards will be strong if you're deprived of sex, and such sex rewards begin to exert control, when the stronger unlearned sex rewards are blocked by social punishment. And second, such a sight might be a cue for a mild sex arousal response — itself something of a reinforcer.

Then what about displaced aggression? Well, the standard notion is that creatures aggress in order to injure the source of harm; but we think the effect on the source of harm is often only a by-product, as mentioned in an early chapter. In other words, we often aggress because of the unlearned internal events that result; perhaps events such as pressure on our teeth when we bite our attacker or the pressure on our nails when we scratch him. So aggression may be maintained by rewards such as teeth and nail pressure, and the effect it has on the aggressor, not by the damage done to the source of the harm.

And often a displaced attack on some other object will produce those same rewarding results just as well as a direct attack on the source of harm. For instance, much research has shown that squirrel monkeys will bite a rubber hose when they receive an electric shock, if that's all there is to bite, even though it was not the hose but rather the human research worker who was the source of the shock. We're saying displaced aggression is a very normal response; we creatures learn to aggress against the source of harm itself only after results like escape from harm have come into play.

So the standard notion is as follows: Aggression directed at the source of harm is the normal state of affairs, with displacement taking place only when the direct response is blocked. But our view is: Displaced aggression is the normal state of affairs, with directed aggression taking place only when the creature has learned to use such aggression to escape harm.

But what is often called displaced aggression may be something else — we may be more likely to aggress to a mild source of harm or frustration, if we've made recent contact with a big source of harm or frustration elsewhere. For instance, failing Chet puts Carol down when dinner is a little late — a mild frustration that would not have caused Chet to aggress if he weren't already in the harmful state of having just failed an exam.

■21 Why does displaced sex occur?
■22 And why does displaced aggression occur?

What

We should at last attempt to define displacement now that we've seen when and why it occurs. We can say an act is displaced when it does not produce its "normal" results, where by "normal" results we mean the results that have caused us creatures to evolve so we can be rewarded by sex and aggression. So "normal results" mean offspring for sex, and escape from harm for aggression. Thus, we might then define displacement as follows:

Displacement: acts that do not deal in a direct way with the basic motive (e.g., fuel, harm, or sexual contact); acts that do not produce the results that controlled the way the species evolved through natural selection (e.g., food, escape, or offspring).

■23 Define displacement.

Sublimation — a special type of displacement

Note those learned sex rewards support more than silly actions, like Chet's going out of his way to sit next to Dawn. They also helped keep Chet working hard on his psych. Freud called this process "sublimation".

Sublimation: a form of displacement where the displaced act produces worthwhile results.

According to Freud, we write poems, build churches, and go to the moon, because we're not able to deal directly with all our sexual or aggressive motives. He went so far as to suggest that all of our complex culture is based on sublimation. To see this, think about what would happen if we had a constant supply of food and sex.

"Great. We wouldn't have to worry about those things. Then we'd get on with the higher life — art, science, meditation, pure love."

Most likely not; instead we'd just eat, have sex, and sleep. Freud may be right: There's only one reason we do anything worthwhile for society — we get learned rewards for it — sublimation.

We should note that there's really no difference between sublimation and displacement, but sometimes you get worthwhile results and sometimes you get other results. We call it sublimation when you get worthwhile results. But sublimation is not really any special process — there's nothing unique to it — in no other way does it differ from displacement.

■24 Define sublimation. Cite an instance.
■25 What would happen if we had a constant supply of food and sex?

The limits of displacement

Freud talked about basic psychic forces, sex and aggression, thinking these forces set up a pressure. And any act that reduced the pressure was okay — it would occur again next time any pressure built up. Here's the problem he saw with displacement: the results of displaced acts do not completely reduce the pressure. The learned rewards for studying psych are not quite like the unlearned rewards for having sex; the learned rewards don't affect the "deprivation conditions" that cause the reward to work in the first place. So we keep doing those acts that get learned rewards, since we're still deprived of the unlearned rewards.

Now Freud did **not** think psychic forces controlled the exact nature of the response. Any old response would do if it reduced the psychic pressure. And he came close to the notion of reward, though he never used the notion himself. We think he would have done better to look at the acts as caused by the rewards they produced and not as caused by the reduction of some sort of psychic pressure.

We feel he also failed to see the correct reason for how things become objects of displacement — why some things are learned rewards and others are not — how neutral events are paired with rewards and become rewards themselves — how talking with Dawn can be a learned reward for Chet. But still he did have much of the basic notion of learned rewards in this theory.

▪26 What problem did Freud see with displacement?

▪27 According to the authors, what is a shortcoming of Freud's view of displacement?

THE ROLE OF SEX

Is sex the big reinforcer?

Sexual rewards control much of what Chet does, in fact much of what nearly everyone in our culture does. Freud's right: our most noble acts are founded on just a few basic rewards, and sex is a big one, even for those who've not come into direct contact with it. Sexual cues still control them — cues set up by the social programs we discussed in the Values chapter.

At the same time, Freud's culture and our's put a heavy counterprogram on sex — superego (guilt) control. In the Morality chapter we saw that this kind of control often fails, with the result that the "guilt-ridden sinner" suffers. We agree with Freud that sex is a big reward, but we feel it's not the only big reward.

■28 What is the common result of moderate but poor super-ego control of the sex response?

■29 How important is sex, according to this text?

One doth not live by sex alone

It seems to us that Freud was less clear about the real nature of sex. There's nothing basic about sex that causes these problems — the guilt-ridden sinner. It's our culture's hang-ups working us over with all of its taboos that produces guilt-ridden people.

Suppose Freud had dealt with people trying vainly to diet for reasons of health or religion — people whose eating was controlled by a weak superego and ego system. Then he might have seen food, rather than sex, as the root of all human problems. People would suffer with guilt about cheating on their diet by eating forbidden foods, just as many still do when partaking in sex. Talk to a weak dieter about high-calorie goodies and you'll also see a lot of weak guilt control.

Freud may not have over-stressed sex, though he did fail to stress other rewards like food. Yet in a sense Freud was right, at least for his time and maybe ours too; there is more faulty super-ego control of sex than of food.

■30 What does "one doth not live by sex alone" mean? Cite an instance.

■31 What would happen if Freud had run into poor superego control of eating? Show how that helps us to see the role of poor super-ego control of sex.

PERSONALITY

Definition

Sid and Juke had been at the books for almost two hours. Juke looked over toward Sid. "You know, this chapter's buggin' me a little, cause it's supposed to be about personality but I haven't run across the word anywhere except the title — I still can't say what that word means."

"That's simple, it means . . ."

"Like this mornin' some dude buggin' me. He say the kind of psych we study don't get at the big things — like 'personality'. I know he's wrong, but he won the debate anyway."

"That's simple. Your personality is what ya do."

"Yeah. I said that. Seems like there's more to it though."

"Well, some things you always do the same way. Your personality is your consistent ways of acting."

"Like Mae's always so earnest. That's part of her personality — her being earnest. But that's just like a social role. The kind of thing we read about in the last chapter."

"Almost, but not quite: Mae switches roles when the cues change, but she doesn't switch personalities. Mae's always earnest. I still see one problem though."

"It makes sense to me. What's the hang-up?"

"We say our personality is our constant way of acting. But Mae drinks water and eats food every day — always constant. Yet that's not her personality."

" 'Course not. We all do that. Your personality is ways that you act that differ from many other people."

"I'll buy it."

Personality: those acts of a person that 1) are fairly constant, though the cues may change, and 2) differ from the ways many other people react to the same cues.

"Okay, I'm ready to give that dude another debate, but I'll never see him now I got my program down."

■32 Define personality.
■33 What's the difference between social roles and personality? Cite an instance of each.

Reification of personality

In the past psychologists reified "personality", making it a thing, a cause of our actions. Why do we do something? Because that's the kind of personality we have — an inquisitive personality, an aggressive personality, etc. They used the concept of personality to explain our actions. But today, many, if not most, psychologists seem to believe the concept of personality is best used to describe what we do, not to explain what we do, since it merely refers to the fact that we do have consistent ways of acting. In fact, we're likely to hinder the growth of our science, when we reify concepts like personality to use them to explain our actions, since that tends to stifle our search for the causes of those actions. Instead, we should be looking for those causes in the genetic and personal history and current environment of the person.

■34 In what way did psychologists use the reified concept of personality? And what was the problem with that approach?

Differences

Sid and Juke talked about how we're all alike and yet we all differ. In Freud's terms, we're mainly the same in our id control. The same unlearned results control us all. Freud thought sex the most basic reward for most of what we do, but he also added aggression as another more-or-less basic reward, when he saw what happened in World War I.

So we are all much the same in that we're reinforced by sex and aggression, according to Freud; but how do we differ? Freud said we differed in the amount of superego (moral) control and ego (rational) control that counteract that id control. For instance, some people are said to have weak superego and ego control; that means they're more likely to act in ways that produce prompt, unlearned rewards such as sex and aggression, without regard for the long range or moral results (weak ego control) and without regard for how their acts might affect others (weak superego control), Chet, for example. But people with strong superego control are more likely to engage in displaced activities rewarded and punished by social results such as the opinions of other people.

■35 According to Freud how do personality similarities and differences relate to his three types of control?

Development

We've defined personality, and we've seen some major ways in which people's personalities (ways of acting) differ. So now the final question is: how did these differing personal styles come about; why don't we all have the same level of ego and superego control?

Freud was one of the first to see a relation between the child and the personality of the adult; in fact, he went so far as to say our adult personality results from what happened to us as children. The child is parent to the adult. The child's relation to its unlearned rewards controls the way the adult will act.

He stressed oral, anal, and genital touch rewards, saying if the child received either too many or too few of those rewards such rewards would have too much control when the child grew into an adult. Adults would spend too much of their lives doing things that got those rewards — got them either as unlearned rewards or through displaced acts leading to related, learned rewards. Freud called this "fixation".

Fixation: excessive control in later life by reinforcers inappropriately contacted in early life.

Freud said those rewards shaped the child's id, ego, and/or superego with effects lasting the life of the person. We agree with Freud: Oral, anal, and genital contact can be strong rewards, with the child's experience affecting the adult. But we differ as to how this works.

When big, unlearned rewards are floating around, they may set up strong learned rewards and punishers. Take oral touch which deals mainly with food intake. Its effect on the child's personality works like this: eating is a social time, setting up social rewards that will stay with the children the rest of their lives. The sight, sound, and touch of other people are paired with food and oral tactual rewards (Freud's oral stage); so these things become learned rewards that help the child acquire more complex response patterns, such as their many social skills maintained by social rewards.

And toilet training can be based on rewards also setting up more social rewards (Freud's anal stage). But many parents rely on punishment for toilet training — "Don't do-do now. Bad girl."

And they also use punishers to stop children from touching their sex organs (phallic stage, 3 — 6 years of age) — "Don't play with yourself, that's awful." And this sets up social punishers such as, "No!" "Don't do that!"

So how does this affect the adult? Parents build up the social rewards and punishers in early childhood. And one of two things happens. They become ingrained if people continue to use them, or they extinguish if people stop giving rewards. Then others continue to control the person with those same well-learned social rewards and punishers for the rest of the person's life. And those social results keep holding on to their power, due to their frequent pairing with other rewards and punishers. But suppose people stopped giving rewards and punishers as the child grows up; then those social results would extinguish — lose their value. But their value is maintained, for instance, when people praise or blame us for something we may have done. So that is one way early childhood can affect the adult — the setting up of social rewards and punishers.

Though Freud saw a strong relation between the young child and the later adult, he had to invent a complex, mental process, with its competing id, ego, and superego, to account for that relationship, since so little was known about the nature of learned rewards at that time. He assumed that some change took place inside the child. He had to think of the id, ego, and superego as things; not just types of control. He thought of them as things that could be changed. Things that would carry these changes to the adult. This helped force him into reification of those processes.

■36 Define fixation.
■37 According to Freud what sort of childhood relations to unlearned rewards would affect the adult personality? What would the effect be?
■38 According to the authors, how can childhood experiences in the following areas affect the adult personality: anal, oral, and genital?
■39 According to the authors, how can these early childhood experiences actually get carried over into the adult's life?

CONCLUSIONS

It's easy to tear apart Freud's theory, as an old turn of the century grandfather, because we've learned a lot about people since then. And it's even tempting to rip it up too, since so many laymen act as if Freud was the latest word.

But we've tried to restate as much of his theory as we can, putting it in the terms of this text. We're trying to bring it up to date with modern psychology, since we feel this is worthwhile, because we believe Freud made many valid statements about cause and effect in human actions. He wasn't afraid to stress the role of sexual rewards for children and women as well as for men (id control). He also dealt with aggressive rewards as a chief cause of human actions (id control). He showed that such rewards were limited by social, moral rewards and punishers (superego control). And he dealt with the fact that it is so hard for long range results to affect our current actions (ego control). He also pointed out what happens to the child greatly affects the later actions of the adult. In fact, we've taken for granted one of his main gifts to human knowledge — the notion that there are, indeed, causes for our actions — that our actions are determined by other factors.

People had a hard time dealing with that notion in Freud's day, as people still do even today. In a later chapter we will also mention one more very worthwhile notion Freud gave us — the notion that we may not be aware or conscious of those factors that do determine our actions. Freud and many of his notions came to gain great acceptance in later years, though they were most often put down and made fun of during the early years. But we are fortunate that Freud persisted, inspite of the social punishers.

On the other hand Freud's theory falters, in that it involves so many reified processes, leading him and others into an attempt to deal with those reified concepts more than with the actions of real people and the causes of those actions found in the real world. But this is not surprising, since it is so tempting to think in terms of reified concepts in our time, and it was even more so during Freud's day.

But to us, the power of his observations outshines the weakness of his theory, so we hope that he will be remembered as the pioneer in observing human nature that he really was.

CHAPTER 22
CONSCIOUSNESS: MEANINGS AND DEFINITIONS

INTRODUCTION

Even long before psychology became a science in its own right, "consciousness" was a much discussed, much argued, and a rarely agreed upon topic. Doubtless much of the debate was due to the fact that contestants were often talking about quite different concepts. As it is and has been employed, "consciousness" can mean any number of things — it applies to a gamut of behavioral events. In this chapter we'll outline some of its common meanings. Then in the two chapters that follow, a more detailed treatment will be given those special aspects of consciousness that always seem to provoke great interest.

CONSCIOUSNESS AS ACTIVATION

You're out!

"Are you ready?" Mae asked.
   "Dammit, Mae! This is dumb!"
   "Come on, Juke. Don't be so squeamish. I know what I'm doing."
   "Okay, okay — I'm ready."
   "Okay. I'm walkin' through the Clark Hall woods, see. Coming home from campus about ten or so at night. I stop to balance the load of books I'm holding. You're some creep that's been waiting in the shadows. You sneak up and grab me from behind in a choke hold. Then I . . ." Mae twisted, at the same time, thrusting her leg backward and to the side in a sweep — hoping to hook Juke's ankle. When Juke saw Mae turn, he relaxed his hold and pulled back his arms. At the same instant, Mae ducked her head. It hit Juke's elbow with a crack. Mae's knees went limp; she slumped to the floor. Out cold.

Activation

A prime feature of living things is movement. The word "animal" comes from the Greek word "anumus" — meaning "to move". Often, movements are clearly induced by stimulus inputs. A sprinter springs from the blocks the instant the starter's gun sounds. If people show no movement on their own and don't react to shouts, nudges, or other strong stimuli — it's time to worry about them. They could be very ill, under the effect of drugs, knocked out, or even dead.

People differ from time to time in terms of how much they move and/or respond to known inputs. They also differ among each other in these respects. A handy way to talk about degree of movement and response to inputs people display is to call it activation.

Activation: the general state, amount, or degree of internal and external body movement and function.

"High" activation means there's more gross movement of body parts and a strong response to inputs. "Low" activation means less of both. Activation has to do with gamut of movement and response that might be observed. At the low end it begins at death's door — a coma — where only vital organs are active and none but the most intense and basic of outside events will cause a response. It extends on the high end to the frantic actions of the athlete and extreme tuned-in state of, well, say a pilot during take-off or landing. Between these two extremes lie other degrees of activation: deep sleep, normal sleep, light sleep or dozing, drowsiness, normal alertness, tenseness, nervousness, jumpiness, and utter mania — wild freaked-out action. These are all just ways of putting labels on the amount or degree of activation. When some people use the term conscious or consciousness, they're talking about activation. It's a very common usage, and what many people mean — or may think you mean — when these words are used.

- 1 What is a prime feature of living things?
- 2 What is the meaning of the Greek word, "anumus"?
- 3 How are we likely to describe someone who neither moves nor shows any response toward stimulus inputs?
- 4 What is the term that's used to describe the degree to which people show movement responsiveness to stimuli?
- 5 What are the two behavioral extremes of activation?
- 6 Give several steps between the two extremes of activation.

CONSCIOUSNESS AS STIMULUS CONTROL

Juke, the unconscious

When Mae came to, she was lying on a couch with wet paper towels on her forehead. Juke was bending over her. *Why's Juke so worried?* she wondered.

"Mae? Mae? You hear me, Mae?" Mae smiled at Juke. It was a silly smile. Why did she feel so giddy? She began to look about her.

"What happened?"

"Got knocked out — that's what happened. Cracked your head on my elbow. I told you it was a fool stunt. Why you want to be some super jock, Kung Fu, I'll never know! A real masher would make quick work of you. But that ain't gonna happen — not as long as I'm 'round it ain't.'"

By this time Mae's head had cleared. She recalled what had happened. Sorry because he hurt someone he didn't mean to, a gentle, concerned, tender Juke was now a scowling big shot — coming on like Smokey the Bear, savior of the weak and frail female. Mae started to fume. Juke would've been smart to let it ride. To back off and not say any more about it. No such luck.

"Why do you have to act like you're getting ready for World War III? Like no one's around to look out for you?"

That was it. Mae's mouth snapped open to reply. She stopped. Instead, she threw the towels from her head and got to her feet, took three steps, and started to reel.

"Hey — where you goin', woman? Come back and sit down before you fall down!" Juke was just adding fuel to the fire. He grabbed Mae by the arm to steady her. She jerked away. Surprised, Juke recoiled. He was worried again.

"What's wrong with you? Hey — I sure didn't mean to hit you. Wouldn't have it happen for the world."

"I know it, you big lummox . . . Juke Jackson, sometimes . . . You think I was knocked out? Well, let me tell you something! When it comes to being 'unconscious', ain't no one more unconscious than you!" Mae turned and headed toward the door, weaving as she walked.

The unconscious

Mae's use of the word unconscious, as she applied it to Juke, doesn't refer to level of activation — the use of the term we talked about before. Rather, she's speaking about a related meaning of consciousness that has to do with stimulus control — the extent to which actions are controlled by the proper cues or discriminative stimuli. From Mae's point of view, Juke's actions aren't being guided by certain — she feels crucial — stimulus aspects of the setting. Juke has clearly missed the point of Mae's efforts to learn self-defense. She's striving for a time when women won't have to play the part of weak and frail creatures who're forced to rely on men for their comfort and safety. Lack of stimulus control in this context is a common failing. Terms such as "out to lunch", "punchy", "dingy", "spacey" — and there are many others — all seem to reduce in meaning to lack of stimulus control.

It makes sense to say that Juke's not "conscious" of concepts — classes of cues — that control Mae's actions. Mae's upset about this. Juke's paying the price for his lack of "consciousness"

- 7 When we look at consciousness as the degree to which a person behaves correctly in the presence of particular cues or discriminative stimuli, this definition boils down to _____ _____. (Two words)
- 8 Give several slang words often used to describe a person who's not under proper stimulus control.

SELF-AWARENESS

What did the other guy look like?

"Jeez, what happened to you? What'd the other guy look like?" Dawn jumped up from the couch. "Let me get some ice." She went across the hall and came back with ice wrapped in a towel. "Sit down — for the love 'a Pete — you look like death warmed over." Mae slumped into the chair. Her head was throbbing. But the wound that hurt most was her pride.

"Juke Jackson is the the most stubborn, biased, rigid, anti-women, super-clod on campus!" Mae said. Dawn placed the ice pack lightly on the lump on Mae's forehead. She winced.

"Well, if that's the way you talked to him, I'm not surprised he socked you."

"No," Mae smiled. "It wasn't like that at all. I was trying out some of the stuff I learned in the self-defense class. Juke was just helping me and I bumped into his elbow."

"Uh huh!" Dawn said. "I see. You and Juke were putting a few wrestling holds on each other and the party got a little rough. Tsk! Tsk!"

"It wasn't like that at all. I was doing the required practice work for the self-defense course — that's all there was to it!"

"Sure. Surrre. I mean, the only person on this whole campus you could find was little old 6'3", 200-pound, ripply-muscled Juke Jackson — that it?"

"No. Well, yes — at the time. I wanted to give it a real test — I assure you there was no other motive!"

"Right on!" Dawn said.

Why self-awareness?

There are two questions full-fledged members of our culture will be asked time after time. And, if they want to remain in good standing, they'd better come up with the right answers. The two questions are: What are you doing, and why are you doing it? Giving correct answers to these queries requires what's often called "self-awareness", or consciousness of self. This, then, is yet a new meaning of the word consciousness.

Self-awareness: being able to give verbal responses that correctly describe what you are doing and the reason you are doing it.

How does a person get consciousness or awareness of self? At first, scholars proposed that it was innate — something we're born with. It was Sigmund Freud who challenged this notion. He stated what should have been the obvious: people often don't have the slightest inkling of what they're doing, let alone, why they're doing it. What Freud was getting at — although he didn't say it quite that way — is that cues and rewards that control huge chunks of our behavior are sometimes beyond our knowledge. If asked, we can't tell what we're doing or why we're doing it. We won't have the self-awareness as far as these acts are concerned at least.

Freud called the work that these unknown cues and rewards perform in the control of actions the "unconscious", giving it the somewhat spooky status of an unknown force or power. Dawn's trying to point out to Mae that the real reasons Mae picked Juke to practice on aren't the ones she gave.

Dawn's got a pretty good case against Mae. She's betting that although Mae may not know it, close contact with Juke is a potent reward for her. Dawn suggests that it's Juke's reward value and not Mae's burning concern for doing her homework that makes Juke the sparring partner of choice. In truth, many cues and rewards act in concert to prompt and maintain what Mae or any of us do at a given time. Yes, Mae had to get in practice time — she's that kind of serious student. But the reason she asked Juke to help out has more to do with sex than it does with duty.

- 9 Knowledge of what we're doing is often called _____.
- 10 It can also be called _____.
- 11 What is ability to give reasons for our actions called? (Two choices.)
- 12 What did Freud call the collective cues and rewards that we're not aware of but yet exert control over our behavior?

REPRESSION

A beast within

All through the rest of the day the scene with Juke, and Dawn's kidding about her motives with Juke, came back to gnaw at Mae. Whether Mae liked to admit it or not, Dawn's logic hit home. Of all the people she might recruit to practice self-defense, Juke was for many reasons the worst choice. Of course, if she could learn to subdue one as big and fit as Juke, she wouldn't have to worry about some gnome of a mugger.

But Juke was too much. He just wasn't the partner a novice should begin with. Dawn was right. Something was fishy. Yes, Mae'd lied to herself — to Juke and Dawn as well. It was sex and not duty that made her choose Juke!

Mae worshipped the truth. Liars, cheats, phonies — all lowest on her list. Now, her name could be added to that list. She was a phoney. What worried her most was that she'd not known it. But, only sick people do that! Was she sick? Was there something wrong with her? In some ways, she was less honest than the mugger slinking in the dark.

The causes of repression

Mae's worried about her mental health. It's her knowledge of Sigmund Freud's theory that causes her to be concerned. Freud was correct in pointing out that rewards and cues, unknown to the person, still exert strong control over actions. He felt knowledge of the role these cues and rewards played could be lost — pushed out of awareness. This happened when the real reasons people did things were not the wholesome ones parents, friends, and others in the culture approved of.

One area where Freud believed this was likely to happen revolved around our behavior toward parents. Suppose contact with your mother or father turned you on in some sexual way? In some cultures, that's okay. In ours it's a mind-blowing thing. Even talking about it's going to make you an outcast. Incest — that's what it's called. And in our culture, it's strictly taboo.

Incest: contact with parents or other blood relatives that is maintained by sexual reinforcers.

But suppose it's true? Suppose contact with a parent is a sexual reward — what then? Freud felt that we're all sexually drawn to the parent of the opposite sex. It begins when we're infants and is a fact for all humans. If all goes well, we'll get over it before we're adults — often we don't though. Yet, the moral laws that hold in our social system flatly reject the very notion. If we're sexually drawn to parents or close relations we're certain to get punished for admitting it. Soon, we're afraid to admit it even to ourselves. When this happens, we lose our hold on this knowledge — awareness of it is lost. This process was called repression by Freud. It seems to happen when telling about what you did or the particular reason you did it would be (or has been) punished by the culture.

Repression: lack of self-awareness of an event of which a person would normally be aware.

When repression takes place, we go right on being aroused — contact with a parent is still a sexual reward for us. But when people ask us what we're doing or why we're doing it, we don't tell the real story. We've repressed it. We give them answers they'll accept — or we say we "don't know". We end up lying and don't even know we're doing it. A pretty sick thing you say. That's what Freud thought too — a sickness that can strike in any instance if our actions or the rewards that control them aren't the right and good ones as far as the culture's concerned.

You can see why Mae's upset. She feels she must be a pretty wretched person — one who gives false reasons for what she does, and doesn't even know it. Juke gets to her sexually — makes her do silly things.

Well, Mae should hold off before she leaps to the nearest couch for treatment. Freud got off the track in a few places. His account wasn't the full story as far as self-awareness is concerned. For Freud, lack of self-awareness was always caused by repression. If not for it, we would know all the rewards and cues that control what we do.

Of course, repression does occur. We all tend to forget things we do that put us in a bad light or make us feel ashamed. But the biggest reason we're not aware of what we do and why we're doing it is more simple than that: we didn't learn it in the first place. Or, in the case of "why" we're doing what we are, the wrong reason may have been learned.

Self-knowledge, like all knowledge, has to be learned. We're not born with the answers. If you don't learn them, you won't have them. Parents are the first agents who give us the answers that'll become our self-awareness, while later on, others get into the act. They all ask the questions: what are you doing, and why are you doing it; and they also give us the answers. So the reasons we all give for what we do are strongly influenced by what others have taught us was the truth, what they have rewarded us for saying.

But what's going on with Mae? Is her problem repression, or did she just not learn to be aware of sexual cues and rewards? We'll have to go back to Mae's childhood, what went on, and what was

discussed. Mae's parents spent a lot of time talking to Mae — teaching her to read, to reason, tuned her in to duty. In truth, they talked little about sex — not that they thought it was bad or nasty — they just didn't get around to the topic in their talks with Mae. Didn't think it was too crucial. In fact, they weren't tuned-in to Mae's sexual behavior. As a result, they failed to tune Mae in to it.

Mae did learn to be aware of duty as a strong reason for her actions. Heeding the call of duty became a strong learned reward. Her parents talked a lot about that. Much of what Mae does today — in college, in the women's movement — is controlled by cues and rewards of duty, work, and service. It's likely she'll give these as reasons for much of what she does — and rightly so. The fact that Juke turns her on — is a strong cue for sex responses on her part — just means she's a woman. Contact with him is a potent reward.

The fact that she doesn't know Juke's power in this respect doesn't mean she's repressed it. It could mean that unlike most women her age in college, she never learned this self-awareness. Perhaps Mae's consciousness is about to change in this respect.

- ▪13 How did Freud account for the fact that we sometimes are not aware of what we do or why we do it?
- ▪14 Freud was wrong. Repression is a myth — it never happens. (Discuss.)
- ▪15 Give your idea of how Freud missed the mark in his theory about control by unknown rewards and cues.

LEARNING CONSCIOUSNESS

Juke finds out

"Man, I don't know what's wrong with that woman — she's crazy. Outta her head. Shoulda' seen her. What's going on Sid? What's her story?"

Sly Sid leaned back in his study chair and put the empty pipe in his mouth, hands behind the back of his neck. "Simple — plain as the nose on your face."

"That simple, huh? Suppose you tell me about it then."

"It's the movement — women's lib; Mae's deep into that."

"So what — I ain't against that. I'm all for rights, man."

"Sure you are — in the abstract. Look, you've got to ask yourself this: why'd Mae sign up for that self-defense course in the first place? And I'll clue ya', it wasn't to be a jock, either. She did it because she wanted to be free — wanted to go places men go, and be safe doing it."

"But she don't have to worry about that. She's a good looking woman. Someone'll always be around to look out for her."

"Wow! Man, you are a clod. That's the whole point — they don't want to depend on men like that. They want to be free, man! For Mae that means not having to depend on you or some other stud to pull her out of the fire."

"That's dumb! What's wrong with taking a little help if you need it?"

"Oh yeah. Well, suppose I told you about this course where the prof graded easier for blacks than he did for whitey — would you go sign up?"

"Course I wouldn't — you know I ain't lookin' for no easy ride or handouts!"

"Well?"

"But that ain't the same thing. Anybody can see that!"

"I'm not sure I see it — and I don't think Mae does either. You got a little thinkin' to do about that."

The verbal community

Sid's right to tune Juke in to the way others see what's going on. He makes a very heavy point: beliefs, viewpoint — the "consciousness" others have about an issue or topic — is their true and right way. It's all they have. Sure, there are other ways to look at it — the fact that these other ways seem strange, odd, stupid, or silly when compared with our own — that's the way consciousness often is. Others feel the same way about ours compared to theirs. Regardless of what we believe, we arrive at our consciousness in the same way. We got rewards for talking and acting these ways in the past.

Today, we believe in the truth of our actions very strongly. But why shouldn't we? Parents, friends, and all those around us whom we love and who maintain us have offered their sanction in the form of social rewards throughout our lives. These people who shape and maintain what we do and say in the culture are called our verbal community.

Verbal community: those persons who both teach and maintain our verbal behavior.

How can Juke change his consciousness? Well, he's in the process. He's become a part of a new verbal community at BSU. Sid's a big portion of Juke's new verbal community. Sid's words and actions are likely to become potent cues and rewards for Juke. His profs — the new books he reads, movies and plays he attends, are all new inputs that will also become a part of his new verbal community. Juke's consciousness is in the process of change.

- ■16 How does self-awareness come about?
- ■17 Exactly how do we acquire reasons for what we do?
- ■18 How does our belief in the correctness of our reasons for doing what we do grow stronger?
- ■19 How do you account for the fact that two people can believe such different things, but each hold such strong convictions about his or her beliefs?
- ■20 What are those who collectively shape and maintain what we say called?
- ■21 How does one get one's consciousness changed? How would you go about changing yours?

A reinforcer for consciousness

That night: "Dawn, Dawn — you awake?"

"Huh, what?" Dawn answered.

"You awake?"

"Huh — oh yeah. Always go to sleep awake."

"Listen, I gotta ask you something, okay?"

"Yeah."

"You really think the only reason I asked Juke to help me practice self-defense holds was — well, sex?" Dawn smiled. "Damn it, Dawn, be straight for once."

"Okay — serious now. Hell, yes. Wait, strike that. Sex wasn't the only reason, but it had to be way out in first place."

"That's awful! How could I be so phony?"

"If you ask me, I think it's kinda nice. Not quite honest, but nice. If you gotta learn that jock self-defense stuff, I can't think of a better way than with some cool dude like Juke."

***

The next day Juke found Mae in the coffee shop after her 11 o'clock class. "Hi," he said. "How's the head?" He was glad to see the knot was gone. Only a small bruise remained.

"Fine. Doing fine. Hoping I'd see you, Juke. I'm sorry I got bugged by you. Wasn't your fault. I just got mad at myself."

"Forget it. I felt dumb myself. Had a little talk with Sid. He told me where you're at — with the self-defense stuff, I mean. That's cool. I'm into helping people make it on their own. Been thinking about it. Don't know who's trying to teach you the holds and counters — the self-defense moves — but I don't think they're doing it right. I'm good at that. Suppose you let me take over?"

"You mean you want to? No, I couldn't let you. I wasted enough of your time. It wouldn't be right, Juke."

"Come on, I want to help. Besides," Juke grinned, "I'm about the best there is."

"I know that, you modest jerk." Mae returned Juke's smile. "There's somethin' else, though. Look, here's the way it is. I'm not sure it'd be all business — on my part at least. I'm trying to say I kinda like your hands on me." Mae cast her eyes down at the table top. Juke shuffled his feet, shifted in his chair, and ran his hand over the back of his neck. All of a sudden he felt like doing a dozen push-ups or running a hundred-yard dash, or just yelling!

CONCLUSIONS

Level of activation, stimulus control, knowledge of one's actions and stimuli that control them — all are commonly called "consciousness". Now you can see how — as was mentioned in the introduction of this chapter — much of the fuss about consciousness comes from failure to define terms.

Just for fun, you might try pinning people who use the terms down to a meaning — get them to define it for you. It's likely you'll find they agree very little — that often they're talking about two or even three "consciousnesses" at once. In the next chapter we'll try to clear things up further by talking about a special case of self-consciousness or awareness.

CHAPTER 23
CONSCIOUSNESS AS
PRIVATE ACTIVITY

INTRODUCTION

Sittin' in the back booth, listenin' to the juke box, n' Lord I'm down

Dawn stared somewhere deep into the empty coffee cup. The spoon rested across the top. She traced tiny circles with her finger on the smooth and shiny convex surface. The voice of the juke box moaned on.

> *You were my best friend, he was my guy,*
> *If only I'd seen then, the look in your eye*
> *I'd known you'd in-tend-ed, to give him a try*

The music seemed to sift through the pores of her skin, filling her up, choking her. That song — she'd heard it a hundred times before today. The tune was lilting — quite pretty, really. But today she truly heard it for the first time. The words spoke for her; cried for her; told of her torment. It was so very sad. In the end the girl takes her own life. *"Cast aching heart and tortured brain 'neath the screaming Amtrack train."* A sob swelled in her throat.

Private events

In past pages, we've seen how "consciousness" can mean a number of things. Consciousness as level of activation — whether you're "knocked out" as opposed to moving around and alert; consciousness as stimulus control — the control of actions by the right cues; and consciousness as knowledge of cues and rewards that account for our actions — being "self-aware" — able to make a statement about what we're doing. These are all things people might mean when they use the word.

But there's yet one more meaning of "consciousness". It involves behavior that goes on inside — something called a "private event".

Private event: something that occurs inside a person's body that only he or she has direct knowledge of.

Most of the things that people do can be gotten to in a direct way — by just looking or listening. This isn't true with private events. There's no direct channel to them. Yet, it's these private events that make up the consciousness that's of greatest interest to most people. This private consciousness is a kind of inside play-by-play of what's going on. Or, it can be a "rehash" of what's happened before — a replay but not always an instant one. Dawn's doing both. She's running a rehash of a recent bad break, and then making further remarks about how the rehash makes her feel.

- ▪ 1 Review: We've talked about three meanings of consciousness in the previous chapter. Give these meanings.
- ▪ 2 How can we tell when consciousness of the three types mentioned above are present?
- ▪ 3 What's the term for the behavior discussed in the above section that's also referred to as consciousness?
- ▪ 4 How does this new consciousness differ from the three other behavioral events that are also called consciousness?

PRIVATE CONSCIOUSNESS

The triangle

Sid came into the Bistro — the little hash house just off campus. He cast his eyes around the dimly lit room, the pictures on the walls, the two long rows of booths, one on either side. A lone figure huddled in the last booth on the right. Sid strained to see more clearly. A girl. It looked like Dawn. But what would she be doing here?

Sid took a few slow paces toward the booth. Whoever it was, she was brooding over a coffee cup, solemn and pensive. He'd never seen Dawn like that.

"Dawn?" he said softly.

"Oh," the girl said, startled. "It's you, Sid. Hi."

"It is you after all," Sid said, relieved. "You ready?"

"Ready? Ready for what?"

"My big line — that's what. Here goes: What's a nice woman like you doin' in a dump like this?" Sid paused, waiting for Dawn to laugh at his hokum — like she always did. A faint smile flickered and was gone. Sid was puzzled by the strange way Dawn was acting. "Can I sit down?" he asked.

"Sure, why not — be my guest. But you'll have to forgive me. I'm afraid I'm not much fun today."

"Something wrong? Trouble at home? Your folks — they're okay, aren't they?"

"No, no, that's not it. Nothing, really. Nothing anyone can do anything about. It's just silly, that's all. I'm a very foolish person. I . . . I get hurt when I shouldn't."

"Why don't you tell me about it. I listen pretty good."

"Oh," Dawn shrugged her shoulders and shook her head. "I don't know — like I said, it's nothing. It's this guy I kinda like. Dated him two or three times. He was nice and we hit it off real good. I really thought something might come of it. Just goes to show you how foolish I am. Well, I just talked to Jill Davis. You know, lives across the hall. She said to me, 'Listen Dawn, Jim Welch just asked me out this weekend. You don't mind do you?' " Dawn sneered while she mocked what the girl had said, adding sing-songy frills to it. Sid could see it clearly now. Dawn was hurt. She was bitter. There was nothing he could do — he felt helpless.

"What did you say?" he asked.

"What could I say? I said, 'Why no, not at all — go right ahead.' I wanted to choke her on the spot!"

"You must really . . . , uh, 'care' for this guy Jim, huh?"

"I don't know how much, but I think I could a lot. If only he . . . I guess it doesn't matter now." A tear ran down Dawn's cheek. She caught it deftly with her small finger. The two of them sat in silence for some seconds. At last Sid looked at his watch.

"It's time for class. Say, you got a class at this hour too, don't you? Wanna walk along?"

"No. You go ahead. I'm just not up to class right now. I'll get someone's notes."

"Sure," Sid said. "Sure. See ya." He hurried out of the diner. The juke box had stopped playing. Dawn dropped in some more coins and pushed A-7 for perhaps the tenth time that day.

The start of private consciousness

It starts with words — with verbal behavior. Not your own but that of your parents or the ones who reared you. Since they brought all the good things — food, drink, comfort — the rewards — they soon became rewards too. Even when they didn't bring gifts or come running to get you out of a tight or thorny spot, they were rewards. No doubt about it, the contact of parents is the first and strongest learned reward youngsters acquire.

But are people other than what they do? No, not really. Parents do a lot, but above all, they talk to children. Thus, these sounds — words and speech — also achieve the status of heavy learned rewards. A baby will do most anything just to hear Momma's voice. As the infant grows larger and stronger, it makes sounds that are loud enough for us to hear. The baby hears them too. Since these sounds sound the same as those produced by parents, they're rewarding, to the parents, of course, but also to the author of the sounds.

When the youngsters start to babble (usually about five or six months) they're making sounds that reward them when they hear them. Just like we might sing to ourselves in the shower, infants reward themselves by babbling. As shower singers, we'd be more rewarded if we sounded like Cat Stevens, or Olivia Newton John. Likewise, tots are more rewarded if what they produce with their small voices sounds like Mom or Dad. Thus, there's a built-in device that keeps pushing babbling sounds toward greater and greater likeness between the child's sounds and those of the parents.

- 5 Review: What is a learned reward?
- 6 Review: How are learned rewards established?
- 7 Trace the sequence of events that causes infants to imitate the sounds made by their parents.

The real story

Too bad we can't turn the clock back a few weeks. We could see things the way they truly were and not be misled by the fiction Dawn has made up for herself. The truth is that this guy Jim — the one Dawn has led Sid to believe has broken her heart — was a dud as far as Dawn was concerned. He was okay, if you like the type — but Dawn didn't. Matter of fact, she thought he was kind of a schlep. More than likely she would've turned him down cold if he'd asked her out again — that's how it was before she found out Jill had some use for him.

But aside from the very real fact that finding out that some-one else is trying to get some-thing (or someone) makes it or them more attractive to us — there's more going on here. Just because Jill's trying to get something Dawn once had and threw away, doesn't shed any light on why Dawn should act like the third act in some Greek drama. But it seems like Dawn enjoyed playing some kind of role, some long-suffering heroine. Too bad the people like Sid who care for her don't know about her role. They take what she says at face value. As a result, Dawn worries them, causes them real — not make-believe — anguish and concern. "Acting as though" in a real world can cause the player trouble, too. The classes Dawn cut aren't "play time". They count. The dimes she keeps chucking in the juke are real — not stage money. And the upset stomach from a zillion cups of bad coffee? Well, the heartache may be a bit phony, but you can bet the heartburn won't be.

In truth, we don't have to worry too much about Dawn. She'll shrug off her blues and come back full tilt. Other people aren't so lucky. They get into it and don't get out. It gets to be a way of life. They end up blowing a job, a marriage, their future — take their lives or the lives of others. All of this with no more sense or reason than Dawn's self-pity jag. We can pin the problem on consciousness — the special kind we spoke of in the first few pages of this chapter. Dawn's private consciousness.

- 8 Review: Explain why seeing someone else approach a person or object may raise the likelihood that you'll also make approach responses.

- 9 Acting as though you're a character in a play can cause real problems for the individual and for others. Explain.

WORDS ARE CUES

To say that sounds or words are rewards to young children is to only tell half of the story. They're also cues. Children soon learn to "mind" their parents. What this means is that verbal units — commands, orders, etc. — given by mom or dad exert stimulus control over the youngster's actions. This's really the whole point to verbal behavior in the first place — it allows us to control each other's actions.

Self-produced verbal cues

Once when she was just a toddler, Dawn started to touch the fan that whirred around in Dad's shop. Just as she was about to put her fingers into the blades, Dad yelled, "No! No! Don't touch!" You better believe Dawn didn't. She knew what it meant, when Dad said that. Then Dawn wandered into the shop later that same day when Dad was in the kitchen. The fan was going around, making a breeze and flashing in the sunlight. She started to reach for the blades. "No! No! Don't touch!" she said to herself. Dawn's words were not only rewards for her — now they were cues as well. Dawn's words controlled her actions. She started minding herself — doing what she said to herself — just like she minded her parents. This, of course, is like the process involved in learning guilt control as described in the Morality chapter.

- ■10 What are the two functions of verbal stimuli? Give two examples of each.
- ■11 Describe a sequence of events that would illustrate the first instance of self-produced verbal cues.

Self-produced cues span the time gap

Thus, we acquire all of our early verbal responses from parents and others who form our close verbal community. We say the things they do, and do so in the same or nearly the same settings. But we're not doomed to be only parrots. Our words begin to control our actions when others aren't there — those who taught us our words in the first place. This helps us greatly. It bridges gaps in time, allowing us to respond long after people have told us what to do. We can replay it whenever we need it. Here's how it works.

You're Dawn, age seven. Your mother's in a bind. Needs things from the market, but can't go herself. "Listen," Mother tells you. "You'll have to be a big girl and go to the store. I want a loaf of bread, quart of milk, and a spool of thread — can you keep that in mind?"

"Sure," you reply. All the way to the store you keep saying over and over, "loaf of bread, quart of milk, and spool of thread; loaf of bread, quart of milk, spool of thread, etc."

When you get the three long blocks away and reach the store, the clerk says, "Can I help you?"

You say, "Sure — I want a loaf of thread, quart of bread, and spool of milk." Oh well, the grocer'll figure it out — and you'll do better next time.

People give us all kinds of speeches we're to learn throughout our lives. We latch on to some for only a short time. Others we keep until we die. Some are in the form of rules — they tell us what we should do or not do under certain conditions; they also tell us what'll happen if we follow them or fail to. One problem with being controlled by our own inside verbal feedback circuit is that we can't listen to it and other people at the same time. Take Sid for instance.

■12 What are rules? What two parts do rules have?
■13 What's one limitation on the control of behavior through self-talk?

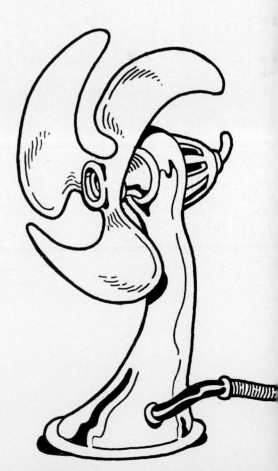

Local high school student wrecks car

Even in high school Sid liked to be cool about things — use science when he could, not leave things up to chance. He studied and studied the steps involved in driving a car. Had them all down so that he could cite chapter and verse. Like some people knew the names of football players or movie stars, or their prayers — Sid knew each word, sentence, and comma in the book he read called *How To Drive A Car.*

When Sid first started to drive he used to have this constant talk-talk with himself. He'd say things like, *Okay, crossing coming up. Reduce speed, test brakes with pumping action, signal with downward waving motion with left hand, shift to lower gear.* All the time he was driving, he kept this little speech going. It worked well for Sid. He was a great driver — until . . .

Well, it was the day that Nan VanWinkle asked him for a ride. Sid'd always liked Nan. He was glad for a chance to show her how mature he was with the car and all. "Sure," Sid said, "hop in." She did.

It all might've been fine, but Nan had this habit of talking all the time. "My, this is a nice car," she said. "What kind is it?"

By then Sid was tooling down the drag in the middle of his talk to himself. *Shift to second gear, release clutch, check for cars at yield sign* — "Chevy, 1954, sedan," Sid blurted out, giving Nan the answer to her question.

"Chevy?" Nan said. "Isn't that the same kind as Bill Foss's?"

Slow down, school zone ahead, check rear view mirror, stop for crossing, pump brakes. "No, Foss's got a Ford."

"A what?" Nan said.

Downshift, pump footfeed, change crank-case, install wiper blades — "Ford."

"Oh," Nan said. "What's the diff? They look about the same to me." That was it for Sid. He wrapped it around the street sign at Oak and Grace. Trooper Dodd scratched his head — said it must have been some kind of failure on the part of the car. The real failure was Sid's words to himself — they couldn't compete with the input from Nan VanWinkle.

■14 Name one type of activity where the limitation on the control of behavior through inside verbal feedback is likely to cause trouble.

Phasing out self-talk

We quit saying things to ourselves when they aren't needed any longer. Sid stopped telling himself what to do when the responses involved came under the control of cues coming from muscles and bones and under better control from the sights and sounds of the highway. When this happened, verbal control was no longer needed and was ousted by a better form of control. Today, Sid can carry on a lively chat with someone else and still drive. It's no trouble at all. Every so often, even now, he, like the rest of us, has to drop back to verbal control when he meets a new challenge on the highway.

Of course, not all speeches get phased out. We keep using them, because people keep asking us to say them — or like math, we never do enough of it to go ahead without saying the rules each time. It'd be something else if we did math all the time. Then we'd do what the rules said without having to say them.

Other verbal recitations having to do with moral or social actions are kept at high strength by the clergy, teachers, police, etc. Doctors and dentists won't let us stop telling ourselves what to do for good health and teeth — lucky for us.

- ▪15 Why is self-talk content phased out?
- ▪16 What type of control takes over from the verbal cues that are phased out?
- ▪17 What's one type of self-talk that's not likely to be phased out for most of us?

Fantasy

The fact that words control actions is to say that they're cues — a point we've made before. But words are also rewards — learned reinforcers. Listening to verbal constructs such as poems or stories is something we may spend a great amount of time doing — even if these words don't tell us how to drive a car, find gold, or bake a cake. These words are rewards all on their own.

To read or listen to a story is in some sense to be there. To see what the people in the story see, hear what they hear, feel what they feel. Our long period of being controlled by words brings us to truly live the scenes the author's words describe, and to respond to described sounds, smells, textures in the same way. The actions these verbal stimuli control are the inside actions that occur when the real stimuli are present — not described events — real ones.

This is a very heavy point — we are really seeing, hearing, or feeling when we respond to the words. The responses are the same acts that are involved when the real scene — the one described by the words — is there. The world given us by the writer or story teller is one that causes us to engage in real seeing, hearing, etc. In terms of how we respond to it — there may be little or nothing that makes our response to the words any different from our response to the things they describe.

- ▪18 What is fantasy?
- ▪19 What kinds of responses occur during fantasy?
- ▪20 How does fantasy control inside behavior of seeing, etc.?
- ▪21 In what sense are seeing in the presence of the object, and seeing when the object is described, alike?

Self-induced fantasy

If we can tell others a story, well — then we can tell ourselves the same story. If hearing another's story or reading his or her book can make us see, hear, or feel what the words describe — then our own verbal description to ourselves can do the same. Now you see how people live who live in a fantasy world.

Their world is much like other worlds. Only the things, people, and settings they respond to are verbal ones.

Dawn's sitting in the Bistro in the middle of a fantasy. It's one of her own making. Not quite all her own though. It has bits and parts from dozens of books she's read, movies she's seen, tales she's heard. The more Dawn tells herself the story, the sadder she gets. The girl in the story — the version she tells herself — is Dawn. If Dawn were to keep it up she could feel so bad she'd never go to class again — flunk out. Then she'd have more time for telling herself stories. She'd feel even worse and give up more.

In the end, Dawn could do like the girl in the song (she's Dawn too) — *"throw aching heart and tortured brain 'neath the screaming Amtrack train"*. It happens. It won't to Dawn, though. Not this time. She's about to quit the fantasy world and join the real one.

- ■22 What is self-induced fantasy?
- ■23 Where do the people and places in our self-induced fantasy come from?

Saved from her slump

It was fifteen minutes after Sid left the Bistro that Ian Drucker saw Dawn and came back to speak to her. Ian was a foreign student and a football player — a native of Belgium. His first term at BSU. In spite of his good looks, Ian didn't seem to get around much. He didn't know much about girls from this country. The truth was that he didn't know what Americans were all about yet. When Dawn saw him coming, she began to play the destroyed woman again. But Ian didn't know enough to go for it — not like poor Sid.

"Hello, Dawn, may I join you?" Ian said.

"Why not," Dawn said. Ian sat down. Dawn was silent — demure. A minute passed, then two. All the time Ian kept smiling at Dawn. It began to get to her. She wasn't used to not talking when a new man was around. Besides, it was hard to look sad with this handsome ninny beaming at you from ear to ear. "Are you finding you like BSU?" Dawn said at last.

"Yes. Very much. So many nice people. The coach, he's been kind to me — a very fine man. Isn't that so?"

"Coach Krub? He's adored — that's all. People say he's a self-styled saint."

"A saint?" Ian said, a puzzled look on his face. "What do you mean?"

"Well, it's just a manner of speaking. You see, Coach Krub . . ." Dawn was coming out of her slump. The zip came back to her speech. This fellow was someone new. What'd he think of the women here? He might be all tied up with some Belgian girl — even married. He didn't wear a ring, though. What was it like in Belgium? What was he really like? Outside the day seemed to get brighter.

* * *

Sid doodled in his notebook through psych class. He couldn't get Dawn out of his mind. The bell rang and the class filed out the door. Sid found himself outside, a fine drizzle wetted his face and cooled his head. *Damn it. Dawn liked someone else — was all hung up. Damn it — why didn't she love him like she did that other guy? But no. She was nice to him. Good old Sid. That's all — just a friend.*

Who was this "Jim" anyway? Some guy with a sports car, a nice pad all juiced up with a fancy stereo rig. Got an old man who's loaded. That's what Dawn likes — someone flashy with loot. Hell with her! Hell with 'em both! Sid walked on in the rain. Then he began to feel sorry for Dawn. *She couldn't help the way she was. She was weak, that's all. She liked him, he knew that. That's it, she was just too weak — too awed by all the others. A little girl in a candy shop.*

CONCLUSIONS

Yes, a visit to your world of private events is a real "trip", and can be a "bummer". Fantasy can take us through some strange twists and turns and return us to the real world at a bad place and in a bad way. There's nothing odd or occult about it though. If we're changed by experience in the real world — learn, have emotions aroused, then we can also learn and become aroused by experience in fantasy. But changes that come from fantasy experience need not affect us badly. Today's miracles — breakthroughs in science, in social reform, in humanitarian effort — were once someone's fantasy.

Talking to yourself in private consciousness (aside from the time it may take that could have been used otherwise) may turn out good or bad, or just be neutral. It all depends on what you say to yourself and on what actions in the external world these words produce.

CHAPTER 24
CONSCIOUSNESS
AND ITS LIMITS

INTRODUCTION

Three straws at the fountain

"Reinforcers, discriminative stimuli, extinction, punishers — that's all we ever talk about in class. Sure, I know they're heavy concepts — but they're too simple. I don't see how they can even begin to account for the depth of human experience." All the time she was talking, Mae couldn't take her eyes off the lavish chocolate malt Dawn had just bought at the soda fountain. "Hey, that looks real good — can I have a taste?"

"Sure. Grab a straw — and I agree with you. Those principles are big if you're talking about learning — but there's more to human existence than learning." Just then Juke appeared. Mae and Dawn had their heads close together, engrossed in their rap session and the malt before them.

"Hi, gang," Juke said.

"Hi, Juke. Get yourself a straw." Juke peeled the paper from a straw and joined in.

"What do you think about what we're learning in psych, Juke? Don't you believe the principles we talk about are too simple?" Mae asked.

"Too simple for what?"

"To account for all that human experience."

"Whatta you mean?"

"Things like — well, meditation, hypnosis, the occult . . ."

"And drugs," Dawn added.

"Oh yeah, that phony b.s. — a big bunch of hot air if you ask me."

"It's not phony," Dawn said. "There're some serious scholars who think you can learn things with drugs you can't learn any other way."

"And meditation," Mae added. "I just joined a meditation group here on campus. They're good people; bright and really into what they're doin'. Nothin' phony about it. They got good data."

"Hot air," Juke said.

"I'm due at a meeting of our meditation group at four. You want to come along, Dawn?"

"I'd like to but I can't — some people I gotta see."

"What about you, Juke? Do you some good to talk to some of the members and see who they are."

"Naw — but thanks."

"Well, later on," Mae said, getting up to leave.

"I'll walk along part way with you," Dawn said. "You goin' our way, Juke?"

"Guess I'll go over to the gym — see you women later."

Beyond normal experience

In the last two chapters we discussed some types of responses that differ, but are still given the name "consciousness". Among these was that quite special consciousness, self-awareness. We learn this latter consciousness from those around us — a verbal community that differs somewhat for each of us. Because of this, the kinds of events we each relate to in self-awareness vary. Still, for any of us, there's a fairly common array of internal and external events whose presence and nature we're most often aware of — a sort of normal range of self-awareness. But this applies only if we're talking about more or less normal stimulus conditions. There are some things we can get into: special stimulus conditions that create a new awareness — consciousness that's outside our normal limits. Hypnosis and meditation are two such uncommon conditions. We'll discuss their power to produce experience that in some sense transcends the normal. The issue here is one our characters debated in the last section: Do responses in these unique stimulus conditions relate to the laws of behavior we've found ample so far; or, must we seek new principles, new levels of analysis? We will deal with this issue soon, but first let's look at something we all know about — an old acquaintance — pain.

- ■ 1 What are two stimulus conditions that are outside our normal limits of consciousness?

PAIN

The nature of pain

Juke would have been wiser to go with Mae, her guru and meditation group than to go to the gym. In any event, he should have known better than to get mixed up in a pick-up basketball game. No better way in the world to get hurt — break a leg or smash your nose. Red, Moose, and the others were playing and they needed someone to make the sides even. Juke wasn't warmed up when he came down on the outside of his ankle, turning it all the way over, the bone knocking sharply against the hardwood.

Juke screamed — then he swore. Red gave him a hand up and followed him as he hobbled over to the bleachers.

"Hell, man — is it bad?"

"Don't know yet. Gotta see if it'll bear any weight." Juke tried it. It hurt some, but mostly it felt numb.

"Can you go on it?" Red asked.

"Dunno. Maybe."

"Come on, we need you on the boards, man! Only four points down — we can take these turkeys! Lace that shoe and bind that ankle so it won't give."

Juke pulled the laces as tight as he could, the high top pressing into the fast swelling flesh. It felt better now when he put weight on it. In five minutes he was back in the thick of the game.

***

Juke didn't know how bad his ankle was hurt until he got out of the shower. By then it was a discolored mess — an ugly, swollen club of a thing. *Better get back to the dorm and get some ice on it — and fast.*

***

Later, back at the dorm, Juke sat in the chair, his tortured ankle resting on pillows stacked high on the bed; ice-packed towels almost obscuring foot and ankle; black, blue and red toes peeping out. They were alone, the two of them — Juke and his pain.

***

Only two things are certain in life — or so the saying goes: death and taxes. But there's one other that the saying doesn't mention — it's pain. To live is to know pain. In some sense pain's the measure of what's real and what isn't — the standard by which the reality of all other experience is judged. Yet, there's something fickle about pain, in spite of its real and often grim nature. What causes pain for some doesn't seem to affect others that way at all — and what's painful for people at one time doesn't bother them at other times. Pain is changed by what people say to us about it. At times we can be talked into — or out of — it. That's pain — quite a puzzle. At once, all too real and yet something you can't quite pin down.

■ 2 In what ways is pain fickle?

Pain as a response

We can start to lessen the pain puzzle right now by saying that pain is a response — a response that most often results when contact is made with punishing stimuli. Punishers that we think of as causing pain are those that damage tissue. However, pain is also caused by the second type of unlearned punisher, the loss of rewards. In some cases we make pain responses to learned punishers — a flashing red light behind you on the freeway, a dear John letter, or the high-pitched whine of bombs as they scream earthward. Hold on for the time being if it bothers you to think of the latter kinds of events — learned punishers — as causing pain; we'll explain this later on.

■ 3 Pain is a r_____.
■ 4 What kinds of stimuli are those that cause pain? How do they acquire their power to produce pain?

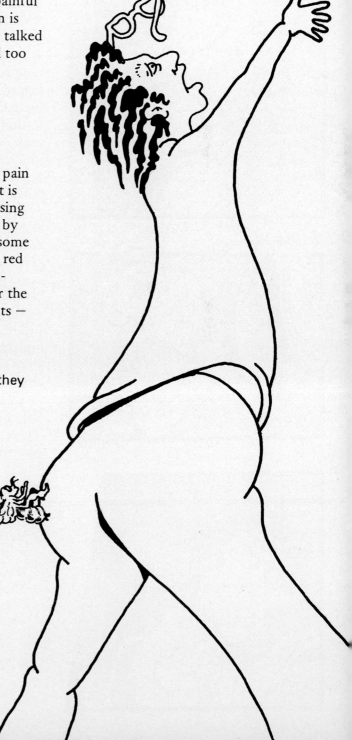

Other responses to punishers

Pain is only one of a number of responses that punishers cause. We'd do well to mention them before we talk about pain as a response. The first and most basic of these is a series of internal events — a surge of action in the autonomic nervous system, in some centers of the brain, and in the endocrine system. These changes turn the creature on, getting it ready for combat or full flight, preparing muscles for fast and intense movement. You'll recall we called this complex of inside changes "arousal" (see Chapter Three), or "activation". It prepares the entire body — muscles, organs, glands — to do what it takes to solve a problem posed by the environment at that moment.

Responses that occur after being aroused by a punisher often take the form of escape, avoidance or aggression. You exhibit escape behavior when you run away or otherwise withdraw from punisher contact; for instance, pulling your hand away from a hot coffee pot, or dumping falling stocks before their value hits rock bottom. Avoidance responses often come after an initial escape response. Sometimes you have to get burned a little by a hot coffee pot or bad stock before you learn to use a pot holder, or refrain from buying the risky stock in the first place.

In both escape and avoidance, people take themselves away from the punishing state of affairs. Aggression achieves the same result — ends or avoids punisher contact. It does this by getting rid of, or in some way cutting off the power of the punisher. In all cases, the same basic sequence occurs: punishers cause arousal, which makes escape, avoidance and aggression more likely.

Punishers cause other responses which fall somewhere between the inside actions of arousal and the outside actions of escape, avoidance, and aggression. These actions can be observed, but it's not clear that they produce results that truly change punisher contact — lessen it in any way, or end it.

Examples of this kind of response to punishers are screaming, yelping, shaking or twitching, and voiding of bowels and bladder. These responses occur with little if any warning when heavy punishers make contact.

- 5 Of responses to punishers other than pain, the most basic is _____. It involves what areas of the body?
- 6 Compare escape and avoidance — how do they differ?
- 7 How are escape and avoidance like aggression? How do they differ from it?
- 8 Some responses to punishers seem to lie somewhere between arousal and escape, avoidance and aggression. Cite some instances.

Pain as self-awareness

We learned before how self-awareness differed from stimulus control. It's one thing to be controlled by certain cues and rewards — it's something else to know that they affect you — to comment to yourself and/or others about what's going on. The former is stimulus control. Actions of all creatures — human or not — come under the control of cues. Self-awareness arises when cues cause us to make statements about how we're being affected by things around us. Thus, self-awareness is a sort of status report we make to ourselves about ourselves.

Sometimes the focus is on how we're doing at a given instant. Seeing our movement on the freeway relative to other cars may cause us to say *I'm going too slow — I'd better speed up.* At other times, self-awareness is a kind of state of our state report. We report to ourselves that we're tired, hungry, cold, sad, confused, nauseous, up-tight, etc. — here the focus is on our own conditions, somewhat apart from what's going on around us.

We're not born with self-awareness. We learn the response mode of self-aware responses — verbal behavior or language — and we also learn to comment about some things and not others. Both of these are taught us by our verbal community.

So how does pain relate to all of this? Well, pain is a self-aware response about the presence of punishers that are causing us to make responses like those we've made to other punishers in the past. These responses include arousal, escape, avoidance, and aggression — and crying, screaming, shaking and twitching, etc., those in-between responses. So pain is a verbal response that all or some of these responses are occurring and that a punisher — either known or assumed — is making contact.

Pain: a self-aware response made when a punisher makes contact, and we comment about its presence and our responses to it.

All punishers cause arousal and tend to evoke cries and other such actions. As we grow older, crying may expose us to punishers that are far worse than the ones that caused us to cry in the first place — thus many adults, and most males, learn not to make these responses.

How we label a punisher is controlled by the type of action we take to limit contact with it. Stimuli we escape from are likely to be called painful. If we later avoid a punisher when it comes near, we don't call it painful — rather we call it frightening. If we attack it after it makes contact, we'll say that it hurt us, and that made us angry. If we attack before it makes contact, we'll say it scared us and we became angry as a result. Punishers for which we've learned no effective escape, avoidance, or aggressive response are the ones that are going to be called just plain painful.

- 9 Review: Contrast stimulus control and self-awareness.
- 10 Explain how self-awareness that's associated with specific outside events differs from state of our state self-awareness.
- 11 Define pain.
- 12 Punishers that cause escape are apt to be called _____. How does this compare with what we'll call those that make contact before we aggress against them? That we avoid by running from before contact? That we avoid by attacking before they make contact? For which there are no escape, avoidance, or aggressive responses?

Physical pain and mental pain

Stimuli that damage tissue cause us to have "physical pain". We call it that because we know that tissue's being harmed; that is when we can see what's happening, or it seems to involve a discrete area of our body. Loss of reward causes the gross responses (escape, avoidance, arousal, aggression), but since there's no proof that tissue's being damaged, and no point of contact, we'll call it mental pain. The effects of learned punishers are also called mental, as opposed to physical, pain. But for all intents and purposes there's not too much difference in the gross responses that occur — punishers tend to have the same effect, learned or unlearned, at that level. To say that unkind words hurt is correct in more than just a poetic sense. Your response to a punch in the stomach and a bad mark on a test may differ very little if we discount strictly local events.

- 13 How do physical pain and mental pain differ? In what sense are they more alike than different?

Only humans have pain

Your pet, Fido, will yelp, whine, and run away if you step on its paw. It will act somewhat the same — though perhaps not escape — if you yell at it or take its food away. Surely the poor thing is in pain! No — no pain. Dogs and other lower animals respond just like humans where punishers are concerned — except they don't have pain. Pain depends on self-awareness. This in turn requires language skills and a verbal community that not only taught you to talk, but also what to talk about — in this case the effects punishers have on you, and how you respond to them — pain.

Pain is limited to humans due to the fact that we need verbal skills and a verbal community that teaches the special self-awareness of punisher action. Therefore, not all humans have pain, since those without the needed verbal skills will never know a painful moment. But this doesn't mean they won't try to escape from punishers, cry out, and appear to be in agony.

People differ both within and among cultures in terms of the kinds of events they label painful. The more verbal communities vary in terms of how they teach pain — the kinds of stimulus contact they teach us to call painful — the more we differ in pain responses. We're the most alike where stimuli that harm outside tissue are concerned. It's easy for our verbal community to see when these parts are being damaged, e.g., burned, cut, or bruised, etc. And it's also easy to see that the other responses to punishers are clearly produced by these stimuli. You pull away, scream, or say "ouch!" at the same time the contact occurs. Other people can't see the harmful stimuli that take place inside, such as those involved in an upset stomach, headache, cancer, or other internal organ damage. There are rarely any

clear-cut escape responses for them to see either, to tip them off that punishers are at work inside. Someone may grimace or cry out, though it isn't likely unless inside conditions produce intense discrete punisher contact. All of these factors make it hard for the verbal community to teach pain responses in a precise manner, no doubt accounting at least in part for the wide range of responses among us where these inside events are concerned.

■14 Why can't lower animals have pain?

■15 What conditions would make a human unable to have pain?

■16 What two events tell the verbal community that punishers are at work?

■17 There is a situation in which we differ least in terms of pain responses. What punishers are involved in that situation? Why do we differ greatly in our response to internal punishers?

HYPNOSIS

Juke gets the evil eye

Sid worked until after ten in the rat lab. He was far from being the only person working in the ancient psych building that late. The place was abuzz — grad students working on thesis projects, profs, even a few other intro psych students like himself. Each cubicle was busy — seemed you could always find people in the lab any hour day or night. Dr. Harper was a more or less constant fixture around the place. He happened to leave the building at the same time as Sid, so he offered him a ride in his old red Volks. Sid didn't have to think twice before accepting. It was a chilly night and there was a good mile and a half to cover from the psych building to the new dorm complex at the edge of campus.

Harper pulled up into the large horseshoe drive, stopping at the dorm entrance. "So this is the new unisex dorm —where men and women live side by side in peace and co-ed bliss. Things sure have changed. When I was in school you couldn't get within a half-mile of the women's dorm after nine — had the lawns and bushes booby-trapped."

"It's okay otherwise, too. The rooms and dining halls are nice. Got fine rec and study areas, too." Sid paused. "Chow's pretty lousy, I'm afraid."

"Guess some things never change," Harper said.

"Say, how'd you like a quick tour?"

"Yeah — It might be nice to take a look around."

After Sid had shown Dr. Harper some of the lounges and study rooms, he stopped by his room. "Come on in and take a look at the living quarters. The light's on — that means Juke's still up."

Once inside they saw Juke, his leg propped high on pillows, his head resting against the back of the chair. They could tell he was having a rough time.

"Hi, Sid. Whatta you say, Doc? You come to see how the natives live?"

"Thought I would — hey, what's wrong?"

"Ankle — turned it over."

"How'd it happen?" Sid asked.

"Foolin' around. Little pick-up ball game. Shoulda known better. It's the weak ankle — serves me right for not having it taped."

"Sure it isn't broken?" Harper said.

"Naw. Just turned. Hurts bad enough to be broke a dozen times."

"Come on," Sid said. "You gotta get some pills or a shot. I'll get one of the counselors to take you to the infirmary."

"No way. If I move it even a little it feels like I'm going through the roof. I'm gonna tough it out right here."

"You can't get any sleep like that. Let me help you get into the sack at least."

"'Preciate it — but I'm okay here."

Dr. Harper was taking a good look at Juke's ankle while Sid and Juke talked. It was swollen and badly discolored. Hard to tell if it was broken — but it didn't look from the outside like there was any bone damage. X-rays could wait until morning. The big thing was to get Juke through the night.

"There's something I'd like to try if you're into it," Harper said. "Might help you get some rest."

"Try? Whatta you mean, Doc?"

"Give you a few suggestions — I do it once in a while for a dentist here in town. Sometimes at the clinic, too. Works real well in most cases."

"Suggestions?" Sid said. "You mean hypnotic suggestions?"

"Right."

"Hypnosis!" Juke said. "You gonna try to put the evil eye on me, Doc?"

"Just going to talk to you a little, that's all. How about it?"

"Doc, I know you're some talker — and a real smart dude. Ain't no way you're gonna talk me outta this pain — no matter how much I wish you could. Look at that ankle. Words ain't gonna do much there!"

Hypnosis and pain

Hypnosis is an often heard of, much studied, but little understood process. It was used by Sigmund Freud at one time, although he gave it up in the end because he found it didn't work well on many patients. Today, hypnosis is used by physicians, dentists, counselors and many other professionals, though there's still much dispute over what may or may not be achieved with it. But one area where it's of proven value is in reducing pain. It's used as an anesthetic agent in surgery, and is of vast importance where allergies or other factors prevent the use of drugs.

* * *

"Come on, Doc. This won't work. You're just wasting your time," Juke said. Sid could tell Juke was ill at ease, and maybe a little scared, too.

"Shush, Juke," Harper said. "Just relax. Now. I want you to look at this watch. That's it. Look at it — back and forth,

back and forth, to and fro, that's it, relax . . ."

* * *

"Now listen, Juke. I'm going to wake you up in a short while. When you open your eyes you'll find your ankle feels much better. You'll let Sid help you into bed. Within five minutes after the lights are out you'll fall into a deep, deep sleep — a restful sleep — you won't wake up until your regular time in the morning. I'm going to count backward from ten. When I reach one, I'll snap my fingers and you'll open your eyes. Ready — ten . . . nine . . . eight . . ."

* * *

Juke woke up the next morning five minutes before the alarm was due to go off. He stretched and yawned. What day was it? Oh yeah. Then he thought about his ankle. He threw back the covers and looked at it. Swelling was down some. He tried to move it up and down, then side-

ways. It felt a little funny, but it didn't hurt. Maybe he just wasn't awake yet. He had to go to the bathroom. Well, now or never. Might as well test it. Juke put some weight on his foot — it still didn't hurt. Just a twinge here and there — but could he wear a shoe? A sneaker, maybe — rip it up a little so it wouldn't bind. Well, looks like he might not miss any classes after all. *Hypnosis — man, that's wild stuff. It worked — but how?* Juke took his psych book from the nightstand and turned to the table of contents. *Wonder what these dudes got to say about hypnosis?*

■18 What famous psychologist used hypnosis in treating clinical patients? Why did he abandon it?

■19 Although there's some debate about what may be achieved through hypnosis, what's one area where it's proved to be very worthwhile?

How does hypnosis work?

Hypnosis is a verbal process. It's just one more instance of how actions come under the strong control of verbal cues. In the past, hypnosis was thought of as a state — a strange condition that was beyond the scope of psychology. Today, we believe otherwise. It appears that the workings of hypnosis can be related to verbal control and principles of social psychology.

As we grow up we come under ever stronger verbal control. We are most prone to respond to the words of parents, physicians, teachers, and others whose training or role we respect — and whose opinions and judgement we trust. It's a big reward when we can please these people. We'll try to do what they say and act the way they want. We trust their judgement far more than our own. If they tell us we can do something we always thought we couldn't, we're likely to take their word for it and give it a try. We'll believe what they tell us is so, even before we believe what we see first hand. It's that simple. And the hypnotist takes over from teachers, parents, etc., cashing in on our long history of being good little boys and girls — taking heed, and doing what we're told.

Of course some people aren't and never have been under good culture control. They have poor verbal skills and don't do what they're told because they don't know what's being asked of them. Others have received great reward for going against the wishes of parents and other agents in the culture. They balk at doing anything they're told. As you might guess, neurotics, psychotics, and the retarded make poor hypnotic subjects. The best subjects? Typical people — like most of us who have minded parents and teachers, and done what the traffic cop said.

It shouldn't come as a great surprise that hypnosis works to change pain responses. Pain is merely self-awareness that amounts to talking to ourselves about internal and external responses that we make to punishers. If we can find something to stop these verbal responses, we can stop self-awareness and therefore pain. Dentists sometimes use noise or loud music that tends to drown out or compete with self-talk. We may remark that we can't hear ourselves think, but what we mean is that we can't hear ourselves talk. Other events distract us from pain responses. A good movie, lively chat, or close scrape with danger keeps us from the self-awareness that is pain. It often happens that people who are badly hurt in auto wrecks or other crises function without pain during the crisis. They may suffer greatly later on, however, when all is quiet. The hypnotist controls the subject's verbal behavior — and thus self-awareness — by choosing those events the subject will comment about and neglecting others. We make responses that go along with the way we're told we are. Is that too much to ask of good little girls and boys, who really want to please the nice hypnotist?

■20 Hypnosis can be related to ＿＿＿＿＿ control and principles of ＿＿＿＿＿ ＿＿＿＿＿.

■21 How do most of us grow up so that we want to please the hypnotist when the occasion arises?

■22 What types of people make poor hypnotic subjects?

■23 Explain how hypnosis stops pain.

MEDITATION

One

One . . . one . . . one . . . one . . . one . . . one . . ., Mae said it again and again to herself.

***

"Just pick a thought," Ken had said. "Simple as that."
"But what kind of thought?"
"Doesn't matter."
"But it must."
"No. Not really — you'll see."

***

One . . . one . . . one . . . one . . . one . . . or was it won — like the tennis game she played last Sunday, that was won; it was one, too — the score, 6—1; love's zero, but it's one, too; makes one out of two. Oh, oh — there she was thinking again — wasn't supposed to think. Why couldn't she stop? This's stupid! Mae opened her eyes. The others were seated in a circle around her, shoes off, cross-legged on the floor, eyes closed, some with lips moving faintly. Others were still; like stone, tranquil faces quiet and serene. Ken approached her from behind and tapped her on the shoulder, motioning with his head for her to leave the circle and join him in the foyer.

"You seem a little dismayed — thought you might like to talk?"
"I don't know what's wrong. Can't seem to shut off the thoughts — they just keep creeping in. No matter how hard I try I just . . ."
"Whoa. Stop right there. Who said you're supposed to try? That's your problem — you're trying."
"But how can you do anything if you don't try?"
"Just do it."
"But . . ."
"You ever hear the story about the centipede who got along just fine until someone asked it how it managed to move a hundred legs at once? Well, when it started to think about how it moved its legs, it got so mixed up it never could walk again. That's your problem — you're trying. Quit it."
"I'll give it a shot."
"Mae."
"Yes."
"One thing. Don't try to 'not try' — okay?"

***

One . . . one . . . one . . . one . . . one . . . one . . . Someone was tapping her shoulder, trying to get her attention. She turned to see that it was Ken again. This time he was smiling.

"That's enough for now — near as I can make out you went about seven minutes straight. How do you feel?"

"Seven minutes? Can't be that long — I just started. Feel? I feel good — no, I feel great! Seven minutes — that's pretty good, huh?"

"Not bad for openers."

"Man, was I gone — where was I? The time went by, but I wasn't here."

"That's what it's all about. Welcome to meditation time."

* * *

Meditation has been practiced in the East for centuries. But there are many kinds of meditation, many schools — all of them using techniques that differ to one extent or another, and with philosophical points of view that vary greatly in extent and kind. Reports of the wonders of meditation were often lavish, but by and large remained untested in any thorough manner by scientists. Part of the problem in making valid statements about the effects of meditation stemmed from the many techniques used among devotees — also the fact that students within schools varied in the degree to which they'd mastered their chosen method. These limits to research vanished when a standard method — transcendental meditation (TM) — came on the scene. Today, an estimated 100,000 people in this country alone adhere to these techniques which were fostered by Maharishi Mahesh Yogi. As a rule, they devote 15 to 20 minutes to TM daily. Students who have received the Maharishi's instruction report benefits of TM which range from "quite helpful" to "miraculous".

- ■24 Why was the thorough research needed to evaluate meditation not possible until recently?
- ■25 What method of meditation has become widely accepted in this country?

Physiological effects of TM

Research has borne out the ancient claims that TM alters body function in a healthful direction. There are marked reductions in the amount of oxygen required and of carbon dioxide expelled during TM as compared to a normal resting state. Oxygen needed is also far lower than during a deep sleep. But what does this mean? Think of your car's engine. The more fuel and air it uses, the more it's moving and subject to strain. Compared to TM levels, our body engine is still racing when we're taking a normal rest or even sleeping. Wear and tear during TM is at an all time low.

Other changes are a reduced heart rate and increased electrical resistance of the skin. The skin has lower resistance when the autonomic nervous system is active — and this takes place when you're upset, up-tight, worried and tense. The heightened skin resistance means that the TM state is a relaxed place to be.

When muscles work, they produce a substance called lactic acid that clogs them up and spills over into the bloodstream. The amount or level of blood lactate, as it's called, determines whether muscles are ready to work. If the level is high then the muscles aren't ready, they're still tired. They'll be ready to go again only when lactic acid's been cleared from them and the blood. During TM, blood lactate levels drop to a point unheard of in either normal rest or in the deepest sleep. Increased blood-flow due to the relaxed state of the blood vessels breaks down lactic acid and clears it from the blood. Muscles are cleansed in fresh lactate-free blood, getting them ready for action after the session's over.

▪26 What are the physiological changes TM brings about in terms of: oxygen-carbon dioxide cycle; skin resistance and heart rate; blood lactate level? What do these changes mean?

▪27 How do these changes compare with those seen during sleep or normal rest?

How does TM work?

By the time we're adults we've had our share of unlearned punishers. Along the way, many things that started out neutral changed into learned punishers through pairing with other punishers. The net result is that we end up an island closed in on all sides by punishers. Actions these punishers cause have been discussed at length in an earlier section. You'll recall that they are arousal, escape-avoidance actions, aggression, and pain. Rarely, however, do all of these responses occur to a single punisher. The direct actions of escape, avoidance, or aggression aren't likely when punisher strength is small or the threat of contact slight. Chances of the self-aware responses of pain or fear occurring are likewise lessened in such cases. But arousal is something else — it's a near certain outcome when punishers are around — whether the other responses occur or not. Further, nothing says we have to be aware of arousal to suffer its effects: increased heart rate, blood pressure, low skin resistance, rapid breathing, and greater levels of oxygen use and carbon dioxide release.

These effects should sound familiar — they're just what TM combats. This gives a hint as to the action of TM: it somehow shuts off or reduces arousal. This happens during meditation, although changes always outlast the session. It may be a matter of hours before devotees return to their old normal up-tight aroused state. This is what makes TM so valuable — so many of us exist in a constant state of arousal, motors racing, systems sparking full blast, slowed down only by nervous rest and fitful sleep. How does TM do it?

Remember that arousal is a complex of internal responses caused by punishers and rewards. Unlearned punisher or reward contact accounts for only a small amount of total arousal. Learned punishers do the most to induce arousal — sights, sounds, the presence of others, our own words to ourselves — yes, it's our own self-awareness that causes the greatest arousal.

Both learned punishers and learned rewards lose their power to arouse us when they are no longer paired with their unlearned counterparts. TM sets up a safe and well-controlled setting where this can quickly come about. The power of learned punishers to evoke arousal wains as practice at TM increases. The end result is a daily amount of time where arousal is at its lowest ebb — far below even the level of deep sleep.

Now you can see that TM isn't so much something people do as it is a process that stops unwanted actions. As Mae's group leader Ken points out, trying to do something — even to not think — is like a trumpet that beckons self-aware responses. When self-awareness enters, increased arousal follows close behind. This defeats the purpose of TM. As is often said about happiness, the desired state in TM isn't something you acquire — rather, it's something that overtakes you. Trying can spoil the whole thing.

- ▪28 Which of the responses to punishers is most certain to occur?
- ▪29 What responses occur in arousal, and how do they relate to the effects of TM?
- ▪30 How do learned punishers lose their power, and how does TM help bring this about?
- ▪31 Why does "trying" interfere with the desired TM effect?

Hypnosis and TM

Seeing people engaged in TM looks a lot like the work of a hypnotist. Are they alike in other respects? Research suggests that they are far from it in terms of the physiological changes taking place. More than that, they differ in terms of how each achieves its effects. In fact, we're not too far off in saying that they work by exactly opposite means.

Hypnosis works when subjects come under the verbal control of the hypnotist. Effects achieved depend on the strong power of words to control responses. Changes are specific to the suggestions the hypnotist makes. The whole point of TM is to stop being controlled by anyone's words, most of all your own. The choice of a word or thought to use as a tool during meditation isn't that important because it doesn't exert any specific control. It's a simple response you make over and over that keeps you from being aroused by other stimuli. The effects of TM are gross and not related to commands given by the student, the guru or anyone else. They're the outcome of a basic process that reduces responses to all learned punishers and rewards during, and to some extent after, the TM session.

- ▪32 Explain how hypnosis and TM achieve their effects through opposite means.

Return to the fountain

". . . then the next thing I knew, it was morning — slept like a baby. That hypnosis is mighty fine stuff," Juke said.

"Fine stuff, huh? Last I heard you thought it was just hot air," Mae said.

"Gotta be how he sprained his ankle in the first place — trying to get his foot out of his mouth," Dawn added.

"I'm here to humble myself and admit my grievous wrong. But one thing I wasn't wrong 'bout though. There ain't nothin' spooky goin' on with hypnosis. The simple principles you women were puttin' down the other day can explain it just fine."

"I guess it's my turn to eat a little crow," Mae said. "The more I get into meditation, the more I see how it fits in with what we've been learning."

"I don't know," Dawn said. "There's too much to explain. What about mental telepathy, astro-projection, auto-kinesis?"

"Pure b.s.," Juke said. "Nothin' to it but hot air."

CONCLUSIONS

In this chapter we've tried to remove the mystery from a few topics that have puzzled and amazed both scientist and lay person alike. The sometimes fickle, sometimes grisly real presence of pain, the frightening power of hypnosis, and the timeless miracles of meditation: all come into focus when viewed from the standpoint of a common set of proven psychological principles. Are these principles also adequate to explain other aspects of human behavior? We believe that they are indeed. This is a judgement that readers must make for themselves in chapters that follow.

CHAPTER 25
EMOTIONS

INTRODUCTION

The group

"I think you're absurd, Doug! You're absurd and overbearing. You got some nerve blaming Edna! Okay, so you got a mistress — you want Edna just to say 'that's nice, anything you say' and let it go at that? You're screwed man! Really warped!" Edna moaned louder, sobbing. Kirt handed her a box of tissues.

"Now just a damn minute! You got some nerve, Jack, what about . . ."

"Hold it, Doug. You'll get your turn but I think Ann has a comment she'd like to share with the group." It was Ted, the group leader, talking.

"Thank you, Ted. It appears to me that this whole issue boils down to an entirely rational dilemma. Let's look at it pros and cons-wise. I feel certain when all the facts are clear, a simple listing should . . ."

"Hell, Ann!" Mona bellowed. "That's crap! You make me sick with all that logical stuff! Bull! What about guts? What about feelings?"

* * *

After the session Ted went into the small office behind the group room to wind down. It'd gone pretty well he thought. There was a knock on the door. "Come on in," Ted said. Kirt, one of the older members of the group, poked his head in.

"Hi. Won't come in. Just wanted to tell you I thought it was a great session tonight. A whole lotta honesty and gut-level stuff there. Really great."

"Yes, I agree. It was productive. One or two felt emotions they've been afraid to deal with — didn't even know they had feelings like that."

"Well," Kirt said. "Just wanted to give you a little feedback."

"'Preciate it — see you next week."

"Right. G'night."

"Nite." Ted leaned back in his chair. *Yes, they all liked it. Seemed to really get into it. What about next week though? It'd be tough to come up with a capper for tonight. Maybe Mona. Have to needle her a little, get her to open up. Should be a lotta action there for a long time. Could last three or four sessions.*

Emotional behavior

In past times writers on the topic of human behavior have always viewed "emotional behavior" as somehow distinct from actions that are geared toward changing the environment. Solving a math problem, running a tractor, hunting, chopping down a tree — these are all actions that have clear-cut results. But what does feeling anger, love, hatred, or envy have to do with changing things? What good are emotions? What do they do for us? Some suggest that we'd be better off without them — they just get in the way — make us feel good or bad, but don't help.

On the other side are those like Ted — the leader of the group we've just eavesdropped on. Groups like Ted's exist in almost every city, town, or burg throughout the country. People who run and support them believe that having emotion is a healthy thing. They go so far as to say that if we don't have emotions — or worse yet, have them and don't know it (or won't admit it) — we run the risk of mental illness.

Ted's trying to incite group members to have new emotions and to admit they're capable of real feelings. Ted would say in so many words that this's his goal. But there seems to be something else going on. Ted appears to assume the role of a showman — trying to come up with a new and better act each session. Can this be part of the treatment?

- 1 What have writers agreed upon about the value of emotion to human survival?
- 2 Some believe that not having emotion can harm people. Discuss.
- 3 What is often the stated purpose of groups who stress the importance of emotions?

Love story

"What's wrong with you, Chet? If your face was any longer you'd be steppin' on it. Why you so pushed outta shape?" Juke and Chet waited in the long line leading to the ticket booth. The wind was cold and gusty, making both men pull up their collars and turn their backs to its chill. Carol and Mae waited for them in the warm lobby.

"I'm hacked — real hacked. Here I am freezing my nubs off, waiting in some line with a bunch a jerk college kids — just to see some slap happy flick."

"Thought you liked flicks, man?"

"Yeah, well I do. But not this loser. Look — it's an old plot, a real tearjerker. Guy falls in love with gal; gal gets fatal disease; gal dies; guy spends the rest of his life pining away for her — sees her face in each snowflake and stuff like that. Smaltz!"

"Well, whatta you wanna do then — bag it?"

"Naw, we're here now. Carol and Mae are all hot to see it. Just hope there's a good cartoon and the popcorn ain't stale — that's all."

* * *

Juke was on his second box of popcorn. So far the movie went the way Chet said it would. Looked like the woman was about to die, okay. She was in the hospital now where her husband had just rushed her. *Oh, oh — big dyin' scene coming up.*

"I'm sorry — sorry for all the times, all the seconds, all . . ." She took her hand and placed it against his lips softly, stopping him from saying more.

"Don't," she said. "Loving is never having to look at your watch." Her eyes closed and she slumped into the pillow.

That was it. Just like old Chet said it'd be. Juke looked around him at the crowd. Sobs and sniffles filled the room. Mae, sitting on his right, clutched his hand and looked straight ahead, her eyes blinking. Carol, who was next to him on the other side, had her head buried in Chet's shoulder. Juke leaned around Carol to speak to Chet. "You sure called the shots — ain't a dry eye in the house." Chet didn't answer. Juke thought he hadn't heard him. He was just about to say something else when the scene changed on the screen, lighting up Chet's face. Chet was crying, making little grunting noises, tears clouding his eyes.

WHAT IS EMOTION?

In an earlier chapter we defined emotion as "a temporary physiological change due to stimulus changes in the creature's world". But as with most terms we define, we may need to say a little more about it to help you get a good grasp of the concept. Most all experts agree that emotion involves our guts — viscera as they're called. These inside actions of the smooth muscles of the stomach, intestines, blood vessel walls, and glands are all involved in emotion. Changes in brain action or function also seem to be a part of emotion, along with heart rhythm or rate changes. But there's more to it than that — all of these changes could and do occur during a brisk game of handball or run down the beach. Then what makes emotion different? There are three main features that distinguish these visceral actions as emotion: the outside setting cues, the inside patterns of physiological events, and the labels we've learned to use.

If we shake and grow red in the face when we've just run a mile — that's one thing. If we do it after we've just been told we're a no good so-and-so — that's something else. The latter's emotional behavior. It's the stimuli, the outside setting cues, that produce the behavior that make us call it that.

Some believe that while increased heart, gland, brain, and other organ actions, the inside patterns of physiological events, are at play in both exercise and emotions, the patterns aren't the same. Likewise, differences between emotions — fear, anger, love, etc. - may have slightly different patterns of organ response.

But regardless of what's going on inside, we will call a response on our part "emotion" if we've been taught to call it that, if we've learned to label it as such. What this means is that two people may report they're angry, but both the pattern and extent of inside action won't be at all the same.

- 4 Name at least six response sites that are involved in visceral responses.
- 5 What other activity can also cause the same general kind of actions as emotion?
- 6 What are the three characteristics of emotion that separate it from other increased visceral actions?

STIMULI THAT CAUSE EMOTION

Unlearned reinforcers

The sudden sight, taste, smell, or touch of unlearned rewards results in a sudden and massive upsurge in visceral responding. A small cube of beef steak placed on the tongue of a man or woman who has fasted for a week causes viscera to "explode" in sudden and intense action. In lower forms, the smell of musk during mating season sparks action from glands and organs. Total activation surges upward; new power to seek out a partner and mate. It seems that by any standard, this is emotional behavior.

Learned reinforcers

Neutral stimuli that have often appeared prior to reward gain the power to incite action from organs and glands of the viscera. A guarded look that reveals a winning card brings a strong surge to the guts of the poker player — emotion that may well shatter the most practiced poker face. The sight of the finish line to the long distance runner; the strokes of his or her writing on a letter; the words "class dismissed" when trapped in a boring lecture; these are cues that cause emotion — a bomb of action — large or small — that goes off inside.

Biological punishers

Things that damage tissue also cause visceral responding. There is increased action from glands, heart, blood vessel walls, and other organs. All this makes it more likely that action will occur to stop the harmful contact. When youngsters are cross — oldsters cranky — this is often due to illness. Somewhere cells are being killed. Thus, being sick or injured causes responses that are "emotional".

Non-biological punishers

The human infant makes visceral responses to non-biological punishers. These stimuli neither harm nor nourish tissue — they are neutral in that respect. Because of the way things happen in nature, some sights, sounds, or other stimuli tend to precede events that hold great harm for a species. Through natural selection, these neutral stimuli become warning stimuli. Once they make contact with the creature they incite visceral responses — emotion. In the human infant loud noises, loss of support (as with the Moro reflex), certain visual cues such as those at play in the visual cliff effect, all cause emotion.

- 7 Review: What is a non-biological punisher?
- 8 Review: How and why do non-biological punishers come about?
- 9 Name three non-biological punishers relevant to the human.
- 10 Review: Briefly outline the visual cliff effect.

Learned warning signals

Neutral events that precede punishers turn into learned warning signals. These cause emotion. A gamut of learned warning stimuli act in this way for all of us. Emotions spoken of as fear, anxiety, anger, dread, loathing, envy, pity, are all gut responses that result from learned warning signals.

- 11 What is a learned warning signal?

THE MANY SOURCES OF EMOTION

It should be clear now that an instance of emotion may stem from any of a number of stimuli. Unlearned rewards, learned rewards, discriminative stimuli or cues, biological punishers, non-biological punishers, learned warning signals — all of these could cause that inside jolt that you or others label emotion. As a rule, we're most likely to call inside responses "emotion" when they're produced by learned stimuli — learned rewards, cues, or learned warning stimuli. It's still true that when our motor revs up inside — and it's not due to running, working or playing hard — it's likely to get the name emotion. Even drugs that have the effect of speeding up visceral action get tagged as emotion-causing agents. We say they make us jumpy, high-strung — very emotional.

- 12 Six different kinds of stimuli may cause the inside responses that are known as emotion. List them.
- 13 Give an example of each of the six kinds and how it would act to produce emotion.
- 14 Which of these six kinds of stimuli are most likely to be the cause of instances we'll categorize as emotional?

WORDS: CUES AND LEARNED WARNING SIGNALS

What's in a word?

"I don't get it — like, you're gonna have to paint me a picture. It's a word and it means something. When I say Marge Cooper's a 'bitch' it means something special. Look here, right in the book. 'Bitch: 1) A female dog or other canine animal; 2) A spiteful or lewd woman; 3) A complaint; 4) A difficult or confounding problem.' Now the guy who put this book out thinks 'bitch' is an okay word, and so do I."

"You're right about one thing — it had to be a man who wrote the book," Mae said. "When I hear that word it does bad things to me. Makes my guts go off and I get uptight. I don't hear a word you say after that."

"So from now on I'm supposed to say Marge Cooper's a spiteful and/or lewd woman, instead a' callin' her a . . .you-know-what?"

"Yes. If you have to say things like that about women, I'd rather hear it that way."

"Man, I don't buy it. I'm all for rights; I go along with you there — but this's somethin' else. You're messin' with my words, and that's part of me. Telling me to change my words is telling me you don't like me."

"That's funny. Minute ago you told me one word was just like another one — as long as they meant the same thing. If that's true, I don't see how it'd be changing you to use some other words."

"What I'm trying to say is that you've got some hang-up; okay, that's your problem. That's like a person with a crippled leg making it against the law to walk without crutches! No man. No way. I like the way I say things. You just have to live with it."

"Okay, have it your way 'nigger'."

"Come on, now. You don't have to act like that."

"You don't like being called a 'nigger'? Well, I don't either. Look it up in your book. You'll find it's there. It means something too — nigger, nigra, colored person, black — what's in a word? Right?"

"You know that ain't the same thing."

"Oh yeah? Maybe that's the way you 'jocks' see things. The jock mentality."

"So you're just mad and gotta put me down."

"Putting you down? I don't know what you mean. You are a member a' the football team, run track and all that good stuff — that's what a 'jock' does isn't it? And while I'm thinking about it — how's that friend a' yours doing? Chuck, you know, the 'fag'? Oh, I forgot. He doesn't like that word — wants to be called 'gay'. I'm sure you don't let a little thing like his feelings stand in your way. Wouldn't want to change your precious words now, would we?"

"Come on, Mae, that's not fair!"

"Maybe it's not. See you roun' the campus — 'jock'." Mae was gone before Juke could reply.

Analysis

Words are cues — they control actions: what, when, how, where — all verbal stimuli that make it more likely some actions will occur rather than others. Those that do occur are, of course, responses that act to change things around us in ways that produce rewards. It's these actions — the movement of muscle and bone — that have a direct role in getting us what we need to survive. But words don't act solely on the outside — they control inside actions that are also quite crucial. The effect of words on the viscera prepare the way for, and support the movement of, the muscles that get the job done.

The call "dinner time" causes a surge inside — a sudden release of stored power — that prompts the tired field hand to rise above fatigue and sprint to the chow line. The words "Look out!" act as a warning signal that causes people to stop what they're doing and quickly look around them. At the same instant, glands and organs inside also respond — prepare to support, in an instant, any movement needed to avert the danger that threatens.

Thus, words often work on both the viscera and the muscles. They control both inside and outside actions that must sometimes work hand in hand for survival.

Like warning signals and cues, verbal stimuli cause visceral responses that make direct action more likely. Those direct actions that are the best bet to occur are those that have been rewarded in that same situation in the past.

But what if things are rigged — what if there's no response that can work — no response that will yield food — no response that will end contact with harmful objects? Or what, in the case of humans, if there are actions that would work — get you out of a tight spot or gain food, water, or sex — but these actions are not allowed by the culture? For instance, breaking a pastry shop window when you're hungry. They are sure to result in massive censure — punishment from others. Then what happens when warning signals and cues increase visceral actions but don't lead to outside moves that bring change? Emotion builds. Visceral action grows and as it grows, it conflicts with other responses and body functions — the person can't work or think about other tasks. Where warning signals are concerned, sleep, sex, and eating are hampered. The person is short-tempered, upset, may cry, shake, show other outward signs of strong visceral action. At this point, friends may begin to notice. Comments about "Bill's nerves", "Sally's bad temper", or "Jack's unchecked emotion" will be heard.

Intense emotional responses can cause someone a great deal of trouble when: 1) They result from stimuli that the person can do nothing to change; things like not knowing what to do or lack of skill or talent to do it, or not knowing that something's wrong. 2) Actions that would or could change stimuli that cause the emotions aren't allowed in the culture. 3) Emotions other people have can cause problems for us all when they lead to fights, cause us to avoid each other, not pool our efforts, or in any way cause us or them to work in ways that lessen our joint chances to survive.

■15 What are the two major types of responses that words control?
■16 What is the outcome of muscle or motor responses that occur to words? Cite two instances.
■17 How do emotional responses work together with muscle responses to aid in survival?
■18 What happens when emotional responses build but don't result in muscle action that helps reduce the stimulus input?
■19 How can this situation cause physical problems? Cite two instances of physical problems it causes.
■20 Under what two conditions are emotions likely to continue to build to the point that they're harmful to the person?
■21 Under what conditions do one person's emotions cause trouble for others?

Mae and Juke's hassle

Many words are neutral as far as emotion is concerned. They are cues for muscle movements — control what we do — but don't cause any amount of visceral action. Other words control very little action — don't tell us what to do, impart knowledge, or help us get rewards. They do result in strong emotional action, though. Most words do a little of both — control visceral action and act as cues for muscles and bones. A problem comes about — words aren't the same for us — their power to cause emotion for each of us varies as a result of our past. This is the crux of the hassle between Juke and Mae.

The poet and the realist

Poet: Oh the midnight holds in cloistered folds the brackish intent
          of sullen whispers . . .
Realist: Sullen whispers! Brackish intent! That's hogwash, pure
          gobble-de-gook! And you're tryin' to tell me that bunch of
          verbal garbage 'means' something profound?
Poet: Yes, Clod. If you weren't such a churlish boor, void of any
          semblance of true feeling, you'd know its meaning.
Realist: Okay, okay . . . If I'm such an emotional dwarf, maybe you'll
          have to translate. Come on, in simple terms even a 'clod'
          can fathom — what does it mean?
Poet: I . . . I don't think I can say. No. It means what it means —
          that's all. I can't translate for you.
Realist: Ha! Figures! Course you can't. There's no way any sense can
          be made of that mess!
Poet: You are a child! You expect a topic outline, I suppose?
Realist: I'd settle for a little straight talk.

***

A word's just like some other one as long as they mean the same
thing — that's Juke's way of looking at it. What he's saying is: if two
words have the same cue function, then they'll control the same
muscle action and are thus equal. He's right — they're equal in terms
of that function at least.

Mae says: two words can be equal in terms of their control of
muscle movements and be unlike in terms of their control of
emotion. She's right too. This's a problem that's bothered a lot of
people. Words that have a lot of power to bring on heavy emotions
are called "loaded" words. "Nigger", "fag", "redneck", "kike",
"dago", "hippie", and "bitch" — they're all loaded words. They have
some cue function — do control muscle responses — but it's often
drowned out by their heavy power to cause emotional response.
Some political words have such faint muscle control function they
mean little or nothing, but are red hot as emotion cues — "liberal",
"conservative", "fascist", "communist", just to name a few.

What responses do you want?

We've made the point that words have a dual function. They control muscle response that changes the world. Words are also cues that produce emotional response. When words are placed in a sentence, increased function of either sort could occur. Cue function for muscles is heightened — we get more precise and/or complex muscle actions by putting single words into larger units.

Words can also be put into phrases, sentences, stanzas, to increase the effect on emotional actions. Poets create compounds of verbal stimuli that cause readers or listeners to have complex emotional responses. Both the poet and others such as the scientist use words in their work. They use the same medium, but differ in intent and purpose. The scientist wants to avoid loaded words and language. Any emotional responses will likely detract from his message — reduce the precision with which words control motor action.

Poets, on the other hand, go just as far the other way. They compose strings of words that may have even less control — as far as giving information is concerned — than any single word did alone. The realist would say that it's word garbage or nonsense — and be right — as far as controlling muscle response goes. If the poet succeeds, the result will be a montage of words that evokes a complex emotional response. The poet has emotions, and then constructs lines and stanzas to evoke like emotions in the reader.

- 22 Words either control muscles (motor responses) or they control viscera (emotional responses). Discuss.
- 23 The fact that two words are synonyms (have the same or approximate dictionary meaning) insures they'll control the same response. Discuss.
- 24 A person who thinks words are of value only if they control muscle action is called a _____.
- 25 A person who puts words together for their power to control emotional responses is a _____.
- 26 A scientist uses words in her or his work to control _____ responses.

FEELINGS AND EMOTION

Group session two

"You're phony! Kirt's a phony blowhard! Ann's some kinda phony know-it-all; thinks she's a brain! Brains hell! She ain't got enough ta blow her nose with! An the biggest phoney a' the whole lot's you, Ted!" Mona turned to Ted, the group leader. She was half snarling. "Want us all to believe what a great, warm, giving human being you are! Crap! What phony crap! All you want outta this deal's the money — fifteen bucks per head. Cattle — that's all we are to you!" Mona grabbed her purse and leaped to her feet, knocking her chair backward. She stomped out of the room and was gone. A deathly hush fell over the group members. They shuffled in their seats, trying to avoid each other's eyes.

"Well," Ted said after a while. "Seems like Mona's had her say. Tell me Edna, what did you feel just now as Mona was raking us over the coals? Can you tell us?"

"Feel? Gosh, I was so shocked. Pity, I guess. I felt sorry for her. No, not quite sorry. Ashamed — that's it. I felt ashamed for her."

"I tell you what I felt! Anger, dammit! I got hot. The nerve of that woman. Been in this group now for two months — she's not made one bit a' effort to help. Sulked around like some prima donna!"

"I agree with Kirt," Ann said. "I thought what she said about Ted was way out of line." There was a pause then. Leon was the only member who'd not spoken.

"What did you feel, Leon?" Edna asked.

"Well, if you really want to know, I guess I felt guilty. Real guilty."

"Guilty?" Kirt challenged. "How do you get that? We didn't do a thing to provoke that."

"Yes. I'm puzzled too. Why do you feel guilty?" Ann said.

"'Cause she's right. We are phoneys — every last one of us. God, what a bunch of pompous phoneys!"

Analysis

A feeling is a statement about what's going on inside of us. You can ask car drivers about gas supplies and they'll check their gauges. When we ask someone how they "feel" we're asking them to make a response that's presumed to be controlled by inside cues. It seems pretty simple, doesn't it? Well, it isn't. There are a lot of problems and vagueness with the concept of feelings.

Feeling: self-awareness of emotional responses, often resulting in a statement about these emotions.

Can there be emotion without feelings?

Guts can churn, glands secrete, nerves fire — all of the inside responses
that are the basic events of emotion — yet, when we ask people what
kind of feelings they're having they may shrug their shoulders and
tell us they don't know what we're talking about. We learn to detect
these inside emotional events when others watch us, guess we're
feeling a certain way and say, "See, there it is — you're having such-
and-such a feeling." We get social reward from them if we detect and
report feelings. Before long we can detect feeling without having
others help us.

It's strange but true — we're closest to these inside responses, but
it takes someone else to teach us to feel them. That's why, in some
cases at least, people never own up to being sad, afraid, or "in love".
It's not that their guts aren't acting like ours — it's just that they've
never been taught to "feel" it.

We teach feelings because it's good to know about each other's
inner status. It's handy just to ask others how they feel or have them
tell us without asking — much more so than watching them — like
others had to who taught them to feel in the first place. Further, if
they can feel, they can take action to change how they feel. Take a
tranquilizer when they feel upset, take a nap when they feel tired,
and go see a funny movie when they feel blue.

Can you have an emotion you can't describe? Sure, in the sense
that you can see a thing you can't describe, you can have things go
on inside that you can't describe. Both of these are stimulus events
we haven't been taught to label. But in a sense we have — we call
such things "indescribable" — that's the kind of emotion it is.

■27 What's a feeling?
■28 How do we acquire feelings?
■29 Can we have emotions without feelings?
■30 How can emotions be indescribable?

KINDS OF EMOTION

People are taught to respond to visceral action and to label it — not only as emotion but as to kind of emotion as well. They give it a name such as joy, fear, sadness, loathing, panic, anger, etc. There's some reason to believe that the pattern of inside action — the kinds of organs involved and the amount of stimuli coming from them — act as cues that control what kind of emotion we call it. For instance, a pattern gets labeled "anger" when we're first taught to feel emotions — from that time on the same pattern will be called anger.

Research has shown that a pattern that causes one person to say he or she's having one kind of emotion isn't likely to be the same pattern other people cue from when they report they're having the same emotion. An inside response that's called fear by one person may be called anger — even joy — when it occurs inside someone else. This seems quite a puzzle. How did it come about?

Don't forget that we all have to be taught to feel our emotions. People who teach them to us can't see what's going on inside — they watch what we do, how we behave. When they see us act a certain way, they say: "If I was to act that way, I'd be feeling . . . (anger, joy, fear, disgust, etc.). Since you act that way, you must be feeling the same kind of thing (having the same kind of inside responses)." But there's ample room for error here: People can make the same outside response, but have inside responses that aren't at all alike. Actors are paid well to do this. And those who observe what we "do" may not look at outside behavior in the same way. Thus two people who watch the actions of someone else may not agree that she or he was acting "angry", "sad", or "happy". One may say the person was acting one way and the other give it some other label. It stands to reason that if they can't agree on the outside action (which they both can see), they're likely to be wrong about inside actions (that they can't even observe).

Both of the above factors can account for the failure of people to report the same emotion when they have the same inside pattern or to report like emotion when patterns differ.

There's even more reason to question the role that patterns of visceral response play in causing us to report one emotion as opposed to another. In some cases it's clear that we're aware of visceral response only to the extent that we know there's a great deal of action there — we know we're having emotion. The name we're likely to give to the emotion results from the setting — the outside scene and the direct action we take there. If we find ourselves challenged, thwarted, and we lash out physically or verbally, the inside turmoil we feel is going to get labeled anger. In some other setting, where we take some other action, the same turmoil will be called something else.

A complete answer to the question — what cues cause us to feel and report a type of emotion? — involves all the factors mentioned. All of us rely to some extent on inside patterns, on the outside setting, and on the kind of actions we take — as cues for labeling emotions. Some rely more on one or two of these than on the other or others.

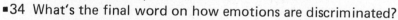

■31 Give the "pattern" notion of how we get cues to differentiate emotions.

■32 When people report the same emotion, they may not have the same inside pattern. Two reasons were given which could help explain this. What are they?

■33 In what way may we get cues to label emotions that don't depend on inside patterns?

■34 What's the final word on how emotions are discriminated?

EMOTIONS AS REINFORCERS

Make me cry — I love it so

Juke was puzzled by the whole thing.

"I don't get it!" He told Sid back at the dorm after he'd said goodnight to Chet and Carol and taken Mae to the elevator. "The place was packed. The biggest bunch of cryin' and moanin' you ever saw — all because of this phony flick. Paid good money just so they could go in there and feel sad!"

"I know what you mean," Sid said. "Got these two aunts. Know how they get their kicks? Goin' to funerals! Yeah! They go to any funeral — even people they didn't know. They carry on, weep and wail with the rest of 'em, just like they'd lost their last friend!"

"But why do they do it? Why?" Juke looked at Sid, waiting for an answer. Sid shrugged his shoulders. For once, Sid couldn't come up with so much as a shred of wisdom or reason that made any sense.

***

No doubt about it — people like emotion, as they go out of their way, pay a high price, put themselves in some bad scenes — all, it seems, so they can have or feel emotions. Emotion is a reward — or can be under the right conditions. What is it that makes it a reward in some cases and a punisher in others? Like Sid, we're somewhat at a loss to come up with iron-clad answers as to why emotional upset is often a strong reward. Others who've looked into this riddle have come up with theories that offer some explanation, but at this point they're scarcely more than wise guesses; no research has been done that would allow us to settle on the correct explanation.

Unlearned non-biological reinforcers

Horses gallop across an open field for no other reason than to gallop; monkeys swing from branch to branch on their way to nowhere — just swinging. The proprioceptive stimuli, the pumping of blood, and other internal events act as rewards. Increases in heart rate and blood circulation bring fresh air and food to some tissues that receive precious little at resting levels of action. Toxins and wastes are cleared by the same process. It's not too far-fetched to propose that these are some unlearned patterns of action serving to keep muscles and organs tuned up.

Humans aren't built to run, swing from branches, or shuffle about on all fours. Still as infants and children they too seem to take measures that stimulate heart rate and blood pressure, engaging in a lot of aimless movement. But as they progress into adulthood, most humans show a steady decrease in movements that seem to do nothing more than exercise the system. Quite likely the internal events that make these actions rewarding to children and to lower animals would make them rewarding to adults as well. But perhaps not if they have to work that hard to get them, or if they are so intense they put a strain on these organs.

Perhaps grown-ups become clever as they get out of shape. They find less strenuous ways of getting the same inside actions. They place themselves in settings that arouse mild to moderate upset; cause a measure of fear, anger, sadness, etc. that make the heart thump and blood course through the system. Whether or not an instance of upset is rewarding would therefore depend on how intense it is. Beyond a certain level, upset would cease to be a reward, and become a punisher. Reward would also depend on how long the upset lasted. Thus, both degree and duration of the emotion are factors that must be dealt with.

The horse can run as hard and as long as is rewarding. Humans control these facets by choosing the proper setting; a suspense or fear-rending movie, a melodrama at the theater. Real life drama comes when we ride the roller coaster, take a sky-dive jump, or hunt the grizzly bear.

For those whose means and systems require cheaper and more sedate actions, a funeral of a person whom you knew only slightly or perhaps didn't know at all, a group therapy setting, encounter group, sensitivity training group, or other situations where emotions are bared. All these things have the features of limited time and intensity. A nice well-ordered dose of emotion — just what the doctor ordered.

Learned social reinforcers

Human contact is a reward whose powers we should never sell short. The degree and kind of social reward that's allowed in our culture is clearly controlled by the setting. Giving or getting heavy social rewards isn't allowed most places. In places where a display of emotion is condoned, social contact of all types is more intense and frequent. You're more likely to get special attention in emotional settings; people are going to be freer in their actions toward each other. More social rewards occur at funerals, sensitivity groups, and other settings — places where the usual constraints on displays of emotion and degree of contact are laid aside. When things get out of hand — emotions are too intense for the social reward that's there — people don't enjoy these scenes. They leave or just stay away in the future, the point being that the social rewards you get are what make you put up with the upset. When upset becomes much greater than reward, the game's not fun anymore; people search for better controlled emotional settings.

Other learned reinforcer values

Even when we don't show it, we're often mildly upset, worried, or harrassed. We can persist this way for days, weeks, or longer. Once we do display emotion — cry, yell, or scream in anger, etc. — others pay attention, perhaps taking part of our load, helping us, or just comforting us; so that when it's all over we feel better.

Since such outbursts frequently result in things getting better, we may have them when we're all alone, and even without that social contact they may be rewarding. We'll feel better afterward. Thus, having emotion may become a learned reward. Getting angry, cursing and kicking things, having a good cry, can make us feel better. It would cease making us feel better if it didn't work once in a while in real ways to change things for the better — that is, if others didn't attend to these outbursts by coming to our aid.

Which of the above theories is the correct one? Any of them could account for the reinforcing effects of emotional upset. And there's no reason to believe they couldn't all work at once — or some for some people and places and some for others. Only further research will answer the question.

- ▪35 Three theories as to why emotions are rewarding were discussed. Explain each of them in a sentence.
- ▪36 Which theory is the correct one? Why?

CONCLUSIONS

Emotions — what good are they? How psychologists used to beat that question to death! As is often true of the noisiest disputes, it turns out that the disputers were often talking about quite different things.

If by emotion one means the inside actions of smooth-muscled organs and glands — we could never do without them. These actions support all behavior. Without them we'd be reduced to a working level somewhat below that of a sloth. No, it's not the inside story, the activation, or the amount of it, that's the problem. It's some patterns of behavior such as aggression, depression, aimless agitation that sometimes go along with upset that do the damage, as we will see in the next chapter.

It needn't be that way, though. These destructive or futile responses can be changed. New ways of coping with aspects of the environment that cause emotion can be learned. Emotion that ends in productive action that benefits us all can never be other than a great thing.

PSYCHOLOGICAL PROBLEMS

One way to account for the success of human creatures on this planet is to look at their power to adapt to ever-changing settings and conditions, making new responses as the environment requires them to.

But the human penchant to adapt is not always a boon, often extracting a great tax. First, humans must have a structure complex enough to allow them to make the wide range of responses adapting calls for. Such structure is delicate by necessity. It can easily become damaged or diseased, causing gross imbalance and malfunction. Second, humans adapt through learning. We know by now that what is learned is over-determined by immediate, as opposed to delayed, results. For the most part this is a good thing — but sometimes short-term gains lead to delayed disaster. Often what yields a quick, happy reward belies tragedy around the bend. Yes, humans can learn the wrong things, and learn them far too well. Thus, humans are prone to have problems both because of structural ills and improper learning.

In the following chapters we'll discuss some of the common psychological problems humans develop. Some appear mainly due to faulty structure — others to learning. But if we look closely, we'll always find both at work. In truth, it's next to impossible to find a case where one doesn't affect the other. Such defects in structure as those causing poor vision can keep us from learning what we should, and at the same time make it likely we'll learn the wrong things — to stay away from school, perhaps. But new adaptive responses can save the day. New solutions arrived at through learning, help us surpass and overcome our handicaps, leaving structural constraints far behind. A small jump in human achievement brought the advent of eye glasses — allowing those afflicted to leap far ahead, surpassing their faulty structure. So goes the human saga . . . But before solutions can be arrived at, problems must be understood. The following chapters present what is, alas, but a sample of those psychological problems that face the beleaguered human.

CHAPTER 26
HANS SELYE AND STRESS

STIMULI

What's a smart kid like you doin' in a place like this? But the question Sid asked himself was absurd. It was the letter. His mother's muted words — words that hid worry and shame.

We've had a rough time this month. I'm sorry I can't send you your usual allowance for the things I know you need — perhaps next month. Your father sends his love, and grows stronger each day — soon he will be back on the job and . . ."

"Come on, Fields, off your dead end! You too, Smitty; come on Brown, let's get with it." It was Conway the foreman. "Hey, where's Severs?"

"Where da' ya think?" Brown said. "In the can . . . ain't that where he always is? Don't you know — he's got loose bowels; least that's what he said. Haw! Haw!"

* * *

Sid shuddered as he looked around the dining hall at the napkin-littered and food-spattered floor. Massive, dark-stained oak tables and square-backed chairs, heavy as lead, filled the huge room. Sometime between now and 3:00 a.m., he would lift, tug, wrestle each table once, twice, maybe more; stack, unstack, restack each chair.

It was the very next morning after the letter came that Sid started looking for work. He needed real money if he was going to help. Most campus jobs wouldn't do. Bud Skillicorn told him about the job with the dining hall maintenance crew.

"They'll bust your butt," Skillicorn warned, "but they give good bread — $3.68 an hour to start."

Sid rubbed his eye against his shoulder, trying to avoid the dust on his hands. His eyes were starting to itch. He could feel raw, angry welts rising on the roof of his mouth. His store of antihistamine tablets was used up two days ago. What next? Sore bones, aching muscles, bruises, swollen hands and feet — wasn't that enough torment for anyone? Just make it until quitting time, back to the dorm, five hours of sleep — no, make that three; he recalled the report that was due. Three hours, get up, do the report, to class — and then? Sidney knew the answer. Right back here — more tables, more chairs, more aches and bruises, and more of Conway, Brown, and the rest.

* * *

Is it true that we "die a little every day"? In some sense, yes.

Even as we're being born, we're plopped into a bath of stimulus energies that begins to tear down the tissues of our bodies. Unless we find some treatment or magic potion to reverse this process — a fountain of youth, perhaps — this envelope of lethal energy will take its toll. It will kill us. The cause of death is likely to be given as "old age".

However, some stimuli destroy cells at a rate well beyond daily wear and tear. When these stimuli impinge in massive force, the effect is called "stress".

Stress: conditions that cause tissue damage far beyond the daily wear and tear of living.

Stressors (stimuli that produce stress) don't gain full control — internal responses launch a counter-attack that softens the effect of the stressors. But here's the rub — or more correctly, "counter-rub" — sometimes these internal mechanisms overshoot and interfere with

other important body processes. Illnesses can develop that in the end may be more harmful than the stressors. These "rebound" problems have been called "diseases of adaptation" by Dr. Hans Selye, a physician and physiologist who has studied stress and its effects for many years.

Stressor: a type of stimulus that occurs in sufficient amount to cause stress.

Diseases of adaptation: physiological problems that arise as a by-product of the body's response to the presence of stressors.

- 1 In what sense can it be said we "die a little each day"?
- 2 When does a stress condition exist?
- 3 What is a stressor?
- 4 What is a "disease of adaptation"?
- 5 On whose research is the concept of "diseases of adaptation" based?

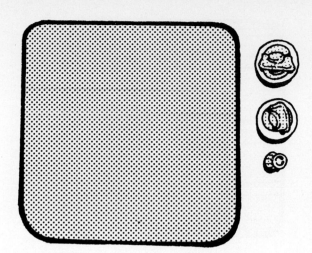

LEARNED AND UNLEARNED STRESSORS

Smitty's eyes darted past Sid then back. "Say, kid, . . . uh . . . you don't have a drink on you, do you . . .?"

"Oh no. I don't drink; I mean, I never carry . . ."

"Yeah," Smitty said, turning his back toward Sid, not letting him finish his statement.

Sid and Smitty stood poised, gathering strength to hoist a table.

"Wait! Wait you guys — let me help." Freddy Severs' chubby legs moved faster than they wanted to, making the roll of gut that hung over his belt shake and wobble. He was too late to find a good hold on the corner of the table. Freddy stumbled, his elbow hitting Smitty a glancing blow on the head, sending the baseball style cap Smitty wore sailing.

"Watch it, Severs!" Smitty screamed.

Freddy's eyes grew large with terror. "I'm sorry. I didn't mean to — honest! Here — let me get your cap." Smitty rubbed his head with one hand and snatched the cap from Freddy with the other.

"Why don't you go take another crap, Severs. Anything, just get the hell outta here!"

***

Sid reached the dorm at 3:20. He ached all over and his head throbbed. His eyes were red itching torture, and now sneezes came in volleys; the dust — that must be it.

"Gawd, you look like death warmed over," the boy on the switchboard said.

"Allergies, " Sid said. He hurried through the lobby. No talk now, just bed. Class at ten — but the report due. He would have to get up by six. He fell into bed without taking off his clothes.

***

Sid woke up an hour later. He struggled with consciousness for a brief moment before he could grasp that something was wrong with him. He clutched at his chest, fighting for air, but there was no room inside. He lunged for the window, punching it open with his forehead and shoulder. The air was cool and plenty

outside, but it wouldn't go into his lungs! They were chock full — blocked with sand or cotton. Air! He had to have it! He stumbled over the bed and burst outside, vaguely aware of two figures in the hallway.

"What's wrong with him!" one voice said.

"He must be loaded," the other answered.

"Hey, man, what's the problem?"

Sidney fell to his knees, resting his head and elbows on the floor. A vice tightened around his chest.

***

"Hi there," the nurse said. Sidney moved his mouth in an effort to answer.

"Don't try it," she said. "You won't have the breath to talk for a while yet. You're still wheezing pretty bad — but at least you don't need the oxygen anymore. Here. This one's amanophlin." She lifted the cotton wad and put the needle into his forearm. "There. We've already given you cortisone." She threw the syringe

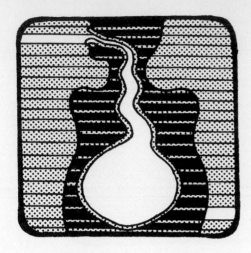

away and opened the door to leave. "Oh, by the way — you're in the university infirmary — in case you wondered. You passed out — acute asthma attack. You were such a lovely shade of blue — seemed almost a pity to spoil it."

***

Stress stimuli may be unlearned. These are energy forms that by their very nature attack and destroy tissues. Knocks, cuts, friction, poisons, radiation, lack of air or nutrients — all are things that kill cells. They are unlearned stressors. Other stimuli don't themselves harm tissue, but are or have been associated with unlearned stressors. When these learned stress stimuli are present, the body tends to respond as if they held the same lethal power as the unlearned stressors they've been associated with in the past. Diseases of adaptation can be caused by either unlearned or learned stressors, or a mixutre of the two.

Unlearned stressors: stimuli which by their very nature destroy tissue.

Learned stressors: initially neutral stimuli that the body comes to respond to as though they are harmful; this occurs because of a past association between these inert stimuli and unlearned stressors.

Sid suffered from both kinds of stressors. The bruises, strains, and fatigue are unlearned stressors. Since Sid isn't husky and is inept at the work (doesn't know how to lift, etc.) he gets a bigger dose of stress than a larger and/or more seasoned person would get at the same job.

In the same way, the makeup of dust is a "poison" for Sid, but may not be for others. Sid's response is inherited — we say he is "allergic", meaning dust is a stressor for him.

Allergy: condition where people are born with a slightly different physical structure that makes stimuli that are harmless for others unlearned stressors for them.

Instances of discord and general hassling that go on among the workers are learned stress stimuli. These scenes make Sid's guts churn, and upset him. For Sid — as with most of us — nasty words, yelling, name calling, are stimuli that have been found in past situations where bad things — punishers — have come down on us. They're generalized learned stressors.

Generalized learned stressors: a class of stimuli in which each member acts as a learned stressor.

- 6 What are unlearned stress stimuli? Name at least five.
- 7 What is a learned stress stimulus? How does it get its power?
- 8 What kinds of unlearned stress stimuli did Sid contact? Name three.
- 9 What kinds of learned stress stimuli did Sid encounter? Name three.
- 10 Name one kind of generalized learned stressor.

GENERAL ADAPTATION SYNDROME

"You're a dope," Dr. Crawford said flatly.

"I feel like a dope — asthma; that's what little twerps and old people get."

"Wrong, Sid, wrong!" Dr. Crawford had a way of rising to his full height of 5'3'' and wagging a well-scrubbed index finger under your nose. "Wrong! It's what happens to dopes like you who think they're Jack Super Smuck, what's-his-name!" He paced once around the room, his hands behind his back; he looked out the window at the students walking across the lawn. "Sid," he said, "your body was trying to tell you something." His voice was calmer now. "All these weeks you go to school all day, work all night — all this time your body's sending you messages. Stop, it's telling you; take it easy, it's telling you; cut it out, it's telling you!"

"I was doing fine."

"Sure you were. Three-sixty-eight an hour — and dying!"

"But asthma's no big deal; right?"

"Ask the boys who carried you in. They seemed to think so."

"I haven't had an asthma attack since I was a kid. It was the dust. I'll just be more careful."

"Just the dust? That's what you think? Well, Sid, it wasn't just the dust. It was abuse, misuse, stress! Stress!" Dr. Crawford stopped short and looked at his watch. "I got to go. Thank about what I've said."

Later that afternoon a nurse brought a book to Sid. There was a note fastened to the cover:

Read this, Sid.
You'll see what I mean about stress —
Crawford.

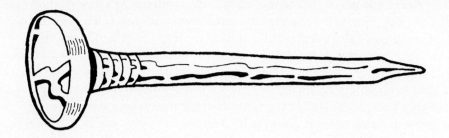

Stress

The book was called *The Stress of Life.* It was based on the research
of a physiologist named Dr. Hans Selye. Sid didn't think it looked
like much fun, but then he didn't have much else to do. He began to
read parts of it.

> *We are creatures caught in the midst of thousands of stimuli. Like
> a goldfish, in his bowl, we are emersed in this energy. It attacks us
> from all sides. Some of these stimuli just bounce off — they do us
> no good or harm. Others can hurt us.*
>
> *A certain amount of this energy can be absorbed without
> causing trouble. Its effects can be mended — but the body takes
> time to do this. As more harmful energy is taken in than the
> system can handle, bad effects mount. The harm done by days,
> weeks, months, comes crashing down. At this point, function is
> impaired — the cumulative effect of these stimuli is called "stress".*

Stress — that was the word Dr. Crawford had used earlier during
his visit. He wasn't aware that it could mean such a specific thing.

> *Although what constitutes a stress situation differs from person
> to person, the reaction to stress is the same. The body goes through
> a series of drastic changes in an attempt to adapt to the stress. This
> series of changes has been called the General Adaptation Syndrome
> (GAS).*
>
> *The GAS has three stages or phases. They are: 1) the alarm
> stage; 2) the resistance stage; and 3) the exhaustion phase.*

General adaptation syndrome (GAS): the characteristic three-phase
response the body makes to the presence of stress.

* * *

Selye speaks of "systemic stress", stress involving large portions of the body. Such stress brings the same response, the GAS. This is true regardless of the nature or form of the energy that produced the stress. A second point Selye makes is that the GAS helps the person adapt; at least, it evolved because it allows the individual to endure and keep going. A third point, and a major one, stemming from Selye's research, is that the GAS doesn't always work to help the person. Sometimes it does great harm. It can be worse in some cases than the stress that brings it on. Medical problems produced by the action of the GAS are called "diseases of adaptation" by Selye.

In calling the response to stress a "syndrome", Selye means that the stages of the GAS from one stressor to another, or for different people, may not be identical — the form, however, is preserved. Thus:

> *The GAS — as the absolutely normal man — is an abstraction which never occurs in its pure form. All agents capable of eliciting the syndrome have some specific actions of their own that they do not share with other types of stress . . ."*

Sidney's asthma attack is a prime example, however, of the GAS at work.

Systemic stress: stressors that affect a large area or part of the body.

* * *

The three parts of the GAS were interesting to Sid. The first, or alarm stage, is an immediate reaction to stress. It's the blowing of the bugle, a physiological call to arms.

> *Massive stress can cause over-response during the alarm stage of the GAS. When a great area of tissue is damaged in a single incident, the GAS may interfere with function. Responses during the alarm stage can be so great that they totally use up all body reserves — often within a matter of a few minutes, even seconds. The end result of this is "physiological shock". Vital functions stop and the person will die unless immediate medical care is forthcoming.*

> *Physiological shock — so that's what they mean by 'going into shock'; of course, people who lose too much blood, get burned or bruised over a large part of their body surface, get bitten by snakes, can go into shock.*

- ▪11 What is the body's reaction to stress called?
- ▪12 What are the three phases of the reaction to stress that Selye describes?
- ▪13 What purpose does the GAS serve in terms of furthering survival?

The alarm stage

Physiological shock — often ending in death — is the result of the over-reaction of the system to stressors. Peter is robbed to pay Paul. Total resources are used for defense, and in the meantime, breathing, heart beat, blood pressure can go begging — shock is a prime cause of death.

    Sid might well have never made it to the hospital alive. Physiological shock as the result of an allergic response is a common killer. This form of shock (called anaphylactic shock) often results from insect bites. The weak venom doesn't bother most of us much, but for others is a deadly stressor.

Alarm stage: the first stage of the GAS; during this stage physiological resources are mobilized and rushed to the point where contact with stressors is going on.

Physiological shock: condition that sometimes occurs during the alarm stage of the GAS where resources are shunted from other systems to the site of the stressor attack; this diversion of resources from other vital functions may cause them to stop and end in death.

Anaphylactic shock: physiological shock brought on by allergic stimuli.

- ■14 What happens when massive stress causes an over-reaction of the GAS, i.e., what is the name of the result?
- ■15 With what stage of the GAS is physiological shock associated?
- ■16 What is the name of shock that is common with allergic reactions?

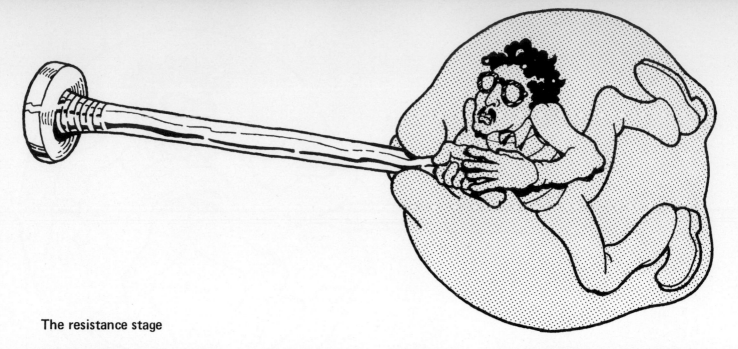

The resistance stage

When Dr. Crawford came in to see him that evening, Sidney was still reading. "Well, what do you think of it?"

"Not bad," Sid said, "but I'm not sure where I fit in — I mean, what does the GAS have to do with me?"

"A lot, Sid. But first, what do you know about the GAS?"

"Well, I know the alarm stage . . ."

"Forget the alarm stage; the resistance stage, that's the one; that's you, Sidney. Asthma, ulcers, chronic spasms of the colon, migraine — outgrowths of the resistance stage."

"I don't get it. I thought asthma was caused by dust, pollens, things like that?"

"Not just that — not that alone. You say your asthma attack was caused by dust — okay. How many times you been around dust in the past few years; pollens, molds, animals that you react to? Dozens of times, hundreds, maybe, but no attack. Why now, after all of these years, an acute attack? And a bad one, Sid, I'm telling you. What you had was no little

wheeze. People die like that all the time. Eh?"

"Well . . ."

"Abuse, Sid. Abuse. Not enough sleep, wrestling those tables all night, putting up with the hassles from that foreman and the rest of that crew; worry about home, worry about grades. That's stress."

* * *

The second stage, the resistance stage, as Selye calls it, comes about if the stress isn't too much all at once — that is, if people don't go into shock and die in the alarm stage. The resistance stage is just a stalling tactic on the part of your body. What happens is that resources are taken from normal functions such as digestion, elimination — even love making — to defense. It prepares the way for an all-out, holding battle. The resistance stage doesn't cure stress or combat it. It just gives you a little more time — lets you live a little longer — survive. But at the expense of other functions. Stress makes it harder for people to digest, to concentrate, to

avoid aggression — and to engage in sexual behavior.

A strange feature of the resistance stage is that it's geared up for the stressor that first sets up the alarm response. Its power to deal with other stressors is reduced below normal. Sid's body was in a life and death battle with the stressors on the job. Thus, defenses against allergic stressors weren't there when needed. Sid suffered an asthma attack that was triggered by dust that wouldn't have fazed him only a few short weeks before.

Resistance stage: second stage of the GAS, during which physiological changes occur that act to lessen the primary effects of stress. It is during this stage that psychophysiological disorders develop.

- ■17 What is the resistance stage? Define.
- ■18 Once in the resistance stage from one stressor, how does the body react to a new type of stress?

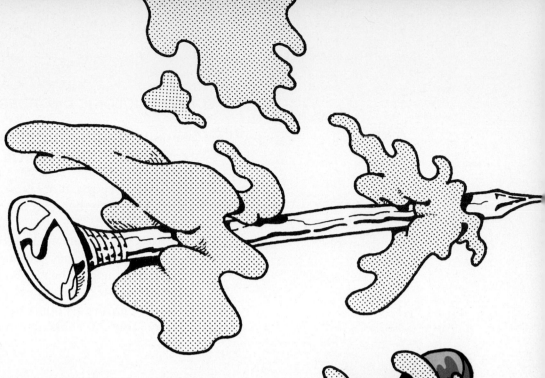

The exhaustion stage

"Okay," Sid said. "I grant what you say is true — it's been getting to me — the lack of sleep, the strains and bruises, the dust, and most of all having to deal with the bad tempers of Conway and the others. In the book, Dr. Selye says that the resistance stage leads to the last stage — the exhaustion stage. Does it follow that I would've ended up that way? I mean . . . that's the end, isn't it?"

"That's right. If people keep coming up against stress stimuli, there's a final point when their systems just can't resist any longer. All defenses collapse; the exhaustion stage occurs, and death. Patients with long-term disease put up a struggle for a time, and then, as the stress keeps up — kaput! It's over; kidneys, liver, lungs, all go at once. But your asthma saved you from all of that!"

If heavy stress keeps up, all defense will sooner or later give out. In the extreme case, the person dies. Often, this "exhaustion stage" doesn't occur because other problems develop — infection, pain in muscles and joints, allergies — that make the person escape the stress setting. As strange as it may seem, these "curses" save lives. They force people to get away, even if it's just to the hospital. Sid's asthma attack may have saved him from far worse medical problems.

Exhaustion stage: the third stage of the GAS, during which all resistance collapses and the organism dies.

- ■19 Describe what happens in the third stage of the GAS.
- ■20 What is the third stage of the GAS called?

* * *

PSYCHOPHYSIOLOGIC DISORDERS

"Are you trying to tell me I'm lucky to have asthma?" Sid asked.

"No — nothing of the sort. All I'm telling you is that your recent attack means something — it means you've been up to your neck in stress. You've kept your asthma under control for years. But now you've bitten off more than you can chew. This attack's just a sign you've been pushing it."

"Unless some changes are made, attacks will become more frequent. cause more damage, with less "bouncing back". Ailments like yours — asthma, ulcers, migraine headaches, and several others are called psychophysiologic problems. They're the result of a scene where people live with massive amounts of stress for a long time. They hang in, take it day after day — like dumb animals. Like you, Sid."

***

Psychophysiologic disorders comprise a group of medical problems that grow out of the "resistance stage" of the GAS. Physiological responses marshalled to combat stressors always impede other normal function to some extent. As the system keeps trying to adapt to the presence of stress, normal function suffers more and more. Problems caused by adaptation responses become medical concerns in their own right — "psychophysiologic disorders" to be exact.

In asthma, for instance, contact with a stressor causes histamines (chemical bodies that attack any foreign substance in the blood) to spread throughout the entire system. It's the action of histamines that cause tissues to swell and become puffy with fluid. When histamines swell tissue, air passages are closed, breathing is impaired.

Psychophysiologic disorders: harmful changes in tissue structure caused by adaptive responses body systems make to the presence of learned stressors.

Psychophysiologic effects can be brief and seldom — but all too often they are long lasting, returning again and again. Once they're chronic, they tend to be more intense and pose a greater threat to health. This happens for two reasons.

First, changes in structure occur when muscles or organs are forced to work in ways they weren't built to work. Sometimes these changes are reversed later — after the stress is gone. But often they can't be reversed — the person's stuck with them for life. With asthma, days, weeks, and months of labored breathing change size and shape of the chest; constant congestion creates an ideal place for germs to grow — colds and other respiratory infections are common. Scar tissues build at involved sites. Ability to breathe is reduced to the point that the patient doesn't have the breath to walk or move about. Even when sitting or lying down, machines are needed to help them get enough air in and out.

Second, learning plays an ever greater role as time and psychophysiologic attacks go on. At first, only unlearned stressors will cause the adaptation response, which in turn causes the psychophysiologic problem. But almost at once, objects or settings that were present when contact with the unlearned stressors was made, become learned stressors. In the future, the body will respond to them as though they were the unlearned stressors they were paired with. They, too, will produce severe psychophysiologic symptoms.

As attacks spiral, the list of learned stressors grows in leaps and bounds. In Sid's case, dust, dander from animal hair, or pollens may comprise the list of unlearned stressors that caused asthma attacks. But after a few attacks, the list of stressors has grown to include many "learned stressors". Now the mere sight of cats or dogs, just sitting on an overstuffed couch, or being near flowers is enough to trigger a full scale asthma attack. Before long, there's nowhere to hide. Stressors — learned or unlearned (it makes no difference) — are all around.

These two features: a change or tearing down of tissue structure that makes them true medical problems; and, the fact that stimuli that were at first "neutral", having only "learned" power to act as a stressor, can trigger an attack, give psychophysiologic disorders their unique status.

Now you see how the notion that problems like asthma, migraine headaches, digestive tract spasms, heart flutters, or other psychophysiologic disorders are "all in the person's head". In the sense that some stimuli that produce these symptoms have only "learned" powers — it's true. On the other hand, there's nothing make believe about the damage to body tissues these attacks foster; the deaths they cause each year. These are all too real.

■21 What are psychophysiologic disorders? Define.

■22 To what stage of the GAS are psychophysiologic disorders related?

■23 Give the sequence of events that produce an asthma attack.

■24 What are the two changes that occur when psychophysiologic attacks become chronic that make them a greater threat to health?

■25 Give some structural changes that can occur with asthma. What is their result in terms of what happens to the sufferer?

■26 Learning plays an ever greater role in psychophysiologic disorders as attacks continue. Explain how this happens.

■27 What are the two features that give psychophysiologic disorders their unique status?

■28 In what way does it make sense to say that psychophysiologic symptoms are "all in a person's head"? In what way is this notion grossly inaccurate?

TYPES OF PSYCHOPHYSIOLOGIC DISORDER

For the most part, it's correct to say that people who get psycho-physiologic problems are those who stick it out — hang-in in the face of stress, whether from learned or unlearned sources. But what controls the type of psychophysiologic disorder that's acquired? These problems can involve any body system. Most common are psychophysiologic disorders of the: 1) skin (rashes, dermatitis, etc.); 2) musculo-skeletal system (backache, muscle cramps, tension headaches, etc.); 3) respiratory system (asthma, bronchitis, etc.); 4) blood and lymph gland systems; 5) cardiovascular system (migraine, hypertension, vascular spasms, etc.); 6) gastrointestinal system (ulcers, colitis, constipation, etc.); 7) genito-urinary system; 8) endocrine system; 9) sensory systems (eyes, ears, balance, etc.).

But why does a person develop one type of disorder as opposed to another, after they have endured enough stress to develop a psycho-physiologic disorder? We're not all that certain of the answer so far. But we do know that once a type of psychophysiologic pattern is settled on, it's the one the person tends to stick with — even in the face of many kinds of learned and unlearned stressors. There seems to be a certain "loyalty" to their special disease. There are many theories that have tried to explain why this occurs.

▪29 Nine systems were mentioned as being commonly involved in psychophysiologic disorders. Name them.

▪30 What does it mean to say that a person tends to be "loyal" to his or her psychophysiologic disorder?

Weak link theory

This theory suggests that the counter-response to stress will affect the system that's weakest. The weakness may appear at birth — or be acquired later through illness. In either event, it is the weakest system, and the target for psychophysiologic disorder. As flare-ups go on, it is weakened further, making it more prone to attack in the future.

▪31 Describe the "weak link theory".

First stress theory

A certain kind of unlearned stressor will attack some organs or systems more than others. The adaptation pattern — and the psycho-physiologic effects produced — are thus controlled by the nature of the stressor. Suppose when Sid was an infant the first full scale stress he came under was caused by allergy — a response to dust. Asthma was the result. In the future when other stressors of any type were present, the same psychophysiologic response was most likely. The response to all stress is somewhat alike, regardless of the stressors that create it. In Sid's case, asthma. Thus, it's the first stressor that controls the kind of psychophysiologic pattern that will occur to all stressors in the future.

■32 Describe the "first stress theory".

Secondary gains theory

Illness often pays off. Let's say that at an early point in a person's life, contact with a stressor causes a psychophysiologic symptom. As suggested above, let's say that the nature of the symptom is controlled by the nature of the stressor. Parents or friends notice the symptom and try to help. In doing so, the person is allowed to get out of school (escape or avoid a scene that's not too pleasant) and also gets more than ample amounts of care, love, and attention — strong rewards. This could set the pattern. When certain types of psychophysiologic symptoms result in big rewards, they're more likely to occur in the future — most likely when the person's involved in a stressful situation.

■33 Describe the "secondary gains theory".

Comparison

These theories are only three of dozens that have been proposed. Those above — or some mixture of them — seem the best bets. When we try to puzzle out why people develop the psychophysiologic disorder they do, we must ask three questions: 1) What caused the first instance of the problem? 2) What maintains the problem — keeps it going? 3) What is the long-term effect of the problem likely to be? The answers to the first two almost always differ — both for a single person, and among people. What first sets up the pattern is rarely the same thing that keeps it going. A safe bet is that stress — either at present or in the past — played a major role. As for the third question — the long-term effects of the problem — the answer is quite clear: unless steps are taken to relieve the problem, only further illness, and perhaps death, will result.

■34 Which theory is the best?
■35 What three questions must be asked in terms of the causes and outcomes of psychophysiologic disorders? What are the answers to these questions?

HANGING IN WITH STRESS

Drugs and liquor

"Look, Sid," Dr. Crawford said, "you've got the facts now. The question is, what are you going to do about your job?"

"Go back, I guess."

"That's smart! That's genius! We'll be seeing you here in bed within a week!"

"No way — I'll take it easy this time."

"When are you going to get it through your thick head that you're not Superman?"

"People get used to things; they adapt. I can get used to it."

"Some things, Sid, you don't get used to. You either get out or they kill you. Look, your folks raised you right; when you make a bargain you try to keep it — that's okay, a good thing most of the time, but now it isn't. It's dumb. Sometimes, Sid, you gotta know how to say, 'Uncle! I give!', and get the hell out!"

Sid shook his head. The idea of quitting was a bitter pill — one he couldn't swallow just yet.

"There's gotta be some other way," he said.

"Sure — how about dope? Drugs? Booze? You could get into that."

* * *

"Come on, Conway," Smitty pleaded, "just ten minutes — that's all. I'll be back before you know it."

"Yeah," Conway sneered. "Then what — you won't do nothin' all night."

"A half-pint, that's all — I swear."

"Forget it," Conway said.

"Let me go — I'm not gonna make it if I don't get a couple 'a snorts — you hear me? I'm tellin' ya!"

Conway looked away from Smitty and sighed. "Go ahead, rummy. Ten minutes."

"Thanks, Conway," Smitty turned to leave.

"Wait," Conway said, reaching into his pocket for some loose bills. "Get me one while you're there — Seagrams — okay?"

"Sure, sure, Conway."

***

Drugs, both legal (nerve pills, pain killers, etc.) and illegal, and alcohol, help to mask the effects of stress. People who use these agents may hang in longer and stay on task although perhaps, at a reduced level of function. As a short-term measure, drugs and alcohol used may be less costly to the person and even to the culture than such things as copping out, or becoming aggressive.

The problem is that drugs do nothing to get rid of other possible reactions to stressors or to soften their long-term effects. Their use makes it less likely that changes in the setting that reduce stress levels will occur. Also, since stress is always present to some degree and in some form or other, many drugs are always going to be big rewards. Drugs and liquor will generalize in their use to other places and settings — even those that most of us would say are not unduly stressful.

■36 How does the use of drugs and liquor help in dealing with a stress situation?

■37 What's wrong with relying on drugs or liquor?

■38 What can be worse than liquor/drug cop-outs?

■39 What is the additional problem with using drugs and liquor in stress situations that stems from the fact that they are reinforcing in their own right?

Coping

"I know what you're saying. It's just that it doesn't seem right. Liquor, drugs — is that all?" Sidney said.

"No, that's not all. There's always a way to cope; ways of changing things that reduce stress. Things like, well, take the dining hall; gadgets to make handling the tables less painful; a more pleasant work setting; fellow workers who aren't bitter, resentful, and mean. But then it may be Conway and the boys are just products of the job. They'd be better if it wasn't such a hard and hopeless place. Yes, there are ways to cope. It could take awhile, though. Is that what you want to do — be the reformer of the BSU food clean up crew?"

"No," Sid said. "That's not what I want to do with my life."

"Good. Then my advice, Sid is, get out. I'll help you get a job you can handle and still make your grades; and needless to say, keep your health as well. The psych people always need bright students to tutor some of the freshmen. It pays well — not quite as much as you're used to."

"That sounds like it might be okay."

"You're still a dope, Sid," Crawford said, as he turned to leave, "but a bright one at least."

***

Stress should not be merely taken as part of a job or setting. There is — and indeed may always be — more stress in any setting than there need be. Taking steps to do away with or reduce the presence of stressors is a job we've all got to assume. But for a given person in a given time and place, "moving on" may be the best means of coping. There's the other side to the story — running away, escaping or avoiding stress by hiding from the world, can become a problem. It, too, can be viewed in a sense as a "disease of adaptation".

■40 What does coping mean in the context of dealing with stress?

Failure

The hall was empty. Conway and the others weren't there to make
fun and yell at him. Freddy passed rows of wooden tables and chairs;
old drinking straws, milk cartons, dirty wadded napkins, pieces of
noodles and other bits and chunks of food were on the floor. How he
hated this job, this filth, these people! Fields — he was okay. But
where was he? He hadn't been there for two nights. Maybe Conway
had fired him. Was he next? Once inside, Freddy turned out the small
light and locked the door. He sat down on the toilet stool, his
trousers intact. It was hot; the sweat popped out on his forehead, but
the dark was soothing. No one could bother him there. "God, God,"
Freddy moaned to himself. "Let me stay here tonight. Don't make
me go out there with Conway and the rest; don't make me lift and
pull and stumble on my own feet! Please!"

There were voices outside. It sounded like Brown and Conway.
Freddy held his breath, he could feel the sweat trickle down his
back into his trousers.

CONCLUSIONS

It goes without saying that we can never truly "win" in our battle
against stress. Sooner or later, bit by bit, it will wear us down. We
will die like our parents and theirs before them — tissue paper beings
in a world of rock and steel. Success at coping is never an all or
nothing thing. Often we're merely trading one type of stress for what
we think will be a weaker, milder form. As we grow smarter both as
individuals and as a culture, we find better stress "bargains" that give
us longer, more healthy, and less stressful lives. Trying to cope is
always a risky business. Sometimes what seems a good bargain — one
that beats stress, for the moment — turns out to merely delay
payment; an overdue note that mounts interest each day. Drugs,
liquor, and "full retreat" as Freddy Severs will find, don't beat stress
at all — they merely mortgage life.

CHAPTER 27
NEUROSES

INTRODUCTION

In the last chapter we learned how long periods of stress can injure health. In this and chapters that follow, we'll find out that some kinds of actions that reduce or get rid of stress create new problems. For instance, running away from stress settings — with little or no regard for where you're running to — can get you in some pretty tough spots. Still, some adopt this form of dealing with stress in a total manner. They are called neurotic. Inept patterns of handling stress take several common forms and are called types of neuroses (singular, neurosis).

Gimmie shelter

Freddy Severs sat on the edge of his chair, in front of him the door marked "M. R. Stein — Clinical Psychologist". The exit door loomed to his left, calling to him. Three or four quick strides and he'd be outside. *What am I doing here? What can these people do for me? They'll ask me a lot of nosey questions about myself — my mother, family, school, sex. Oh no! What if they ask me if I ever played with myself! What would I say then?*

"Mr. Severs." It was the woman — the one who took his name and gave him the forms to fill out. "Dr. Stein will see you now."

Freddy takes a test

Back at her desk, Carol LaPorte typed up a folder from the sheet the man inside had filled out. Severs, Frederick C.; Age: 32; Employed: Dining Hall Crew, Big State University. She took the test booklet and answer sheet out of the file. Dr. Stein always gave new clients the MMPI — The Minnesota Multiphasic Personality Inventory. It was a good test to begin with — that's what Dr. Stein said.

***

"I know there's nothing to be afraid of," Freddy said. "I mean, sometimes, I know it. But that don't matter — I just keep finding more things that bother me. Boy, you don't know how hard it was just to come here."

"Maybe I do, Mr. Severs. In any event, we'll talk more about it on your next visit. Right now I'd like you to take a test."

"A test?" Dr. Stein could see Freddy's body stiffen.

***

"What do the results show, Dr. Stein?"

"Well, see these three points on the profile?" Carol leaned over to see what Dr. Stein was talking about. Three dots were well above the line that read "70". Each dot was above one of three sets of letters — "HS", "HY", and "D". "These three scales make up what's known as the neurotic triad. They tell us, Carol, that our Mr. Severs is most likely a neurotic!"

THE MMPI AND NEUROTICS

A test is a standard group of stimuli — as a rule in the form of questions, problems, etc. — that are given to subjects or clients in a standard way. The MMPI allows for answers made by the client to be compared to those given by people who have needed and received treatment in the past — people who have shown by their actions that they have problems. It is presumed that a person who answers standard questions the same way as a neurotic will behave the same in other ways as well. The fact that Freddy had high scores on the neurotic triad means that he answered these questions the same way as known neurotics. This suggests that Freddy may have some of the same hang-ups and can also be helped by the same kind of treatment.

Minnesota Multiphasic Personality Inventory (MMPI): a psychological test used in mental health settings, designed to indicate the presence of behavior patterns that are likely to cause (or be the current cause of) psychological problems.

- 1 Briefly tell what a psychological test is.
- 2 What do the initials MMPI stand for?
- 3 What comparison does the MMPI allow?
- 4 What is the assumption about the answers of current subjects taking the test and those on whom the test was first constructed?
- 5 What is the practical advantage of this relationship if it holds?

What's a neurotic?

"A neurotic? What does that mean? Seems you hear it so often — I mean, I'm a psych major, or at least I was, and I'm still not sure," Carol said.

"What I mean," Dr. Stein said, "is that the term neurotic is misused a lot. A neurosis is a syndrome — a group or cluster of actions that seem to go with each other. There are about four that define the neurotic syndrome — things neurotics tend to do, or ways they act. The big one, of course, is anxiety."

Syndrome: a group or cluster of behaviors, all or most of which, certain clients or patients tend to exhibit.

Freddy's anxiety attack

Freddy passed by a sign that said, Crosstown Freeway. The highway die-way they called it. Freddy shuddered when he recalled how the cars whizzed by so fast. The big trucks — they were the worst! Great beasts that could crush his small car like a bug! Freddy hadn't been on the freeway in months. It took hours now for him to get across town; taking the side roads, the old routes people used before the freeway was built. Lately even that wasn't safe. It terrified him. Now it was too late — nearly five o'clock, and Friday! Before he could do anything about it, he was in heavy traffic. The choking feeling came, like walls were closing in on him. *God — get me out of here!*

The light changed. Cars were turning in front of him from the left lane. *Hurry, damn it! Hurry cars, before the light changes!* Finally, the last car cleared. *Now!* Freddy stepped on the gas — but nothing happened. The engine had died. Freddy ground the starter. Horns began to blow behind him. He could see angry faces in the rear view mirror. The noise was so bad that he couldn't hear the engine; didn't know if it was catching or not. Just as he got it started, the light changed to red. There was a quiet side-street to his right. The car jumped and jerked around the corner. When he reached the quiet end of the block, Freddy turned off the engine and parked. Sweat fogged his glasses. If his hands would quit shaking he could wipe the lenses. He slumped over, head against the steering wheel; his heart pounded, his breath came in short, stolen gasps.

Anxiety

Anxiety is a complex response that involves conscious feelings, thoughts, and changes in heart beat, sweat glands, and breathing. Shaking or muscle tremors are part of it as well. In some ways it's somewhat like normal fear that any of us might have when we're in danger. But unlike fear, it occurs in places or with things that can't do any real harm to anyone. Often, the neurotic seems to carry it with her/him as a constant partner. In such cases, it is called "free-floating anxiety".

   Freddy is having an anxiety attack — a very severe siege of anxiety. Such sieges are common for him. But then, as you will see later, anxiety is the major symptom in Freddy's type of neurosis. For other kinds of neurotics, anxiety is not so pronounced. It's always there to some extent, and is the prime defining factor for all neuroses.

Anxiety: complex response involving irregularities in heart, blood vessel, gland, and muscle actions. Thoughts or feelings of being afraid may be, but are not always, present.

Free-floating anxiety: persisting anxiety that is not tied to a specific setting or object; it often takes the form of lingering thoughts or feelings that something bad is about to happen.

- 6 Roughly define a syndrome.
- 7 Why are neuroses called a syndrome?
- 8 What is the first and major factor that defines neurosis?
- 9 What is anxiety in terms of physiological responses and its relation to normal fear?
- 10 What is anxiety called that doesn't seem to be related to any specific place or thing?

Freddy beats Freddy again

"Anxiety," Carol said. "Yes, I could see that Mr. Severs seemed scared of something — but then a lot of people get uptight when they're waiting to see a doctor."

"Quite true. We all get that way from time to time — but for Mr. Severs, I'm afraid it's a way of life."

"But why is he worse that way than the rest of us? Was he born that way?"

"Could be. More than likely, he wasn't though. He learned it. You see, the real answer has to do with what neurotics do about it when they're afraid — as compared to, say — well, you, for instance. And that's really the second feature of the neurotic."

"What's that?" Carol asked.

"It's called 'self-defeating behavior'."

* * *

Freddy locked the car. He would leave it for the time being. There was still too much traffic. But when would he get it back? He could think about that later. He looked at his watch — only thirty minutes to make it to work. He could get a taxi. But the idea scared him — riding in a car with a strange driver. He didn't trust taxi drivers anyway — they talked rough; mean — like Conway and Brown. He could walk, but he'd be late. What would Conway say then? No, he couldn't face that. He just wouldn't go to work. People get sick don't they? How could Conway know if he was really sick or not?

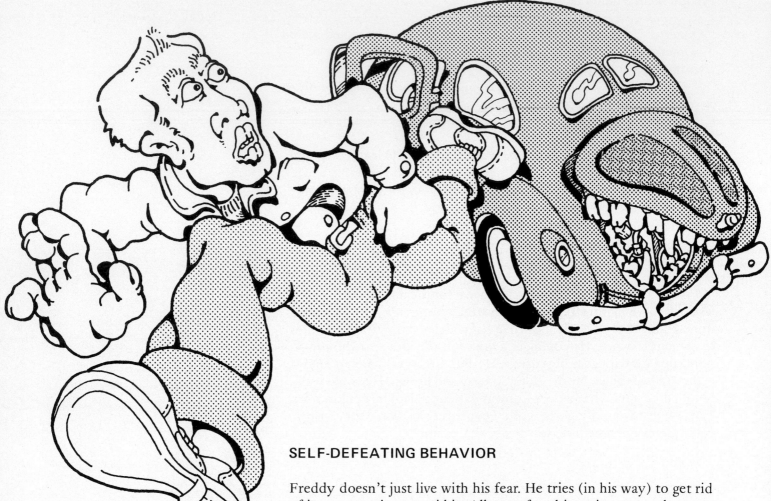

SELF-DEFEATING BEHAVIOR

Freddy doesn't just live with his fear. He tries (in his way) to get rid of it — escape it, or avoid it. All too often his actions are only stop gap. They just postpone the threat. He takes the path that's most handy. Such action leads to worse problems and fear in the future — it is self-defeating.

Neurotics are their own worst enemies. They make new troubles and cause greater upset by using halfway measures in dealing with a problem. They never solve a thing — just push the moment to settle-up out of the way for a time. But it always comes back — often with a vengeance!

We've all been rightly accused of putting off things until tomorrow, taking the easy way out, not facing the music — but for the neurotic, it's always that way. Give Freddy enough time and he'll do himself in — "self-defeating behavior".

Self-defeating behavior: part of the neurotic syndrome; using inadequate measures to deal with problems, thus merely postponing consequences and often making them worse.

■11 What is the second important factor that defines neurosis?

Avoidance

A new problem often calls for a new approach. To escape a problem by going elsewhere; to deny it, act like it isn't there; to take the bull by the horns in a frontal assault and with open aggression; or to just bring things out into the open and laugh about it — these are just a few ways of dealing with problems. Neurotics try to solve all of theirs in the same way — most often to escape or avoid them in the quickest and least stressful manner; something that's worked in the past. They are loyal to a tried and true technique. The same fear that makes them run in the first place, keeps them from taking a chance on new ways of solving conflicts. In this sense, drunks, junkies, and bullies are neurotic. They, too, are locked in on one way of dealing with the world.

■12 What is the third important type of action that defines neurosis?
■13 In what sense are drunks, junkies, and bullies like the neurotic?

Social reinforcers

"Poor Mr. Severs," Carol said. "He seems such a sad man. No, not quite that — harrassed, that's it. Does he have to be that way?"

"Yes, I'm afraid neurotics are in some state of turmoil most of the time. But that doesn't rule out social reward. They get pity, attention, a lot of "good strokes" as a result of their problems. As a matter of fact, I guess they're a real proof for the old saying, 'It's an ill wind that blows no good fortune'."

"You mean they like being the way they are?"

"No, not at all — but it does pay off from time to time. People feel sorry for them; want to help. It's a poor excuse for respect or for love — but then you can't be neurotic and have it all."

***

Most of the neurotics' actions are to free themselves from a threat. They look at life in terms of getting away or staying away from bad scenes. When they aggress it is to remove a person or thing that could, by some logic, harm them; maybe by causing them to lose what they have. The other side of the coin is also worth looking into. It's also true that much of what they do and say gets them help and comfort from others. A lot of the "woe is me" talk is likely to find people of mercy who respond to it. But they fail even here. People get tired of their sad talk and begin to avoid them — score a new loss and add something more to worry and fret about.

■14 What does the saying, "It's an ill wind that blows no good fortune", mean? And how does it relate to the neurotic's behavior?
■15 How do the neurotic's efforts in getting social reinforcers finally fail?

KINDS OF NEUROSES

So there you have it — the neurotic — a mixture of these things: anxiety, self-defeating behavior, a rigid, hung-up way of trying to solve problems. And then you can add in the social reward they get for failing: for bad talk and self-put-downs.

"But there are other kinds of neurotics aren't there?"

Yes, there are eight patterns of neuroses that stand out.

enough to get a special label. We'll deal with the hysterical and hypochondriacal neuroses at some length, and then mention the others briefly.

Juke gets a break

"Juke! Hey, Juke! Cummere! Look, Juke," Coach Krub said. "You're only a freshman, but I'm goin' ta give you a break. How'd you like to be on the specialty team — punt returns — the deep slot?"

"Like it? Come on man, yeah, I'd like it! But, what happened to Moss?"

"Who? Uh, Moss . . . Yeah, injured — got a bad muscle tear."

Juke was puzzled by what he saw on the coach's face.

***

"Hey, Red. What happened to Moss?" Juke asked the big tackle later.

"Wudda ya mean?" Red said, squirting a mouthful of water back into the fountain.

"I mean he ain't gonna be doin' punt returns."

"Yeah? Come to think about it, I kinda don't blame him. Did you check out what happened last week against Duke? They high-lowed 'im — damn near broke him in two — old Moss got his bell rung good."

"No stuff?"

"Damn sure did."

***

Juke found Moss sitting in the whirlpool after practice. "How's the leg, Moss?"

"Oh, hi there, Juke. Doin' okay — just okay."

"Say, Moss. Coach asked me to run back punts in your place — that cool by you?"

"Sure, Juke. 'At's the way it

gotta be, I guess. Someone's gotta do it. I sure wish I could do it — man, I'd give anything. Leg won't let me do it though — plain as that. Look here." Moss lifted his big hulk out of the whirlpool and stood up. He took two steps before his leg buckled. His hip and thigh slapped like thunder as he dropped against the concrete floor.

"Hey, man! Cool it!" Juke rushed to help him up. "I can see your leg's gone out!"

"Yeah. Nothin' I can do about it. Piss! Sure wish it was gonna be me out there runnin' 'em back Saturday."

Juke looked at Moss's solemn blue eyes, blinking back tears. "Me too," Juke said. "Me too." Juke meant what he said.

Hysterical neurosis

Hysterical neurotics seem to have less turmoil and upset than others. They have found an escape that really works — a cop-out that gets them out of a whole bad scene such as a job, challenge; even a life! Yes, in one form of this response, people bag it — leave loved ones, jobs, bills, in-laws. They just seem to forget

the whole mess. The disassociative hysteric type of hysterical neurotic, as they're labeled, may go to a new town, take on a new name, and start a new life, failing to recall all details of the past. After awhile — could be when things get too hot in the new life — they may go back to their first

life. Their recall returned, they will be at a loss to explain their absence.

Hysterical neurosis: a type of neurosis where stress settings or problems are escaped or avoided by loss of memory or the development of physical dysfunction.

Other cases are less extreme; only chunks of time are wiped out. As you might guess, things that took place during these lost periods of time are things they didn't or don't want to deal with. They get away with it since in our culture we blame people less for what they did if they can't recall it or didn't "know what they were doing". Public and self-blame is lessened if not avoided all together. Some learn to deal with problems this way even as children. They forget things they don't want to handle as though they don't exist.

Disassociative type: one of the two types of hysterical neuroses, in which the person develops loss of memory, in some cases even to

the point of forgetting who he or she is. In other cases only selective blocks, or chunks, of time are forgotten.

In the second form of the hysterical neurosis, people become blind, deaf, lose feeling in arms or legs; they become paralyzed, or find they can't walk or move head or limbs. This is called the conversion type of hysterical neurosis. You can see that these ailments would be cause to let someone miss work, renege on a duty, or cop out. It's a good ploy — it lets the person get out of some tough job or task, but still save face.

Is Moss's bum leg a type of conversion hysteria? We can't say. Both Juke and the coach seem

to think there's something funny going on. One thing's for sure, Moss isn't faking it. He believes there's something wrong with his leg. He may be fooling others, but he's fooling himself as well — so it is with the hysterical neurotics. They're not faking. The disassociative person really can't remember; the conversion person really can't make arms, legs, eyes or ears perform.

Conversion type: a type of hysterical neurosis where the sufferer develops loss of movement of various parts of the body, or loss of sensitivity or total function of eyes, ears, skin, or other sense organs.

Dr. Stein says that the hysterical neurotic is a dying breed. What she means by this is that this type of problem isn't as common as it used to be. Why? We don't know for sure, but it's a good bet that it has something to do with the fact that people know more about how their bodies work than they used to. Hysteric symptoms are a little too hokey for today's hip patients to adopt.

■16 What type of neurotic seems to have less turmoil and upset than others? Why is this so?

■17 There are two types of hysterical neuroses. What are they?

■18 Briefly describe the pattern of the disassociative hysteric.

■19 What reason is given for the hysteric's forgetting the past? What cultural factors make forgetting a good cop-out?

■20 Briefly define what physical problems the conversion hysteric is likely to have.

■21 How is the conversion hysteric neurotic different from someone who is just playing sick?

■22 The hysterical neurotic is a dying breed. What does this statement mean?

Oh dad, poor dad

Oooooooohhh — my liver, my life, my legs, my lungs! They're failin'
me! They're failin' me! My heart is sad, my breath is bad, and I think
I'm goin' crazy!

The Hypochondriac Song (traditional)

"Hi, Dad."

"Dawn! There you are! Come here, give your old dad a kiss."

"Dad, what are you doing in town? Why are you here? Is something wrong?"

"Oh no . . . nothing, nothing to worry your pretty head about . . . It's only . . . I . . ."

"Dad — you're crying! What's wrong?"

"It's my health, dear. Your old dad's not too well. The old heart, I'm afraid."

"But what about the tests at Mayo's last year — surely they would've found it if anything was wrong."

"At that time we all thought the problem was my liver — of course, that's where they all looked. They missed it."

"But, if there was something really bad . . ."

"Dawn, if it should go bad, well . . . I just want you to know how much . . ."

"Dad, it's going to be okay — you'll see."

"That's my little Dawn — always the bright side. Yes, that's my Dawn, all right! That's right darlin', life's for the living — for the young. Enjoy it; for when it goes, well . . ."

"Dad!"

"I'm sorry, honey. I just can't help the tears."

Hypochondriacal neurosis

All people who seem unduly worried about their bodies aren't always neurotics. There's a wide range in the amount of time and worry each of us allots to her or his health, some too much, others far too little. Don't forget that neurosis is a way of life. The factors we spoke of earlier (anxiety; self-defeating behavior, etc.) are strongly at work. For the hypochondriac they all happen to pivot around concern for health. These people are as a rule very bright, and do a lot of reading; most of it about disease. (There's a joke about one who died of a misprint!) The social reward from those — nurses, doctors, friends — who hear their tale of woe plays a bigger role in this type of neurosis than in most others.

Hypochondriacal neurosis: form of neurosis where anxiety revolves around an often remarkable knowledge of medical symptoms, and the persistent belief that the person's symptoms are a sure sign of various diseases.

- ▪23 There is reason to believe that Dawn's father is a neurotic. What kind would he be called?
- ▪24 There's a joke about the hypochondriac who died of a misprint. Why is this joke relevant?
- ▪25 Why is positive social reinforcement more of a factor in hypochondriacal neurosis than in other kinds?

Other types of neuroses

Unlike those with more severe psychological problems, neurotics know enough to know that something's wrong — that they're not making out too well in life. Just what the problem is and how they might solve it — well, that part eludes them. Though able to function quite well at times, they're far from having things together. The strange thoughts and actions neurotics may engage in are many and often quite bizarre, as we've seen. Let's look at some other types of neuroses.

Phobic neurosis

Anxiety is again the chief symptom with this problem; a very focal kind of anxiety that's triggered by a certain object or situation. Phobic neurotics are for the most part aware of what they're afraid of, and that they have no reason to fear what's really a quite harmless stimulus setting or object, but this insight doesn't lessen the fear. These people will move heaven and earth in trying to steer clear of the dreaded phobic stimulus. In taking such absurd escape and avoidance meaures, they show the other neurotic symptoms such as self-defeating behavior, etc., that were discussed in a prior section. Some common phobic or fear objects and settings for phobic neurotics are closed places, water, and height. These objects are given a Greek prefix which is placed before the word "phobia", making words like claustrophobia, aquaphobia, acrophobia, etc.

Phobic neurosis: neurosis where acute anxiety occurs when the person makes contact with the "phobic" stimulus — a harmless object or setting that triggers the anxiety.

Depressive neurosis

This type of neurotic seems to have a great knack for finding something to be sad about. Sometimes there's a "reason" of sorts — the person cites some recent personal loss or problem. Often the sadness descends from nowhere; the person is at a loss to tell why he or she should be depressed. In other cases, the down comes when something — girl or boy-friend, cherished golf club, wallet or purse — is lost. These are losses that none of us would relish, but we would surely shrug it off after awhile. The neurotic drags it out for weeks, months, even years. It's this feature that brands the depressive neurotic.

Depressive neurosis: type of neurosis characterized by excessive or drawn-out depression under circumstances that don't warrant such a response.

Depersonalization neurosis

Feeling out of it — like we don't belong, don't know what's going on — isn't a rare thing anymore. These feelings come and go and are normal. Depersonalized neurotics are a different case. They complain of a more or less constant feeling of being detached or divorced from the real world.

Their homes, friends, surroundings — even their own bodies or faces — seem strange or foreign to them. Anxiety results. They worry about these strange feelings, settling into a constant, nagging, blanket of fear.

Depersonalization neurosis: neurosis whose main component is a near constant feeling of unreality or apartness.

Neurasthenic neurosis

Those who suffer from this neurosis complain of being tired, fatigued, spent — as though they'd just finished a twenty-mile hike. The neurasthenic differs from the conversion type of hysterical neurotic who may also complain about weakness or tiredness. Hysterics accept it all with little or no anxiety. Neurasthenics are distressed, anxious and baffled over why they feel so puny.

Neurasthenic neurosis: neurosis where the primary complaint involves feelings of tiredness or fatigue that have no medical basis for occurring.

Obsessive-compulsive neurosis

Obsessions — thoughts that intrude to disturb and alarm by their nature and frequency; and compulsions — pointless actions that the person can't seem to stop; make up the two features that describe obsessive-compulsive neurosis. Sometimes the compulsive act occurs without obsessive thoughts, the doer only seldom aware that she or he is doing it. Obsessions that don't end in deeds — thinking about doing something that you don't do — such as suicide, leaving your mate, quitting your job — also occur. Often, obsessive-compulsive pairs are closely tied. Near constant fearful thoughts about dirt or germs, and compulsive hand-washing, is an example. As with all neuroses, anxiety plays a major role. Compulsive actions seem to reduce anxiety.

Obsessive-compulsive neurosis: a type of neurosis characterized by highly frequent thoughts and/or actions that the person can't seem to control.

▪26 There are eight types of neuroses. What are the five types of neuroses that were described in the previous section? Briefly describe each of them.

▪27 Hypochondriacal neurosis revolves around notions of body malfunction. What other two neuroses have this theme?

▪28 What are obsessions? Compulsions?

▪29 Does each compulsion have an obsession? Can they occur separately? Discuss.

ANXIETY NEUROSIS

Whatever happened to Freddy?

"Whatta you say, college boy?" Smitty said.

"How're ya feelin'?" Conway asked.

"Still a little weak, but okay."

"I guess you're lookin' for this." Conway handed Sid his check.

"Thanks. Sorry I didn't work out too well — I mean, I know it takes time to train people and all that."

"Forget it. Don't blame you for gettin' the hell out."

"Fuggin'-'a'," Smitty said.

"Hey," Sid said, looking around, "where's Freddy?"

"Beats me," Conway said. "Hasn't been here for two weeks. One night he just didn't show."

"Probably got locked-up in a crapper somewhere. Ha! Ha!" Smitty said.

***

"Carol, did Mr. Severs show today? No? How many has he missed now? Three, huh? Thanks. *Poor alone, afraid Mr. Severs,* Dr. Stein thought. *Where is he now? What's he doing?* Dr. Stein pulled a folder from her desk and opened it. The top sheets of a sheaf of papers read:

Anxiety Neurosis — Notes: *The anxiety neurotic's problem is one of learning too well to tune-in to signs of anxiety or fear. He or she becomes an expert at picking up the faintest body sign — drop of sweat, muscle twitch, pulse, breath — that may give cause to escape, avoid, to run! To get away from 'it'. But what is 'it'? Of what is he or she most deathly afraid? Fear itself. It is fear of fear.*

At this same instant in a rooming house on the other side of town, another author is also at work. Shaking hands pull a notebook from a dresser drawer. There is a title printed in block letters on the cover:

THE JOURNAL OF FREDERICK C. SEVERS — HIS LIFE

Tuesday, December 10: Today is the tenth day that I have not left the third floor of Mrs. Coats' boarding house. I live on the third floor. I have, in fact, not left my room except to go to the bathroom. I share it (the bathroom) with Mr. Donlee who works nights for the railroad, I believe. Sometimes the man who lives downstairs (I don't know his name) uses my bathroom. One day he almost pulled the lock out of the eye when I was in there. I thought my heart would never stop pounding. Oh, God, why doesn't he stay down there where he belongs? It isn't fair! I still have the dozen cans of Spam left and about as many cans of pork and beans. There are a few cans of other things, too. I ate the last of the canned peaches. They sure were good.

Picking up on anxiety cues:
Like all of us, the anxiety neurotic is subject to changes in body states that result from past punishment episodes. These body states occur when the subject comes in contact with a setting similar to the one where he/she was punished in the past.
Example: changes in heart rate, breathing, sweating when a student has to give a speech in front of the class. The student has been made fun of or criticized for speaking to groups before. The student becomes aware of these body signs. So does the anxiety neurotic.

Normal coping: *But what happens? Most of us go through with it — give the speech anyway. The next time we aren't so afraid. The body cues aren't so pronounced. Note: The fear cues are extinguished.*

Neurotic avoidance: *Neurotics don't cope. Instead, they make an escape-avoidance response, i.e., they cop out. In the example of the speech, they beg off, play sick, or get out of it some way.*

Wednesday, December 11: I thought I would die today! He walked right in on me. I was sure the door was locked — but no, bam, in he came. "Sorry," he said — that was all. But he didn't look very sorry. I've decided; from now on I'll only go at night. The rest of the time I'll just hold it.

Thursday, December 12: Today I watched TV all day. I didn't have to go at all, but I'm afraid for the morning. It's always worse then. Someone came to my door and listened outside it today. I think it was the landlady. I hope she doesn't start up on me again like she used to.

Friday, December 13: Mrs. Coats came to my door again. She called my name twice. I didn't say anything and she went away. I relieved myself in the wash basin. I hope I don't have to do anything else. Today's Friday the 13th!

Reinforced avoidance behavior: *Since the cop-out gets the person out of a tight spot, copping-out is reinforced. The person's more likely to cop out in the future.*

Lowered threshold: *Here's the catch — picking up on body signs was the signal the neurotic used to make an escape/avoidance response. He/she copped out; this reinforced copping-out; it also lowered the level at which body cues will have to occur to be detected in the future — thus, the threshold is lowered. It takes less upset to make him/her run.*

The cycle:
1. *Pick up on anxiety cues.*
2. *Cop out.*
3. *Reinforces cop-out, lowers threshold at which body cues can be detected.*
4. *Detected at a lower level in the future.*
5. *More likely to cop out, etc.*

Role of thoughts: *What does thinking have to do with anxiety neurosis? Thoughts of fear or being afraid, act like a goad; act as a stimulant on body function. They become more afraid because they think they're going to get afraid. Thus thoughts feed into cycle; increase heart rate, blood pressure, etc.*

Saturday, December 14: I did it today. I had to use a shoe box.

Sunday, December 15: Mrs. Coats called outside my door again. She left and came back with someone. I think it was Mr. Donlee. I heard them talking outside about me. I wish they'd go away for good.

Monday, December 16: It's a blue Monday. Mrs. Coats pounded on my door. She said that if I didn't open it she'd go get the police — then she went away.

The anxiety neurotic

Anxiety neurosis is in some ways the purest form of neurosis; it is also the hardest to deal with for both patient and therapist. When you ask them what's wrong, anxiety neurotics may complain of quite specific fears — things like close places, high buildings, airplanes. Thus, they appear at first blush to have a simple phobia — a strange fear of a harmless thing or place. Then it gets more complex. As you learn more you find they're not only afraid of high buildings, closed places, bugs, but a thousand other things as well — and each day the list grows.

Their pattern is to escape, to cut and run; avoid all situations, people, places that cause them anxiety. The problem is that this works — it does reduce anxiety — as a short-term measure at least. It also has the harmful side-effect of making escape and avoidance more likely to occur and at a lower level of anxiety in the future. In running, the anxiety neurotic becomes more afraid, more prone to run again. As if they didn't have it bad enough, they then use free time they've gained through copping-out to think up new things to fear.

As with other forms of neurosis, thoughts play a big role in making anxiety worse and causing a "vicious cycle". Thoughts spur physical changes such as increased heart beat and blood pressure. This in turn causes other changes such as sweating and nervous shaking. The person becomes aware of these changes which gives rise to more thoughts and panic, goading internal actions to a still higher level.

What happens to anxiety neurotics? It depends. If they're lucky they'll get into a situation where they can't run; where they must try to cope. If this happens often enough, they're on their way back. Sadly, for some it never happens. Like Freddy Severs, they end up alone, wretched, and afraid. A total retreat from life.

Anxiety neurosis: a type of neurosis characterized by massive anxiety that seems to become attached to an ever-increasing number of things and settings.

"Not bad," Dr. Stein said. "These notes make pretty good sense. Pity poor anxiety neurotics, caught in a trap of their own design. God what a life! To run because you're scared, only to be more scared the next time — and why? Because you run!"

***

Freddy Severs crouched in the closet. He could hear the strange voices outside.

They were beating down the door.

■31 What type of neurotic pattern can we assume Freddy Severs has adopted?

■32 The anxiety neurotic has fear of fear. What does that mean?

■33 What do the anxiety neurotics pick up on that's their cue to run away?

■34 Normal people also pick up on these cues. How does their response to them differ from the neurotic's? Why does it work out better for them?

■35 Two things happen when the anxiety neurotic cops out in a tight spot. What are they?

■36 What is a lowered threshold?

■37 Give the cycle that characterizes the anxiety neurotic's behavior.

CONCLUSIONS

Old neurotics never die, they just . . . What? "Limp along", I guess. Unless they receive some fairly intense therapy they're doomed to spend their years on the fitful edge of life. As they get older they become merely older neurotics. The neurotic actions we spoke of don't go away on their own. They're too well learned; they do work — after a fashion. Still, most neurotics make it — survive. But some don't.

The old myth has it that the state of neurotics might wax and wane — sometimes better, sometimes worse — but they somehow always pulled it out in the final reel; rallied and survived. We know better now. Some neurotics get worse each year, consumed and beaten down by their mistakes, cop-outs, fretful worry and upset. Neurotics can become psychotic, be removed from the outside world and placed in the structured confines of the state hospital or asylum. Freddy Severs is on that threshold now.

CHAPTER 28
BEHAVIOR PROBLEMS

INTRODUCTION

If you've not studied psychology before now you've likely made the common error of calling anyone who behaved strangely from time to time a "neurotic". After reading the last chapter you now know that neurosis is in some sense "a way of life". It pervades almost all contacts the neurotic has with the world and its challenge.

The label, "neurotic", should not be applied lightly. But people do act "strange", have odd ways of acting and talking that, while not a large part of their behavior, are so bizarre that they evoke great comment. What then do we call these people if not neurotic? What label is applied? Since the actions in question are only a small part of total behavior, we don't label the people. We label the actions that cause these people and others trouble, evoke scorn, and raise eyebrows. We call these actions "behavior problems". We will deal with their origin and nature now.

PRODUCTION DEFECT OR BEHAVIOR PROBLEM?

He was large for fourteen — big boned, solid, not an ounce of fat on him. The scene changed to a close-up of his fists — strong, wedge-shaped, thin at the wrists, scarred knuckles, bluish-red and white flesh grown back in a mottled design. Two foreign hands came into the scene. They took off the white web belts that held his wrists down against the arms of the chair. His hands were free now, as the camera pulled back to give a full view of the action. He moved his fingers, then ever so slightly his hands. A strange look came on his face. Then — wham! The sound told the whole story. His right fist flew into the air and came to roost soundly on the right side of his head and ear. Wham! Now the left fist. Wham! The right again. Wham! Wham! Wham! Wham! Wham!

"Sweet Jesus!" Juke said.

"Oh no!" Dawn hid her face with her book. Sid and Chet looked on, deathly quiet, eyes blinking at the swift action flashing from the screen.

* * *

"He was slow — had some kind of mental defect. That's all. No big deal," Chet said.

"You talk like he was some kind of . . . of . . . 'thing' — didn't you see his face? He was pleading — pleading for help." Dawn was still trembling from the movie they'd seen in psych class a short time before.

"I don't know about any a' that," Juke said. "But what the boy was doin' sure ain't natural. The dude doin' the talkin' said he was already blind from it — knocked the retinas loose from the back a' his eyeballs."

"He said there was a lot of brain damage, too. All of it from the blows," Sid said.

"So he's crazy! A retard; nuts — it's all the same. The thing is, he's not playin' with a full deck."

"That's not very funny, Chet!" Dawn said. "I don't care what you say. I think he was trying to tell us something — trying to . . . reach out."

"Haw!"

"Dawn's right; there's more to it than that," Sid said.

"You two are somethin' else! Tryin' to reach out — come on! Look, sometimes you pick up the paper and you read where Ford or GM screwed up — turned out a bunch a' cars that didn't have the right parts. So they call 'em all back in and put the right parts in. Well, they don't know how to do that with people yet. The kid in the movie isn't right, that's all. If he was he wouldn't do such nutty things. No person in his right mind is gonna keep doin' things that hurt his chances to survive. It goes against all laws of human nature."

"But . . ."

"Right on!" Juke said.

"I don't know," Sid scratched his head.

* * *

Common sense tells us that there can be people with bad or missing parts — just like cars or TVs. We know that cars won't perform right if they're not "all there". Chet reasons that what's true of cars must be true of people. When people don't act right, they too must have missing or faulty parts.

Chet's logic is bad. Though people with missing parts may act strange — it doesn't follow that all people who act strange have missing parts. A lot of data show we don't have to look inside to account for this "crazy" behavior — doing things that hurt our bodies, cause us pain, make it tough to get along with others — we learn these strange acts just as we learn anything else. Learned acts that cause us this kind of trouble are called behavior problems. Anyone can pick them up — Dawn, Sid, Juke, and yes, Chet, even you.

Behavior problems: learned patterns of behavior that produce results harmful to the person or make him or her unacceptable to society.

- 1 Outline what may be called the "missing parts" theory of "crazy" behavior.
- 2 How do behavior problems originate?

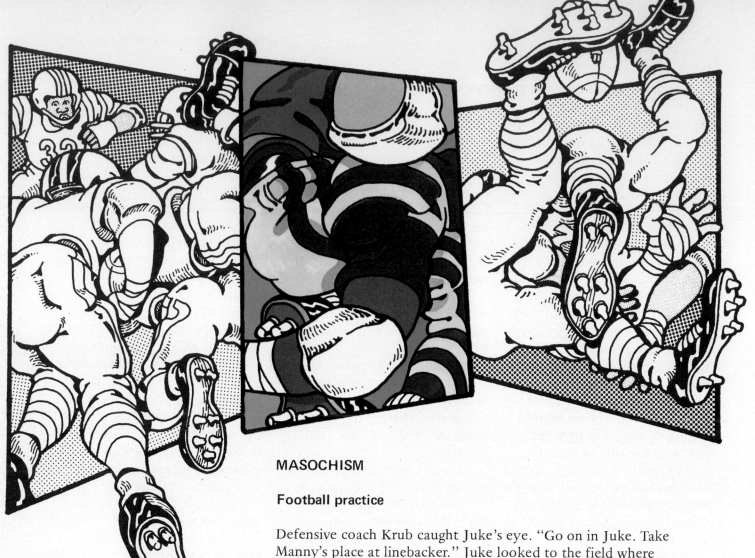

MASOCHISM

Football practice

Defensive coach Krub caught Juke's eye. "Go on in Juke. Take Manny's place at linebacker." Juke looked to the field where scrimmage was in progress, then back to Coach Krub, a puzzled look on his face.

"But that's defense, Coach."

"Tell me about it. Get humpin'! 'Bout time you big offense stars found out where the game's really played."

"Right," Juke put on his helmet and sprinted in. "I got it, Manny," he said to the player he replaced. The blue team broke huddle. It was only a practice scrimmage, but the blues acted like it was the Super Bowl. Tubbs, the 230-pound blue fullback, came barreling dead at him — the ball tucked in his middle.

"Sweet Jesus," Juke mumbled. He took two quick steps, arched his back and lunged forward to meet Tubbs head on. Juke grunted — that's all he could be sure of. The rest was sheer pain; flailing arms, a thousand knees, lumps of plastic pads and bone, all in an eyeblink.

"Way ta' go, Juke baby!" Hands were grabbing him under the pads, pulling him to his feet.

"Nice goin'." Clark patted Juke on the rump.

"Man, you cooled that honky out," Burski said. "Dropped him like a load a' dead beef!"

"Yeah? Yeah!" Juke said and smiled. He looked at his arms and

legs, rubbing them, half expecting them to be gone. He was still numb; a thousand bones could be broken for all he knew. His head throbbed beneath his helmet. The blue team broke huddle.

"Come on!" Burski yelled at them. "Me and old Juke's got a little somethin' for you!"

"Come an' get it — Poppa's waitin'," Juke heard himself say. A chill went up his back. He felt great. *Maybe Coach Krub was right — defense, that's where it's at.*

Analysis

"People work to get as much pleasure and as little pain as they can." That's the way it's taught. That's "human nature" — at least as far as many believe. Only it isn't always that way.

For a long time now writers have talked about people who seemed to like things that harmed their bodies; things that others wouldn't touch with a ten-foot pole, because they caused so much pain. They called these people masochists.

Masochism: condition where stimulus contact that others experience as painful and work to avoid, becomes a learned reinforcer for a particular person.

They also made the point that they were pretty screwed up. Sometimes, like Chet, they said these poor souls acted that way because of "something missing" or "bad parts".

Today we know better. Research has shown us how almost anyone can get to like anything — that is, it can get to be a reward for them. How? Well, Juke's on his way. Let's look at what's going on. Juke gets in front of Tubbs. Juke gets clobbered. Does it hurt? Does his head chime? Does he feel like a Mack truck just did a number on him? You can bite your bullet, and believe he does. So that's fun?

But let's see what else happens. **Juke makes a big play. He gets the job done.** As a result, his team says, "Good goin', Juke." His coach says, "That's heads up, Juke." Juke looks in the mirror and says, "Hey, you're one tough fella." It's social reward at work. So thus far here's how it goes. Clobbered———⟶ Reward. So, we can expect being clobbered, the pain, etc. will get to be a cue for social reward. In the future Juke may really dig getting clobbered as long as it's often followed by social rewards.

Big and little guys

Little guy: Okay. That's okay for you big guys. You can play football. When you get hit it doesn't hurt you like it does me. I'm just a little guy.

Big guy: That's bull. I get just as many lumps as you — more even. You'd know that if you studied physics. Size's got nothing to do with it.

Little guy: That don't add up. If it hurt you like it does me, you'd quit. You'd join the Skittle Bowl team like me.

Big guy: You're missin' it. It's not what we both get, which is lumps. It's what I get that you don't get.

Little guy: You mean?

Big guy: That's right. Social rewards. I'm big enough to push the other guys outta the way, and make those TD's. I get the roar of the crowd. . .

Little guy: The siss, the boom. . .

Big guy: and the bah. Don't forget that, runt. Since you're puny, you don't succeed; ergo, no sis, no boom. . .

Little guy: No bah?

Big guy: I'm afraid not. Since your lumps never lead to rewards they don't get to be cues for reward.

Little guy: So that's why I don't like it when I'm creamed by a 280-pound tackle, why I found it less than wholesome? I always knew there was a good reason I didn't like being torn limb from limb!

Big guy: Oh yes. I, on the other hand, adore it. Oh bliss!

Little guy: Gee. That puts it in a new light. Say — is there anything I can do for you?

Big guy: Well — if you have any big friends. . .

***

Say little guy, don't give up so soon. You, too, can become a contact crunch freak — be hooked on pain. Don't forget; in our culture, a small guy who makes it in a "big guy" jock scene is likely to get even more social reward. Why? Because he's a small guy! "Gosh, he's only 97 pounds, but all of it tiger! What spirit! What pluck!" What b.s.

- 3 Define masochism.
- 4 The fact that humans tend to do all they can to reduce contact with painful stimuli and try to increase contact with stimuli that feel good, has been called h_____ n_____.
- 5 What is a person called who seems to defy his/her "human nature" in terms of seeking out painful stimuli?
- 6 What did early writers give as a reason for the masochist's behavior?
- 7 What is the modern position on the cause of masochism?
- 8 Outline how usually painful stimuli become rewards.
- 9 What will make painful stimulation remain a powerful reward?
- 10 Big guys don't get injured as badly from a tackle as a little guy would. Support or reject this notion.
- 11 What is the primary reason that painful stimulation is more likely to become a reward for a big guy than for a little guy?

SELF-ABUSE AND SOCIAL REINFORCEMENT

Let's return to the boy in the psych movie. Does he beat himself because of the "bad parts" theory of Chet's; or, did he learn to do this? There is no direct link between retardation and self-abuse, although most children who exhibit this type of behavior are retarded (they test out with below normal I.Q.s). More than likely the child learned to "like" hitting himself the same way Juke or his jock crowd learns to enjoy the crunch of contact on the field. It got him a lot of social rewards. Let's have an instant replay, and you'll see for yourself.

Replay: How James Smith learned self-abuse

James, age 18 months — scene: clinic.
M.D.:   Mrs. Smith, I know you're worried about James. He's just learning to walk, and speech isn't coming as fast as it should. I'm afraid you have to steel yourself for the future. The truth is, James may never be normal.

James, a few weeks later — scene: home.
Mr. Smith: Gosh Ruth, you can't be with Jimmy all the time. Don't worry so much about him. Let him do a few things on his own. At least let him try.
Mrs. Smith: Bill! How can you talk like that? You know he's . . . do I have to say it? Look, now you've made him cry! There, there Jimmy, it's all right.

James, some months later — scene: home.
Mrs. Smith: There, Jimmy. You play with your blocks while I clean the rug. I'll be right back. Jimmy! Jimmy! What are you doing? You shouldn't hit against your head like that. You could hurt yourself. Here, come on. I'll just take you with me. I can carry you and run the vacuum cleaner too, I guess. You do love your mommy, don't you!

James, a year later — scene: home.
Mrs. Smith: I'm sorry, Bill, I just can't go. Who'd look after Jimmy?
Mr. Smith: But Ruth. You have to go. We can get a sitter — one of the college kids. You know, an older one.
Mrs. Smith: Oh, Bill — we can't take a chance. Suppose he'd get one of his spells. If the sitter was just the least bit . . . why, Bill, we could come home and find Jimmy a mass of blood — maybe even dead! No, Bill, you go without me.

***

There you have it. Jim's self-abuse leads to his mother's doting presence. She's right on the spot, giving out these warm social rewards. Later on, after they put Jim in the state home, Jim's actions will result in the same kind of attention from a nurse or ward person. Jim's only trick will be to hit himself. He will have done it for so long, it will have paid off so well in social reward that by that time we can say that if Jim likes to do anything, he'll like to hit himself. He'll be a real masochist, and may soon be a dead one.

Of course, all kids — even normal ones — have times when they may hit themselves, bang their heads on the wall or floor, pick at their skin. Why don't "normal" kids develop this problem? Well, some do. Some kids who're fine in other ways can learn to do this if they get attention for it. Most youngsters learn other tricks — games, sports, skills that get a lot more social reward than self-abuse. The child who's called "slow" or retarded is kept under the eagle eye of parents. They're always tuned-in — on the lookout for strange or bizarre behavior. When they see it, they're all too likely to reward it — although never meaning to — by paying attention.

- ■12 What can be said about the intelligence of youngsters who are self-abusive to the point of inflicting serious bodily harm?
- ■13 How are the boy in the film and a football player alike?
- ■14 In what way might parents contribute to the development of self-abusive behavior in a child?
- ■15 What tends to defeat the "bad parts" theory in terms of who develops self-abusive behavior?
- ■16 Why are normal youngsters less likely to develop self-abusive behavior than retarded children?

LEARNING MALADAPTIVE BEHAVIOR

In comp class:

"I don't see why it has to be triple-spaced," Chet said.

"I've told you that . . . several times, Mr. LaPorte. It's to allow you room to rewrite later on."

"But that's only if I mess up and have to rewrite."

"All have in the past, Mr. LaPorte, save only one or two that I can recall."

"So. Some didn't have to. That's my point. Why can't I do it double-spaced?"

In phys ed class:

"That's it, LaPorte. You signed up for this course — you run. Got it?"

"No. I don't see the point. I knew how to run before I even heard a' this lousy course. If I gotta take a phony jock course, I want to learn some sport I can use later on."

"Phys ed I is a fitness course — it's the first course. We want you fit before you move on, okay?"

"No. I'd rather drop it than have to put up with a lot a' crap."

"Drop the course, then; no skin off my nose!"

***

"Chet," Juke said. "Mind if I tell you somethin'?"

"Sure — what is it?"

"Nah. Forget it. It's nothin'."

"Come on. What is it?"

"Okay — but remember you asked. Chet, 'bout a fourth of the time you're the greatest dude ever walked the earth, but the rest of the time you're a real pain."

"Whatta you mean — 'pain'?"

"I mean 'pain', that's what — an' I don't mean in the head. Like, why you gotta fuss and argue all the time — about nothin'?"

"If you mean why do I stand up for my rights; all I can say is that you, of all people, should know why!"

"Rights, man? Got nothin' to do with rights!"

"Who'n the hell asked you anyway?"

***

Why does Chet have to make it so hard? Why doesn't he just do what people ask him to, and let it go at that? Chet says he's just sticking up for his rights. Juke doesn't buy that excuse. It's not a matter of rights. Chet balks, argues, questions, drags his feet anytime he's told to do something. His plan or scheme — his way — is always far better. As Juke says — Chet is a real pain. But it's easy to call him names such as "conceited" or "negative", cross him off and steer clear. In some ways, Chet's not to blame. He has a behavior problem, one that he learned a long time ago. Time for a replay. . .

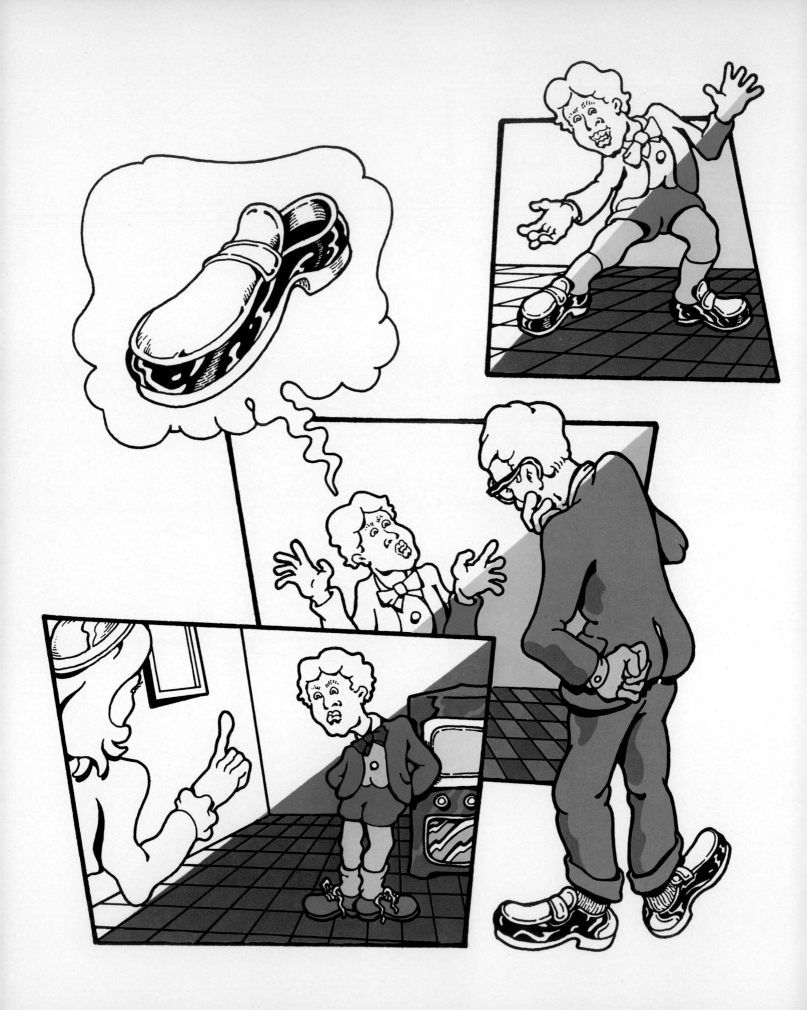

Chet, age 4; scene: at home, getting ready for church.

Mom: Chet, tie your shoes, just like we practiced all last week. You're a big boy now; big boys tie their own shoes.

Chet: (Chet fiddles with shoes, quits, is sullen.) I don't wanna tie my shoes.

Mom: Young man, I've had about enough out of you . . .

Dad: Hold on Sal — Chet's part of the group here. He's got a right to give his views. Now, son, why is it you don't want to tie your shoes?

Chet: I don't like these shoes — they're ugly.

Dad: I see. Well, what kind of shoes would you like? Say, maybe you'd like some like Dad's? See, loafers — no strings; just slip your foot in and out — that simple.

Chet: I want some — like Dad's. Mom, I want . . .

Dad: "Loafers" — can you say that, son?

Chet: Loafers.

Dad: That's good, Chet. See there, Sal? The little guy knows his own mind, that's all. He knows what he likes. He wants shoes like Dad's!

Mom: But someday he's got to learn to tie shoe laces.

Dad: He can learn that any-time — and he will, when he finds a pair of lace shoes he likes. Sorry fella, you'll just have to wear these today. Here, let Dad tie them for you; it's getting late. There. See, they're really not that bad, are they? (Dad hugs Chet.)

Chet: (Chet smiles and snuggles.) Can I have shoes like yours, Daddy?

Dad: Sure you can, son. First thing Monday. You just wait.

* * *

A lot went on there. What started the whole thing rolling? If you look closely you'll see. It was Chet's lack of skill. Tying shoes was hard for Chet to learn; not that it wasn't just as tough for a lot of us. But sooner or later, our folks told us that we'd better do it — or else. Chet learned something pretty slick on this day. He found that if you refuse to do something you don't know how to do, and, if you give some kind of trumped up reason why you shouldn't have to — then you often get out of it. One thing Chet picked up from Dad was the old, "you're stepping on my rights" routine. It works on all comers. More than likely, they'll back off if you scream, "My rights are being worked over!"

Today, Chet has a real behavior problem. He's stubborn, won't go along and try to make things work. Anytime someone asks or tells him to do something, he goes into his routine. Why does he still do it? To tell the truth — and here's Chet's real problem — he doesn't do anything very well. His little trick has worked so well over the years — with parents, teachers, clerks, etc., that he's been able to cop out. He got out of most places where the rest of us hung in and learned what we were supposed to.

Chet didn't hang-in, didn't learn it. Now he's a klutz. Chet's one skill is to argue. That's what he does best, so it's what he does most of the time. It gets him some social reward too. But more than that, it gets him out of a lot of bad duty — tasks that he's not really sure he could do.

■17 How do deficits in skills contribute to behavior problems?

■18 "Things that are rewards are good for us, or they wouldn't be rewards in the first place." Defend or refute this notion.

■19 Review question: What is rationalization?

■20 Cite an instance of rationalization in the behavior of a character(s) in the chapter.

DELAYED GRATIFICATION

"Mae, I don't know what I'm going to do," Dawn said.

"You sick?"

"Am I! I've made dates with three dudes for the game. What'll I do?"

"You've heard of Greyhound?"

"Come on, Mae. I'm panicked!"

"How can I help you? You're insane! Why'd you pull such a dumb stunt?"

"I don't know. They're all such cool guys, gosh . . ."

"The girl who couldn't say no, huh?"

"I guess I am. Tell me, Mae, do you think there's something wrong with me?"

***

For someone with Dawn's gifts and talents, a college campus is a candy store. She just can't help trying to grab all the goodies in sight. This causes her a lot of trouble, and sometimes others suffer as well. In this sense, Dawn has a behavior problem. But she's not alone there. At times we all behave in ways that bring us senseless grief later on.

All humans have a sort of built-in defect — rather, let's say that one feature of their makeup accounts for a large portion of behavior problems. It's the fact that rewards that can be gotten right away tend to exert far stronger control than those (often much greater) that don't come until later. It often turns out that doing what it takes to get the "fast quick one" makes us lose out on better ones later on — or worse, puts us in line for heavy punishers.

Success — the whole human trip — depends on our learning that sometimes we've got to avoid acting in ways that get the fast, cheap payoffs, and instead behave in ways that yield greater long-term benefits. Some writers call it learning to delay gratification.

As we move from infancy to become full-fledged members of the culture, delay of gratification assumes ever greater importance — it's both needed and expected if we're going to make it.

Delayed gratification: refraining from actions that produce immediate reinforcers and behaving instead in ways that produce better, although delayed, outcomes.

As we progress, learning to delay does not occur in an across-the-board fashion: we learn to do it well in some places and settings, but not so well, or not at all, in others. People have a behavior problem if they keep running into the bad effects from selling out to the fast rewards.

We've seen how this works. The quick glory on the gridiron could make Juke a cripple; cause him to miss out on the gentle long-lasting joys of later life that require a somewhat intact body. The youngster in the psych film is also selling out for quick reward. If he could learn other skills — to talk, read, play with toys, and other children — he'd get a far greater reward. But for some reason — perhaps a problem in structure or development that occurred — he hasn't learned other skills. Nor as long as he sticks to his one sure-fire response — self-abuse — is it likely he'll ever learn other ways.

▪21 What general feature of human structure makes us prone to develop behavior problems?
▪22 Why does this not usually result in behavior problems for lower animals?
▪23 What is delayed gratification? Define.
▪24 Delay of gratification is a general pattern of behavior — if we learn it in one setting it will always quickly generalize to other settings. Discuss.

CONCLUSIONS

Some of us get hooked on the short-term reward of smokes, drugs, liquor, running headlong into the horrors of cancer, addiction, and brain damage, waiting around the corner. Responses to food and sexual rewards must be tempered in amount or form, or they too will create the long-term ills of obesity and over-population.

"Doing what comes naturally" may work fine in the simple life of lower creatures. The time for that has long since passed for the human. Our future as individuals and as a culture clearly depends on acting in ways that produce the best long-run rewards. Behavior problems — copping out, the quick and easy reward — can only spell our doom.

CHAPTER 29
PSYCHOSES

NEUROSES, BEHAVIOR PROBLEMS, AND PSYCHOSES

Carol goes to the state hospital

"I'm not saying you'll like it there, Carol — but it would be fine training. Good for you to see what happens to people if we fail here at the clinic."

"I think I'd like to try it."

"Good. It's settled then. I'll phone the people out there and tell them to expect you."

***

Carol hurried across the breezeway and stopped in front of a heavy metal door marked "Ward 10". She pushed the button that sounded the buzzer in the nursing station. The door opened.

"Hi there." It was Jim, the head attendant.

"Room for me inside?"

"Always room for one more; come on."

A small, old woman, her hair neatly pulled back, faced the wall. Her right hand moved in a clockwise motion — as though scrubbing the pock marked plaster surface. Her hand was empty, holding no cloth, or sponge.

"Hello, Mrs. Kline. How's the work going?"

"Not good. Slow today. Things just won't get clean."

"My, you look nice. That a new dress you have on?"

"Mom sent it — from New Orleans."

"My! My!"

***

"Jim, does Mrs. Kline's mother ever come to see her?"

"Mother? What mother? Ruth, does old Kline there have a mother?"

"Naw — that's just a story she tells. She's an orphan. Been here since she was seventeen."

"She told me her mother gave her the new dress."

"Some mother! Momma Jim. I gave her that dress out of a batch the Women's Club sent."

"Oh, " Carol said.

***

"Hello, Mr. Saal. How're you today?" Mr. Saal sat on the end of the bench, his legs drawn up under him, dark eyes, gaunt face, a thin man in his early thirties. "Mr. Saal? Aren't you going to speak to me? Mr. Saal?" He stared at an ancient ball of gum stuck to the wall.

***

Carol walked down the hall to the ward room. A TV set high above on a platform flashed in silence, lighting the dim room. A quiz show. Six or seven middle-aged women sat on benches against the wall, watching the mute images. Their eyes turned to Carol as she came nearer.

"Hi, honey," one of them said.

"You're new here — what's your name?" a new voice asked. A gray-haired woman in house shoes grabbed Carol's arm. She wore ankle socks; long gray and black hairs bristled from unshaven legs. "Cigarette! Cigarette! Gimmie a fag, dammit!" she screeched.

"What's your name?"

"Hi, baby."

"Cigarette! Gimmie a Camel!"

"What's your name?"

Carol wanted to run. She tore loose from the hands that tugged at her clothing; grappling bodies. Beyond the door in the quiet hall now — she was safe. "God, this is nothing like working the out-patient clinic. Some healer I am! A gutless wonder! Just people; poor, sad, used up, run-down people. Sick and low — psychotics, and I run from them like they were lepers!"

Contrast

As we saw in the last chapter, behavior problems are learned. They evolve, as other learned acts, through reward. Experts also agree that learning is likewise the basis for neuroses. It's true that neurotic parents tend to produce neurotic children, but it's believed that association and not heredity is to blame. If both behavior problems and neuroses are learned, what is the difference between them? Two main factors emerge: extension of the problem actions into total living, and intensity of harmful results.

A behavior problem concerns and affects only a small part of the person's total behavior. It doesn't slosh over into other areas. Neurotic patterns extend into all parts of life; they color all aspects of the world the neurotic sees, hears, and deals with. Neurosis is a way of life. Also, the "intensity" or degree of harm, pain, and loss that neurotics cause themselves is far greater than that caused by behavior problems. It is truly the greater "price" neurotics pay that makes their patterns unlike behavior problems.

But neurotics and those with behavior problems seem to get by. They work, produce, even create; have children, vote, and make it pretty much on their own. Others with psychological problems aren't so lucky. They get to the point that friends, parents, or agents of the public question their skill to survive alone. There is real concern that they could get hurt, or threaten the welfare of others. Some of these people haven't been able to learn the skills that the culture requires. They've always been "behind" others their age from the very start. They are called "retarded" and we will deal with them at length in a later chapter.

A second type of person who can't make it alone is called a psychotic. It's not that these people are retarded — they've learned some social and common-knowledge skills, but for some reason they haven't acquired other quite basic ways of dealing with the environment. At this point we can't say for sure why it turned out this way. We don't know what kept them from gaining the skills they need — skills others seem to have mastered with little trouble. There's reason to believe that some of these severe psychological problems — psychoses as they're called — stem from biological factors. Genes that cause faulty structure to begin with, or disease that attacks and impairs present structure, are often mentioned.

As you will soon see, there are many kinds of psychoses. In some, biology plays a large part; and in others, may not figure in at all. In any case, learning contributes greatly. Psychotics are far from being the passive creatures with "burned out" brains as they're often portrayed in fiction. They are by no means immune to rewards and punishers. Some of what they do appears to occur for the same reason as behavior problems. They learn the "wrong" things — things that get them some quick reward, but have bad long-term effects, both on their lives and on the lives of those they live among. In what follows, we'll try to look at some of these basic skills psychotics lack. We'll also focus on some of the things they do learn — very likely as a result of these deficits in basic skills. It's often these latter problems that cause them to need so much special care.

Psychoses: types of severe psychological problems in which behavioral function is so grossly inappropriate that the person must receive almost constant attention and care.

- 1 Review: Define neuroses.
- 2 Review: Define behavior problems.
- 3 How are neuroses and behavior problems acquired?
- 4 In what two ways do neuroses differ from behavior problems?
- 5 What is meant by "extension" and "intensity" in the context of distinguishing neuroses from behavior problems?
- 6 Neuroses and behavior problems are learned, but there's reason to believe that b____ _____ factors play a part in some kinds of _____.
- 7 What two kinds of biological factors are often mentioned as possible causes for psychoses?
- 8 Psychotics have "burned out" brains. Discuss.

BIOLOGICAL PSYCHOSES

We've said that some psychoses have distinct biological bases. Others have been less tied to problems of structure and function of the body, but biology is believed to be at least a partial causal factor. Still others are thought solely the result of environmental factors and learning. It seems safest to assume that both biology and environment play a major role in all of these most severe of psychological problems.

Psychoses result in quite direct ways from the effects of poisons, drugs, alcohol, disease, injury to the brain or nervous system, and poor nutrition. Even here the form of the behavior that results stems from the person's past personality and learning.

Some psychoses appear to be caused in part by biological changes that occur at certain points in normal development. The vast physical changes in the body that take place at puberty are believed by some to be a major factor in some forms of schizophrenia. The "change of life" or menopause is related to another kind of psychosis — "involutional melancholia" — where depression is the main problem. Psychoses are also a common event in old age — "senile psychosis".

Involutional melancholia: a psychosis whose major symptom is depression. Since it comes on at about the same time of the menopause in women and reduced potency in men, there is some reason to believe it has a major biological basis.

Senile psychosis: psychosis that accompanies advanced age.

- 9 What is the best statement as to whether biology or environment is most to blame for psychosis?
- 10 What biological causes have a more or less direct role in producing psychoses?
- 11 What three types of psychoses occur at certain developmental points? At what developmental point do they occur?
- 12 Define the following: involutional melancholia, senile psychosis.

PSYCHOGENIC PSYCHOSES

The best known psychoses as far as the public is concerned are those believed to be caused by learning. These psychoses are called "psychogenic psychoses".

Psychogenic psychoses: psychoses whose major cause is thought to involve what has happened to the person.

Let's look at some of them.

Schizophrenia

Schizophrenia is not a single psychosis, but a group of psychoses that seem to share some common features. Despite the fact that they're all known as "schizophrenia", they are — or can be — about as different as night and day in terms of the gamut of behavior seen.

Schizophrenia: a class of psychoses marked by lowered or "flat" emotional response, loss of interest in most reinforcers and activities and perhaps the presence of delusions and hallucinations.

Schizophrenics are best described as being out of touch: under poor stimulus control may be a good way to put it. Most things that frighten, turn on, or interest normal people don't seem to matter to schizophrenics. They often let hair go uncombed, clothes unwashed, and bodies unbathed. They are said to have "flat affect". This means they don't show emotion in settings where it's normal; on the other hand, emotional response may be quite heavy; so much as to be out of line or inappropriate to the occasion.

Flat affect: failure to exhibit appropriate emotional response, usually by showing little response at all.

Besides being turned down (flat affect) and tuned out (poor stimulus control), some schizophrenics seem to have their own private thing going. They believe strange things — delusions — and may hallucinate. It's true that some schizophrenics are in their own world — having fantasies, grooving on themselves, therefore lost to us most of the time. But most of them are nowhere — not having a private thing, not conscious. They've lost (or never had) that special "consciouness of private events" that we spoke of in a past chapter. They just don't "exist" for themselves.

There are many sub-types of schizophrenia. Paranoid schizophrenia is one you often hear of. People with this problem have delusions of grandeur. They act like they're famous or very special and because of this should receive special treatment. For example, they may think they're Napoleon or Jesus Christ.

Paranoid schizophrenia: schizophrenia marked by active delusions, most often of grandeur and persecution.

Delusions of persecution are also a hallmark of the paranoid schizophrenic. This delusion — the belief that people are out to get you — is well known, often given to mental patients in the movies.

The hebephrenic schizophrenic assumes a childish state; laughs and giggles and acts silly, has tantrums or cries for no good reason. The catatonic schizophrenic, on the other hand, has two distinct forms. In one form the catatonic is a person who's raving mad — manic, rushing about, apt to be violent. In the other form, the catatonic never moves, assuming a pose and holding it, statue-like, silent, forboding, in a stupor, remaining that way for months or years.

Hebephrenic schizophrenia: schizophrenia marked by childish actions and affect, as though the person had regressed to an earlier age.

Catatonic schizophrenia: schizophrenia taking two forms: one form agitated and manic; the second form lethargic, stupored, and perhaps motionless for long time spans.

Affective psychoses

The term "affective" refers to emotions or "mood". People with affective psychoses show extremes in these responses. They bubble over, wound up and frantic; they tune-out, become turned off, down and depressed. In either case, there's no good reason for them to behave as they do.

The best known of the affective psychoses is manic-depressive psychosis, which has three types. First, there's the manic type. A person with this problem can't seem to sit still. Both mouth and limb are in constant motion, running in hectic action, an ever new project or crusade in the works; all this wild movement acted out to a "score" of machine gun, non-stop verbiage — a 33 1/3 record souped up to 78!

The second type of manic-depressive psychosis — depressed type — is so low, so sad, so mired down in a salty quagmire of tears and "woe is me", that they can scarcely move. They find no point in eating, talking — no point to life. Sometimes their rate reaches dead zero. They chug to a stop, caught in hopeless stupor.

The third type of manic-depressive psychosis — circular type — is the one most people think of when they hear the term "manic-depressive". The person shows marked swings from "manic" to "depressed" phases of mood. Months of manic action where wild deals are made, earth shaking projects begun, lofty plans talked to death, are followed by full retreat — depression; sadness, loneliness, regret, guilt, stupor. But then the cycle begins anew. The wild-eyed mania descends. So it may go, year after year.

Affective psychoses: psychoses marked by distinct irregularities of emotional response or mood. Reasoning, judgement, and other features are relatively unaffected.

Manic-depressive psychosis: affective psychosis existing in three forms or types. In the manic type, people work at high speed and energy, exaggerate, and take on any challenge. In the depressed type they become depressed, have no energy, and no ambition; often they vegetate. In the circular type excursions between the manic and the depressed phases take place at intervals.

Paranoid psychoses

Paranoia is the best known of the paranoid psychoses, or paranoid states, as they are now more formally called. The paranoid is bright, has great skill and talent, is known to be glib, and charming; can make you feel like a million, really turn your head around. But when pushed or threatened, paranoids get up-tight. The show — their "act" of a cool, loose, "easy-rider" — is over. Once their cover's blown, the tightly woven delusions of grandeur, of persecution, come springing out like so many kinky coils of steel.

The paranoid's logic is tight; can't be assailed. But the premise it's based on is clearly cock-eyed. When they're not in a tight life-episode, paranoids get along pretty well; they may do so for years. Then as things close in they get more and more brittle and at last shatter, the state hospital often following.

Paranoia: paranoid psychosis marked by distinct delusions of grandeur and persecution. The paranoid should be distinguished from the paranoid schizophrenic who has somewhat the same delusions but also has the response patterns common to schizophrenia.

Paranoia is by no means the same as paranoid schizophrenia. A person with the latter is a schizophrenic first; out of touch, words and deeds don't jibe, gaping holes in logic. It just happens that paranoid delusions are also a major feature — thus giving rise to the label paranoid schizophrenic. There's some hope for the person with paranoia. For the paranoid schizophrenic, the future looks far more dim.

▪13 Psychoses that are thought to stem primarily from environmental factors are called p_____ psychoses.

▪14 Define schizophrenia.

▪15 What is flat affect?

▪16 What does it mean when it's said that the schizophrenic's "turned down" and "tuned out"?

▪17 All schizophrenics have great amounts of private experience. Discuss.

▪18 What does it mean to say that schizophrenics may not "exist" for themselves?

▪19 Three kinds of schizophrenia were mentioned. Define each of them.

▪20 What are the two forms of catatonic schizophrenia?

▪21 What are delusions of grandeur? Of persecution? With what form of schizophrenia are they associated?

▪22 What are affective psychoses? Define.

▪23 What are the three types of manic-depressive psychoses? Describe them.

▪24 Which type is best known to the public?

▪25 Which is the best known of the paranoid states or psychoses?

▪26 What marks paranoia?

▪27 How does paranoia differ from paranoid schizophrenia? Which is the worse of the two?

RESPONSE BIAS

The trouble with Harold

Carol went to the back of the ward to regroup after her panic. Like most wards, Ward 10 had a hard time keeping patients in clean clothes. A clothes dryer and washer donated by a service club eased the problem. It ran most of the day, seven days a week. Now the hum and whir of the machines were perfect cover. Carol could cry here, fix her eyes, and go out to face the patients again. She watched the clothes as they tumbled in the dryer, tears still beaded on her cheek. Blue work pants caught her eye as they spun in the dryer. There was something odd going on. She looked closer. "Oh no!" she shrieked. There were arms in a shirt, and legs in the trousers — a face and a head in there, too! There was a man inside. Blood streamed out of gashes on his face and head.

***

"Hi. Are you the one who found Harold this morning?"

"I'm afraid so. How is he?"

"Fine — believe it or not. His luck's holding. After all he's been through, I think he must be made of steel. Listen, I'm Bob Moore. I may be Dr. Moore soon as I get the thesis out of the way. I'm with Psych Service. Oh, and by the way, thanks for getting Harold out before he got mangled too bad. He could get killed that way one of these days."

"Then he does it often?"

"Third time this week."

"But why? Why does he do it?"

"Sure wish I knew. I got some ideas, but so far that's all they are. Gonna have to observe Harold a lot more, I'm afraid. Which brings me to you. How'd you like to help?"

"Me? Well sure — of course. But I don't know much."

"That's okay. Mostly you'll be watching him; taking data."

"In that case — great. You got a deal — that is, if I can clear it."

"Leave that to me. But first of all, I'm going to get some fresh psychological test results on Harold."

***

"Harold, I want you to look at this card and tell me what you see."

"Snakes. See, here's a green one. The red one's gonna eat 'em up."

"Uh huh. How about this card?"

"Snakes, a bunch of 'em!"

"This card?"

"Snakes."

"And this?"

"More of 'em — snakes."

***

"Hi, Bob. Just called to let you know I'm through testing Harold King. The report's in the works; should get it in a coupl'a days. It didn't take long at all — the old boy's not got much to work with. Saw nothin' but snakes on all the cards. What? Can't say for sure. He didn't answer enough to compute an I.Q. I'd say normal, though. Well listen, here's the way I look at it. His perceptual system is typical paranoid schiz. He sees the whole world as threatening. That's why he's self-destructive; got a lot of hostility and . . . Bob? Bob? Are you on the line?"

The role of reinforcement history

A lot has been said about how psychotics must see, hear, or observe things around them. Strange acts are thought to be the result of a bizarre way of looking at things. Research has told us this approach is futile. We'll never know what the patient "sees". We can't get inside others and see, feel, or hear through their senses. But that's beside the point. What we should care about is why psychotics act the way they do in the presence of stimuli where normals behave otherwise.

One way to look at Harold's answers to the question "What do you see?" is to think of it as not being controlled by the card at all. Harold says he sees "snakes" all the time. He has a high rate of saying he "sees snakes". Further, this response will occur just about any time you ask him what he sees, no matter what object you're pointing to or holding before him.

This is a way of getting at what's going on that seems to make more sense. Instead of saying that Harold "perceives" the cards in some strange way, we say that he doesn't see them at all. That is, the stimuli on the cards play no role in the control of his response. Thus, we can predict that Harold will make the response that was rewarded in the same setting in the past. In this sense, Harold's response is the result of reinforcement history. When responses that are normally controlled by particular cues occur as a result of reward alone — we call this "response bias".

Response bias: a response that occurs because of its lengthy history of reinforcement in a wide range of settings and stimuli, and **does not** occur as a result of any special sensory activity or experience.

One of the strangest and most puzzling things psychotics do — one of the things that likely had a lot to do with landing them in a state hospital in the first place — is to "hallucinate", or have "hallucinations". In the past an hallucination was loosely defined as: sensing (seeing, feeling, hearing, smelling, etc.) something (or someone) that's not there. Once again the mistake of assuming experience pops up. To say that people see, hear, feel, or are having any other experience — based merely on the way they act is to court error.

We don't ever know what people experience. What we do know is how they behave. So, let's define hallucination this way:

Hallucination: actions appropriate to the presence of a stimulus object or setting, that occur in its absence.

Quite likely, some people who have hallucinations are seeing images or hearing voices — much as when we dream, or are fooled by a magician's slight of hand. But the hallucinations psychotics have — at least by the time they get to the open ward in the state hospital — are seldom this way. They are far more likely the result of response bias. What these people say and do, is not the result of "visions" or phantom voices. It is response bias — a long and strong reinforcement history at work.

But how does response bias come about? One way is that some people have only a few responses that get them rewards. They tend to emit the same old responses without regard to setting or cues. This strengthens the notion that psychosis is the result of glaring deficits in basic skills and response patterns.

▪28 Why is it risky to talk about what people experience?

▪29 What is the occurrence called when responses that are controlled for most people by cues, are controlled by reinforcement history?

▪30 If a response is not controlled by cues in a situation, what is likely to be the controlling factor?

▪31 What is one set of conditions that might tend to produce psychosis?

▪32 How does the presence of response bias strengthen the notion that psychosis is caused by behavioral deficits?

▪33 Define response bias.

▪34 Define hallucination.

▪35 Hallucinations may have two different causes. What are they?

▪36 Why is it incorrect to define hallucinations as always being the result of visions or other experience?

SOCIAL REINFORCEMENT AND PSYCHOTIC ACTS

"Here's the way I see it, Carol. I think Harold does the clothes dryer thing for social rewards."

"That's hard to believe. There should be an easier way for him to get social rewards."

"For you and me — sure. But for Harold? Look at him. Not handsome, clever, glib; can't amaze with card tricks, charades, do shadow pictures. There's more to it than that, too. Harold's one of many. He has to work hard for the slightest little bit of notice he gets from the ward people. After all, there're forty more 'Harolds' on the ward. And for the most part, only one attendant. He's got to come up with a real act to win out."

"Yeah, well, I'd say he's got a doozy!"

***

All too often the psychotics are pictured as people wrapped up in their own private worlds, immune to social control — beyond the effects of social reward. Indeed, most psychotics aren't handy at picking up on many of the social cues that control our actions. Just the same, human contact, attention, social rewards that work so well on us also turn their heads around, too.

But in the state hospital, where there are so many patients and so few staff, contact is seldom or rare for some patients. Ward persons can't pay attention to all, so they attend only to "certain" patients. And who are these elite? The ones who say or do strange "crazy" things, or threaten their own health and safety or that of others. Thus, their attention boomerangs — a potent reward, it merely tends to increase the very behavior they're trying to stop.

Yes, state hospitals tend to create their own monsters. A lot of the truly "crazy" acts are the result of misplaced social rewards given by the staff. This doesn't mean attendants and others who treat and care for the patient mean to reward bad behavior. Often they are harsh, and may treat patients in ways that would be punishing for others. We can't overlook the great power of social contact. To a lonely patient, a slap can be as a kiss to others.

It's well known that the way patients are treated in state hospitals or other settings is a major cause of many psychological and behavioral problems. Such problems are called "iatrogenic" — a word that roughly means "produced by the treatment".

Iatrogenic: produced by the treatment; in the context of psychological or behavioral problems, such problems produced by the structure and treatment in mental or state hospitals.

A good feel for the havoc misplaced social reward can cause is a first step in stopping the spread of iatrogenic disorders.

- ■37 Are psychotics always insensitive to social rewards? Discuss.
- ■38 What could the statement: "We create our own monsters", have to do with the behavior of ward attendants as they interact with the patients?
- ■39 What effect does the patient/attendant ratio have on the occurrence of bizarre behavior in state hospitals?
- ■40 How do attendants unintentionally "shape-up" bad behavior?
- ■41 Define iatrogenic.
- ■42 What is a first step in stopping the spread of iatrogenic disorders in a state hospital?

* * *

"But if Harold keeps hurting himself, we have to keep treating his wounds. Doesn't that mean we have no choice but to feed into his deal?"

"Right. Looks like he's got us. We can't very well ignore him as he whirls around in the dryer."

"What do you want me to do?" Carol asked.

"For the time being, nothing — just hang on."

PSYCHIC NEEDS AND MENTAL HEALTH

Dawn's view

"The poor soul!" Dawn said. They were having a cup of coffee at Carol's and Chet's. Carol had just told her about Harold. "I know it's true — there're people who're that lonely."

"Hard to believe, though," Carol said.

"Not really. Love's one thing none of us can do without. You know the worst fate in the world's 'solitary' — locked up all alone — no one to talk to. People go insane."

"But Harold — I don't know. He doesn't seem to suffer much."

"He's past that. He's mad and hostile — mad at everyone who won't love him. Instead of hurting them, he takes it out on himself."

"You think so?"

"Yes, I do."

"But Harold — "

"Why don't you try being kind to him — show him some care and maybe a little love."

"I don't know."

"Try it. You gotta do something!"

All it takes is love

The talk she had with Dawn kept gnawing on Carol the next day. What she said made sense. It wasn't too far from what Bob had said either. The poor man! She'd tried to stay away from Harold thus far. Just watch him and take data — that's all. Bob didn't say she should do anything else. Maybe she could try to give Harold a little kindness — treat him like a real person. Why hadn't she before now? Was she really just trying to follow orders? Or — was that a cop-out? Was she afraid — disgusted by what she saw when she looked at him? No. That wasn't it. It wasn't!

Carol had to try to make contact with Harold. He'd been quiet all morning — most of the time watching TV and working a puzzle. He hadn't shown the slightest sign of upset. Surely it wouldn't do any harm to just go say hello. Carol walked over to him and put her hand lightly on his shoulder. Harold turned toward her. When he saw her, his mouth dropped.

"Hello, Harold — do you like puzzles?" Harold jumped up like he'd been bitten by a snake. Pieces of the puzzle scattered all over; then — Zoom! He was gone, making a beeline to the back of the ward. By the time Carol caught up with him, he was in the dryer, his blue eyes peering out the window.

"Oh no!" Carol cried.

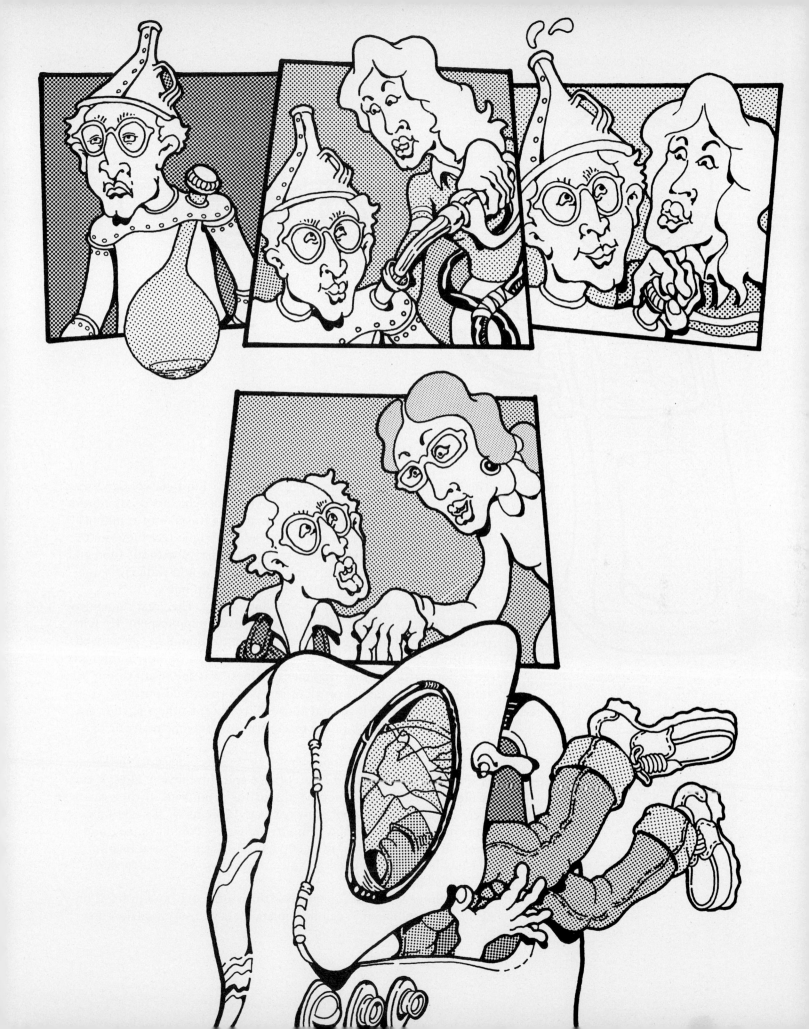

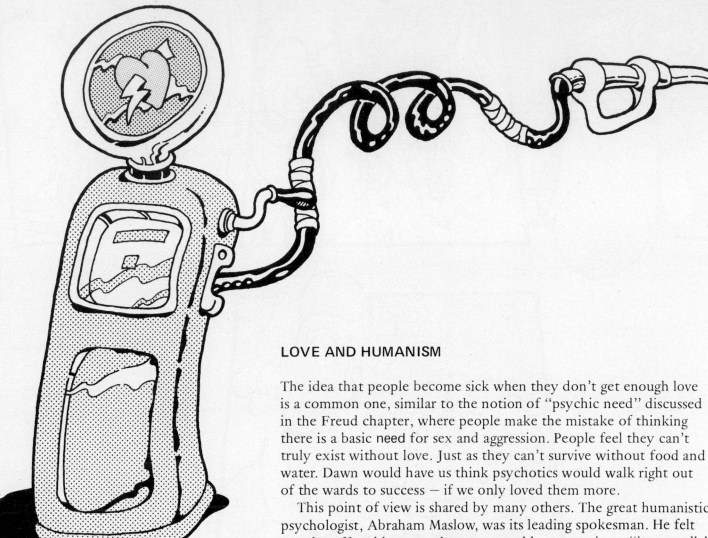

LOVE AND HUMANISM

The idea that people become sick when they don't get enough love is a common one, similar to the notion of "psychic need" discussed in the Freud chapter, where people make the mistake of thinking there is a basic need for sex and aggression. People feel they can't truly exist without love. Just as they can't survive without food and water. Dawn would have us think psychotics would walk right out of the wards to success — if we only loved them more.

This point of view is shared by many others. The great humanistic psychologist, Abraham Maslow, was its leading spokesman. He felt people suffered because they were unable to tune-in to "inner wells" of knowledge, skills, and feelings that, according to him, all humans were born with. He said that mental illness was the result of our joint human failure — failure on all of our parts to extend ourselves to each other, to offer love, and above all to accept others as they are. People slighted greatly in the receipt of love become neurotic or psychotic.

Treatment for these poor people, as Maslow viewed it, should consist in giving them total acceptance and total love — always, even while the bizarre and sometimes disgusting symptoms of their sickness were in full effect. Was Maslow correct? It seems we'll never know. None of us — even Maslow himself, perhaps — could ever be good enough, patient enough, calm enough to offer the "total love" Maslow believed was needed. Since thus far we've all fallen short, the theory is untested.

One thing is certain — giving less than total love, and doing it only when you feel like it — can be a mistake. It will surely make things

worse. To some it appears that Maslow was well off the track in his thoughts on the value and nature of love and human contact. It's true love's a big reward for most of us. We'll do some pretty silly things if they result in a little human contact. But it's one thing to say that social contact's a reward and something else to say we "need" it. Many things — dope, liquor, cigarettes — are heavy rewards. But who's ready to say we need them? It's a bad concept. It's like saying we have a "love tank" — just like autos have gas tanks. When you're low, you've just got to get it filled. If you don't — you'll suffer for it later.

Once love and human contact is viewed as one of many kinds of rewards — although a truly strong one, indeed — things seem to make more sense. If we love people — children, wives, husbands, students, patients — paying attention when they're doing bad things, we will only make those bad things increase. But loving them when they're doing good things — well, that's something else again. If we give this giant reward for appropriate acts, it can do wonders; perhaps then love is enough!

■43 Are what people "need" and what is reinforcing always the same?

■44 Give another way to look at the notion of "needing love".

■45 What is the "empty love tank" theory? Criticize it.

■46 When is "love" likely to work to benefit the patient or individual?

■47 Who was Abraham Maslow?

ONE CAUSE OF A PSYCHOTIC RESPONSE

Discriminative stimulus or reinforcer?

"Gosh, Bob — I don't know what to say. I'm sorry. I didn't know Harold would get that way. He must hate me or something. One kind word from me and whiz — off to the dryer."

"Don't blame yourself — Harold's okay. Besides, maybe you didn't have a thing to do with it."

"I'm telling you — it was strange. Just like I told him to go jump in the dryer."

"Just like you told him — hmmmm. You know somethin', that makes good sense — like you told him."

"But Bob, . . . I'd never . . ."

"No, no, I don't mean it that way. Look, will you try it again?"

"You mean make Harold jump in the dryer!"

"Don't worry. We'll be waiting. He won't get hurt."

"Just go up and speak to him?"

"That's right — just like you did before — right?"

"Okay. Here goes." Harold was sitting alone, glumly staring off into space. Carol touched him on the shoulder. "Hello, Harold." He was off and running toward the dryer. In a couple of minutes Bob and Jim brought him back. Harold paced for a few minutes. Then he quieted down and started to watch the TV.

"How was that, Bob?" Carol asked.

"Great — just great. Now let's try it again."

"Again?"

"Again."

***

In the next few days they tried it out many times. At first only with Carol. Later, they got staff from other wards — people Harold hadn't seen before — to play Carol's role. It was the same in all cases.

Harold lit out for the dryer room, and each time someone was there to keep him from getting hurt.

"Hooray! Looks like we got it figured out."

"And just how do 'we' have it figured out — if you don't mind telling me?"

"Well, we know socials are big rewards for Harold. He'll do anything for a few social strokes — most of all from a stranger or a woman. The thing I forgot is that attention's a stimulus — it can be a cue as well as a reward."

"I'm sorry — I just don't get it."

"Look at it this way. Harold there's an actor. He does his act — that is, he does something crazy — and he gets an actor's reward — applause. Only in his case it's just the nurse who cleans him up or the doc who sews up his cuts. But Harold's an actor. Now an actor only acts when there's an audience?"

"I don't know. When people are around I guess."

"No. There're people around Harold all the time."

"I don't know then."

"What does an audience do besides just being around?"

"They watch the actor — pay attention to . . . hey! I think I see what you're getting at. When I go up to Harold, I'm telling him that I'm ready to watch him."

"Right!"

"So it's like I'm also telling him it's time to do his thing — is that what you mean?"

"That's it! Attention's a cue for him to do it."

"But I thought you said attention's a reward?"

"It's both. Don't you see? Socials are also the cues that tell him there's more there to get if he'll just perform."

Stimulus control and reinforcement priming

There is reason to believe that psychotics are under very poor stimulus control. Much of their bad talk and actions are bad only in the sense that they don't take place in the right setting. Taking off clothes is fine at home, not in public. Talking out loud is okay if there's someone else in the room and you're talking to them. When you're alone — well, you've heard what's said about people who talk to themselves.

Social cues, those subtle stimuli that mean so much in leading us to respond the right way, might as well not exist for many psychotics. But sometimes, psychotics may behave as they do because certain stimuli — ones that we might not expect — do exert control. Harold's dryer trick seems such a case. The same kind of stimulus that serves as a reward is also a cue for the response. We tend to think that a type of stimulus will serve only one role. But there's no reason it can't do both jobs. This type of thing can be called "reinforcement priming". If we're thirsty and think the pump's dry — we'll just sit by. If a bead of water drips from the pump, it's a strong cue — a cue that tells us that water's around and we can get it if we get busy.

Reinforcement priming: when a substance or stimulus that is a reinforcer for a response also serves as a discriminative stimulus when delivered to produce that same response.

- ▪48 What does stimulus control have to do with whether or not an act is inappropriate? Cite two instances.
- ▪49 What is a good general statement about degree of stimulus control and psychotics?
- ▪50 Are there any exceptions to the above?
- ▪51 Review question: How does a stimulus become a reward? A learned reward? A cue?
- ▪52 If a stimulus is both a cue and a reward, what does this mean in terms of the function it will perform?
- ▪53 What is reinforcement priming?
- ▪54 Give the two examples of reinforcement priming mentioned in the chapter. Now, can you think of another on your own?

CONCLUSIONS

In this chapter we've found out one quite curious thing when looking at the cause of "psychoses" as opposed to the cause of "psychotic behavior". It's clear that some, if not all psychoses occur after disease, brain damage, or other biological events harm the physiological structures. Biology in this sense is the cause of the psychosis. Even so, if we look closely, we find that the things psychotics do — their bizarre behavior — is both maintained and learned in the same fashion as other behavior — through rewards.

Research into biological bases of psychoses goes ahead. Perhaps some day soon we'll find ways to prevent these biological problems, or perhaps change them once they do occur. In the meantime, we're not without hope — not without weapons. Learned actions can be unlearned. Psychotic behavior can be replaced with "normal" or appropriate actions. It is, after all, the psychotic's actions we object to in the first place, not his or her biology. A normal person is, for all intents and purposes, one who acts normal. In later chapters we'll learn more of this approach.

POST SCRIPT

Carol came in early the next day. She couldn't wait to find Bob. "I've been thinking about what you said about Harold. It makes good sense."

"I feel good about it, too."

"Where do we go from here with Harold?"

"That's a good question. I'm not quite sure."

"But can't he get some kind of treatment? Isn't there a cure for him?"

"I don't know about a 'cure'. What's wrong with Harold, well, I don't think it helps to think of it as a disease. It's not something that's ever going to be cured in that sense. What we can do is try to teach Harold to behave the way 'normal' people do. Give up his weird antics."

"But if he behaves like normals, won't he be normal? I mean, who would know the difference?"

"That's just the point. The approach I've got in mind puts the focus on what Harold does. If we can get him to do what normal people do — and that doesn't include jumping in clothes dryers — then he'll be normal."

"What is it?"

"It's called 'behavior modification'."

CHAPTER 30
RETARDATION

INTRODUCTION

"We don't take what we do lightly here at the Co-Op School." It was Ceil Bennett, director and founder of the school who was talking. Mae had come to see about volunteer work. "The kids you'd be working with are retarded — rejects from the public school system. You can bet they're not a piece of cake when it comes to trying to help them. But we're here to try. If we don't do our best, there's no point to it.

"If you come to work with us, there'll be no pay, no one'll say you're great, and so far as I can see, fringe benefits are ziltch! Now — that's the good part. You want to hear more?"

"I guess not — your 'hard sell' got me. When do I start?" Mae asked.

Ceil Bennett laughed, unwound a little and leaned back in her chair. "I'd like to say yesterday — but Monday'll have to do."

"I'll be here." Mae got up to leave. She paused in front of Ceil's desk. "One thing I'd like to ask. A girl; she looked about ten or eleven years old. I saw her when I came in; she had this way of looking at me . . ."

"A black girl — with a missing front tooth?"

"Why yes, that's the one."

"Casey — Casey Clark — so she got to you that quick, eh? Welcome to the club."

PSYCHOSES, RETARDATION, AND CULTURAL DEPRIVATION

As we learned in the last chapter, psychotics are a good bet to spend at least part of their lives in an institution. Mental retardation (often shortened to retardation) is a second major biosocial problem whose victims likewise require placement in an institution or at least a specially structured life setting. The "retarded", as they are often referred to, appear vastly unlike psychotics when the extremes in each group are compared. When we look at certain cases it may, in practice, be a toss-up as to whether they should be labeled "retarded"

or "psychotic". It's possible though to list some standard ways the two differ.

As was mentioned in the last chapter, psychotics may have behavior deficits, but these deficits aren't as a rule across the board. Psychotics have islands of "normal" skills and may be quite talented in some areas. In contrast, behavior deficits in all areas mark the retarded. Gross deficits in social and intellectual behavior and a lowered level of motor coordination are the rule.

Strange words and actions are the best known features of

psychosis. Actions of the retarded, on the other hand, are not so much strange as they are limited, showing lack of skill, and little knowledge.

For many psychotics there are periods in their lives when they behave in a manner that's "normal" for their age and situation. The retarded are as a rule saddled with their problem from birth. They are behind from the very start and never catch up with "normal" peers.

Some psychoses have well-known physiological bases; most occur along with some biological

symptoms. Others, it is believed, are entirely learned. It's likely that all retardation will sooner or later be linked to a physiological state that's a more or less direct cause of the problem.

The retarded should not be confused with those persons who've not had the chance to learn what our culture requires them to know. When lack of knowledge or skills stems from not having the training or experience that is standard in the culture, this deficit is called "cultural deprivation". The retarded, on the other hand, have been exposed, but have simply not learned. It's the failure to benefit from the normal training and experience that the culture provides that defines the retarded. It marks them distinctly from both the psychotic and the culturally-deprived.

Retardation (mental retardation): general failure to benefit from normal training and experience, such that the minimum mastery of the skills and knowledge the culture requires is not attained.

Cultural deprivation: failure to master the skills and knowledge the culture requires because of a lack of exposure to the normal training and experience commonly provided.

- 1 The psychotic and retarded were compared using four criteria. What were they and how did they compare?
- 2 Define retarded.
- 3 Define culturally-deprived.
- 4 How do the retarded differ from the culturally-deprived?

CAUSES OF RETARDATION

Genes and retardation

Mae showed up promptly on Monday. Ceil was pleased to see her, but wasted no time in small talk, She started her at once on what she called her "two-dollar tour".

The Co-Op School had once been a family home. It was large — twelve rooms in all. Now most of the rooms were no longer rooms as such. They were a maze of four or five small booths, one for each child. They entered one of the booths. Ceil motioned to Mae that they'd have to be quiet.

"This's Tim," Ceil said in a whisper. Tim sat on one side of a board hinged from the wall that served as a makeshift table. Two students who looked up just long enough to nod were seated across from him. Tim was eight or so, judging by his looks. His eyes seemed half open; his mouth in a fixed pose, his lips parted. Then he smiled. For a few seconds he was just like any other child.

"What's wrong with Tim?" Mae asked when they were outside. "He looks strange. Well, he looks retarded — I guess that's what I mean."

"He's a PKU case — phenylke-tonuria. They found out about it when he was ten months old. By then things had happened that the doctors couldn't reverse. His system's pretty well under control now, though."

"PKU. I've read about that.

It's curable with the right diet and drugs — isn't it?"

"I don't know about that. It seems there are changes that can't be reversed with drugs — any kind of medical treatment — but the process can be stopped. The sooner they detect it the better."

***

Some types of mental retardation are caused by the inheritance of faulty structure. One such case is PKU. It arises when body structure is deficient in producing a certain enzyme.

Due to the shortage of this enzyme, certain chemical reactions can't fully occur. The result is an incomplete product which is, in fact, a potent toxin that attacks tissue throughout the body, doing permanent damage, especially to brain and nerve cells. Through early examination the deficit can be detected and the enzyme can be added through drug treatment and special diet. Once the system is in balance, work with the PKU child can begin. It involves teaching these children what they missed out on during the acute phase when the toxins were active.

Phenylketonuria (PKU): metabolic condition that arises from the inheritance of faulty structure and causes mental retardation.

Some doctors believe that other types of retardation will be traced to biochemical needs that are unique to a given person. Such unique needs vary widely from person to person and are thought to be inherited. One example is in the area of vitamins.

Standards set up that state daily vitamin needs may not apply to all people. Those who were born with a need for more than the amount most of us thrive on, will suffer a shortage. Treatment that follows this approach has to do with giving massive doses of vitamins "megavitamin treatment", as it is called.

Megavitamin treatment: treatment for mental retardation that involves giving the patient massive doses of selected vitamins.

So far, a few published studies have found good results. Other studies have not found any benefit. Since there's no good way to tell if a child needs more vitamins, what kinds, or how much, this treatment is a "shot in the dark" venture at this point.

The future may bring new data to bear on the topic of genes and retardation. For now, only a small portion of the retarded can be said to be as they are because of inheritance.

- 5 Name one known instance of retardation that's caused by genetic factors.

- 6 What is the structural problem that causes PKU?
- 7 What problems does the lack of this enzyme produce?
- 8 Name another way in which genetics may be associated with retardation.
- 9 What is the structural prob-

lem here and how is an attempt being made to remedy it?
- 10 What is the name of the treatment that involves the use of large doses of vitamins? Why might this approach be called a "shot in the dark"?

Congenital retardation

Ceil moved through the hodge-podge of booths like she had radar — half the time looking back at Mae, giving her facts and figures about the school and its clients. Forward progress came to an abrupt halt. A girl of about four gave out with a small yelp before she ran to Ceil. She clutched her leg with stubby fingers. Ceil lifted her up and held her against her hip.

"And this little showboat is Sissy. Say hello to Mae, Sissy."

"Hevro," the girl said.

"Hello there," Mae answered. The little girl lit up like a neon sign, coyly smiling at Mae, her head nestled on Ceil's shoulder. Mae noticed her eyes. They had the heavy folds of the mongoloid — something she'd read about. The stubby fingers, chunky build, and plastic movements confirmed Mae's beliefs.

Later, Mae asked about Sissy. "She was mongoloid, wasn't she?"

"Yes. She's one of our stars here. But I suspect you figured that out for yourself. We've got one other here — Jimmy. You'll

meet him later. He's almost as big a hit as Casey — not nearly the 'ham', though. Mongoloids are likely to be the 'pets' wherever you find 'em."

"Why's that?" Mae asked.

"As you can see, they like and give a lot of love; they smile and laugh a lot of the time. Compared to some of our kids — and to most retarded — they learn fast. You can teach them a lot with just a little patience."

***

Mongolism or Down's Syndrome (so named after its discoverer) is known by the discrete and fairly standard body features it produces. These include: a thick tongue, somewhat flattened face, stubby fingers, and limbs that appear plastic, lacking normal bone and muscle tension. Best known are the mongoloid's thick or heavy looking eyelids — the result of an extra fold of skin. Yet, for all these faults in structure, mongolism is not a genetic problem — it is not inherited. It occurs after conception at the time the newly

formed embryo begins the phase of rapid cell division and growth. Thus, mongolism can rightly be called a "congenital" problem — meaning that it occurs sometime between the event of normal conception and the birth of the infant.

Mongolism (Down's Syndrome): congenital problem that occurs as the newly formed embryo begins to divide into new cells. Infants born with this condition have abnormal body features including a thick tongue, heavy dual-folded eyelids, flattened face, etc.

Congenital: taking place sometime between normal conception and birth.

Other congenital birth defects are caused by diseases the mother suffers while she carries the baby. A deformed or retarded child is a likely result when a mother has German measles during the first four months of her term. The risk here is so great that most doctors suggest abortion. Venereal disease in a pregnant woman is another cause for birth defect and retardation. Contact with poisons of many kinds when pregnant can cause birth defects. And drug abuse brings, along with other ill effects, the spectre of a birth defect and a retarded child.

- ■11 What is Down's Syndrome? How is it related to the mongoloid?
- ■12 In what sense is Down's Syndrome a congenital problem?
- ■13 Define mongolism.
- ■14 Define congenital.
- ■15   Name four other possible causes of congenital birth defects that may be related to retardation.

STEREOTYPING AND BRAIN DAMAGE

Mae's program

Ceil paused outside one of the booths. "And now the moment we've both been waiting for." They went inside. Two students were in the booth with a young black girl. Ceil nodded to the two students. "Mae, this is Casey. She's the one you asked about the other day, isn't she?"

"Yes. Yes, she is. Hello, Casey."

"Hello — what's your name? My name's Casey."

"Her name's Mae," Ceil said. "Casey, tell Mae what you've been doing here."

"I've been doing my numbers — see." She held up a sheet of paper; sums were written beneath the problems dittoed on the paper. The numbers were big and well formed.

"That's very good, Casey," Mae said, handing back the paper.

"Casey, Mae's going to be working with you some. You think you'll like that?"

"When? When?" Casey said.

"Soon," Mae said. "I hope very soon."

The schedule called for Mae to work with Casey an hour each day. Thirty minutes more were spent in getting ready for the session and in plotting the data after it was over.

The program Ceil had outlined for her to use with Casey was a simple one. It had to do with teaching her color names. Mae was surprised to find that Casey didn't know her colors — any ten-year-old would know that. But Casey only looked ten. She was thirteen. "Don't be fooled by Casey," Ceil had said. "She talks well, can carry on a pretty good give and take with you; she does the right things, has good manners, and hygiene. But these skills mask some real holes. She doesn't know a lot of things we take for granted in someone who acts as alert as she does and tries as hard."

They started with five colors — red, green, yellow, blue, and orange. The colors were wooden blocks, all the same size and texture. They were put in front of her in a row. Casey was supposed to pick up the right one when Mae named the color. If Casey picked up the right one, Mae praised her: "That's good; good girl, Casey." Sometimes she hugged her too, or just touched her lightly — a huge treat for Casey, and not a small one for Mae.

If she picked up the wrong block, Mae said, "No, Casey," and quickly picked all the blocks up and held them in her lap for fifteen seconds. When she did this, Mae wasn't to look at Casey. She had to avoid all social contact for this brief time. It was hard for Mae to tell Casey she was wrong because the child looked so forlorn. And worst of all was the waiting. Mae wanted to rush right into the next trial so

Casey could be right — and the gloom change to sunshine. At the end of fifteen seconds, Mae would put the blocks down again and turn to Casey.

After each trial — whether Casey was right or wrong — Mae picked up all the blocks and put them down in a new place in the row, so Casey couldn't rely on the placement as a cue rather than the colors. In that way when she was correct most of the time, it would be color and not place that would control her response.

Mae ran twenty trials, one after the other — took a rest — and then started a new block of twenty trials. Five such blocks, or a hundred trials, were run each day she worked with Casey.

***

You can see what was going on in the training Mae is giving Casey. Praise, hugs, touching — this is social reward. Mae thus rewarded correct responses. The "no" when Casey makes a wrong response is a cue — and it looks like it's a strong one. It's, of course, a punisher too. Also, the fifteen-second wait after a wrong response is a mild punisher called a "time out" or "time out from positive reinforcement". Casey has to wait a bit before she has a chance to win back her friend's esteem. She's given a time out from the situation where she can earn these rewards. Giving reward for correct actions and ignoring and/or punishing wrong ones causes the subject to make a discrimination. Casey's program is a form of "discrimination training".

Time out (time out from positive reinforcement): a procedure where the chance to earn reinforcement is delayed for a short period of time as a consequence of making an error. Time out tends to act as a mild punisher, thus suppressing errors.

Discrimination training: reinforcing a response in the presence of one discriminative stimulus, while not reinforcing it in the presence of other discriminative stimuli. Discrimination training typically results in the person making the response only in the presence of the correct discriminative stimulus.

- ▪16 What general type of procedure or training is involved in rewarding a correct response and extinguishing or punishing incorrect ones?
- ▪17 What's a time out? Define.
- ▪18 Define discrimination training.

Stereotyping

It didn't take long for Mae to get the drift of what was going on. Casey wasn't learning. That became clear enough. Mae looked at the record of right and wrong trials. Sometimes she got four or five right in a row. Other times she might go as many as fifteen or even twenty trials without more than one or two correct. All in all, Casey was right only about a fifth of the time — just what you'd expect by chance.

Anyone could do that well — even blindfolded. Maybe Casey just needed more practice. At least that's what Mae hoped. So she ran more trials. Then a funny thing happened. Casey started picking up the block on the far right — and only that block. It didn't matter what color Mae asked for — Casey picked the one on the far right. She stuck with it for sixty trials. Mae took a break then.

Casey broke the pattern on the first trial on the very next series. She picked the one on the far left. It was the correct one. Mae hugged and kissed her and rejoiced. *It's about time!* she thought. But her joy was short-lived. Now Casey wouldn't get off the far left again. Next it was the middle one. She kept on it for the rest of the session.

***

Mae spent three hours in the stacks before she found a book that would answer her questions. Later in the dorm she turned to the section she was looking for.

Sometimes the retardate adopts fixed or rigid response patterns. All cues, signs, informative input, go unheeded as the individual proceeds in an unvarying mode of action. Position biases, repetitive speech and mannerisms are common. This condition — without doubt the result of brain malfunction — is often referred to as "stereotyping".

"Stereotyping" — that's what it's called — "the result of brain malfunction". That's serious. There isn't much you can do about brain damage!

Stereotyping: a mode or manner of responding where the person keeps making the same response regardless of the presence of discriminative stimuli that could result in perfect control and correct responses.

***

Mae slept badly that night. The next day she went to the Co-Op School early so she could check Casey's file. She didn't know what all of the terms meant, but one entry was all too clear.

9-12
. . . considering the history of acute encephalitis at the age of three years along with the neurological and behavioral results, it is concluded that the patient's current low performance is attributable to brain damage of a moderate to severe degree.
Dx. Chronic Brain Syndrome (undifferentiated)

That was it. Mae felt a numbing fog of despair descend on her. Casey would never learn her colors. She'd never learn much more than she had. Casey was brain damaged.

■19 Define stereotyping.

Brain damage

One mode of behaving often seen in the retarded is stereotyping. It's the term used to describe a situation where the subject persists in making the same response in the face of changing cues and reward features. Fixing on a position — right, left, middle, etc. — as Casey did is common. Stereotyping has been known to occur in cases of known "brain damage".

Brain damage: damage to brain cells that kills them or vastly impairs their normal function.

Brain damage means what you might predict. Some cells or portion of brain tissue are in a morbid state, they're dead. This can result from a variety of things. It can happen when the head is hit or knocked in auto wrecks, or pierced from gunshot wounds. Damage in such cases is said to be due to "trauma".

Trauma: injury to body tissues that results from impact and collision with various objects.

Drugs, liquor, poisons, lead in paint and other toxins also kill neural and brain cells. In the final stages of the disease, syphillis germs attack neural cells. Other disease creates changes in the body that affect the medium around the brain. A shortage of oxygen to the brain — known as "anoxia" — kills brain cells. It's a leading cause of birth defect, and often takes place when the infant's being delivered.

Anoxia: condition where cells are damaged due to the failure of oxygen to reach them.

Once gone, brain tissue isn't replaced by the body. It won't grow back like muscle, skin and bone. Disease kills brain tissue.

Like many cells, brain cells die if they're heated even a few degrees above normal. Thus, any disease that produces a high fever can cause brain damage. Encephalitis — the disease Casey is alleged to have suffered — infects and inflames the fluid (cerebrospinal) that surrounds the brain. If severe enough, it will cause damage to the brain proper.

Encephalitis: infection of the fluid that surrounds the brain and spinal cord.

Cerebrospinal fluid: fluid that surrounds the brain and spinal cord.

But what does all of this have to do with stereotyping? Does brain damage cause it? And most of all, does the presence of brain damage mean that no new learning can occur?

- ■20 Define brain damage.
- ■21 Define trauma.
- ■22 Define anoxia.
- ■23 Define encephalitis.
- ■24 Define cerebrospinal fluid.
- ■25 Cite two instances of trauma.
- ■26 What chemical agents are known to kill brain cells?

Time and area of brain damage

The next day Casey greeted Mae like she always did — a kitten whose owner was at last home. Seeing the bright and happy face, eager to start the session, brought tears to Mae's eyes. Casey was ready to pick up the blocks again — blocks that for her would never have color. She was doing it to please Mae. But for Casey it was pointless. It wasn't a chance to learn; it was a cruel game where she might at one moment find hugs and kindness and at the next indifference.

***

Mae was lucky to find Ceil in her office after the session.

"Hello," Ceil said. "Come in! Is something wrong, Mae?"

"I couldn't get to first base with Casey. She couldn't learn the colors," Mae said slowly, trying to hide her sadness. "She kept picking the right one; then the left, the middle — no matter what color name I gave her. Stereotyping, I think they call it."

"Yes that's right. So?" Ceil was still confused by Mae's manner.

"So, I found out that it's sometimes due to brain damage. I checked Casey's records. You can see for yourself." Ceil took Casey's folder and read the part Mae pointed to. Then she looked up at Mae.

"It says Casey may be brain damaged — is that what you mean?" Ceil didn't bat an eye.

It was Mae who was confused now. How could Ceil be so calm about it? "If Casey's brain's damaged, it means she can't learn. It means we're hurting her — torturing her — asking her to do things she just can't do! She wants to learn, wants to do what we want her to, but . . ." Mae looked down at the floor and tried to swallow.

"So that's it. Well, that makes sense. Wait here a minute." Ceil left the office and returned with a stack of folders. "Look here," she said, opening one of the folders and leafing through it until she found the page she wanted. "This's Ted — diagnosis: brain damage." She tossed Ted's folder on her desk and opened the next one. "Susie — indications: brain damage. Louise: brain damage. Jackie: brain damage. Look, all of them." She dropped the stack in Mae's lap. Most of the kids here — dx: brain damage. Now do you see?"

"No, I don't — not at all. Do you mean the doctors are wrong — they're not really brain damaged?"

"No, that's not what I mean — though I'm not sure they're right about it all the time. They go mostly on what the child does; how he or she acts. When x-rays and brain waves don't show damage, they're likely to say a kid's brain damaged — just because he or she acts a lot like others they've seen who have proven damage. But that's really not the point, is it?"

"No, Casey's the point. What if she is brain damaged? What are we doing to her? Is there any way we could be more cruel?"

"Yes, there is — a lot more cruel. It's to quit on Case — Look. Let's say she is brain damaged — so what? Are you sure you're not? I'm not? In these days of DDT, exhaust fumes, dope, booze, atom bombs, bad air, football, wreckless drivers! We're all likely to have some brain damage. It's a matter of degree. Besides — and here's the real point — brain damage does not mean you can't learn. I've heard of cases — seen a few first hand — where people lost big chunks of their brain. Sure it knocked 'em at first. Maybe turned 'em into a basket case for a time. But slowly, with patience and training, they came back. They lived to go ahead with their job, homes, raise their kids. They may come out of it just as good as they were before. No — even if Casey's brain damaged, the worst thing we could do is give up on her. No! Worse than that is to let her cop out and give up."

* * *

Brain damage — a chilling thought. Like Mae, most of us feel that it's the end of the line. Ceil points out that it doesn't have to be that way. The effect of brain damage and whether it can be reversed, depends on a number of things. The amount of damage — the total number of cells destroyed — is a prime factor. Of greater concern is the part of the brain involved. The human brain differs from the brains of other creatures in the degree of special functions some parts assume. When a part with a special function is destroyed, that function can't be taken over by other intact portions. Vision, hearing, speech, are all functions that depend on the intact presence of special brain tissue. When these parts are lost, the functions also go.

Other portions of the brain are involved in a gross way in behavior. Loss of this tissue can cause impaired action at first. With training, the old skills return. The role the damaged tissues played is taken over by intact portions. Besides how much and where, when the damage occurred can be a crucial factor.

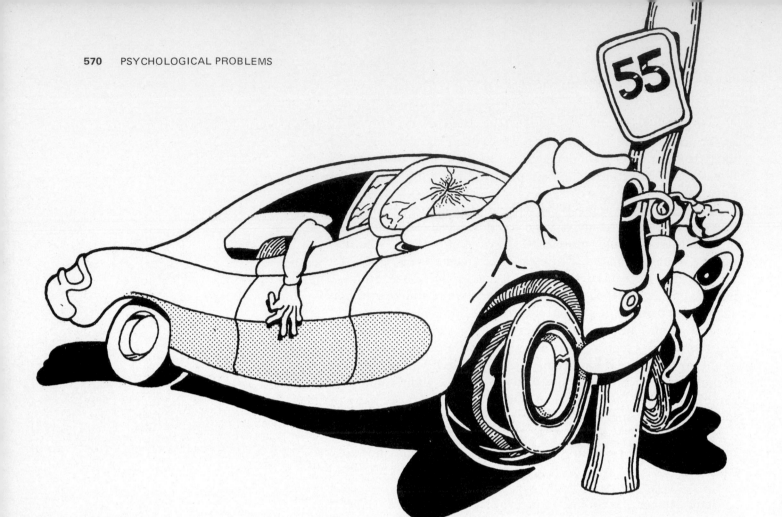

All things equal, adults who suffer brain damage have a better chance to regain lost skills and functions than children. Infants or very young children suffer the most. In their case, it is not a matter of relearning. They never had the skills. And, after injury, they may never learn them. Part of the problem with children is due to the delay in training that is caused by the disease or injury that caused brain damage. While muscles and bones are growing, damaged brain and neural tissue don't allow some skills and functions to keep pace. Further, the skills that aren't learned are very basic ones — those that are building blocks for the normal skills our culture demands. Later on, advanced skills can't be learned because the basic ones are missing.

■27 What effect does the extent of brain damage have to do with impairment of function?
■28 What does location have to do with brain function?
■29 What is the relationship between age and the effect of brain damage on function?
■30 What does the delay in learning basic skills have to do with the increased problem of brain damage in the young?

STEREOTYPING AND STIMULUS CONTROL

"But what about the stereotyping?" Mae said.

"Stereotyping's no big deal here. We run into it pretty often with these kids. It never, never means we should back off and quit."

"Well, what does it mean, then?" Mae asked.

"It means there's something wrong with the program. You don't have stimulus control. In your program with Casey, neither the colors nor the color names are getting control of her response. It's the reward alone that's controlling it."

"She picks up one of the blocks when I tell her — it's just the wrong one, for the most part. Lately, I've been getting the stereotyping."

"Let me put it another way. Suppose Casey was color blind — something wrong with the structure of her eye so she couldn't respond to color stimuli. Put yourself in her place. You see this woman across from you. She tells you to pick up the red one. She motions to a row. She looks at you and waits. You're supposed to pick up one of them. You humor her by picking up one of the blocks. This seems to be what she wants at first. She keeps asking you to do it again. You happen to pick up the one on the far right. Wow! She goes crazy — gives you all kinds of hugs and kisses. That must be the one she wants — the one on the right. That's the one to pick up

next time!"

"Yes, I can see that. But what about the next time, when the one on the right side isn't the correct one? Tell her 'no' and turn away. It almost kills her."

"So into each life a little rain must fall — picking the one on the right does pay off on an average of one out of five times. And too, the one on the right could just by chance happen to be on the right three or four times in a row. You know, the block that's the same color as the name you call ends up there by chance. It happens — right?"

"But what about the shift? Like, when she shifts from stereotyping on the right side to the middle?"

"Well, if you look real close, I think you'll find she does this only after she's gone dozens of trials without making the right response. Stereotyping to the right side, say, is extinguished. She tries a new placement. If this happens to be correct a few times in a row — she's likely to stereotype on it."

"Then Casey's color blind?"

"No. No. At least, I doubt it. If a few other things don't work, we'll check that out. It's not likely, though. Only a small percentage of the kids are color blind. No, it's just a gross lack of stimulus control."

* * *

Ceil's way of looking at stereotyping seems to take all the

mystique out of it. Authors in the past have gotten a lot of mileage out of pointing up the "strangeness" of the retarded. Ceil brings it all down to earth — and right back home. The truth is, we all suffer from stimulus control problems — that is, our actions don't always fit with what the cues in the setting are trying to tell us will be rewarded.

Going forty in a twenty-mile zone, picking out a horror of a scarf or tie to go with our outfit, telling an off-color joke to our spouse's fuddy Uncle Oswald — these, too, are stimulus control problems. We've got them for the same reason Casey has hers. The correct responses haven't occurred often enough in the presence of the unique cues. As a result, they just haven't been reinforced.

It's only after several times of being paired with the right responses and rewards that the stimulus becomes a good strong cue. Only then will it exert tight control. We'll do better and Casey's stereotyping will end when the correct response occurs in the presence of the right stimuli and then — and only then — yields reward.

■31 Cite at least three ways normal people may be said to have stimulus control problems.

■32 When will stereotyping end?

TEACHING THE RETARDED

"I'll tell you what's wrong. We've got too much going on at once — too many cues floating around. See, there are five verbal cues — the color names; and there're five colors — the five colored blocks. They're cues too. That's a lot. We've got to make it easier for Casey. It's not that she or any other person who's retarded can't learn — it's just that they don't learn under normal conditions. We'll have to change things. Make it easier."

"I don't see how making it easy for her gets us or her anywhere. She still won't know what she should — what other kids her age know."

"That's right — but there's more to it. I didn't say we wouldn't make it harder later on. I can see your next question's going to be: How? Well, we've got a few tricks. Some special techniques. You'll see."

* * *

For all we may say about the causes of retardation, the truth is that seldom do we know in a specific case what's really wrong with the structure. The result we see is the outcome of a merging of factors, and not due to structure alone. Difference in structure can affect health. This in turn thwarts or slows training. Lack of certain skills can further impair growth by keeping the child from normal sports, games and social contact. This reflects backward on body growth. It's a case of the "for want of a nail, the shoe was lost; for want of a shoe, the horse was lost; . . ."

What we do know is that the retarded can learn. The problem is that they often can't learn in those settings provided for the normal child in our culture. They aren't able to benefit from teaching methods that prevail in our schools. In the past few years, behavioral science has developed new methods that allow us to teach the retarded person in a direct and certain manner. With these new tools the question is not so much: what can the retarded learn? It's rather: what are we willing to invest in their training? With these new methods the limits believed to be a part of the "sentence" of being retarded may well dissolve as fiction.

■33 For all we've said about causes, what can we usually say about a specific case of retardation?

■34 The role faulty structure plays in the outcome we see as retardation was likened to the saying, "for want of a nail, the shoe was lost; . . ." Tell how this relates.

■35 With the new methods developed in behavioral science, what is the real question we must ask regarding the training of the retarded?

■36 If the retarded can learn, why is it they usually don't?

CONCLUSIONS

It's easy enough to see that our knowledge of the causes of retardation, as with the causes of psychoses, needs much filling in. New facts are found daily — yet, it will be some time before our grasp comes close to being complete. We've mentioned a few well known genetic and congenital causes of retardation. We've also dealt with brain damage, and given some notion of its effect on behavior.

These things are good to know, but at this point in time it's not likely we could do anything about faulty structure — even if we could pinpoint the damage or defect. Medical science for the most part can do little to change this structure. What we can do — must do — is "go over the top" of the known or presumed defect in structure. We do this by using new and more powerful training techniques that have recently been developed. It is, after all, the getting there — the mastering the skills needed to survive in our culture — that matters, not the route but the techniques that are used. In the next chapter we'll discuss some of these techniques. We'll look at some of the behavioral methods that have been so effective with the retarded and psychotic.

THERAPIES

We've seen how creatures develop across the ages, evolving as conditions change. And we've seen how they develop within their life spans — growing and learning — taking on new form and function. Sometimes these phylogenetic and ontogenetic factors act in concert to cause problems — problems that constrain proper actions and threaten survival. We discussed the nature of these problems in the last section. Now it's time to think about how we can deal with them — or better still, avoid them in the first place.

As you know, humans are prone to develop complex and vast psychological problems; but we're not helpless in the face of this threat. We know something of how these problems arise; we know they're always caused, at least in part, by our common human structure, and helped along in some cases by the special structure that's unique to each of us.

But, so far, we've not had much success at changing structure for the sake of therapy. Even at this moment, scientists are trying to find ways to repair faulty and damaged structure and to prevent such problems in the future. Still, we have a while to wait.

But our problems also result from the wrong sort of learning. Here we can do more right away — something that won't change structure, but may buffet or in some way negate its constraints. New learning can replace old — new effective actions can replace the feeble ones of the past.

Treatment for psychological problems has taken both approaches in the past. Structure has been altered through drugs, surgery, and other gross physical measures, in an attempt to deal with psychological problems. Other approaches to therapy have involved verbal exchanges between therapist and patient — or among therapists and patients. In either case, this type of therapy is called psychotherapy.

You won't be surprised to find that we view psychotherapy — and indeed, all therapy to some extent — as having a large component of learning. Even where drugs and surgery are employed, patients must learn responses that are in some sense new and foreign to their altered structure. In the following chapters we present two approaches to therapy which most clearly spell out the role of learning, arranging for that learning to occur in the most direct manner.

CHAPTER 31
B. F. SKINNER
AND BEHAVIOR
MODIFICATION

INTRODUCTION

Basic and applied psychology

A clear day, bright sunshine, but cool. Sid watched gusts of wind chase dead leaves across the courtyard three stories below. His eyes returned to stare at the empty seat in front of him. It was the one Dawn sat in — that is, when she made it to class. *What's wrong with that woman?* Sid thought. *Twice this week she's cut Harper's class. She better get her act together.* Sid rested his chin in cupped hands, tuning back in to attend to Dr. Harper's lecture.

"And so, we turn from basic to applied science. Just how do the concepts we've learned so far in the term relate — if in fact they do? It's time to try to answer the question that all science and scientists must contend with after they've shown us their data; after they've told us their theories: So what? Will they better our lives, make us happy, help us survive? The mechanics of reinforcement, extinction, punishment — are these tools that nature alone may use? Or, may we put them to our own purpose — to change our own lives, perhaps our destiny? It's time to see how the principles we've studied may be applied to change behavior in a way that will profit both the individual and the culture. The approach we'll discuss at our next class meeting is 'behavior modification'. Class dismissed."

B. F. Skinner's operant psychology

The greatest force in modern psychology is embodied in the person
of B. F. Skinner, whose major research and theory were first presented
in 1938 in his book, *The Behavior of Organisms*. Both in that volume
and throughout the years, Skinner has embraced a single basic tenet:
Behavior makes sense only when related to the outcomes it creates for
the behaving creature. A simple notion, but one deeply rooted in the
hard clay of biological evolution. Actions allow creatures to do
something about their world, changing those aspects that foster
survival, freeing them from the sometimes fatal dole of a passive life.
Thus, for Skinner, the true meaning of actions can be found in how
those actions operate to alter a creature's world. This led him to call
his approach "operant psychology".

Skinner and his students have succeeded in showing how the
simple premise that "behavior is controlled by its consequences" is
indeed a basic truth that applies to all behavior. Operant research has
further proven that the principles of behavior first shown with pigeons
and rats in the humble Skinner box, apply to other creatures —
the human among them. These laws and principles have, of course,
been the ones we've discussed in previous chapters. We'll now see
how they're applied in behavior modification.

- 1 Whose teachings have provided the greatest force in modern
  psychology?
- 2 What is Skinner's single basic tenet? In what is it deeply rooted?
- 3 What term did Skinner apply to his psychology? How does this
  name describe his approach?

Behavior modification

"It's not that I don't enjoy your class, Dr. Harper — I cut other classes, too! I mean . . ." Dawn stammered.

"I think I know what you mean. You're trying to tell me that you cut classes and you wish you didn't — that it?"

"Something like that."

"If that's the case, seems like we should do something about it."

"But I try, Dr. Harper, I really do. At the start of each week I swear I'm not going to cut a single class. Then the next thing I know, something comes up — a phone call, or someone drops by, or . . . well . . ."

"Sounds like a perfect set-up to try out some behavior modification."

"Some what?"

"You know, I mentioned it in class."

"Errr . . ."

"Oh — that's right! You didn't make it to the last class, did you? That's okay. I'll explain it to you. See, by employing the concepts of operant psychology, we can design a program to help you manage your class-attending behavior — self-control. Get it? The first thing we've got to do . . ." Harper was off and running, gesturing wildly, as he always did when he was enthused. Dawn wondered what she was letting herself in for.

* * *

Behavior modification, or b mod, as it's called, is the applied branch of the science of behavioral psychology and operant psychology in particular. The concepts applied largely come from B. F. Skinner's operant approach. By now we know that actions change when they produce certain events or outcomes — are reinforced or punished. By and large, rewards and punishers are supplied by nature; and in human society, by others acting intuitively or in accord with common sense. In b mod, outcomes — rewards, etc. — are used in a direct, planned manner to produce desired changes, changes in what humans and other creatures do.

Behavior modification: the application of principles of behavioral psychology, and operant psychology in particular, to change actions in a desired manner or direction.

Psychologists first used b mod more than a decade ago to curtail problem behavior in psychotics, the retarded, and others confined in state homes or hospitals. Later, it was also found to be of great service in dealing with the problems of less impaired persons. Now it's a mainstay in resolving conflicts of normal people of all ages — children, teen-agers, adults, and the elderly. It works with all kinds of problems: in marriage, in business, in educational settings, in prisons, and in child-rearing.

One of the greatest promises of behavior modification lies in its use in helping people manage their own behavior. This is often called self-control. Dr. Harper is suggesting to Dawn that she use b mod to change her class-attending behavior. An exciting prospect! We'll hear more of her program later on.

- ▪ 4 What is the applied branch of operant psychology?
- ▪ 5 Where and with whom was b mod first used? With what kinds of people and problems is it currently used?
- ▪ 6 What is one of the greatest promises of b mod?
- ▪ 7 Thought question: How does b mod relate to the helping approach Carol used in raising little Chet?

EXTINCTION PROCEDURES AND B MOD

Harold goes mod

The morning trudged on. Carol tried hard to keep on task, typing the few letters Dr. Stein had given her. But her eyes always returned to the clock on the wall. First thing after lunch she'd meet Bob Moore at the state hospital to talk over the b mod program he'd designed for Harold. The best part was she'd be a part of the team that would carry out the treatment. That was something to think about!

***

"The basic problem with Harold is clear enough — he gets paid off for doing bizarre things. Jumping into the dryer's the worst in a long list of tricks he's learned, to get him a few socials," Bob Moore said. "Harold's bad stuff is reinforced; and the reward's attention. In this sense, social rewards are the cause of Harold's actions. Now, it follows that the action will stop if we take away the cause. So we'd have to ignore Harold, when he did his thing."

"How can we do that? We can't turn our backs and act like he isn't in the dryer. He's just flesh and bone. Even Harold's got his limits," Carol said.

"And there's the rub," Bob answered wryly.

***

Extinction isn't a new concept for us. In a previous chapter we learned that it's both a procedure and a process. Taking away the reward is a procedure that reduces response frequency — the extinction process.

Extinction procedures are widely applied in b mod practice. Much of what we'd like to see changed about ourselves and others involves problem behavior: things we do that harm us or cause us to lose rewards in the long run. We can often stop these actions by using extinction.

Problem behavior is maintained by its results, just like other acts. If we wish to use extinction, we must first find the reward maintaining the unwanted response. Then we can start the extinction procedure; we can take steps to insure that the problem behavior stops yielding the reward. Once this is done, response frequency will dwindle — the extinction process. Harold's actions are rewarded by attention. Bob and Carol will use the extinction procedure by ignoring Harold's unhealthy acts.

But is this wise? Carol points out that Harold could die in the clothes dryer if they leave him to his own devices. Of course, she's right. In fact, many problem behaviors maintained by attention are like this — ignoring them can be so costly or harmful that we can't risk it. In fact, that's why and how they're shaped, in many cases. It's impossible for others to ignore such harmful acts so the unfortunate people may find themselves inadvertently locked in a deadly game where they're doing unhealthy things — dangerous things that can't be ignored and so are guaranteed attention. It looks like our heroes are trapped. If they ignore Harold he could wipe himself out, and if they move in — stopping him before he gets hurt — they're paying attention to, and rewarding his bizarre routine. Quite a dilemma; but one b mod has faced before — and surpassed. There are perhaps more ways to skin a cat than even Skinner dreamed of.

***

"This should do it — put Harold's responses on extinction and still not worry about injury. Take a look inside," Bob said.

Carol opened the dryer door. All of the metal surfaces were covered with thick pieces of foam rubber.

"Took off the line to the coils so they won't heat up. Fixed the timer, too. Harold'll get a five-minute ride, but no cuts or scrapes — and no burns."

"So Harold's got a ticket to ride. Now we really can ignore him."

"At least we can make it look like we are," Bob said.

- 8 What must you find out before extinction procedures can be applied to a problem behavior?
- 9 The careless use of an extinction procedure could spell disaster in cases where attention maintains a problem behavior. Why?

Baseline

Carol had always kept careful records on how often Harold jumped into the clothes dryer, even long before the program began. Bob showed her how to plot these data on a graph as he seemed to feel getting such data was crucial. Carol couldn't see why it mattered. After all, they knew Harold had a problem. Once was enough — why did she have to keep track of how often it happened? Now that it looked like they were ready to start, Bob wanted more data — "baseline", he called it.

"Why do we have to watch Harold any longer? Can't we just get on with it — start extinction?"

"No, we need more baseline data. We've changed things. It's not the same dryer — not at all. Sooner or later we'll want to change the dryer back to the way it was. Could be that the changes we've made will take all the fun out of it for Harold and he'll quit — even without extinction. Then when we restore the dryer, he might go right back to it. No, we've got to observe him a few days more, and treat him just like always. If he jumps in the dryer one of us or the ward people will get him out and take him to the nurse's station. They'll check him over just like they've done in the past. If Harold stops his antics, then we may be wrong — attention may not be what causes him to act

that way. But, it's a good bet we're on the right track if he keeps it up, even with the dryer changed. Then we can start treatment."

***

Baseline data serve as a standard to which treatment outcomes are compared. It might appear a simple matter to tell if treatment is doing any good, yet nothing is further from the truth. Opinions based on unstructured observation are always suspect, no matter who gives them — the patient, friends, ward people, or even the pros — psychologists, physicians, nurses, etc. Good baseline data help do away with any questions. They are precise — taken in a manner to insure that they reflect the patient's actions, and not the opinions of the staff or other viewers. Data are taken in the same precise way during treatment, so we can compare treatment data to the baseline. This makes it fairly simple for us to decide if a treatment is helping or hindering.

Baseline: systematic observations taken prior to treatment which are used to evaluate the extent and nature of treatment effects.

We use a treatment because we think it will have a good result. It follows that we'll assume that outcomes occurring when the

treatment begins are caused by it. Perhaps we can't assume this — not if we make other changes along with the treatment. Bob's point is that dryer changes may affect Harold's actions.

In Harold's case, if extinction were begun at the same time the dryer was changed there'd be no way of knowing whether outcomes were due to extinction or to the dryer. They must therefore see what effect the dryer makes before the treatment begins. Bob's suggesting that two baselines need to be used — one with the old dryer, and the other after changes. If the dryer has no great effect on Harold's actions, then treatment may proceed.

There wasn't a chance that Harold could get hurt after the changes in the dryer were made. Still, they had to act the same — rush to the dryer each time Harold got in, retrieve him, and take him to the nurses' station, then back to the ward. It was clear within a week that the changes didn't slow him down. In fact, they seemed to work the other way, increasing response frequency somewhat. It looked more than ever like attention was the cause of Harold's response.

- ■10 Define baseline.
- ■11 Why is baseline needed?
- ■12 When may two baselines be needed?

Treatment begins

At last it was time to begin extinction. Carol, Bob, and some of the others sat unobserved inside a nearby office watching Harold and the dryer. They didn't have to wait long. Soon Harold came to the dryer, opened the door and jumped in, closing the door behind him. He whirled around for five minutes, then the machine stopped. Nothing else happened, and no one came to get him. At last he pushed the door open and climbed out, returning to the ward area.

That day Harold repeated the sequence fifteen times. This bothered Carol. He'd never gone into the dryer that often in a week — let alone a single day. Something was wrong.

"I don't get it, Bob. It looks like extinction's only making Harold worse. It doesn't make sense."

"It looks that way I admit — but don't panic. Harold always got hurt before. Sometimes he was so wracked up he could hardly move. That kept return trips down for a while. Now when he gets out, he's no worse for the trip. He's in good shape to do it again right away. But that's only part of the answer. Responses always increase at first when they're placed on extinction. That's one reason some people who try extinction give it up. It looks like it's making

things worse. You'll see. We have to wait it out, that's all. Meanwhile, Harold's in no danger."

***

Bob was right. The frequency dropped down to five on the next day, to three on the third day, and to zero on the fourth. A day later it happened once more — then nothing for two weeks.

"You called it right, Bob. Harold's stopped. But now what? Is that it?" Carol asked.

"Not quite. The next step's the tricky one. We've got to change the dryer back like it was."

"But if Harold jumps in it, he could get hurt."

"Right you are — and we'd have to move in to stop him before it was too late. We'd be right back where we started. But if he doesn't try it we're okay. Let's hope that's the way it is. The ward people are on my back to get their dryer in working order. Now or never, I guess."

***

Carol found Bob sitting in his office, feet propped up on the desk.

"I've got all the data plotted like you asked me. A solid month now and no problems from Harold. It all seems a little too easy."

"Too easy, huh? What about all those weeks we put in?"

"I guess I don't mean easy — though I can't say it ever seemed like work to me. Simple — that's what I mean. It seems too simple."

"I'll admit we got a few breaks here and there with Harold. But it is simple. And not just with Harold — with most problem behavior. Harold did his thing because he got rewarded for it. Why didn't he do something else — something worthwhile? Well, maybe he couldn't. That's one way to look at it at least. If only Harold had good skills that paid off — but if that were true, would he be here in the first place?"

"Not all of Harold's behavior is bad. He watches TV, plays cards. I saw him reading a book the other day."

"Sure — and who pays attention when he does? No one. That's the point — and that's how b mod works. It changes rewards, shifts them around. It puts the heavy rewards on good actions, and removes them from problem acts. Like you said, simple — in theory, at least. But pretty tough to pull off sometimes."

"Then we've only started with Harold?"

"That's right. Now comes the hard part — and it may last for years — teaching Harold good behaviors and making sure others reward him for them."

***

If you're not certain of the many phases of Harold's b mod treatment, it might help to take a brief look at Carol's graph.

The frequency of jumping in the dryer is given on the vertical scale to the left. The days of the baseline and treatment program are indicated along the horizontal axis at the bottom. When extinction began (Week 4), response frequency shot up to 15 on the first day. Responses dwindled in the next days and soon hit zero.

And that's the way it was. Restoring the dryer had no effect (Week 7) — Harold was through with it. Extinction wins again!

■13 When an extinction procedure begins it often looks like it's not working. Why?

■14 Describe a behavior modification procedure using extinction.

■15 Explain what's meant by the statement: "B mod works by shifting rewards

from one response to another."

■16 Thought questions: What's the difference between extinction and punishment by the removal of a reward? How could you use extinction for a specific act while keeping the rate of reward very high? Can you think of an instance where you should use such a procedure in your own personal life?

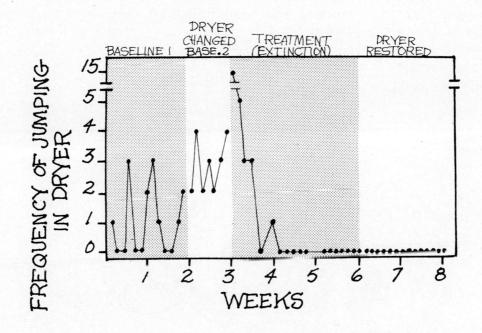

TASK ANALYSIS AND SELECTION

Making it easier for Casey

Mae Robinson found out about b mod at nearly the same time as Carol — and for the same reason. Standard training methods had not helped Mae's charge, Casey Clark, just as they had failed with Harold. But Mae stuck with Casey, though Casey might never learn her colors. Neither the color of the blocks nor the color names controlled her response. She was stereotyping — locked onto whatever block was in a certain place in the row of five blocks — not attending to any aspect of color. Mae was ready to believe Casey's brain was too impaired for her to learn. But Ceil Bennett had an answer — try b mod.

"Casey's not the first youngster here at the Co-op School who's given us trouble with stereotyping," Ceil said. "We're far from licked with her. There are a lot of things we can try."

"You said something about making it simpler for her — what'd you mean by that?"

"Come on," Ceil said. "Let's go get Casey and I'll show you."

Ceil sat Casey in the chair and got the colored blocks. But Ceil used only two blocks — the red and green; not the five Mae had worked with. She put this pair of blocks in the same place on the table before Casey.

"You can see I've started with only two blocks instead of the five you were using," Ceil explained to Mae. "There are two color stimuli, and their names — red and green — four stimuli in all — a far simpler task. We give her one a bit harder — more complex — when she masters this. Task analysis and selection are important factors in all teaching — but with the retarded they're crucial."

* * *

Things go a lot better if you start with something your subjects already know when you're training a new skill. Success yields success. Start with tasks they can do, changing the nature of the task slowly, until you're teaching the one you were heading for. To some extent good teaching is just proper task selection. Good teachers make sure youngsters know how to add and subtract before moving on to more complex math skills. Good coaches teach basics before starting on the fine points of their sport. But correct task selection depends on proper task analysis in the first place — and this is where b mod and behavioral techniques have it over other approaches. Their system of analyzing what's going on in a learning setting is much tighter, and more fruitful.

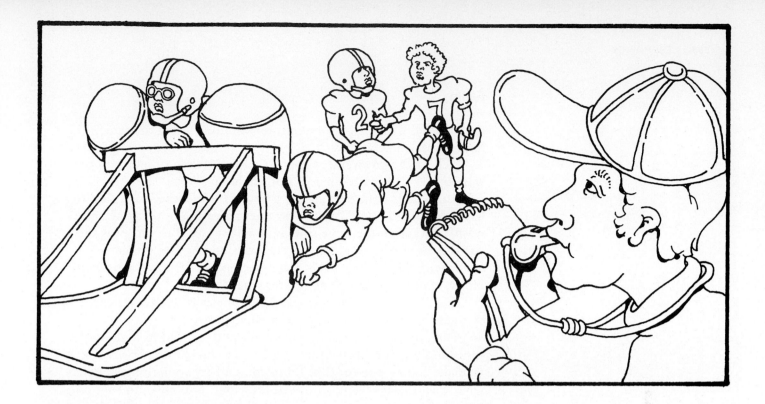

Task analysis: breaking down a complex behavior into its basic components.

Task selection: presenting the various basic components of a complex task in a sequence and manner that lead to mastery of the complex behavior.

The operant approach sticks close to things that can be observed — responses, stimuli, and of course, rewards and other outcomes. All tasks — no matter how complex — can be broken down into basic units that are made up of three elements: 1) the response, or responses involved; 2) stimuli that control responses; and 3) the outcome or consequences the responses produce. Thus, when we look at a task from the point of view of behavior mod, we ask: What responses is the subject supposed to make? What stimuli should control these actions? What does the subject get for his effort?

Ceil Bennett analyzes Casey's task in just this way. First she asks if the reward used with Casey is a strong one. Here there's little doubt — social rewards really turn her on. No, her failure to learn isn't due to weak rewards. What about the response? Can Casey make the movements involved? No problem here either. Picking up a block is a simple act for her. That leaves the stimuli. Ceil sees that Casey's acts must come under the joint control of both the color name (a verbal cue given by Mae), and the visual cue of the block whose color matches the color name. But there are five blocks and five color names — a very complex task. Perhaps starting with a simpler one would help — just two colors and two names at first. She could break down the task into still simpler units.

But task selection is also a

practical matter. Ceil wants to get on with Casey's training, and starting with a simpler task before moving on would take more time. You'll soon see that Ceil was a bit hasty, and will be forced to use another b mod technique to get Casey on the right track. But knowing that she needs to use this new technique also is a result of good task analysis. Without doubt, the success b mod enjoys — the fact that it often works where other approaches fail — is largely due to the rigor it applies in task analysis and selection.

- ■17 Define task analysis.
- ■18 Define task selection.
- ■19 Tasks must be broken down into three elements. What are they?
- ■20 Thought question: What would you do by way of task analysis and task selection in this course?

Fading

Ceil worked with Casey for about ten minutes, using the same method Mae had employed.

"Pick up the green one, Casey," Ceil said. When Casey's response was correct Ceil praised her. If not, she'd say, "No, Casey," waiting fifteen seconds before giving her a new trial. In either case, Ceil took back the blocks after Casey chose one, making sure that one color wasn't always on the same side on the next trial. "Color" was the cue they wanted to control the response, and not "right-left" placement. After a few trials, Casey stereotyped on the right hand block, choosing that one no matter what Ceil asked for.

"Well," Ceil said. "How about that." Mae was slightly relieved; Ceil was getting the same results that she had gotten.

"The problem's stimulus control — I'm certain of it. Making the task simpler than it is now won't buy us a thing. Somehow we've got to make color a cue for Casey. I'm going to try something — watch." On the next trial Ceil put the two blocks out, but one — the red one — was about six inches closer to Casey than the green one. "Pick up the red block, Casey," Ceil said. Casey did as Ceil said. On the next trial the correct block was again closer to Casey than the wrong one. It was the one she picked up. Mae didn't know why Ceil was doing this. It was clear that color had nothing to do with the correct responses. "Closeness" was the cue controlling her actions. But Ceil kept it up. Casey was right for eleven trials in a row.

"Now," Ceil said, "I'm going to 'fade'." On the next trial the correct block was closer to Casey than the other one — but it wasn't quite as close as it had been on the last trial. During the next few trials Ceil reduced the closeness more — each time by a fraction of an inch. Within twenty trials, the two blocks differed very little in terms of how close they were to Casey. Casey hadn't made a mistake. On the the next trial, Ceil placed the blocks so that they were equally close to Casey.

"Here goes — with just a little luck . . ." Ceil called for the green one. Casey's response was correct on that trial, and the next twenty as well. Not a single error! "It worked." Ceil said. "She's got it now. What I did's called 'fading'. In this case, cue control was shifted from spatial cues to color cues. Now color controls the response — and that's what we wanted!"

"So Casey wasn't color blind," Mae said.

"And brain damage — that is, if the reports are right about her — didn't stop her from learning it either — not after b mod got into the act, in any event."

"Now what? Where do we go from here?" Mae asked.

"Add a new color next session. And by the end of the week, you could have her doing what you started out with — five blocks and five names. But keep in mind that you should go slowly. You can add new colors, but from time to time you may have to drop back and do some fading like I did."

*   *   *

Two techniques are so widely used in b mod that no treatment of the topic can proceed without their mention — shaping and fading. You can look at shaping as a kind of on the spot, task analysis and selection. It begins with a response you want to see your client or pupil make — one that he or she isn't making now. First you reward a response the person can make — one that's somewhat close to the one you want. You keep rewarding it until a response appears that's still closer. When this happens, you hop on it and forget the old one. And so it goes through many approximations until you get what you wanted. Mae used shaping to get Cecil the rat to make the lever-press response. And that's where shaping first started. Shaping, or the method of successive approximation, was explained in an earlier chapter (Learning: Factors Affecting Learning). It has been used for decades in training rats and pigeons in the lab. But it can be applied in many more unique settings. People using behavior modification saw its value as a means of getting human clients to learn new responses, and started using it quite early in the game. Now it's a mainstay in the b mod arsenal.

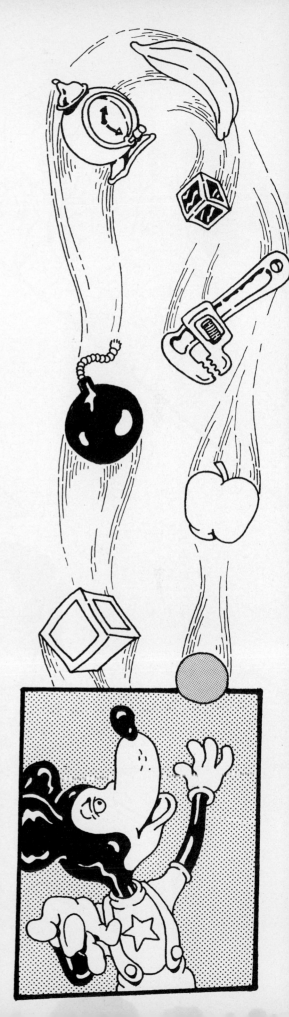

You may notice a likeness between shaping and fading — the technique Ceil used with Casey. Both involve gradual change. What changes in shaping is the response that's reinforced; whereas, in fading, the change is in the nature of the controlling stimuli. Fading change can occur in many ways, but the method used by Ceil is a common one. First, a type of stimulus is found that controls the desired response — makes the subject respond correctly. This stimulus is paired with the stimulus you want to acquire control. Then for a time, both are used. Soon the first stimulus is gradually removed or faded out by easy, sometimes subtle, degrees, leaving the other stimulus at full strength. That stimulus will acquire the control you wanted as the first fades, if the procedure was well-designed and carried out.

Fading: a technique coming from operant research and used in behavior modification. In fading, stimulus control is gradually shifted from a stimulus that exerts present control to one that did not exert control before the procedure was employed.

Closeness of the correct block was the spatial cue that gained quick control of Casey's response. Ceil arranged it so that the closer block was also correct in terms of the verbal color cues Casey got. As closeness cues were faded out, Casey's response came under the control of color cues. At last only color cues remained, but by this time had gained control of Casey's response. As you can see, stimulus control was shifted from one type of stimulus to another — in this case, from closeness to color. Fading — like shaping — is a technique that b mod people lifted right out of the operant psychologist's lab. It has served its new masters well.

- ■21 Review: Define shaping.
- ■22 Define fading.
- ■23 What are two techniques that are used widely in b mod?
- ■24 How are shaping and fading alike?
- ■25 What changes in each of the above?
- ■26 Explain how fading works. Give an example.

B MOD AND SELF-CONTROL

Dawn's behavioral contract

Dawn took her glasses from her purse and put them on. As a rule she tried not to wear them when men were around. No time to think about that now — she didn't want to miss a single comma of the contract Harper had written and was now urging her to sign.

> *I, Dawn Baker, agree to and promise to comply with the following rules:*
> 1. *I am to be present at all class meetings of all classes for which I'm enrolled in the current term.*
> 2. *Dr. Harper may check with instructors or professors and get a daily attendance report from them.*
> 3. *I will pay Dr. Harper $2.00 for any class meeting of any course I do not attend.*

That was the main part of the contract. There were other parts to the document where terms were defined in greater detail — things like at what point being late for class became a cut, etc. Dawn finished reading the contract and handed it back to Harper.

"Well?" he asked.

"I don't know. Two dollars — that's not much money. Do you think it'll work?"

"I think so — and I had a good reason for the two dollar fine. But I'll tell you that later. What about it — you going to sign?"

"I'll sign it, but . . ."

"Right here," Harper said. "Blood won't be needed."

***

"It's for you," Mae said, handing Dawn the phone.

"Hello — Dawn? This is Harper. You owe me. Cut lit and psych today — that'll be four bucks. You can drop it by tomorrow."

***

Dawn scrounged the bottom of her coke glass in quest of the last bit of fluid. She turned coyly toward Bret Davis, captain of the fencing team and owner of the finest blue eyes on campus. She was about to plunge into those azure pools when she noticed the clock on the wall behind him.

"Wow! Phys ed class — I'm late!" She sprang from her chair, gathering her books in one sweep.

"So what — what's a gym class? Bag that woman jock scene."

"Sorry Bret, gotta run. Bye now."

"But . . ." Bret Davis watched with awe as Dawn hit full stride by the time she cleared the door, crossing the soggy lawn, dodging puddles — Crazylegs Baker on the move.

Behavioral contracts

Behavioral contracting is one technique we're certain didn't come from the lab. Contracts have been with us a long time, almost as long as verbal behavior itself. They've been used down through the ages as a means of control among people who have something to gain from each other's actions. But b mod has found a new use for the contract — self-control. Clients who wish to stop doing harmful things or start spending their time in more useful ways have turned to behavioral contracts.

Aside from their purpose, behavioral contracts are a lot like any contract, describing in precise detail what the contractee is supposed to do, and prescribing exact rewards or penalties that occur when these terms are met, or not met. Contracts work best if someone other than the contractee checks to see if promises are kept and then gives out the rewards or penalties that are due. But some get along fine when they themselves carry out the terms, rewarding or punishing themselves when needed.

Some clinics and centers using b mod techniques have set up services with a staff trained to help clients prepare such agreements. The contracting service carries out its terms after a contract is prepared and the contractee signs it. Clients in turn pay a fee for the assistance they receive. Clients take out contracts for hundreds of different reasons: to lose weight; finish theses or other school work; keep on exercise programs . . . And yes, contracts to keep people from cutting class or missing work, like Dawn has just signed, are quite common.

Every day, counselors and therapists use behavioral contracts more and more in the area of suicide. Patients sign suicide contracts in which they agree not to attempt to take their lives during the term detailed in the contract. It seems all too simple — yet it works. In fact, recent data suggest that it rarely fails, succeeding with people who would surely be lost if other types of control were used.

■27 What b mod technique can we be sure didn't come from the lab?

■28 What two things do behavioral contracts make clear?

■29 Give examples of the kinds of self-control programs that contracts are sometimes used for.

■30 How do contracting services in clinics or centers work?

■31 Thought question: What sort of contracting for self-control would you find helpful? Is there anyone you could contract with? Why don't you try it?

THE PAYOFF

"I'm proud of you, Dawn," Harper said. "A full month and not a single cut."

"I'm kinda proud, too. And surprised. Didn't think losing two dollars mattered that much. Which reminds me, you said you had a reason for choosing that amount — is there some kind of magic to it?"

"No — no magic. But there is a lesson. If you take the weeks in the term, figure out the number of class meetings per week, multiply and then divide the quotient into the amount of tuition your folks pay for each credit hour involved . . . Well, take my word for it, it comes out to about two dollars. That's how much you throw away each time you miss a class."

"Two bucks, huh? Hey, if that's true, why didn't it keep me from cutting before the contract — I was losing it then, too, wasn't I?"

"Of course — and that's the lesson. You were wasting your money all along, but you wouldn't have noticed it until it was too late — next term, maybe, or the summer — or who knows, twenty years from now when someone asked you a question about something you'd have known if you'd gone to classes. See, it's just like I'm always saying. All b mod does is take those long delayed results of our actions and move them up front, next to the response, where they'll do some good — control some behavior. Results juggling — that's one way of looking at b mod."

CONCLUSIONS

In dealing with behavior modification in this chapter we've entered into the realm of applied psychology. We've attempted to show how behavioral principles — most of them coming from B. F. Skinner's operant analysis — are used to reduce behavior problems and build in desired skills. We've seen the principle of extinction at work in reducing self-injuring actions in a psychotic patient. We've looked at task analysis and selection in general, and related to the training of a retarded youngster; and we've seen the role of the operant techniques of shaping and fading in behavior modification. And last, we watched behavioral contracting at work as a technique in behavior modification — a technique long in the public domain but put to new uses in behavior modification.

A point we can derive from this and previous chapters is that human problems of excess and neglect occur because appropriate actions fail to make contact with rewards — and also because unwanted acts get rewarded by accident, ignorance, or default. Behavior modification is an attempt to re-align rewards with desired actions, and remove them from unwanted or problem behaviors.

CHAPTER 32

JOSEPH WOLPE AND BEHAVIOR THERAPY

INTRODUCTION — AT THE ZOO

They captured Gore and Dodo that same day in the jungle, scarcely a mile apart — the heavy fibers of hemp net falling on them, a huge passive hand squelching all struggle.

* * *

Chet flipped through the pages without seeing them, propped up in bed, his ears tuned to sounds in the kitchen — Carol closing the fridge door; Carol clinking glasses, rattling dishes; the bump and surge as Carol started the dishwasher — Carol.

What was that woman doin' in there? "Carol! Carol!" Chet yelled. "You ever comin' ta bed?"

* * *

Sunlight marked the start of Gore's life in the zoo, tumbled from the wooden crate, harsh rays striking like a hammer blow — blinding. Gore crouched and waited — something, someone was nearby; a stranger, yet not a stranger; a creature like Gore's parents, like Gore's brothers and sisters, like Gore — still a stranger. Gore sniffed. The odor tugged at it, something out of the past that gently beckoned Gore to approach. But no — not now. Other sights, sounds, odors — foreign and alarming — took charge, spurring Gore like steel barbs to intense, nervous pacing.

As time passed, Gore became more calm, at last pausing, finding food. Had it been there all the while? The other approached, daring to come closer this time, touching its muzzle against Gore's shaggy mane, licking and sniffing down the length of Gore's body. Gore stiffened, then relaxed, returning the gesture. For a brief time Gore was back in the jungle again.

* * *

The sun had come and gone many times but Dodo didn't eat the food, instead grinding it into the sandy earth beneath its restless paws; ignoring sleep and the stranger that came near, boldly nudging Dodo, once, twice, a third time. Dodo lashed out, the blow catching the startled beast on the ear, sending it screeching, scurrying away. It would keep a safe distance, not being so bold again. No matter — Dodo was too busy looking, pacing, scratching, clawing at the walls and ground. There would never be anything else.

* * *

Carol heard Chet call, his voice piercing the comforting sounds of the kitchen. The feelings in her stomach worsened, that sick and queasy trembling inside. She knew all too well what caused it, the nausea, the sinking dread. Chet was waiting, waiting for her to perform — to lie, to fake an orgasm — or to tell the truth and begin the fight — always the fight.

***

"How they doin' — calmed down any?"

"That one over there's doin' fine. Been eatin' good — even took a mate. Wouldn't surprise me to find some young 'uns outta that pair 'fore long."

"Yeah?" The two zoo keepers smiled at each other. "What about the other one?"

"Ain't gonna make it — won't eat — meaner 'n the devil too — whops the tar outta the other one when it tries to sidle up. Acts like it's scared to death — 'fraid we got a loser there."

"A real dodo, huh?"

"Yeah."

***

Elsewhere we've discussed how warning stimuli cause changes in glands, heart, blood vessels, and other organs inside the body, preparing the way for fast and intense action that an onrushing crisis may soon require. The person or creature's ready for fight or flight. In this aroused state, the creature's not good for much else; in fact, other life functions — the gentler responses that sustain the body and prolong the species — simply can't occur while warning stimuli are in command.

Now you can see why Gore and Dodo despaired in their zoo homes. New scents, sights, climate, strange walls on all sides, foreign objects and creatures — strong warning stimuli. These prepared Gore and Dodo to run or fight. But run where? Attack what or whom? But no matter — while in this state their bodies couldn't respond to food or sexual stimuli. At last Gore, the survivor, calmed down. The heavy arousal responses slackened. Gore ate, and took a mate, insuring a future Goredom in the new home.

Not so with Dodo — in a grip that strangled its insides and drove it to constant frenzy — not responding to food, refuge, and the mate its new home offered. Like many wild creatures placed in the confines of a zoo, Dodo's arousal would not abate or slacken. And like them, Dodo died, hungry and alone.

The crisis described above isn't solely one of Gore's and Dodo's — it's a human problem as well, often an acute one. In more than a poetic sense, humans are born and will spend their entire lives in a zoo, surrounded by hostile forces, foreboding stimuli on all sides. But humans also have an edge. Unlike other creatures, we humans don't have to depend solely on the endowment we've gained from natural selection; we're not at the mercy of our genes. We've devised techniques to combat the effects of warning stimuli intruding into our lives and detracting from our partaking of and enjoying human rewards. One such technique is called "behavior therapy".

Behavior therapy: a therapy approach based on learning principles, that seeks to change both outside actions and feelings by altering arousal responses.

- 1 Review: What is arousal?
- 2 How does arousal help survival?
- 3 In what way may arousal interfere with survival?
- 4 Define behavior therapy.

LEARNED PUNISHERS IN SEXUAL BEHAVIOR

Fear and loathing in the bedroom

"I don't like coming to you like this, Dr. Stein. I hate being, as they say, 'part of the problem'."

"Has it always been like this — was there ever a time when you liked sex?"

"It hurt at first. But that didn't bother me so much. Chet either. I guess we both thought it'd pass," Carol said.

"And did it?"

"Yes — very soon, really. Then I noticed that I was starting to like it."

"How did you feel about that?"

"Good at first — it was something new happening to me — to my body. But Chet — I mean — it upset me too, made me nervous and tense when it was over. I found that I wanted it to last longer."

"And that made you feel bad?"

"Yes. I felt ashamed, and guilty, like I'd done something wrong. I know it doesn't make any sense — I'm legally married, and all that. I still feel that way, though."

"Tell me, how did your parents look at sex?"

"I . . . well, that's funny. I guess I don't know. They never talked about it — not that I recall. Mom told me she and Dad wanted me to be a 'nice' girl. They used to say that a lot."

"I want your most candid answers to these questions — okay? What's it like when you have sex with your husband?" Carol was silent for a moment as she composed her reply.

"Well, first there's the dread — a kind of nagging feeling; like something not all that pleasant's going to happen soon. I know it's not a kind thing to say — but I feel just like I used to when I was waiting to get a tooth filled."

"Do you always know in advance when you're going to have sex?"

"Oh yes — Chet's like that. Let's me know as soon as he comes in after class or work that he'd like to do it later on . . . may I say something before we go any further, Dr. Stein?"

"Of course."

"I know I've got hang-ups about sex — guess I've always had them. I was prepared to live with that. But lately it's worse — really bad. It's the orgasm thing."

"Orgasm thing?"

"Chet thinks I should have an orgasm when we make love — it's gotten to be a big deal with him. He always has to know. But I don't — and I never have. Sometimes I lie and say I did, but Chet seems to know. Then I try to convince him it doesn't matter . . . only . . ."

"Only what, Carol?"

"The truth is that it does matter — I do want it. I feel cheated — if only Chet would take longer, try a little harder."

"Have you ever talked to him about it?"

"I couldn't, I just couldn't. Chet doesn't like to talk about sex outside the bedroom, and . . . well . . ."

"What is it?"

"There just isn't time in the clinches, Dr. Stein."

* * *

Sex stimuli are warning signals for most people who live in our culture. Like Carol, we're punished in both direct and subtle ways during childhood and young adulthood for a host of acts — both words and deeds relating to sex organs or sex acts themselves. As a result, contact with sexual stimuli or the stimuli produced by a person's own actions during sex can serve as strong warning stimuli when we're adults. These may be so strong that they override the effects of the unlearned rewards of sexual contact, sometimes causing the person to avoid or escape sexual stimuli, foregoing all acts that produce them. You don't need beatings for sexual acts when you're young, for this to happen. Punishers needn't be that heavy — others work just as well — scorn, the withdrawal of love, or threats of that nature, disdain by others who label such acts "lewd", "loose", "immoral", or "perverse".

Carol's parents only wanted her to be nice. Their program was subtle, perhaps unplanned and beyond their awareness in part — but it had its effect. Carol was a "nice" girl. A good thing, too. That's the kind of girl Chet wanted for his bride — but not for his wife, as it turns out. Now he wants Carol to forget past training; he wants her to enjoy sex as much as he — well, almost as much. He berates her for not having an orgasm, though he's not willing to take any role beyond standard manly assistance in helping her. But more must be done for Carol's gut level responses toward sex, and her own sexual behavior, to let her come into contact with the strong rewards that can come from sexual union.

- 5 What type of stimuli are likely to be warning stimuli for us?
- 6 How do these warning stimuli acquire their power?

Behavior therapy

"If it's any comfort, you aren't the only one with these problems. A lot of people — men as well as women — hassle with them."

"You said 'problems' — how many do I have?"

"Well — two that I see. The first is pretty much par. No one reared in our culture avoids it completely. It's the sex hang-up you're aware of — a result of the fact that we treat sex as a taboo for the whole of a person's young life, and then all of a sudden — just because of a few words spoken to them by clergy or a J. P. — we expect them to check signals and chuck the past. Yes, you've got sex hang-ups; but who doesn't? The other problem has more to do with you as a unique person, and of course, with Chet and the kind of man he is. But there's more to it than your dealings with Chet."

"I don't understand — a real problem, neurosis or something like that?"

"No, no — you're a fine person, Carol; bright, sensitive, easy to work with, good mother, great worker and employee. You never cause any fuss, always think of the other guy first — and that's your problem."

"But I was always taught to be that way. Surely you're not telling me it's wrong?"

"No, not as a rule. Looking out after the other person's fine — most of us don't do it nearly enough. But what about you? You have wants, goals, desires, and yes, rights. And they're as good as anyone else's. Then, why is it you always submerge your wants to those of other people — to Chet's childish whims, to your parents' requests, the other shopper in the market, the pushy driver at the four-way stop?"

"I'm just trying to make things go — have them work out. Someone's got to give in."

"Sure — and unless you start standing up for yourself, it's always going to be you. But there's one thing you don't mention — level with me, now. Doesn't it hurt your feelings, make you angry, maybe think a little less of yourself and others, when you're always the one that gives in?"

"Yes, sometimes . . . no, pretty often I guess — but I get over it."

"Meanwhile, are you really in top form?"

"I suppose not."

"And there's the other side. Are you truly kind to others when you let them take advantage of you? Are you teaching them the right thing — that they can walk over people and get away with it? Give 'em a break — let them be the giver for a change! Giving's a fine thing, a great opportunity. Why don't you give Chet and the others a chance to find that out?"

"I see what you mean. I've thought about what you've said many times — but I'm afraid. I don't want them to dislike me. To hate me. I just can't do it."

"Well, I want to give you a little help — behavior therapy holds the answer for you."

***

In the last chapter we discussed behavior modification, a treatment based on learning principles. Behavior therapy is another treatment approach using learning to view problems and design treatment. The practice of behavior therapy was first introduced by Dr. Joseph Wolpe; and like b mod it's rather new to the area of clinical treatment.

Wolpe based his approach on the premise that anxiety was the basis of a host of clinical problems; he felt it interfered in many aspects of living — in marriage, on the job, in school failure . . . By now we know that anxiety is arousal — arousal caused by learned punishers or warning stimuli. These stimuli are themselves harmless; they do no damage, and they may not precede other harmful events at present. Yet, because of their past pairing with other punishers they produce anxiety responses, hindering the person in many pursuits.

Wolpe reasoned that new learning could rid patients of their anxiety since these internal responses were acquired in that fashion in the first place. As a result, his techniques were geared toward getting the patient to respond in a new way to anxiety-provoking stimuli. The approach has proven a great success. Some problem behaviors are often cleared up in a few short sessions — problems that before Wolpe, called for years of costly therapy, often ending in little or no improvement. So-called "hopeless" cases often yield with little effort to Wolpe's approach.

But we would mislead you if we were to restrict the content of behavior therapy to a discussion of Wolpe. The bandwagon he first started to roll a few short years ago has been joined by countless others, and has ranged far and wide. Indeed, behavior therapy today involves dozens of techniques for use with more problems and in more settings than we can attempt to list. Along the way, Wolpe's theories have been challenged, although in practice his techniques remain largely intact. We shall discuss here the two techniques, "systematic desensitization" and "assertive training" — tried and true methods, and long-time behavior therapies.

- 7 What two major therapies are based on learning principles?
- 8 Who introduced behavior therapy?

SYSTEMATIC DESENSITIZATION

Carol's systematic desensitization program

"The first thing we're going to deal with is your anxiety in the sexual setting. It comes from two sources, as I see it. The first is your sex training — how your parents and others viewed sex, and the extent to which they imposed their views on you. The way you respond to sexual stimuli is the result of this training, whether you're conscious of it or not."

"Then we'll talk about my parents and how it was when I was a child? I think I'll like that."

"Sorry — but I'm afraid not. Behavior therapy doesn't work that way. We'll spend little if any time talking about how you acquired your anxiety — although it helps to know whether the source is active or stems largely from the past. Which brings us to the second source of your tenseness in the bedroom."

"The orgasm?"

"Yes, in part. I mean the way you get uptight trying to please him, trying to have an orgasm so

he won't feel bad or think he's a poor lover — end up pouting and acting hurt — punishing you. And let's be honest — the concern isn't solely for Chet. You get tense because you want it for yourself — and haven't been able to so far. That's fine, but worrying about it just makes it less likely."

"So you start to tighten up as soon as your husband tells you he'd like to have sex later on. Then it gets worse during dinner."

"That's right. Lately it gets so bad I can't eat — I just pick at my food."

"The next part of your routine is when you give little Chet his bath and put him down for the night; after that the dinner dishes."

"That's when it really starts — I find all kinds of things to do in the kitchen; shelves to dust, sweep the floor two or three times."

"Stalling."

"Yes — that's all it is."

* * *

"Okay, Carol. Just relax. Close your eyes if that'll help, but mostly I want you to listen to what I say and try to imagine it — the more vivid the better. Try to see the scene, hear the sounds, smell the odors — and above all, try to feel what I tell you is happening to your body. Good. Now, I want you to imagine that you're home getting dinner ready. The door opens, and in comes Chet . . ."

* * *

The behavior therapy approach began with systematic desensitization — a technique that soon proved robust and flexible. It was first used with phobias — intense fears of certain harmless objects, places, or other stimuli. Systematic desensitization worked well with all phobic responses. It didn't seem to matter if the client was labeled neurotic or not. The method was soon extended to other kinds of fear or anxiety responses that weren't strictly phobic.

There are four basic steps to systematic desensitization as Wolpe first put forth, although most workers today feel they don't need all of these steps. The first step is to find out what kinds of stimuli cause the anxiety responses. The therapist asks questions of the client in an attempt to pinpoint the precise stimuli that are at work. They urge clients to be as specific and complete as they can, helping the therapist to zero in on those aspects of a setting that produce the anxiety response.

Most often it's not one but many stimuli that cause the problem. The second step involves ranking those stimuli in order of power, since some cause greater upset than others. Such an ordering of stimuli is called an "anxiety stimulus hierarchy".

Anxiety stimulus hierarchy: an ordering of anxiety stimuli in terms of their power to provoke the response.

Next, the therapist teaches the client to relax. Wolpe stressed the point that few of us ever truly relax — that, in fact, we don't know we're tense because we've never been that relaxed. Often he used a large part of the first treatment sessions to teach the client to relax.

The last step in the treatment is the crucial part — where the real work goes on. The therapist asks the clients to imagine themselves in the scenes the therapist describes, remaining in a relaxed state all the time. These scenes depict places and things that have caused the client anxiety in the past. Wolpe believed the least potent stimulus should be imagined first, followed by the next most potent — and so on, up through the hierarchy. He thought that by overcoming the anxiety a step at a time from the weakest to the strongest stimuli, the therapist could recycle, in the office, when the patient became upset. He or she could again approach the disturb-

ing cue, face it, and then go on to the next step in the hierarchy. When the last item is reached, and the client can imagine it and face the situation, without showing any anxiety, the treatment is complete — the client cured.

These four simple steps make up the entire technique — finding out what the anxiety stimuli are; putting them in a hierarchy; teaching the client to relax; and having the client imagine stimuli in the hierarchy while relaxed. Too simple, you say? The results show otherwise — we'll find out how it works in a moment.

- ▪ 9 Review: What is a phobia?
- ▪10 Define anxiety stimulus hierarchy.
- ▪11 With what kind of problem was systematic desensitization first used?
- ▪12 Briefly describe the four steps of the systematic desensitization procedure as Wolpe outlined them.

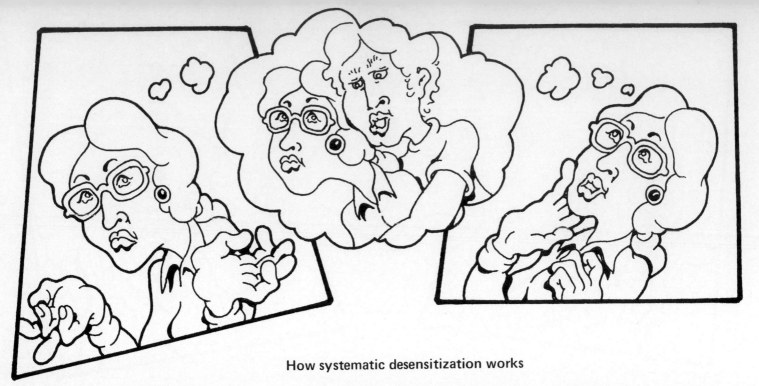

How systematic desensitization works

It is commonly believed that relaxation and the ordering of stimuli in a hierarchy are crucial steps in the desensitization procedure. Recent research, however, has not found this to be the case — neither relaxation nor the order that stimulus events are imagined seems to matter. The technique works just as well when the clients aren't relaxed, and when they confront the strongest stimuli right away, without going through the graded steps of a hierarchy.

Imagining a situation, it appears, is the crucial factor in the treatment. We know, of course, that to imagine is to be controlled by words — either your own, as in fantasy — or in this instance, by those of the therapist. When we imagine, we make the same responses as if we were really there — see, hear, or feel whatever the words depict, the same inside movements occur, just as they do when the real stimuli make contact. We respond in other ways as though we're there, too, becoming anxious to an imagined scene if the real one would have caused us to respond that way. In short, having clients imagine stimuli that make them anxious has the same effect as placing them in the real setting — at least in terms of the anxiety responses produced. Through imagining you can have clients in your office while you expose them to stimuli from home, or work, or social settings that cause them problems.

Why should facing these stimuli by imagining rid them of their power when facing them in real life hasn't? But that's just the point — clients haven't faced them in real life. What they've done is avoid them in the first place, or make a hasty retreat, escaping after the slightest contact. In the Neuroses chapter we spoke of how anxiety neurotics avoided or escaped all settings that caused them the slightest anxiety. Normal people like Carol or ourselves don't, as a rule, run from things that cause us anxiety — most often we face and combat them. Although, at times, we do escape and avoid certain settings or activities that make us uptight — things like giving speeches, attending

stuffy social functions, and playing games or sports that we don't do well in. We try to limit contact with these situations just as Carol tries to do with sex. Perhaps we don't lose out too much if we avoid speech-making and social functions; but most of us would say that losing out on sex is a more drastic sacrifice. No, Carol's not an anxiety neurotic, but her problem could rob her of rich human rewards, and perhaps wreck her marriage.

Keep in mind that these anxiety-causing stimuli are learned — they are punishers and warning stimuli that gained their power because they had been paired with or led to other punishers in the past. They quickly lose their power if we make contact with them, wait them out, and no great harm befalls us. What better place to do this than in the comfort of our friendly therapist's cozy office, where we're only imagining the scenes that cause us anxiety? It's certain that there's no threat, no punishers, that we're going to have to deal with there. Facing the stimuli and seeing them through to a safe non-punished climax is what does the trick. It doesn't matter at all that the stimuli are imagined, and that bad outcomes are out of the question in the therapist's office. We are, in effect, forced to have contact with them — contact though only imagined, that is far beyond what we would subject ourselves to on our own. This forced contact is what makes desensitization work.

■13 What is the crucial factor in the systematic desensitation technique?

■14 Why does imagining the stimuli that cause anxiety sap their power, when contact with them in real life seems to cause so much trouble?

■15 Briefly describe in your own words how systematic desensitization works.

ASSERTIVE TRAINING

"I don't know what's wrong with you, man! You gotta get a little gumption! No way you deserve a 'C' on that paper — that's an 'A' job if I ever saw one."

Sid tried to avoid Mae's eyes that seemed to pin him to the back of the booth, giving him no place to run to. "I'm sure Dr. Ray had some good reason for giving me that grade. Who am I to question him?"

"Who're you? 'Who am I?' he says. I'll tell you who! You're the victim — that's who!"

"Look, Mae. Don't make a big deal out of it. It's okay. It doesn't matter."

"Of course it doesn't. That's why you're so uptight. I bet you've been worryin' all day."

"You're right, Mae. I am hurt — and mad, too. I worked my tail off on that paper. It knocked me for a loop when I saw that big red hook marked on my paper. A 'C' — how can he give me that?"

"Go see the dude — make a fuss!"

"I can't do that. Question his ability — his right to give me a bad mark? He's a PhD — a famous scholar — and I'm just a student."

"Come off it, Sid — quit puttin' yourself down! You're smart and you know it. You're also a taxpayer — least your folks are. You got rights, man! Use 'em! What can he do to you? Askin' him about his grading standard's not outta line."

"I don't know — I don't know what he'll do. I'm scared. Mae, I don't want to bug him about my grade."

"Sid, you're a jerk. Come on, let's go. I'm gonna take you to the campus store and buy you a book I saw there."

"A book? How's that goin' to help?"

"You'll see. It's on something called 'assertive training'."

* * *

In our highly social world, it's the "squeaky wheel" that gets the most oil. Some people appear keenly aware of this, their constant complaints getting them more than their share of attention. In contrast, there are those patient souls who never question the treatment they receive, often suffering unduly as a result. We may admire those who never complain; but the simple truth of the matter is that a little squeaking in our own behalf is required if we're to get along.

So, why do we balk at standing up for our rights or asking for our share? Of course it goes back to past training. Challenging the powers that be — parents, teachers, cops, bullies — has sometimes been punished. As a result most of us think twice, before we take on heavyweight people — yet, we'll do it when we must. But not some people. It's out of the question for them — they just can't assert themselves. The very thought of mixing it up with authority figures causes tenseness, spoiling their calm, making them unfit for more gentle and loving tasks.

But not speaking out can cause problems too — above and beyond the loss of rights or privileges. Those who feel slighted but don't complain often harbor private feelings of dislike or even downright hatred for others whom they feel have wronged them. These thoughts keep them stirred up — in near constant arousal. If only they'd speak up, they might find those they blame had nothing to do with it — or perhaps were simply not aware of what they'd done. Complaining could also give others a chance to give their side of the story, perhaps putting their actions in a new light. The point is that we'd all do better in the long run if we dealt with conflicts in a more direct way, keeping it all out front. It all makes good sense — alas, if only like Sid, we weren't such chickens!

But we needn't despair. Behavior therapy has a way of dealing with this problem. It's called "assertive training". With Mae's help, Sid's about to get a crash course.

Assertive training: behavior therapy technique designed to help clients become more active in speaking out in their own behalf or otherwise protecting their rights and interests.

▪16 Define assertive training.

▪17 Why are most of us reluctant to one extent or another to challenge authority?

▪18 What is often a harmful by-product of failing to take our own part?

TECHNIQUE

Overlearning

". . . and so Dr. Ray, in light of what I've just said, I . . ." Sid turned away when a couple entered the lounge.

"Go on. Don't let them bother you. You're doin' fine," Mae said.

"It's no good — it's silly. Sayin' these words — how's that goin' to do any good? And I'm supposed to pretend you're Dr. Ray. But you're not — you don't look a thing like him."

"Relieved to hear it," Mae said. "But for right now, you're gonna do what the book says. Keep sayin' the words. Let's go through it four or five more times. Then I want you to go home n' do it lookin' in a mirror."

"Mae, this's stupid — it won't work!"

"You better hope it does — 'cause there's somethin' you don't know. I sneaked off and made a call while you were waitin' in line at the bookstore. You're on at Dr. Ray's office at ten in the morning."

"What?"

"You got it — you're booked in to see him at ten."

"Mae, you rat fink — you're puttin' me on!"

"Man, I don't bluff. Check it out if you don't believe it. You're on for the morning."

"Mae, you did it to me. I'm gonna bomb — come off like some pushy oaf," Sid whined.

"Yeah, that could happen, if you don't get with it. Once more, from the top, okay?" Sid shook his head over what seemed to him a sealed doom. He took a deep breath, and sat up in the lounge chair.

"Hello, Dr. Ray, I'm Sid Fields, one of the students in your twelve o'clock section and . . ."

***

It's easy to see why Sid has doubts about the good that will come from the practice he's going through. It appears contrived — far away from the real thing. Clients often feel that way when they first begin behavior therapy and assertive training. But you can't argue with success — it works. And of course, there are good reasons why.

This phase of the assertive training technique is called "overlearning". Sid's saying the words he'll later use when he has the showdown with his prof. He's learning a speech — in fact, overlearning it — to the extent that he won't have to think about what he's saying when the time comes.

Anxiety responses disrupt sex and eating patterns — a point we made earlier. But the disruptive effects of anxiety go beyond this, tending to compete with all actions that aren't geared toward getting the person away from anxious stimuli. We're more likely to forget things, lose track of what we're trying to do or say, when we're anxious than at other times. But not all responses are so easily disrupted — a well-learned response sequence has a better chance of staying intact. This suggests that overlearning can protect responses we intend to make when anxiety stimuli are present.

Overlearning: method used in assertive training where responses made in an anxiety setting are rehearsed repeatedly.

Sid's like a combat soldier receiving basic training. Constant drill makes it more likely that troops will perform during battle as they're supposed to. Because of overlearning Sid has a better chance of doing what he came to do when he faces his prof, even if his heart's beating like a drum.

- ■19 Define overlearning.
- ■20 What kinds of responses is anxiety most likely to disrupt? Least likely to disrupt?
- ■21 How does overlearning help protect a response from disruption by anxiety?
- ■22 In what sense is Sid's program during this phase of the treatment like basic training for combat troops?

Imagining

That night Sid went ahead with the assertive training on his own. He was far from certain that it was the answer for him but he did know one thing: Mae wasn't going to let him wriggle off the hook. His fate was sealed — he'd have to go through with it. The next section of the assertive training book was titled, "Making Believe".

Once you have overlearned the words and deeds you want to execute when your moment of truth arrives, it's high time to put them to work. Is that a groan I hear? Shame on you! That will teach you to jump to conclusions. No, not in the real *situation — only when you imagine. You must imagine yourself at the location and in the company of characters who will be there when the time arrives. You must put yourself in this position — seeing, hearing, touching, experiencing each aspect of what will most likely take place — all on the make-believe stage of your thoughts. It's of greatest importance that you imagine yourself there, saying the lines you have learned and carrying out your part to the slightest detail, to the absolute letter.*

Imagining, as we learned, is the crucial element in systematic desensitization. It's also involved in Sid's assertive training, and in many other behavior therapy techniques. Imagining serves two distinct purposes in Sid's program. The first is the same as it serves in systematic desensitization. Imagining yourself in the setting where you must later perform, strips anxious stimuli of their power to produce anxiety. Sid's anxiety will weaken each time he imagines himself presenting his case in Dr. Ray's office. When the real thing comes along, he'll be less upset than he would have dreamed possible.

The second value of imagining is that it allows Sid to learn actions that, unlike his speech, can't be directly rehearsed. You can learn skills by imagining. If you can imagine yourself doing some task that you don't know how to do, you'll do better at it next time you try it out for real. One researcher showed this with two groups of subjects who tried to find their way to a goal by tracing through a puzzle maze with their fingers. Sometimes they made mistakes by going into blind alleys; and, at first, each group made about the same number of mistakes. After the test, one group was told to go home and think about working the maze — just take a half-hour each day and imagine they were working it. The second group didn't get any instructions; it was presumed that they went home and forgot about the task. A week later both groups came back to try their hands (fingers) at the same maze. The group that had imagined working the maze made far fewer errors. They had learned by imagining.

So you can see that there are three basic elements to Sid's program: 1) he overlearns all responses he's going to make later on; 2) he imagines himself in the setting, thereby reducing anxiety; and 3) allowing him to learn actions he can't practice in a direct manner. There are many types of assertive training programs used by behavior therapists for many purposes, but these three features are common to most of them.

■23 What does the second part of the assertive training technique involve?

■24 In what way does assertive training use the same technique as systematic desensitization?

■25 Totally, what are the three elements of the assertive training technique?

People power

Carol waited until after dinner — the quiet time after little Chet was down for the night, the way she'd rehearsed it for the past few days.

"Chet, I had a talk with Dr. Stein awhile back."

"Yeah?" Chet said. He was sitting at the desk, trying to read over some class notes, and also keep track of the program on the TV across the room.

"It was about us, Chet. I talked to her about us."

"About us — whatta you mean? What about us?"

"Our problem with sex." Chet slammed down his notes and glared at Carol.

"You talked to that woman about what we do? Where do you get off with that — puttin' what goes on between you and me on parade! Bring on the TV crews! Talkin' about that to a stranger!" Chet was on his feet now, ranting, pacing wildly. "Guess you told her what a beast I am, lusting after you, making you do awful things!"

"The fact is that I'm not going to tell you a thing until you sit down and quit acting like a madman. This is one time you're going to listen." Carol heard herself say the words, they tumbled out without effort, perfect and well formed — she was in control. . .

* * *

Sid bounded down the steps of the all-purpose classroom building, passing the surge of students on their way to and from classes. Some turned to look at him. It pleased him to have people notice him; but why today? Could they sense his glow — a strange feeling of being in charge? He loped across the green — the shortest way to the snack bar where Mae waited to hear a report on his meeting with Dr. Ray. The news was good. Earlier, on his way to Dr. Ray's office, he was a doomed man — James Cagney on his way down the long hall to the hot-seat. It was Sid's game from the instant he sat down in the chair across from Dr. Ray, who peered at him over bifocal glasses. He laid his case out like a trial lawyer, point by point, step by step. Dr. Ray listened — not that he had a chance to do otherwise. Words came to Sid in full phrases — like the ones he'd practiced with Mae, and in the mirror — better though. More terse, precise, clear and to the point — "el-o-quent" . . . eloquent.

* * *

Carol looked up at the ceiling, thinking, Chet's hand resting lightly on her shoulder. He was asleep now. Sometimes she liked to study him when he slept. She thought of the picture album Chet's mother showed her when they were first married. Pictures of Chet — as an infant; a toddler; in grade school, his arm around his two chums; Chet as a burr-headed serious looking Boy Scout; a cocky fag-smoking high schooler. Looking at Chet now, she could see them all — they were still here — and others, too. She'd met a new Chet tonight, gentle and kind — a patient Chet. But wasn't that part of her husband there all the while? Of course. Perhaps the fault was hers, the trouble during their marriage. She'd put no demands on Chet, never told him what she wanted, what she wanted him to be. She hadn't helped him, that much was clear — merely accepted him in her smug, resigned way; a martyr, chained by her virtue to some spoiled child. No more. Chet could change, would change — but first she must.

CONCLUSIONS

Joseph Wolpe, as we stated in this chapter, is the father of behavior therapy. He wasn't the first to venture into this problem area, or to try a learning approach; yet his influence all but eclipsed the early efforts of others. Today, the presence of behavior therapy has grown in both size and scope.

For all intents and purposes, behavior therapy began with systematic desensitization, a technique fostered by Wolpe that strips anxiety stimuli of their power, freeing patients from the crippling effects of constant arousal. The crucial element in systematic desensitization is imagining, which brings clients in contact with anxiety stimuli to the extent needed to neutralize them.

Imagining also plays a major role in assertive training and other behavior therapy techniques. Like behavior modification, perhaps the greatest value of behavior therapy is that it allows us to be more than helpless captives of static features of environment, genetic structure, and past training. These approaches give us a means to change our actions and our future.

NOTES

Preface

Brown, R., & Herrnstein, R. J. *Psychology.* Boston: Little, Brown, 1975.
A very intelligent, thoughtful, and original treatment of general psychology.

The following two books are fine examples of writing in the style advocated by Flesch:
Camus, A. *The stranger* (S. Gilbert, trans.). New York: Random House, 1946.
Vonnegut, K., Jr. *Breakfast of champions.* New York: Delacorte Press/ Seymour Lawrence, 1973.

Christensen, F. *Notes toward a new rhetoric.* New York: Harper & Row, 1967.
Everyone should read this fantastic book. It's been of great value in helping us smooth out our writing style.

English, B., & English, C. *A comprehensive dictionary of psychological and psychoanalytic terms.* New York: David McKay, 1958.
Much more than a dictionary, the book usually gives a good deal of useful information about the terms presented. All psychology majors should have this one.

Flesch, R. *How to test readability.* New York: Harper & Brothers, 1951.
A very brief book and a nice introduction to Flesch's notions about readable writing.

Flesch, R. *The art of readable writing.* New York: Harper & Row, 1974.
The crucial parts of Flesch's method may tend to get a little lost in some of the less crucial details, but the book should still be read by any serious writer.

Keller, F. S. *The definition of psychology* (2nd ed.). Englewood Cliffs, New Jersey: Prentice-Hall, 1973.
Clearly written. An excellent introduction to the history of psychology and its many points of view.

Pronko, N. A., & Bowles, J. W., Jr. *Empirical foundations of psychology.* New York: Reinhart, 1951.
Well-written. Cites a large amount of data and represents a point of view compatible with the present book. Unfortunately, it's out of print but you may be able to find it in your library.

Psychology today: An introduction (3rd ed.). Del Mar, California: CRM Books, 1975.
One of the best of the many eclectic general survey texts, and a pioneer in the elaborate use of graphics in intro psych books.

Salzinger, K. *Psychology: The science of behavior.* New York: Springer, 1969.

The study objectives are numbered questions at the end of each sub-section of all chapters. You might want to take a second now to glance at them to get a feeling for what we're talking about. Here's a fairly good way to use these study objectives: First just read the chapter over fairly quickly without much concern for the objectives. Then reread the chapter, this time making sure you can answer each question. Now when you run across an objective you can't answer, look over the section until you find the answer. If you still can't find it, make a mark by it and check with another student or your teacher so you get a correct answer. You'll find this works pretty well.

* * *

*Often we use such phrases or terms as "*cite *an instance of", or "*dis-cuss*", in the study objectives. But your quizzes and exams may be of a multiple-choice format. In that case, you'll be expected to "*recognize *an instance of", or "*recognize *a correct statement about".*

* * *

We've become quite interested in writing style, since we've just spent the major part of the last sixteen months of our lives writing this book. Some of the guidelines we've adopted seem a little contro-versial, though we feel they've greatly improved our writing style. (We've adhered more rigorously to those guidelines in the main part of the text than in this note section.)

First of all, we wish to make our writing easy to read, interesting, and clear. In so doing, we've run across the objection that we're coddling you — an objection we've encountered before, in using programmed instruction, and in our behavioral approach to higher education where we do everything we can to insure that the student has a good chance of mastering the material in the course. The stan-dard objection is that we should be careful not to make things too easy, as somehow that might prevent you from developing the moral muscles you'll need to deal with the rough, real world once you've completed the course.

We're not moved too greatly by such arguments, as we know of no data to indicate that suffering through difficult texts and courses does indeed prepare you for the difficulties you'll encounter in less well-designed instructional systems, or with less well-designed materials. On the contrary, we feel that then maybe you'll be better able to deal with the harsh realities of a less-planned instructional program later on if you've learned a good deal from our course or materials, and if you've found them rewarding. So we've thought of ourselves as word technologists, trying to arrange our words to accomplish their imme-diate objectives as best we could.

Rudolf Flesch gave us our first major guideline source for writing. He recommends that we make the reading as easy as possible, not because students can't understand more complex reading, but just because they'll be able to read easy reading more quickly, and may, in fact, also comprehend more of it. Flesch points out that short words and short sentences are major components of a style that's easy to read. And there are data to support this. We tried for an average word length of about 1.4 syllables, and an average sentence length of about 16 words. This puts our writing in the fairly easy, or fiction, category. By the way, scientific writing is way down at the bottom of the readability scale; in fact it's at the very bottom — the most difficult thing we humans have devised for other humans to read.

Flesch also suggests that readability is a function of how interesting the material is, as well as how easy it is to read. For interest, he recommends using "personal words" and "personal sentences". Personal words are pronouns such as I, me, we, he, you, and she, but not neuter pronouns such as it, or them. They're also first names and words like "people" and "folks". Personal sentences are sentences with quotation marks, questions, commands, requests, exclamation marks, and those that are grammatically incomplete. Basically, personal sentences are conversational sentences. You tend to give your writing style a warmer and more personable feel if you follow those suggestions. On the average we've tried to keep the personal words in the range of 10% to 17%, and the personal sentences in the range of 42% to 58%. This puts our writing in the range of very interesting to dramatic, or from The New Yorker *style to fictional style. Once again, scientific writing is rated at the very bottom of the interest scale — rated dull. By the way, Flesch shows many instances of well-respected writing that are in accord with his suggestions. A couple of examples we've noted are Camus',* The Stranger, *and Vonnegut's,* Breakfast of Champions — *both written with incredible simplicity and beauty, both very easy to read.*

Flesch suggests some other guidelines. 1) Write the way you talk, with informal English. Whenever you write about a general principle, show an application of a specific case, tell a pointed anecdote, focus on a typical member of a group. As E. B. White says, "Don't write about Man, write about a man." 2) Use contractions. 3) Vary the length of your sentences. Have many very short sentences and a few that are fairly long, *even though you have an average length that is also fairly short. 4) Most long, complex, words can be expressed just as well with a few short words. 5) Don't write with just nouns and adjectives glued together with the verbs is,* was, are, *and* were, *use action verbs. We've found these guidelines of great value, though many people with* traditional *training in writing strongly object to them.*

The writing of Francis Christensen is another major source of influence. Christensen's book deals with syntactic maturity of writing style. The free modifier is a major concept in Christensen's analysis. The free modifier is a non-restrictive modifying clause that can occupy more than one location in a sentence. For instance, "We followed Christensen's guideline, because we wanted to have a mature style," *or* "because we wanted to have a mature style, *we followed Christensen's guidelines."* "Because we wanted to have a mature style" *is the free modifier modifying the main clause "followed Christensen's guidelines." It's a free modifier since it can go either at the beginning or at the end of the main clause.*

Christensen says to put most of the free modifiers in a cumulating position (at the end of a sentence), since that makes the sentence much easier to read. Sometimes you can place modifiers at the beginning; rarely, though, in the middle of the sentence. In many cases, we've tried to have about 35% of our words in the form of free modifiers, as Christensen has collected data indicating that this is the style of many good professional writers.

*Now this syntactic maturity (35% free modifiers) tends to go **against reading ease (short sentences). So we've written with those** two opposing constraints operating. Sometimes we've rationalized our longer sentences saying, they're easier to veiw since we've put the free modifier in the cumulating position. (That previous sentence is a 21-word example.) Which is more effective, is an empirical question — one someone might answer with an interesting experiment.*

***

We've made some effort to write our dialogue as people, in fact, do talk. Most of us don't always use perfect grammar or perfect pronunciation; and we often use contractions, so we've tried to write that way. But we had to back up somewhat since it turns out to be fairly hard to read words written as people really pronounce them.

We've also allowed our characters to shift in and out of language styles from time to time, since we humans aren't always that consistent. Audience cues greatly control the form of our language. Students talk one way in the dorm and often another way in the classroom. Blacks talk one way with Blacks and often another way with Whites. The thoughtful editing and the suggestions several Black students gave to our attempts at Black English are responsible for any success we've had with this fascinating language style. Of course, the shortcomings of those attempts are ours. These students also said they preferred reading a text that made at least some attempt to present dialogue in the way people really speak; and that's what we've tried to do.

***

From time to time, we use technical terminology in the notes section, terms that may not have yet been introduced in the main part of the text. The terms are defined in the Glossary at the back of the book so you can check them out if you have any question. For more information, you can also go to the Index to find out in which chapters the contents are discussed.

1 Introduction

Albert, E. The roles of women: A question of values. In S. M. Farber & R. H. L. Wilson (Eds.), *The potential of woman.* New York: McGraw-Hill, 1963.
The author, for many years considered the leading authority on sexual roles and sexual practice, examines some of the psychological variables relevant to the behavior of women, and contrasts them to male behavior.

Bachrach, A. J. *Psychological research: An introduction.* New York: Random House, 1962.
A simply and clearly written work

dealing with some of the key issues in psychological research.

Bird, C. *Born female: The high cost of keeping women down.* New York: Pocket, 1969.

Boring, E. G. *A history of experimental psychology.* Englewood Cliffs, New Jersey: Prentice-Hall, 1950.

By far the most complete history of psychology, detailing philosophical and other roots that led to modern psychology.

Churchman, C. W. *The systems approach.* New York: Dell, 1968.

Ginsburg, B. E. All mice are not created equal: Recent findings on genes and behavior. *Social Service Review,* 1966, *60,* 121-134.

Harshbarger, D., & Maley, R. F. (Eds.). *Behavior analysis and systems analysis: An integrative approach to mental health programs.* Kalamazoo, Michigan: Behaviordelia, 1974.
One of the first collections of articles to illustrate and describe how a systems approach is applied to programs whose aim is to deliver mental health services to the public.

Kuhn, T. S. *The structure of scientific revolutions.* Chicago: University of Chicago Press, 1970.
The author analyzes the history of science in terms of models or paradigms that fortuitously evolve and determine the direction of inquiry.

Lindsay, J. A. *A short history of sci-*

ence. Garden City, N.Y.: Doubleday Anchor, 1959.

Newman, H. A., Freeman, F. N., & Holtzinger, K. J. *Twins: A study of heredity and environment.* Chicago: University of Chicago Press, 1937.

Thomsen, D. E. General relative's catch 22. *Science News,* 1975, *107* (16), 262-263.

Tiger, L. The possible biological origins of sexual discrimination. *Impact of Science on Society,* 1970, *20,* 29-44.
The author, in this fascinating book, goes back to the beginnings of society and traces how biological features inherent in the human female have interacted. Demands of culture and the environment are viewed as a possible force in creating some of the practices of sex discrimination we see today.

Wann, T. W. *Behaviorism and phenomenology: Contrasting bases for modern psychology.* Chicago: University of Chicago Press, 1964.

Wechsler, D. *The measurement and appraisal of adult intelligence.* Baltimore: Williams & Wilkins, 1958.

Whaley, D. L., & Surratt, S. L. *Attitudes of science.* Kalamazoo, Michigan: Behaviordelia, 1967.
This book explains science as a practical method of inquiry, as a way of looking at events. Four basic guiding rules or principles are detailed as the attitudes of science.

Philosophers continue to haggle about what the universe is really like — just as they've always done, from the very start. Questions are asked like: What's real and what's illusion? What's the extent and nature of the cosmos? But lately, things have changed. These issues — once the domain of metaphysicians and philosophers — are becoming more and more the grist for hard-nosed physicists. One topic that has aroused their interest recently is determinism — cause and effect. What does it boil down to?

Some time ago one philosopher came up with what appears to be the most we can safely say about cause and effect. Our belief that one event causes another is based solely on the fact that the two generally occur together — the "cause" always occurring just before the "effect". Thus, if pushed to the wall, we can't say anything about "how" or even "if" one causes the other — or if the two are connected at all. The only thing we truly know is that the two typically occur together, and have done so in the past. Throwing a rock at a window, we watch the pane shatter on contact; but we can't say that the rock had anything to do with the breaking window.

But recently, physicists — not metaphysicians, philosophers, or mystics — have begun to question determinism. Those who are concerned are the theoretical physicists, who, like Einstein, are attempting to define and describe the architecture of the universe — how space, time, and events are interrelated. Dr. Rainer Sachs of the University of California at Berkeley found a baffling paradox when he tried to fit determinism into the geometry of four-dimensional space as formulated by Einstein's theory of general relativity — a formulation on which much of the experimentation in modern physics is based, and which has allowed the science to progress in leaps and bounds. But strange things happen when determinism is included in the model. Events from the past could suddenly appear full-blown without warning — perhaps a giant photon coming from nowhere, blowing us all to smithereens. There's no way determinism can work. Thus physics that condones determinism is based on a model that's indeterministic — a fine state of affairs. Sachs has tried to remedy things by altering the model so that determinism can be included. However, these altered models are so restrictive they won't permit much of what actually is done in modern physics to occur. Sachs feels that the problem is hardly a small one.

***

We've defined psychology as the study of behavior; however, there are many other ways that psychology has been and may be defined. One way that was prevalent in the past was to refer to the construct of the mind. The movement over the past years has been steadily away from the "mind", and toward behavior as the focus of study. Other approaches have stressed the stimulus side of things, speaking of psychology as the study of experience. But what is experience and what isn't? It's more than mere contact with the environment — more than just being there — but how much more? Because of these problems, definitions of this sort have also fallen away. It's clear that "contact" itself doesn't always change people or at least doesn't seem to change them in the same way. Clearly, we must look at more than the environment alone in the study of psychology. It appears that the only immutable aspect is behavior. All psychologists are interested in behavior, whether they talk about it in those terms or not. The ultimate question must be, what did the person do? Obviously behavior is the primary subject matter.

***

The argument in psychology between function and feeling is a long-standing one. Some psychologists are clearly interested in *feelings — they want people to be happy, to accept themselves. The changes they attempt through therapy have this as a goal. Other psychologists have their eye on survival. Do people's actions contribute to their survival? Does their behavior fit in with what must go on if the individual and the culture are to survive? Drawn to extremes, of course, both positions become ridiculous. It seems silly to completely disregard people's feelings. We know that feelings influence actions. Workers whose lot in life makes them unhappy may not be productive or desirable. On the other hand, we can't always encourage people to do what makes them happy — or less unhappy. Yet some psychotherapists seem entirely concerned with getting clients to accept themselves without giving much thought to whether or not they should accept themselves. The behavior of some people is so destructive — that the people who act that way should never accept themselves. It seems the last thing we should to is help them accept themselves, thus condoning, and perhaps abetting their behavior.*

But, it's beginning to appear that the quarrel between function and feelings, as with many quarrels in psychology, is pointless. We're finding that feelings do not occur independent of one's actions. How a person feels about things is a function of past outcomes, past history of rewards. It's possible with proper cultural practices, for people to learn to engage in functional acts, and to enjoy them as well. This, of course, is the great hope of behavioral psychologists — to put people together so their good feelings accompany appropriate action.

2 Biophysical Structure

Bronowski, J. *The ascent of man.* Boston: Little, Brown, 1974.

Crick, F. H. C. The genetic code. *Scientific American,* 1962, *207,* 66-74.

Darwin, C. *The origin of the species by means of natural selection or the preservation of favored races in the struggle for life and the descent of man and selection in relation to sex.* New York: Modern Library, 1936.

Dobzansky, T. *Genetics and the origin of species* (3rd ed.). New York: Columbia University Press, 1951.
The author has long been considered one of the leading authorities in genetics and evolution. Reading this book helps in getting a feel for much of the modern thought on the topic of heredity and evolution.

Evolution: A theory evolving. *Science News,* 1975, *107* (8), 113-128.

Fox, S. W. *Terrestrial origins of macromolecules and of cells.* NASA Accession No. N66-248-42, Rept. No. NASA-CR-74819, 1965.

Fox, S.W. Spontaneous generation, the origin of life, and self assembly. *Current Modern Biology,* 1968, *2* (3), 235-240.
The author has for many years been a leader in a controversial area of biochemistry. Fox's basic premise is that modern cells generated spontaneously from elements which were present when the earth first began.

Guyton, A. C. *Function of the human body.* Philadelphia: Saunders, 1969.
This popular volume on physiology is used in many college-level physiology courses.

Hondos, W. Evolutionary interpretation of neural and behavioral studies of living vertebrates. In F. O. Schmidt (Ed.), *The neuro-sciences: Second study program.* New York: Rockefeller University Press, 1970.

Jukes, T. H. *Molecules and evolution.* New York: Columbia University Press, 1966.

Measuring evolution: A new approach proposed. *Science News,* 1975, *107* (17), 265-280.

Quagliano, J. B. *Chemistry* (2nd ed.). Englewood Cliffs, New Jersey: Prentice-Hall, 1964.

Skinner, B. F. *About behaviorism.* New York: Knopf, 1974.
The most clearcut statement by the author, compiling many features in-

cluded in other books and articles written since 1938.

Thomas, L. *The lives of a cell.* New York: Viking Press, 1974.
This extremely entertaining and somewhat offbeat book is written about simple organisms from a somewhat naive viewpoint. The author's insights are relevant not only to biology and to simple organisms, but also to higher forms, including the human.

Watson, J. D. *Double helix.* New York: Atheneum, 1968.
A personal account of the discovery of the structure of DNA.

From time to time you'll run across an objective that is described as a thought question. Your teacher may not treat this in the same way as the other questions. For instance, they may not be on the quiz or they may require short essay answers or they might be reserved for class discussion. In any case, you would be well-advised to find out the course policy concerning such objectives.

***

The concepts of complexity and instability shouldn't be taken as inherent in the general scheme of nature. Their use in this chapter is merely to present a way of looking at the many diverse events that occur at different levels and stages of existence. Structure doesn't necessarily become more unstable as complexity increases. There are levels at which complexity reaches a level of organization where it becomes quite stable. It may remain in that form for eons, forever, in fact. At the level of the atom, we find that some elements that have more electrons, protons, and neutrons, than others are far more stable. This instability is not necessarily related just to the number of sub-atomic parts contained in the atom. We find the same thing in chemistry. Simple compounds are often extremely unstable, whereas, more complex compounds have great integrity. We find these exceptions to the Principles of Complexity and Instability at the biochemical, molecular, cellular and multicellular levels as well.

But the exceptions don't obscure the rule — in one sense they bear it out. For even the most stable compounds show variation in structure, tending in some cases to be more complex. This new complexity is often destroyed as quickly as it originates. So that osscilation may go on for ages, each stage destroyed by instability, never reaching a new stage of stable complexity. But one fine day, a new stable, more complex form arises. And so it starts again.

***

Where did life first come from? Scientific theories seem to fall into two basic camps: 1) Life came from outer space. Particles from distant parts of our galaxy or other galaxies came into our solor system to take root on earth. 2) Life began as spontaneous generation from inert chemicals that were present at the time the earth was formed. Those scientists holding the theory of outer space origin suggest that the length of time since the beginning of the earth isn't sufficient for inert chemicals to have produced the complex forms of life seen today. As you've seen, the thesis the authors favor is based on work of the spontaneous generation idea. Sidney Fox's notion is that a very primitive cell, or "protocell", generated relatively fast from the debris present on the crust of the earth and in the atmosphere when it first formed. Through the ages since then, this primitive cell has evolved to the form of the contemporary cells, cells with nucleic acid or genes. Workers at Fox's lab, as well as at other locations, have reinforced the theory by creating protocells from the constituents that most agree were present when the earth was formed.

* * *

The distinction between germinal cells and other cells must be made to further qualify the thesis that mutation is less likely to occur in complex creatures as opposed to simple ones. The germinal cell in the human is the cell that's produced by the union of the sperm and egg. From this single cell all other parts of the human come, as cells divide and differentiate. Mutation during this process is extremely rare, both within the germinal cell itself and among the many cells that divide from it.

Once full growth is reached, cells are replaced as they're destroyed, or otherwise become inactive. Mutation does occur during the regeneration process.

Some suggest that mutation in single human cells is in fact about as prevalent as in single cells of less complex creatures. There is, however, a relationship between complexity of the cell and likelihood of mutation. The more complex the cell, the less likely it will be to mutate. One reason this is true is because cells that are the most complex reproduce less frequently than less complex cells. It has long been a doctrine that human brain cells once destroyed will never be replaced. This has been questioned recently but, in any event, it's clear that regeneration of complex brain cells is extremely minimal. Other human cells such as the cells of the skin and particularly those cells of the mouth, lips, and other parts of the body that are likely to have contact with the abrasive environment reproduce quite rapidly. Most mutations are found in these cells. Skin cancers are far more common than cancers of other tissue, followed closely by epithelial tissue of the mouth, anus, and respiratory system. Most scientists believe that cancers are the result of mutations. However, an alternative theory is that they are produced by aberrations in the biochemical messengers that control cell production.

But for all the above, the primary thesis that mutation becomes too costly for complex creatures remains quite true. Mutation ceases to be a method of adaptation for complex creatures as it indeed is for many lower organisms, and for all microorganisms.

* * *

There's a basic similarity between natural selection of organisms by the environment and the selection of responses by reward and punishment. We can view the latter as a further extension of the more basic process of natural selection. Recent advances in biochemistry indicate that modifications in cellular structure may occur as a result of learning, with these modifications being quite like those alterations that take place in nucleic acids of cells when they mutate. This suggests that we may be able to look at learning as a kind of short-term mutation, an alteration in cell structure, occurring as a result of experience.

A certain number of mutants will always survive. Physicians often give many antibiotics at once to get around possible immunity of the creature to some. Their attempt is to kill all the organisms in hopes **that the mutants who are insensitive to one drug will be killed off by** *the others in the package. Biochemists point out, however, that what the physicians may be doing is creating a strain of supermicrobes, immune to all known antibiotics. They argue that regardless of how many antibiotics one gives, there may someday remain a microbe that might have died of starvation or old age — but all the antibiotics to which it is immune killed off all the competition. This supermicrobe could strike so fast and be so lethal, immune to all of our antibiotics.*

3 Physiological Processes

Békésy, V. & Rosenblith, W. A. The mechanical properties of the ear. In S. S. Stevens (Ed.), *Handbook of experimental psychology.* New York: Wiley, 1951.
A clearcut account of how the ear operates, including many of the remarkable aspects ot this fine piece of evolutionary engineering.

Deutsch, J. A., & Deutsch, B. *Physiological psychology.* (Rev. ed.). Homewood, Illinois: Dorsey Press, 1973.

Eccles, J. C. The synapse. *Scientific American,* 1965, *213,* 56-66.
This researcher is the leading expert on the nature of the synapse.

Gardner, F. *Fundamentals of neurology* (5th ed.). Philadelphia: Saunders, 1968.

Hernandez-Péona, R. Reticular mechanisms of sensory control. In W. A. Rosenblith (Ed.), *Sensory communication.* Cambridge, Mass.: The M.I.T. Press, 1961.
The author's research in reticular formation and the role that it plays in selection of sensory input, has had great impact in many areas of biology and psychology.

Kandel, E. R. Nerve cells and behavior. *Scientific American,* 1970, *223,* 57-70.
An intriguing article which seeks to relate the activity of nerve cells and the nature of neurons to behavior as it's seen occurring in everyday existence.

Katz, B. The nerve impulse. *Scientific American,* 1952, *185,* 55-64.
This researcher has for years been a student of nerve conduction. This summary of his work is a comprehensive account of the nerve impulse — of what takes place when nerves conduct.

Milner, P. M. *Physiological psychology.* New York: Holt, Rinehart & Winston, 1970.

Morgan, C. T. *Physiological psychology* (3rd ed.). New York: McGraw-Hill, 1965.
The standard physiological psychology

source book for the past several decades.

Ranson, S. W., & Clark, S. L. *The anatomy of the nervous system: Its development and function* (10th ed.). Philadelphia: Saunders, 1959.
This is a standard text for courses in physiology and anatomy, and is commonly used in medical schools, as well as all other places where these topics are taught and studied.

Walter, W. G. *The living brain.* New York: Norton, 1953.

Our treatment of the nervous system has been extremely low key. This differs from the way it's often presented in introductory psychology texts, and differs also from the way it's typically talked about in the popular media. Ironically, it seems that those who reify the power of the human brain are those scientists who study it and those lay people who know the least about it. Both tend to give the brain too much autonomy and responsibility. They talk about it like a small boy speaks of his dad. The brain can do anything! The point we hope we've made is that the brain is an evolutionary product. It's not something that functions autonomously, independent of the environment — a little man, or homunculus, that directs actions — a switch person inside us.

Yet, even with those constraints, we could have said much more about the brain and nervous system. This is the tradition of introductory psychology texts. We question the value of this tradition. It's perhaps more appropriate for a course in physiology or anatomy. Few of us will have either the skill or the opportunity to attempt to change what our friends, children, wives, husbands, or clients do through direct or indirect intervention into the nervous system. If we're going to make a difference we'll probably have to restrict ourselves to forms of input that are restricted to external contact — not brain surgery. It is these aspects — the principles of human learning — we've, therefore, chosen to stress.

* * *

In defining stimulus, we're saying that simply everything is a stimulus, almost but not quite a useless concept. All energy configurations are stimuli. We define a stimulus as a physicist would, rather than in terms of the subjective response of the observer. That then allows us to study the subjective response of the observer as a function of stimulus dimension as specified by the physicists.

4 Evolution and Behavior

Altman, J. *Organic foundations of animal behavior.* New York: Holt, Rinehart and Winston, 1966.
A classic book. Extremely well-written. Presents a fascinating analysis of the details of the behavior of simple creatures for those students who are seriously interested in such matters.

Fraenkel, G. S., & Gunn, D. L. *The orientation of animals, kineses, taxes, and compass reactions.* New York: Dover, 1961.

Goodwin, G. G. *The animal kingdom; the strange and wonderful ways of mammals, birds, reptiles, fishes, and insects* (Ed. F. Drimmer). New York: Greystone, 1954.

Hinde, R. A. *Animal behaviour; a synthesis of ethology and comparative psychology* (2nd ed.). New York: McGraw-Hill, 1970.

Lorenz, K. Z. The evolution of behavior. *Scientific American.* 1958, *199* (6), 67-78.

Most of the articles cited from *Scientific American* are written for the educated layman. This means they're usually somewhat more interesting to, and more easily read by, such readers in comparison to the original technical articles on which these reports are based. But in some instances, they may still be fairly difficult reading.

Orr, R. T. *The animal kingdom.* New York: Macmillan, 1965.

In general, biological structures of increasing complexity evolve as natural selection tends to select more and more complex structures that deal more effectively with their environment. But, at the same time, there are many simpler structures which seem to be thriving as they've adapted quite well to their environment. It may be that more complex structures are needed to deal with more complex or changing environments. But, simpler structures can survive in some relatively stable or simpler environments.

***

We can look at basic stimulus control also in terms of the concepts of operant and respondent behavior, covered in the next chapters. We can look at basic stimulus control as respondent control, if the light is an unconditioned stimulus eliciting or evoking the unconditioned approach response. Of course, this might also be a conditioned stimulus response.

Or, we can look at this as operant control: if the light is a cue for the operant response of approaching that light, with the food acting as the reward. We can also see this as an instance of feedback stimulus control (to be covered later), since each response affects the subsequent stimulus input (the intensity of the light) that in turn affects the next response.

5 Motivation of Learned Acts

Bachrach, A. J. *Psychological research; an introduction.* New York: Random House, 1972.

A brief introduction to what psychological research is really about. For the introductory student.

Geis, G. L., Stebbins, W. C., & Lundin, R. W. *The study of behavior: Reflex and operant conditioning* (Vol. 1). Englewood Cliffs, New Jersey: Prentice-Hall, 1961.

One of the best of the programmed texts. Students like it. An introduction to the basic concepts of reflex and operant conditioning.

The next two books present some of the basic principles of behavior as they relate not only to animals but also to humans:

Malott, R. W. *Contingency management in education.* Kalamazoo, Michigan: Behaviordelia, 1972.

Whaley, D. L., & Malott, R. W. *Elementary principles of behavior.* New York: Prentice-Hall, 1971.

You might look at the next two books for an interesting account of some of the reinforcers that can control the creative behavior of scientists. Both are very well-written and easy to read. Solzhenitsyn, S. I. *The first circle* (T. P. Whitney, trans.). New York: Bantam Books, 1969.
Watson, J. D. *The double helix.* New York: Atheneum, 1968.
This is an interesting account of the reinforcers controlling the creative behavior of some of the world's most famous scientists.

Tinbergen, N. The curious behavior of the stickleback. *Scientific American,* 1952, *187* (6), 22-26.

The study of basic learning processes with animals is one of the most active areas of psychological research in the United States today, with the albino rat the most commonly used species, and the Skinner box the most commonly used apparatus. The Skinner box consists of an enclosed experimental cubicle used to keep the experimental animal fairly close to the response and reward devices, and to keep distracting or irrelevant factors from affecting the experiment. The box contains a response device which the animal learns to operate. This device is often connected to an electrical recording apparatus so that the experiment can be run automatically.

***

The reward of knowledge for knowledge sake, science for science sake, is a special type of reward to be dealt with in a later chapter — a learned reward, not a biological one. Knowledge becomes a reward because it's often paired with other more basic rewards such as dealing successfully with the world about which you are knowledgeable, thereby obtaining fuel and escaping harm.

We're not too comfortable with the term "non-biological" when referring to stimuli such as cues or rewards that affect behavior. We don't mean to imply that non-biological stimuli do not affect the biology of the creature involved. We mean that they don't have an effect that has direct biological significance for the organism's survival. They don't directly constitute a fuel supply or a harmful stimulus condition.

***

Needless to say, by action we mean biologically generated action and not mechanical action, in our definition of motivation. For instance, being knocked over by a tornado is motion, but we wouldn't call it action in the sense that we're using the word since it was a mere mechanical event. By action we mean things that could not be done by the body of a dead person.

It's always hard to define terms, especially in our definitions of unconditioned and conditioned stimulus and response, when you try to be succinct and clear, as well as precise. We've used the term "cause". That should exert proper stimulus control over most of the student readers of our book, as it would seem to tap into their intuitive repertoire. However, the more philosophically-inclined faculty may be uncomfortable with that word in general, and in this context in particular. One problem is that "cause" may imply the sufficient, as well as the necessary, conditions for an event to occur. We only wish to use it in the sense of "necessary" condition. The word "elicit" is commonly used in this context but introductory students don't readily understand it. The word "evoked" may be a little clearer.

We expressed the definition of operant conditioning in terms of "a change in response". But definition should also imply the maintenance of a response during steady state. In other words, it's a change in the rate of response over what would be the case if the results weren't there. Suppose the results weren't there? Then the response rate would decrease if those results were acting as a reward, and increase if those results were acting as a punisher.

In many cases, Dodo is clearly a fictional creature. For instance, a complex species that has inherited the complex capacity to learn would most likely not mutate one that failed to learn. We invented Dodo to show what would happen if a creature was similar to Gore, but was without the crucial features under study.

***

Most people have a great deal of difficulty with the distinction between feedback stimulus control and operant conditioning. Here's the point we're trying to make: A feedback stimulus functions either as an eliciting stimulus or as a cue; while in operant conditioning, the stimulus resulting from the response functions as a reward or punisher.

Now you may have a hard time with this distinction for two reasons: 1) People tend to equate feedback with reward in their everyday use of the term; so you may be reading that meaning into our analysis in spite of our efforts to keep it out. And 2) the other source of difficulty may be that the results of a response may, indeed, function both as a feedback stimulus and as a reward at the same time. But we should still distinguish between the two functions of that stimulus much as we do between the reward function and the cue function of stimuli in a stimulus-response chain. There, each response produces an event which serves to reward that response and functions as a cue for the next response.

Consider the following instance: the captain piloting her ship by compass, with the observing response of looking at the compass being rewarded by the sight of the compass. It's a reward because of the cue function it will then serve in controlling her steering response. So the feedback provided by the compass can serve as a cue for the next steering response while it also serves as a reward for the observing response of looking at the compass.

However, this compass feedback need not function as a reward for the steering response itself (just the observing response.) The captain need not learn how to avoid oversteering and understeering, etc., as a result of the rewards and punishers for looking at the compass. She can still get her boat safely into port. The experience of steering and looking at the compass may be a learning experience affecting the way she steers the ship next time out, but it need not function as such a learning experience to still be a good example of effective feedback stimulus control.

6 Motivation Indirectly Related to Biological Need

Azrin, N. H. Pain and aggression. *Psychology Today,* May 1967, pp. 27-33.
The articles referred to in *Psychology Today* are usually well-written, entertainingly presented, clear, and authoritative.

Azrin, N. H., Hutchinson, R. R., & Hake, D. F. Extinction-produced aggression. *Journal of Experimental Analysis of Behavior,* 1966, *9,* 191-204.

Bateson, T. G., & Reese, E. P. The reinforcing properties of conspicuous stimuli in the imprinting situation. *Animal Behaviour,* 1969, *17,* 692-699.

Hess, E. H. Imprinting in animals. *Scientific American,* 1958, *198* (3), 81-90.

Hess, E. H. *Imprinting.* New York: Van Nostrand Reinhold, 1973.

Hinde, R. A. *Animal behaviour; a synthesis of ethology and comparative psychology* (2nd ed.). New York: McGraw-Hill, 1970.

Skinner, B. F. *About behaviorism.* New York: Knopf, 1974.
One of Skinner's clearer presentations of behaviorism, containing interesting material about aggression and imprinting.

Skinner, B. F. The shaping of phylogenic behavior. *Journal of the Experimental Analysis of Behavior*, 1975, *24,* 117-120.
Often articles published in psychological journals such as these, are fairly difficult to read; but we recommend them if you really want to get the details of the way scientific analysis and research work.

Tinbergen, N., & the editors of *Life. Animal behavior.* New York: Time, 1965.
The books from this series published by *Time* are all clearly written and highly recommended.

Our view has changed concerning the relation between biological causes of behavior and learned behavior. Like many learning theorists we have a tendency to stress the plasticity of behavior, its malleability, a notion that all or nearly all actions are learned — few, if any, are biologically or structurally predetermined. Like most learning theorists we've had a tendency to minimize the type of unlearned reinforcers affecting behavior. We've tended to suggest that any exotic reinforcer would probably turn out to be a learned reinforcer — that, on closer scrutiny, it might turn out that such an event was reinforcing because it had been paired with other more obvious basic reinforcers, such as attaining fuel or escaping a harmful condition.

For instance, such a view might suggest that there are no direct, immediate unlearned reinforcers for aggression; but rather, it's the effect aggression has on the external environment that causes that aggression. In other words, aggression helps the aggressor get fuel and escape harm. So any more immediate rewards would be learned rewards, due to their pairing with those basic unlearned rewards.

In general, that still seems to us to be a fairly reasonable position — it's parsimonious. It's an attempt to simplify things, to understand a wide variety of divergent bits of data in terms of some more elegant or simple process. In other words, we would look for the ubiquitous process of the establishment of learned reinforcers rather than assume that nature has, in fact, prewired so many dozens or hundreds of specific, unlearned reinforcers.

But our position has changed somewhat since we've been looking at behavior from the point of view of evolution through natural selection. It now seems much more plausible to us that creatures might readily evolve so that certain events are unlearned reinforcers, because those events have often been associated with other biological conditions such as fuel or harm — conditions that more directly affect the creature's survival. Therefore, creatures that find such events innately reinforcing or punishing may be more likely to survive and pass those reinforcer-punisher preferences and aversions on to their offspring.

So we're no longer as concerned with some of the issues of past decades. Are novelty or bright lights, or motion, unlearned rewards or are they learned rewards due to their previous pairing with other reinforcers. Is a sweet taste an unlearned reward or might it be a learned reward resulting from pairing with other rewards? Consider laboratory rats. They prefer non-nutritively sweetened saccharin water to plain water. Could the reinforcing value of the sweet taste be due to the sweet taste of their mother's milk or the lab chow they were raised on? We no longer feel compelled to find such an interpretation since it now seems as plausible to us that such reinforcers might be innately determined. But then we find ourselves on another quest for parsimony.

With this new view, we ask the question, how could some particular stimulus help the species survive and thereby become an unlearned reinforcer? To put it another way, how might that stimulus have been paired with some other events — direct biological consequences dealing with fuel or tissue damage? In other words, we're now ready to look for an association between the unusual reinforcer and the more obvious, direct biologically significant consequences throughout the evolution of the species. We no longer merely survey the evolution of the behavior of the individual organisms. Now we look at phylogenetic as well as ontogenetic development of reinforcer and punisher power.

It seems that frustrated pigeons peck at pictures, and mirrors, and other pigeons behind plastic walls, perhaps with a higher probability than they peck at just a plain wall itself, thereby indicating that it's more than the pressure on the beak that makes a particular response reinforcing. It may be that the visual stimulus also reinforces the looking response and perhaps brings the bird into closer proximity with the target, thereby increasing the probability of a peck at the target versus a peck at something else, or versus no peck at all. But we must confess this may be straining ever so slightly to account for this as a reinforced operant response.

***

We don't mean that emotional-physiological responses are a direct cause or a sufficient condition for high-energy activity when we speak of emotion as an energizer. We mean that those emotional-physiological reactions merely support such high-energy actions. The creature may not only engage in fight or flight, but may also freeze in an immobile position when in the presence of danger. We suspect that most often what will help the creature survive will determine the stimulus conditions in which it will fight, flee, or freeze. This may result from evolutionary and learning factors.

7 Learning: Basic Elements

Eriksen, C. W. *Behavior and awareness.* Durham, North Carolina: Duke University Press, 1962.
This classic volume is one of the first attempts to deal with the elusive topic of consciousness and its relationship to what is learned.

Hunter, W. S. The delayed reaction in animals and children. *Behavior Monographs,* 1913, *2.*
In this series, Hunter compared the ability of various animals to make a delayed reaction response, believing animal intelligence was being measured.

Kimble, G. A. *Foundations of conditioning and learning.* Englewood Cliffs, New Jersey: Prentice-Hall, 1967.
A standard textbook in conditioning and learning.

Laties, V. G., Weiss, B., & Weiss, A. B. Further observations on overt mediating behavior and the discrimination of time. In P. B. Dews (Ed.), *Festschrift for B. F. Skinner.* New York: Appleton-Century-Crofts, 1970.

Rozin, P. & Kalat, J. Specific hungers and poison avoidance as adaptive specializations of learning. *Psychological Review,* 1971, *78,* 459-486.

Skinner, B. F. *About behaviorism.* New York: Knopf, 1974.

Whaley, D. L, & Malott, R. W. *Elementary principles of behavior.* Englewood Cliffs, New Jersey: Prentice-Hall, 1971.

We've included the Law of Repeated Delayed Results in this chapter. In truth, however, we don't know if repeated delayed results in and of themselves will even cause learning to occur. One thing is certain — delayed results do affect our behavior. If they didn't we'd be in a great deal more trouble than we are. In teaching this law we may have erred as others have done. Learning theorists in the past have gone afield in at least two distinct ways. They've tended to make learning too mechanical — trying to make psychology replete with laws as simple and as unitary as the laws of Newtonian physics. Others have made learning far too speculative, subjective, and conditional — what's learned depends on what the subject wants to learn.

But how could repeated delayed results work? Presumably, they could have a statistical effect. Let's say that a particular response is never followed by immediate rewards, but is consistently followed by a delayed reward. It seems reasonable that the response would be affected over time and many repeated pairings by the rather weak influence of the delayed result. These faint though consistent results could have a cumulative effect. Yet, if we look at the research that's been done, we find that results don't seem to have any effect at all if they occur more than a few seconds after a response. If this is true, delayed results, no matter how often repeated, wouldn't matter. It's also possible that the experimental design used in establishing the limit was insensitive to the very faint effects that might occur.

It's our guess that delayed results alone don't work at all. We believe that learning as a result of delayed outcomes depends on some form of mediation. Psychologists may ultimately find that all results must be mediated, even those that don't violate the fraction-of-a-second limit, if they're to have any effect at all. It is, therefore, the form of mediation that should be questioned and not whether or not mediation is necessary.

In the typical learning situation, when the result follows immediately after the response, mediation of a chemical or biochemical nature occurs. The response produces bodily changes that last for a brief period of time — long enough to come in contact with other effects the results create in the body. Mediation beyond the fraction-of-a-second limit must occur through other media. In the bait-shy effect, for instance, it's believed that the mediation is achieved by traces of the stimulus that linger after the stimulus has been consumed. Poisoned food is a stimulus that obviously doesn't completely disappear when it's consumed. Tastes, odors, effects on the gastrointestinal system may last for many hours — long enough for delayed results to make contact.

Other stimuli don't create such long-lasting effects. Effects don't outlast the stimulus in most cases. Thus far we haven't found anything like the bait-shy effect occurring to extroceptive stimuli such as light or sound. One exception with extroceptive stimuli occurs in the case of ionizing irradiation. However, X-rays and other forms of ionizing radiation are known to affect the gastrointestinal system and to have very little effect on most other systems. Avoidance learning that occurs to these stimuli could be mediated by the gastrointestinal system, much as in the bait-shy phenomenon. Where other stimuli are concerned it appears that mediation must be carried on by responses, although these may be either internal or external. In either case, these sequences of responses must be fairly consistent if they're to provide the mediation needed to bring current action into contact with delayed results. So, at this point we present the Law of Repeated Delayed Results as a tenuous one.

8 Learning: Factors Affecting Learning

Deese, J., & Hulse, S. H. *The psychology of learning* (3rd ed.). New York: McGraw-Hill, 1967.
A classic in the area of learning.

Gilbert, R. N., & Sutherland, N. S. *Animal discrimination learning.* New York: Academic Press, 1969.

Honig, W. K. (Ed.). *Operant behavior: Areas of research and application.* Englewood Cliffs, New Jersey: Prentice-Hall, 1966.
Some of the most detailed and sophisticated analyses of the operant approach to behavior extant.

Kimble, G. A. *Hilgard and Marquis' conditioning and learning* (2nd ed.). Englewood Cliffs, New Jersey: Prentice-Hall, 1961.
A very popular rewrite of the classic conditioning and learning sourcebook.

Malott, R. W. *How I learned to relate to my laboratory rat through humanistic behaviorism: A laboratory manual.* Kalamazoo, Michigan: Behaviordelia, 1973.
A laboratory rat manual used in many beginning animal courses in introductory psychology and animal behavior. The experiments are planned so as to require only the simplest of Skinner boxes.

Reynolds, G. S. *A primer of operant conditioning.* Glenview, Illinois: Scott, Foresman, 1968.

Shettleworth, S. J. Constraints on learning. In D. W. S. Lehrman, R. A. Hinde & E. Shaw (Eds.), *Advances in the study of behavior (No. 4).* New York: Academic Press, 1973.

Skinner, B. F. *The behavior of organisms; an experimental analysis.* Englewood Cliffs, New Jersey: Prentice-Hall, 1938.

Whaley, D. L., & Malott, R. W. *Elementary principles of behavior.* Englewood Cliffs, New Jersey: Prentice-Hall, 1971.

This book was the beginning of operant psychology's influence on the study of animal and human behavior. Since its publication, Skinner has produced many volumes and numerous articles, all of which expound, delineate, and extend basic tenets of operant behavior.

You may find it interesting to note the different ways in which we can conduct the business of science. We can make discoveries in the highly controlled setting of the experimental laboratory. In other instances, we draw discoveries from our observations made in a variety of uncontrolled settings. The first method is exemplified by the Skinner box, the apparatus described in this chapter and developed by Skinner. The Skinner box is a contrived environment, a rigid and standard one where controlled scientific experiments are conducted. Most often there's only one response that the experimenter is interested in observing. The space is restrictive, and care is taken to make the box as barren as possible.

The approach is to restrict the environment and thus eliminate all variables except those under study. The experimenter can discern the relationship between the lever-press response and the variables such as schedules of reinforcement, the periodic presence of specific cues, etc. This approach has yielded excellent results. We owe the formulation of most of the principles that we've talked about in the learning chapters to the Skinner box.

Since Skinner first discovered these principles, much research has been conducted demonstrating that they hold for humans as well as for rats and pigeons.

In sharp contrast to Skinner's approach is the one employed by Darwin which led to his theory of evolution. Darwin studied many creatures in their natural environments, and shunned laboratory research. From these thousands of observations, Darwin was able to distill the prime relationship between an organism and its environment, stating it as the Principle of Natural Selection. Darwin's Skinner box was the whole world, and his subjects creatures of all species. Each time a new member was found to fit the pattern, Darwin's theory was strengthened.

How different these two approaches are, yet both have served science well. Can it be said that one is more important to science than the other? Perhaps it can.

There's a great lack of people with the skill to proceed as Darwin did. Few of us have the observational and inductive skills to discern such relationships by his method. Skinner's method is, on the other hand, a quite safe one that almost any scientist can well employ. It is, in fact, an approach used by most scientists today. It doesn't require scientists to have Darwin's genius before they're able to produce valuable facts and relationships.

Sigmund Freud is often likened to Darwin in terms of his inventive genius. But if we look closely, we see that Freud had much more in common with Skinner. He saw few patients compared to clinical psychologists and psychiatrists today. He did, however, spend many many hours with each of his clients, restricting them to a controlled setting — the psychoanalyst's couch — a setting where Freud could exert full control over interactions with the client.

Perhaps the future will produce other Darwins. In the meantime, science proceeds daily in small increments, moving carefully from the controlled laboratory to the world.

9 Learning: Learning Results and Generalization

Blough, D. S. Generalization gradient, shape, and summation in steady-state tests. In P. B. Dews (Ed.), *Festschrift for B. F. Skinner.* New York: Appleton-Century-Crofts, 1970.

Hanson, H. M. Effects of discrimination training on stimulus generalization. *Journal of Experimental Psychology,* 1959, *58,* 321-334.

Harlow, H. F. The formation of learning sets. *Psychological Review,* 1949, *56,* 51-65.
In this paper, Harlow puts forth the empirical findings which have done much to explain the ability of humans and other organisms to come under control of extremely abstract concepts.

Kelleher, R. T. Conditioned reinforcement in second order schedules. *Journal of the Experimental Analysis of Behavior,* 1966, *9,* 475-486.

Kelleher, R. T., & Gollub, L. A review of positive conditioned reinforcement. *Journal of the Experimental Analysis of Behavior,* 1962, *5,* 543-597.

Logan, F, *Fundamentals of learning and motivation.* Dubuque, Iowa: Brown, 1970.

Malott, R. W. *How I learned to relate to my laboratory rat through humanistic behaviorism: A laboratory manual.* Kalamazoo, Michigan: Behaviordelia, 1973.

Reynolds, G. S. Potency of conditioned reinforcers based on food and on food and punishment. *Science,* 1963, *139,* 838-839.

Sidman, M. By-products of aversive control. *Journal of the Experimental Analysis of Behavior,* 1958, *1,* 265-280.

Skinner, B. F. *The behavior of organisms.* Englewood Cliffs, New Jersey: Prentice-Hall, 1961.

Skinner, B. F. *About behaviorism.* New York: Knopf, 1974.

Terrace, H. S. Stimulus control. In W. K. Honig (Ed.), *Operant behavior: Areas of research and application.* Englewood Cliffs, New Jersey: Prentice-Hall, 1966.

Watson, J. *Behaviorism.* New York: Norton, 1930.

Whaley, D. L., & Malott, R. W. *Elementary principles of behavior.* Englewood Cliffs, New Jersey: Prentice Hall, 1971.

Wolfe, J. B. Effectiveness of token rewards for chimpanzees. *Comparative Psychology Monographs,* 1936, *12* (No. 5).

Some writers in the field of learning speak of the loss of the power *of a learned reward as extinction. We talk about extinction as a procedure in which reinforcers are employed, and a response that was rewarded is no longer rewarded. And the extinction process, of course, results when the response fails to occur after many unreinforced occurrences.*

A phenomenon that appears to be similar happens when learned reinforcers are no longer paired with unlearned reinforcers. The creature makes a response which results in the learned reward, or reinforcer. Responses continue to produce the learned reinforcer, but it's never paired with a primary reinforcer, and thus it loses its reinforcing property. As a result, the organism soon stops responding; however, the learned reinforcer keeps occurring. You can see that this isn't the same as extinction where the unlearned reinforcers are withdrawn. This point of view, of course, leads us to say that the only way we can talk about a response extinguishing where it has been maintained by a learned reinforcer is if the learned reinforcer is withheld — then we can call it extinction.

10 Sensory Processes

Cornsweet, T. N. *Visual perception.* New York: Academic Press, 1970. An excellent and authoritative text on visual perception, though not necessarily easy reading.

Fraenkel, G. S., & Gunn, D. L. *The orientation of animals, kinesis, taxes, and compass reactions.* New York: Dover, 1961.

Galanter, E. Contemporary psychophysics. In G. Mandler (Ed.), *New directions in psychology* (Vol. 1). New York: Holt, Rinehart & Winston, 1962. This moderately difficult chapter is an excellent introduction to an approach to sensory and perceptual processes; quite compatible with the analysis of this book.

Geldard, F. A. *The human senses* (2nd ed.). New York: Wiley, 1972. A fine intermediate-level text dealing with sensory processes.

Hinde, R. A. *Animal behaviour; a synthesis of ethology and comparative psychology* (2nd ed.). New York: McGraw-Hill, 1970.

Mueller, C. G., & Rudolf, N. *Light and vision.* New York: Time-Life Books, 1967.

Stevens, S. S., & Warshovsky, F. *Sound and hearing.* New York: Time-Life Books, 1967.

What is a stimulus? The sun sends photons down to earth where they bounce off of objects and strike our retina, causing a sensory response. What was the stimulus: the sun, the object, or the photon? The way we use the term is that the object is the stimulus. We're able to deal with this stimulus at a distance or make a distal sensory response to it because of the effect it has on photons, causing them to be reflected into our eyeballs. In a sense, it's not the photons we deal with. They're more the medium than the message.

* * *

A sensory response is the terminal output of a sensory receptor. Sensory control is the control of those sensory systems exerted by physical stimuli. When we talk about terminal response, we're talking about the terminal response of the sensory system itself while it's still in the afferent side and prior to the brain.

It may be straining the point a bit to say that a tissue-damaging event serves as a cue for the escape response, when, in fact, it's that aversive stimulus the creature is escaping. It's as if we had a rat in a Skinner box where we turned on an electric shock on the grid floor and allowed the rat to escape the shock by pressing a response lever. The shock is analogous to a motivation operation rather than a cue. A cue would be involved if, when the shock came along, the bar presses were ineffective unless the green light was on — the green light then being the cue.

But it may be appropriate to say motivational states also have cue properties, as people have in the past said. Perhaps a response wouldn't be effectively controlled by such events without those stimulus properties. For instance, there are people and organisms that don't sense tissue damage. In those cases they won't make effective escape responses. So, in a sense, tissue damage does have a sensory property which must control our behavior if we're to escape damage.

11 Perception

Bower, T. G. R. The visual world of infants. *Scientific American,* 1966, *215* (6), 80-92.
This research on size constancy and shape constancy is also interesting to look at in terms of point of view of this chapter.

Cornsweet, T. N. *Visual perception.* New York: Academic Press, 1970. This intermediate to advanced text on vision is clearly one of the very best in the field.

Gibson, E. J., & Walk, R. D. The visual cliff. *Scientific American,* 1960, *202* (4), 64-71.

Graham, C. H. Visual perception. In S. S. Stevens (Ed.), *Handbook of experimental psychology.* New York: Wiley, 1951.

Hochberg, J. E. *Perception.* Englewood Cliffs, New Jersey: Prentice-Hall, 1964. A brief book for the introductory or intermediate student.

Kaufman, L., & Rock, I. The moon illusion. *Scientific American,* 1962, *207* (1), 120-130.
The study of the moon illusion where the moon looks larger when it's closer to the horizon is interesting to interpret from the point of view of this chapter.

The following two references are more detailed treatments of the point of view presented in this chapter. They're fairly difficult reading.
Malott, M. K., & Malott, R. W. Perception and stimulus generalization. In W. C. Stebbins (Ed.), *Animal psychophysics.* New York: Plenum, 1971.
Malott, R. W., & Malott, M. K. Perception revisited. *Perceptual & Motor Skills,* 1969, *28,* 683-692.

Mussen, P. H., Congor, J. J., & Kagan, J. *Child development and personality* (4th ed.). New York: Harper & Row, 1974.

Nissen, H. W. Phylogenetic comparison. In S. S. Stevens (Ed.), *Handbook of experimental psychology.* New York: Wiley, 1951.

The following was expurgated from the main part of the text but saved for the most dedicated of students:

"Either I don't get that visual cliff thing or the authors are crazy," Dawn said, concerned that it might be the former, but hopeful it might be the latter, since she wanted to be one up on the authors. "It seems to me like this whole visual cliff thing is in the wrong chapter; it should be in 'Motivation Indirectly Related to Biological Need' not 'Perception'. At least, that's the way it seems to me."

"Afraid I'm not tracking you," Mae replied, annoyed at having her quiet reading disturbed, yet looking forward to helping Dawn catch the authors at their own tricky game. "What do you mean?"

"Well, perception is a type of cue control," she paused to get agreement where she knew she could.

"Right," Mae obliged.

"But they're trying to find out why the view over the cliff is a punisher, not why the cliff 'appears' deep. They're saying, 'We don't know how it 'appears' to the creature. In a sense, that question of how it appears doesn't mean much. All we know is how the creature reacts to the sight. It reacts as if the sight were a punisher, an aversive stimulus. So the creature tries to avoid it; or to escape it.' So they're asking, 'Why's that sight a punisher?' And that's a motivation question. They're not asking, 'Why does this view appear deeper than that one?' That'd be a perception question."

"Okay, the perception question can be asked like this: 'What arrangement of its features causes a stimulus to act as a cue for a response?' A cue control question. And here they're asking what arrangement of features of a stimulus cause it to act as a punisher? A motivation question."

"But still it seems like the visual cliff can be thought of as a perception problem — not sure how though," Mae mused.

"Yeah, I feel awkward about it too. But I don't know how to get it straight."

Both women thought for a while. Then Mae spoke. "Maybe it's both a motivation problem and *a perception problem. Like some stimuli act as punishers when they combine, and I'll bet that when they combine they act as cues for some response, some response like, 'That sure looks like a cliff all right,' for human adults. But I guess we can't really say the visual cliff looks like a real cliff, not if we just look at the avoidance response, or at some emotion response. All we can say is the visual cliff is a visual punisher just like a real cliff."*

"But maybe the creature can't tell the two aren't the same. Suppose you used the real cliff as a cue for some learned response; then the creature would make the same response when it saw the visual cliff; otherwise, they weren't the same cues. So maybe the visual cliff is also a perception problem. But maybe not too. They need some other response under the control of those complex cues to be sure what they've got — they can't just do it with an escape or emotion response."

***

To see if the visual cliff is a perceptual effect, we would need to do an experiment like the following: We'd need to isolate the two potentially relevant stimulus dimensions; for instance, angle of regard, and (to pull a lot of variables together), distance of the object being viewed. This would be analogous to a Muller-Lyer illusion experiment where we had length of line as one stimulus dimension, and angle of the arrowheads as the other stimulus dimension; where we change the apparent length of line when we change the angle of the arrowheads. Now the angle of regard is analogous to the arrowheads, and the distance of the object is analogous to length of line. So, we might change the apparent distance or depth when we changed angle of regard. The problem is, what's the difference between distance and depth, that is, horizontal distance vs. vertical depth? In other words, how does angle of regard influence the effect a distant object has?

* * *

The brightness constancy phenomenon is surely affected by the stability of differences in light reflections between an object and the background, under differing light intensities. But there is also a mechanism controlling the entrance into the eyeball of the absolute amount of photons reflected. Pupil dilation and contraction keep the amount of photons that strike the retina within a fairly stable range. This process may also be very important in accounting for brightness constancy. This could be determined with an organism with an artificially fixed pupil size, under a wide range of light intensities.

* * *

Concerning the distinction between sensory and perceptual stimulus control, one might ask, isn't color almost always going to involve complex perceptual control, since it will always be contrasted to some background? Probably most of our responses to many stimulus features are, in fact, under perceptual control. The only time there wouldn't be perceptual control of a response to color would be where there is a neutral background such as black or white — though how much of an effect the background color has will no doubt vary with the value of the background colors and their saturation and intensity. This then raises the question, how do we ever know what the real color of an object is if color contrast is always an illusion? What we mean by the real *hue, perceived color, is a response to that object when it's against a neutral, non-interactive background. That is our reference response or baseline, not that the hue of the object in that condition is any more real than its hue under other conditions.*

* * *

Our responding to the color of an object is a sensory response with regard to a distance from the object. It may be a perceptual response with regard to the color of those stimuli surrounding the object. In that sense, we may be making both a sensory and a perceptual response in a natural environment; but it would be reasonable to make that distinction, for purposes of analysis, even in a natural environment. In other words, one set of variables, distance and color of the object, aren't really interacting; so they exert sensory controls with regard to each other; whereas the color of the object and the color of the background are interacting, therefore, exerting perceptual control with regard to each other. "Interact" is the crucial word here.

We have dealt exclusively with **visual** perceptual phenomena in this chapter as very little work has been done in the multi-dimensional stimulus control exerted by other modalities. We would, however, think of such phenomena, equal loudness contour, for instance, as being a perceptual phenomenon since there is an interaction between intensity and frequency of tone in the control over the response of matching tones according to their loudness.

On the other hand, we would not so classify work where the researcher studies the absolute threshold response to a pure tone as a function of the intensity of masking noise. The experimenters are manipulating two stimulus dimensions, tone intensity and noise intensity; however, those two dimensions do not truly interact in the same sense that stimulus dimensions interact in perceptual control. The masking noise doesn't cause the observer to respond to the tone as if it were some other tone, as would be the case with a perceptual illusion and other general perceptual interactions. Instead, the masking noise simply hinders the observer's detection of that tone.

***

The fairly standard behavioral approach is to say there's no such thing as a "sensation" or "perception", and we're inclined to agree with this. However, this standard approach, then, often goes on to say that since there's no such thing as sensation or perception, it doesn't make sense to distinguish between sensory psychology and perceptual psychology, or sensory processes and perceptual processes. We disagree with that. As we've indicated, they do seem to point to different types of stimulus control. On the other hand, the words "sensing" and "perceiving" seem generally to be used interchangeably and don't seem to mean much more than the notion that we're under some general control of some stimuli. Or, a behaviorist might ask, why even bother with trying to objectify terms like "sensory" and "perceptual" processes, since they seem so vague and fuzzy, and mentalistic, and are used in so many different ways by so many people? Why bother with them if we don't do behavioral analyses, and try to make distinctions between terms like "mind" and "spirit", as people use those terms also? The answer is that there's a fairly consistent use of the terms, sensory and perceptual, that tends to stand out against the ambiguity. The distinction between sensory control and perceptual control is of considerable methodological importance, as the research procedure best-suited for studying sensory control is the discrimination procedure, while the procedure best-suited for studying perceptual control is the generalization procedure.

In perceptual research we ask the question: How does changing one stimulus dimension affect the organism's response to another stimulus dimension? For instance, when we study an illusion. Under those conditions there is no correct answer, so we can't reinforce *correct responses and extinguish incorrect responses — we can't use a differential reinforcement procedure, a discrimination training procedure. So we must use a stimulus generalization procedure. We train the observer on one set of conditions and then test the response to novel stimulus combinations during extinction. This is a stimulus generalization procedure.*

On the other hand, a discrimination procedure can be maintained throughout testing when studying the effects of a single dimension of a stimulus in a sensory control experiment. There, we're asking the subject to tell us, for instance, whether or not a stimulus value is zero or greater than zero. That question has a correct answer; therefore, responses can be reinforced. We're not asking the observer how something appears to that observer, as is the case with perceptual research where we can't reinforce any response the observer makes, since we don't really know how it "appears" to the observer.

12 Development of Basic Responses

Baer, D. M. The control of developmental process: Why wait? In J. R. Nesselroade and H. W. Reese (Eds.), *Life-span developmental psychology: Methodological issues.* New York: Academic Press, 1973.

The following three books are clear presentations of the use of the helping approach in rearing your children:
Becker, W. C. *Parents are teachers: A child management program.* Champaign, Illinois: Research Press, 1971.
Patterson, G. R. *Families; application of social learning theories to family life.* Champaign, Illinois: Research Press, 1971.
Patterson, G., & Gullion, M. E. *Living with children: New methods for parents and teachers* (Rev. ed.). Champaign, Illinois: Research Press, 1968

Bijou, S. W., & Baer, D. M. *Child development: Volume 1. A systematic and empirical theory.* Englewood Cliffs, New Jersey: Prentice-Hall, 1961.
A brief introductory or intermediate text of considerable interest.

Gesell, A. Infant vision. *Scientific American,* 1950, *182* (2), 20-22.

McIntire, R. W. *Child Psychology: A behavioral approach to everyday problems.* Kalamazoo, Michigan: Behavior-

delia, 1975.
This well-written book gives you much worthwhile information about how to use a helping approach in rearing your children.

Pronko, N. H., & Bowles, J. W., Jr. *Empirical foundations of psychology. New York: Rinehart, 1951.*
This book contains a description of Spelt's experiment on the conditioning of the human fetus *in utero*; and a great deal of information concerning the role of heredity and experience in the development of the child.

Schmidt. W. H. O. *Child development: The human, cultural, and educational context.* New York: Harper & Row, 1973.

Skinner, B. F. *Walden two.* New York: Macmillan, 1962.
This utopian novel about a commune has many controversial implications for child-rearing. You'll enjoy reading it.

Spelt, D. K. The conditioning of the human fetus *in utero. Journal of Experimental Psychology,* 1948, *38,* 338-346.

Spiro, M. E. *Kibbutz: Venture in utopia.* New York: Schoken, 1956.

Well-written book about a real commune very similar to the one described by Skinner in his novel.

Staats, A. W. *Child learning, intelligence, and personality: Principles of a behavioral interaction approach.* New York: Harper & Row, 1971.

This excellent and readable book had a considerable influence on the nature of this, and the next two chapters. You might wish to read page 58 of that book for further explanation of why it's worthwhile to accelerate the development of motor behaviors, etc.

We should note that evolution is not necessarily always going on with all species. Some species, such as the shark, may have, in fact, stopped evolving. And, perhaps the human species has also, more or less, stopped evolving, as far as biological evolution is concerned.

We said the world causes phylogenetic development by selecting those members of the species *that have evolved response patterns that help them survive. In another sense, the environment really* selects the response patterns *that help the species survive; and those response patterns just happen to have a particular biological structure attached to them; and that biological structure just happens to be heritable. So, in a real sense, the environment makes direct contact with the individual or species by selecting response patterns that are viable, thereby programming the heritable structure in the case of phylogenetic development, and programming whatever structure is involved in learning in the case of ontogenetic development.*

In this and other chapters, we often distinguish between our physical world and our social world. We don't mean to imply that the social world is not also physical, but rather that the social world is a subset of the physical world — a subset involving other creatures.

***

In suggesting that we should help our children learn how to get a maximum amount out of life and give a maximum to life, we're not suggesting that we should train them to be selfish, individualistic, robber barrons with little concern for the best interests of others. In fact, the survival of our species may be greatly enhanced by a culture that trains its members to be very effective in looking out for the welfare, not only of their contemporaries and themselves, but also the welfare of future generations.

From our point of view, eugenics seems to have made a negative contribution to the field of psychology with the possible exception of the field of mental retardation. It may, however, have made a much more positive contribution to the field of physical medicine. But, in all areas there must be great concern for the civil liberties of potential parents subjected to eugenic control.

13 Development of Language

Developmental psychology today. Del Mar, California: CRM, 1971.

Garcia, E., Guess, D., & Byrnes, J. Development of syntax in a retarded girl using procedures of imitation, reinforcement, and modeling. *Journal of Applied Behavioral Analysis,* 1973, *6,* 299-310.

Hockett, C. F. Logical considerations in the study of animal communications. *Animal sounds and communication,* 1960, *7,* 392-429.

Linden, E. *Apes, men, and language: How teaching chimpanzees to "talk" alters man's notion of his place in nature.* New York: Saturday Review Press, 1974.
This book is pleasant reading and deals, in an interesting manner, with the research on teaching language to chimps.

Lyons, J. *Noam Chomsky.* New York: Viking Press, 1970.

Mussen, P. H., Conger, J. J., & Kagan, J. *Child development and personality* (4th ed.). New York: Harper & Row, 1974.

Ostwald, P. F., & Peltzman, P. The cry of the human infant. *Scientific American,* 1974, *230* (3), 84-90.

Rumbaugh, D. M., Gill, T. V., & Von Glaersfelz, E. C. Reading and sentence completion by chimpanzee (Pam). *Science,* 1973, *182,* 731-733.

Skinner, B. F. *Verbal behavior.* Englewood Cliffs, New Jersey: Prentice-Hall, 1957.

Skinner, B. F. *Contingencies of reinforcement: A theoretical analysis.* Englewood Cliffs, New Jersey: Prentice-Hall, 1969.
This book includes an interesting analysis of rule-governed and contingency, or intuitive, control of behavior. In general, it's quite relevant to many of the sections of the present text, and highly recommended for the dedicated student, though it's not easy reading.

Skinner, B. F. *About behaviorism.* New York: Knopf, 1974.

Staats, A. W. *Learning, language, and cognition; theory, research, and method for the study of human behavior and its development.* New York: Holt, Rinehart & Winston, 1968.
We highly recommend this thoroughgoing analysis of language which greatly influenced the present chapter.

Whaley, D. L., & Malott, R. W. *Elementary principles of behavior.* Englewood Cliffs, New Jersey: Prentice-Hall, 1971.
A more detailed analysis of the criteria stimulus control must meet to be classified as language control. These criteria are, of course, much more elaborate than the one presented in the definition in the present chapter, though this definition does get at much of the essence of language. However, it probably doesn't rule out some forms of stimulus control that we might not wish to call language.

From time to time, we'll use the term "normal conditions". For instance, we talk about "language acquired through the normal process of being raised by vocal parents." In this context, we don't mean "healthy", or "correct", or "the right way", when we use the word "normal"; we simply mean "standard", or "common", or "typical".

What are the reinforcers for following rules when the normal rewards aren't enough to insure doing complex tasks the right way? By normal rewards we mean the rewards that will result from the completion of the task. One source of reinforcer for following complex rules of this sort is the social reinforcement given by others as we make progress along the way. Another source is the mere completion of the component responses involved in following that rule. We've all had a history of reinforcement by task completion when we carefully and correctly followed the details of a set of instructions.

So following the details of a set of instructions should themselves come to be a learned reinforcer.

***

Thinking may take forms other than talking, but it's simply covert or private behavior of various sorts. For instance, thinking about tumbling might involve covert muscle movements so slight they couldn't be observed by an outside observer. Of course, we can also think out loud — when we talk to ourselves out loud. And we can also engage in public thinking when the muscle movement becomes so large that an outside observer can actually see us move our limbs, as when pianists rehearse a piece of music by moving the fingers appropriately.

14 Development of Intelligence

Psychology Today had a special section on the controversy surrounding whether or not intelligence is inherited. The articles were:
Dobzhansky, T. Differences are not deficits. *Psychology Today,* December 1973, pp. 97-101.
Jensen, A. The differences are real. *Psychology Today,* December 1973, pp. 80-86.
Rice, B. The high cost of thinking the unthinkable. *Psychology Today,* December 1973, pp. 89-93.

Engelmann, S. The effectiveness of direct verbal instructions on IQ performance and achievement in reading and arithmetic. In J. Hullmuth (Ed.), *Disadvantaged child, compensatory education: A national debate,* 1970, *3,* New York: Brunner/Mazel.

Garcia, J. I. Q.: The conspiracy. *Psychology Today,* April 1972, pp 40-43. An excellent article showing what intelligence tests are made of and how they're made. It takes a lot of the mystery, mystique, and magic out of those simple pieces of paper, at the same time taking the mystery, mystique, and magic out of the concept of intelligence itself.

Herrnstein, R. J. I.Q. *The Atlantic Monthly,* 1971, *228* (3), 43-64.

Herrnstein, R. J. *I.Q. in the meritocracy.* Boston: Little, Brown, 1973.

Jensen, A. R. Skinner and human differences. In J. H. Wheeler (Ed.) *Beyond the punitive society; operant conditioning: Social and political aspects.* San Francisco: W. H. Freeman, 1973.

Kamin, L. J. *The science and politics of I.Q.* New York: Erlbaum/Wiley, 1974. This book presents a very strong attack against the notion that something called intelligence is inherited, and against the data that has been put forth to support that notion.

Koenig, P. Field report on psychological testing of job applicants: "They just changed the rules on how to get ahead." *Psychology Today,* June 1974, pp. 87-103.

Staats, A. W. *Child learning, intelligence, and personality: Principles of a behavioral interaction approach.* New York: Harper & Row, 1971.

Tyler, L. E. *Intelligence: Some recurring issues.* New York: Van Nostrand Reinhold, 1969. A collection of classic papers dealing with the problem of intelligence, or intelligent behavior.

At first we had planned to deal extensively with the arguments and data raised and resurrected by Jensen, et al. But the developmental approach that evolved out of the two preceding chapters seemed to dictate a much different chapter, leaving inadequate space to deal with the complex analyses of the logical positions and data-base in support of the heritability of intelligence. However, a great contribution to this field has been made by Kamin. In his book, among other things, he points out the considerable weaknesses of the identical-twin-raised-apart studies that purport to prove intelligence is inherited. Previously, these studies have often been considered to be crucial.

***

Infants who grow up in institutions show little orienting behavior. This is true when you compare institutionalized retarded infants to home-reared retarded infants, or when you look at normal infants raised in a foundling home or institution. They tend to simply lie in their cribs, not orienting toward adults. In other words, they have not learned those responses because those responses have not been rewarded through large amounts of adult contact, attention, etc.

15 Jean Piaget and the Development of Cognitive Behavior

Engelmann, S. E. Relationship between psychological theories and the act of teaching. *Journal of School Psychology,* 1967, *5* (2), 93-100.

Engelmann, S. E. Does the Piagetian approach imply instruction? In D. R. Green, M. P. Ford, & G. B. Flamer (Eds.) *Measurement and Piaget; proceedings.* New York: McGraw-Hill, 1971.

Gagne, R. M. Contributions of learning to human development. *Psychological Review,* May 1968, pp. 177-191.

Ginsburg, H., & Opper, S. *Piaget's theory of intellectual development; an introduction.* Englewood Cliffs, New Jersey: Prentice-Hall, 1969.

Hall, E. A conversation with Jean Piaget and Barbel Inhelder. *Psychology Today,* May 1970, pp. 25-32.

Mpiangu, B. D., & Gentile, J. R. Is conservation of number a necessary condition for mathematical understanding? *Journal for Research in Mathematics Education,* 1975, *6* (3), 179-192.

Piaget, J. How children form mathematical concepts. *Scientific American,* 1953, *189* (5), 74-79.

Piaget, J., & Inhelder, B. *The child's conception of space.* New York: Norton, 1967.

Schmidt, W. H. O. *Child development: The human, cultural, and educational context.* New York: Harper & Row, 1973.

Watson, J. S. Conservation: An SR analysis. In I. E. Sigel & F. H. Hooper (Eds.), *Logical thinking in children: Research based on Piaget's theory,* New York: Holt, Rinehart & Winston, 1968.

Keep in mind that Piaget and many other cognitive-developmental psychologists do correlational *research rather than* experimental *research. Yet, we often make the error of thinking they're doing experiments just because of the complex nature of their dependent* variables (events observed and measured in an experiment in order to see if other events will cause them to change). Piaget sets up a complex task; then he observes that the performance on that task is correlated with the age of the children. The fact that he may vary some features of that task doesn't make it an experiment.

The testing situation provides an analogue, since, there, you might measure people's performance on intelligence tests as a function of their age. You're treating age as if it might be a causal variable; and you should not lose sight of this no matter how complex the intelligence test situation becomes. Your test might have some item such as the length of a number a person can repeat after hearing it read. In that case, you'd have to test the person with numbers of differing lengths before finding the longest number the person could correctly repeat. By presenting numbers of different lengths, you're varying some feature of the test items. But you're not doing an experiment; you're just using a complex process to measure the dependent variable. The closest thing you would have to an independent variable (an event the researcher changes or varies during the course of an experiment in order to see what effect these changes will have on the dependent variable), is the age of the people you're testing.

On the other hand, you could be doing an experiment if you measured the percentage of people who can correctly repeat the number as a function of the length of that number. In that case, the length of the number is the independent variable which you can indeed vary; and the percent of people who are correct is the dependent variable. That differs from the situation where you're measuring the length of the number recalled as a function of the age of the people. In the first case, the length of the number you presented is a true independent variable — you're varying it; while in the second case, age of the people is merely a variable you're selecting, as you can't vary the age of the individual people. You must take 'em as you find 'em.

***

In Piaget's work, the overall dependent variable is the child's performance on a series of complex and graded tasks. From his point of view the causal variable is the non-varied but correlational variable of the child's age. For this to be a true experiment he would have to get a hold of, and really vary some factor presumed to be causal. For instance, he could vary the nature of the learning experiences the children have had prior to exposure to the test situation where he required them to solve problems. Then he would be doing a true experiment, because he would have a true independent variable.

Mpiangu and Gentile studied the relation between concepts of conservation and mathematics. Their research was of an experimental nature demonstrating the value of being able to draw causal conclusions from experimental data where the correlational data might easily mislead us into inferring causal connections though they may not really be there. In other words, learning the concept of conservation may often precede learning certain sorts of mathematics in the *natural world of the child. But this doesn't mean there is a causal relation between the two events. Only an* experimental *analysis can demonstrate that. And their analysis showed that children did* not *need to learn conservation* before *learning arithmetic. This indicates that some of Piaget's stages of development might not always progress in a fixed sequence.*

***

For the purposes of this chapter, we've defined "object constancy" much more narrowly than need be the case for general consideration. So here's a more general definition — general object constancy: responding in a manner appropriate to an object regardless of surrounding stimuli, the point of view of the observer, or the object's color or brightness. This, then, brings color and brightness constancy within the domain of object constancy.

***

Over-generalization of the sort that produces anthropomorphic language is considered a sign of immaturity on the part of the youthful speaker, but a sign of maturity on the part of the older speaker and writer. Take, for instance, the poet whose stock in trade is the metaphor — the extended stimulus generalization.

***

Perhaps conservation of fluid involves two types of concept control. We've looked at the multi-dimensional concept of volume as a function of width and height. But perhaps there's a second concept at work — one based on the fact that the pouring operation can be reversed. With enough training the operation of pouring may, itself, function as a cue that the two volumes are equal. Then children could say the two volumes were equal, if they had seen the pouring operation between the two glasses.

They might be able to match the two volumes even though they might not be able to identify the equal volumes in those glasses of different shapes without the cue of the pouring operation.

16 Social Reinforcement

Berne, E. *Games people play.* New York: Grove, 1964.
Well-written and insightful. Shows how social reinforcement is operative in many places where we'd least expect, though the author doesn't analyze the excellent examples in terms of social reinforcement.

Berscheid, E., & Walster, E. Beauty and the beast. *Psychology Today,* March 1972, pp. 42-46.

These two articles describe a fascinating example of the power of social reinforcement to control the lives of people for better or for worse as seen in Mel Lyman's commune.
Felton, D. The Lyman family's holy siege of America. *Rolling Stone,* December 32, 1971, pp. 40-60.
Felton, D. The Lyman family's holy siege of America. *Rolling Stone,* January 6, 1972, pp. 40-60.

Hart, B.; Allen, K.; Buell, J.; Harris, F.; & Wolf, M. Effects of social reinforcement on operant crying. *Journal of Experimental Child Psychology,* 1964, *1,* 145-153.

Hartup, W. W. Friendship status and the effectiveness of peers as reinforcement agents. *Journal of Experimental Child Psychology,* 1964, *1,* 154-162.

Kesey, K. *One flew over the cuckoo's nest.* New York: Viking, 1964.
An interesting example of how a person's behavior or the behavior of the controller may be controlled through social reinforcement.

Malott, R. W. *Humanistic behaviorism and social psychology.* Kalamazoo, Michigan: Behaviordelia, 1973.
Social reinforcement can affect our lives in ways we wouldn't normally expect. Written in a style somewhat like the present book.

Middlebrook, P. N. *Social psychology in modern life.* New York: Knopf, 1974.

Skinner, B. F. *Science and human behavior.* New York: Macmillan, 1953. (See especially Section 4, "The Behavior of People in Groups") An excellent book relevant to this and many other chapters in the present text. Though written for introductory students, it isn't easy reading; professional psychologists often gain new insights upon rereading it.

Social psychology: Explorations in understanding. Del Mar, California: CRM, 1974.

Williams, C. D. The elimination of tantrum behavior by extinction procedures. *Journal of Abnormal Social Psychology,* 1959, *59,* 269.

Zimmerman, E. H., & Zimmerman, J. The alteration of behavior in a special classroom situation. *Journal of the Experimental Analysis of Behavior,* 1962, *5,* 59-60.
The above reference attests to the powerful effect of learned reinforcers.

These next five chapters deal with social psychology or social behavior. You might define social behavior as that behavior whose rewards are mediated through or elicited by behavior of other organisms.

* * *

It sometimes seems to debase human beings to suggest that we're just running around trying to collect as many social rewards as we can get from our friends. Well, to some extent, that baseness depends on what we do to get their approval — what behaviors our friends reinforce. Choose your friends wisely. Choose people whom you wish to emulate. But, even so you may find them reinforcing subservient behavior or adulatory behavior. So you'll not only have to look at how your friends behave, but also at what they reinforce.

* * *

We can understand most of the data of social psych in terms of social rewards. When you look at any social psych data, ask, " what are the rewards involved?" Also ask, "how can we describe the events in terms of behavior?"
The fact that we are learned rewards for each other is the glue that holds all social systems together. Social rewards play a major role in keeping us going in almost any situation even though there is some nominal long-range reward that's of more value. For instance, why did you decide to go to college? *Was it really a rational decision?*

Maybe. But we'll bet there were many immediate social results and much programming in support of "your" decision to do something that might have little "payoff" until several years from now. First there are the obvious ones — Mom and Dad. They're proud of you if you go to college and ashamed of you if you don't. Then there are your friends. Many of them are going on. They also reward your conforming, and punish non-conforming. If you don't do what they do, then you're subtly implying that they aren't doing the right thing. You can say that something may be right for them even though it's not right for you. But in their heart of hearts, they know you're giving them a sneaky put-down with your failure to do as they do. And so they punish that with an explicit disapproval if you don't shape up. Even such coerced compliance is rewarding to your friends. Of course, they would deny that they're controlling your compliance. And if they could be convinced, then your compliance might be somewhat less rewarding to them.

People differ a great deal in the extent to which they go out of their way to seek social rewards. This could mean that social rewards are not important for some people. But we doubt it. More likely, some simply haven't learned good skills at seeking social reward. Others become very skilled at getting such rewards and so appear to depend on them more. Perhaps they do in that such rewards control more of their behavior. But the less-skilled would be too if they knew how. So perhaps we shouldn't talk about some people having a higher need for approval.

In theory, we'd think social rewards might be stronger for some people than for others, since those people may have had more of their rewards mediated by other people. But social rewards are very strong for all people in our culture, since we've all had so many of our rewards mediated by other people. On the other hand, people may vary in the extent to which solitary acts like reading have become rewarding. And sometimes social and solitary rewards do compete for a person's time.

***

Dress codes may be an example of the effects of social reward through approving imitation. It's rewarding when people dress like we do and wear their hair like we do. That means that they must approve of us, doesn't it? So, in fact, we tend to reward people's conforming to our clothing and hair style. And, in fact, we may even punish non-conforming behaviors:

"Would you look at that? I haven't seen any man with such short hair in years."

"Gee, you look funny in a dress. That's the first time I've ever seen you in one."

And sometimes it's even formalized into dress codes in schools.

"Thou shalt not wear thy hair long enough to touch thy shoulders if ye are male," "Thou shalt not wear jeans." "Thou shalt not wear skirts above thy knees."

Yes, indeed! Even school administrators need to know their students love them and like to see that shown in appropriate dress and hair style; and like the teenagers themselves, they punish non-compliance.

Now we may all agree that some of these arbitrary social conventions should not exert as much control over our behavior as they do, either as the person on whom the rule is being imposed or as the person who's imposing that rule. But denying that we're influenced by such insidious social rewards doesn't, in fact, get rid of that influence. Being aware of those factors that control our behavior may be a first step in our getting control over them, and thereby getting control over the kind of people we'll become.

***

We all find it rewarding to show our accomplishments for the approval of others — to put our newly made mud pies on display. It's rewarding just thinking about showing our creations to our friends. They'll comment with approval about what a great job we've done. And so, in fact, we arrange for them to really see our mud pies. Sometimes we're very subtle, we just casually leave them lying about in hopes that someone will notice and say a few good words about them.

But people may differ from each other a great deal in the extent to which they think about those potential rewards, and in the extent to which such rewards control their actions. Perhaps some people have a less rewarding history for showing their mud pies. Too bad, since it may be that knowing how to get social reinforcement for your mud pie building, is a useful feature to becoming a good and productive mud pie maker.

Some of the most productive people we've known are tremendous egomaniacs. They seem to spend a large part of their social time making sure others are aware of the great mud pies they've made. But their bragging may be useful in maintaining their high rate of production, even though it may be irritating to their audience if they are not at least somewhat subtle in the ways they set the occasions to receive their praise. So perhaps one of the things we should all learn to do is to be able to tactfully get a great deal of approval for everything we accomplish. That rewarding approval will make it more likely that we'll accomplish more things in the future.

17 Social Values

Bandura, A., & Walters, R. *Social learning and personality development.* New York: Holt, Rinehart & Winston, 1963.

Clark, B. S. The acquisition and extinction of peer imitation in children. *Psychonomic Science,* 1965, *2,* 147-148.

Hicks, D. J. Imitation and retention of film-mediated aggressive, peer, and adult models. *Journal of Personality and Social Development,* 1965, *2,* 97-100.

Klineberg, O. *Social psychology.* New York: Holt, 1954.

Notz, W. W. Work motivation and the negative effects of extrinsic rewards: A review with implications for theory and practice. *American Psychologist,* 1975, *30,* 884-891.

The concept of culturally determined values is a crucial part of the next three chapters. In the case of attitude change, we'll see that values concerning such issues as the liberation of women and their roles in our social system, result from cultural programming. In the next chapter we'll see our moral values also result from our history of reward and punishment as programmed by others. And, in the third chapter, we'll see how culturally based values can interact with the roles we play, causing us to be one sort of person or another.

Establishing the right values in the members of a culture may be one of the most crucial functions of that culture. The social system, the culture itself, it would seem, will be more likely to survive if the members of that culture place a high value on that culture, and the other members within that culture.

It would seem that the culture should establish values of caring for others in that culture, values of sharing, of helping — anti-rip-off values. The culture that doesn't do this may have a hard time surviving. So setting up these values is often one of the functions of the culture's major social systems — like the church, the school, and the home.

18 Attitude Change

Asch, S. E. Opinions and social pressure. *Scientific American,* 1955, *193* (5), 31-35.
An interesting research report to be viewed in terms of social reinforcement and its powerful impact.

Ben, D. J. *Beliefs, attitudes, and human affairs.* Belmont, California: Brooks/Cole, 1970.

Farber, S. M., & Wilson, R. H. L. *The potential of women.* New York: McGraw-Hill, 1963.

Kelman, H. C. The processes of opinion change. *Public Opinion Quarterly,* 1961, *25,* 57-78.

Our presentation of attitude change in terms of compliance, identification, and internalization stages is loosely based on Kelman's work in this area.

Kiesler, C. A., Collins, B. E., & Miller, N. *Attitude change: A critical analysis of theoretical approaches.* New York: Wiley, 1969.

McLaughlin, B. *Learning and social behavior.* New York: The Free Press, 1971.

Zimbardo, P. G., & Ebbeson, E. B. *Influencing attitudes and changing behavior.* Reading, Massachusetts: Addison-Wesley, 1960.

A traditional approach is to treat "attitude" as a person's tendency to look at things in a certain way. We differ somewhat from this traditional approach in two ways. First, the traditional approach may imply that attitude is a thing causing us to perceive the world one way or another. There seems to be a slight tendency to reify the concept of attitudes. What we've tried to do is show how our actions result from certain forms of stimulus control involving statements we may say to ourselves that act as cues for those actions, and involving certain sorts of rewards and punisher values — values often determined by our culture. In other words, we're treating attitudes as a process or relationship between cues, actions, and their results.

In fact, our approach to most topics tends to differ from the traditional approach to social psychology and psychology in general, in that we go out of our way to avoid reifying concepts, instead dealing as much as we can with observed events and the processes relating them. We do sometimes make inferences about unobservable processes like thinking. However, these inferences are in the form of extrapolations from observable processes made under the assumption that these same laws governing external processes also describe those internal, private, unobserved, or covert behavioral processes. In other words, we're dealing with behavior and the laws of behavior, whether we look outside or inside the organism — a simple empirical generalization.

This is a position sometimes referred to as radical behaviorism, which can be contrasted with methodological behaviorism that says we can't observe private events and therefore should act as if they don't exist.

A second way in which we differ from much of the traditional approach to the concept of attitude and social psychology is that traditional social psychology is phenomenological. That approach stresses the concept that our actions are the result of the way we perceive the world. So they would say our attitude affects the way we perceive the world, and our perception of the world affects what we actually do.

One problem with the phenomenological approach is that it also tends to reify concepts like perception, when in fact, there's no such thing as our perception of things which might cause us to act in some way. There are only our actions resulting from various cues and our history of reward and punishment. The effect a particular visual stimulus has on us, the way it operates as a cue, or warning stimulus, or whatever, can only be understood if we know our phylogenetic and ontogenetic history with regard to that stimulus. We're left with a false sense of security if we rely on the explanation that we're responding to a particular stimulus the way we do because of the way we perceive it. So we try not to rely on phenomenological explanations of behavior.

The concept of reference group is also useful in looking at attitudes. A reference group is a group you identify with. The values or reinforcers of that group are your rewards, since you think of yourself as a member of that group. This may be true for the following reasons. Let's say one of your reference groups is college students (you can have more than one reference group). Well, you won't be too surprised if American college students have much the same values. You've all had much the same histories, grown up around the same time, seen the same movies, and TV programs, gone through the same wars, the same impeachments, the same music, and seen the same heroes and heroines come and go. Why wouldn't you have the same values? And besides, your parents have pretty much the same values as your roommate's parents, at least more so than the parents of the kid pumping gas down at the local gasoline station (unless that kid happens to be your roommate).

So you'll be more willing to adopt an attitude if you know that

that attitude has been endorsed by your reference group. You know this new attitude will most likely be consistent with your other attitudes, attitudes you share with that reference group. We can see this in the following case: Suppose we run across some psychological concept we don't know too much about. We haven't yet had the time to sit down and figure out what we really think about that concept. Then we might want to know what some respected scholar has decided about that concept. We might even tend to base our attitudes on the fact that the scholar believes the concept is valuable, or worthless, or whatever, even though we don't know the basis for the scholar's opinion. The reason for this is that in the past we've found that this scholar's opinion tended to agree with ours. We belong to the same reference group.

We can see the same thing with college students as they relate to their teachers. If you tend to respect your teacher, you may be eager to know his or her attitude about some subject, to help you form your own attitude. This needn't be blind allegiance to authority, especially since no two authorities in a university seem to agree about things anyway. Instead, it means you may be fairly safe in adopting an attitude of a specific teacher, if that teacher has put a good deal of thought into forming that attitude, and if you've found you've agreed with that teacher's attitudes in the past. You and your teacher may form a common intellectual reference group.

And here's a final reason why you may find yourself adopting the attitudes of your reference group: Knowing a value is held by your reference group serves as a cue that expressing this value on our part will be reinforced by our reference group. For instance, your fellow college students will tend to reward acts in keeping with values like theirs, and punish those that aren't. We may rush right down to the local soda shop to join the Pepsi generation if we see an advertisement saying, "All of the really hip young college students turn on to Pepsi-Cola," knowing that'll put us in with the in crowd.

***

Now we often think our internalized values have a logical and rational consistency. And often that is the case. But people can have strong internalized values that might seem to conflict. For example, many scientists feel a belief in science conflicts with beliefs in religion and/or the supernatural or divine creator. They would feel there is no way those two sets of statements can be logically consistent. On the other hand, there are some good scientists who put great faith in traditional religion.

19 Morality

Aronfreed, J. *Conduct and conscience; the socialization of internalized control over behavior.* New York: Academic Press, 1968.

Berkowitz, L. *The development of motives and values in the child.* New York:

Basic Books, 1964.

Brown, R., & Herrnstein, R. J. *Psychology.* Boston: Little, Brown, 1975.

The present chapter is loosely based on Kohlberg's notions of stages of moral development which, in turn, are based on Piaget's notions.

Kohlberg, L. The development of children's orientation toward a moral order: In sequence in the development of moral thought. *Vita Humana,* 1963, *6,* 11-33.

Kohlberg, L. The child as a moral philosopher. *Psychology Today,* September 1968, pp. 25-30.

Kohlberg, L., & Turiel, A. *Research in moral development: The cognitive-development approach.* New York: Holt, Rinehart & Winston, 1971.

Kohlberg, L. Continuities in childhood and adult moral development revisited. In T. B. Baltes & K. W. Shaie (Eds.), *Life-span developmental psychology: personality and socialization.* New York: Academic Press, 1973.

Legal and moral control are more or less the same in some ways: Both are based on either written or oral codes (though most laws are written in our society with the exception of some common law, and many moral codes are oral or only implied, with exceptions like the Ten Commandments). And, both are based mainly on punishment (though they needn't be: we could give insurance rebates to law-abiding drivers, and we could more often reward moral action).

* * *

Here's a problem with internal guilt control. It's often too weak. The learned punisher got its value through pairing it with other punishers, both learned and unlearned. And what happens when you build up a learned punisher that way? That newly acquired punisher is less strong than the original one. Big Chet's "NO!" (learned punisher) was less punishing than his hit (unlearned punisher). Little Chet's "NO!" was an even weaker punisher since it was a learned punisher due to its pairing with big Chet's weakened "NO!" Little Chet's "NO!" will not work as well at stopping immoral acts.

20 Social Roles

Asch, S. E. *Social psychology.* Englewood Cliffs, New Jersey: Prentice-Hall, 1952.

Costanzo, P. R., & Shaw, M. E. Conformity as a function of age level. *Child Development,* 1966, *37,* 967-975.

McDavid, J. W., & Harali, H. *Psychology and social behavior.* New York: Harper & Row, 1974.

Reisman, D., Glazer, N., & Denney, R. *The lonely crowd; a study of the changing American character.* Garden City, New York: Doubleday, 1953.

Whyte, W. *Street corner society.* Chicago: University of Chicago Press, 1943.

Winder, C. L., & Rau, L. Paternal attitudes associated with social deviance in pre-adolescent boys. *Journal of Abnormal and Social Psychology,* 1962, *64,* 418-424.

Here's another way a non-conformist can be programmed (or even your everyday, garden-variety conformists like us: with the concept of the negative reference group *— a variation on the concept of* reference group. *The negative reference group is a group you do* not *identify with. You may know damn well you should vote against Jones if you hear that the hard-hats think we should elect Jones. If you're a non-conformist, you have a history of reward for going* *against popular opinion. You've learned that the majority is often wrong — or about twenty years behind the times. So all the nonconformist has to hear is "Most people believe that . . ." That does it. He or she is certainly not most people. Most people, ugh. Mom and Dad tell you that your hair looks nice for a change, and you run to the mirror to see what's wrong.*

21 Sigmund Freud and Personality

Freud, S. *Psychopathology of everyday life.* New York: New American Library, 1951.
This reprint of Freud's work may be one of his clearest and most straightforward books. It contains many examples showing how our behavior is determined by events in our environment though we are often unaware of it.

Hall, C. S. *A primer of Freudian psychology.* New York: New American Library, 1954.

Hall, C. S., & Lindzey, G. *Theories of personality* (2nd ed.). New York: Wiley, 1970.
A classic in the field, in terms of its excellent coverage of the standard theories of personality.

Krasner, L., & Ullmann, L. P. *Behavior influence and personality: The social matrix of human action.* New York: Holt, Rinehart & Winston, 1973.

Lundin, R. W. *Personality: A behavioral analysis* (2nd ed.). New York: Macmillan, 1974.

Skinner, B. F. *Science and human behavior.* New York: Macmillan, 1953. See especially Chapter 24, "Psychotherapy."

22 Consciousness: Meanings and Definitions

Case, S. *The tyranny of words.* New York: Harcourt, Brace, & World, 1938.
This very simply written book, by a journalist rather than a behavioral scientist, is quite readable and, because of the research done on the topic, is also an extremely valuable source book. The primary thesis presented is that emotions and conscious feelings are controlled by words, and that these mean more in terms of controlling behavior than the actual dictionary meanings of the words.

Festinger, L. *A theory of cognitive dissonance.* Stanford, California: Stanford University Press, 1957.

Freud, S. *An outline of psychoanalysis* (J. Strachey, trans.). New York: Norton, 1949.

Gazzaniga, M. S. The split brain in man. *Scientific American,* 1967, *217,* 24-29.

This exciting research deals with the behavioral outcomes of operations performed for medical reasons on human subjects where the fibers that connect the two hemispheres of the brain were severed.

Lindsley, D. B. Psychophysiology and motivation. In M. R. Jones (Ed.), *Nebraska Symposium on Motivation.* Lincoln: Nebraska University Press, 1957. Lindsley is best known for defining activation by means of the electroencephalogram, or potentials collected from the surface of the brain.

Ornstein, R. E. *The psychology of consciousness.* San Francisco: W. H. Freeman, 1972.

Skinner, B. F. *Verbal behavior.* Englewood Cliffs, New Jersey: Prentice-Hall, 1957.

Skinner, B. F. *Contingencies of reinforcement.* Englewood Cliffs, New Jersey: Prentice-Hall, 1969.

Skinner, B. F. *Beyond freedom and dignity.* New York: Knopf, 1971.
The most popular of Skinner's books to date. Its primary thesis is that concepts like freedom and dignity have, through reification, come to control our behavior and to lead us into wrong and perhaps harmful directions.

Skinner, B. F. *About behaviorism.* New York: Knopf, 1974.
This book offers excellent insights into how self-awareness and awareness of internal events can act as powerful stimuli.

Stone, I. *The passions of the mind: A novel of Sigmund Freud.* Garden City, New York: Doubleday, 1971.
This is an extremely engrossing biography of Sigmund Freud written by a well-known writer of popular fiction. It's quite well done and consistent with other far more difficult-to-read biographies.

Tart, C. (Ed.). *Altered states of consciousness.* New York: Wiley, 1969.

Torbert, W. R. *Learning from experience: Toward consciousness.* New York: Columbia University Press, 1972.

Activation and arousal are both terms used to describe the general amount of activity taking place within an individual. An internal state of high activation signals a readiness to take overt action, although such action may not be occurring at the time. However, activation can be defined instrumentally in several different ways. One researcher uses electroencephalograph (EEG) potentials to indicate arousal level. Low levels yield slow regular waves. This pattern becomes jumbled, or desynchronized, as activation increases. Activation may also be defined by blood pressure level, degree of electric conductance of the skin, heart rate, or in terms of other "peripheral measures", as they're called. The importance of activation to behavior is quite obvious on one level. Without some degree of activation the individual is not going to make any response at all. Sleep would describe the actions of such a person. Over the years there have been many arguments regarding the nature of activation and its relevance to behavior. Is it a good thing or is it harmful? Research demonstrates that it may be either. Sometimes, and for some people, performance may be improved by higher activation. In other instances, increasing activation may lower performance, causing us to make more errors or to act in rigid, insensitive ways. Obviously, the effect increased activation has on people depends on two important factors: 1) the level of activation already present; and 2) the nature of the task. Performance on tasks that take a great amount of concentration and subtle discrimination may be interfered with by high levels of activation. Performance on simpler tasks that require strength, endurance, etc. may be helped by higher activation levels.

* * *

Self-awareness depends on a verbal community that labels our behavior and requires us to also label it so that we may later describe what we're doing, to ourselves and others. In point of fact there's no way to tell through observation if a person is self-aware. Seeing that others are quite deliberate, and under very tight stimulus control is no proof of self-awareness. But if this is true, does self-awareness help? Self-awareness gives our behavior a greater chance of generalizing to other situations. By being aware, we're able to compare our behavior to other people's, characters in plays or books, to descriptions of behavior elsewhere.

***

The term "verbal community" was first introduced by B. F. Skinner. It's crucial to the understanding of consciousness and indeed to all forms of verbal behavior. At first your verbal community may be comprised of parents or relatives. Later, it's extended to teachers. As we grow older we come under the control of peers who comprise a large portion of our verbal community. In fact, by the time we reach the fourth or fifth grade, peers may take over as our main verbal community, exerting such tight control that they may compete with other segments of our verbal communities — like our parents and teachers. As reading skills develop we may come under the control of the many varied verbal communities contained in books. Movies and TV are also part of our verbal community. Finally, as we begin to talk to ourselves in critical ways, becoming self-aware, we become our own verbal community. In much the same way that others approved and disapproved of our behavior, told us what we were doing wrong, and what we might do to change our behavior, we take over this function.

23 Consciousness as Private Activity

Asch, S. Effects of group pressure upon the modification and distortion of judgements. In H. Proshansky & B. Seidenberg (Eds.), *Basic studies in social psychology.* New York: Holt, Rinehart & Winston, 1965.
The work, dealing with the astounding effects the judgements of people around us have on our perceptions and attitudes, is a standard in psychology.

Atkinson, J. W. (Ed.). *Motives in fantasy action and society.* Princeton, New Jersey: Van Nostrand, 1958.

Bandura, A., & Walters, R. H. *Social learning and personality development.* New York: Holt, Rinehart & Winston, 1963.

Eriksen, C. W. *Behavior and awareness.* Durham, North Carolina: Duke University Press, 1962.

Haber, R. N. Eidetic images. *Scientific American,* 1969, *220* (4), 36-44.

Jacobson, L. E. The electro-physiology of mental activities. *American Journal of Psychology,* 1932, *44,* 677-694.
This early researcher established that imagination results in movements that correlate with the activity that is being imagined. Jacobson concluded, and others have affirmed since then, that to imagine is, in some sense, to respond as though one were doing the things that were imagined in reality.

Maltz, M. *Psycho-cybernetics.* Englewood Cliffs, New Jersey: Prentice-Hall, 1960.
This extremely popular work, long on the best-seller list, deals with how imagination and fantasy may play a positive role in human endeavor.

McGuigan, F. J. *Thinking: Studies of covert language processes.* New York: Appleton-Century Crofts, 1966.
An unbiased account of studies which have been undertaken to examine the

internal vocal responses that occur during different types of problem-solving behavior.

Millenson, J. R. *Principles of behavioral analysis.* New York: Macmillan, 1967.

Osborn, A. F. *Applied imagination.* New York: Scribner, 1957.

Skinner, B. F. *Science and human behavior.* New York: Macmillan, 1953.

Skinner, B. F. *Verbal behavior.* Englewood Cliffs, New Jersey: Prentice-Hall, 1957.

Skinner, B. F. *Contingencies of reinforcement.* Englewood Cliffs, New Jersey: Prentice-Hall, 1969.

Whorf, B. L. *Language, thought, and reality.* Cambridge, Mass.: Technology Press, and New York: Wiley, 1956. Whorf's initial influence on philosophy is now beginning to be felt more in behavioral science as we learn more about the nature of language and its effects on human beings. The author's primary thesis is that the structure of the language used by a society determines the existence of concepts within that culture.

In this chapter we saw how our behavior comes under the control of our own verbal cues, permitting us to follow instructions we provide ourselves in a variety of situations. Like all instructions, instructions to ourselves cause us to make responses which are then reinforced by the situation. We follow a road map because in making the responses indicated on the map, we're reinforced by reaching our destination. We follow instruction in a "How to Play Tennis" book because if we do as the book says, we'll perform better and perhaps gain some measure of social reinforcement from the gallery. The purpose instructions serve is to get us to make responses in the first place. Reinforcement for making these responses arises from other sources. Once the responses are made, the reinforcers take over, and instructions will no longer be needed. Even so, we may continue to give ourselves instructions.

At any given time we may be functioning under instructional control but may be capable of getting along without it. Unless we're forced to attempt the response without aid of instructions we may never know that they're no longer needed. An example can be seen in the following instance: A friend of mine had been working out in a gymnasium for some months. He kept his workout togs in a locker secured with a combination lock. Like most of us, he worked the combination lock by remembering the numbers, and dialing them in sequence. He became ill and didn't use the locker for a month. Later, when he resumed his lunch-hour workouts he found that he'd forgotten the combination. Just as he was about to walk away the thought struck him that he might try to work the lock by forgetting all about the numbers and just turning the dial. He took the lock in his hands and twisted the dial without once even trying to think of the combination. After three swift turns the lock opened. How did it work? Independent of the numbers, the movements involved in opening the lock had been rewarded over the many months before. These lock-opening movements had come under the control of reinforcement. The numbers weren't needed any longer, and perhaps hadn't been for months.

Many books have been written whose main thesis revolves around similar phenomena. They may be entitled "Pleasing Your Creative Self", or some such similar compelling statement. They suggest that we'd all be more creative if we somehow escaped from rules, regulations, and instructions. In some instances this is entirely true. We might solve some problems, perform some acts more easily, if we forget we know anything about it and let our muscles take over. But, in other cases this is quite clearly not true. The magic these books promise won't take place unless the specific responses involved in the creative act, whatever it may be, have taken place and have been rewarded over a long period of time. Yes, after a long period of following tedious instructions, we may benefit, at least occasionally, if we forget those rules and regulations, and try new intuitive approaches. But for those people who haven't been through a long regime, it's doubtful that freedom will yield other than immature responses.

24 Consciousness and its Limits

Barber, T. X. *Hypnosis: A scientific approach.* New York: Van Nostrand Reinhold, 1969.
This researcher has done countless studies in the area of hypnosis, attacking the area in a very straightforward way, using empirical studies and building on the results of this mass of studies. Extremely cogent and compelling conclusions are drawn from the evidence.

Buss, A. H., & Portnoy, N. W. Pain tolerance and group identification. . *Journal of Personality and Social Psychology,* 1967, *6,* 106-108.

Cannon, W. B. *Bodily changes in pain, hunger, fear, and rage* (2nd ed.). New York: Appleton-Century-Crofts, 1929.
This is the newer edition of the classical work in which bodily changes, primarily those of a physiological and neurological nature, are related to environmental stressors.

Gildard, F. A. *The human senses* (2nd ed.). New York: Wiley, 1972.

Hilgard, E. R. *Hypnotic susceptibility.* New York: Harcourt, Brace & World, 1965.
This study found that the people most susceptible to hypnosis are those who appear to be the most well-adjusted, and under control of the verbal community.

Hilgard, E. R. Pain as a puzzle for psychology and physiology. *American Psychologist,* 1969, *24,* 103-113.
Hilgard, one of the best known and most respected contemporary psychologists, does an extemely thorough job of examining the problems in understanding pain as a psychological phenomenon in this article.

Lindsley, D. B. *The role of nonspecific reticulo-thalamocortical systems and emotion in physiological correlates of emotion.* New York: Academic Press, 1970.

Melzack, R., & Wall, P. D. Pain mechanisms: A New theory. *Science,* 1965, *150,* 971-979.
It's the thesis of the writers that pain, to a great extent, depends on learning. In this particular article the primary author further advances physiological theories of pain.

Milgram, S. Behavioral study of obedience. *Journal of Abnormal and Social Psychology,* 1963, *67,* 371-378.
This work has recently caused much furor within the psychological community. It points out quite clearly that subjects will do what they're told even

if it appears to be jeopardizing their welfare, health, and perhaps their lives. The story of the Milgram studies was made into a television special shown to a nationwide audience.

Orne, M. T. On the social psychology of the psychological experiment: With particular reference to demand characteristics and their implications. *American Psychologist,* 1962, *17,* 776-783.

Ornstein, R., & Naranjo, C. *On the psychology of meditation.* New York: Viking, 1971.

Science and the sources of pain. *Science News,* 1974, *106* (17), 261.

Skinner, B. F. *Science and human behavior.* New York: Macmillan, 1953.

Skinner, B. F. *Verbal behavior.* Englewood Cliffs, New Jersey: Prentice-Hall, 1957.

Skinner, B. F. *Contingencies of reinforcement.* Englewood Cliffs, New Jersey: Prentice-Hall, 1969.

Skinner, B. F. *About behaviorism.* New York: Knopf, 1974.

Tart, C. T. (Ed.) *Altered state of consciousness.* New York: Wiley, 1969.

Wagner, A. R. Frustration and punishment. In R. N. Haber (Ed.), *Current research in motivation.* New York: Holt, Rinehart & Winston, 1966.

Wallace, R. K., & Benson, H. The physiology of meditation. *Scientific American,* 1972, *226,* 84-90.
This is the source reference for almost all introductory psychology books as far as the physiology of meditation is concerned. It represents, to date, the very best controlled research in this area.

Yogananda, P. *The autobiography of a yogi.* Los Angeles, California: Self-Realization Fellowship, 1951.

Zborowski, M. *People in pain.* San Francisco: Jossey-Bass, 1969.
This is a somewhat offbeat volume which deals with pain and differences in pain as a result of national origins.

Zimbardo, P. G., Rapaport, C. & Baron, J. Pain control by hypnotic induction of motivation states. In P. G. Zimbardo (Ed.), *The cognitive control of motivation.* Glenview, Illinois: Scott, Foresman, 1969.

One of the most difficult things to attempt to get across is that pain is strictly a self-aware response. It doesn't obtain in creatures that aren't capable of self-awareness, that don't have a verbal community to teach them the pain responses. It's clear that we learn pain from people around us. It's not by accident that headaches and other such ailments run in families. Of course, it may be said that the structure that causes headaches may be inherited — therefore children will have headaches like their parents because they inherited a similar structure. But we don't find similar pain patterns just among persons of the same family. We also find them within some cultures but not in others. Some cultures never seem to feel despair; their suicide rate is almost non-existent. Members of other cultures take their lives with great frequency and with very little provocation. In our culture the thing that rewards pain detection is the fact that having pain gets us out of many unpleasant situations. This seems a paradox yet all evidence seems to point to its truth.

The use of drugs and alcohol plays a similar role. Let's say a person detects a pain. He or she then takes aspirin, which reduces stimulation. The act of taking the medicine is thus rewarded. Later on, aspirin or other pain killers may be taken whenever similar stimulation occurs.

But something else has happened, too. Pain is more likely to be felt at a lower level of stimulation on the next occasion. As a result the pain killer will be taken even more prematurely than before. And so it goes, pain felt at lower levels, and pain killers taken more often. It's easy to see how people get into these cycles, and how the mere taking of pain killers only causes more pain in the end.

In general, pain killers are most effective and cause the least trouble when we take them to keep going; that is, when we take them to finish a job or complete a project. They hold the most danger for us when we take them as an escape. We use pain killers not only to escape from the stimulation within, but also use taking them as an excuse to go home, quit work for the rest of the day, or as an excuse not to get out of bed.

* * *

Pain as we've noted is a learned concept. The verbal community teaches us to tune in, to discriminate, and to be aware of certain internal and external events associated with tissue damage. This isn't to say that pain responses aren't also subject to stimulus generalization. Once a pain response is learned to one form of stimulation, it may generalize to stimulation in other parts of the body. We may qualify the quality of internal stimulation by calling it a stabbing pain. We mean that the stimulation feels like it felt when our skin was jabbed with a knife or hat pin. In a similar way, pain can be called "dull" or "biting", or by any other generalized descriptions. Once taught, therefore, the concept of pain may extend to other stimulus situations as an automatic process.

* * *

We've spoken of the verbal community and its role in the teaching of pain. When the verbal community sees us behaving in ways that suggest we're being harmed, we're told we're in pain. Later on, when we behave as before, we'll label our situation painful — and, unfortunately, experience pain. But there is a limit to how far the verbal community can go in teaching pain, or any self-awareness for that matter. By and large, the verbal comments can't get past our skin. Since they can't get inside and see what's taking place, there's a limit to how much those in our verbal community can teach us about our inner world. Since we rely on the verbal community to teach us all self-awareness, there's a limit to what we may know about ourselves.

But recently science has found a way to give the verbal community new eyes, new ears — new sensors. It's called biofeedback. Biofeedback involves the use of certain mechanical and electronic devices which detect internal responses, responses that can't be detected by the unaided observer, and that for the most part, the subject is unaware of. These devices deliver correlates of the internal responses to the outside, portraying them in some new stimulus mode, such as visual or auditory, which observers can respond to. Observers can tell immediately with these devices when blood pressure is rising or lowering, temperature is altering, sphincters are changing position, or very small muscle groups are responding. Once these events are displayed, observers can reward subjects for certain movements and not reward others. Reward in biofeedback usually consists of a signal, some simple stimulus such as a light or tone that tells the individual what's happening. This is, of course, "feedback", thus the term, "biofeedback".

Through biofeedback individuals can be trained to control internal responses. By reinforcing desired responses, they can cause these responses to occur more often. The sensors, in essence, allow the verbal community access to a once obscure region.

A second part of the biofeedback procedure includes making the subjects self-aware, so that they know when these responses are occurring. Thus, the subject is first taught to make the responses in question occur more often — perhaps to increase or decrease blood pressure or heart rate. But this is done entirely through feedback or signals that are made contingent on the correct response. It's a simple trick from this point to teach the individual to become aware of what's going on inside. All that remains to be done is to solicit self-awareness responses from the subjects and reward them when they're accurate. Soon the individual will not only be able to control the particular internal response but will also become aware that such control is needed. This methodology is exciting for it offers the promise of allowing individuals with medical problems such as diabetes, to become aware of their blood-sugar level without the necessity of having it tested and to then take the proper food or medication to alter the problem. Persons with other problems can become aware of them long before they become serious.

In some ways biofeedback can be viewed as a short-cut method to the techniques that have long been used by Eastern cultures — in Yoga for instance. The Yoga teacher or guru is an individual who has developed a great skill in spotting the external manifestations of inside responses — responses that he wishes his pupil to learn to control. Thus, the guru is, in essence, a specialized verbal community. He becomes so through years of training. Like an expert swimming or football coach, the guru knows what subtle responses to look for and reward. The guru can label the pupil's responses with accuracy and more subtlety, and therefore allow the pupil to develop subtle self-awareness and control of these responses. You can see that these procedures all involve the same basic principles that we've talked about in this book. Normal self-awareness, biofeedback, control and awareness, and the Yogi controlling physiology and anatomy, are all the result of verbal communities at work.

25 Emotions

Azrin, H. H., Hutchinson, R., & Sallery, R. D. Pain-aggression toward inanimate obejcts. *Journal of the Experimental Analysis of Behavior,* 1964, *7,* 223-228.

Black, P. *Physiological correlates of emotion.* New York: Academic Press, 1970.

Cannon, W. B. The James-Lange theory of emotions: A critical examination and an alternative theory. *American Journal of Psychology,* 1927, *39,* 106-124.

Cannon challenges the James-Lange theory, expressing the point of view that emotions are of a phylogenetic origin and intrinsic to the nature of the organism and the environment in which it lives. The author believes emotions are not the product of behavior, but rather the elicitor of behavior.

Chase, S. *The tyranny of words.* New York: Harcourt, Brace & World, 1938.

Darwin, C. *The expression of the emotions in man and animals.* Chicago: University of Chicago Press, 1965.

Harlow, H. F. The formation of learning sets. *Psychological Review,* 1949, *56,* 51-65.

James, W., & Lange, G. G. *The emotions.* Baltimore: Williams & Wilkins, 1922.
James suggests that emotion follows after the response is made, and is not the cause of the response but rather a product of it.

Korzybski, Alfred. *Science and sanity: An introduction to non-Aristotelian systems and general semantics* (4th ed.). Lakeville, Conneticut: International Non-Aristotelian Library Publishing Company, 1958.
Korzybski has formed an entire school in semantics, the primary thesis of which is that the structure of the language restricts us in our ability to make meaningful discriminations and to appropriately deal with the environment. In some sense, the author presents the other side of the thesis that Whorf presented at about the same time, and suggests that the restrictions in our language have caused us to become prone to mental illness.

Ornstein, R. E. (Ed.). *The nature of human consciousness.* New York: Viking Press, 1973.

Razran, G. H. S. A quantitative study of meaning by a conditioned salivary technique (semantic conditioning). *Science,* 1939, *90,* 89-90.

Razran, G. H. S. Semantic, syntactic, and phonetographic generalization of verbal conditioning. *Psychological Bulletin.* 1939, *36,* 578.
This research shows how words become conditioned emotional cues and how generalization of emotional responses occurs across semantic as opposed to physical dimensions of stimuli.

Schachter, S. The interaction of cognitive and physiological determinants of emotional states. In L. Berkowitz (Ed.), *Advances in experimental social psychology.* New York: Academic Press, 1965.

Schachter, S., & Singer, J. E. Cognitive, social, and physiological determinants of emotional states. *Psychological Review,* 1962, *69,* 379-399.
A new dimension in understanding the nature of emotions. Schachter points out that the emotions we experience are controlled by external cues, and in some situations, totally so. Thus, the most we can say is that there is an interaction between internal events and external cues which produces the consciousness of certain emotions.

Watson, J. B., & Rayner, R. Conditional emotional reactions. *Journal of Experimental Psychology,* 1920, *3,* 1-14.
This study demonstrates a clearcut case of how phobias may be established through aversive conditioning.

The group in this chapter was portrayed in a somewhat negative light. Needless to say, this doesn't need to be the case. Groups often serve a useful purpose and do help many individuals overcome difficulties. Whether or not a group helps depends in great measure upon the purpose of the group, and how well the purpose is expressed. The purpose may be to get members to "open up", to become emotional. But, does it always help to bare emotions? In some cases, it undoubtedly does. Learning to be more assertive, saying what you believe to other people, may be a very valuable thing. But it depends, of course, on what your beliefs are and on how appropriate they are.

Many people find it very hard to communicate the most simple personal desires and needs to other individuals. They find it hard to complain although they're suffering in a most offensive and unnecessary manner. Getting people to the point that they can air their opinions, giving good information and feedback to others can help in many ways. For one thing, it allows them to communicate with others, who may very well be sensitive to their wants once they find out what they are. Likewise, it allows for reality testing — for people to come in contact with the views and beliefs of other people; and therefore, allows an opportunity to correct any faulty assumptions or notions that they may have developed.

But as we saw in this chapter, too often the purpose of the group can become perverted. One quite reinforcing thing is to be involved in emotional upheaval of some sort; that is, as long as the emotional upheaval is a safe one. This is what makes movies and books pleasing — they're controlled and have natural boundaries. Emotions that we experience are vicarious and can be terminated merely by walking out of the movie or putting the book down — escaping to the real world.

Emotional trips in groups can get out of hand. Members can learn the wrong things. They can learn to punish, to become overly emotional to the point that they behave inappropriately in an outside setting. They may learn values and attitudes that are rewarding and fun to talk about, but clearly don't help in the outside world — and, in fact, may get in the way. However, if properly handled, groups can be quite exciting. What's more important, they have value. They continue to help many individuals, allowing them to be more functional and effective citizens.

26 Hans Selye and Stress

American Psychiatric Association. *Diagnostic and statistical manual of mental disorders.* Washington, D. C., 1968.

Brady, J. V. Ulcers in executive monkeys. *Scientific American,* 1958, *199,* 95-100.
The author establishes that ulcers can be reliably produced by learned stressors and psychological variables. Brady also discovered that temporal and other factors of the situations play a big part in the problem.

Gray, J. *The psychology of fear and stress.* New York: McGraw-Hill, 1971.

Janis, I. *Psychological stress.* New York: Wiley, 1958.

Jellinek, E. N. *The disease concept of alcoholism.* New Haven, Conn.: Hillhouse Press, 1960.
The disease concept of alcoholism is examined and its inadequacies are dealt with.

Lachman, S. J. *Psychosomatic disorders: A behavioristic interpretation.* New York: Wiley, 1972.
This learning approach is quite compelling.

Obermeyer, J. B., & Seligman, M. E. P.

Effects of inescapable shock upon subsequent escape and avoidance responding. *Journal of Comparative and Physiological Psychology,* 1967, *64,* 29-33.

O'Kelly, L. E., & Steckle, L. C. A note on long-enduring emotional responses in the rat. *Journal of Psychology,* 1939, *8,* 125-131.

Ruff, G. E., & Korchin, S. J. Adaptive distress behavior. In M. H. Applye & R. Trumbull (Eds.), *Psychological stress.* Englewood Cliffs, New Jersey: Prentice-Hall, 1962.

Seligman, M. E. P. Can we immunize the weak? *Psychology Today,* June 1969, pp. 42-44.
Seligman presents the premise of learned helplessness in this article. The author's primary thesis is that organisms learn to stop making adaptive responses if historically these responses have not been successful. In short, organisms learn to quit trying and, in essence, lie down and die. Seligman suggests here that we may be able to immunize people to stress situations by arranging the proper type of early training.

Selye, H. *The stress of life.* New York: McGraw-Hill, 1956.
Since the presentation of the theories in this volume, Selye has become the authority on stress.

Simms, J. H., & Baumann, D. D. The tornado threat: Coping styles of the north and the south. *Science,* 1972, *176,* 1386-1391.
The authors show how styles of coping with threat differ from culture to culture or from community to community, and that these styles of coping are determined by the behavior patterns of that particular region.

Trotter, R. J. Stress: Confusion and controversy. *Science News,* 1975, *107* (22), 356-357.
This article points out a new emphasis on stress. New data have come to light which suggest that stress is not a generalized factor, but is due to specific psychological stimuli; that is, to stimuli that have been established and gained their power through learning. In some sense Selye's position is challenged by these new data and the relevance of psychological variables to psychosomatic and psychophysiological disorders becomes more important.

Weiss, J. M. Effects of coping responses on stress. *Journal of Comparative and Physiological Psychology,* 1968, *65,* 251-260.

Weiss, J. M. Psychological factors in stress and disease. *Scientific American,* 1972, *226,* 104-113.

As its leading researcher, Hans Selye has been the undisputed authority on stress for the past several decades. Selye considers stress the result of contact with the many punishing stimuli in the environment — stimuli that for the most part are avoidable. In a real sense to live is to know stress. Selye believes learned stimuli also play an important part in stress reactions. Their primary importance is seen in what Selye calls "diseases of adaptation", the psychophysiological problems we discussed above. He views learning and other adaptive responses as secondary to the harmful effects of natural stressors. Recently, Selye's position has been challenged by John Mason. Both he and Selye presented their position at a symposium sponsored by the Kittay Scientific Foundation. Mason believes that learned stressors may play a bigger role in stress than the unlearned stressors that Selye has written about. Mason cited research in which hormone levels were measured in male rhesus monkeys before and while they were confined in restraining chairs. Although this kind of stress may not be as extreme as electric shock or starvation, it is, nonetheless, a stressor that raised hormonal changes significantly. Mason suggests that the primary changes in these hormonal levels might be due to learned stimuli — stimuli that cause arousal because of their past history of being paired with other punishers. In subsequent experiments, Mason and his co-workers introduced precautions that minimized such reactions. They kept novelty and certainty at a minimum, allowing lengthy periods of adaptation to the experimental set-up. They strictly limited other psychological stimuli coming from the outside. For instance, animals were kept in private and sound-resistant booths. Cubicles were entered only rarely for cleaning and samples.

In a similar study in which Mason and his associates used starvation as a stressor, discomfort was minimized by offering non-nutritive fruit-flavored pellets to reduce the discomfort of empty gastrointestinal tracts. With these measures, stress was reduced to an all time low level. It appeared that the stress was more a factor of learned stimuli (or at least stimuli that had no direct biological significance), than it was of the physical conditions that Selye believed were the primary causes of stress.

Mason sees his results not so much as a challenge to Selye as a further extension of Selye's work. A further finding, however, questions one of Selye's basic assumptions. Mason's data suggest that specific learned stressors produce changes that are specific to that stressor. One stressor, for instance, might attack the pituitary-adrenal-cortical system, while another stressor activates another organ or hormonal system. These findings seem to fit better with what we know about psychophysiological problems. It may turn out that psychophysiological problems aren't the result of adaptation to unlearned stressors, but are the direct result of psychological stressors.

27 Neuroses

Adamson, R. E. Functional fixedness as related to problem solving: A repetition of three experiments. *Journal of Experimental Psychology,* 1952, *44,* 288-291.

American Psychiatric Association. *Diagnostic and statistical manual of mental disorders.* Washington, D. C., 1968.

Breuer, J., & Freud, S. *Studies in hysteria* (J. Strachey, trans.). New York: Basic Books, 1957.
Freud's classical work in hysteria. As a result of their interactions and the production of this volume, Freud and Breuer had serious disagreements over the cause of hysteria. Freud felt that sexual traumas in youth were the cause of hysteria, whereas Breuer felt that there were other causes as well.

Diven, K. Certain determinants in the conditioning of anxiety reactions. *Journal of Psychology,* 1937, *33,* 291-308.

Gantt, W. H. *Experimental basis for neurotic behavior.* New York: Hoeber, 1944.

Goldiamond, I. Perception. In A. J. Bachrach (Ed.), *Experimental foundations of clinical psychology.* New York: Basic Books, 1962.
A signal detection analysis of wide areas of behavioral phenomena, allowing them to be looked at in a direct

manner, and paving the way for more effective research and treatment.

Green, D. M., & Swets, J. A. *Signal detection theory and psycho-physics.* New York: Wiley, 1966.
These authors successfully take signal detection theory from engineering and apply it to classical psychophysics.

Hathaway, S. R., & Meehl, P. E. *An atlas for the clinical use of the MMPI.* Minneapolis: University of Minnesota Press, 1951.

Jones, K. L., Shainberg, L. W., & Byer, C. O. *Drugs and alcohol.* New York: Harper & Row, 1969.

Kutash, S. B. Psychoneuroses. In B. B. Wolman (Ed.), *Handbook of clinical psychology.* New York: McGraw-Hill, 1965.

Martin, B. *Anxiety and neurotic disorders.* New York: Wiley, 1971.

Masserman, J. *Behavior and neurosis.* Chicago: University of Chicago Press, 1943.
A series of investigations and speculations characteristic of Masserman's experimental ingenuity and perceptiveness in drawing inferences from this work.

Russell, W. R., & Nathan, P. W. Traumatic amnesia. *Brain,* 1946, *69,* 280-300.

Sandler, J., & Davidson, R. S. *Psychopathology: Learning theory, research, and application.* New York: Harper & Row, 1973.
An excellent review of the behavioral literature in psychopathology, which makes an outstanding appeal for the superiority of this way of looking at problems.

Slater, E. The neurotic constitution. *Journal of Neurological Psychiatry,* 1943, *6,* 1-16.

Ullmann, L. P., & Krasner, L. *A psychological approach to abnormal behavior.* Englewood Cliffs, New Jersey: Prentice-Hall, 1969.
The first abnormal psychology textbook written from the behavioral standpoint. It's excellent in its scope and consistent in its outlook.

Whaley, D. L. *Psychological testing and the philosophy of measurement.* Kalamazoo, Michigan: Behaviordelia, 1973.

Perhaps labeling Freddy Severs neurotic may seem too mild since he appears to be growing worse and worse, and his behavior is becoming so bizarre and maladaptive. Indeed, when Freddy is taken away it's quite likely that he'll be diagnosed a simple schizophrenic, or perhaps be given a catchier title — pseudo-neurotic schizophrenic. The point is that the distinction between neuroses and psychoses is a very fuzzy one in some cases. Although this point has been hotly argued in the past; in fact, there have been long debates as to whether or not there is continuity between neuroses and psychoses or whether they're two distinct problem states. The answer, of course, is that some neuroses are not likely to get worse, but this depends upon the afflicted person, the other strengths and skills of his or her particular life situation, and many other factors.

It seems that any severe problem, whether we call it a character disorder, neurosis or psychosis, can become a factor that can cause a person to become severely debilitated — so debilitated, in fact, that the person will have to be maintained in an institution, for perhaps a lifetime. Regardless of label, the entire problem of classification is quite a delicate one. In the end, it's probably true that the ultimate importance of classification is the treatment the label indicates. If this isn't true it seems totally irrelevant as to whether a person is called a neurotic, psychotic, behavior problem, said to have a character disorder, or whatever. What seems to be important is the degree of debility present, and what measures must be taken to get the individual back to the point where he or she can function in society.

28 Behavior Problems

Sandler, J. Masochism: An empirical analysis. *Psychological Bulletin,* 1964, *62,* 197-204.
Sandler reviews the experimental work that has been done on masochism, presenting research in which monkeys are trained to become masochists.

Sandler, J., & Davidson, R. S. *Psychopathology: Learning theory, research, and applications.* New York: Harper & Row, 1973.

Ullmann, L. P., & Krasner, L. *Case studies in behavior modification.* New York: Holt, Rinehart & Winston, 1965. The first of a series of readings in which behavior modification and behavior therapy are applied to clinical problems.

Ullmann, L. P., & Krasner, L. *A psychological approach to abnormal behavior.* Englewood Cliffs, New Jersey: Prentice-Hall, 1969.

Whaley, D. L., & Malott, R. W. *Elementary principles of behavior.* Englewood Cliffs, New Jersey: Prentice-Hall, 1971.

To people unfamiliar with the problem, it's difficult to imagine how youngsters could develop such severe self-injuring behavior that they detach retinas, cause permanent brain damage, and inflict disfiguring wounds to their bodies. Such bizarre behavior, they often feel, must be the result of physical abnormality.

As we've pointed out in this chapter, most youngsters who develop self-injuring behaviors at this level, do indeed have some abnormal diagnosis. They're often retarded and may have other handicaps as well. But it's not likely that the fact of their retardation has anything in a direct way to do with self-injury. The data gathered in dozens of cases indicate that social reinforcement of the behavior is the perpetuating cause.

The deficits that these youngsters have preclude their getting social reinforcement in normal ways. Further, they're most always in the presence of adults who are caring for them, and this is likely to be doubly true once, for any reason, they exhibit some self-injury tendency. Yet, most kids, even all-American healthy boys and girls, go through some fleeting periods in their development when they demonstrate some self-injurious behavior.

29 Psychoses

American Psychiatric Association. *Diagnostic and statistical manual of mental disorders.* Washington, D. C., 1968.

Coleman, J. C. *Abnormal psychology and modern life.* Glenview, Illinois: Scott, Foresman, 1964.

Costello, C. G. Classification and psychopathology. In C. G. Costello (Ed.), *Symptoms of psychopathology: A handbook.* New York: Wiley, 1970.

Heckel, R. B., & Salzberg, H. C. How to make your patients chronic. *Mental Hospitals,* 1964, *15,* 37-38.
The authors explain their views on iatrogenic diseases and how typical mental institutions perhaps cause more problems than they help.

Heston, L. The genetics of schizophrenia and schizoid disease. *Science,* 1970, *167,* 249-256.

Kallman, F. J. The genetics of mental illness. In S. Arieti (Ed.), *American Handbook of Psychiatry.* New York: Basic Books, 1949.

Kallman, F. J. *Heredity in mental health and disorder.* New York: Norton, 1953.
A review of the significant studies which have attempted to define the relationship between heredity and mental illness. The account is somewhat compelling, although the research for the most part does not substantiate the author's conclusions.

Rosenthal, D. *Genetic theory and abnormal behavior.* New York: McGraw-Hill, 1970.

Sanders, M., Smith, R. S., & Weinmon, B. S. *Chronic psychosis and recovery.* San Francisco: Jossey-Bass, 1967.

Skinner, B. F. *Science and human behavior.* New York: Macmillan, 1953.

Skinner, B. F. *Beyond freedom and dignity.* New York: Knopf, 1971.

Szasz, T. S. The myth of mental illness. *American Psychology,* 1960, *15,* 113-118.
This hallmark book questions the validity of traditional clinical diagnosis. The author suggests that mental illness is to a great extent the product of society's definitions and does not relate to actual behavioral or physical differences or physical attributes that can be independently observed.

Ullmann, L. P., & Krasner, L. *A psychological approach to abnormal behavior.* Englewood Cliffs, New Jersey: Prentice-Hall, 1969.

30 Retardation

Anderson, V. E. Genetics in mental retardation. In H. A. Stevens & R. Heber, (Eds.), *Mental Retardation.* Chicago: University of Chicago Press, 1964.

Arehart-Treichel, J. Correcting enzyme defects in the test tube. *Science News,* 1975, *107* (13), 211-212.
This is a brief report on new technology in which genetically-minded biochemists are experimenting with the correction of enzyme defects.

Bensberg, G. J. (Ed.). *Teaching the mentally retarded.* Atlanta, Georgia: Southern Regional Education Board, 1965.

Clark, H. B., Rosebury, T., Baer, A. M., and Baer, D. M. Time out as a punishing stimulus in continuous and intermittent schedules. *Journal of Applied Behavior Analysis,* 1973, *6* (3), 443-455.

Fay, J., & Doll, E. A. Organic impairment simulating mental deficiency. *American Journal of Orthopsychiatry,* 1949, *19,* 112-119.

Ferster, C. B., & Appel, J. B. Punishment of S^Δ responding in matching to sample by time out from positive reinforcement. *Journal of the Experimental Analysis of Behavior,* 1961, *4,* 45-56.

Hunt, J. McV. The psychological basis for using preschool enrichment as an anecdote for cultural deprivation. *Merrill-Palmer Quarterly of Behavior and Development,* July, 1964, *10* (3), 209.

Jordan, T. E. (Ed.). *Perspectives in mental retardation.* Carbondale & Edwardsville, Illinois: Southern Illinois University Press, 1966.

Kutsky, R. J. *Handbook of vitamins and hormones.* New York: Van Nostrand Reinhold, 1973.

Lindsley, O. R. Direct measurement and prosthesis of retarded behavior. In R. L. Jones (Ed.), *New directions in special education.* Boston: Allyn & Bacon, 1970.
A strategy and tactics for attempting to remediate behavioral problems of the retardate.

Meade, Johnson & Co. *Phenylketonuria.* Evanston, Illinois: Meade, Johnson & Co., 1958.

Reitan, R. M., & Davison, L. A. (Eds.). *Clinical neuropsychology: Current status and applications.* Washington, D. C.: Halsted Press, 1974.

Russell, E. W., Neuringer, C. & Goldstein, G. *Assessment of brain damage; a neuropsychological key approach.* New York: Wiley-Interscience, 1970.

Sarason, S. B., & Doras, J. *Psychological problems in mental deficiency* (4th ed.). New York: Harper & Row, 1969.

Swartz, D. P. Gestational and perinatal factors in brain damage. In T. E. Jordan (Ed.), *Perspectives in mental retardation.* Carbondale & Edwardsville, Illinois: Southern Illinois University Press, 1966.

Zigler, E. Rigidity and social reinforcement effects in the performance of institutionalized and noninstitutionalized normal and retarded children. *Journal of Personality,* 1963, *31,* 258-269.

The definition of mental retardation included here is of a general nature, encompassing what we believe to be the crucial aspects of the problem. The most accepted definition, however, is more technical in nature, published by the American Association of Mental Deficiency (AAMD): "Mental retardation refers to significantly subaverage general intellectual functioning existing concurrently with deficits in adaptive behavior and manifested during the developmental period."

The degree of intellectual functioning is discerned by referring to a standard intelligence test, either the Stanford Binet or the Wechsler. Individuals scoring two standard deviations below the mean on tests (IQ of approximately 50 to 67) are termed mildly mentally retarded. Those scoring three standard deviations below the mean (IQ: 30-50) are labeled moderately mentally retarded. Those scoring four standard deviations below the mean (IQ: 20-30) are labeled severely mentally retarded, and those scoring five standard deviations below the mean (IQ: 19 or below) are labeled profoundly mentally retarded.

The second part of the AAMD definition of retardation deals with adaptive behavior. Adaptive behavior is defined as "the effectiveness or degree with which the individual meets the standards of independence and social responsibility expected of individuals of his age and cultural group. Since expectations vary from different age groups, adaptive behavior will vary at different ages." During infancy and early childhood, for instance, the following are important factors, and deficits in them are grounds to label the individual "retarded" provided intellectual functioning and intelligence tests scores are also sufficiently subnormal. These are: 1) sensory-motor development skills, 2) communication skills (including speech and language), 3) self-help skills, and 4) socialization (ability to interact with others).

During childhood and early adolescence the important factors are: 1) application of basic academic skills in daily life; 2) application of appropriate reasoning and judgement; 3) mastery of the environment and social skills; 4) participation in group activities, and interpersonal relationships. During late adolescence and adult life vocational and social responsibilities become factors. Thus, within the concept of adaptive behavior is also included the third part of the AAMD definition, mainly that of the developmental period. Though we've implicitly covered all the factors in the chapter it's good to review them more specifically here.

***

Stereotyping has long been noted as a feature of behavior of the retarded; but more than that it's been linked to brain damage. Much has been said about what causes stereotyping, and all too much of it is speculation. The most prevalent explanation is not at all a scientific one, nor even a neurological one for that matter; but rather, has to do with the consciousness and intentions of the retarded or brain-damaged individual. It's generally believed that the person becomes rigid in response patterns because he or she is unable to discriminate to solve a problem. The person thus reverts to a rigid and stereotypic pattern of responding as a defensive move primarily to save ego and to prevent undue frustration. It's quite true that if you watch individuals who cannot but fail to discriminate properly, and continue to make errors, they often become quite anxious and frustrated. Settling on a rigid way of responding seems to reduce this anxiety to some extent.

Actually, this whole explanation is far too mystical and far far too mentalistic for modern consideration. The simple truth of the matter is that stereotyping occurs because the relevant stimuli in the situation are not controlling the individual's behavior. What's controlling the behavior is the reinforcement schedule or the reinforcement itself. The discriminative stimuli in the situation are not exerting the control. What occurs, after all, is a stereotyped response which gets rewarded. The percent of times the stereotyped response is rewarded is, of course, determined by the particular discrimination problem.

In Casey's situation, initially, you can see that if there are five colored blocks, which are changed in a regular manner, Casey is going to be right at least one out of five times. All things equal this will be true whether she sticks with one block or keeps switching position choices. What causes Casey to stereotype is often that quite by chance the same position will be reinforced one or two, or even three times in a row. Three reinforcements after that it will be reinforced on an average of at least once out of every five times. So you can see why stereotyping occurred in the first place and why it maintains.

Then how is stereotyping broken up since there also exists the probability and even the reality that the position Casey chooses may not be reinforced for many times in a row. The random changing of the position of the block and the names of the colors insures that *this must happen occasionally. When it does happen, Casey may switch from her stereotyped position to a new one. If this one is reinforced, her stereotyping will change to the new position.*

Explaining Casey's behavior in terms of what she's thinking or trying to do seems a bit far-fetched. We can rest assured that Casey has very little conversation with herself and that her behavior can't be explained in terms of motives, intent or other features of consciousness that apply only to people with normal verbal behavior. Rather it can be explained quite easily in terms of the simple analysis given above.

31 B. F. Skinner and Behavior Modification

Bandura, A. *Principles of behavior modification.* New York: Holt, Rinehart & Winston, 1969.
This most complete textbook on behavior modification presents the gamut of its application covering virtually all of the relevant literature.

Carey, J. J. *The college drug scene.* Englewood Cliffs, New Jersey: Prentice-Hall, 1968.
An interesting account of drug use as it appeared at the time of the writing. We believe things have changed somewhat since then. This is a classical paper for it showed how extinction procedures may be used to get rid of what were felt to be otherwise intractable behavior problems.

Carlson, C. S., Arnold, C. R., Becker, W. C., & Madson, C. H. The elimination of tantrum behavior of a child in the elementary classroom. *Behavior Research and Therapy,* 1968, *6,* 117-119.

Catania, A. C. *Contemporary research in operant behavior.* Glenview, Illinois: Scott, Foresman, 1968.

Goldfried, M. R., & Merbaum, M. (Eds.), *Behavior change through self control.* New York: Holt, Rinehart & Winston, 1973.

Naylor, J. C., & Briggs, G. E. Effects of task complexity and task organization on the relative efficiency of part and whole training methods. *Journal of Experimental Psychology,* 1963, *65,* (3), 217-224.

Reese, E. P. *Experiments in operant behavior.* New York: Naiburg, 1960.

Skinner, B. F. *The behavior of organisms.* Englewood Cliffs, New Jersey: Prentice-Hall, 1938

Skinner, B. F. *Cumulative record.* Englewood Cliffs, New Jersey: Prentice-Hall, 1959.

Skinner, B. F. B. F. Skinner . . . an autobiography. In P. B. Dews (Ed.), *Festschrift for B. F. Skinner.* New York: Appleton-Century-Crofts, 1970.

Terrace, H. S. Discrimination learning with and without errors. *Journal of the Experimental Analysis of Behavior,* 1963, *6,* 1-27.

Watson, D. L., & Tharp, R. G. *Self-directed behavior: Self-modification for personal adjustment.* Monterey, California: Brooks/Cole, 1972
This is the first of a series of books to espouse the now commonly accepted practice that people can modify their own behavior, through the use of behavioral principles.

Wolf, M. M., Birnbrauer, J. S., Williams, T., Lawler, J. A note on apparent extinction in the vomiting behavior of the retarded child. In L. P. Ullmann & L. Krasner (Eds.), *Case studies in behavior modification.* New York: Holt, Rinehart & Winston, 1965.

Some people are thankful for behavior modification because it gives them a means of controlling their own behavior. For others, however, the idea that behavior techniques are needed to control one's behavior is extremely repugnant, smacking of moral weakness and lack of character. It's this issue that Skinner deals with in his book, Beyond Freedom and Dignity *— the fact that we place such a great store in so-called "will power" and our own personal self-control.*

Self-control is greatly misunderstood by most of the public, as well as by many psychologists. In a behavioral sense, we never have any choice as to what actions we'll take, even when we may find ourselves doing what we want to do, and even when it may seem that we have other options. Those other options may be physical or logical options, but not behavioral options. People who've been trained to be neat, to keep personal belongings in good order and repair and to keep things tidy, will find doing these things quite easy — in fact, they'll probably find it punishing if they're not allowed to keep things neat. It's also likely that they won't understand someone else with less tidy habits. Above all, they won't be able to see why such a person would have to undergo a behavior modification program for something that's so natural and, after all, only good sense.

But, this is the case with much that we learn. We forget how and where we learned it and often, how difficult it was for us to learn. But self-control, whether it's the result of a long past history or of current conditions that just happened to be benevolent, is nonetheless the result of environmental influence.

32 Joseph Wolpe and Behavior Therapy

Eysenck, H. J. *Experiments in behavior therapy.* New York: Pergamon, 1963.

Farber, I. E., & Spence, K. W. Complex learning and conditioning as a function of anxiety. *Journal of Experimental Psychology,* 1953, *45,* 120-125.
The authors establish a relationship between anxiety and learning, making the point that people who have a higher level of anxiety, although not massive anxiety, tend to learn better than those who do not have this level of anxiety.

Feshback, S., & Loeb, A. A. A further experimental study of a response interference vs. a drive facilitation theory of the effect of anxiety upon learning. *Journal of Personality,* 1959, *27,* 497-506.
The authors examine the relationship between anxiety and learning, trying to take into account those theories that have said it is a facilitator as well as those findings that have suggested it has interfered with learning.

Frank, C. *Assessment and status of the behavior therapies and associated developments.* New York: McGraw-Hill, 1967.
Extremely viable insights and analyses by one of the first people to employ behavior therapy.

Jacobson, L. E. The electro-physiology of mental activities. *American Journal of Psychotherapy,* 1932, *44,* 677-694.

Krueger, W. C. F. The effect of over-learning on retention. *Journal of Experimental Psychology,* 1929, *12,* 71-78.

Levine, L., & Loth, D. *The frigid wife.* New York: Messmer, 1962.

This literary description of frigidity offers some insights into the problem, but doesn't deal in any systematic way with the psychological factors that produce it.

Malmo, R. B. Anxiety and behavioral arousal. *Psychological Review,* 1957, *64,* 276-287.
Malmo talks about the relationship between anxiety, behavioral arousal, and performance and presents the famous inverted U-function, which, in our opinion, is to date, the best statement of the relationship between arousal and performance.

Malmo, R. B., & Ansel, P. Anxiety produced interference in serial rote learning with observation on rote learning after partial frontal lobectomy. *Journal of Experimental Psychology,* 1948, *38,* 440-454.
Malmo's hypothesis that anxiety is an inverted U-function is further substantiated by this research in which rote learning is interfered with as anxiety increases toward the highest levels, although it's facilitative at lower levels.

Masters, W. H., & Johnson, V. E. *Human sexual inadequacy.* Boston: Little, Brown, 1970.

McGuigan, F. F. *Thinking: Studies of covert language processes.* New York: Appleton-Century-Crofts, 1966.

Morris, D. *The human zoo.* New York: McGraw-Hill, 1969.

Postman, L. Retention as a degree of overlearning. *Science,* 1962, *135,* 666-667.
A definitive statement about the relationships of overlearning.

Skinner, B. F. *About behaviorism.* New York: Knopf, 1974.

Solomon, R. L., Kamin, L. J., & Winne, L. C. Traumatic avoidance learning: The outcome of several extinction procedures with dogs. *Journal of Abnormal and Social Psychology,* 1953, *48,* 291-302.
This is one of a series of classical works that outlines avoidance behavior and its relation to extinction — how avoidance learning resists weakening through non-reinforced trials.

Wilkins, W. Desensitization: Social and cognitive factors underlying the effectiveness of Wolpe's procedure. *Psychological Bulletin,* 1972, *79,* 311-317.
An excellent review of all of the desensitization studies. In it the exciting theory is seriously indicted. The conclusion is that only social and cognitive variables matter and that relaxation and the hierarchy are irrelevant in the treatment.

Wolpe, J. The systematic desensitization treatment of neuroses. *Journal of Nervous and Mental Disease,* 1963, *132,* 189-203.
Wolpe discusses systematic desensitization treatment, its rationale, and the procedure whereby it may be employed.

Wolpe, J. *The practice of behavior therapy.* New York: Pergamon, 1966.

Wolpe, J. Fur phobia: A hair of the hound. *Psychology Today,* June 1969, pp. 34-37.

Wolpe, J., Salter, A., & Reyna, L. J. (Eds.). *The conditioning therapies.* New York: Holt, Rinehart & Winston, 1964.
The most effective techniques of behavior therapy, primarily those taking the form of desensitization and assertive training, are presented in this text.

GLOSSARY

Absolute threshold: the lowest intensity that will reliably produce a response.

Absorption: change in physical or chemical structure when a stimulus makes contact.

Achievement test: a psychological test based on samples of behavior that relate in a direct way to past occasions for learning.

Actions: an action is equivalent to a response. Sometimes it implies a sequence of complex acts or responses.

Activation: the general state, amount, or degree of internal and external body movement and function.

Affective psychoses: psychoses marked by distinct irregularities of emotional response or mood. Reasoning, judgement, and other features are relatively unaffected.

Afferent nerves: nerves that transfer sensory stimuli coming from the outside, to inside structures.

Aggressive reinforcer: an event that becomes a reinforcer when the creature is exposed to conditions that may be bad for it —

either 1) the removal of a fuel source, 2) a harmful state, or 3) events that have been paired with such conditions in the history of the species.

Alarm stage: the first stage of the GAS; during this stage physiological resources are mobilized and rushed to the point where contact with stressors is going on.

All or None Law: neurons either fire as totally as they are capable or they don't fire at all. There is no graded response.

Allergy: condition where people are born with a slightly different physical structure that makes stimuli that are harmless for others unlearned stressors for them.

Amniotic sac: the sac filled with protective fluid which holds the fetus.

Analysis: the task of finding out and describing the precise set of conditions that give rise to specific events.

Anaphylactic shock: physiological shock brought on by allergic stimuli.

Anatomy: study of the structure of plants and animals.

Anoxia: condition where cells are damaged due to the failure of oxygen to reach them.

Anthropomorphism: describing animals and objects in human terms.

Anxiety: complex response involving irregularities in heart, blood vessel, gland, and muscle actions. Thoughts or feelings of being afraid may be, but aren't always, present.

Anxiety neurosis: a type of neurosis characterized by massive anxiety that seems to become attached to an ever-increasing number of things and settings.

Anxiety stimulus hierarchy: an ordering of anxiety stimuli in terms of their power to provoke the response.

Application: the bringing together of the needed conditions in order to produce certain desired events or outcomes.

Asexual reproduction: reproduction process that produces an offspring with one parent.

Assertive training: behavior therapy technique designed to help clients become more active in speaking out in their own behalf or otherwise protecting their rights and interests.

Atomic evolution: a process occurring in nature where through fusion of nuclei, simple atoms evolve into more complex ones.

Attending: a person attends to a stimulus when that stimulus exerts some form of stimulus control over the person's actions.

Attitude: the combined efforts of beliefs (verbal discriminative stimuli), actions (responses), and values (reinforcers).

Axon: part of the neuron cell body that transfers stimuli across the greatest distances.

Bait-shy effect: creatures tend to avoid eating a substance that tastes or smells like poisoned food previously eaten just once before.

Baseline: systematic observations taken prior to treatment which are used to evaluate the extent and nature of treatment effects.

Basic stimulus control: control exerted by a stimulus over the form or path of a response.

Behavior modification: the application of principles of behavioral psychology, and operant psychology in particular, to change actions in a desired manner or direction.

Behavior problems: learned patterns of behavior that produce results harmful to the person or make him or her unacceptable to society.

Behavior therapy: a therapy approach based on learning principles, that seeks to change both outside actions and feelings by altering arousal responses.

Belief: a verbal statement that functions as a discriminative stimulus, pointing the way to those actions that get valued results.

Binocular convergence: two eyes converge or turn in on a thing to fixate on it.

Brain damage: damage to brain cells that kills them or vastly impairs their normal function.

Brightness constancy: an object is the same brightness even though the overall level of light may change, causing it to reflect less light.

Catatonic schizophrenia: schizophrenia taking two forms: one form agitated and manic; the second form lethargic, stupored, and perhaps motionless for long time spans.

Centralization of function: as multi-celled organisms become more complex, cells specialize in a new function, and give up old functions. Functions given up are taken on by other cells specialized in those functions. Cells that provide like function tend to be located at places in the organism best suited to serve the whole.

Cerebrospinal fluid: fluid that surrounds the brain and spinal cord.

Chromosome: package that contains genes; each human cell has 46 chromosomes, half of which are represented in reproductive cells (sperm or egg).

Color contrast: a shift in the apparent color of an object away from the color of the background.

Compliance: when an outside reinforcer controls an action, and neither the value of the direct results of that action nor belief statements about that action exert control.

Concept: a class of stimuli that may differ in many features, but share at least one common feature.

Concept formation: learning to respond the same to a class of stimuli that form a concept, while not responding to others outside that class.

Conditioned response: response evoked by a stimulus only after pairing that stimulus with one that already causes the response.

Conditioned stimulus: something that evokes a response after a few pairings with another stimulus that already causes that response.

Congenital: taking place sometime between normal conception and birth.

Conversion type: a type of hysterical neurosis where the sufferer develops loss of movement of various parts of the body, or loss of sensitivity or total function of eyes, ears, skin, or other sense organs.

Creative behavior: a new response or set of responses that is in some sense appropriate to the setting in which they occur. These responses should be new to the person though not necessarily new to others.

Cue (discriminative stimulus): a stimulus in whose presence a response is likely to yield reinforcement.

Cultural deprivation: failure to master the skills and knowledge the culture requires because of a lack of exposure to the normal training and experience commonly provided.

Delayed gratification: refraining from actions that produce immediate reinforcers and behaving instead in ways that produce better, although delayed, outcomes.

Delayed stimulus matching: the presentation of the sample and then its removal, with a delay period before the comparison stimuli are presented.

Dendrite: that part of the neuron that receives a stimulus input.

Depersonalization neurosis: neurosis whose main component is a near constant feeling of unreality or apartness.

Depressive neurosis: type of neurosis characterized by excessive or drawn-out depression under circumstances that don't warrant such a response.

Deprivation: period of time during which there is no contact with a reinforcer.

Determinism: the notion that an event is produced or results from the active presence of a precise set of conditions.

Developmental sequence: the normal order in which behavior develops for a given species.

Differentiation of function: as single-celled organisms develop into multiple-celled ones, some cells develop specialized structure which allows them to provide a function that helps the total organism survive.

Disassociative type: one of the two types of hysterical neuroses, in which the person develops loss of memory, in some cases even to the point of forgetting who he or she is. In other cases only selective blocks, or chunks, of time are forgotten.

Discrimination training: reinforcing a response in the presence of one discriminative stimulus, while not reinforcing it in the presence of other discriminative stimuli. Discrimination training typically results in the person making the response only in the presence of the correct discriminative stimulus.

Discriminative stimulus: a stimulus in whose presence a response is likely to yield reinforcement.

Diseases of adaptation: physiological problems that arise as a by-product of the body's response to the presence of stressors.

Displacement: acts that do not deal in a direct way with the basic motive (e.g., fuel, harm, or sexual contact); acts that do not produce the results that controlled the way the species evolved through natural selection (e.g., food, escape, or offspring).

Distal sensory response: response to a stimulus not in direct contact with a creature.

Efferent nerves: nerves that transfer stimuli to muscles or glands, causing them to respond.

Egg: female cell that will unite with male sperm to form a new creature.

Egocentric behavior: behavior controlled by stimuli from the immediate point of view of the person behaving rather than from the point of view of others, even when the latter is called for.

Ego control: rule-governed control, based on reason and logic — a conscious weighing of the results of our acts, both present and future, good and bad.

Emotions: temporary physiological changes due to stimulus changes in the creature's world — both internal and external world.

Encephalitis: infection of the fluid that surrounds the brain and spinal cord.

Endocrine system: stimulus transfer system that involves chemicals dispersed by glands into the bloodstream, where contact is made with other tissues through blood circulation.

Exhaustion stage: the third stage of the GAS, during which all resistance collapses and the organism dies.

Extinction procedure: withholding the reinforcer that has followed a response.

Extinction process: a reduction in response frequency that occurs when the response no longer yields a reinforcer.

Evolution: a change, that occurs across generations, in the ability of a type of creature to deal with its environment.

Fading: a technique coming from operant research and used in behavior modification. In fading, stimulus control is gradually shifted from a stimulus that exerts present control to one that did not exert control before that procedure was employed.

Fatigue: a slowing down or complete stop in response frequency, often accompanied by reduction in general activity (rest) followed sometime thereafter by a return to the previous response and activity level.

Feedback stimulus control: control of the form or path of a response by stimuli resulting from a preceding response where the control is exerted.

Feeling: self-awareness of emotional responses, often resulting in a statement about these emotions.

Fetus: a prenatal creature in its more advanced stages of development: the prenatal human after the sixth to eighth week of pregnancy.

Flat affect: failure to exhibit appropriate emotional response, usually by showing little response at all.

Fixation (visual): lining up an object with the center of the retina.

Fixation: excessive control in later life by reinforcers inappropriately contacted in early life.

Focus: adjustment of the lens to form a clear image on the retina.

Free-floating anxiety: persisting anxiety that is not tied to a specific setting or object; it often takes the form of lingering thoughts or feelings that something bad is about to happen.

Frustration: withholding reinforcers where they have been obtained before.

Gene: substructure of a cell that functions to maintain more or less constant form or structure between parent and offspring.

General adaptation syndrome (GAS): the characteristic three-phase response the body makes to the presence of stress.

Generalized learned stressors: a class of stimuli in which each member acts as a learned stressor.

Grammar (syntax): the ordering of words in sentences to form larger units of stimulus control.

Guideline control: control by a statement of the discriminative stimulus, the response, and the natural results.

Guilt control: self-punishment of acts similar to those that have been or would be punished by others.

Habituation: decreased motion or response to a state of affairs (often a harmful state) due to prolonged exposure to that state.

Hallucination: actions appropriate to the presence of a stimulus object or setting, that occur in its absence.

Hebephrenic schizophrenia: schizophrenia marked by childish actions and affect, as though the person had regressed to an earlier age.

Helping approach: we should go out of our way in a planned, careful, and thoughtful manner to influence the development of our children along worthwhile paths.

Hypochondriacal neurosis: form of neurosis where anxiety revolves around an often remarkable knowledge of medical symptoms, and the persistent belief that the person's symptoms are a sure sign of various diseases.

Hysterical neurosis: a type of neurosis where stress settings or problems are escaped or avoided by loss of memory or the development of physical dysfunction.

Iatrogenic: produced by the treatment; in the context of psychological or behavioral problems, such problems produced by the structure and treatment in mental or state hospitals.

Id control: prompt, unlearned reinforcers and punishers exert greater control over us than delayed social reinforcers and punishers.

Identification: the learning and keeping of an attitude due to social reinforcers, with the values of that attitude becoming learned reinforcers.

Illusion: stimulus control when two or more features interact causing us to make an error in our response to a stimulus.

Imitation: a type of stimulus control in which the form of the response matches the form of the discriminative stimulus.

Imprinting: changing a neutral stimulus into a reinforcer by exposing the newborn to that stimulus.

Incest: contact with parents or other blood relatives that is maintained by sexual reinforcers.

Individual differences: the idea that people differ in very basic ways along various characteristics.

Instinctive reinforcer: a reinforcer for a response that either helps a creature survive in the future or helps its offspring survive; most often the reinforcer acts only during certain crucial times — times when some events in the creature's world trigger biochemical changes within the creature; and those bio-chemical changes in turn alter the effect some neutral event has on the creature, causing the neutral event to stop being neutral and start acting as a reinforcer.

Intelligence test: a psychological test designed to sample behaviors that relate in an indirect way to past occasions for learning. The sampled behaviors are useful in many settings, but those samples do not often include physical or social skills.

Intermittent reinforcement: occasional, rather than consistent reinforcement of a response.

Internalization: the learning and keeping of an attitude due to its closeness to other attitudes — with close attitudes that agree being reinforcing and close attitudes that disagree being punishing.

Interneurons: neural cells that form pathways to serve as a relay function in stimulus transfer.

Intuitive control: the control of behavior by direct reinforcers and punishers, that normally result from the acts without the aid of rules.

Involutional melancholia: a psychosis whose major symptom is depression. Since it comes on at about the same time of the menopause in women and reduced potency in men, there is some reason to believe it has a major biological basis.

Language control: complex stimulus control where the arrangements of various stimuli (like words) function as discriminative stimuli for various acts and combinations of acts.

Law of Complexity and Mutation: as multiple-celled creatures tend to develop complex differentiated cells and systems of centralized function, mutations become less likely.

Law of Immediate Results: a result has the most effect on the response that came just before it (a response is most controlled by the results that occurred just after it).

Law of Intermittent Reinforcement and Speed of Extinction: the more intermittent the rewards that have maintained a response in the past, the more often it will occur without being reinforced before it extinguishes.

Law of Repeated Delayed Results: a result occurring some time after the response that produces it, may gain control over that response, if the delayed pairing of response with result occurs often enough.

Learned response class: a group of responses that may differ widely in form, but are likely to occur in the same setting because they have produced the same reinforcer under those conditions in the past.

Learned response generalization: the tendency for responses that have little or no unlearned relationship to occur in the same setting because they have produced the same result there in the past.

Learned results: reinforcers and punishers that begin as neutral stimuli, and gain their power through association with other reinforcers or punishers.

Learned stimulus control: control of the form, path, or rate of a response by stimuli that have no unlearned control. These stimuli gain control by being present when that response is reinforced.

Learned (or complex) stimulus generalization: pattern of responding acquired through learning where a response occurs in the presence of stimuli that may differ in many gross features, but share at least one controlling feature.

Learned stressors: initially neutral stimuli that the body comes to respond to as though they are harmful; this occurs because of a past association between these inert stimuli and unlearned stressors.

Learning: a change in behavior that occurs as a result of experience.

Learning view: development of responses results from learning.

Legal control: control by a statement of the discriminative stimulus, the response, and the added physical results.

Manic-depressive psychosis: affective psychosis existing in three forms or types. In the manic type, people work at high speed and energy, exaggerate, and take on any challenge. In the depressed type they become depressed, have no energy, and no ambition; often they vegetate. In the circular type excursions between the manic and the depressed phases take place at intervals.

Masochism: condition where stimulus contact that others experience as painful and work to avoid, becomes a learned reinforcer for a particular person.

Maturation view: development of responses follows a biologically predetermined sequence.

Mediation: sequences of more or less standard responses and events that fill the time between a response that produces the reinforcer and the occurrence of that reinforcer.

Megavitamin treatment: treatment for mental retardation that involves giving the patient massive doses of selected vitamins.

Meiosis: the splitting of the human reproductive cell to form sperm and eggs with half (23) of the full complement of chromosomes of the parent.

Microorganism: simple life forms; often single-celled creatures.

Minnesota Multiphasic Personality Inventory (MMPI): a psychological test used in mental health settings, designed to indicate the presence of behavior patterns that are likely to cause (or be the current cause of) psychological problems.

Mitosis: asexual reproduction where the creature divides to form two identical organisms.

Molecular evolution: evolution of the molecular structure.

Mongolism (Down's syndrome): congenital problem that occurs as the newly formed embryo begins to divide into new cells. Infants born with this condition have abnormal body features including a thick tongue; heavy dual-folded eyelids, flattened face, etc.

Moral control: control by a statement of the discriminative stimulus, the response, and the added verbal, social, or supernatural results.

Moro reflex: the newborn infant makes a clutching response when its head loses support and falls backward. This response consists of stretching out its arms and bringing them together over its chest.

Motivation: factors that: 1) increase the effect stimuli have as reinforcing stimuli; 2) increase the effect they have as unconditioned or as conditioned stimuli; and 3) simply raise the over-all rate of motion.

Motor skills: skills of muscular movement.

Mutation: change in the composition of the gene that results in altered structure in offspring as compared to the parent.

Nativist: a person who tends to believe that people are born with basic skills that cannot be acquired through learning or experience.

Natural approach: any planned intervention on our part is either not needed, fruitless, or a source of problems.

Natural control: control over a creature's actions due to the normal results of those actions.

Natural selection: features of a creature help it survive in the world of nature, allowing the creature to pass that feature on to its offspring.

Nerves: axons that run in bundles alongside each other.

Nervous system: stimulus transfer system made of specialized cells that form pathways through which electrochemical energy is conducted.

Neurasthenic neurosis: neurosis where the primary complaint involves feelings of tiredness or fatigue that have no medical basis for occurring.

Neuron: cell specialized for rapid and far reaching stimulus transfer.

Object constancy: responding in a manner appropriate to an object, even though that object is out of sight.

Obsessive-compulsive neurosis: a type of neurosis characterized by highly frequent thoughts and/or actions that the person can't seem to control.

Ontogenetic development: the development of a single creature during its lifetime. Often the creature becomes more complex as it develops.

Operant conditioning: a change in the likelihood of a response due to the results of that response.

Organ: substructure of a complex creature where cells form together to provide a function or functions that help the entire organism survive.

Orienting response: a response to a stimulus that changes the position of the creature's body relative to that stimulus, often putting the creature's receptors in a better position to sense that stimulus.

Overlearning: method used in assertive training where responses to be made in an anxiety setting are rehearsed repeatedly.

Pain: a self-aware response made when a punisher makes contact, and we comment about its presence and our response to it.

Paranoia: paranoid psychosis marked by distinct delusions of grandeur and persecution. The paranoid should be distinguished from the paranoid schizophrenic who has somewhat the same delusions but also has the response patterns common to schizophrenia.

Paranoid schizophrenia: schizophrenia marked by active delusions, most often of grandeur and persecution.

Parasite: an organism that exists because of functions provided by others, but does not contribute to their survival.

Parsimony: this guideline states that scientists should always look for the simplest way to explain data; they should invent new concepts only when existing concepts clearly can not account for all the data.

Perception: stimulus control by two or more interacting stimulus features, where the value of one

stimulus feature affects the nature of our reaction to another feature.

Personality: those acts of a person that 1) are fairly constant, though the cues may change, and 2) differ from the ways many other people react to the same cues.

Phenylketonuria (PKU): metabolic condition that arises from the inheritance of faulty structure and causes mental retardation.

Phobic neurosis: neurosis where acute anxiety occurs when the person makes contact with the "phobic" stimulus — a harmless object or setting that triggers the anxiety.

Phylogenetic development: the development of a species from an earlier form, through evolution. Often it develops into more complex structures and functions.

Physiological shock: condition that sometimes occurs during the alarm stage of the GAS where resources are shunted from other systems to the site of the stressor attack; this diversion of resources from other vital functions may cause them to stop and end in death.

Physiological system: group of organs and supporting structures, that provide a special function for a creature.

Physiology: study of the function of living things and their organs.

Pleasure Principle: reinforcers and punishers control all that we do.

Pre-language control: simple stimulus control where specific stimuli are discriminative stimuli for specific acts.

Pre-moral control: social control where the act is controlled solely by the direct (perhaps physical) results to the person; similar to legal control — not really moral control, but rather pre-moral control.

Prenatal period: the period from conception to the birth of the creature.

Principle of Complexity: as matter exists and survives at any level (atoms, molecules, cells, creatures, cultures, etc.) changes occur that tend to make some units at that level more complex.

Principle of Instability: as a system reaches a certain point in complexity, it becomes unstable which tends to limit further complexity — at least at the level of that system.

Private event: something that occurs inside a person's body that only he or she has direct knowledge of.

Proprioceptive stimuli: inner stimuli produced by the tension (or position) of the muscles.

Proximal sensory response: response to a stimulus in direct contact with a creature.

Psychologenic psychoses: psychoses whose major cause is thought to involve what has happened to the person.

Psychology: the study of behavior.

Psychophysiologic disorders: harmful changes in tissue structure caused by adaptive responses body systems make to the presence of learned stressors.

Psychoses: types of severe psychological problems in which behavioral function is so grossly inappropriate that the person must receive almost constant attention and care.

Punisher: an outcome (often a harmful one) that reduces the occurrence of actions it closely follows.

Punishment: a reduction in actions that takes place when these actions lead to outcomes that harm tissue or remove reinforcers.

Purposivism: the notion that events have purposes causing them to occur.

Rational moral control: moral control where rules acting as discriminative stimuli for specific acts are derived from a larger moral code; punishers and reinforcers for following the specific rules have their effect because they are stated in terms of the larger moral code.

Rationalization: faulty thinking so that the truth about our actions can not serve as a discriminative stimulus for punishment of those actions.

Receptors: specialized cells well suited to absorb certain forms of energy.

Recruitment: as summated action of receptors grows, more neurons in a bundle begin to fire.

Reflex: a stimulus-response relation. It refers to the idea that a stimulus elicits a response. It can be either an unconditioned reflex (an unconditioned stimulus and response) or a conditioned reflex (a conditioned stimulus and response).

Reify: to invent things that help to explain how real things relate. Reification is the turning of a relation between real things into a thing itself.

Reinforcement priming: when a substance or stimulus that is a reinforcer for a response also serves as a discriminative stimulus when delivered to produce that same response.

Reinforcer: a change in conditions, stimuli, or events occurring right after a response and causing that response to be learned.

Repression: lack of self-awareness of an event of which a person would normally be aware.

Resistance stage: second stage of the GAS, during which physiological changes occur that act to lessen the primary effects of stress. It is during this stage that psychophysiological disorders develop.

Respondent conditioning: the procedure of pairing two stimuli with the result that one stimulus (conditioned stimulus) acquires the power to cause the response already caused by the other stimulus (unconditioned stimulus).

Response bias: a response that occurs because of its lengthy history of reinforcement in a wide range of settings and stimuli, and **does not** occur as a result of any special sensory activity or experience.

Retardation (mental retardation): general failure to benefit from normal training and experience, such that the minimum mastery of the skills and knowledge the culture requires is not attained.

Reward: an everyday term meaning roughly the same thing as reinforcer.

Role: a consistent way of acting under the control of a specific set of discriminative stimuli.

Rule: a statement that 1) describes the nature of the response; 2) describes the relevant setting or stimulus conditions; and 3) describes the results of the response in that setting.

Rule control: stimulus control in which rules function as discriminative stimuli.

Rule-governed moral control: moral control where a rule covering many different actions serves as a cue. The results that control that act are punishers or reinforcers given directly by that person or by someone else.

Satiation: a reduction in the power of a reinforcer as a result of repeated frequent exposure to it.

Schizophrenia: a class of psychoses marked by lowered or "flat" emotional response, loss of interest in most reinforcers and activities and perhaps the presence of delusions and hallucinations.

Science: the systematic study of how events or occurrences are related to the production of other events or occurrences.

Self-awareness: being able to give verbal responses that correctly describe what you are doing and the reason you are doing it.

Self-defeating behavior: part of the neurotic syndrome; using inadequate measures to deal with problems, thus merely postponing consequences and often making them worse.

Senile psychosis: psychosis that accompanies advanced age.

Sensory process: stimulus control by one stimulus feature in relation to other features that do not affect our reactions to that controlling feature.

Sexual reproduction: reproduction process where offspring are produced with two parents.

Shaping (method of successive approximation): procedure where a person or animal is taught to make a new response by reinforcing any responses that approximate or are part of the correct performance. This is done to increasingly narrow requirements until the desired behavior is attained.

Size constancy: the size of an object tends to have proper stimulus control over our actions whatever the distance of the object.

Social control: control over a person's actions through the efforts of others.

Social reinforcer: a reinforcer that involves another person's actions.

Sperm: male cell that will unite with female egg to form a new creature.

Spontaneous recovery: event taking place during an extinction procedure — a temporary and somewhat fleeting return in responding after an initial stoppage.

Stereotyping: a mode or manner of responding where the person keeps making the same response regardless of the presence of discriminative stimuli that could result in perfect control and correct responses.

Stimulus: any event in our physical world.

Stimulus generalization: a response that occurs in the presence of one stimulus is likely to occur in the presence of a stimulus that is similar to the first.

Stimulus generalization gradient: as a new stimulus differs from the one on which stimulus control was first established, its power to control a response is comparably lessened.

Stimulus matching procedure (matching-to-sample): a sample stimulus is presented along with a set of comparison stimuli. A reinforcer is given for the response of selecting the comparison stimulus that matches or is the same as the sample stimulus.

Stimulus transfer: conduction of a stimulus energy from one part or structure of a creature to other parts or structures.

Stimulus transform: a change of stimulus from one form of energy to another.

Stress: conditions that cause tissue damage far beyond the daily wear and tear of living.

Stressor: a type of stimulus that occurs in sufficient amount to cause stress.

Sublimation: a form of displacement where the displaced act produces worthwhile results.

Superego control: social reinforcer and punisher control by the culture's values — usually through guilt control.

Symbiosis: a situation where two or more organisms have a greater mutual chance to survive as a result of the function they provide for each other.

Synapse: connection between two neurons.

Synaptic vesicles: clumps of matter occurring in the end bouton that release chemicals when an impulse comes down the axon.

Syndrome: a group or cluster of behaviors, all or most of which, certain clients or patients tend to exhibit.

System: the placing of tasks, personnel, and machines into a unit to achieve a somewhat complex end result or function.

Systematic stress: stressors that affect a large area or part of the body.

Tactual stimulus: stimulus having to do with touch.

Task analysis: breaking down a complex behavior into its basic components.

Task selection: presenting the various basic components of a complex task in a sequence and manner that lead to mastery of the complex behavior.

Test validity: a test is valid if it predicts the behavior it was designed to predict.

Theory of evolution by natural selection: the process of mutation causes a variety of life forms, with some forms surviving, while others die as the state of nature selects among them. And the offspring of those that survive may inherit some of these helpful structural changes. Thus a species acquires more and more helpful new features over time, with creatures evolving that are well suited for their world.

Time out (time out from positive reinforcement): a procedure where the chance to earn reinforcement is delayed for a short period of time as a consequence of making an error. Time out tends to act as a mild punisher, thus suppressing errors.

Transmitter agents: chemicals released at the synapse that govern the nature of synaptic transfer.

Trauma: injury to body tissues that results from impact and collision with various objects.

Unconditioned response: response evoked by a stimulus even without prior experience.

Unconditioned stimulus: something that evokes a response without prior experience.

Unlearned response class: group of responses that are alike in the sense that they tend to produce the same result, and are subject to unlearned response generalization.

Unlearned response generalization: the tendency for new responses to occur spontaneously, even in a fairly fixed stimulus setting.

Unlearned stressors: stimuli which by their very nature destroy tissue.

Values: people's values are their reinforcers and punishers and the strengths of those reinforcers and punishers.

Verbal community: those persons who both teach and maintain our verbal behavior.

Warning stimuli: stimuli in whose presence punishment is likely to occur.

INDEX